# ESIC UDC

## Phase I - Preliminary Examination

Latest Edition
Practice Kit

**20 Tests**
08 Mock Test
12 Sectional Test

Based On Real Exam Pattern

✓ Thoroughly Revised and Updated

✓ Detailed Analysis of all MCQs

**Title**                         : ESIC UDC Phase I - Preliminary Examination

**Author Name**          : Mr. Rohit Manglik

**Published By**           : EduGorilla Community Pvt. Ltd.

**Publishers Address**  : 12/651, First Floor Opp. Arvindo Park, Near Jama Masjid,
                                    Indira Nagar, Lucknow, Uttar Pradesh-226016, India


## Copyright EduGorilla

**ISBN : 978-93-90239-70-2**

**Second Edition**




## Disclaimer EduGorilla



**Compiled and created by EduGorilla Community Pvt. Ltd**

**Printed By EduGorilla Community Pvt. Ltd.**

**ROHIT** MANGLIK
CEO, EduGorilla

**Dear Applicants,**

People say *"Success comes to those who work hard."* But I've seen people working hard for their exams day in and day out for marginal success. While others succeed in their examinations by putting in just half the work. So are they God Gifted? No! I believe that it's because they work *smart* and not just *hard*. Similarly, for your exams, you should strategize your preparation so as to increase the likelihood of success. Well with EduGorilla get ready to increase your *chances of selection* in your exam by *16x*.

EduGorilla helps you in not only working *hard* but also working in a *smart and strategic* manner. With EduGorilla's preparation package, you get a chance to make your exam preparation easy, and a fun learning path towards selection. Finding the right path to your preparations can be difficult if you don't know in which direction to head. Don't worry, we have you covered! EduGorilla will be your guide to success in your journey. With our Preparation Package, you can prepare strategically and beat the exam in just one attempt.

EduGorilla's Preparation Package includes-

• **Test Series**        • **Books**

Our preparation package is handcrafted as per the latest changes, expert opinions, and students' discretion. Thus, enabling you to get through each stage of the selection process for your exam.

Our Books are designed by the teachers and experts of the respective exam with a combined 150+ years of experience; to provide you with easy, efficient, and effective learning. Our books are smart, in the sense that not only do they give you the answers to the questions but also provide similar questions for practice.

EduGorilla's competent Test Series gives you real-time experience and confidence through which you can clear your offline or online exam in just one attempt. We currently host 83,000+ mock tests for 1,440+ competitive and academic exams.

Thus, EduGorilla misses no chance to assist you in your preparation and covers all stages of the exam, so that you don't have to look anywhere else.

We provide complete preparation packages for defense, banking, teaching, and other National & State-Level exams. Hence, it doesn't matter which exam you aspire to because you will reach your success.

**ALL THE BEST !**

Let EduGorilla be your Guide to Success.

*Rohit Manglik,*
*Founder and CEO, EduGorilla*

# INTRODUCTION

EduGorilla focuses on guiding students to succeed in their examinations. With that in mind, our book, titled "ESIC UDC : Phase I - Preliminary Examination", has been drafted through the collective efforts of our distinguished experts with 150+ years of combined experience. This book consists of questions that are created following the latest changes in the syllabus and exam pattern. We compiled the book on the basis of questions that are most likely to appear in the ESIC UDC. Through EduGorilla's "ESIC UDC : Phase I - Preliminary Examination" your chances of success will increase 16x.

EduGorilla does this through our Complete Preparation Package. This package consists of well-conceptualized and structured content in the form of questions that are tailor-made according to your needs and will help you practice for exams in a smart way by pinpointing all the necessary information. It also provides hints and solutions, along with a smart answer sheet for your self-evaluation. You can assess your shortcomings and work accordingly on areas that may require more of your attention.

EduGorilla promises to help you succeed in your examination and accomplish your dream goals. We believe in our aspirants and see them at the top of the merit list. And the first step towards the top is to start preparing with us. EduGorilla's "ESIC UDC : Phase I - Preliminary Examination" includes the following attributes.

➤ Well-Researched Content

➤ Top-Notch Quality

➤ Detailed Answers and Analysis

➤ Smart Answer Sheet

➤ Exam Relevant Questions

Therefore, EduGorilla fortifies your preparation and makes it durable enough to help you stand tall and beat the examination.

**ESIC UDC**
Scan QR code for Eligibility, Exam Pattern, Syllabus and more.

**Book ID: 0272**

# TABLE OF CONTENTS

# Mock Test 01

## General Intelligence & Reasoning

**Q.1** Select the related shape from the given option.

**A.**

**B.**

**C.**

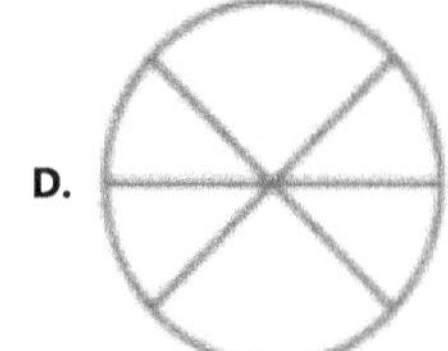

**D.**

**Q.2** Select the related shape from the given option.

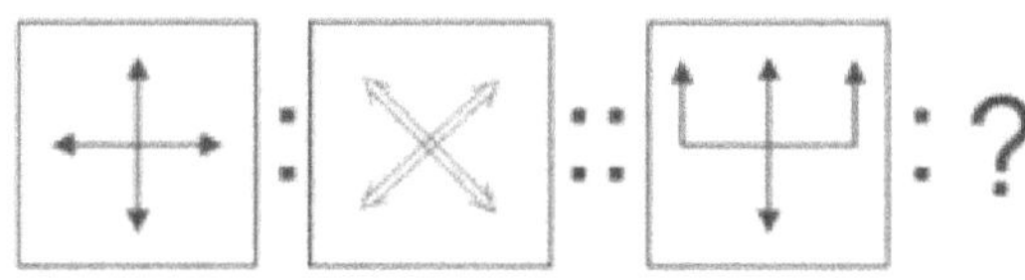

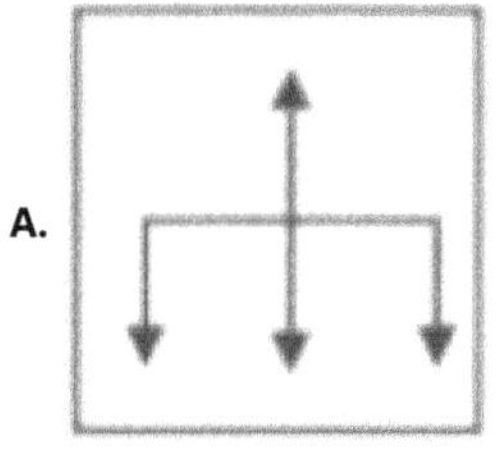

**A.**

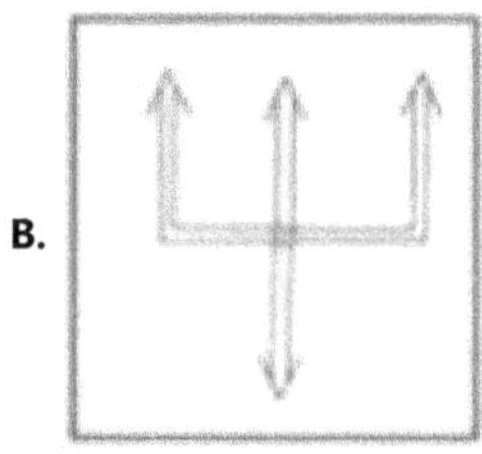

**B.**

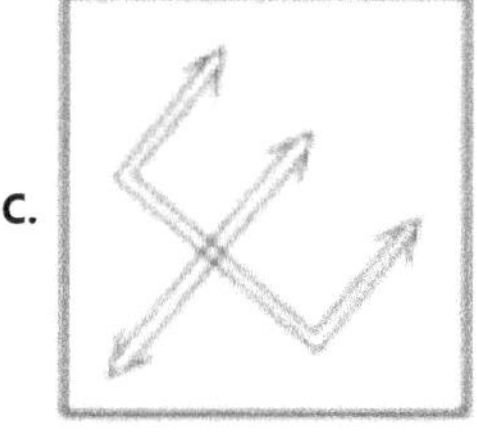

**C.**

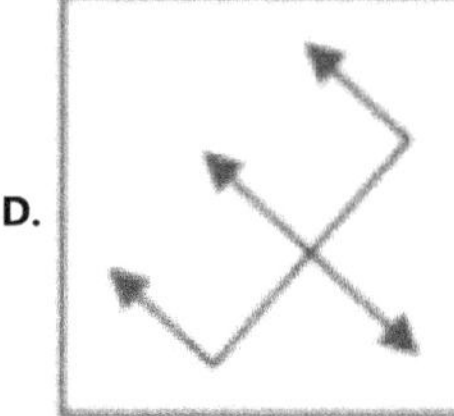

**D.**

**Q.3** Choose the correct option from the following question.
HJIK: MONP : : PRQS: ?

**A.** UVWX    **B.** UWVX    **C.** UXWV    **D.** UWXV

**Q.4** In the following question select the odd word pair from the given alternatives.

**A.** Book : Paper      **B.** House : Bricks
**C.** Court : Lawyer      **D.** Body : Organs

**Q.5** 'Iron' is related to 'Solid' in the same ways as 'Mercury' is related to _______:

**A.** Solid    **B.** Gas    **C.** Liquid    **D.** Vapor

**Q.6** Choose the correct option from the following question.
China: Buddhism :: Germany: ?

**A.** Roman Catholicism      **B.** Islam
**C.** Hinduism      **D.** Christianity

**Q.7** Find out the missing number from the following question.
6, 13, 32, 69, 130, ?

**A.** 221    **B.** 201    **C.** 336    **D.** 186

**Q.8** Find the wrong term from the following question.
9234, 8345, 2394, 8541

**A.** 8541    **B.** 9234    **C.** 2394    **D.** 8345

**Q.9** Choose the correct option from the following question.
343 : 678 : : 512 : ?

**A.** 1024    **B.** 1536    **C.** 1000    **D.** 1016

**Q.10** In the following question, select the odd one from the given alternatives.

**A.** 2, 4, 72    **B.** 1, 2, 9    **C.** 5, 3, 152    **D.** 3, 4, 90

**Q.11** In a certain code language, " $NUMBER$" is written as " $156897$" and " $BARREN$" is written as " $847791$". How is " $RUBBER$" written in that code language?

**A.** 759597    **B.** 758897    **C.** 795957    **D.** 795579

**Q.12** Choose the Odd one out among the following options.

**A.** Brush    **B.** Colour    **C.** Painting    **D.** Artist

**Q.13** In a family, there are 5 members and all are going to a picnic. D is the mother of T. M is the brother of T. M and T are children of U. V is M's child. If T is a female, then how T is related to V?

**A.** Aunt    **B.** Nephew    **C.** Sister    **D.** Cousin

**Q.14** Which figure in the given question will complete the pattern of the question figure?

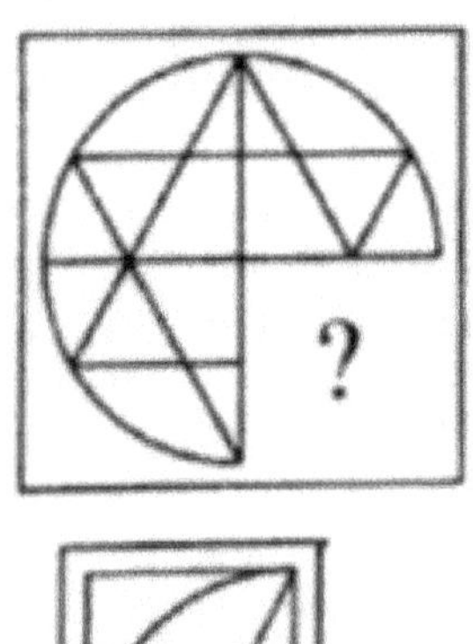

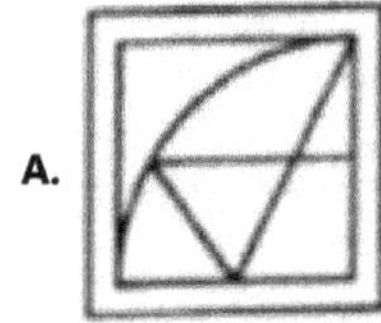

**A.**

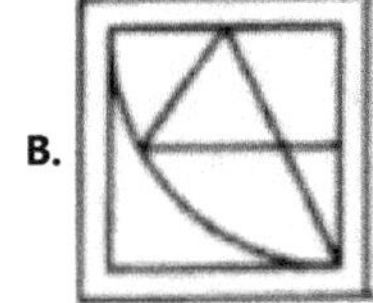

**B.**

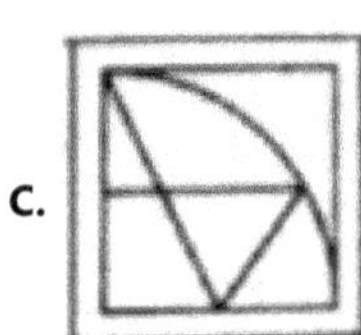

**C.**

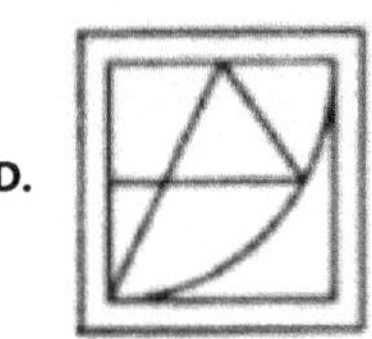

**D.**

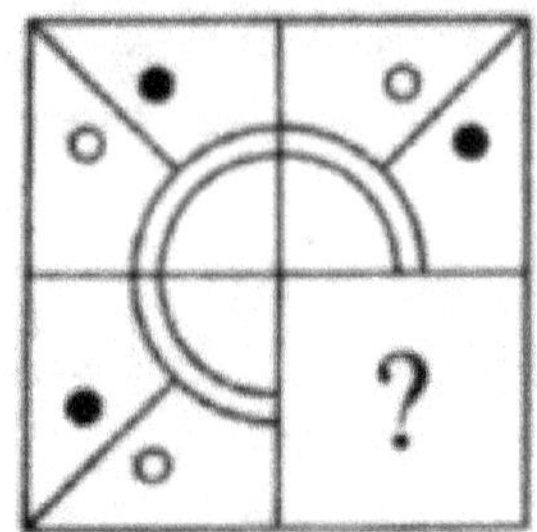

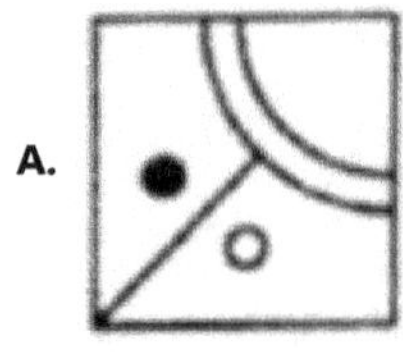

**A.**

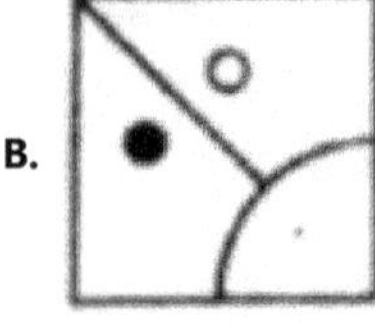

**B.**

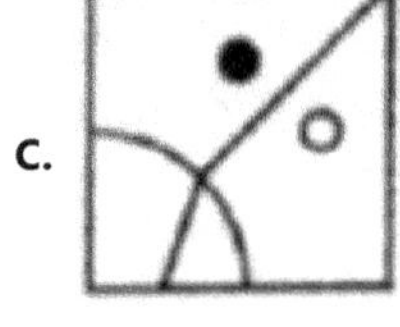

**C.**

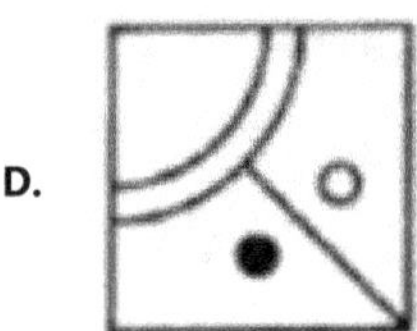

**D.**

**Q.15 Direction**: In the following question below are given some statements followed by some conclusions. Taking the given statements to be true even if they seem to be at variance from commonly known facts, read all the conclusions and the conclusions and then decide which of the given conclusion logically follows the given statements.

**Statements**:

I. No circle is square.

II. Some squares are rectangle

**Conclusions**:

I. Some circles are rectangle

II. No circle is rectangle

**A.**   Only conclusion (I) follows

**B.**   Only conclusion (II) follows

**C.**   Both conclusion follow

**D.**   Either conclusion (I) or conclusion (II) follows

**Q.16** Which figure represents the relation among Bitter gourd, Pineapple, and Vegetable?

**A.**
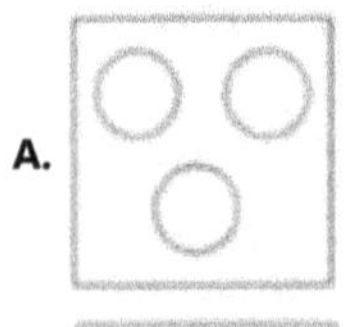

**B.**
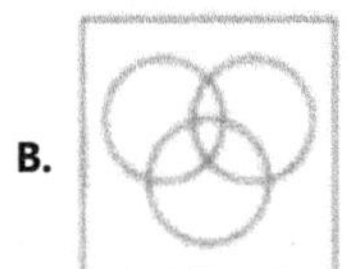

**C.**
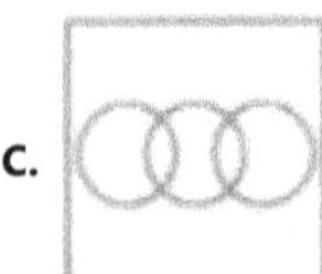

**D.**

**Q.17** Which figure in the given question will complete the pattern of the question figure?

**Q.18** Three different positions of a dice are shown below. Which number appears on the face opposite the number 6 ?

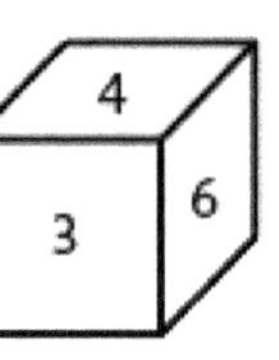 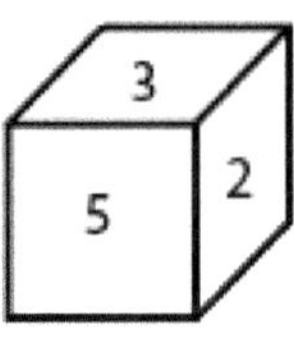 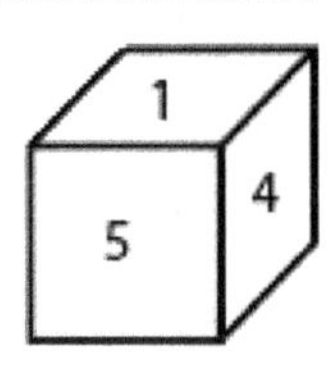

**A.** 4          **B.** 5          **C.** 2          **D.** 1

**Q.19** If ' + ' means ' - ', ' × ' means ' + ', ' ÷ ' means ' ÷ ' and ' - ' means ' × ' then what is the value of:

86 × 12 + 53 − 18 ÷ 49

**A.** 81          **B.** 46.48          **C.** 78.53          **D.** 47.17

**Q.20** Three different positions of the same dice are shown below. Which number is on the face opposite the face showing 4?

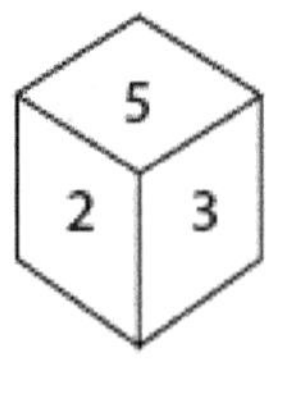 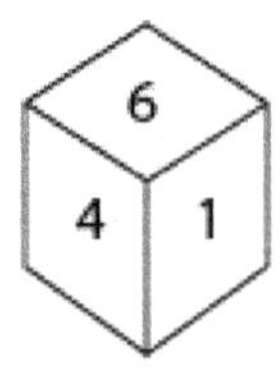 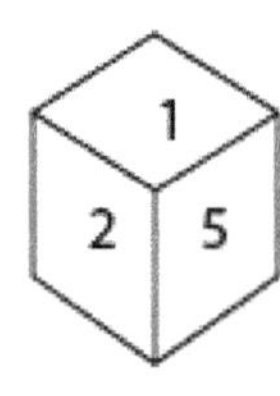

**A.** 2          **B.** 5          **C.** 3          **D.** 6

**Q.21 Direction:** In the following question, a word is represented by only one set of numbers are given in any one of the alternatives. The sets of numbers given in the alternatives are represented by two classes of alphabets as in the two given matrices. The column and row of Matrix I are numbered from 0 to 4 and those of Matrix II from 5 to 9. A letter from these matrices can be represented first by row and then the column number e.g. in the matrices for questions 1 to 5, K can be represented by 65,77, etc. H can be represented by 30,11 etc. Similarly, you have to identify the correct set for the word given in each question.

|   | 0 | 1 | 2 | 3 | 4 |
|---|---|---|---|---|---|
| 0 | A | E | S | T | H |
| 1 | T | H | A | E | S |
| 2 | E | S | T | H | A |
| 3 | H | A | E | S | T |
| 4 | S | T | H | A | E |

|   | 5 | 6 | 7 | 8 | 9 |
|---|---|---|---|---|---|
| 5 | P | O | R | K | L |
| 6 | K | L | P | O | R |
| 7 | O | R | K | L | P |
| 8 | L | P | O | R | K |
| 9 | R | K | L | P | O |

Matrix I      Matrix II

LEAST

**A.** 85, 01, 00, 40, 41      **B.** 32, 21, 44, 87, 44

**C.** 10, 34, 21, 32, 97      **D.** 00, 66, 33, 20, 34

**Q.22 Direction:** In the following question, a word is represented by only one set of numbers are given in any one of the alternatives. The sets of numbers given in the alternatives are represented by two classes of alphabets as in the two given matrices. The column and row of Matrix I are numbered from 0 to 4 and those of Matrix II from 5 to 9. A letter from these matrices can be represented first by row and then the column number e.g. in the matrices for questions 1 to 5, K can be represented by 65,77, etc. H can be represented by 30,11 etc. Similarly, you have to identify the correct set for the word given in each question.

|   | 0 | 1 | 2 | 3 | 4 |
|---|---|---|---|---|---|
| 0 | A | E | S | T | H |
| 1 | T | H | A | E | S |
| 2 | E | S | T | H | A |
| 3 | H | A | E | S | T |
| 4 | S | T | H | A | E |

|   | 5 | 6 | 7 | 8 | 9 |
|---|---|---|---|---|---|
| 5 | P | O | R | K | L |
| 6 | K | L | P | O | R |
| 7 | O | R | K | L | P |
| 8 | L | P | O | R | K |
| 9 | R | K | L | P | O |

Matrix I      Matrix II

POLAR

**A.** 66, 31, 95, 33, 43      **B.** 86, 97, 24, 88, 11

**C.** 79, 87, 59, 31, 76      **D.** 00, 86, 32, 89, 57

**Q.23** Which figure must continue series of figure?

Question figure      Answer figure

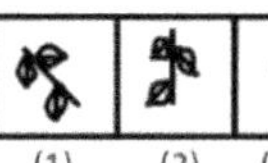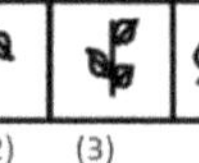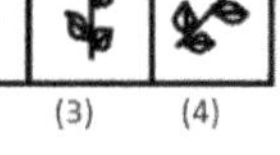

(a)   (b)   (c)   (d)     (1)   (2)   (3)   (4)

**A.** (1)      **B.** (2)      **C.** (3)      **D.** (4)

**Q.24** What will come in the place of question mark (?).

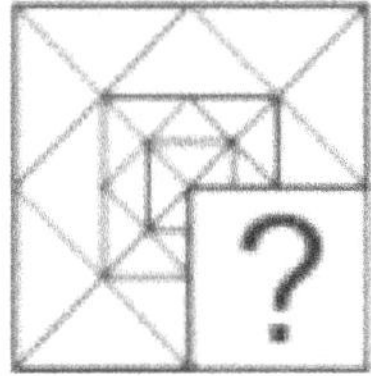

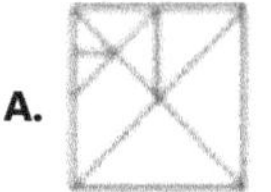 **A.**    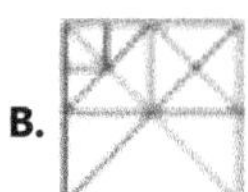 **B.**    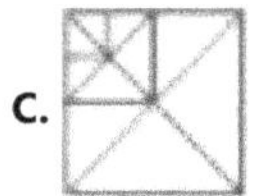 **C.**    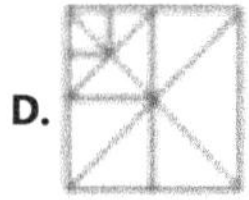 **D.**

**Q.25** From among the figures, select the figure which satisfies the same conditions of placement of the dots as in question figure.

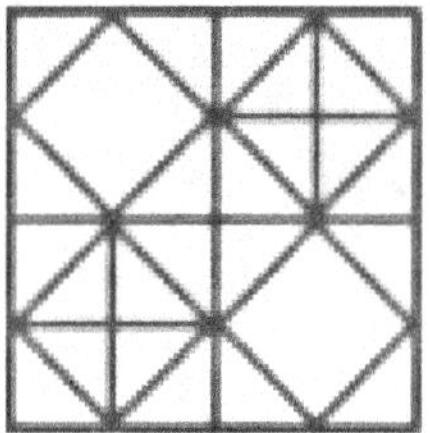

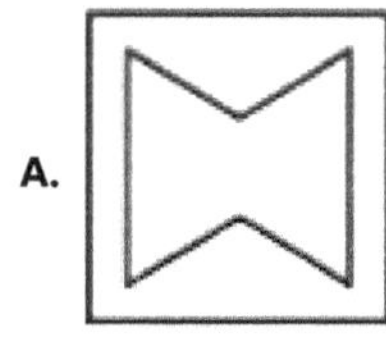

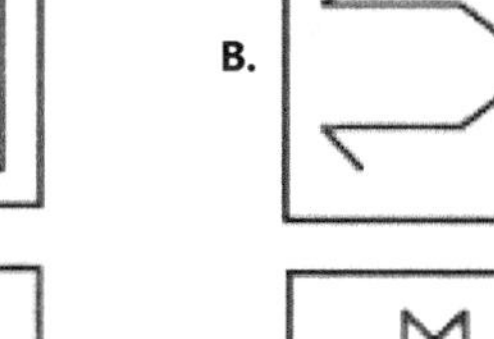

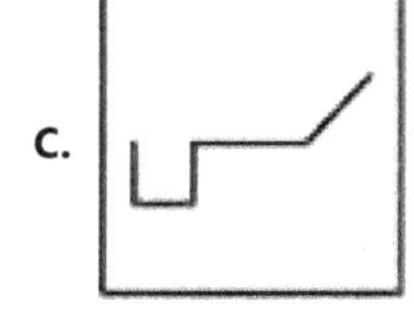

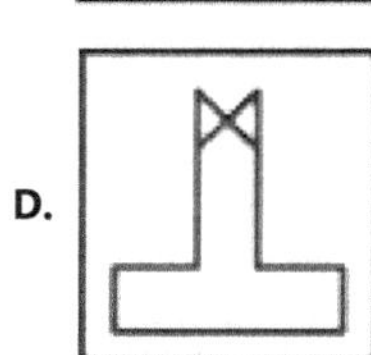

A.    B.    C.    D.

## General Awareness

**Q.26** Recently which place has Bihar got invor the ongoing cleanliness survey 2021?

*[Delhi Forest Guard, 2021], [UPSSSC Rajasva Lekhpal, 2015]*

**A.** 1st    **B.** 10th    **C.** 12th    **D.** 13th

**Q.27** Which scientist of Bihar and his team have invented a new technology to identify bacteria?

*[UPSSSC Rajasva Lekhpal, 2015]*

**A.**    Dr. Amar Tripathi

**B.**    Ravi Bhushan Pandey

**C.**    Dr. Ujjwal Verma

**D.**    Dr. Radhakrishna Prasad

**Q.28** Who has been appointed as the new the Chairperson of SEBI for a period of 3 years?

**A.**    Arundhati Bhattacharya

**B.**    Kalpana Morparia

**C.**    Gita Gopinath

**D.**    Madhabi Puri Buch

**Q.29** ________ has partnered with Aditya Birla Wellness to launch 'Wellness Plus Credit Cards'.

**A.** ICICI bank      **B.** YES bank

**C.** HDFC bank      **D.** IDBI bank

**Q.30** RBI has formed working group to regulate digital lending frauds. How many members are there in a working group?

**A.** Three    **B.** Five    **C.** Six    **D.** Eight

**Q.31** The 51st International Film Festival of India will be celebrating the work of legendary filmmaker ________.

**A.** Soumitra Chatterjee      **B.** Uttam Kumar

**C.** Satyajit Ray      **D.** Aparna Sen

**Q.32** The Centre has sanctioned Rs 37.87 crore for the facelift of Parshuram Kund pilgrimage site in ______.

**A.** Arunachal Pradesh
**B.** Manipur
**C.** Telangana
**D.** Maharashtra

**Q.33** Dr Najma Heptulla has virtually released a book titled "Making of a General-A Himalayan Echo". The book has been authored by ______.

**A.** Lt General Konsam Himalay Singh
**B.** Nirmal Chandra Suri
**C.** Lt General Sarath Chand
**D.** Lt General Anil Chauhan

**Q.34** The 1896 session of the Indian National Congress is noted for which of the following?

**A.** Sang the national anthem for the first time
**B.** Sang the national song for the first time
**C.** The tricolor was waved for the first time
**D.** None of these

**Q.35** Which of the following Governor General is called the liberator of the Indian press?

**A.** Lord William Bentinck
**B.** Sir Charles Metcalf
**C.** Lord Auckland
**D.** Lard ellenborough

**Q.36** By whom was the Carthage system used in the context of maritime trade?

**A.** Dutch
**B.** French
**C.** English
**D.** Portuguese

**Q.37** S Vijayalakshmi is associated with which sport?

**A.** Badminton
**B.** Table tennis
**C.** Chess
**D.** Hockey

**Q.38** 'Sandy Storm' is an autobiography of which cricketer?

**A.** Dilip Vengsarkar
**B.** Mohinder Amarnath
**C.** Sandeep Patil
**D.** Roger binny

**Q.39** When is World Biodiversity Day celebrated?

**A.** 22 March
**B.** 22 April
**C.** 22 May
**D.** 22 June

**Q.40** Who can change the number of Supreme Court judges?

**A.** Presidential order
**B.** Parliament by law
**C.** Supreme Court notification
**D.** Central government notification

**Q.41** To work as the Chief Justice of the Supreme Court, a person should work in the High Court for at least how many years?

**A.** 10 years
**B.** 12 years
**C.** 15 years
**D.** 20 years

**Q.42** Which of the following statements is correct in relation to the vast plains of India?

1. The world's largest alluvium deposit is found in India.
2. Bangar has new alluvium as compared to Khadar region.
3. Khadar region is located in low altitude areas.

**A.** 1 and 2 only
**B.** 2 and 3 only
**C.** 1 and 3 only
**D.** 1, 2 and 3

**Q.43** The Dempier – Hodges line is related to which of the following?

**A.** Gulf of Cambay
**B.** Palk Strait
**C.** Andaman and Nicobar Islands
**D.** Sundarbans

**Q.44** Which is the largest salt producing state of India?

**A.** Rajasthan
**B.** Gujarat
**C.** Tamil Nadu
**D.** Odisha

**Q.45** Sixth Schedule of Indian Constitution deals with the administration and control of Scheduled Areas and Scheduled Tribes in which four states?

**A.** Manipur, Mizoram, Tripura, Nagaland
**B.** Assam, Meghalaya, Tripura, Mizoram
**C.** Assam, Meghalaya, Arunachal Pradesh, Nagaland
**D.** Assam, Meghalaya, Mizoram, Nagaland

**Q.46** Who among the following is the author of the famous book 'Meghdoot'?

**A.** Kalidas
**B.** Chetan Bhagat
**C.** Arundhati Bhattacharya
**D.** Dadabhai Norwegian

**Q.47** In which state of India is the Kamakhya Temple located?

**A.** Jharkhand
**B.** Chhattisgarh
**C.** Arunachal Pradesh
**D.** Assam

**Q.48** Which badminton player clinched the 'Indonesia Masters title'?

**A.** Carolina Marin
**B.** Ratchanok Intanon
**C.** P V Sindhu
**D.** Nozomi Okuhara

**Q.49** Rupinder Pal Singh has announced his retirement from International play, He is associated with which sports?

**A.** Cricket
**B.** Hockey
**C.** Football
**D.** Badminton

**Q.50** Which river of India is called Vridha Ganga?

**A.** Krishna
**B.** Godavari
**C.** Kaveri
**D.** Narmada

# Quantitative Aptitude

**Q.51** What will come in the place of question mark (?).

$$19 \div \left[1 - \frac{1}{2} + 2\frac{2}{3}\right] = ?$$

**A.** $\frac{1}{6}$
**B.** 6
**C.** $\frac{1}{2}$
**D.** $\frac{1}{19}$

**Q.52** The average age of three boys is $15$ years. If their age is in the ratio of $3:5:7$, what will be the age of the youngest boy?

**A.** 5 Year
**B.** 9 Year
**C.** 7 Year
**D.** 8 Year

**Q.53** The average marks obtained by 40 students of a class is 86. If the 5 highest digits are removed, the average is reduced by one point. State the average marks of the top 5 students.
**A.** 93    **B.** 52    **C.** 47    **D.** 85

**Q.54** A player in cricket had an average of 10 innings. In the 11th innings, he scored 108 runs and this increased his average run number by 6. Now, what is their average run number?
**A.** 20    **B.** 11    **C.** 45    **D.** 48

**Q.55** The ratio of the number of students in the three classes is 2: 3: 4. If 12 students are increased in each class, then the ratio becomes 8: 11: 14. How many students were there in the first three classes together?
**A.** 164    **B.** 165    **C.** 163    **D.** 162

**Q.56** The ratio of the annual income of A and B is 4: 3, and the ratio of their annual expenditure is 3: 2. If each of them saves 6000 at the end of the year. So what is the annual income of A?
**A.** 22000    **B.** 15000    **C.** 10000    **D.** 24000

**Q.57** Due to a shortage of labor in a factory, its production decreases by 25%. By how much% should the working period be increased so that production remains the same?
**A.** $53\frac{1}{3}\%$    **B.** $23\frac{1}{3}\%$    **C.** $40\frac{1}{3}\%$    **D.** $33\frac{1}{3}\%$

**Q.58** In an examination, 40% of the students fail in Mathematics, 30% fail in English. 10% fail in both subjects. So, tell the% of students who passed in both the subjects.
**A.** 36%    **B.** 20%    **C.** 50%    **D.** 40%

**Q.59** If $a + b = 1$ and $a^3 + b^3 + 3ab = k$ then the value of $k$ is :
**A.** 1    **B.** 2    **C.** 8    **D.** 7

**Q.60** Father is aged three times more than his son Ronit. After 8 years, he would be two and a half times Ronit's age. After further 8 years, how many times would he be of Ronit's age?
**A.** 2 times    **B.** $2\frac{1}{2}$ times
**C.** $2\frac{3}{4}$ times    **D.** 3 times

**Q.61** If there is a loss of 30% after selling a pen for Rs. 56, then at what price will it be sold to get a profit of 20%?
**A.** Rs. 96    **B.** Rs. 84    **C.** Rs. 72    **D.** Rs. 48

**Q.62** What value will come in place of the question mark (?) In the question given below?
$40\%$ of $265 + 35\%$ of $180 = 50\%$ of $? + 80\%$ of $?$
**A.** 80    **B.** 95.58    **C.** 130    **D.** 125.5

**Q.63** Mohan can do any work separately in 10 days and Sohan in 15 days. Sohan works alone for 3 days, and after that, he leaves the work, then in how many days will Mohan complete the remaining work?
**A.** 8 days    **B.** 5 days    **C.** 6 days    **D.** 9 days

**Q.64** While working 8 hours a day, Ashu can prepare a book for 18 days. If the same work is to be completed within 12 days, how many hours will Ashu be working every day?
**A.** 12 hours    **B.** 10 hours    **C.** 11 hours    **D.** 13 hours

**Q.65** The speed of a boat in still water is 12 km/hr more than that of current. If the speed of the current is $1.25x$ km/hr and the time taken by the boat to cover 160 km in downstream is 5 hours then find the value of ' $x$'.
**A.** 8    **B.** 6    **C.** 4    **D.** 10

**Q.66** The length of a rectangle is 4 cm more than its breadth. If the area of the rectangle is 45 cm², what is the perimeter of the rectangle?
**A.** 21 cm    **B.** 24 cm    **C.** 25 cm    **D.** 28 cm

**Q.67** A person can ride a boat in the opposite direction of the stream at a speed of 10 km/h. And its speed in the direction of current is 16 km/h. Show the speed of the boat in calm water.
**A.** 17 km/h    **B.** 13 km/h    **C.** 30 km/h    **D.** 29 km/h

**Q.68** What should come in place of question mark (?) in the following question?
$$464 \div (16 \times 29) + 4\frac{1}{2} = ?$$
**A.** 1.5    **B.** 2.5    **C.** 2    **D.** 5.5

**Q.69** Which of the large number should be reduced from 10,000 so that the remainder is complete or divided by 32, 36, 48, and 54?
**A.** 9136    **B.** 3868    **C.** 3123    **D.** 3785

**Q.70** What is the largest number from which 2, 3, and 4 respectively are left when divided into 38, 45, and 52?
**A.** 12    **B.** 6    **C.** 13    **D.** 14

**Q.71** What should come in place of the question mark (?) In the following question?
$$14 \times ? + 695 = 36\% \text{ of } 2400 + 755$$
**A.** 72    **B.** 66    **C.** 75    **D.** 80

**Q.72** Three circle each of radius 3.5 cm touch one another. The area subtended between them is:
**A.** $6(\sqrt{3}\pi - 2)$ square unit
**B.** $6(2\pi - \sqrt{3})$ square unit
**C.** $\frac{49}{8}(2\sqrt{3} - \pi)$ square unit
**D.** $\frac{49}{8}(\sqrt{3} - \pi)$ square unit

**Q.73** What is the value of $\alpha(\alpha \neq 0)$ for which $x^2 - 5x + \alpha$ and $x^2 - 7x + 2\alpha$ have a common factor?
**A.** 6    **B.** 4    **C.** 3    **D.** 2

**Q.74** A rectangular field costs Rs. 225 for ploughing at the rate of 75 paise per square meter. if ratio of length and breadth is 4: 3 find its perimeter.
**A.** 50    **B.** 60    **C.** 80    **D.** 70

**Q.75** The selling price of an article is Rs. 1920 and the discount given is 4% The marked price of the article is:

**A.** Rs. 2400   **B.** Rs. 2000   **C.** Rs. 1600   **D.** Rs. 1200

# English Comprehension

**Q.76** Choose the most appropriate option to change the passive voice form of the given sentence.

Close the windows for fear of rain.

**A.** The windows be closed for fear of rain.
**B.** Let the windows be closed for fear of rain.
**C.** The windows may be closed for fear of rain.
**D.** Due to fear of rain, close the windows.

**Ques (77-79):Direction:** Read the following passage and answer the question that follows.

In 18th-century Germany, Baron Munchausen regales his friends, over drinks, with stories of his many adventures. These include his supposed travel to the moon. Long before Neil Armstrong and Edwin Aldrin stepped out of Apollo 11 onto the surface of the moon 50 years ago, on July 20, 1969, the aspiration to travel to this shiny orb in the sky has fired human imagination. A Flight To The Moon by George Fowler, From The Earth To The Moon – and its sequel, Around The Moon – by Jules Verne, The First Men In The Moon by HG Wells, Prelude To Space by Arthur C Clarke... are only a few of the many fictionalised accounts that have, for centuries, reflected this aspiration. In the 1954 Explorers On The Moon, iconic comic book character, Tintin, reaches the moon. While some writers imagined the moon's surface to be barren and uninhabited, others have written about it being populated with lunar beings. Even when Apollo 11 mission was being planned and worked on, in 1963, Apollo At Go by Jeff Sutton, presented a realistic fictionalised portrayal of the upcoming landing.

The successful landing of Apollo 11 and Neil Armstrong and Buzz Aldrin's walk on the moon, opened up another exciting possibility – could the common man or non-space-scientist reach for the moon? Literally? What had hitherto been in the realm of speculation was now a reality and we weren't satisfied with just second-hand information anymore. Between 1969 and 1972, the US sent six successful manned missions to the moon, and with each victory, the lunar destination seemed a little closer within the reach of the common man.

**Q.77** When did the US send first successful manned trip to the moon?

**A.** 1972   **B.** 1963   **C.** 1969   **D.** 1954

**Q.78** Who was the first person to speak of travel to the moon?

**A.** Munchausen        **B.** Armstrong
**C.** Sutton            **D.** Branson

**Q.79** Which of the following statements is not true according to the passage?

*[SSC Sub Inspector (CPO), 2019]*

**A.** Man's walk on the moon inspired scientists to plan more expeditions.
**B.** All the writers wrote about the moon being inhabited by weird creatures.
**C.** Someday the common man could make a trip to the moon.

**D.** Man has always been attracted to the moon.

**Q.80** In the following question choose the word which best expresses the meaning of the given word.

Uncouth

**A.** Ungraceful          **B.** Rough
**C.** Slovenly           **D.** Dirty

**Q.81** In the following question choose the word which best expresses the meaning of the given word.

Error

**A.** Misadventure        **B.** Misgiving
**C.** Ambiguity          **D.** Blunder

**Q.82** Improve the bracketed part of the sentence.

Women walk miles on the blazing sands in search of an (elite) pot of water.

**A.** Elusive            **B.** Elated
**C.** Effusive          **D.** No Improvement

**Q.83**

Find the opposite meaning of Heresy.

**A.** Agreement          **B.** Error
**C.** Mindful           **D.** Rash

**Q.84** Find the word just opposite of Provoke.

**A.** Insult            **B.** Anger
**C.** Encourage         **D.** Soothe

**Q.85** Select the most appropriate meaning of the given idiom/Phrase.

To cry out against

**A.** To complain loudly against
**B.** To fall
**C.** To throw aside
**D.** To remain without

**Q.86** Fill in the blanks.

Scarcely had the day dawned ______ we left for the mountains.

**A.** than   **B.** when   **C.** then   **D.** so

**Q.87** Fill in the blanks.

I wonder ______ we shall reach there in time.

**A.** when   **B.** if   **C.** where   **D.** while

**Q.88** Select the most appropriate meaning of the given Idiom/Phrase.

A Perfect Storm

**A.** To take risks
**B.** A perfect enemy
**C.** The worst possible situation
**D.** To spoil something

**Q.89** In the following question, select the correctly spelled word from the four alternatives.

**A.** Distributesd        **B.** Deteriorating
**C.** Distresssed        **D.** Drestic

**Q.90 Direction:** In the following questions, some part of the sentence is highlighted in bold. Which of the options given below the sentence should replace the part printed in bold to make the sentence grammatically correct.

The manager was sleeping during day time in his cabin **than suddenly his room filled with light.**

A. and than suddenly his room filling with light.
B. as suddenly his room filled through light.
C. when suddenly his room filled with light.
D. then suddenly his room filled by light.

**Q.91 Direction:** In the following question, out of the four alternatives, choose the one which can be substituted for the given words/ sentence.

One who collects coins

A. Archaeologist          B. Numismatist
C. Philatelist          D. Connoisseur

**Q.92 Direction:** In the following question, out of the four alternatives, choose the one which can be substituted for the given words/ sentence.

One who is skillful

A. Diligent          B. Different
C. Disciplined          D. Dexterous

**Q.93** Improve the bold part of the sentence.

The man disappeared after he **was rescuing** a boy from drowning.

A. was rescued          B. has been rescued
C. had rescued          D. No improvement

**Q.94** Correct the underlined part of the sentence.

I am waiting for three-quarters of an hour.

A. I am waiting since
B. I have waited since
C. I have been waiting for
D. No improvement

**Q.95 Direction:** In the following question, a disarranged sentence is given in which words are lettered P, Q, R, and S. Arrange these to form a meaningful sentence.

P: tramp.
Q: I was
R: as free
S: as a

A. QRSP          B. QPRS          C. PQRS          D. PRSQ

**Q.96 Direction:** In the following question, a disarranged sentence is given in which words are lettered P, Q, R, and S. Arrange these to form a meaningful sentence.

P: the narcissus
Q: bloom
R: is the
S: first to

A. PSQR          B. PRSQ          C. RSQP          D. RPQS

**Q.97 Direction:** Fill in the blanks with a suitable form of a verb.

This medicine is __________ from a tropical plant.

A. deprived          B. derived
C. derisive          D. None of these

**Q.98 Direction:** Fill in the blanks with a suitable form of a verb.

The new law will __________ the entire community. Everyone will be affected.

A. impact          B. impede
C. impress          D. None of these

**Q.99 Direction:** Fill in the blanks with a suitable article.

She wants to become ______ engineer.

A. a          B. an
C. the          D. None of these

**Q.100** Find out the Adjective.

Exhaustion

A. exhausted          B. exhaustive
C. exhausting          D. exhaust

# // Smart Answer Sheet //

**Correct** — Indicates percentage of students who answered questions correctly.

**Skipped** — Indicates percentage of students who skipped questions.

| Q. | Ans. | Correct | Q. | Ans. | Correct | Q. | Ans. | Correct | Q. | Ans. | Correct | Q. | Ans. | Correct |
| --- | --- | --- | --- | --- | --- | --- | --- | --- | --- | --- | --- | --- | --- | --- |
| | | Skipped | | | Skipped | | | Skipped | | | Skipped | | | Skipped |
| 1 | C | 48.88 % / 46.42 % | 17 | D | 47.4 % / 52.5 % | 33 | A | 52.23 % / 38.04 % | 49 | B | 61.88 % / 36.63 % | 65 | A | 45.39 % / 39.57 % |
| 2 | C | 88.02 % / 10.48 % | 18 | B | 27.02 % / 69.08 % | 34 | B | 42.14 % / 44.39 % | 50 | B | 41.9 % / 45.46 % | 66 | D | 51.76 % / 37.46 % |
| 3 | B | 58.82 % / 35.64 % | 19 | C | 67.06 % / 32.22 % | 35 | B | 49.17 % / 42.65 % | 51 | B | 65.09 % / 30.84 % | 67 | B | 76.71 % / 21.0 % |
| 4 | C | 57.4 % / 41.14 % | 20 | B | 63.41 % / 32.32 % | 36 | D | 42.06 % / 45.65 % | 52 | B | 41.53 % / 33.97 % | 68 | D | 42.34 % / 37.91 % |
| 5 | C | 80.14 % / 15.74 % | 21 | A | 53.26 % / 38.28 % | 37 | C | 63.64 % / 30.59 % | 53 | A | 61.36 % / 35.46 % | 69 | A | 60.9 % / 36.12 % |
| 6 | D | 57.91 % / 38.69 % | 22 | C | 44.41 % / 41.07 % | 38 | C | 20.73 % / 70.36 % | 54 | D | 61.16 % / 33.77 % | 70 | B | 56.2 % / 42.66 % |
| 7 | A | 66.8 % / 30.57 % | 23 | A | 68.38 % / 30.51 % | 39 | C | 64.07 % / 31.19 % | 55 | D | 44.23 % / 34.8 % | 71 | B | 67.59 % / 30.86 % |
| 8 | D | 59.34 % / 36.74 % | 24 | C | 69.51 % / 30.3 % | 40 | B | 52.95 % / 46.27 % | 56 | D | 82.49 % / 16.41 % | 72 | C | 67.5 % / 30.37 % |
| 9 | D | 44.42 % / 33.17 % | 25 | C | 64.99 % / 30.21 % | 41 | A | 31.17 % / 67.67 % | 57 | D | 45.17 % / 35.24 % | 73 | A | 54.13 % / 33.74 % |
| 10 | D | 59.49 % / 35.79 % | 26 | D | 64.59 % / 33.35 % | 42 | C | 56.94 % / 32.76 % | 58 | D | 44.26 % / 50.24 % | 74 | D | 31.5 % / 67.39 % |
| 11 | B | 63.84 % / 35.86 % | 27 | C | 55.76 % / 38.28 % | 43 | D | 41.09 % / 31.98 % | 59 | A | 40.5 % / 50.48 % | 75 | B | 42.21 % / 42.36 % |
| 12 | D | 65.93 % / 32.42 % | 28 | D | 60.08 % / 38.06 % | 44 | B | 57.04 % / 39.01 % | 60 | A | 56.59 % / 34.74 % | 76 | B | 46.61 % / 48.79 % |
| 13 | A | 53.65 % / 32.98 % | 29 | B | 69.88 % / 30.08 % | 45 | B | 19.15 % / 73.42 % | 61 | A | 48.75 % / 45.48 % | 77 | C | 31.45 % / 68.5 % |
| 14 | D | 53.08 % / 40.13 % | 30 | C | 47.4 % / 48.14 % | 46 | A | 41.51 % / 53.05 % | 62 | C | 63.86 % / 30.63 % | 78 | A | 14.8 % / 82.51 % |
| 15 | D | 69.63 % / 30.11 % | 31 | C | 46.72 % / 41.13 % | 47 | D | 12.82 % / 80.64 % | 63 | A | 52.5 % / 46.0 % | 79 | B | 19.29 % / 69.86 % |
| 16 | D | 60.26 % / 38.4 % | 32 | A | 17.02 % / 81.08 % | 48 | B | 53.5 % / 39.36 % | 64 | A | 64.24 % / 34.43 % | 80 | B | 86.79 % / 10.32 % |

| Q. | Ans. | Correct | |
|---|---|---|---|
| | | **Skipped** | |
| 81 | D | 85.96 % | |
| | | 13.26 % | |
| 82 | A | 55.37 % | |
| | | 44.0 % | |
| 83 | A | 40.02 % | |
| | | 45.14 % | |
| 84 | D | 64.8 % | |
| | | 35.0 % | |

| Q. | Ans. | Correct | |
|---|---|---|---|
| | | **Skipped** | |
| 85 | A | 67.88 % | |
| | | 30.09 % | |
| 86 | B | 48.15 % | |
| | | 44.53 % | |
| 87 | B | 80.8 % | |
| | | 14.67 % | |
| 88 | C | 45.29 % | |
| | | 35.6 % | |

| Q. | Ans. | Correct | |
|---|---|---|---|
| | | **Skipped** | |
| 89 | B | 54.22 % | |
| | | 44.48 % | |
| 90 | C | 77.08 % | |
| | | 19.14 % | |
| 91 | B | 77.99 % | |
| | | 17.62 % | |
| 92 | D | 51.99 % | |
| | | 34.03 % | |

| Q. | Ans. | Correct | |
|---|---|---|---|
| | | **Skipped** | |
| 93 | C | 48.79 % | |
| | | 32.88 % | |
| 94 | C | 54.42 % | |
| | | 43.48 % | |
| 95 | A | 67.48 % | |
| | | 31.07 % | |
| 96 | B | 55.73 % | |
| | | 31.14 % | |

| Q. | Ans. | Correct | |
|---|---|---|---|
| | | **Skipped** | |
| 97 | B | 52.73 % | |
| | | 39.42 % | |
| 98 | A | 41.25 % | |
| | | 58.75 % | |
| 99 | B | 49.33 % | |
| | | 35.39 % | |
| 100 | A | 40.19 % | |
| | | 37.49 % | |

## Performance Analysis

| | |
|---|---|
| **Avg. Score (%)** | 65.0% |
| **Toppers Score (%)** | 70.0% |
| **Your Score** | |

# //Hints and Solutions//

**1.**

Hence, the correct option is (C).

**2.**

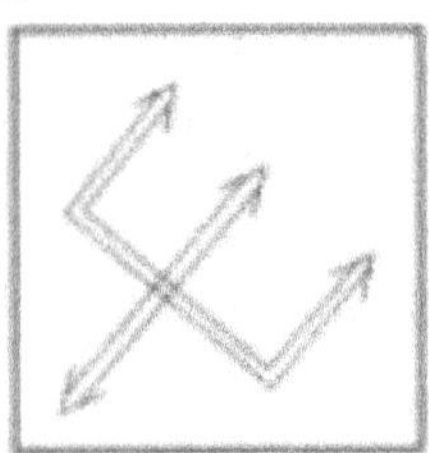

Hence, the correct option is (C).

**3.** As you can see :

H    J    I    K

$+5\downarrow$  $+5\downarrow$  $+5\downarrow$  $+5\downarrow$

M    O    N    P

Similarly,

P    R    Q    S

$+5\downarrow$  $+5\downarrow$  $+5\downarrow$  $+5\downarrow$

U    W    V    X

Hence, the correct option is (B).

**4.** (1) Book: Paper → books are made of paper.

(2) House: Bricks → house is made of bricks.

(3) Court: Lawyer → Lawyer is a part of the Court.

(4) Body: Organs → Body is made of organs.

Hence, the correct option is (C).

**5.** Iron is found in solid-state. Similarly, Mercury is found in a liquid state.

Hence, the correct option is (C).

**6.** Just as Buddhism is the main religion of China, Christianity is the largest religion in Germany with 57% of the population of the whole country.

Hence, the correct option is (D).

**7.** The pattern is,

$1^3 + 5 = 6$

$2^3 + 5 = 13$

$3^3 + 5 = 32$

$4^3 + 5 = 69$

$5^3 + 5 = 130$

$6^3 + 5 = 221$

Hence, the correct option is (A).

**8.** The sum of the digits of all the numbers is 18. But the sum of the digits of 8345 is 20, so this designation is incorrect.

$9 + 2 + 3 + 4 = 18$

**8 + 3 + 4 + 5 = 20**

$2 + 3 + 9 + 4 = 18$

$8 + 5 + 4 + 1 = 18$

Hence, the correct option is (D).

**9.** According to the pattern,

$343 × 2 = 686 - (2)^3$

$= 686 - 8$

$= 678$

Similarly,

$512 × 2 = 1024 - (2)^3$

$= 1024 - 8$

$= 1016$

Hence, the correct option is (D).

**10.** In the first three options, the third term in the series is the sum of the cubes of the first two terms. However, this is not the case in the fourth option.

$2^3 + 4^3 = 72$

$1^3 + 2^3 = 9$

$5^3 + 3^3 = 152$

$3^3 + 4^3 = 91$

Hence, the correct option is (D).

**11.** The codes for "$NUMBER$" and "$BARREN$" are as follows:

| N | U | M | B | E | R |
|---|---|---|---|---|---|
| 1 | 5 | 6 | 8 | 9 | 7 |

And,

| B | A | R | R | E | N |
|---|---|---|---|---|---|
| 8 | 4 | 7 | 7 | 9 | 1 |

According to the information given above,

| R | U | B | B | E | R |
|---|---|---|---|---|---|

| 7 | 5 | 8 | 8 | 9 | 7 |
|---|---|---|---|---|---|

Therefore, the code for " $RUBBER$ " will be $758897$.

Hence, the correct option is (B).

**12.** Options (A),(B) and (C) depicts the tools used to make a drawing whether an artist can be anyone.

Hence, the correct option is (D).

**13.** As M and T are children of U and D is the mother of T → U is the husband of D

T is a female and V is M's child → T is aunt of V

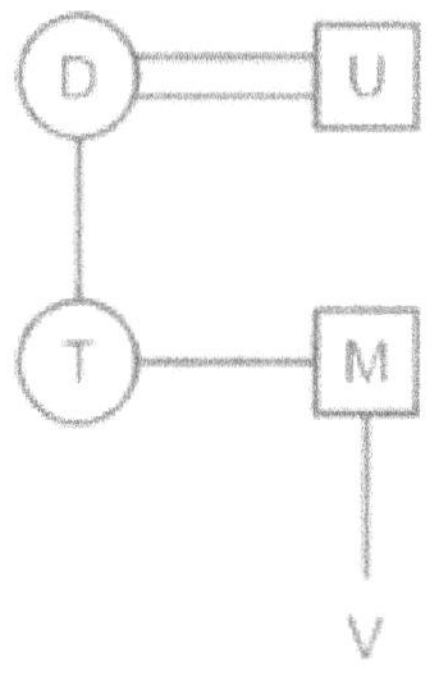

Hence, the correct option is (A).

**14.**

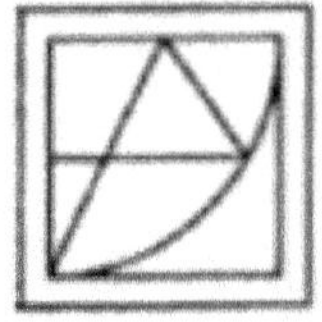

Hence, the correct option is (D).

**15.** The least possible diagram of this question is as follow,

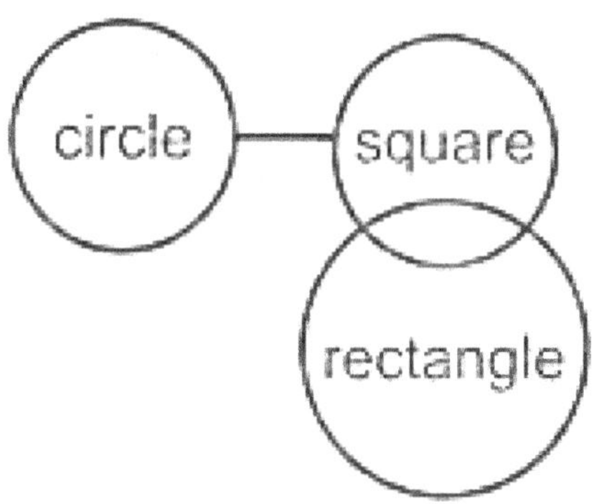


I. Some circles are rectangle → False (It is possible but not defined).

II. No circle is rectangle → False (It is possible but not defined).

But, conclusion I and II makes a complimentary pair.

Thus, either conclusion (I) or conclusion (II) follows.

Hence, the correct option is (D).

**16.** Bitter gourd is a type of vegetable. While pineapple is a type of fruit.

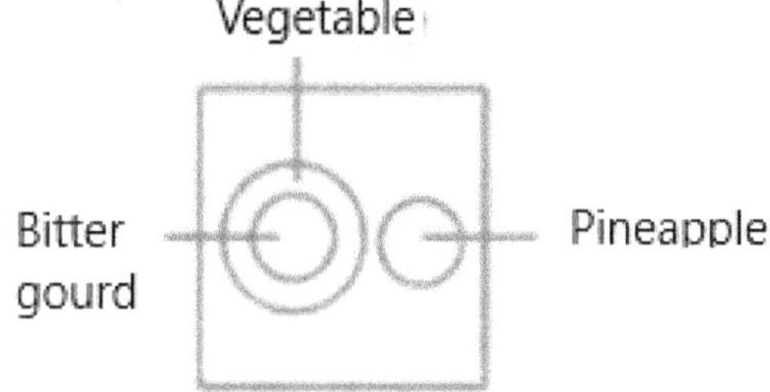


Hence, the correct option is (D).

**17.**

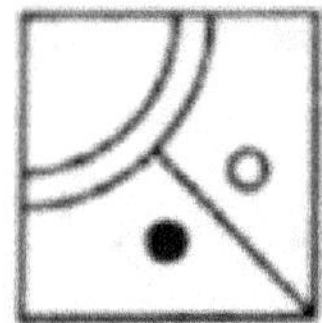

Hence, the correct option is (D).

**18.** As per the diagram, we can see that, face 3 and 4 are adjacent, face 3 and 5 are adjacent, and face 4 and 5 are adjacent, so face 3,4 and 5 are adjacent face. But as per diagram 1, face 4, and face 6 are adjacent faces.

Thus from the above, it is clear that face 5 is the opposite face of face 6.

Hence, the correct option is (B).

**19.** Changing operators as a given format.

| Symbols | Meaning |
|---|---|
| + | - |
| × | + |
| ÷ | ÷ |
| - | × |

Given expression: 86 × 12 + 53 − 18 ÷ 49

After interchanging symbols: 86 + 12 - 53 × 18 ÷ 49

= 86 + 12 − 19.46

= 78.53

Hence, the correct option is (C).

**20.** From figure (1) and figure (3), we can say that 3 and 1 are conjugate to 2 and 5.  And both the number 3 is on the downside conjugate to 2 and 5. 1 is on the upper side conjugate to 2 and 5. Now, figure (2) clearly says that number 4 is on the right (down) side of number 6 and also 4 is on the opposite side of 5.

Hence, the correct option is (B).

**21.** $L \rightarrow 59,66,78,85,97$

$E \rightarrow 01,13,20,32,44$

$A \rightarrow 00,12,24,31,43$

$S \rightarrow 02,14,21,33,40$

$T \rightarrow 03,10,22,34,41$

$\text{LEAST} \rightarrow 85,01,00,40,41$

Hence, the correct option is (A).

**22.** $P \rightarrow 55,67,79,86,98$

$O \rightarrow 56,68,75,87,99$

$L \rightarrow 59,66,78,85,97$

$A \rightarrow 00,12,24,31,43$

$R \rightarrow 57,69,76,88,95$

$POLAR \rightarrow 79,87,59,31,76$

Hence, the correct option is (C).

**23.**

In each step, one leaf is getting added on either side of line and after each two steps, the figure is rotating through an angle of 45° clockwise. During rotation, no leaf is added.

Hence, the correct option is (A).

**24.**

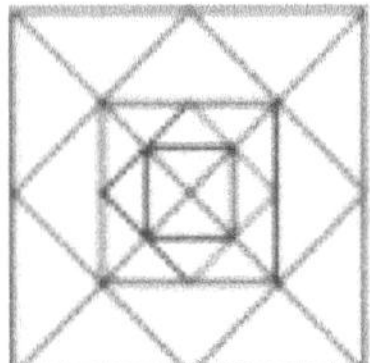

Hence, the correct option is (C).

**25.**

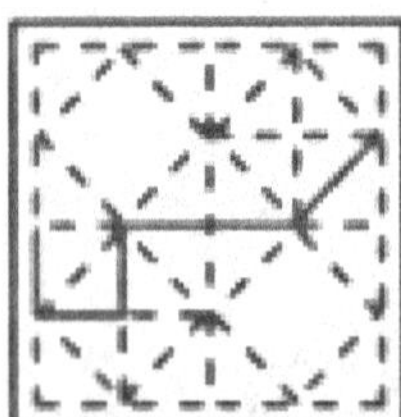

Therefore, the correct answer is 'option (C)'.

Hence, the correct option is (C).

**26.** The Central Government released the State Ranking of Swachhta Survekshan $2021$, in which Bihar is ranked $13^{th}$ among the states with more than $100$ municipal bodies, while Gaya district has been ranked $289^{th}$ out of $659$ districts across the country in the district ranking of all India. The same

Supaul has got $300^{th}$, Patna $313^{th}$ and Muzaffarpur $351^{st}$.

Hence, the correct option is (D).

**27.** Dr. Ujjwal Verma, a young scientist from Bihar and his team, has invented a new technology to identify bacteria. Dr. Ujjwal Verma, a resident of Kadamkuan Patna and Professor of Electronics and Communication Engineering at Manipal Institute of Technology, Karnataka, has seen the chemical change of sugar by putting sugar in threads and putting it in a culture dish to feed the bacteria.

Hence, the correct option is (C).

**28.** Madhabi Puri Buch has been appointed as the new the Chairperson of SEBI for a period of $3$ years.

The government has announced Madhabi Puri Buch as new the Chairperson of SEBI for a period of $3$ years. Buch is a former whole-time member of SEBI. She will succeed Ajay Tyagi, whose five-year term comes to an end. This is the first time that a woman and a person from the private sector have been chosen for a key post with SEBI.

Hence, the correct option is (D).

**29.** Yes Bank has announced its partnership with Aditya Birla Wellness Private Limited to launch the 'YES BANK Wellness' and 'YES BANK Wellness Plus' Credit Cards. It aimed at the holistic health, self-care, and wellness of consumers. This is an innovative step to encourage and promote self-care, mental and physical well-being.

Hence, the correct option is (B).

**30.** The Reserve Bank of India has constituted a working group to develop and regulate digital lending through online platforms and mobile applications. The working group will study all aspects of digital lending activities in the regulated as well as by the unregulated financial sector. The six-member panel has four RBI internal members and two external members. The panel will submit its report within three months. Jayant Kumar Dash, executive director, RBI, will be chairman of the group. Other three internal members are Ajay Kumar Choudhary, chief general manager-in-charge, Department of Supervision, P Vasudevan, chief general manager, Department of Payment and Settlement Systems, RBI, and Manoranjan Mishra, chief general manager, Department of Regulation.

Hence, the correct option is (C).

**31.** The 51st International Film Festival of India will pay tributes to the legendary filmmaker Satyajit Ray. This was announced during the Golden Jubilee edition of IFFI in 2019, by Secretary of Ministry of Information and Broadcasting Amit Khare, as part of the Centenary celebrations of Satyajit Ray. IFFI will showcase his selected films, Charulata, Ghare Baire, Pather Panchali, Shatranj Ke Khilari, and Sonar Kella as part of this tribute.

Hence, the correct option is (C).

**32.** The Centre has sanctioned Rs 37.87 crore for the facelift of Parshuram Kund pilgrimage site in Arunachal Pradesh''s Lohit district. Parshuram Kund is one of the most sacred places in the country which is visited by a large number of pilgrims throughout the year and thousands of people take a holy dip in the Lohit river during Makar Sankranti.

Hence, the correct option is (A).

**33.** Manipur Governor Dr Najma Heptulla has released a book titled "Making of a General-A Himalayan Echo" virtually on January 8, 2021. The book has been authored by (Retd) Lt General Konsam Himalay Singh. In this book, he has conveyed his dreams and views as well as also highlighted about Manipur. This book is the memoir of Lt Gen (Dr) Himalay Singh. Konark Publishers Pvt Ltd is the publisher of the book.

Hence, the correct option is (A).

**34.** India's national song 'Vande Mataram' was sung at the first session of the Congress in 1896. Vande Mataram is an excerpt from Bankim Chandra Chatterjee's novel Anand Math. It was the national anthem of India till 1937.

Hence, the correct option is (B).

**35.** Sir Charles Metcalf was the Governor-General of India from March 20, 1835, to March 4, 1936. He gave complete freedom to the press, hence he is also called the liberator of the Indian press.

Hence, the correct option is (B).

**36.** The Carthage system refers to the trade license issued by the Portuguese for maritime trade. In the 20th century, the British also introduced a system called "Navisert".

Hence, the correct option is (D).

**37.** S Vijayalakshmi is associated with Chess.

Subbaraman Vijayalakshmi born 25 March 1979 is an Indian chess player who holds the FIDE titles of International Master (IM) and Woman Grandmaster (GM), the first female player in her country to achieve these titles. She has won more medals than any other player for India in the Chess Olympiads.

Hence, the correct option is (C).

**38.** Sandeep Patil is a former Indian cricketer, Indian national age-old cricket manager, and former Kenya national team coach who guided the half-century. Who guided the Minos to the semi-finals of the 2003 World Cup. He was a middle-order batsman and an occasional medium-speed bowler. His autobiography is titled Sandy Storm.

Hence, the correct option is (C).

**39.** International Biodiversity Day is celebrated on 22 May. Its purpose is to protect biodiversity.

Hence, the correct option is (C).

**40.** Parliament has the right to make laws. Parliament can change the number of judges by law. Initially, there were 7 judges in the Supreme Court. This number increased to 10 in 1956, 13 in 1960, 17 in 1977, and 25 in 1985. Currently, the number is 31.

Hence, the correct option is (B).

**41.** A key qualification to become a judge of the Supreme Court is that the person has served as a judge of a High Court for at least 10 years.

Hence, the correct option is (A).

**42.** The vast Gangetic plains in North India are the largest alluvium deposits in the world, fertile soil is deposited on it by rivers flowing from the Himalayas. Khadar region is formed from new alluvium, it is a low altitude area.

Hence, the correct option is (C).

**43.** The Dempier-Hodges line is an imaginary line, drawn in 1829–30, the line represents the northern boundary of the Sundarbans delta. The line lies parallel to the 24 Parganas district of West Bengal.

Hence, the correct option is (D).

**44.** India produces 160 million tonnes of salt every year, India is the third-largest salt producer in the world. Gujarat, Rajasthan, Andhra Pradesh, and Tamil Nadu are the 4 major salt-producing states of India. Odisha also produces about 30,000 tonnes of salt in Ganjam, Puri, and Balasore.

Hence, the correct option is (B).

**45.** The Sixth Schedule of the Indian Constitution deals with the administration and control of Scheduled Areas and Scheduled Tribes in the states of Assam, Meghalaya, Tripura, Mizoram. Because the Sixth Schedule of the Constitution makes separate arrangements for the tribal areas of Assam, Meghalaya, Mizoram, and Tripura. Article 244 A was added to the Constitution through the 22nd Constitutional Amendment Act, 1969. It empowers the Parliament to establish an autonomous state for some tribal areas of Assam and the local legislature or the Council of Ministers or both.

Hence, the correct option is (B).

**46.** Kalidas is the author of the famous book 'Meghdoot'. Kalidas was a great Sanskrit poet and dramatist. He has composed works based on the mythology of India. His plays and poems are mainly based on the Vedas, Ramayana, Mahabharata, and Puranas.

Hence, the correct option is (A).

**47.** The Kamakhya Temple is a Hindu temple at Nilachal hills in Guwahati, Assam. it is dedicated to the mother goddess Kamakhya. it is one of the oldest and most revered centers of Tantric practices. This temple was constructed between the 8th-17th centuries.

Hence, the correct option is (D).

**48.** Ratchanok Intanon, the Badminton player of Thailand, defeated Spain's Carolina Marin in the women's singles final match of the Indonesia Masters tournament in Jakarta. This is her second win in the Indonesian Masters event after her triumph in 2010.

Ratchanok Intanon became world champion in women's singles in 2013 and became the first Thai player to become No.1 in women's singles. Carolina Marin is the present Olympic Champion and three-time World Champion.

Hence, the correct option is (B).

**49.** Rupinder Pal Singh has announced his retirement from International play, He is associated with Hockey.

He was a part of the Indian Men's Hockey Team that won the bronze medal at the Tokyo Olympics 2020. He represented India in 223 matches. He represented India in the 2014 Commonwealth Games, 2014 Asian Games at Incheon, 2016 Olympic Games held at Rio de Janeiro, and at the 2018 Commonwealth Games.

Hence, the correct option is (B).

**50.** Godavari river of India is called Vridha Ganga.

The Godavari is India's second-longest river after the Ganga. Its source is in Triambakeshwar, Maharashtra. It flows east for 1,465 kilometers, draining the states of Maharashtra, Telangana, Andhra Pradesh, Chhattisgarh, and Odisha.

Hence, the correct option is (B).

**51.** $19 \div \left[1 - \frac{1}{2} + 2\frac{2}{3}\right] = ?$

$\Rightarrow ? = 19 \div \left[1 - \frac{1}{2} + 2\frac{2}{3}\right]$

$\Rightarrow ? = 19 \div \left[3 - \frac{1}{2} + \frac{2}{3}\right]$

$\Rightarrow ? = 19 \div \left[3 - \frac{3}{6} + \frac{4}{6}\right]$

$\Rightarrow ? = 19 \div \left[3 + \frac{1}{6}\right]$

$\Rightarrow ? = 19 \div \left[\frac{19}{6}\right]$

$\Rightarrow ? = 19 \times \left[\frac{6}{19}\right]$

$\Rightarrow ? = 6$

Hence, the correct option is (B).

**52.** Let the age of three boys be $3x, 5x$ and $7x$ respectively. And the average age is $15$ years.

While the average age $= \frac{3x+5x+7x}{3}$

$15 = \frac{15x}{3}$

$\Rightarrow x = 3$

Therefore, the youngest boy's age $= 3 \times 3 = 9$ Year

Hence, the correct option is (B).

**53.** As given, the average marks obtained by 40 students of a class is 86.

$\text{Average} = \frac{\text{Sum of all digits}}{\text{Number of students}}$

First of all, we will just add the sum of the digits $= 86 \times 40 = 3440$

Now the sum which will be formed after taking out those five digits is $= 35 \times 85 = 2975$

Difference of both $= 3440 - 2975 = 465$

Now the average of five digits $= \frac{465}{5} = 93$

Hence, the correct option is (A).

**54.** Given,

$n^{th}$ inning = 11

Run scored = 108

Increase in average = 6

Desired average run number = Runs scored in last inning n - (n - 1) × Increase in average

$\Rightarrow 108 - (11 - 1) \times 6$

$\Rightarrow 108 - 60$

$\Rightarrow 48$ run

Hence, the correct option is (D).

**55.** Let the number of students in the three classes is $2x, 3x$ and $4x$.

The number of students will be $(2x + 12)$, $(3x + 12)$ and $(4x + 12)$ after increasing 12 students in each class.

So, $\frac{2x+12}{3x+12} = \frac{8}{11}$

$\Rightarrow x = 18$

So the number of students $= 2x + 3x + 4x$

$\Rightarrow 2 \times 18 + 3 \times 18 + 4 \times 18$

$\Rightarrow 162$

Hence, the correct option is (D).

**56.** Let A have income $4x$ and expenditure $3x$.

And B has income $3x$ and expenditure $2x$.

According to the given formula,

Income - Expenditure = Saving

$\Rightarrow 4x - 3x = 6000$

$\Rightarrow x = 6000$

Annual income of A $= 6000 \times 4 = 24000$

Annual income of B $= 6000 \times 3 = 18000$

Hence, the correct option is (D).

**57.** Given that, due to shortage of labor in a factory, its production decrease = $25\%$

Hence the working period $= \frac{25}{100-25} \times 100$

$\Rightarrow 33\frac{1}{3}\%$

Hence, the correct option is (D).

**58.** Given that, 40% of the students in an exam fail in Mathematics, 30% fail in English. 10% fail in both subjects.

Total unsuccessful students = 40% + 30% - 10% = 60%

Hence, students passing in both the subjects = 100 - 60 = 40%

Hence, the correct option is (D).

**59.** Given that,

$$a + b = 1$$

On cubing both sides,

$$\Rightarrow (a + b)^3 = 1^3$$

$$\Rightarrow a^3 + b^3 + 3ab(a + b) = 1$$

$$\Rightarrow a^3 + b^3 + 3ab = 1$$

$$\Rightarrow k = 1$$

Hence, the correct option is (A).

**60.** Let Ronit's present age be $x$ years.

Then, father's present age $= (x + 3x)$ years $= 4x$ years

$$\therefore (4x + 8) = \frac{5}{2}(x + 8)$$

$$\Rightarrow 8x + 16 = 5x + 40$$

$$\Rightarrow 3x = 24$$

$$\Rightarrow x = 8$$

$\therefore$ Required ratio $= \dfrac{(4x+16)}{(x+16)}$

$$\Rightarrow \frac{48}{24} = 2$$

Hence, the correct option is (A).

**61.** It is given that, there is a loss of 30% after selling a pen for Rs. 56.

We know that,

$$CP = \left[\frac{100}{(100 - \text{Loss percent})}\right] \times SP$$

$$SP = \left[\frac{(100 + \text{Profit percent})}{100}\right] \times CP$$

Therefore, according to the question,

$$CP = \left[\frac{100}{(100 - 30)}\right] \times 56$$

$$= \left(\frac{100}{70}\right) \times 56$$

$$= \text{Rs. } 80$$

Now, $SP = \left[\dfrac{(100 + 20)}{100}\right] \times 80$

$$= \left(\frac{6}{5}\right) \times 80$$

$$= \text{Rs. } 96$$

$\therefore$ The pen will be sold at Rs. 96 to get a profit of 20%.

Hence, the correct option is (A).

**62.** $40\%$ of $265 + 35\%$ of $180 = 50\%$ of $? + 80\%$ of $?$

$$\Rightarrow \frac{40 \times 265}{100} + \frac{35 \times 180}{100} = \frac{50 \times ?}{100} + \frac{? \times 80}{100}$$

$$\Rightarrow 106 + 63 = \frac{?}{2} + \frac{? \times 4}{5}$$

$$\Rightarrow 169 = \frac{? \times 5 + ? \times 8}{10}$$

$$\Rightarrow 13 \times ? = 169 \times 10$$

$$\therefore ? = \frac{169 \times 10}{13} = 130$$

Hence, the correct option is (C).

**63.** Given, Mohan can do any work separately in 10 days and Sohan in 15 days.

Work done by Sohan in 1 day $= \dfrac{1}{5}$

Work done by Sohan in 3 days $= \dfrac{3}{15} = \dfrac{1}{5}$

Hence remaining work $= 1 - \dfrac{1}{5} = \dfrac{4}{5}$

Mohan does 1 work in 10 days.

so, $\dfrac{4}{5}$ will do the work $= 10 \times \dfrac{4}{5} = 8$ days

Hence, the correct option is (A).

**64.** Given:

Working $8$ hours a day, Ashu can prepare a book for $18$ days.

So, working $1$ hour a day, Ashu can complete the work in $= 18 \times 8 = 144$ days

$\therefore$ Number of hours Ashu should work to complete the work in $12$ days $= \dfrac{144}{12} = 12$ hours $/$ day

Hence, the correct option is (A).

**65.** Given,

The speed of the current is $1.25x$ km/hr.

And the speed of a boat in still water is $12$ km/hr more than that of current.

According to the question,

The speed of a boat $+$ The speed of the current $= \dfrac{\text{Distance}}{\text{(Time taken by the boat)}}$

$$1.25x + 1.25x + 12 = \frac{160}{5}$$

Or, $2.5x = 20$

Or, $x = 8$

Hence, the correct option is (A).

**66.** Let be the length and breadth of a rectangle $x$ cm and $(x + 4)$ cm respectively.

Given,

The area of the rectangle $= 45$ cm²

$x(x + 4) = 45$

$\Rightarrow x^2 + 4x - 45 = 0$

$\Rightarrow (x + 9)(x - 5) = 0$

$\Rightarrow x = 5$

So, the length $= x = 5$ cm

And the breadth $= x + 4$

$\Rightarrow 5 + 4 = 9$ cm

Perimeter = 2(length + breadth )

$\Rightarrow 2(9 + 5)$

$\Rightarrow 28$ cm

Hence, the correct option is (D).

**67.** The boat moves 10 km/h in the opposite direction of the stream to the person. And its speed in the direction of the stream is 16 km/h

According to the given formula,

Speed of boat in calm water

$= \dfrac{\text{(Speed in the current of the stream + Speed in the opposite direction of the stream)}}{2}$

Speed of boat in calm water $= \dfrac{10+16}{2} = 13$ km/h

Hence, the correct option is (B).

**68.** Given,

$464 \div (16 \times 29) + 4\frac{1}{2} = ?$

$\Rightarrow 464 \times \dfrac{1}{16 \times 29} + 4.5 = ?$

$\Rightarrow 1 + 4.5 = ?$

$\Rightarrow ? = 5.5$

Hence, the correct option is (D).

**69.** The number is 10,000, as given.

By factor

$32 = 2 \times 2 \times 2 \times 2 \times 2$

$36 = 2 \times 2 \times 3 \times 3$

$48 = 2 \times 2 \times 2 \times 2 \times 3$

$54 = 2 \times 3 \times 3 \times 3$

Thus the LCM of 32, 36, 48 and 54 = 2 × 2 × 2 × 2 × 2 × 3 × 3 × 3

$\Rightarrow 864$

Thus, that number is very large = 10,000 - 864 = 9136

Hence, the correct option is (A).

**70.** Suppose the largest number is $x$, and by dividing 38,45 and 52, 2,3 and 4 are left respectively.

Absolute Number = $x$

$\Rightarrow$ HCF of $(38 - 2), (45 - 3), (52 - 4)$

$\Rightarrow$ HCFof $36, 42, 48 = 6$

$\Rightarrow x = 6$

Hence, the correct option is (B).

**71.** Given,

$14 \times ? + 695 = 36\%$ of $2400 + 755$

$\Rightarrow ? \times 14 + 695 = \dfrac{36}{100} \times 2400 + 755$

$\Rightarrow ? \times 14 = 864 + 755 - 695$

$\Rightarrow ? = \dfrac{924}{14}$

$\Rightarrow ? = 66$

Hence, the correct option is (B).

**72.**

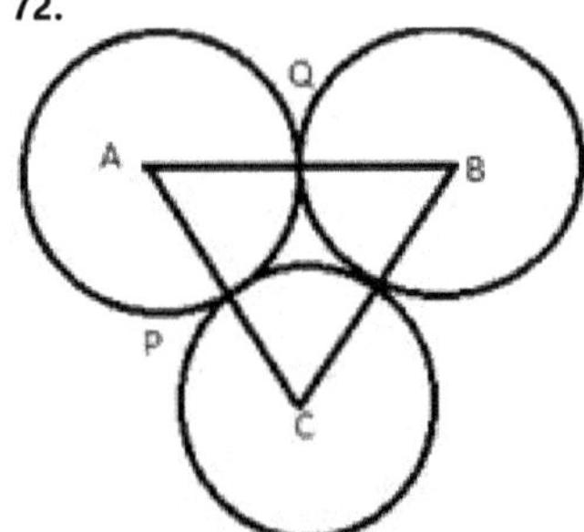


Given,

Radius of circle = $3.5$ cm

Side of equilateral triangle = 3.5 + 3.5 = 7 cm

In equilateral triangle, the angle $(\theta)$ will be 60°.

Area of sector APQ $= \dfrac{(\pi r^2 \theta)}{360}$

Area enclosed = Area of equilateral triangle -3 × Area of sector APQ

$= \dfrac{\sqrt{3}}{4} \times (7)^2 - 3 \times \pi \times (3.5)^2 \times \dfrac{60}{360}$

$$= \frac{\sqrt{3}}{4} \times 49 - 3 \times \pi \times 3.5 \times 3.5 \times \frac{1}{6}$$

$$= \frac{49}{8}\left(2\sqrt{3} - \pi\right)$$

Hence area enclosed be $= \frac{49}{8}\left(2\sqrt{3} - \pi\right)$ square unit

Hence, the correct option is (C).

**73.** Given,

Let $(x - a)$ is the factor of both quadratic equation.

Then $x = a$ will satisfy both the equation.

So, $a^2 - 5a + \alpha = 0$ ........ (i)

$a^2 - 7a + 2\alpha = 0$ ........ (ii)

Substracting equation (i) from equation (ii)

$$2a - \alpha = 0$$

$$\Rightarrow \alpha = 2a$$

Now from equation (i)

$$a^2 - 5a + 2a = 0$$

$$\Rightarrow a^2 - 3a = 0$$

$$\Rightarrow a = 3, a \neq 0$$

$$\Rightarrow \alpha = 2a = 6$$

Hence, the correct option is (A).

**74.** Area of field $= \dfrac{225}{75} = 300$

Suppose the length of a rectangular field is $4x$ and $3x$.

According to question,

$$\Rightarrow 4x \times 3x = 300$$

$$\Rightarrow 12x^2 = 300$$

$$\Rightarrow x^2 = 25$$

$$\Rightarrow x = 5$$

Perimeter of a rectangular field $= 2(l + b)$

$$\Rightarrow 2(4 \times 5 + 3 \times 5) = 2(35)$$

$$\Rightarrow 70$$

Hence, the correct option is (D).

**75.** Given, the selling price of an article is Rs. 1920 and the discount given is $4\%$.

Let the marked price of the item is $x$.

$$\Rightarrow 96\% \text{ of } x = 1920$$

$$\Rightarrow \frac{x \times 96}{100} = 1920$$

$x = $ Rs. $2000$

Hence, the correct option is (B).

**76.** The imperative sentences which are used to give orders should start with 'let' in the passive voice and the form of the verb should be 'be + V3'.

Therefore, the correct passive voice of the sentence will be option B, i.e., 'Let the windows be closed for fear of rain'.

Hence, the correct option is (B).

**77.** US send first successful manned trip to the moon on July 20, 1969.

According to the passage, "Long before Neil Armstrong and Edwin Aldrin stepped out of Apollo 11 onto the surface of the moon 50 years ago, on July 20, 1969 , the aspiration to travel to this shiny orb in the sky has fired human imagination."

Hence, the correct option is (C).

**78.** As can be read from the first two lines, it was Baron Munchausen who first spoke of travel to the moon in the 18th century, much before than the actual manned mission was sent to the moon.

Hence, the correct option is (A).

**79.** According to the passage, some writers imagined the moon's surface to be barren and uninhabited whereas others have written about it being populated with lunar beings.

Hence, the correct option is (B).

**80.** Uncouth: Rude or socially unacceptable

Rough: Not smooth, soft or level

Ungraceful: Lacking grace; clumsy

Slovenly: Lazy, careless, and untidy

Dirty: Not clean

Hence, the correct option is (B).

**81.** Error: Mistake

Blunder: To make a stupid mistake

Misadventure: An unfortunate incident

Misgiving: A feeling of doubt or apprehension about the outcome or consequences of something

Ambiguity: The quality of being open to more than one interpretation

Hence, the correct option is (D).

**82.** Elusive: Difficult to find, catch, or achieve

The sentence is:

Women walk miles on the blazing sands in search of an elusive pot of water.

Here Elusive is used as an adjective.

Hence, the correct option is (A).

**83.** Hersey: An (religious) opinion or belief that is different from what is generally accepted to be true

Agreement: The state of agreeing with somebody

Error: Mistake

Rash: An area of small red spots that appear on your skin when you are ill or have a reaction to something

Hence, the correct option is (A).

**84.** Provoke: To cause a particular feeling or reaction

Soothe: To make somebody calmer or less upset

Insult: To speak or act rudely to somebody

Anger: The strong feeling that you have when something has happened or somebody has done something that you do not like

Encourage: To inspire with courage

Hence, the correct option is (D).

**85.** To complain loudly against, is the correct meaning of the given idiom.

**Example:**

People around the world are crying out against the government's civil rights abuses.

Hence, the correct option is (A).

**86.** The sentence suggests that the blank should contain a word that is a conjunction as it joins the two sentences.

The sentence uses the conjunction phrase 'Scarcely had ..... when. It is used to show two things happening right after one another.

e.g. Scarcely had I finished my lunch when the teacher came back.

The appropriate word that completes the phrase is 'when'.

Hence, the correct option is (B).

**87.** The sentence suggests that the blank should contain conjunction as it binds the two sentences.

The conjunction should also reflect the possibility that the sentence implies, with conditional conjunction, in this case- if.

The only option that gives the intended meaning is 'If'.

Hence, the correct option is (B).

**88.** "A Perfect Storm" means "The worst possible situation".

**Example:**

Through some perfect storm of wars, downturns, and disasters, the once-sunny outlook turned dark.

Hence, the correct option is (C).

**89.** "Deteriorating" is correctly spelled. This word means "To become worse".

Example:

The political tension is deteriorating into civil war.

Hence, the correct option is (B).

**90.** Among the given phrases, the correct replacement of the highlighted phrase will be "when suddenly his room filled with light".

'When' will be used in the form of conjunction for indicting the 'time' in simple tense.

The preposition 'with' is used as "by means of" comes before an INSTRUMENT (light) whereas 'By' as a preposition indicates the way of doing something (action).

Hence, the correct option is (C).

**91.** Numismatist is the study or collection of currency, which includes coins, tokens, paper money, and relatable objects. The meanings of the other words are:

Archaeologist: A person who studies human history, particularly the culture of historic and prehistoric people, through discovery and exploration of remains, structures, and writings, etc.

Philatelist: A person who collects or studies stamps

Connoisseur: An expert judge in matters of taste

Hence, the correct option is (B).

**92.** Diligent = Quietly and steadily continuing a task despite any difficulties

Different = Unlike in nature, quality, form, or degree.

Disciplined = Obeying the rules.

Dexterous = Skillful in physical movements; especially of the hands

Hence, the correct option is (D).

**93.** Two complete events occurred, rescue happened first hence it will be expressed in the past perfect tense, 'had rescued' will be the correct usage.

Hence, the correct option is (C).

**94.** If some action has started in the past and is still continuing, then present perfect continuous tense should be used instead of present continuous tense. So, the phrase 'am waiting' needs to be replaced with 'have been waiting' to make the sentence contextually correct.

Thus, the correct formation would be, 'I have been waiting for three – quarters of an hour'.

Hence, the correct option is (C).

**95.** Q is first because it has the subject, the comparison is always in order 'as free as'. Thus, S follows R.

Then the sentence is: "I was as free as a tramp."

Hence, the correct option is (A).

**96.** P is first, since it contains the subject followed by the auxiliary verb in R, the is followed by first-degree adjective S and not a verb.

The sentence is:

The narcissus is the first to bloom.

Hence, the correct option is (B).

**97.** If something is "derived from" something else, it means it came from there; originated there.

To take something, especially something necessary or pleasant, away from someone: He claimed that he had been "deprived" of his freedom/rights.

A "derisive" noise, expression, or remark expresses contempt. There was a short, derisive laugh. Synonyms: mocking, ridiculing, jeering,

This medicine is derived from a tropical plant.

Hence, the correct option is (B).

**98.** The verb "impact" means to affect something.

"Impede" something to delay or stop the progress of something synonym hinder, hamper.

 If something "impresses" you, you feel great admiration for it. What impressed him most was their speed.

The new law will impact the entire community. Everyone will be affected.

Hence, the correct option is (A).

**99.** The indefinite article (an) is used before a noun that is general or when its identity is not known.

Then the sentence is,

She wants to become an engineer.

Hence, the correct option is (B).

**100.** Exhaustion: The state of being extremely tired

An adjective is a word that tells us more about a noun. It "describes" or "modifies" a noun. And the adjective form of Exhaustion is **Exhausted.**

Hence, the correct option is (A).

# Mock Test 02

## General Intelligence & Reasoning

**Ques (1-2):Direction:** Study the following figure and answer the question given below.

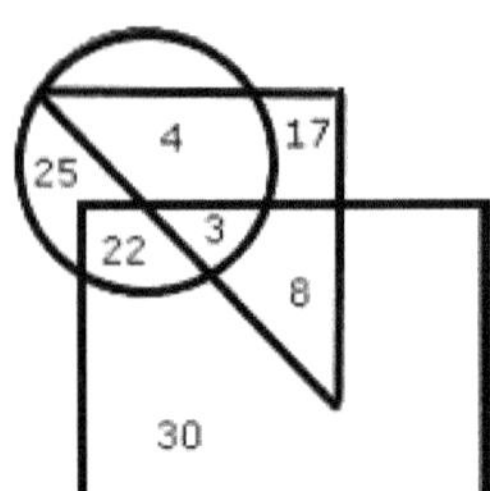

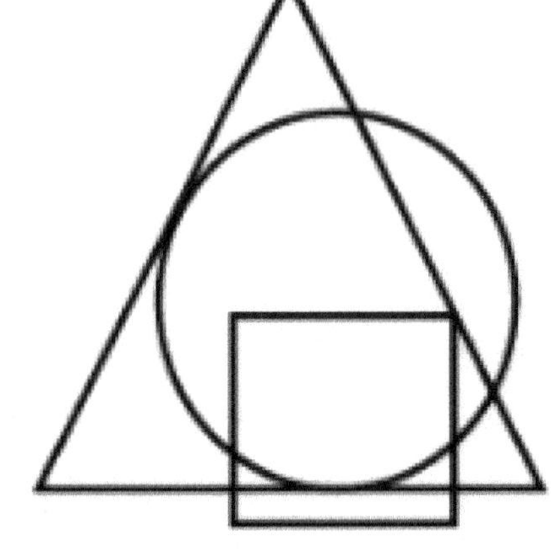
**B.**

**Q.1** How many doctors are neither artists nor players?

**A.** 17     **B.** 5     **C.** 10     **D.** 30

**Q.2** How many doctors are both players and artists ?

**A.** 22     **B.** 8     **C.** 3     **D.** 30

**Q.3 Direction:** From amongst the figures marked (A), (B), (C) and (D) select the figure which satisfies the same conditions of placement of dots as in figure (X).

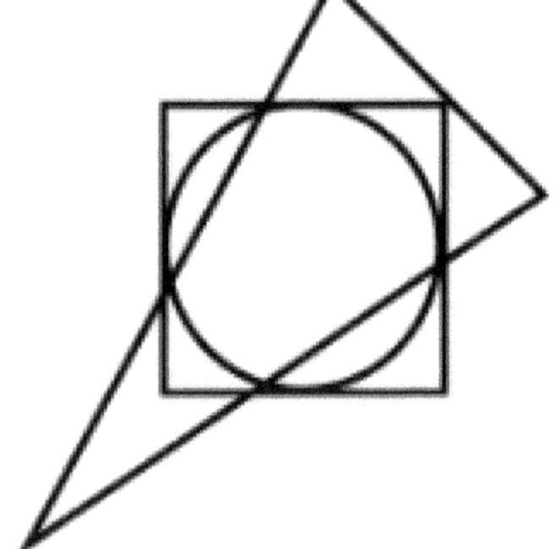
**C.**

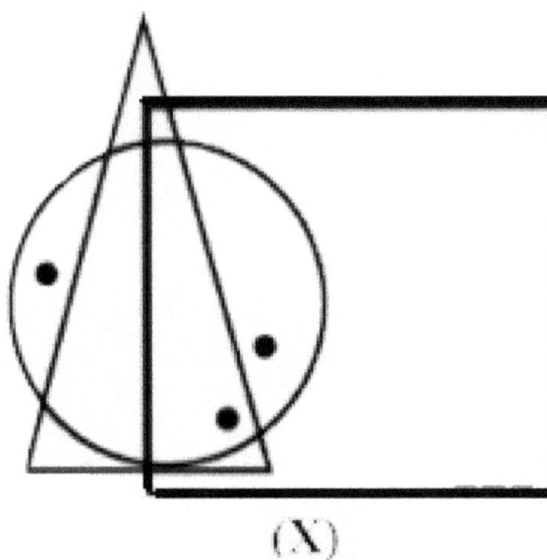

(X)

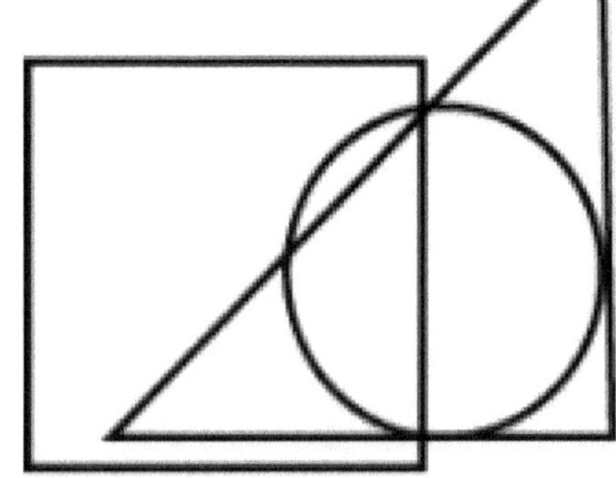
**D.**

**A.**

**Q.4 Direction:** In the following question, select the related word from given alternatives.

India : Bengal Tiger :: USA : ?

**A.** Kangaroo     **B.** Emu

**C.** Bison     **D.** Snow Leopard

**Q.5**

**Direction:** Two positions of a dice are shown. When 4 is at the bottom, what number will be on the top?

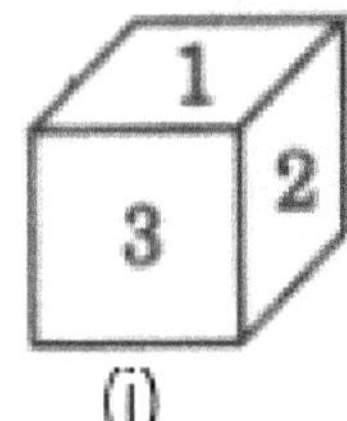 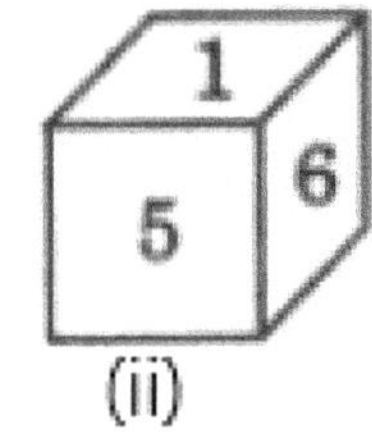
(i)  (ii)

**A.** 1　　**B.** 2　　**C.** 3　　**D.** 4

**Q.6** If "DINNER" is coded as 8 then how will "LETTER" be coded as

**A.** 0　　**B.** 10　　**C.** 1　　**D.** 2

**Q.7** Select the odd letters from the given alternatives.

**A.** BDF　　**B.** JBA　　**C.** HBF　　**D.** BFF

**Q.8** In the following question, select the odd word pair from the given alternatives.

**A.** Mother - Sister　　**B.** Father - Son
**C.** Son - Daughter　　**D.** Friend - Sister

**Q.9 Direction:** A series is given with one term missing. Select the correct alternative from the given ones that will complete the series.

10, 12, 8, 10, 6, 8, 4, ?, 2, 4, 0

**A.** 5　　**B.** 7　　**C.** 6　　**D.** 3

**Q.10 Direction:** A series is given with one term missing. Select the correct alternative from the given ones that will complete the series.

KLCQ, PPFS, UTIU, ?

**A.** AYLW　　**B.** AXLW　　**C.** ZXLW　　**D.** ZXMW

**Q.11 Direction:** Which of the following terms follows the trend of the given list?

PQPQPQPQPQ, RQPQPQPQPQ, RSPQPQPQPQ, RSRQPQPQPQ, RSRSPQPQPQ, ________.

**A.** RSRSRSPQ　　**B.** PQPQPQPQ
**C.** RQPQPQPQ　　**D.** RSRSRQPQ

**Q.12** In certain language, CHIT is coded as CIHT. How is READ coded in that language?

**A.** RDEA　　**B.** ARED　　**C.** RAED　　**D.** DEAR

**Q.13** If 'cloud' means 'blue', 'land' means 'brown', 'street' means 'black', 'flower' means 'red' and 'bird' means 'flying' then tell where the red would be planted?

**A.** Brown　　**B.** Blue　　**C.** Black　　**D.** Flying

**Q.14**

**Direction:** A dice is rolled twice and the two positions are shown in the figure below. What is the number of dots at the bottom face when the dice is in position (i)?

(i)　　　(ii)

**A.** 1
**B.** 5
**C.** 6
**D.** Cannot be determined

**Ques (15-16):Direction:** Study the following information carefully and answer the question given below:

In a family, P is married to R. They have 3 daughters, S, U, and V. S is married to X, U is married to K and V is married to L. J is the daughter of S and X. K and U have one daughter D. V, with L, has 2 daughters and each daughter has one brother.

**Q.15** How many female members are present?

**A.** 7　　**B.** 9　　**C.** 8　　**D.** 4

**Q.16** What is the total number of family members present?

**A.** 10　　**B.** 16　　**C.** 13　　**D.** 12

**Ques (17-19):Direction:** In the following question, you are given a figure (X) followed by four alternative figures (1), (2), (3) and (4) such that figure (X) is embedded in one of them. Trace out the alternative figure which contains figure (X) as its part.

**Q.17**

Find out the alternative figure which contains figure (X) as its part.

 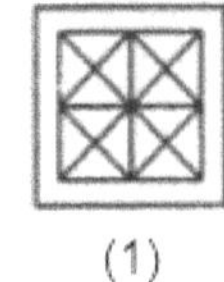 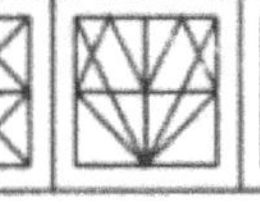 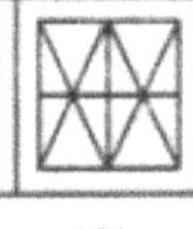 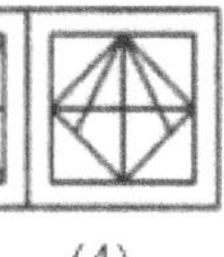
(X)　　(1)　　(2)　　(3)　　(4)

**A.** (1)　　**B.** (2)　　**C.** (3)　　**D.** (4)

**Q.18** Find out the alternative figure which contains figure (X) as its part.

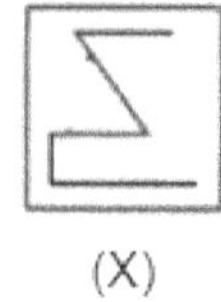 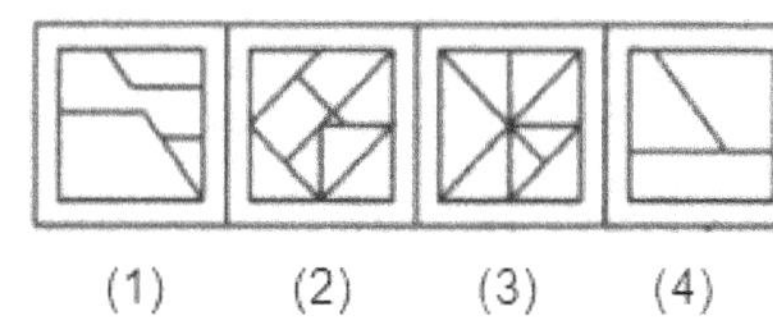
(X)　　(1)　　(2)　　(3)　　(4)

*[SSC Sub Inspector (CPO), 2020]*

**A.** (1)　　**B.** (2)　　**C.** (3)　　**D.** (4)

**Q.19**

Find out the alternative figure which contains figure (X) as its part.

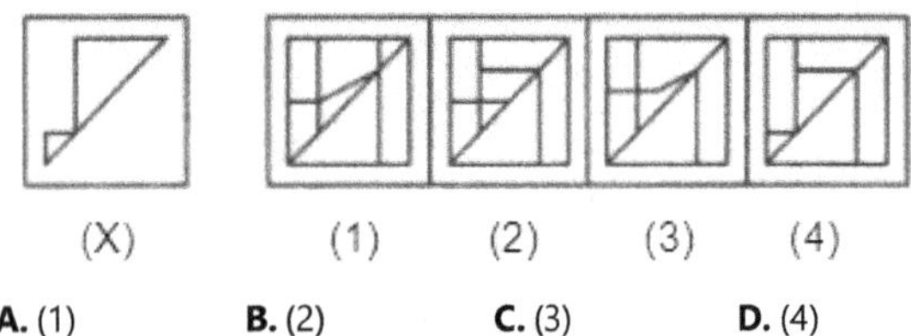

**A.** (1)  **B.** (2)  **C.** (3)  **D.** (4)

**Q.20 Direction:** If a mirror is placed on the line AB, then which of the following figures is the right – image of the given figure?

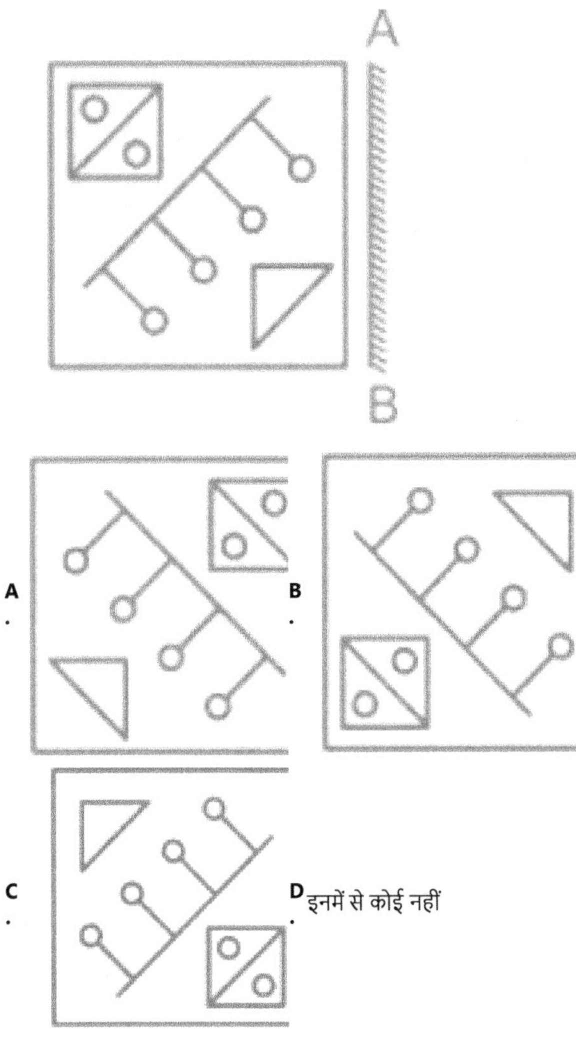

D. इनमें से कोई नहीं

**C.** 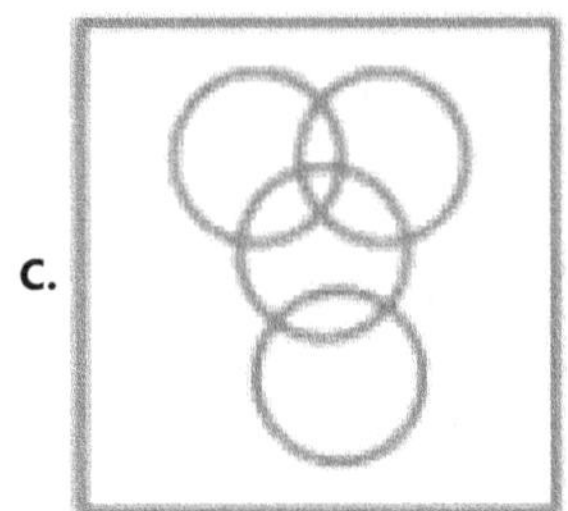  **D.** 

**Ques (22-24):Direction:** The columns and rows of Matrix I are numbered from 0 to 4 and those of Matrix II from 5 to 9. A letter from these matrices can be represented first by its row and then the column number e.g., in the matrices for questions 1 to 4, M can be represented by 14, 21 etc.; 0 can be represented by 20,32 etc. Similarly you have to identify the correct set for the word given in the question.

**Matrix-I**

|   | 0 | 1 | 2 | 3 | 4 |
|---|---|---|---|---|---|
| 0 | F | A | N | O | I |
| 1 | I | O | F | A | N |
| 2 | A | N | O | I | F |
| 3 | O | F | I | N | A |
| 4 | N | I | A | F | O |

**Matrix-II**

|   | 5 | 6 | 7 | 8 | 9 |
|---|---|---|---|---|---|
| 5 | S | E | H | B | T |
| 6 | H | S | E | T | B |
| 7 | B | T | S | E | H |
| 8 | E | H | T | B | S |
| 9 | T | S | E | H | B |

**Q.21 Direction:** Identify the diagram that best represents the relationship among the classes given below.

Wheat, Tea, Plant and Coffee

**A.** 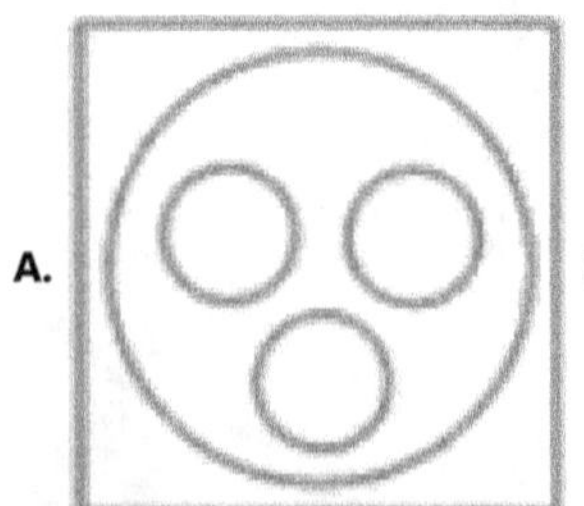  **B.** 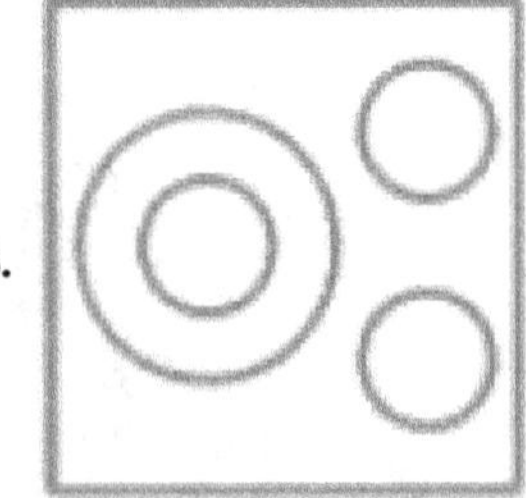

**Q.22 NEST**
**A.** 02, 56, 55, 59  **B.** 14, 67, 66, 67
**C.** 21, 76, 77, 76  **D.** 33, 85, 88, 86

**Q.23 FAITH**
**A.** 43, 42, 41, 78, 89  **B.** 24, 31, 10, 59, 57
**C.** 31, 34, 23, 76, 79  **D.** 12, 20, 40, 68, 65

**Q.24 FINE**
**A.** 31, 32 33, 82  **B.** 24, 19, 21, 78
**C.** 12, 10, 13, 67  **D.** 00, 04, 02, 56

**Q.25 Direction:** Study the diagram given below and answer the following question.

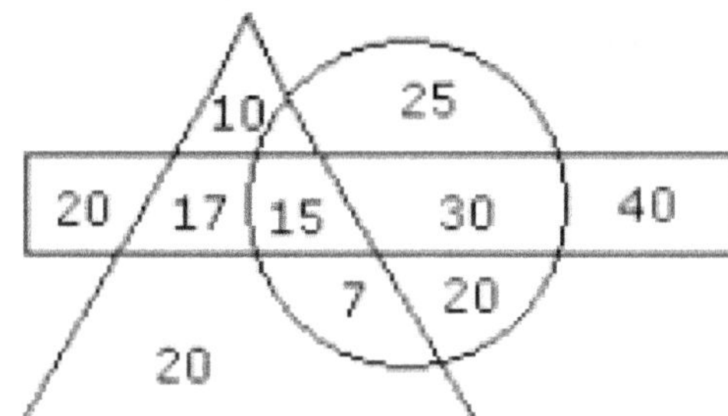


△  ⟶ Persons who takes tea

○  ⟶ Persons who takes coffee

▭  ⟶ Persons who takes wine

How many persons who take tea and wine but not coffee?
**A.** 20        **B.** 17        **C.** 25        **D.** 15

# General Awareness

**Q.26** The first train was successfully test-fired between which country's railway link from Bihar's Madhubani district?
**A.** Nepal        **B.** Bhopal
**C.** Bihar        **D.** Allahabad

**Q.27** Where has the only Genome Sequencing Lab in the Bihar started?
*[Delhi Forest Guard, 2021]*

**A.** Patna        **B.** Darbhanga
**C.** Gaya        **D.** Vaishali

**Q.28** Who has been named the 2022 Laureus Sportsman of the Year?
*[Delhi Forest Guard, 2021]*

**A.** Marcel Hug
**B.** Max Verstappen
**C.** Rafael Nadal
**D.** Robert Lewandowski

**Q.29** In which of the following countries did Prime Minister Narendra Modi start 'Ramayana Circuit' on May 11, 2018?
*[Super TET Paper - I, 2019]*

**A.** Nepal        **B.** Indonesia
**C.** Sri Lanka        **D.** Myanmar

**Q.30** Which of the following sports is the term" butterfly stroke" associated with?
**A.** Tennis        **B.** Volleyball
**C.** Wrestling        **D.** Swimming

**Q.31** Who is the author of the book "The Kingdom of God is Within You"?

**A.** Leo Tolstoy        **B.** Henry David
**C.** Mahatma Gandhi        **D.** John Ruskin

**Q.32** What is the disinvestment target for 2020-21?
**A.** 1,73,000 crores        **B.** 2,10,000 crores
**C.** 65,000 crores        **D.** 1,05,000 crores

**Q.33** Which among the following defines the model in which the banks sell the insurance products of their partner insurance company?
**A.** Bancassurance        **B.** Banking Assurance
**C.** Bank Assurance        **D.** Insurance Banking

**Q.34** Who was the first Tirthankara of Jainism?
**A.** Arishtanemi        **B.** Parshvanath
**C.** Ajitanath        **D.** Rishabha

**Q.35** Who among the following led the Khasi Tribal Movement against the British?
**A.** Raja Jagannath        **B.** Sewaram
**C.** Gomadhar Kunwar        **D.** Tirut Singh

**Q.36** Who was the founder of "The Asiatic Society"?
**A.** Sir William Jones        **B.** Sir John Marshall
**C.** R. D. Banerjee        **D.** Sir William Bentick

**Q.37** The objective of Union Budget 2020-21-
I. Achieving smooth delivery through digital governance
II. Improvement in physical quality of life through National Infrastructure Pipeline
**A.** Only I        **B.** I, II only
**C.** II only        **D.** Neither I nor II

**Q.38** Fiscal policy is concerned with _______.
**A.** Public revenue
**B.** Public expenditure and debt
**C.** Bank rate policy
**D.** Both (A) and (B)

**Q.39** Right to Education became a fundamental right on _______.
**A.** March 15, 2010        **B.** April 1, 2010
**C.** July 17, 2010        **D.** October 10, 2010

**Q.40** By which of the following institution is the "Moortidevi Sahitya Puraskar" awarded?
**A.** Ministry of HRD, Central Governmnet
**B.** Sahitya Academy
**C.** Bharatiya Jnanpith Trust
**D.** Bharatiya Vidya Bhavan

**Q.41** Who is the author of 'India Vince Freedom'?
**A.** Maulana Azad        **B.** Dominic Lapierre
**C.** Abdul Gaffar Khan        **D.** Jawaharlal Nehru

**Q.42** Jamini Roy distinguished himself in the field of _______.
**A.** Badminton        **B.** Painting
**C.** Theatre        **D.** Sculpture

**Q.43** 'Saddle Peak' the highest peak of Andaman and Nicobar Islands is located in _______.

**A.** Great Nicobar  
**B.** Middle Andaman  
**C.** Little Andaman  
**D.** North Andaman

**Q.44** Who was appointed as the Chief Executive Officer of IDFC First Bank Ltd?

**A.** Aditya Puri  
**B.** Sandeep Bakshi  
**C.** V. A. Prasanth  
**D.** V Vaidyanathan

**Q.45** The Insurance Regulatory and Development Authority of India has been granted the powers to frame rules for the insurance sector in India under _______ of the Insurance Act 1938.

**A.** Section 114  
**B.** Section 114A  
**C.** Section 112  
**D.** Section 115A

**Q.46** What is the name of India's research station in the Arctic region?

**A.** Dakshin Gangotri  
**B.** Maitri  
**C.** Himadri  
**D.** None of these

**Q.47** Article 19 of the Indian Constitution provides _______.

**A.** 6 freedom  
**B.** 7 freedom  
**C.** 8 freedom  
**D.** 9 freedom

**Q.48** When is World Theater Day celebrated?

**A.** 25 March  
**B.** 26 March  
**C.** 27 March  
**D.** 28 March

**Q.49** "Law of demand" implies that when there is excess demand for a commodity, then _______.

**A.** Price of the commodity falls  
**B.** Price of the commodity remains same  
**C.** Price of the commodity rises  
**D.** Quantity demanded of the commodity falls

**Q.50** On which of the following rivers is the Alamatti Dam constructed?

**A.** Kaveri  
**B.** Seeleru  
**C.** Krishna  
**D.** Tungabhadra

# Quantitative Aptitude

**Q.51** A group of $150$ men can do work in a certain number of days. If the first day all men work together, second-day $4$ men leave the work, the third day another $4$ men leave the work and so on. In this process, the group takes $8$ days more. Find the number of days taken by the group.

**A.** 15 days  **B.** 35 days  **C.** 45 days  **D.** 25 days

**Q.52** The roots of quadratic equation $2x^2 + x + 4 = 0$ are:

**A.** Positive and negative  
**B.** Both Positive  
**C.** Both Negative  
**D.** No real roots

**Q.53** If $x = 3 - 3^{\frac{1}{3}} + 3^{\frac{2}{3}}$, then find the value of $x^3 - 9x^2 + 36x + 10$.

**A.** 50  **B.** 60  **C.** 80  **D.** 0

**Q.54** A dishonest shopkeeper makes cheating of $25\%$ at the time of buying the goods and $37.5\%$ cheating at the time of selling the goods. He promises to sell his goods at $15\%$ loss. Find the profit percentage.

**A.** 60%  **B.** 70%  **C.** 50%  **D.** 80%

**Q.55** Find the number of prime factors in the expression $18^2 \times 17^3 \times 45^3 \times 23^2 \times 29$.

**A.** 20  **B.** 21  **C.** 22  **D.** 23

**Q.56** What is the difference in interest when a person invests a sum of Rs. $1500$ for $2$ years at Simple rate of interest of $10\%$ and the same money for same time and the rate is compounded yearly?

**A.** Rs. 5  **B.** Rs. 15  **C.** Rs. 25  **D.** Rs. 35

**Q.57** A trader bought two cycles for Rs. 1800, if he sold first cycle at 15% profit and second at 25% profit, he earns a profit of Rs. 351, and if he sold first cycle at 25% profit and second at 15% profit, he gain Rs. 18 more. Find the cost price of both the cycles.

**A.** Rs. 990 and Rs. 810  
**B.** Rs. 810 and Rs. 990  
**C.** Rs. 900 and Rs. 900  
**D.** Rs. 1000 and Rs. 800

**Q.58** A train crosses a platform half of its length with a speed of $72$ km/hr in $1$ minutes, then find in how much time it will cross another train of double length which is standing on the platform with $60\%$ of its speed.

**A.** 100 second  
**B.** 150 second  
**C.** 200 second  
**D.** 250 second

**Q.59** The roots of $100x^2 - 20x + 1 = 0$ is:

**A.** $\frac{1}{20}$  
**B.** $\frac{1}{10}$  
**C.** $\frac{1}{10}$  
**D.** None of the above

**Q.60** If $3x - 4y = 5$ and $xy = 3$, then find $27x^3 - 64y^3$

**A.** 125  **B.** 665  **C.** 225  **D.** 985

**Q.61** A square ABCD, L is the midpoint of side AB, M is the midpoint of side BC, N is the midpoint of side CD and O is the midpoint of side AD, then find the ratio of area of shaded region PQRS to the area of square ABCD.

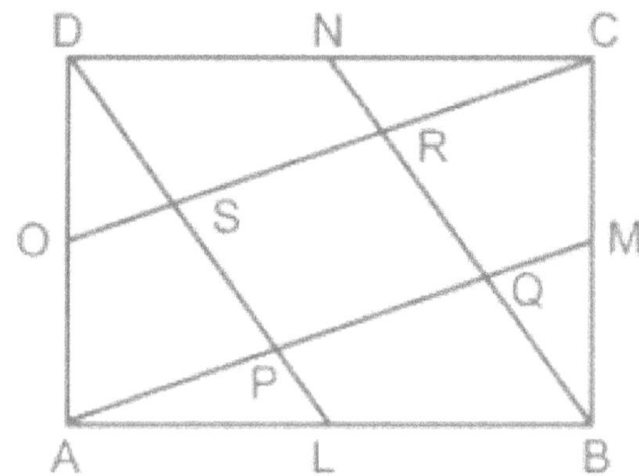

**A.** 1 : 4      **B.** 1 : 5      **C.** 1 : 6      **D.** 1 : 8

**Q.62** A child goes around an equilateral triangular park. From A to B his speed is $10$ km/hr, from B to C his speed is $12$ km/hr and from C to A his speed is $15$ km/hr. Find his average speed.

**A.** 10 km/hr      **B.** 12 km/hr      **C.** 15 km/hr      **D.** 8 km/hr

**Q.63** A, B and C starts a business, A invests money for $4$ months and claim $\left(\frac{1}{8}\right)^{th}$ of the profit and B invests money for $6$ months and claim $\left(\frac{1}{3}\right)^{th}$ of the profit, while C invests Rs. $1560$ for $8$ months. How much money did A invests?

**A.** Rs. 520      **B.** Rs. 620      **C.** Rs. 720      **D.** Rs. 820

**Q.64** A person bought two bicycles for Rs. $1600$ and sold the first at $10\%$ profit and the second at $20\%$ profit. If he sold the first at $20\%$ profit and the second at $10\%$ profit, he would get more. The difference in the cost price of the two bicycles was:

**A.** Rs. 25      **B.** Rs. 75      **C.** Rs. 50      **D.** Rs. 40

**Q.65** What value should come in place of '?' in the following equation?
$$52^2 - 42^2 +?^2 = 64^2 - 56^2 + 3^2 - 2^2$$
**A.** 2      **B.** 3      **C.** 4      **D.** 5

**Q.66** A student find the average of ten $2$ digit numbers, and while copying numbers by mistake, he writes one number with its digit interchanged, as a result of that his average is $3.6$ less that the correct answer, then find the difference of the digits of the number in which he made the mistake.

**A.** 2      **B.** 3      **C.** 4      **D.** 5

**Q.67** The ratio of income of A, B and C are in the ratio $4:5:6$ and the ratio of expenditure is $2:3:4$ if savings of B is $\left(\frac{1}{3}\right)$ of its income, then find the ratio of their respective savings.

**A.** $15:16:14$       **B.** $16:14:15$
**C.** $14:15:16$       **D.** $16:15:14$

**Q.68** Simplify $\dfrac{(0.73)^3+(0.27)^3}{(0.73)^2+(0.27)^2-0.73\times0.27}$ =?

**A.** 0.27      **B.** 0.4087      **C.** 0.73      **D.** 1

**Q.69** In an alloy $83\%$ is copper and remaining percentage is zinc, and in another alloy $87\%$ is copper and remaining percentage is zinc. In what ratio the two alloys be mixed so that the new mixture must have $14\%$ zinc. Find the percentage of copper in the new mixture.

**A.** 65%      **B.** 75%      **C.** 55%      **D.** 85%

**Q.70** What approximate value should come in place of '?' in the following equation?
69% of 699 + 19.96 × 19.68 – 45.5% of 99.9 =?
**A.** 745      **B.** 845      **C.** 645      **D.** 945

**Q.71** There are two candidates in an election. 10000 voters did not cast their vote. 80% of casted votes are valid. Winning candidate won by 2000 votes and losing candidate got 20% of total votes. Find the total number of voters.

**A.** 15000      **B.** 25000      **C.** 35000      **D.** 20000

**Q.72** Three taps $A, B$ and $C$ can fill a tank in $12, 15$ and $20$ hours respectively. If $A$ is open all the time and $B$ and $C$ are open for one hour each alternately, the tank will be full in:

**A.** 6 hours      **B.** $6\frac{2}{3}$ hours
**C.** 7 hours      **D.** $7\frac{1}{2}$ hours

**Q.73** If letters of the work KUBER are written in all possible orders and arranged as in a dictionary, then the rank of the word KUBER will be:

**A.** 67      **B.** 68      **C.** 65      **D.** 69

**Q.74** Three numbers which are co-prime to each other are such that the product of the first two is $551$ and that of the last two is $1073$. The sum of the three numbers is:

**A.** 75      **B.** 81      **C.** 85      **D.** 89

**Q.75** Which of the following fraction is the largest?

**A.** $\frac{7}{8}$      **B.** $\frac{13}{16}$      **C.** $\frac{31}{40}$      **D.** $\frac{63}{80}$

# English Comprehension

**Ques (76-80):Read the passage given below and then answer the question given below the passage. Some words may be highlighted for your attention. Read carefully.**

Research predicts that digital payments in India will exceed USD 500 billion by 2020, up from USD 50 billion in 2016. It's just one way in which Fintech is changing the face of the financial services industry. Fintech – the technological innovations in the design and delivery of financial services and products – is revolutionizing customer expectations. Emerging technologies such as Artificial Intelligence (AI), big data and analytics, the blockchain, cloud, Internet of Things (IoT), and robotics are disrupting traditional finance.

AI and machine learning are transforming customer experience with personalized services and improvements in back-office efficiencies. Banks use big data and analytics in their fraud, risk management, and regulatory compliance. IoT is revolutionizing insurance. But its growth is **conservative** in comparison to big data, cloud and machine learning used in payments and alternative lending. Big data and machine learning are spotting trends and providing better investment insights. Robots are venturing into investment and changing how wealth advisory services are delivered. The effect of machines on investment management professionals is a pressing question.

The real challenge is finding the right talent pool to complement the **agility** of the technologies. Investment management firms must compete with other industries using disruptive technologies to attract the best people. Investment teams and technical teams will need to be integrated to create checks and balances on the models and processes. Proper integration is a counter to the potential lack of transparency and interpretability in these models' decision-making processes.

**Q.76** How are the emerging technologies transforming customer experiences?

**A.** Through innovations in the design and delivery of financial services and products.

**B.** By improving the back-office efficiencies.

**C.** By using complex algorithms that need a longer learning curve.

**D.** Both (A) and (B)

**Q.77** Which of the following is the major challenge faced in models' decision-making processes?

**A.** The growth is conservative in India.

**B.** There is a lack of transparency and interpretability.

**C.** They are disrupting traditional finance.

**D.** Both (A) and (B)

**Q.78** What is the meaning of the word agility used in the passage?

**A.** The way of behaving or happening in an unusual and unexpected manner.

**B.** The process of making a problem or situation worse.

**C.** The ability to deal with new changes or situations quickly.

**D.** A typical example.

**Q.79** According to the passage, how are robots helping the investment?

**A.** By instilling cultures of ethical decision making.

**B.** By reducing fees and improve the quality of service for investors.

**C.** By enhancing digital payments in India.

**D.** By changing how wealth advisory services are delivered.

**Q.80** Which of the following is the closest antonym for the word conservative used in the passage?

**A.** Conventional

**B.** Progressive

**C.** Hostile

**D.** Winsome

**Q.81 Fill in the blank with an appropriate word.**

All the winners prize ______ tomorrow.

**A.** will be given

**B.** will given

**C.** will be given

**D.** will have given

**Q.82 Read the sentence to find out whether there is any grammatical error in it. The error, if any will be in one part of the sentence. If there is no error choose option 4 'No error' as the answer.**

The Japan-administered islands (a) / are also claimed in China,(b) / which calls them the Diaoyu. (c) / No error (d)

**A.** (a)      **B.** (b)      **C.** (c)      **D.** (d)

**Q.83 In the following question, four words have been given out of which one word is incorrectly spelt. Find the incorrectly spelt word.**

**A.** Prudence

**B.** Tact

**C.** Haox

**D.** Dupe

**Q.84 In the following question, out of the four alternatives, select the alternative which is the best substitute of the phrase.**

That which cannot be easily read

**A.** Illegible

**B.** Eligible

**C.** Illegitimate

**D.** Legislature

**Q.85 In the following question, a sentence has been given in Active/Passive voice. Out of four alternatives suggested, select the one, which best expresses the same sentence in Passive/Active voice.**

Rohan was asking a question.

**A.** A question had been asked by Rohan

**B.** A question has been asked by Rohan

**C.** A question was being asked by Rohan

**D.** A question was asked by Rohan

**Q.86 Fill in the blank with an appropriate word.**

America ______ the powerful president.

**A.** have      **B.** has      **C.** is      **D.** does

**Ques (87-91):In the following passage, some of the words have been left out. Read the passage carefully and select the correct answer for the given blank out of the given alternatives.**

Unlike Egypt in the 1970s, Syria has had neither the military ability nor the international __(1)__to launch a campaign to get its territory back. President Bashar al-Assad tried to kick-start a U.S.-mediated peace process with Israel during the Obama __(2)__, but it failed to take off. And now, the Syrian government, after fighting eight years of a civil war, is __(3)__ and isolated, and the U.S. move is unlikely to trigger any strong response, even from the Arab world. But that is the least of the problems. Mr Trump's decision flouts international norms and consensus and sets a dangerous __(4)__ for nations involved in conflicts. The modern international system is built on sovereignty, and every nation-state is supposed to be an equal player before international laws irrespective of its military or economic__(5)__.

**Q.87** Which of the following word fits the blank labelled as (1)?

**A.** Clot      **B.** Clout      **C.** Bull      **D.** Foul

**Q.88** Which of the following word fits the blank labelled as (2)?

**A.** Regimen

**B.** Regulate

**C.** Presidency

**D.** Resolve

**Q.89** Which of the following word fits the blank labelled as (3)?

**A.** Debilitated      **B.** Denominated
**C.** Divulged      **D.** Deluge

**Q.90** Which of the following word fits the blank labelled as (4)?
**A.** Pretension      **B.** Prejudiced
**C.** Precedent      **D.** Portend

**Q.91** Which of the following word fits the blank labelled as (5)?
**A.** Foresight      **B.** Paltry
**C.** Crony      **D.** Might

**Q.92** Choose the word SIMILAR in meaning to the given word.
Bewitching
**A.** Daring      **B.** Fascinating
**C.** Deriding      **D.** Tailgating

**Q.93 In the following question, choose the word opposite in meaning to the given word and mark it in the answer sheet.**
Profane
**A.** Discord      **B.** Criticism
**C.** Religious      **D.** Applause

**Q.94 In the following question, a word has been written in 4 different ways out of which only one correctly spelt. Select the correctly spelt word.**
**A.** Idiocyncrasy      **B.** Idiocyncresy
**C.** Idiosyncresy      **D.** Idiosyncrasy

**Q.95 In the following question, a word has been written in 4 different ways out of which only one correctly spelt. Select the correctly spelt word.**
**A.** Liason    **B.** Liaison    **C.** Liaeson    **D.** Liaision

**Q.96 In the following question, a word has been written in 4 different ways out of which only one correctly spelt. Select the correctly spelt word.**
**A.** Dilema      **B.** Delemma
**C.** Dilemma      **D.** Delema

**Q.97 Directions:** Rearrange the given 5 sentences A, B, C, D and E in proper sequence to form a meaningful paragraph and mark the correct sequence from the given options as your answer.
A. Ashoka Chakra is imprinted in the centre with twenty-four spokes equally spaced.
B. The flag is made of Khadi.
C. The National Flag of India is tri-colour flag with saffron, white and green colour.
D. It is in navy blue colour.
E. It has the saffron colour on the top, white in the centre and green at the bottom with equal width and length.
**A.** BADEC    **B.** ADCEB    **C.** BEADB    **D.** CEADB

**Q.98 Directions:** Rearrange the given 5 sentences A, B, C, D and E in proper sequence to form a meaningful paragraph and mark the correct sequence from the given options as your answer.
A. Indian culture is popular across the world.

B. Indian culture is considered as the oldest and most diverse cultures of the world.
C. Indian people are highly devoted to their culture and religion.
D. People of different religions and cultures live here with strong bond.
E. The Indian literature, philosophy, art and music have heavily been influenced by Indian culture and "Dharmik" religions throughout the history of India.
**A.** ABCDE    **B.** ABECD    **C.** BACED    **D.** CDEAB

**Q.99 In the following question, out of the four alternatives, select the alternative which is the best substitute for the phrase.**
A person who insists that a particular type of behavior is very important.
**A.** Fiend    **B.** Maniac    **C.** Lunatic    **D.** Stickler

**Q.100** In the following question, out of the four alternatives, select the alternative which is the best substitute of the phrase.
That which cannot be erased
**A.** Invincible      **B.** Indelible
**C.** Incorrigible      **D.** Inaudible

# // Smart Answer Sheet //

**Correct**   Indicates percentage of students who answered questions correctly.

**Skipped**   Indicates percentage of students who skipped questions.

| Q. | Ans. | Correct / Skipped | Q. | Ans. | Correct / Skipped | Q. | Ans. | Correct / Skipped | Q. | Ans. | Correct / Skipped | Q. | Ans. | Correct / Skipped |
|---|---|---|---|---|---|---|---|---|---|---|---|---|---|---|
| 1 | A | 62.63 % / 35.77 % | 17 | C | 64.24 % / 35.47 % | 33 | A | 66.72 % / 32.06 % | 49 | C | 56.61 % / 33.63 % | 65 | D | 45.48 % / 42.09 % |
| 2 | C | 46.81 % / 31.7 % | 18 | D | 61.55 % / 31.78 % | 34 | D | 77.39 % / 21.25 % | 50 | C | 63.68 % / 30.09 % | 66 | C | 53.0 % / 41.45 % |
| 3 | A | 55.47 % / 31.38 % | 19 | D | 56.95 % / 34.14 % | 35 | D | 52.12 % / 44.32 % | 51 | D | 63.64 % / 33.45 % | 67 | D | 68.87 % / 30.61 % |
| 4 | C | 63.29 % / 32.34 % | 20 | A | 48.63 % / 41.76 % | 36 | A | 45.28 % / 39.11 % | 52 | D | 83.6 % / 13.5 % | 68 | D | 77.0 % / 17.76 % |
| 5 | A | 58.29 % / 35.88 % | 21 | A | 69.57 % / 30.3 % | 37 | B | 55.15 % / 39.48 % | 53 | D | 86.99 % / 10.3 % | 69 | B | 42.95 % / 44.84 % |
| 6 | A | 46.89 % / 35.7 % | 22 | A | 49.06 % / 38.2 % | 38 | D | 42.2 % / 33.93 % | 54 | B | 54.38 % / 39.57 % | 70 | B | 44.84 % / 37.7 % |
| 7 | B | 51.41 % / 43.79 % | 23 | B | 50.53 % / 41.54 % | 39 | B | 48.97 % / 46.22 % | 55 | B | 43.89 % / 53.61 % | 71 | B | 61.04 % / 36.9 % |
| 8 | D | 40.96 % / 43.03 % | 24 | D | 48.82 % / 44.16 % | 40 | C | 48.88 % / 47.19 % | 56 | B | 67.74 % / 31.81 % | 72 | C | 44.87 % / 33.17 % |
| 9 | C | 67.39 % / 30.09 % | 25 | B | 68.75 % / 30.12 % | 41 | A | 79.96 % / 18.4 % | 57 | A | 29.66 % / 69.27 % | 73 | A | 45.63 % / 35.39 % |
| 10 | C | 54.62 % / 33.47 % | 26 | A | 41.69 % / 31.87 % | 42 | B | 45.88 % / 51.97 % | 58 | C | 50.02 % / 48.69 % | 74 | C | 60.06 % / 36.68 % |
| 11 | D | 44.52 % / 44.44 % | 27 | A | 53.25 % / 30.46 % | 43 | D | 63.05 % / 36.7 % | 59 | C | 84.21 % / 12.83 % | 75 | A | 53.75 % / 39.71 % |
| 12 | C | 58.51 % / 30.71 % | 28 | B | 65.58 % / 31.55 % | 44 | D | 65.69 % / 33.91 % | 60 | B | 53.8 % / 36.74 % | 76 | D | 44.21 % / 33.47 % |
| 13 | A | 60.24 % / 30.83 % | 29 | A | 49.2 % / 34.82 % | 45 | B | 59.3 % / 38.13 % | 61 | B | 43.86 % / 35.75 % | 77 | D | 52.76 % / 43.2 % |
| 14 | C | 41.67 % / 48.85 % | 30 | D | 81.8 % / 12.72 % | 46 | C | 53.93 % / 34.64 % | 62 | B | 63.39 % / 36.36 % | 78 | C | 61.69 % / 32.55 % |
| 15 | C | 50.08 % / 37.95 % | 31 | A | 62.02 % / 31.4 % | 47 | A | 57.01 % / 33.37 % | 63 | C | 46.87 % / 40.3 % | 79 | D | 69.71 % / 30.28 % |
| 16 | C | 62.22 % / 36.43 % | 32 | B | 85.52 % / 10.07 % | 48 | C | 79.08 % / 10.74 % | 64 | C | 51.73 % / 45.61 % | 80 | B | 58.46 % / 35.13 % |

| Q. | Ans. | Correct / Skipped |
|---|---|---|
| 81 | A | 83.07 % |
| | | 11.15 % |
| 82 | B | 41.89 % |
| | | 30.76 % |
| 83 | C | 89.45 % |
| | | 10.21 % |
| 84 | A | 55.01 % |
| | | 31.68 % |

| Q. | Ans. | Correct / Skipped |
|---|---|---|
| 85 | C | 77.45 % |
| | | 22.17 % |
| 86 | B | 76.41 % |
| | | 16.67 % |
| 87 | B | 41.99 % |
| | | 37.69 % |
| 88 | C | 64.61 % |
| | | 33.19 % |

| Q. | Ans. | Correct / Skipped |
|---|---|---|
| 89 | A | 45.09 % |
| | | 52.33 % |
| 90 | C | 66.98 % |
| | | 31.64 % |
| 91 | D | 49.47 % |
| | | 43.39 % |
| 92 | B | 80.68 % |
| | | 18.68 % |

| Q. | Ans. | Correct / Skipped |
|---|---|---|
| 93 | C | 84.02 % |
| | | 15.51 % |
| 94 | D | 43.55 % |
| | | 49.95 % |
| 95 | B | 59.95 % |
| | | 34.67 % |
| 96 | C | 53.02 % |
| | | 45.17 % |

| Q. | Ans. | Correct / Skipped |
|---|---|---|
| 97 | D | 47.16 % |
| | | 45.03 % |
| 98 | A | 52.24 % |
| | | 31.79 % |
| 99 | D | 84.42 % |
| | | 12.65 % |
| 100 | B | 42.85 % |
| | | 56.81 % |

## Performance Analysis

| | |
|---|---|
| Avg. Score (%) | 58.5% |
| Toppers Score (%) | 65.0% |
| Your Score | |

# //Hints and Solutions//

**1.** The number of doctors who are neither artists nor players is 17.

Hence, the correct option is (A).

**2.** The number of doctors who are both players and artists is 3.

Hence, the correct option is (C).

**3.**

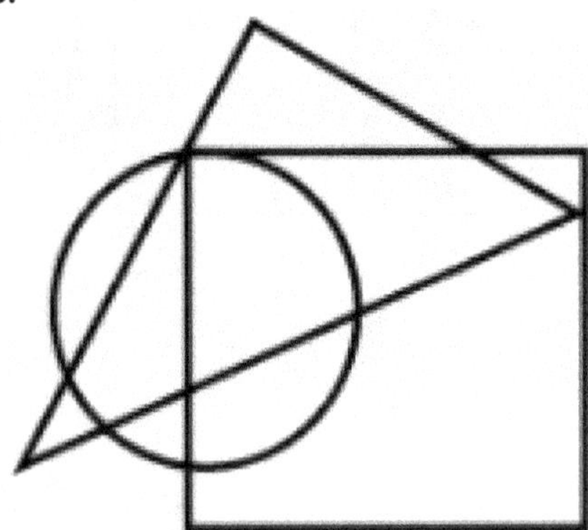

There are three dots in figure (X) one in the circle alone, second in the region common to square and circle only and third in the region common to cell the three figures.

Only figure (A) contains all the three types of regions.

Hence, the correct option is (A).

**4.** Bengal Tiger is National Animal of India.

Similarly, Bison is National Animal of USA.

So, Bison is related to USA.

Hence, the correct option is (C).

**5.** From figures (i) and (ii), we conclude that 2, 3, 5 and 6 he adjacent to 1. Therefore, 4 lies opposite 1. Hence, when 4 is at the bottom, then1 must be on the top.

Hence, the correct option is (A).

**6.**

| A | B | C | D | E | F | G | H | I | J | K | L | M |
|---|---|---|---|---|---|---|---|---|---|---|---|---|
| 1 | 2 | 3 | 4 | 5 | 6 | 7 | 8 | 9 | 10 | 11 | 12 | 13 |
| N | O | P | Q | R | S | T | U | V | W | X | Y | Z |
| 14 | 15 | 16 | 17 | 18 | 19 | 20 | 21 | 22 | 23 | 24 | 25 | 26 |

D is 4th letter, I is 9th letter, N is 14th, E is 5th and R is 18th letter.

| D | I | N | N | E | R |
|---|---|---|---|---|---|
| 4 | 9 | 14 | 14 | 5 | 18 |

18 + 4 = 22  .....i)

9 + 5 = 14  .....ii)

14 + 14 = 28

i) + ii) = 22 + 14 = 36

36 – 28 = 8

Code for "DINNER" is 8.

Similarly,

| L | E | T | T | E | R |
|---|---|---|---|---|---|
| 12 | 5 | 20 | 20 | 5 | 18 |

12 + 18 = 30  .....i)

5 + 5 = 10  .....ii)

20 + 20 = 40

i) + ii) = 30 + 10 = 40

40 – 40 = 0

So, code for "LETTER" is 0.

Hence, the correct option is (A).

**7.** If we give number to each letter according to its alphabetical order we find that,

BDF = 246 = All alphabets have even number

JBA = 1021 = Only first two alphabets have even numbers

HBF = 826 = All alphabets have even number

BFF = 266 = All alphabets have even number

Hence, the correct option is (B).

**8.** All options except 'Friend - Sister' represents blood relation while 'Friend - Sister' doesn't represents blood relation.

Hence, the correct option is (D).

**9.** Here by observing the given series,

10 + 2 = 12

12 – 4 = 8

8 + 2 = 10

10 – 4 = 6

6 + 2 = 8

8 – 4 = 4

4 + 2 = 6

6 – 4 = 2

2 + 2 = 4

4 – 4 = 0

So, "6" is the missing term.

Hence, the correct option is (C).

**10.** Given Series: KLCQ, PPFS, UTIU, ?

The logic followed for the Series:

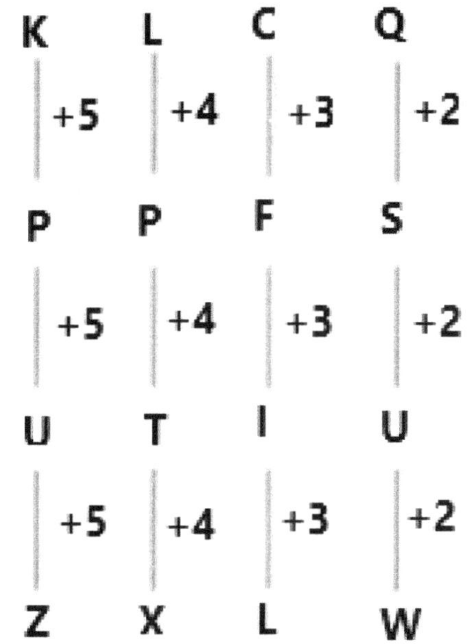

So, the next term will be ZXLW.

Hence, the correct option is (C).

**11.** The logic followed is:

The letters are increased by 2 as in alphabetical series, starting from the first letter.

PQPQPQPQPQ, **R**QPQPQPQ, **RS**PQPQPQ, **RSR**QPQPQ, **RSRS**PQPQ, **RSRSR**QPQ.

Hence, the correct option is (D).

**12.**

Similarly,

Hence, the correct answer is (C).

**13.** Here cloud = blue, land = brown, street = black, flower = red and bird = flying,

Here, red indicates flower, hence flower will be planted on land.

And land means brown.

Hence, the correct option is (A).

**14.** From figures (i) and (ii) we conclude that 3, 4, 1 and 5 dots appear adjacent to 2 dots. Therefore, 6 dots must appear

opposite 2 dots. Since, there are 2 dots on the top face when the dice is in position (i), therefore, the number of dots at the bottom face must be 6.

Hence, the correct option is (C).

| Symbol in Diagram | Meaning |
|---|---|
| ○ | Female |
| ☐ | Male |
| ═══ | Married Couple |
| ─── | Siblings |
| │ | Difference of a Generation |

**15.**

Members: K, L, P, R, S, F, U, V, and X.

In a family, P is married to R. They have 3 daughters, S, U, and V. S is married to X, U is married to K and V is married to L.

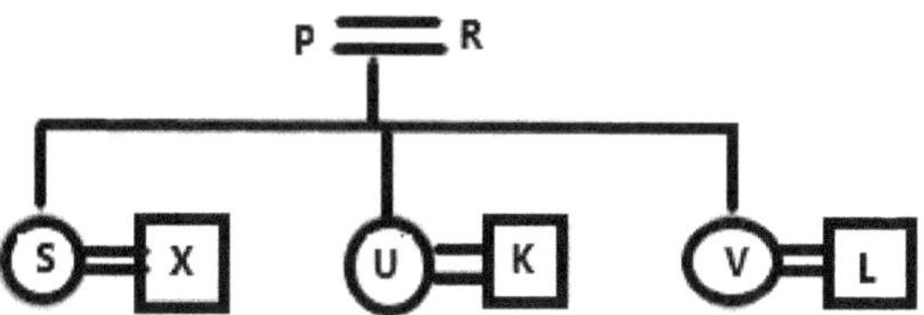

J is the daughter of S and X. K and U have one daughter D. V, with L, have 2 daughters and each daughter have one brother.

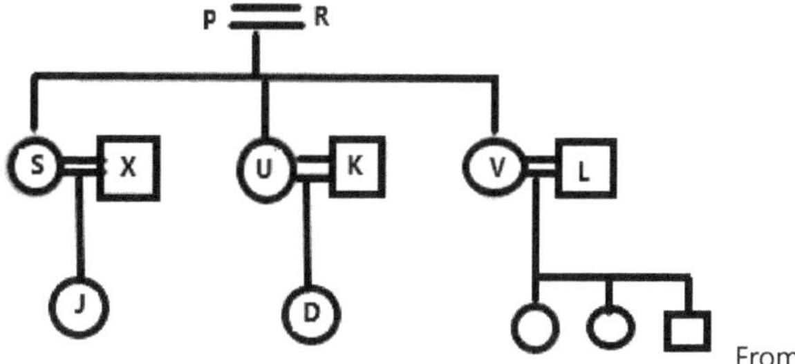

From the family tree, we see that the number of females is 8.

Hence, the correct option is (C).

| Symbol in Diagram | Meaning |
|---|---|
| ○ | Female |
| □ | Male |
| ═══ | Married Couple |
| ─── | Siblings |
| │ | Difference of a Generation |

**16.**

Members: K, L, P, R, S, F, U, V, and X.

In a family, P is married to R. They have 3 daughters, S, U, and V. S is married to X, U is married to K and V is married to L.

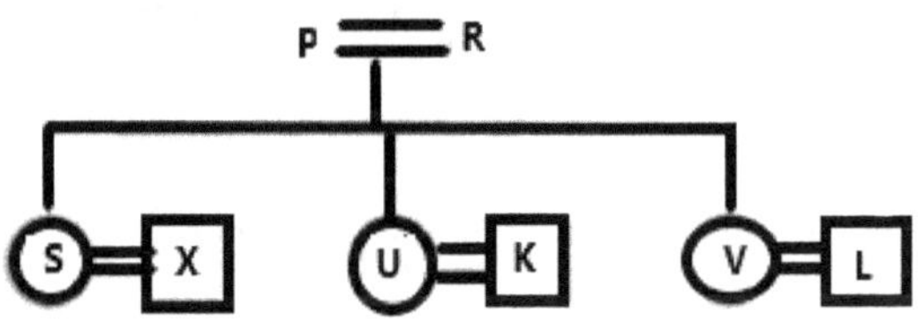

J is the daughter of S and X. K and U have one daughter D. V, with L, have 2 daughters and each daughter have one brother.

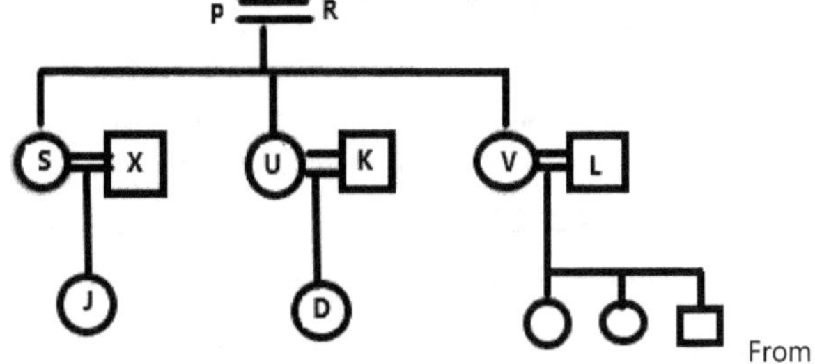

From the family tree given above, we see that the total number of members is 13.

Hence, the correct option is (C).

**17.**

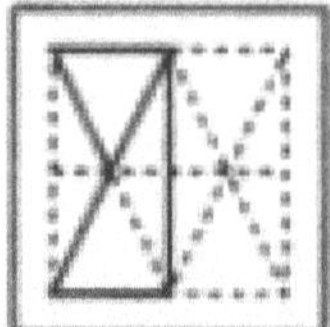

Hence, the correct option is (C).

**18.**

Hence, the correct option is (D).

**19.**

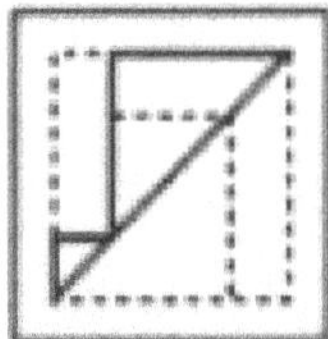

Hence, the correct option is (D).

**20.**

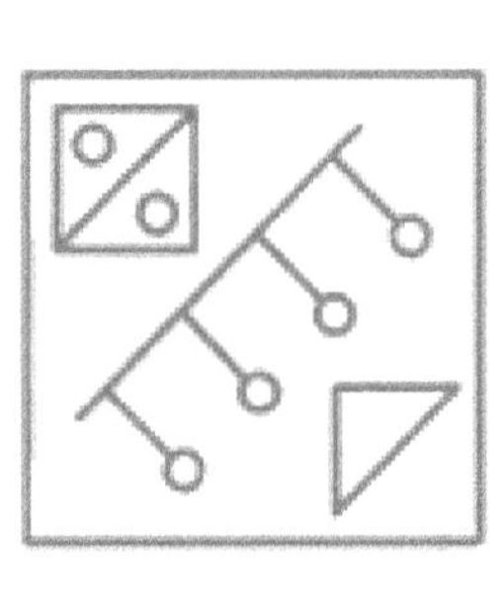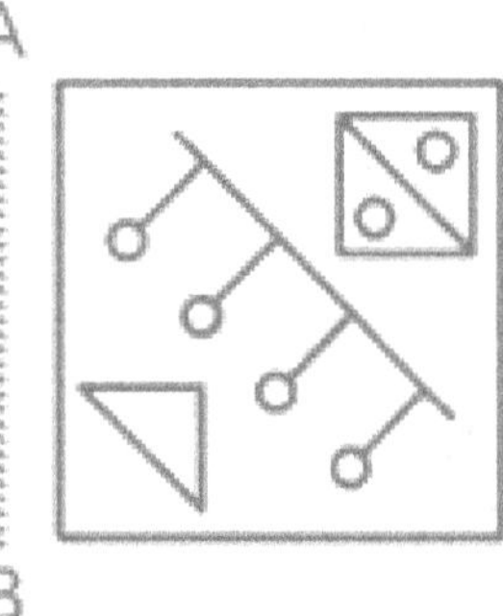


So, figure 2 is the mirror image of the question figure.

Hence, the correct option is (A).

**21.** Given elements: Wheat, Tea, Plant and Coffee

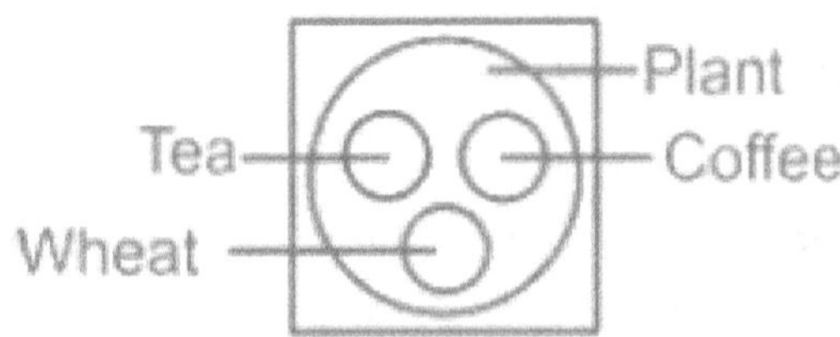


Hence, the correct option is (A).

**22.** From matrix I, N can be coded as 02, 14, 21, 33 or 40.

From matrix II, E can be coded as 56, 67, 78, 85 or 97.

From matrix II, S can be coded as 55, 66, 77, 89 or 96.

From matrix II, T can be coded as 59, 68, 76, 87 or 95.

Hence, the correct option is (A).

**23.** From matrix I, F can be coded as 00, 12, 24, 31 or 43.

From matrix I, A can be coded as 01, 13, 20, 34 or 42.

From matrix 1,I can be coded as 04,10, 23, 32 or 41.

From matrix II, T can be ceded as 69, 68, 76, 87 or 95 . From matrix II, H can be coded as 57,65,79,86 or 98.

Hence, the correct option is (B).

**24.** From matrix I, F can be coded as 00, 12, 24, 31 or 43.

From matrix I, I can be coded as 04, 10, 23, 32 or 41.

From matrix I, N can be coded as 02, 14, 21, 33 or 40.

From matrix II, E can be coded as 56, 67, 78, 85 or 97.

Hence, the correct option is (D).

**25.** 17 persons take tea and wine but not coffee.

Hence, the correct option is (B).

**26.** The first train was successfully test-fired between Nepal country's railway link from Bihar's Madhubani district.

Train service between Jainagar in Bihar and Kurtha in Nepal is expected to start soon after the speed test of the train. Rajesh Kumar, Chief Public Relations Officer of East-Central Railway (ECR) said that the speed trial was successfully carried out by locomotive at a speed of $110$ km per hour on the kilometer-long newly-gauge converted railway section between Jaynagar of Samastipur division and Kurtha in Nepal. During this senior high officials of IRCON and Nepal Railways were present.

Hence, the correct option is (A).

**27.** Patna has the only Genome Sequencing Lab of the state started. Bihar's first and only genome-sequencing facility at Patna-based Indira Gandhi Institute of Medical Sciences (IGIMS), has become non-operational since last week due to a lack of reagents. No samples are being tested in the state at the moment to ascertain the omicron variant of COVID- $19$.

Hence, the correct option is (A).

**28.** F1 champion Max Verstappen has been named the 2022 Laureus Sportsman of the Year.

Jamaican Olympic sprinter Elaine Thompson-Herah has been named Sportswoman of the Year.

Hence, the correct option is (B).

**29.** On May 11, 2018, Prime Minister Narendra Modi and Nepalese Prime Minister KP Sharma Oli jointly flagged-off a direct bus service between the two sacred cities Janakpur and Ayodhya, as part of the Ramayana Circuit.

The bus service seeks to promote religious tourism and built a strong foundation for people-to-people contact between the two countries. As per the mythological story 'Ramayana', Ayodhya is Lord Rama's birthplace, while, Janakpur is the birthplace of goddess Sita.

Hence, the correct option is (A).

**30.** The butterfly is a swimming stroke swum on the breast, with both arms moving simultaneously, accompanied by the butterfly kick (also known as the "dolphin kick"). While other styles like the breaststroke, front crawl, or backstroke can be swum adequately by beginners, the butterfly is a more difficult stroke that requires good technique as well as strong muscles.

Hence, the correct option is (D).

**31.** Leo Tolstoy is the author of the book "The Kingdom of God is Within You".

The book is based on the Tolstoyan proponents of nonviolence, nonviolent resistance, and the Christian anarchist movement.

The book was published in Germany in the Russian language in the year 1894.

The book was his true transformation process of Luke 17:21 from the bible.

Hence, the correct option is (A).

**32.** The disinvestment target for the financial year 2020-21 is Rs 2,10,000 crore. This target is 223% higher than the revised estimate of Rs 65,000 crore in 2019-20.

Hence, the correct option is (B).

**33.** Bancassurance is defined as the model in which banks act as the corporate agents of the insurance companies.

The banks sell the insurance products of the concerned insurance company to their customers.

Insurance companies tap into the large customer base of banks through this model of distribution.

Hence, the correct option is (A).

**34.** Rishabha was the first Tirthankara of Jainism.

He was also known as Adinatha and Adish Jina.

He was the first among the twenty-four Tirthankara of Jain tradition.

He was born to the fourteenth and last Kulakara King Nabhi and his Queen Marudevi in Ayodhya.

He established the first ascetic order and taught people the path to moksha.

Arishtanemi was the twenty-second Tirthankara in Jainism.

Parshvanath was the twenty-third Tirthankaras of Jainism.

Mahavir Jain was the twenty- fourth Tirthankaras of Jainism.

Ajitanath was the second Tirthankara of Jainism.

Hence, the correct option is (D).

**35.**

| Tribal Revolt | Year | Leaders |
| --- | --- | --- |
| Khasi | 1829-32 | Tirut Singh |
| Bhils | 1817 | Sewaram |

| Ahom | 128-33 | Gomadhar Kunwar |
| Chaur | 1766-72 | Raja Jagannath |

Hence, the correct option is (D).

**36.** Sir William Jones founded "The Asiatic Society".

He founded "The Asiatic Society" on 15th January 1784.

The Asiatic Society of Bengal is located in Kolkata.

The Asiatic society possesses an art collection that includes paintings by artists Peter Paul Rubens and Joshua Reynolds.

The society's library contains around 10,0000 general volumes, and its Sanskrit section has more than 27,000 books, manuscripts, coins, prints, and engravings.

Hence, the correct option is (A).

**37.** The central government has released a report of the task force on the National Infrastructure Pipeline for 2019-2025. The purpose of this pipeline is to make living easier by providing access to clean and affordable energy, safe drinking water, health care for all, bus terminals, airports, modern railway stations and world-class educational institutions.

Hence, the correct option is (B).

**38.** Fiscal policy is concerned with public revenue, public expenditure, and debt.

Fiscal policy is the part of government economic policy which deals with, expenditure, taxation, borrowing and the management of public debt in the economy.

It is basically concerned with the flow of funds in the economy.

The two main instruments of fiscal policy are government taxation and changes in the level and composition of taxation and government spending can affect the following variables in the economy: Aggregate demand and the level of economic activity; the pattern of resource allocation: and the distribution of income.

It maintains the balance of payment equilibrium and promote economic development.

It also encourages investments and price stability.

Hence, the correct option is (D).

**39.** The right to Education became a fundamental right on April 1, 2010.

The Right to Education Act (RTE), is an Act of the Parliament of India enacted on 4 August 2009.

The Right to education is a fundamental right that is given to every citizen of India by the Constitution of India.

The Right to education not only gives the right to get an education in any region of India but also in Schools, Colleges, and Universities.

All children between the age of 6 to 14 have the right to get free and compulsory education under Article 21A of the Indian Constitution.

Hence, the correct option is (B).

**40.** The "Moortidevi Sahitya Puraskar" was instituted by Bharatiya Jnanpith Trust.

The Moortidevi Award is an India literary award given to an author.

The award is stated only to Indian writers writing in Indian languages included in the Eighth Schedule of the Constitution of India, and in English with no self-nominations.

Hence, the correct option is (C).

**41.** The author of the book (India Vince Freedom) is Maulana Azad. It is told in this book that one of the makers of modern India tells the story of Partition of India with intimate knowledge and feeling like never before.

Hence, the correct option is (A).

**42.** Jamini Roy distinguished himself in the field of Painting.

Jamini Roy was a Bengali, Indian painter.

Jamini Roy was the first awardee of the Lalit Kala award.

He was honoured with Padma Bhushan in the year 1954.

He created a painting in a unique style by combining his own style with the qualities of native folk paintings.

His paintings were a combination of the nominal brush strokes of the Kalighat style with elements of tribal art from Bengal.

Hence, the correct option is (B).

**43.** 'Saddle Peak' the highest peak of the Andaman and Nicobar Islands is located in  Diglipur, a town in North Andaman Island.

It is the highest point of the archipelago in the Bay of Bengal with a length of 731 meters (2,418 feet) followed by Mount Thullier at 2,106 feet (642 meters) on Great Nicobar and Mount Harriet at 1,197 feet (365 meters) on South Andaman.

It is surrounded by Saddle Peak National Park.

Hence, the correct option is (D).

**44.** Private sector lender, IDFC Bank's name has been changed to 'IDFC First Bank Ltd' with effect from 12 January 2019.

IDFC Bank and Non-Banking Financial Company (NBFC) 'Capital First' completed their merger on 18 December 2018.

V Vaidyanathan, Founder of Capital First Ltd, was appointed as Managing Director and Chief Executive Officer of the IDFC First Bank Ltd.

Hence, the correct option is (D).

**45.** The Insurance Regulatory and Development Authority of India came up in India in 2000 with the objective of regulating the insurance sector in the country.

It was given the powers to regulate the insurance companies in India as per the provisions of Section 114A of the Insurance Act 1938.

Hence, the correct option is (B).

**46.** The name of India's research station at the North pole is Himadri.

Himadri station is India's first Arctic research station located at Spitsbergen, Svalbard, Norway.

It was inaugurated on the 1st July 2008 by the Minister of Earth Sciences.

It is located at a distance of 1,200 kilometres from the North Pole.

Its main aim is to monitor the fjord dynamics and atmospheric research and research on aerosol radiation, space weather, food-web dynamics, microbial communities, glaciers, sedimentology, and carbon recycling.

Hence, the correct option is (C).

**47.** Article 19 of the Indian Constitution provides 6 freedoms.

Following are the 6 fundamental freedom provided under Article 19 of the Constitution of India are:

Freedom of speech and expression.

Freedom to assemble peacefully without arms.

Freedom to move freely throughout the territory of India

Freedom to form associations or co-operative societies.

Freedom to reside and settle in any part of the territory of India.

Freedom to practise any profession or to carry on any trade, business or occupation.

Hence, the correct option is (A).

**48.** World Theater Day is celebrated on 27 March. It is celebrated by the International Theater Institute. The first World Theater Day message was written by Jean Cousteau in 1962.

Hence, the correct option is (C).

**49.** "Law of demand" implies that when there is excess demand for a commodity, then the price of the commodity rises.

The law of Demand is that when the price of the product decreases with an increase in the consumption of the product and vice-versa.

| When price rises | a. | If the price of a commodity rises and the demand falls then the market will have an excess supply of that commodity. |
| --- | --- | --- |
| | a. | For the excess supply, the price of the commodity will go down until it reaches its equilibrium point. |
| When demand rises | b. | If the demand rises then the market will demand more commodity and there will be a short of supply or excess demand. |
| | c. | Taking advantage of excess demand the producers will raise the price of the product until it reaches its equilibrium price. |

Hence, the correct option is (C).

**50.** The Alamatti Dam is constructed on the Krishna river in the Bijapur district of North Karnataka.

The Almatti Dam is a hydroelectric project on the Krishna river.

The Almatti Dam was opened in July 2005, with a height of 524.26 feet and a length of 1565.15 feet.

It is the main reservoir of the Upper Krishna Irrigation Project.

It is operated by Karnataka Power Corporation Limited.

Hence, the correct option is (C).

**51.** Let $x$ days are taken by $150$ men to finish the work

$\Rightarrow$ Total work $=$ men $\times$ days $= 150 \times x = 150x$

$\Rightarrow$ Work done in one day $= \dfrac{1}{150x}$

Now,

$\Rightarrow$ Work done by $150$ men on first day $= \dfrac{150x}{150}$

$\Rightarrow$ Work done by $146$ men $(= 150 - 4)$ on second day $= \dfrac{146}{150x}$

And so on, this happen for $(x + 8)$ days

$\Rightarrow \left(\dfrac{150x}{150}\right) + \left(\dfrac{146}{150x}\right) + (x + 8)$ times $= 1$

$\Rightarrow \left(\dfrac{1}{150x}\right) \{150 + 146 + \cdots . (x + 8)$ times $\} = 1$

$\Rightarrow \left(\dfrac{1}{150x}\right) [\{(\dfrac{(x+8)}{2} 2 \times 150) + (x + 8 - 1)(-4)\}] = 1$

$\Rightarrow \{\dfrac{(x+8)}{2}\}(300 - 4x - 28) = 150x$

$\Rightarrow (x + 8)(272 - 4x) = 300x$

$\Rightarrow 272x - 4x^2 + 2176 - 32x = 300x$

$\Rightarrow 4x^2 + 60x - 2176 = 0$

$\Rightarrow x^2 + 15x - 544 = 0$

$\Rightarrow x^2 - 17x + 32x - 544 = 0$

$\Rightarrow (x - 17)(x + 32) = 0$

$\Rightarrow x = 17$

$\therefore$ Number of Days taken $= 17 + 8 = 25$ days

Hence, the correct option is (D).

**52.** Given,

$2x^2 + x + 4 = 0$

$\Rightarrow 2x^2 + x = -4$

Dividing the equation by $2$, we get

$\Rightarrow x^2 + \dfrac{1}{2}x = -2$

$\Rightarrow x^2 + 2 \times x \times \left(\dfrac{1}{4}\right)^2 = -2$

By adding $\left(\frac{1}{4}\right)^2$ to both sides of the equation, we get

$$\Rightarrow (x)^2 + 2 \times x \times \frac{1}{4} + \left(\frac{1}{4}\right)^2 = \left(\frac{1}{4}\right)^2$$

$$\Rightarrow \left(x + \frac{1}{4}\right)^2 = \frac{1}{16} - 2$$

$$\Rightarrow \left(x + \frac{1}{4}\right)^2$$

$$= \frac{-31}{16}$$

The square root of a negative number is imaginary, therefore, there is no real root for the given equation.

Hence, the correct option is (D).

**53.** $\Rightarrow x = 3 - 3^{\frac{1}{3}} + 3^{\frac{2}{3}}$

$$\Rightarrow x - 3 = 3^{\frac{2}{3}} - 3^{\frac{1}{3}} \quad - (1)$$

On cubing both sides,

$$\Rightarrow x^3 - 9x^2 + 27x - 27$$

$$= \left(3^{\frac{2}{3}}\right)^3 - \left(3^{\frac{1}{3}}\right)^3 - 3 \times 3^{\frac{2}{3}} \times 3^{\frac{1}{3}}\left[3^{\frac{2}{3}} - 3^{\frac{1}{3}}\right]$$

$$\Rightarrow x^3 - 9x^2 + 27x - 27 = 9 - 3 - 9(x - 3) \quad (\because$$
BY equation $(1)$ )

$$\Rightarrow x^3 - 9x^2 + 27x - 27 = 6 - 9x + 27$$

$$\Rightarrow x^3 - 9x^2 + 36x - 27 = 33$$

$$\Rightarrow x^3 - 9x^2 + 36x + 10 = 0$$

Hence, the correct option is (D).

**54.** Let cost price of $1000\,gm$ of goods be Rs. $1000$

A dishonest shopkeeper makes cheating of $25\%$ at the time of buying the goods,

$\Rightarrow$ Quantity bought by the shopkeeper for Rs. $1000$

$$= 1000 + 25\% \text{ of } 1000 = 1250\,gm$$

A shopkeeper makes $37.5\%$ cheating at the time of selling the goods,

$\Rightarrow$ Quantity sold by the shopkeeper for Rs. $1000$

$$= 1000 - 37.5\% \text{ of } 1000 = 625\,gm$$

But, he promises to sell the goods at $15\%$ loss,

$\Rightarrow$ Selling price of $625\,gm$ good

$$= 1000 - 15\% \text{ of } 1000 = Rs.\,850$$

$\Rightarrow$ Selling price of $1250\,gm$ good

$$= \left(\frac{850}{625}\right) \times 1250 = \text{Rs. } 1700$$

$\therefore$ Profit percentage $= \left(\frac{Selling price - cost price}{cost price}\right) \times 100$

$$= \left(\frac{1700 - 1000}{1000}\right) \times 100 = 70\%$$

Hence, the correct option is (B).

**55.** The expression $18^2 \times 17^3 \times 45^3 \times 23^2 \times 29$, can be written as

$\Rightarrow 18^2 \times 17^3 \times 45^3 \times 23^2 \times 29 = 3^4 \times 2^2 \times 17^3 \times 3^6 \times 5^3 \times 23^2 \times 29$
$= 3^{10} \times 2^2 \times 17^3 \times 5^3 \times 23^2 \times 29$

$\Rightarrow$ Number of prime factors $= 10 + 2 + 3 + 3 + 2 + 1$ [adding all the powers of prime numbers]

$\therefore$ Number of prime factors $= 21$

Hence, the correct option is (B).

**56.** $\Rightarrow$ Simple interest for $2$ years $= \dfrac{(Principal \times rate \times time)}{100}$

$$= \frac{(1500 \times 10 \times 2)}{100}$$

$$= \text{Rs. } 300$$

Compound interest when compounded yearly at the rate of $10\%$

$\Rightarrow$ Compound Amount $=$ Principal $\left\{1 + \left(\frac{rate}{100}\right)\right\}^2$

$$= 1500\left\{1 + \left(\frac{10}{100}\right)\right\}^2$$

$$= \text{Rs. } 1815$$

$\Rightarrow$ Compound interest $= 1815 - 1500$

$$= \text{Rs. } 315$$

$\Rightarrow$ Required difference $= \text{Rs. } (315 - 300)$

$$= \text{Rs. } 15$$

$\therefore$ Difference is Rs. $15$

Hence, the correct option is (B).

**57.** Let $C_1$ be the cost price of first cycle and $C_2$ be the cost price of second cycle.

Now, he sold first cycle at 15% profit and second at 25% profit, he earns a certain profit

$\Rightarrow$ Total Profit = Rs. 351

Now,

$\Rightarrow$ Profit = profit% of cost price

$\Rightarrow 351 = 15\%C_1 + 25\%C_2$

$\Rightarrow 15C_1 + 25C_2 = 35100 \qquad ---- (1)$

Also, he sold first cycle at 25% profit and second at 15% profit, he gain Rs. 18 more,

$\Rightarrow 25\%C_1 + 15\%C_2 = 351 + 18$

$\Rightarrow 25C_1 + 15C_2 = 36900 \qquad ---- (2)$

Subtracting equation (1) from (2), we get

$\Rightarrow 10(C_1 - C_2) = 1800$

$\Rightarrow (C_1 - C_2) = 180$

$\Rightarrow C_1 = 180 + C_2 \qquad ---- (3)$

Now,

$\Rightarrow 15(180 + C_2) + 25C_2 = 35100$

$\Rightarrow 2700 + 40C_2 = 35100$

$\Rightarrow C_2 = 810$

Now,

$\Rightarrow C_1 = 180 + 810 = $ Rs. 990

$\therefore$ Cost price of cycles are Rs. 990 and Rs. 810

Hence, the correct option is (A).

**58.** Let the length of the train be $2x$ km.

$\Rightarrow$ Length of platform $= \left(\dfrac{1}{2}\right) \times 2x = x$ km

As train crosses a platform half of its length with a speed of $72$ km/hr in $1$ minute,

$\Rightarrow$ Speed $= 72$ km/hr

$= 72 \times \left(\dfrac{5}{18}\right)$

$= 20$ meter/second

$\Rightarrow$ Time $= 1$ minute $= 60$ second

Now,

$\Rightarrow$ Distance $=$ speed $\times$ time

$\Rightarrow x + 2x = 20 \times 60$

$\Rightarrow 3x = 1200$

$\Rightarrow x = 400$ meter

Now,

$\Rightarrow$ Length of another train $= 2 \times 2x = 4x = 4 \times 400 = 1600$ meter

$\Rightarrow$ Speed $= 60\%$ of $20 = 12$ meter/second

$\Rightarrow$ Time in crossing another train $= \dfrac{distance}{speed}$

$= \dfrac{(1600+800)}{12}$

$= \dfrac{2400}{12}$

$= 200$ second

$\therefore$ Time taken to cross the train is $200$ second

Hence, the correct option is (C).

**59.** Given,

$\Rightarrow 100x^2 - 10x - 10x + 1 = 0$

$\Rightarrow 10x(10x - 1) - 1(10x - 1) = 0$

$\Rightarrow (10x - 1)(10x - 1) = 0$

$\Rightarrow (10x - 1)^2 = 0$

$\Rightarrow 10x - 1 = 0$

$\Rightarrow x = \dfrac{1}{10}$

Hence, the correct option is (C).

**60.** We know,

$a^3 - b^3 = (a - b)(a^2 + ab + b^2)$

$(a - b)^2 = a^2 + b^2 - 2ab$

Now let us simplify, $27x^3 - 64y^3$ using the formula $a^3 - b^3 = (ab)(a^2 + ab + b^2)$

Where $a = 3x$ and $b = 4y$

$= (3x)^3 - (4y)^3$

$= (3x - 4y)((3x)^2 + 3x.4y + (4y)^2)$

$= (3x - 4y)(9x^2 + 12xy + 16y^2) - \cdots (1)$

Given Data, $3x - 4y = 5$

Squaring on both sides of this equation,

$\Rightarrow (3x - 4y)^2 = 5^2$

It is of the form $(a - b)^2 = a^2 + b^2 - 2ab$, where $a = 3x$ and $b = 4y$

$\Rightarrow 9x^2 + 16y^2 - 24xy = 25$

Now we add and subtract $12xy$ to the equation, we get

$\Rightarrow 9x^2 + 16y^2 - 24xy + 12xy - 12xy = 25$

$\Rightarrow 9x^2 + 16y^2 - 36xy + 12xy = 25$

$\Rightarrow 9x^2 + 16y^2 + 12xy = 25 + 36xy$

Substituting the given Data: $xy = 3$ in the above equation we get,

$\Rightarrow 9x^2 + 16y^2 + 12xy = 25 + 36 \times 3$

$\Rightarrow 9x^2 + 16y^2 + 12xy = 25 + 108$

$\Rightarrow 9x^2 + 16y^2 + 12xy = 133$

Now, substituting $9x^2 + 16y^2 + 12xy = 133$ and $3x - 4y = 5$ in equation $(1)$, we get

$\Rightarrow (3x - 4y)(9x^2 + 12xy + 16y^2)$

$\Rightarrow 27x^3 - 64y^3 = 5 \times 133$

$\Rightarrow 27x^3 - 64y^3 = 665$

Hence, the correct option is (B).

**61.**

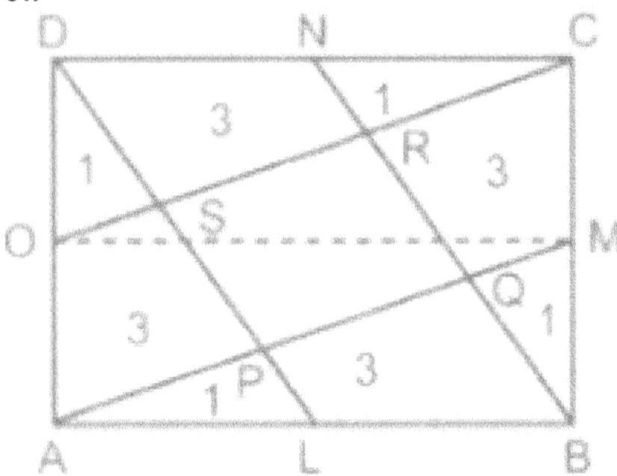

L and N are the midpoints, so DL ∥ BN.

Similarly, OC ∥ AM,

In ΔAQB, L is the midpoint of AB and LP ∥ BQ.

So, P is a midpoint of side AQ.

$\Rightarrow$ AP= $\left(\dfrac{1}{2}\right) \times$ AQ

$\Rightarrow \dfrac{AP}{AQ} = \dfrac{1}{2}$

Also, ΔAPL and ΔAQB are similar

$\Rightarrow$ Ratio of area of ΔAPL and ΔAQB = 1 : 4

$\Rightarrow$ Area of ΔAPL = 1

$\Rightarrow$ Area of PLQB = 3

By symmetry,

$\Rightarrow$ Area of ΔAPL = ΔQMB = ΔNRC = ΔDOS = 1

$\Rightarrow$ Area of PLQB = RCMQ = DSRN = OSPA = 3

Now, Join mid points O and M,

$\Rightarrow$ Area of ΔAMB = ΔAOM = ΔMOC = ΔDOC = 5

$\Rightarrow$ Area of ABCD = 5 + 5 + 5+ 5 = 20

$\Rightarrow$ Area of AMCO = 5 + 5 = 10

$\Rightarrow$ Area of PQRS = area of AMCO – area of APSO – area of CRQM
= 10 – 3 – 3 = 4

∴ Area of shaded region : Area of ABCD = 4 : 20 = 1 : 5

Hence, the correct option is (B).

**62.** Let the distance covered on each side be $x$ km

As,

$$Speed = \dfrac{Distance}{time}$$

Time taken to cover side AB $= \dfrac{x}{10}$ hr

Time taken to cover side BC $= \dfrac{x}{12}$ hr

Time taken to cover side CA $= \dfrac{x}{15}$ hr

Now,

$\Rightarrow Avg.\,speed = \left(\dfrac{total\ distance}{total\ time}\right)$

$= \dfrac{(x+x+x)}{\left(\frac{x}{10}\right)+\left(\frac{x}{12}\right)+\left(\frac{x}{15}\right)}$

$= 3x \times \dfrac{60}{(6x+5x+4x)}$

$= \dfrac{180x}{15x}$

$= 12$ km/hr

Hence, the correct option is (B).

**63.** As, A claim $\dfrac{1}{8}$ of the profit and B claims $\dfrac{1}{3}$ of the profit so, let the profit be $24$ units

$\Rightarrow$ Profit of A $= \left(\dfrac{1}{8}\right) \times 24 = 3$ units

$\Rightarrow$ Profit of B $= \left(\dfrac{1}{3}\right) \times 24 = 8$ units,

$\Rightarrow$ Profit of C $= 24 - 3 - 8 = 13$ units

Also, A invests money for $4$ months, B invests for $6$ months and C invests for $8$ months.

We know,

$\Rightarrow k \times$ Profit $=$ Time $\times$ investment, where $k$ is a constant

|  | A | B | C |
|---|---|---|---|
| Profit | 3 | 8 | 13 |
| Time | 4 | 6 | 8 |
| Investment | $\dfrac{3k}{4}$ | $\dfrac{8k}{6}$ | $\dfrac{13k}{8}$ |

Given,

$\Rightarrow C\,'$s investment $=$ Rs. $1560$

$\Rightarrow \dfrac{13k}{8} =$ Rs. $1560$

$\Rightarrow k = 960$

Now,

$\Rightarrow$ A's investment $= 3\frac{k}{4}$

$= \left(\frac{3 \times 960}{4}\right)$

$=$ Rs. $720$

$\therefore$ Investment of A is Rs. $720$

Hence, the correct option is (C).

**64.** Total cost price Rs. $= 1600$ Let CP $_1 = 600$ and CP $_2 = 1000$

Case I, When he sells first at $10\%$ profit and second at $20\%$ profit:

$\therefore$ Profit on CP $_1 = 10\%$ on $600 =$ Rs. $60$

Profit on CP $_2 = 20\%$ on $1000 =$ Rs. $200$

Total Profit = ₹ 260 ...(i) Case II, When he sells first at $20\%$ profit and second at $10\%$ profit:

$\therefore$ Profit on CP $_1 = 20\%$ on $600 =$ Rs. $120$

Profit on $_2 = 10\%$ on $1000 =$

Rs. $100$

Total Profit $=$ Rs. $220 \ldots (ii)$

Difference in Profit

$=$ Rs. $40$

When difference in profit is Rs. $40$, then difference in cost price would be Rs. $(1000 - 600) =$ Rs. $400$.

When difference in profit is Rs. $5$, then difference in cost price would be:

Rs. $= \left(\frac{400}{40} \times 5\right)$

$=$ Rs. $50$.

Hence, the correct option is (C).

**65.** Given,

$\Rightarrow 52^2 - 42^2 + ?^2 = 64^2 - 56^2 + 3^2 - 2^2$

$\Rightarrow ?^2 = (64^2 - 56^2) + (3^2 - 2^2) - (52^2 - 42^2)$

$\Rightarrow ?^2 = 960 + 5 - 940$

$\Rightarrow ?^2 = 25$

$\therefore ? = \sqrt{25} = 5$

Hence, the correct option is (D).

**66.** Let the digits of the number be $'xy'$

$\Rightarrow$ Number $= 10x + y$

After interchanging the digit, the number becomes $10y + x$

$\Rightarrow$ Difference in average after interchanging the digits $= 3.6$

As, there are $10$ numbers,

$\Rightarrow$ Difference between the numbers will be $= 3.6 \times 10 = 36$

$\Rightarrow$ Difference in numbers $9x - 9y = 36$

$\therefore$ Difference in digits, $(x - y) = 4$

Hence, the correct option is (C).

**67.**

|  | A | B | C |
|---|---|---|---|
| Income | 4 | 5 | 6 |
| Expenditure | 2 | 3 | 4 |

Making ratios of income and expenditure of B equal by multiplying income by $3$ and expenditure by $5$,

|  | A | B | C |
|---|---|---|---|
| Income | 12 | 15 | 18 |
| Expenditure | 10 | 15 | 20 |

Saving of B is $\frac{1}{3}$ of its Income,

$\Rightarrow$ If the income of B is $3$, then the expenditure is $2$ and the savings is $1$,

On multiplying the income by $3$ and the expenditure by $2$, we get

|  | A | B | C |
|---|---|---|---|
| Income | 36 | 45 | 54 |
| Expenditure | 20 | 30 | 40 |
| Saving | 16 | 15 | 14 |

$\therefore$ The ratio of their savings $= 16 : 15 : 14$

Hence, the correct option is (D).

**68.** Given,

$$\frac{(0.73)^3 + (0.27)^3}{(0.73)^2 + (0.27)^2 - 0.73 \times 0.27}$$

let $a = 0.73$ and $b = 0.27$

$$= \frac{(0.73 + 0.27)\left[(0.73)^2 + (0.27)^2 - 0.73 \times 0.27\right]}{(0.73)^2 + (0.27)^2 - 0.73 \times 0.27}$$

$[\because a^3 + b^3 = (a + b)(a^2 + b^2 - ab)$

$= 0.73 + 0.27$

$= 1$

Hence, the correct option is (D).

**69.** $\Rightarrow$ Copper in the new alloy $= 100 - 14 = 86\%$

Using allegation method,

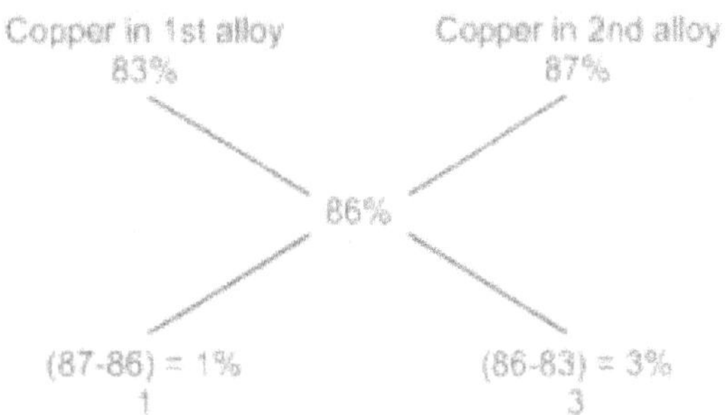


$\Rightarrow 1:3$ is the ratio in which the two mixture must mixed so that the new mixture has $86\%$ copper,

$\Rightarrow$ Percentage of copper in new mixture $= \left(\dfrac{3}{4}\right) \times 100 =$ $75\%$

Hence, the correct option is (B).

**70.** 69% of 699 + 19.96 × 19.68 – 45.5% of 98 = ?

Take approximate value as,

$\Rightarrow 69 \approx 70$

$\Rightarrow 699 \approx 700$

$\Rightarrow 19.96 \approx 20$

$\Rightarrow 19.68 \approx 20$

$\Rightarrow 45.5 \approx 45$

$\Rightarrow 99.9 \approx 100$

After putting approximated values, equation now becomes,

$\Rightarrow$ 70% of 700 + 20 × 20 – 45% of 100 = ?

$\Rightarrow$ 490 + 400 – 45 = ?

$\therefore$ ? = 845

Hence, the correct option is (B).

**71.** Let the total number of voters be 100x

$\Rightarrow$ Votes casted = 100x – 10000

80% of casted votes are valid,

$\Rightarrow$ Valid votes = 80% of (100x – 10000) = (80x – 8000)

Winning candidate won by 2000 votes and losing candidate got 20% of total votes,

$\Rightarrow$ Losing candidate got = 20% of 100x = 20x

$\Rightarrow$ Winning candidate got = 20% of x + 2000 = 20x + 2000

According to the question,

$\Rightarrow$ (80x – 8000) = 20x + 2000 + 20x

$\Rightarrow$ x = 250

$\Rightarrow$ 100x = 25000

$\therefore$ Total votes polled = 25000

Hence, the correct option is (B).

**72.** $(A+B)$'s 1 hour work $= \dfrac{1}{12} + \dfrac{1}{15} = \dfrac{9}{60} = \dfrac{3}{20}$

$(A+C)$'s 1 hour work $= \dfrac{1}{12} + \dfrac{1}{20} = \dfrac{8}{60} = \dfrac{2}{15}$

Part filled in $2$ hours $= \dfrac{3}{20} + \dfrac{2}{15} = \dfrac{17}{60}$

Part filled in $6$ hours $= 3 \times \dfrac{17}{60} = \dfrac{17}{20}$

Remaining part $= 1 - \dfrac{17}{20} = \dfrac{3}{20}$

Now it is the turn of $A$ and $B$ and $\dfrac{3}{20}$ part is filled by $A$ and $B$ in $1$ hour

Total time taken to fill tank $= (6+1)$ hours

$= 7$ hours

Hence, the correct option is (C).

**73.** Total words starting with B $= 4! = 24$

Total words starting with E $= 4! = 24$

Total words starting with KB $= 3! = 6$

Total words starting with KE $= 3! = 6$

Total words starting with KR $= 3! = 6$

If Starting word will be KUBER, then rank of KUBER, $= 24 + 24 + 18 + 1$

$= 67$

Hence, the correct option is (A).

**74.** Since the numbers are co-prime, they contain only 1 as the common factor. Also, the given two products have the middle number in common. So, middle number = H.C.F. of 551 and $1073 = 29$

First number

$= \dfrac{551}{29}$

$= 19$

Third number

$= \dfrac{1073}{29}$

$= 37$

$\therefore$ Required sum $= 19 + 29 + 37$

$= 85$

Hence, the correct option is (C).

**75.** L.C.M. of $8, 16, 40$ and $80 = 80$

$\dfrac{7}{8} = \dfrac{70}{80}, \dfrac{13}{16} = \dfrac{65}{80}, \dfrac{31}{40} = \dfrac{62}{80}$

Since, $\dfrac{70}{80} > \dfrac{65}{80} > \dfrac{63}{80} > \dfrac{62}{80}$,

So, $\dfrac{7}{8} > \dfrac{13}{16} > \dfrac{63}{80} > \dfrac{31}{40}$

So, $\dfrac{7}{8}$ is the largest.

Hence, the correct option is (A).

**76.** According to the passage, there are various technologies that are emerging - Artificial Intelligence (AI), big data and analytics, the blockchain, cloud, Internet of Things (IoT), and robotics. AI and machine learning are transforming customer experience with personalized services and improvements in back-office efficiencies. Fintech – the technological innovations in the design and delivery of financial services and products – is revolutionizing customer expectations.

Hence, the correct option is (D).

**77.** The passage mentions the major challenges in the last paragraph. Options (A) and (B) are not the challenges that the models' decision-making processes are faced with. According to the last line, 'Proper integration is a counter to the potential lack of transparency and interpretability in these models' decision-making processes'. The word counter means the opposite in effect. So, the line conveys that proper integration is a solution to the challenge of having a lack of transparency and interpretability in these models.

Hence, the correct option is (D).

**78.** The word agility is used to describe the quality of moving fast and quickly. In the given context which talks about the agility of the passage, it means that the emerging technologies have the ability to deal with new changes and challenges in a quick manner.

The way of behaving or happening in an unusual and unexpected manner – an aberration, anomaly, deviation, divergence.

The process of making a problem or situation worse – exacerbation.

A typical example – standard, prototype, paradigm, model.

Hence, the correct option is (C).

**79.** Robots are venturing into investment and changing how wealth advisory services are delivered. Blockchain may redefine how financial institutions operate.

Hence, the correct option is (D).

**80.** In the given context, the word conservative means restrained and traditional in style. Let us look into the meaning of the given words:

Progressive – new and modern which encourages change in the society

Conventional – ordinary and traditional

Hostile – showing unfriendliness and opposition

Winsome – pleasing and attractive in simple (often child-like) ways

The word conventional is, in fact, a synonym. We are looking for an antonym (a word having the opposite meaning).

Hence, the correct option is (B).

**81.** The sentence is in the simple future tense. Therefore will be given should be used.

Hence, the correct option is (A).

**82.** The error lies in part (b) of the sentence as the preposition 'in' is incorrect and must be replaced with 'by' as something is 'by' someone. It means formally request or demand say that one owns or has earned (something). It should read as are also claimed by China.

Hence, the correct option is (B).

**83.** The correct spelling for this is "hoax" which means "a humorous or malicious deception."

Prudence: the quality of being prudent; cautiousness.

Tact: skill and sensitivity in dealing with others or with difficult issues.

Dupe: deceive; trick.

Hence, the correct option is (C).

**84.** The correct word here is "illegible" which means "that which cannot be easily read."

Eligible: having the right to do or obtain something; satisfying the appropriate conditions.

Illegitimate: not authorized by the law; not in accordance with accepted standards or rules.

Legislature: the legislative body of a country or state.

Hence, the correct option is (A).

**85.** The sentence is in active voice thus in the passive voice the object 'question' must be written before the subject 'Rohan.' In active voice :

Subject+verb+object

In passive voice:

Object+verb+subject

The tense here is past continuous thus 'was being asked' is the correct verb to be used here.

Hence, the correct option is (C).

**86.** Have is used with some pronouns and plural nouns. For example: 'Nurses have a difficult job.' Has is used with the third person singular. For example: 'The washing machine has a leak in it'.

Hence, the correct option is (B).

**87.** The sentence suggests that the blank must contain a noun.

Also, given the context, the word should mean 'influence'.

The only word that fits the blank is **clout.**

Hence, the correct option is (B).

**88.** The sentence suggests that the blank must contain a noun.

Also, given the context, the word should mean 'the period when Obama was the President of the U.S.'

The only word that fits the blank is the **presidency**.

Hence, the correct option is (C).

**89.** The sentence suggests that the blank must contain a verb.

Also, given the context, the word should is similar to 'isolated'. Since it is referring to a war-torn country, the word must mean 'reduced in strength' by war.

The only word that fits the blank is **debilitated.**

To divulge is to disclose something. A deluge is a severe flood.

Hence, the correct option is (A).

**90.** The sentence suggests that the blank must contain a noun.

Also, given the context, the word should mean a dangerous 'trend'.

The only word that fits the blank is **precedent.**

To portend is to be a sign of something likely to happen.

Hence, the correct option is (C).

**91.** The sentence suggests that the blank must contain a noun.

Also, given the context, the word should mean 'strength'.

The only word that fits the blank is **might.**

Paltry means are very small. Crony means a close friend.

Hence, the correct option is (D).

**92.** The word 'bewitching' means 'fascinating, magical.'

Daring - involving or taking risks.

Deriding - to laugh at someone or something in a way that shows you think they are stupid or of no value.

Tailgating - drive too closely behind (another vehicle).

Hence, the correct option is (B).

**93.** 'Profane' means not relating to that which is sacred or religious. It means relating to or believing in a religion.

Hence, the correct option is (C).

**94.** The correct spelling is 'idiosyncrasy'. To have an idiosyncrasy is to have a special quality, something that may be considered an odd habit.

E.g. One major idiosyncrasy about Monica was her obsession with cleaning and organization.

Hence, the correct option is (D).

**95.** The correct spelling is 'liaison'. To liaison is to create communication and cooperation between committees and/or organizations.

E.g. Joseph managed the liaison between his father and his mother-in-law's company.

Hence, the correct option is (B).

**96.** The correct spelling is 'dilemma'. To be in a dilemma means to be in trouble or to have a problem that is confusing and thus hard to make a decision on.

E.g. Abraham was in a dilemma about whether to tell Rose about their daughter's divorce.

Hence, the correct option is (C).

**97.** After reading the given sentences we can easily make out that the paragraph talks about 'National Flag'.

Except for sentence C, none of the other sentences is of independent nature. Also, sentence C introduces the topic, hence it will be the starting sentence of the paragraph. Sentence E follows C, as it tells the positions of the colours mentioned in sentence C. Sentence A will follow E, as components of the flag are being discussed and sentence A is taking it further. D will follow A as sentence D tells the colour of the 'Ashoka Chakra'. Sentence B completes the paragraph.

Hence, the correct option is (D).

**98.** After reading the given sentences we can easily make out that the paragraph talks about 'Indian culture'.

Sentence A forms the forms the base for the paragraph by telling that it is 'popular across the world'. Sentence B will follow B as it implicitly telling the reason why the 'Indian culture' is popular. Sentences C and D both talk about 'Indian people', hence will come together. Since 'people are highly devoted to their culture and religion', hence 'people here live with strong bond'. Thus, sentence D will follow C. The paragraph is concluded by sentence E which tells about the factors that have influenced the culture.

Hence, the correct option is (A).

**99.** Firstly, let us find the meanings of the given options-

**Stickler-** A person who insists on a particular type of behaviour.

**Fiend-** A cruel person.

**Maniac-** A person having wild behaviour.

**Lunatic-** A person who is mentally ill.

Clearly, **stickler** best expresses the meaning of the above-mentioned phrase.

Hence, the correct option is (D).

**100. 'Indelible'** means 'that cannot be erased'.

The meanings of the other words are-

**Invincible:** too strong to be overcome.

**Incorrigible:** incapable of being corrected.

**Inaudible:** a sound that cannot be heard.

Hence, the correct option is (B).

## General Intelligence & Reasoning

**Q.1 Direction:** In the question, two statements are given, followed by two conclusions, I and II. You have to consider the statements to be true even if it seems to be at variance from commonly known facts. You have to decide which of the given conclusions, if any, follows from the given statements.

**Statement:** Ramesh's friend helped him to get a loan.

**Conclusions:**

I: Ramesh's friend was supportive.

II: Ramesh had many friends.

**A.** Only conclusion I follows

**B.** Only conclusion II follows

**C.** Both conclusion I and II follows

**D.** Neither I or II follows

**Q.2**

> Find out which of the figures (1), (2), (3) and (4) can be formed from the pieces given in figure (X).

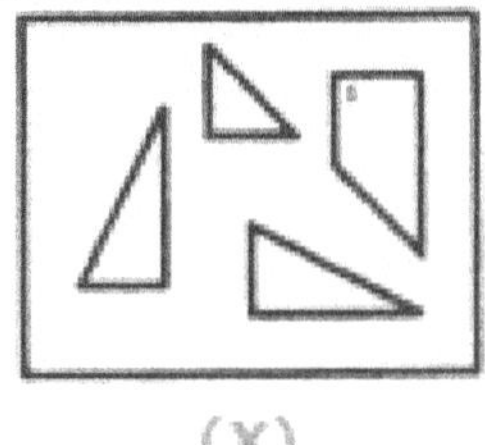

(X)

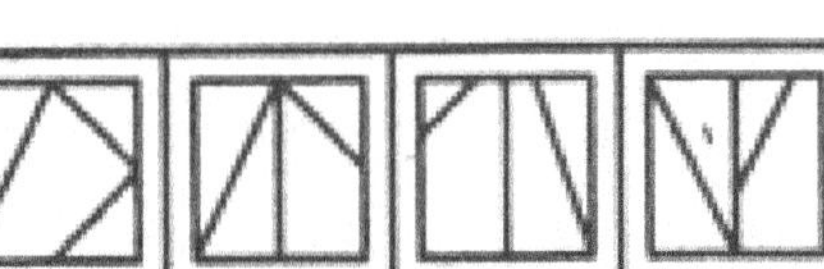

(1)  (2)  (3)  (4)

**A.** 1  **B.** 2  **C.** 3  **D.** 4

**Q.3 Directions:** In the following question, select the related letters/number from the given alternatives.

713T: 812V :: 2280: ?

**A.** 327P  **B.** 327Q  **C.** 127P  **D.** 129Q

**Q.4**

**Directions:** Study the following number sequence and answer the question following it.

6 5 6 5 5 6 6 7 6 5 7 5 6 6 5 7 7 5 6 6 7

If 1 is added to number at even places and 1 is subtracted from number at odd places, how many times do we get three consecutive same number?

**A.** 0  **B.** 1  **C.** 2  **D.** 3

**Q.5** In each of the following question find out the alternative which will replace the question mark.

Trail : Jury::?

**A.** Dispute : Arbiter

**B.** Poll : Contestant

**C.** Championship : Spectator

**D.** Conference : Speaker

**Q.6** In the following question, four groups of three numbers are given. In each group, the second and the third number is related to the first number by a Logic/Rule/Relation. Three are similar on the basis of some Rule/Relation/Logic. Select the odd one from the given alternatives.

2 10 20, 3 15 30, 4 16 40, 5 25 50

**A.** 2 10 20  **B.** 4 16 40  **C.** 5 25 50  **D.** 3 15 30

**Q.7** If 'MISTAKE' is coded as 9765412 and 'NAKED' is coded as 84123, how is 'STAIN' coded?

**A.** 89483  **B.** 65478  **C.** 68194  **D.** 98175

**Q.8 Direction:** Based on the statement(s) given below, choose the best possible conclusion(s) that follows:

**Statement:**

A class teacher has badly scolded Vihaan in front of all the students.

**Conclusions:**

I. Vihaan has not completed his homework.

II. A class teacher wanted Vihaan to feel embarrassed in front of all the students.

**A.** Only conclusion I follows

**B.** Only conclusion II follows

**C.** Both conclusions I and II follow

**D.** Neither conclusion I nor II follows

**Q.9** In the following question, select the odd word pair from the given alternatives.

**A.** Conclusion - Introduction

**B.** Farewell - Salutation

**C.** Adieu - Greeting

**D.** Culmination - Wrap

**Q.10** In a certain code language, "LEAVE" is written as "MGDXF". How is "MINED" written in that code language?

**A.** NEQJK  **B.** NKQEG  **C.** NKGQE  **D.** NKQGE

**Q.11** In the following question, four words have been given out of which three are alike in some manner, while the fourth one is different. Choose the word which is different from the rest.

**A.** Bengali  **B.** Maithili  **C.** Hausa  **D.** Bodo

**Q.12** If FAN is written as '84', HIT is written as '1440' then how 'BUN' is written?

**A.** 80  **B.** 588  **C.** 450  **D.** 200

**Q.13** In the following question, select the related word from the given alternatives.

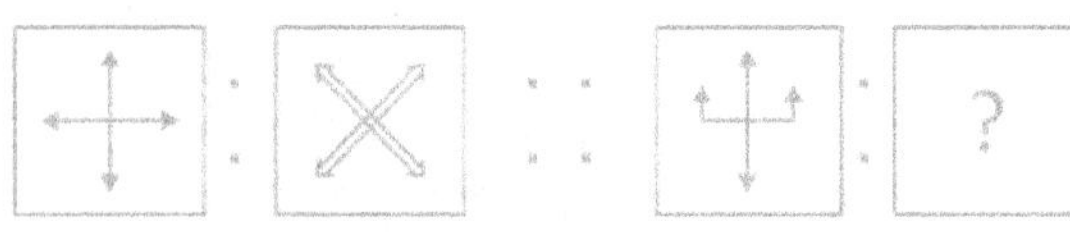

**A.** 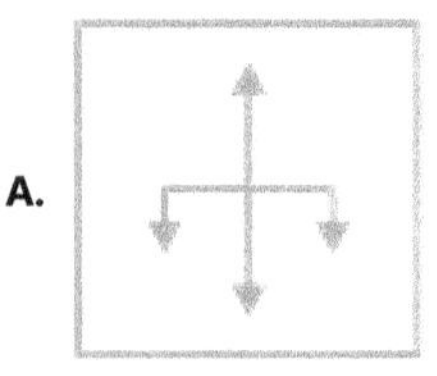

**B.** 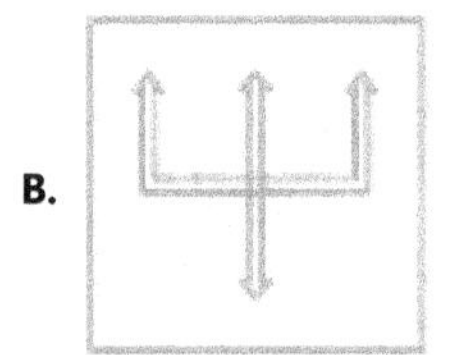

**C.** 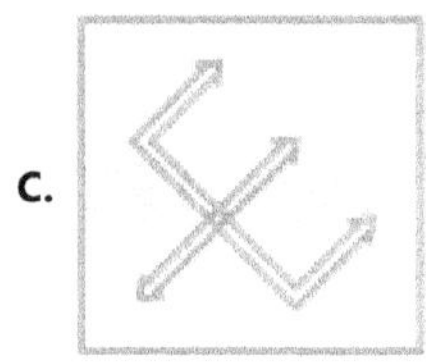

**D.** 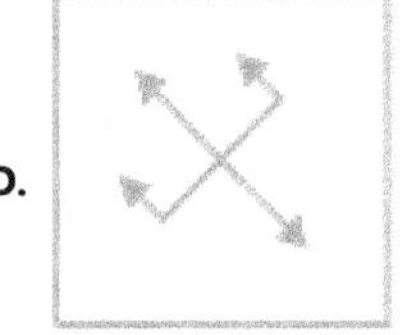

**Q.14** Find the missing term : 3, 5, 9, 17, ?

**A.** 33     **B.** 42     **C.** 26     **D.** 65

**Q.15** P and Q are sisters, R and S are only brothers, P's son is S's brother. In which of the following ways is P related to R?

**A.** Mother     **B.** Daughter
**C.** Grandmother     **D.** Aunt

**Q.16** Which figure in the given question will complete the pattern of the question figure?

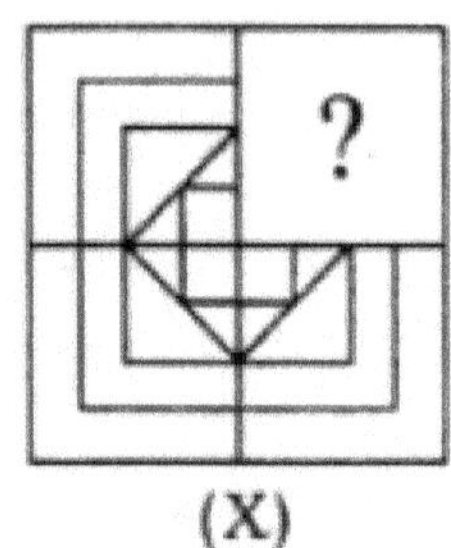

**(X)**

**A.** 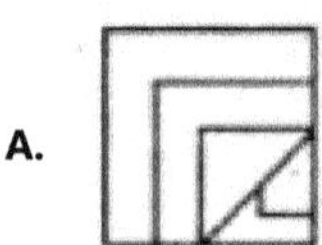

**B.** 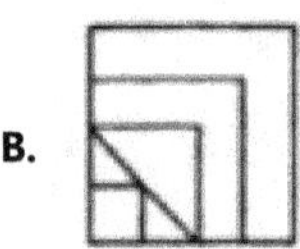

**C.** 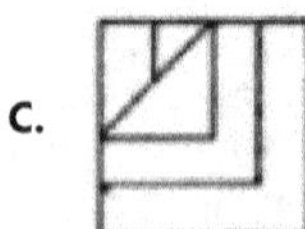

**D.** 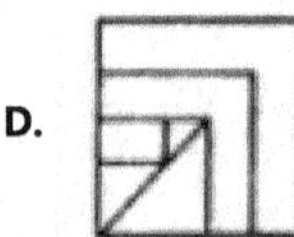

**Q.17 Direction:** Identify the diagram that best represents the relationship among the given classes.

Singer, Musician, Businessman

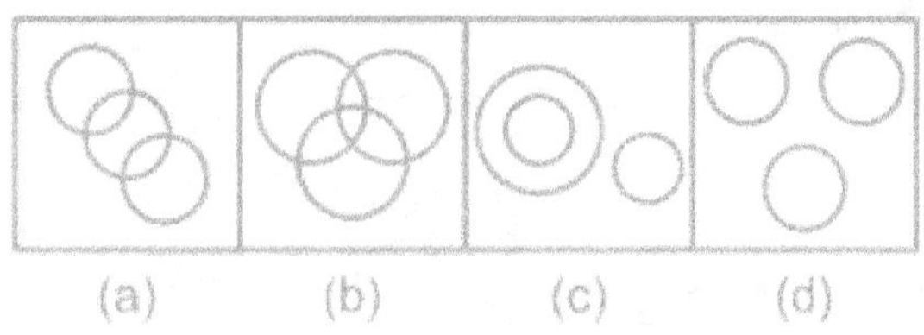

**A.** (a)     **B.** (b)     **C.** (b)     **D.** (c)

**Q.18**

A number of friends decided to go on a picnic and planned to spend Rs. 96 on eatables. Four of them, however, did not turn up. As a consequence, the remaining ones had to contribute Rs. 4 each extra. The number of those who attended the picnic was

**A.** 8     **B.** 12     **C.** 16     **D.** 24

**Q.19** Select a figure from amongst the Answer Figures which will continue the same series as established by the five Problem Figures.

**Problem Figures:**

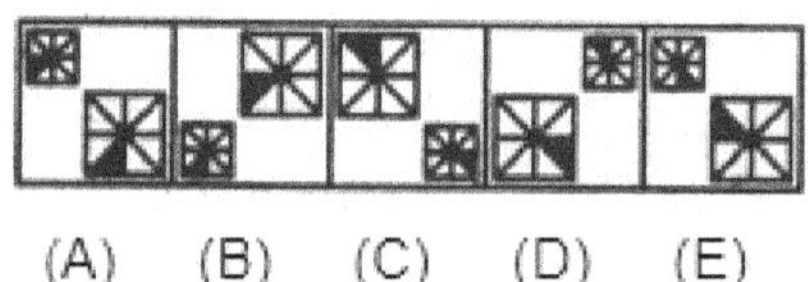

(A)    (B)    (C)    (D)    (E)

**Answer Figures:**

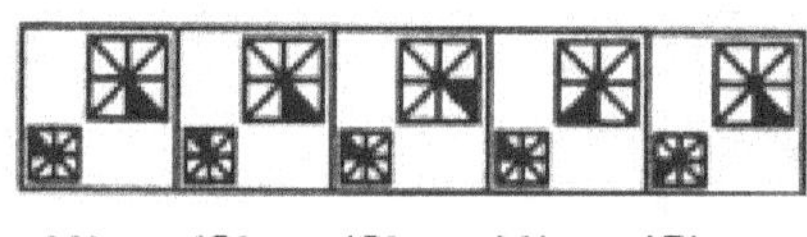

(1)    (2)    (3)    (4)    (5)

**A.** (1)     **B.** (2)     **C.** (4)     **D.** (3)

**Q.20** Correct the following equation by interchanging the two signs.

$8 \times 4 + 5 \div 2 - 1 = 11$

**A.** × and +     **B.** × and ÷     **C.** + and -     **D.** ÷ and -

**Q.21** The following question needs or may not need brackets at certain places to make them correct. Find out at which places it needs bracket.

$30 - 6 - 4 - 2 = 30$

**A.** 30 - (6 - 4) - 2     **B.** (30 - 6) - 4 - 2
**C.** 30 - 4 - (6 - 2)     **D.** 30 - (6 - 4 - 2)

**Q.22** Find the minimum number of straight lines required to make the given figure.

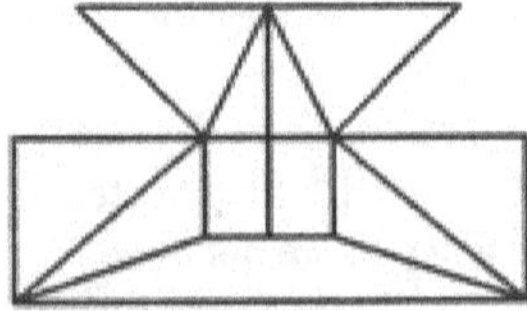

*[Intelligence Bureau Security Assistant, 2017]*

**A.** 16     **B.** 17     **C.** 18     **D.** 19

**Ques (23-24):Direction:** Study the following information carefully to answer the given question.

Amar, Brijesh, Pinky, Deep, Eshwar, Nancy, Gurkamal and Harsh are sitting around a circle facing the center. Nancy is third to the right of Pinky and second to the left of Harsh. Deep is not an immediate neighbor of Pinky or Harsh. Eshwar is to the immediate right of Amar, who is second to the right of Gurkamal.

**Q.23** Who is second to the left of Pinky?

**A.** Amar     **B.** Eshwar     **C.** Brijesh     **D.** Deep

**Q.24** Who is to the immediate right of Pinky?

**A.** Amar     **B.** Bijesh     **C.** Deep     **D.** Ishwar

**Q.25** How many triangles are there in the given figure?

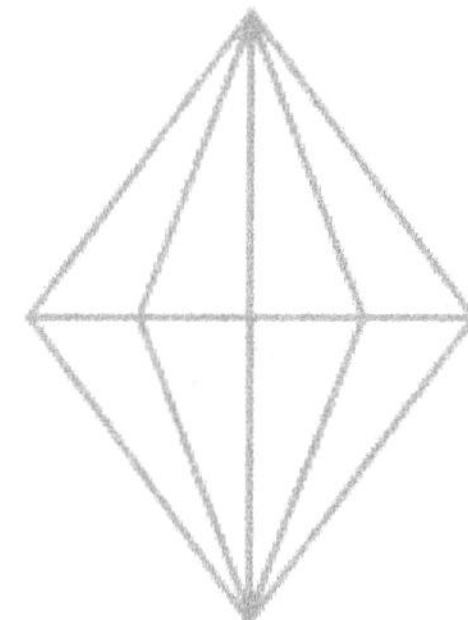

**A.** 13     **B.** 32     **C.** 21     **D.** 24

# General Awareness

**Q.26** The country's first-ever radio channel for the visually impaired, named 'Radio Aksh' has been launched in which city?
*[Delhi Forest Guard, 2021]*

**A.** Delhi     **B.** Nagpur
**C.** Allahabad     **D.** Agra

**Q.27** Who was appointed as the new chairman of the Central Board of Film Certification (CBFC) in August 2017?
*[Super TET Paper - I, 2018]*

**A.** Anupam Kher     **B.** Shekar Kapoor
**C.** Javed Aktar     **D.** Prasoon Joshi

**Q.28** As on March 2018, which of the following is the India's fastest supercomputer?
*[Super TET Paper - I, 2019]*

**A.** Summit     **B.** Sierra     **C.** Mihir     **D.** Pratyush

**Q.29** San Jose is the capital of which of the following countries?
**A.** Jamaica     **B.** Guinea-Bissau
**C.** Moldova     **D.** Costa Rica

**Q.30** The salaries and allowances of the judges of High Court are charged on the _______.
**A.** Consolidated Fund of the State
**B.** Consolidated Fund of India
**C.** Contingency Fund of the State
**D.** Public Fund of India

**Q.31** Sitara Devi is associated with _______.
**A.** Manipuri dance     **B.** Kathak dance
**C.** Garba dance     **D.** Hindustani Vocal

**Q.32** Which mint is known for producing standardized weights and measures in India?
**A.** Noida     **B.** Mumbai
**C.** Hyderabad     **D.** Kolkata

**Q.33** What is the full form of "ATA"?
**A.** Advanced Technology Attachment
**B.** Active Terminal Access
**C.** Array of Transfer Access
**D.** Automated Teller Architecture

**Q.34** The rate at which RBI borrows money from commercial banks within the country is known as:
**A.** Reverse Repo Rate
**B.** Base Rate
**C.** Savings Deposit Rate
**D.** Bank Rate

**Q.35** Where is the headquarters of Small Industries Development Bank of India (SIDBI)?
**A.** Kolkata     **B.** New Delhi
**C.** Mumbai     **D.** Lucknow

**Q.36** Which of the following article of Indian Constitution is related to the appointment of Attorney General of India?
**A.** Article 52     **B.** Article 63
**C.** Article 76     **D.** Article 110

**Q.37** The Rourkela steel plant was built on the bank of which of the following river?
**A.** Bhadra river     **B.** Brahmani river
**C.** Damodar river     **D.** Bhima river

**Q.38** Jallikatu is the traditional game of which state?
**A.** Karnataka     **B.** Andhra Pradesh
**C.** Tamil Nadu     **D.** Kerala

**Q.39** 'Carolina Marin Martin', is related to which game?
**A.** Hockey     **B.** Shooting
**C.** Golf     **D.** Badminton

**Q.40** "Playing It My Way" is the autobiography of which of the following persons?
**A.** Yuvraj
**B.** Dr. A.P.J. Abdul Kalam
**C.** Narendra Modi
**D.** Sachin Tendulkar

**Q.41** The decision of Non-Cooperation Movement was adopted by the Indian National Congress in its _______ in 1920.
**A.** Benaras Session     **B.** Calcutta Session
**C.** Lucknow Session     **D.** Madras Session

**Q.42** In which Rock Edict Ashoka mentions about the casualities of Kalinga War and declares the renunciation of war?
**A.** Maski Edict     **B.** Rock Edict XIII

**C.** Rock Edict XI          **D.** Rock Edict X

**Q.43** In India, the Black Revolution is associated with self-dependence in the production of________.
**A.** Oil seeds production
**B.** Crude petroleum
**C.** Black box
**D.** No option is correct

**Q.44** What did Wilhelm Conrad Roentgen discover ?
**A.** Conservation of electric charge
**B.** Electric bulb
**C.** X-Rays
**D.** Thermodynamics

**Q.45** Sarojini Naidu became the first Indian woman President of the Indian National Congress in _______ session of the INC.
**A.** Kanpur          **B.** Calcutta
**C.** Lucknow          **D.** Surat

**Q.46** Trishna wildlife sanctuary is located in which of the following state?
**A.** Assam          **B.** Telangana
**C.** Tamil Nadu          **D.** Tripura

**Q.47** When is World Humanitarian Day observed?
**A.** 17 August          **B.** 18 August
**C.** 19 August          **D.** 20 August

**Q.48** Which of the following has adopted a resolution titled 'Global solidarity to fight the coronavirus disease 2019 (COVID-19)', calling for intensified international cooperation to defeat the pandemic?
**A.** ASEAN
**B.** United Nations General Assembly
**C.** SCO
**D.** EU

**Q.49** Ustad Bismillah Khan is famous for _______ and was awarded _______.
*[Allahabad High Court Review Officer (RO), 2019]*

**A.** Shehnai, Bharat Ratna
**B.** Sitar, Bharat Ratna
**C.** Flute, Padma Shri
**D.** Sarod, Bharat Ratna

**Q.50** Who among the following won the Player of the Match Award in the final between Australia and New Zealand in recently concluded T20 Men's Cricket World Cup 2021?
**A.** David Warner          **B.** Kane Williamson
**C.** Adam Zampa          **D.** Mitchell Marsh

# Quantitative Aptitude

**Q.51 Direction:** What will come in the place of question mark (?) in the following question.
345.86 + 321.86 + 123.14 + 189.14 = ?
**A.** 768          **B.** 980          **C.** 1048          **D.** 1145

**Q.52** Every month, Swati manages to save 12% of her monthly income. But, last month, she was able to save only Rs. 7020, which is 90% of her monthly savings. What is her monthly salary?
**A.** Rs. 48000          **B.** Rs. 54000
**C.** Rs. 65000          **D.** Rs. 72000

**Q.53** In an examination, the average marks scored by 60 students is 55. On complaint by three students, it was found that their marks were wrongly entered as 6, 6 and 3 instead of 96, 60 and 39 respectively. What is the correct average marks scored by the students in the examination?
**A.** 56          **B.** 57          **C.** 58          **D.** 59

**Q.54** After the first round of counselling, the ratio of the filled seats to the unfilled seats in a college is 7 : 3. If there were 60 more seats in the college, and 24 more seats remained unfilled, then the ratio of filled to unfilled seats would be 9 : 4. How many seats are there in the college?
**A.** 600          **B.** 640          **C.** 700          **D.** 720

**Q.55** Rohit bought two alloys of zinc and copper in the ratio of 3 : 1 and 5 : 2 respectively. He bought 28 kg of both the alloys. He mixed both the alloys. Find the ratio of copper and zinc in new alloy?
**A.** 17 : 41          **B.** 15 : 41          **C.** 41 : 15          **D.** 41 : 17

**Q.56** In a race of 1000 m, A can beat B by 100 m, in a race of 800m, B can beat C by 100m. By how many meters will A beat C in a race of 600 m?
**A.** 57.5 m          **B.** 127.5 m          **C.** 150.7 m          **D.** 98.6 m

**Q.57** LCM of two numbers 32 and their HCF 8 is. One number is 8 , find the second number.
**A.** 24          **B.** 16          **C.** 32          **D.** 40

**Q.58** The value of $16 - [5 - 2\{14 \text{ of } 2 - (8 \div 4 \times 2 - 1 + 3)\}]$ is:
**A.** 51          **B.** 55          **C.** 53          **D.** 57

**Q.59** Distance between Surat and Delhi is 324 km. Two bikes start from Surat and Delhi towards each other at a same time and meet after 4 hours. Speed of one bike is 9 km/hr faster than other. Find the speed of slower bike.
**A.** 45 km/hr          **B.** 36 km/hr          **C.** 30 km/hr          **D.** 24 km/hr

**Q.60** If $x^2 - 12x + 33 = 0$, then what is the value of $(x - 4)^2 + \left[\frac{1}{(x-4)}\right]^2$?
**A.** 16          **B.** 14          **C.** 18          **D.** 20

**Q.61** Find the unit digit of given expression: $x^3 - 3x^2 + 63$ if $(x - 4) = 0$.
**A.** 7          **B.** 0          **C.** 9          **D.** 2

**Q.62** All the face cards are removed from a pack of playing cards. The remaining cards are well shuffled and then a card is drawn from it. What is the probability that the drawn card is an ace?
**A.** $\frac{1}{5}$          **B.** $\frac{1}{4}$          **C.** $\frac{1}{10}$          **D.** $\frac{2}{10}$

**Q.63** An article was sold at 21% gain. Had it been sold for Rs. 640 more, then the gain would have been 37%. What is the cost price (in Rs) of the article?

**A.** 3250          **B.** 4000          **C.** 5700          **D.** 6500

**Q.64** The price of a product after getting 20% discount is Rs. 3,024 which includes 5% tax on selling price. What was the marked price (in Rs.) of the product?

**A.** 3780          **B.** 2742          **C.** 3600          **D.** 2880

**Q.65** In how many years will Rs. 25,000 yield Rs. 8,275 as compound interest at 10% per annum compounded annually?

**A.** 2          **B.** 4          **C.** 3          **D.** 5

**Q.66** Rs. 3500 are invested for 3 years in a scheme of simple interest at a rate of 16% per annum. What will be the amount (in Rs.) obtained after 3 years?

**A.** 5050          **B.** 7200          **C.** 5180          **D.** 4500

**Q.67** A 15 m long bus crosses a 75 m long bridge in 6 seconds. In how much time will it cross a man running in the same direction at a speed of 9 km/hr?

**A.** 0.6 sec          **B.** 0.8 sec          **C.** 1.0 sec          **D.** 1.2 sec

**Q.68** Speeds of a boat along the current and against the current are 12 km/hr and 6 km/hr respectively. What is the speed (in km/hr) of the current?

**A.** 2          **B.** 3          **C.** 4          **D.** 9

**Q.69** Find the value of $(x - y)$, if $(3^5)^x \div (9)^{2x-1} = 243$ and $(5)^{x-2y} \times (5)^{x+y} = 625$.

**A.** 0          **B.** 1          **C.** 2          **D.** 3

**Q.70** What is the area (in cm$^2$) of the rhombus having side as 5 cm and one of the diagonal as 8 cm?

**A.** 25          **B.** 24          **C.** 26          **D.** 23

**Q.71** A cone, a hemisphere and a cylinder stand on the same base and have same height. The ratio of their volume is

**A.** 2 : 1 : 3          **B.** 1 : 2 : 3          **C.** 3 : 1 : 2          **D.** 1 : 3 : 2

**Q.72** The point where the triangle forms the right angle in the right-angled triangle is known as the ________.

**A.** In-centre          **B.** Circum-centre
**C.** Centroid          **D.** Ortho-centre

**Q.73** A and B invested Rs. 24000 and Rs. 8000 for a period of 2 year. After 2 year, they earned Rs. 48000. What will be the shares of A and B out of this earning?

**A.** Rs. 36,000, Rs. 12,000
**B.** Rs. 40,000, Rs. 10,000
**C.** Rs. 25,000, Rs. 40,000
**D.** Rs. 20,000, Rs. 12,000

**Q.74** Pipe A can fill the tank in 15 min and B can fill the tank in 45 min then in how many minutes both can fill 50% of the tank.

**A.** $\frac{45}{2}$          **B.** $\frac{45}{4}$          **C.** $\frac{45}{8}$          **D.** 45

**Q.75** A train of 500 m crosses a bridge in 1 min with the speed of 90 km/hrs while a person crosses the same bridge in 3 minute 20 seconds. Speed of person in km/hr is:

**A.** 10 km/hr          **B.** 15 km/hr          **C.** 12 km/hr          **D.** 18 km/hr

# English Comprehension

**Ques (76-80):Direction: Read the following passage and answer the question given below.**

With the latest proposal, the U.S. plans to "shame" China by bringing the Azhar listing to a public debate at the UNSC. And if that fails, it is reportedly considering a UN General Assembly statement condemning Azhar. The listing of Azhar is an unfinished task India is justified in pursuing. However, the latest U.S. move comes with some concerns. To begin with, there is no indication that China is ready to change its stand, particularly in the face of coercion or threat from the U.S., and it could veto this proposal as well. There appears to be little to be gained at present by forcing China further into Pakistan's corner, especially as New Delhi has said it would pursue the Azhar listing with China with "patience and persistence", in keeping with its desire not to sacrifice the bilateral relationship over the issue. It is equally unlikely that a world power like China would be moved by the threat of public humiliation. New Delhi must applaud the strong support the U.S. and the other UNSC members have provided on the issue of cross-border terror threats, and on the vexed issue of Azhar's listing. But it must be careful not to stake too much on an immediate win at the UNSC vis-a-vis China, and keep its expectations realistic.

**Q.76** Which of the following would be a way to 'shame' China that U.S. may be planning to use?

A. Bringing the Azhar listing to a public debate at the UNSC

B. Applauding the strong support against Azhar by the other UNSC members

C. A statement at the UN General Assembly condemning Azhar

**A.** A and C          **B.** Only A
**C.** A and B          **D.** A, B and C

**Q.77** Which of the following could be the implications of forcing China's hand in the issue of Azhar listing?

**A.** It may further force China towards alliance with Pakistan
**B.** It may choose to veto the proposal again
**C.** It may complicate the bilateral relationship between India and China
**D.** All of the above

**Q.78** Consider the following statements. Which of these are correct?

I. The U.S. is justified in pursuing listing of Azhar as global terrorist at the UNSC.

II. Coercion methods may not work well with a world power such as China.

III. China has vetoed the attempts to list Azhar at the UNSC in the past.

**A.** Only I          **B.** I and II
**C.** II and III          **D.** I, II and III

**Q.79**

Consider the following word from the passage. Which of the following options give its plural form?

Forum

**A.** Forums      **B.** Fora
**C.** Forii      **D.** Both 1 and 2

**Q.80** Which of the following conclusions can be made about India's stance regarding China?

**A.** India should lessen the intensity of its demand of the listing of Azhar

**B.** India does not wish to jeopardize its bilateral relationship with China

**C.** India should thwart the U.S. ambitions to shame China

**D.** India should ally with U.S. and other supporting UNSC members to coerce China

**Q.81 In the following sentence, a part of the sentence is underlined. Below are given alternatives to the underlined part, which may improve the sentence. Choose the correct alternative. In case no improvement is needed, choose the option 'No improvement'.**

<u>Having seen</u> the war, Arnold thought there was nothing that could faze him.

**A.** Being into      **B.** Having been
**C.** Being      **D.** No improvement

**Q.82 Read each sentence to find out whether there is any grammatical error in it. The error, if any will be in one part of the sentence. If there is no error choose option 4 'No error' as the answer.**

Under Trump, the U.S. has bolted from (1)/ or threatening to leave a number of agreements, (2)/ including the Trans-Pacific Partnership free-trade pact. (3)/ No error (4)

**A.** 1      **B.** 2      **C.** 3      **D.** 4

**Q.83 In the following sentence, three words or phrases have been printed in bold. One bold part in the sentence is not acceptable in Standard English. Choose the inappropriate word. If there are no errors in the bold parts, mark (4) i.e. 'No error' as the answer.**

The judge was **known** to be **ostentatious** and thus they **petitioned** to him for justice.

**A.** Known      **B.** Ostentatious
**C.** Petitioned      **D.** No error

**Q.84 Fill in the blank.**

The Bible has proclaimed that he ______ loves his fellow men is loved by God in return.

**A.** Whom    **B.** Whose    **C.** Who    **D.** That

**Q.85** In the following question, a sentence has been given in Active/Passive voice. Out of four alternatives suggested, select the one, which best expresses the same sentence in Passive/Active voice.

Are you looking for a shop which sells sweets?

**A.** Are the shop which sells sweets was looked by you?
**B.** Are the shop which sells sweets was looked for by you?
**C.** Is the shop which sells sweets being looked for by you?
**D.** Is the shop which sells sweets being looking for by you?

**Q.86** A sentence has been given in Active/Passive Voice. Out of the four alternatives suggested, select the one which best expresses the same sentence in Passive/Active Voice.

Who had eaten the last piece of cake?

**A.** By whom had the last piece of cake been eaten?
**B.** By whom was the last piece of cake eaten?
**C.** Whom was the last piece of cake been eaten by?
**D.** By whom has the last piece of cake been eaten?

**Q.87** A sentence has been given in Direct/Indirect speech. Out of the four alternatives choose the one which best expresses the same sentence in Direct/Indirect speech.

Ted said, "The flowers have been taken care of."

**A.** Ted said that the flowers had been taken care of.
**B.** Ted said that the flowers have been taken care of.
**C.** Ted said that the flowers were being taken care of.
**D.** Ted said that the flowers were to be taken care of.

**Q.88** In the following question, a sentence has been given in Direct/Indirect speech. Out of the 4 alternatives suggested, select the one which best expresses the same sentence in indirect/Direct speech.

The strange lady asked the man if he was Catholic or Jewish.

**A.** "Are you Catholic or not?" The strange lady asked the man
**B.** "Aren't you Catholic or Jewish?" The strange lady asked the man.
**C.** "Are you Catholic or Jewish?" The lady asked the man.
**D.** "Are you Catholic or Jewish?" The strange lady asked the man.

**Q.89 Fill in the blank.**

As I was late for the rehearsal dinner of my friend, I ______ haste.

**A.** Prepared      **B.** Gave
**C.** Followed      **D.** Made

**Ques (90-94):In the following passage, some of the words have been left out. Read the passage carefully and select the correct answer for the given blank out of the given alternatives.**

While the country celebrates the missile test as a scientific achievement, it must also __(1)__ on the possibility that this might goad its none-too-friendly neighbor Pakistan into a competitive __(2)__. Also, in the absence of a __(3)__ threat to India's space assets from China or any other country with Anti-Satellite missile capabilities, whether the 'deterrence' sought to be achieved by this test would lead to a more stable __(4)__ security environment is not certain. There are other questions, too. Will the test __(5)__ space weaponization? Prime Minister Narendra Modi, while announcing the success of the test, was clear that India wanted to maintain peace rather than indulge in warmongering.

**Q.90** Which of the following word fits the blank labeled as (1)?
**A.** curb    **B.** dwell    **C.** entail    **D.** curtail

**Q.91** Which of the following word fits the blank labeled as (2)?
**A.** pallor    **B.** succor    **C.** frenzy    **D.** prestige

**Q.92**
Which of the following word fits the blank labeled as (3)?
**A.** credible      **B.** crescendo
**C.** vestige      **D.** palliative

**Q.93** Which of the following word fits the blank labeled as (4)?

**A.** penury  **B.** prevalent
**C.** posterior  **D.** strategic

**Q.94** Which of the following word fits the blank labeled as (5)?

**A.** swirl  **B.** spur  **C.** advent  **D.** refute

**Q.95 In the following question, out of the four alternatives, select the word opposite in meaning to the word given.**

Benediction

**A.** Oppressive  **B.** Clinch
**C.** Curse  **D.** Deceitful

**Q.96** In the following question, a word has been written in 4 different ways out of which only one correctly spelt. Select the correctly spelt word.

**A.** Sangine  **B.** Sanguine
**C.** Sanguin  **D.** Sangvine

**Q.97** Select the word which means the same as the group of words given.

One who does not drink alcohol.

**A.** Vegetarian  **B.** Faithful
**C.** Religious  **D.** Teetotaler

**Q.98 Rearrange the given 5 sentences A, B, C, D and E in proper sequence to form a meaningful paragraph and mark the correct sequence from the given options as your answer.**

A. They believe that they can be happy if they possess certain things or be with certain people or reach a professional height.

B. Happiness is a very simple term which is used commonly.

C. Not many! Most people look for happiness outside.

D. Even a small kid can tell the meaning of happiness.

E. But how many of us really know the meaning of true happiness and how to attain that state?

**A.** BDAEC  **B.** BDECA  **C.** BECDA  **D.** ECABD

**Q.99 Rearrange the given 5 sentences A, B, C, D and E in proper sequence to form a meaningful paragraph and mark the correct sequence from the given options as your answer.**

A. However, as the severity of the problem increases it becomes more and more difficult to deal with it.

B. It is thus important to be alert and avert the problem from arising in the first place.

C. Cancer, a condition that is caused by excessive growth of cells, can be cured if detected at an early stage.

D. As painful as the condition is, the treatments used to cure it are equally agonizing.

E. It is also essential not to neglect its symptoms to get rid of it at the earliest.

**A.** DBECA  **B.** CDABE  **C.** ADEBA  **D.** CADBE

**Q.100 Select the word that best defines the phrase.**

Giving undue favours to one's own kith and kin.

**A.** Patriotism  **B.** Nepotism
**C.** Jingoism  **D.** None of these

# // Smart Answer Sheet //

**Correct**   Indicates percentage of students who answered questions correctly.

**Skipped**   Indicates percentage of students who skipped questions.

| Q. | Ans. | Correct / Skipped |
|----|------|--------------------|
| 1 | A | 65.42 % / 31.15 % |
| 2 | B | 58.5 % / 31.73 % |
| 3 | B | 61.27 % / 33.3 % |
| 4 | B | 59.85 % / 33.34 % |
| 5 | A | 76.97 % / 19.91 % |
| 6 | B | 44.79 % / 41.66 % |
| 7 | B | 44.85 % / 32.81 % |
| 8 | D | 43.35 % / 47.24 % |
| 9 | D | 42.28 % / 39.06 % |
| 10 | D | 44.25 % / 40.45 % |
| 11 | C | 29.55 % / 69.22 % |
| 12 | B | 47.7 % / 45.65 % |
| 13 | C | 48.94 % / 39.74 % |
| 14 | A | 53.0 % / 42.14 % |
| 15 | A | 68.95 % / 30.72 % |
| 16 | B | 61.54 % / 30.08 % |

| Q. | Ans. | Correct / Skipped |
|----|------|--------------------|
| 17 | B | 51.23 % / 45.38 % |
| 18 | A | 59.01 % / 40.96 % |
| 19 | A | 55.95 % / 39.48 % |
| 20 | B | 87.84 % / 11.0 % |
| 21 | D | 55.71 % / 40.32 % |
| 22 | B | 47.89 % / 36.15 % |
| 23 | A | 59.77 % / 35.05 % |
| 24 | B | 54.69 % / 31.21 % |
| 25 | D | 42.92 % / 37.8 % |
| 26 | B | 63.53 % / 32.54 % |
| 27 | D | 48.38 % / 40.46 % |
| 28 | D | 40.61 % / 30.85 % |
| 29 | D | 77.6 % / 14.84 % |
| 30 | A | 45.32 % / 43.28 % |
| 31 | B | 56.02 % / 36.81 % |
| 32 | B | 65.78 % / 31.67 % |

| Q. | Ans. | Correct / Skipped |
|----|------|--------------------|
| 33 | A | 43.16 % / 35.76 % |
| 34 | A | 61.48 % / 36.15 % |
| 35 | D | 42.69 % / 44.24 % |
| 36 | C | 44.12 % / 32.35 % |
| 37 | B | 59.4 % / 33.65 % |
| 38 | C | 40.93 % / 56.61 % |
| 39 | D | 53.82 % / 41.97 % |
| 40 | D | 59.05 % / 40.0 % |
| 41 | B | 68.2 % / 31.57 % |
| 42 | B | 60.1 % / 36.11 % |
| 43 | B | 63.73 % / 33.28 % |
| 44 | C | 61.41 % / 30.47 % |
| 45 | A | 55.53 % / 30.99 % |
| 46 | D | 68.9 % / 30.71 % |
| 47 | C | 64.88 % / 33.63 % |
| 48 | B | 57.59 % / 31.65 % |

| Q. | Ans. | Correct / Skipped |
|----|------|--------------------|
| 49 | A | 55.08 % / 35.43 % |
| 50 | D | 65.03 % / 33.61 % |
| 51 | B | 64.48 % / 31.15 % |
| 52 | C | 63.23 % / 32.93 % |
| 53 | C | 68.02 % / 30.95 % |
| 54 | D | 43.66 % / 31.82 % |
| 55 | B | 25.72 % / 67.31 % |
| 56 | B | 68.7 % / 30.89 % |
| 57 | C | 44.63 % / 55.21 % |
| 58 | B | 43.99 % / 37.71 % |
| 59 | B | 48.37 % / 31.14 % |
| 60 | B | 62.12 % / 33.2 % |
| 61 | C | 45.29 % / 42.39 % |
| 62 | C | 22.99 % / 76.41 % |
| 63 | B | 57.12 % / 36.08 % |
| 64 | C | 69.67 % / 30.06 % |

| Q. | Ans. | Correct / Skipped |
|----|------|--------------------|
| 65 | C | 64.79 % / 32.25 % |
| 66 | C | 49.81 % / 50.07 % |
| 67 | D | 62.01 % / 31.16 % |
| 68 | B | 50.38 % / 44.25 % |
| 69 | B | 46.76 % / 32.95 % |
| 70 | B | 57.74 % / 36.89 % |
| 71 | B | 63.66 % / 35.54 % |
| 72 | D | 58.22 % / 36.79 % |
| 73 | A | 64.76 % / 33.49 % |
| 74 | C | 60.78 % / 35.1 % |
| 75 | D | 55.75 % / 36.83 % |
| 76 | A | 44.59 % / 45.09 % |
| 77 | D | 60.51 % / 38.76 % |
| 78 | C | 55.95 % / 30.4 % |
| 79 | D | 51.01 % / 46.21 % |
| 80 | B | 43.47 % / 39.67 % |

| Q. | Ans. | Correct | | Q. | Ans. | Correct | | Q. | Ans. | Correct | | Q. | Ans. | Correct | | Q. | Ans. | Correct |
|----|------|---------|---|----|------|---------|---|----|------|---------|---|----|------|---------|---|----|------|---------|
| | | Skipped | | | | Skipped | | | | Skipped | | | | Skipped | | | | Skipped |
| 81 | D | 67.26 % | | 85 | C | 62.37 % | | 89 | D | 64.73 % | | 93 | D | 54.8 % | | 97 | D | 65.97 % |
| | | 31.04 % | | | | 33.88 % | | | | 30.01 % | | | | 39.19 % | | | | 30.17 % |
| 82 | B | 59.03 % | | 86 | A | 46.2 % | | 90 | B | 29.77 % | | 94 | B | 66.99 % | | 98 | B | 16.11 % |
| | | 38.39 % | | | | 50.26 % | | | | 70.0 % | | | | 30.69 % | | | | 81.66 % |
| 83 | B | 25.3 % | | 87 | A | 58.87 % | | 91 | C | 58.09 % | | 95 | C | 64.62 % | | 99 | D | 18.14 % |
| | | 73.87 % | | | | 34.41 % | | | | 30.13 % | | | | 33.37 % | | | | 74.58 % |
| 84 | C | 87.49 % | | 88 | D | 61.37 % | | 92 | A | 65.97 % | | 96 | B | 81.36 % | | 100 | B | 64.87 % |
| | | 12.05 % | | | | 37.31 % | | | | 33.52 % | | | | 11.44 % | | | | 30.79 % |

## Performance Analysis

| | |
|---|---|
| **Avg. Score (%)** | 65.5% |
| **Toppers Score (%)** | 68.0% |
| **Your Score** | |

# //Hints and Solutions//

**1.** From the information above, we can easily conclude that Ramesh's friend extended support to Ramesh in the hour of need. Therefore, conclusion I follows.

But the information above is not sufficient for us to conclude the number of friends Ramesh had. Therefore, conclusion II does not follow.

Hence, the correct option is (A).

**2.** By observation and analysis,

Hence, the correct option is (B).

**3.** The pattern is as follows,

$$7 \xrightarrow{+1} 8 \quad 1 \xrightarrow{} 1 \quad 3 \xrightarrow{-1} 2 \quad T \xrightarrow{+2} V$$

Similarly,

$$2 \xrightarrow{+1} 3 \quad 2 \xrightarrow{} 2 \quad 8 \xrightarrow{-1} 7 \quad O \xrightarrow{+2} Q$$

Thus answer must be 327Q.

Hence, the correct option is (B).

**4.** Given series: 6 5 6 5 5 6 6 7 6 5 7 5 6 6 5 7 7 5 6 6 7

After making changes: 5 6 5 6 4 7 5 8 5 6 6 6 5 7 4 8 6 6 5 7 6

Thus we get only 1 time 3 consecutive 6.

Hence, the correct option is (B).

**5.** As Jury settles the Trial.

Similarly,

The job of the Arbiter is to settle the Dispute.

So, correct answer is Dispute : Arbiter.

Hence, the correct option is (A).

**6.** The logic in each group is:

The second number is multiplication of the first number with 5.

The third number is multiplication of the first number with 10.

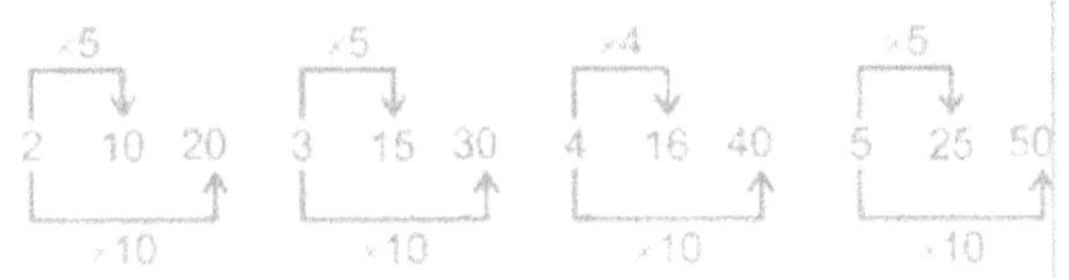

So, the odd group is 4 16 40.

Hence, the correct option is (B).

**7.** The logic is:

| M | I | S | T | A | K | E |
|---|---|---|---|---|---|---|
| 9 | 7 | 6 | 5 | 4 | 1 | 2 |

| N | A | K | E | D |
|---|---|---|---|---|
| 8 | 4 | 1 | 2 | 3 |

Similarly,

| S | T | A | I | N |
|---|---|---|---|---|
| 6 | 5 | 4 | 7 | 8 |

Hence, the correct option is (B).

**8.** Conclusions:

I. Vihaan has not completed his homework.

Since the reason for scolding is not mentioned in the statement so conclusion I can't be concluded from the statement. Thus, conclusion I doesn't follow.

II. A class teacher wanted Vihaan to feel embarrassed in front of all the students.

Intentions of the class teacher can't be determined from the statement so conclusion II doesn't follow.

Hence, the correct option is (D).

**9.** As 'Conclusion' is at the end while 'Introduction' is at the start of anything.

Similarly, 'Farewell' is done at the end while 'Salutation' is done at the beginning of any function.

'Adieu' is at end of while 'Greeting' is at the start of anything.

But, 'Culmination' while 'Wrap' both mean at the end of something.

Therefore, "Culmination - Wrap" is the odd word pair from the given alternatives.

Hence, the correct option is (D).

**10.**

Similarly,

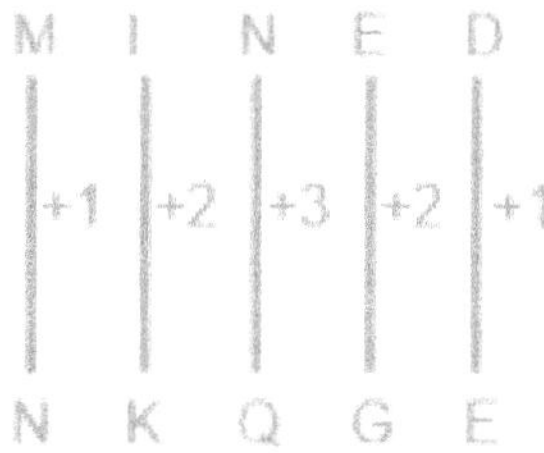

So, MINED is written as "NKQGE".

Hence, the correct option is (D).

**11.** Here, all except Hausa are languages of some Indian state. Hausa is a language of Nigeria.

Thus, "Hausa' is the correct alternative.

Hence, the correct option is (C).

**12.** Consider A = 1, B = 2, C = 3 ........... Z = 26

FAN $\Rightarrow$ F = 6, A = 1, N = 14

$\Rightarrow$ FAN = 6 × 1 × 14 = 84 (Multiply the values)

HIT $\Rightarrow$ H = 8, I = 9, T = 20 = 8 × 9 × 20 = 1440, in the same manner

BUN $\Rightarrow$ B = 2 U = 21, N = 14. So, 2 × 21 × 14 = 588.

Thus value of BUN will be 588.

Hence, the correct option is (B).

**13.** From first to second figure,

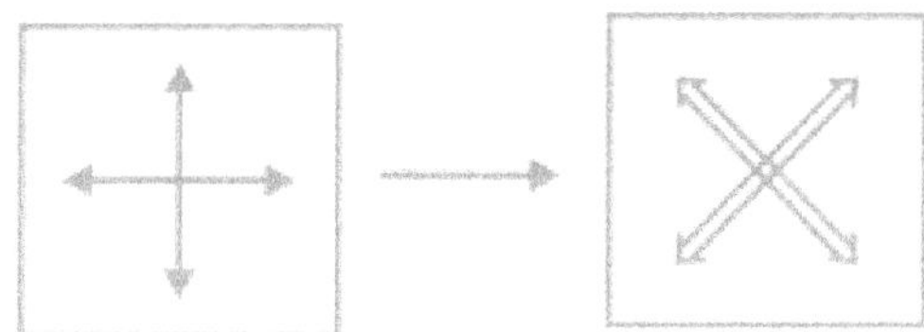

The second figure is the replication of the first figure in both pairs and we get the second one by rotating the first one by $45°$.

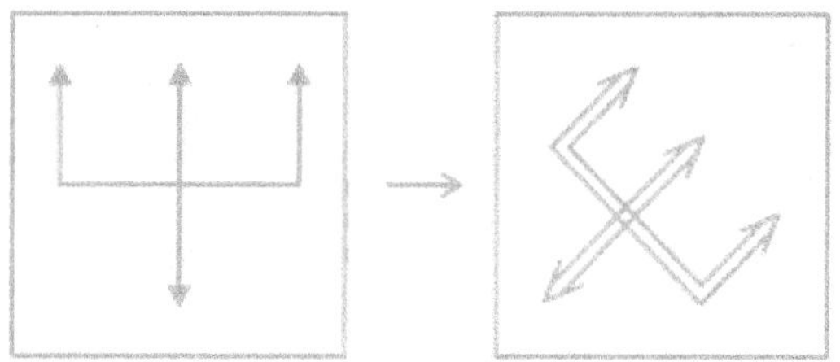

Hence, the correct option is (C).

**14.** 1st term : 3

2nd term : 3 + 2 = 5

3rd term : 5 + 4 = 9

4th term : 9 + 8 = 17

So,

5th term : 17 + 16 = 33

Hence, the correct option is (A).

**15.** From the given information,

| Symbol in Diagram | Meaning |
|---|---|
| ○ | Female |
| □ | Male |
| ——— | Married Couple |
| ——— | Siblings |
| \| | Difference of A Generation |

Based on given data, we can draw family tree-

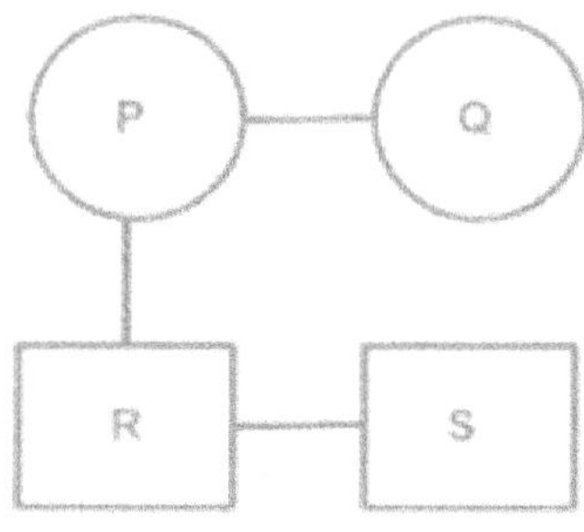

So, P is the mother of R.

Hence, the correct option is (A).

**16.** Here the other three designs of the figure are identical. 'By rotating the given figure $90°$ clockwise,

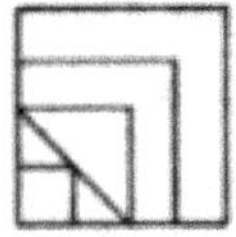

Hence, the correct option is (B).

**17.**

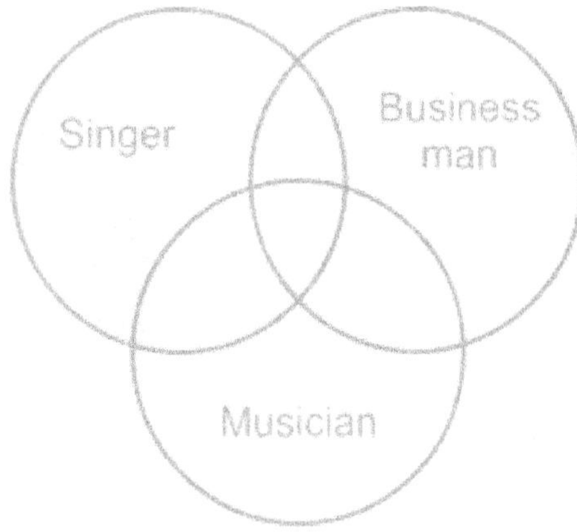


Hence, the correct option is (B).

**18.** Let the number of persons be $x$. Then,

$$\frac{96}{x-4} - \frac{96}{x} = 4$$

$$\Rightarrow \frac{1}{x-4} - \frac{1}{x} = \frac{4}{96}$$

$$\Rightarrow \frac{x-(x-4)}{x(x-4)} = \frac{1}{24}$$

$$\Rightarrow x^2 - 4x - 96 = 0$$

$$\Rightarrow (x - 12)(x + 8) = 0$$

$$\Rightarrow x = 12$$

So, required number $= x - 4 = 8$.

Hence, the correct option is (A).

**19.** Both the larger and the smaller squares move to the adjacent corner ACW in each turn. Also, the shading in the smaller square moves 1, 2, 3, 4, 5, ... steps ACW sequentially and the shading in the larger square moves 1, 2, 3, 4, 5,.... steps CW sequentially.

Hence, the correct option is (A).

**20.** Given equation is 8 × 4 + 5 ÷ 2 - 1 = 11

Let's check each of the option,

A. Interchanging × and +

Equation will become, 8 + 4 × 5 ÷ 2 - 1 = 17 ≠ 11

B. Interchanging × and ÷

Equation will become, 8 ÷ 4 + 5 × 2 - 1 = 11

C. Interchanging + and -

Equation will become, 8 × 4 - 5 ÷ 2 + 1 = 30.5 ≠ 11

D. Interchanging ÷ and -

Equation will become, 8 × 4 + 5 - 2 ÷ 1 = 35 ≠ 11

So, by interchanging × and ÷, we get correct answer.

Hence, the correct option is (B).

**21.** Given equation is 30 - 6 - 4 - 2 = 30

Let's check each option,

1. 30 - (6 - 4) - 2 = 30 - 2 - 2 = 26 ≠ 30

2. (30 - 6) - 4 - 2 = 24 - 4 - 2 = 18 ≠ 30

3. 30 - 4 - (6 - 2) = 30 - 4 - 4 = 22 ≠ 30

4. 30 - (6 - 4 - 2) = 30 - (6 - 6) = 30

So, 30 - (6 - 4 - 2) is the correct answer.

Hence, the correct option is (D).

**22.** The figure may be labelled as shown.

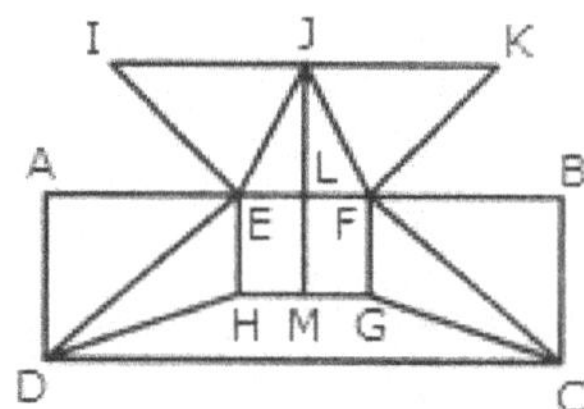


The horizontal lines are IK, AB, HG and DC i.e. 4 in number.

The vertical lines are AD, EH, JM, FG and BC i.e. 5 in number.

The slanting lines are IE, JE, JF, KF, DE, DH, FC and GC i.e. 8 is number.

Thus, there are 4 + 5 + 8 = 17 straight lines in the figure.

Hence, the correct option is (B).

**23.** People: Amar, Brijesh, Pinky, Deep, Eshwar, Nancy, Gurkamal and Harsh are sitting around a circle.

1) Nancy is third to the right of Pinky and second to the left of Harsh.

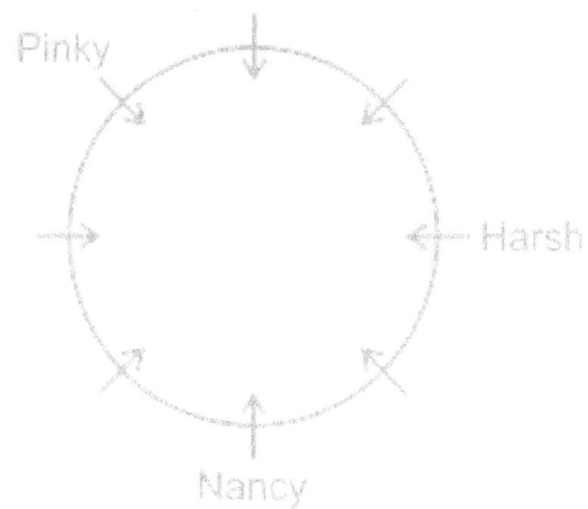

Hence, the correct option is (A).

**24.** People: Amar, Brijesh, Pinky, Deep, Eshwar, Nancy, Gurkamal and Harsh are sitting around a circle.

1) Nancy is third to the right of Pinky and second to the left of Harsh.

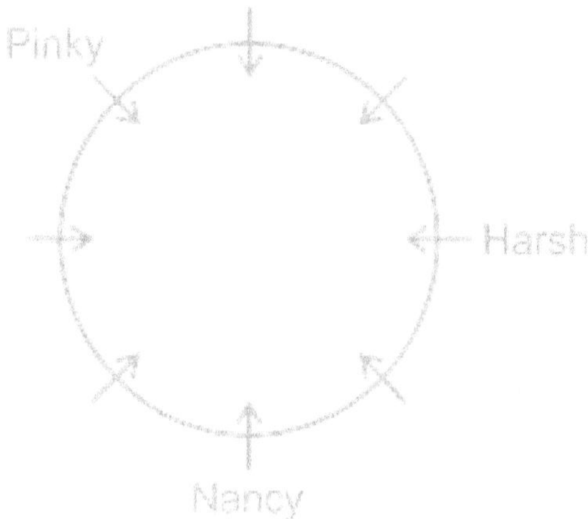

2) Deep is not an immediate neighbour of Pinky or Harsh.

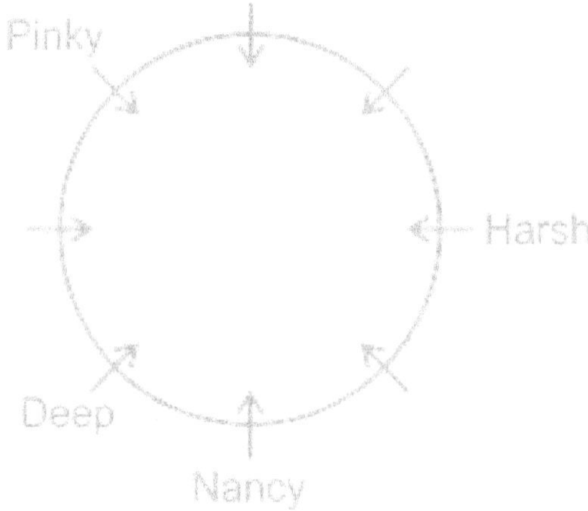

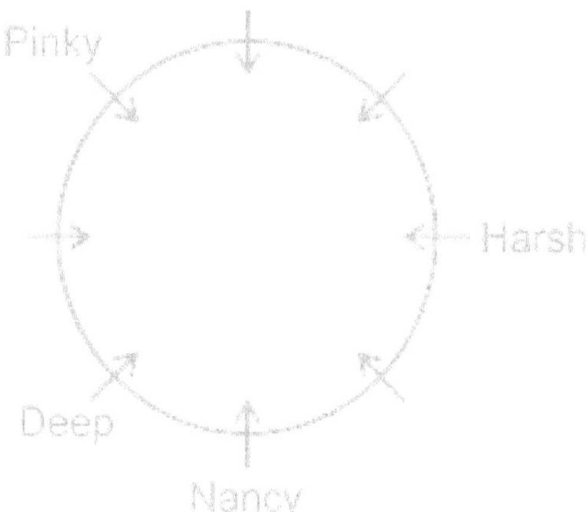

2) Deep is not an immediate neighbour of Pinky or Harsh.

3) Eshwar is to the immediate right of Amar, who is second to the right of Gurkamal.

Here the only position possible for Aman is to the immediate right of Harsh.

Thus the vacant place is occupied by Brijesh.

3) Eshwar is to the immediate right of Amar, who is second to the right of Gurkamal.

Here the only position possible for Aman is to the immediate right of Harsh.

Thus the vacant place is occupied by Brijesh.

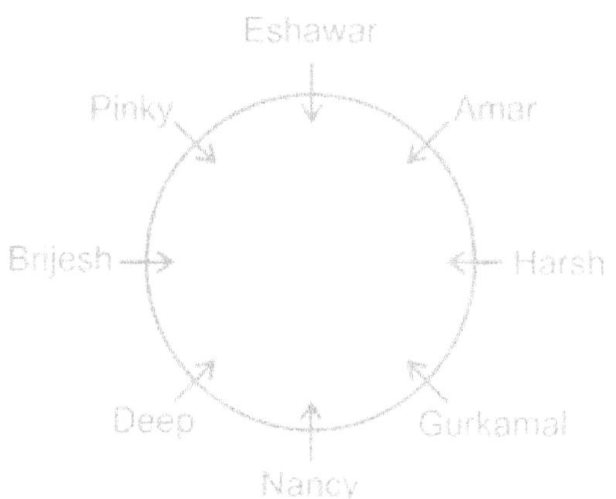

Thus Brijesh is to the immediate right of Pinky.

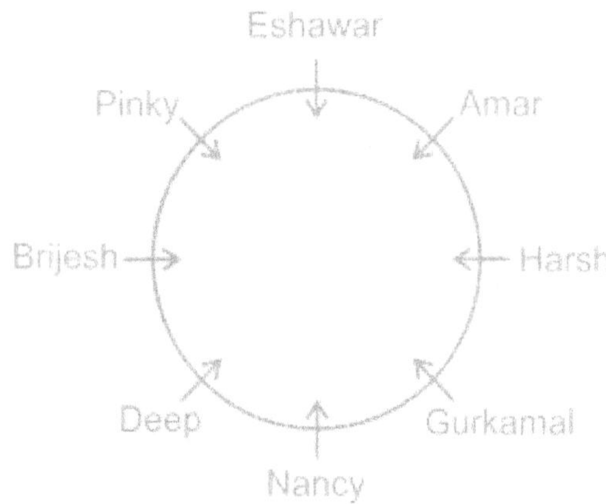


Thus Brijesh is to the immediate right of Pinky.

Hence, the correct option is (B).

**25.**

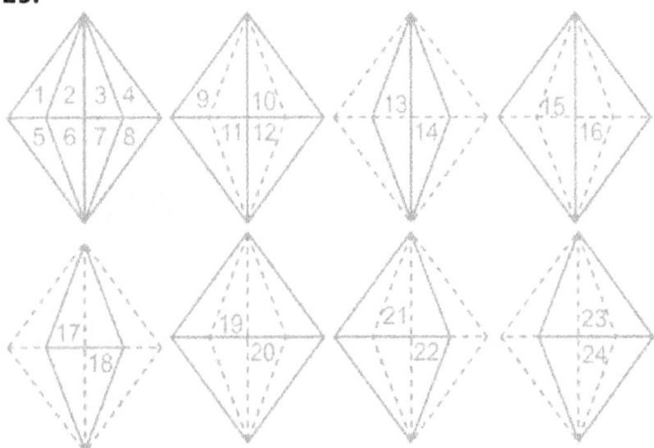

Hence, the correct option is (D).

**26.** The country's first-ever radio channel for the visually impaired, named 'Radio Aksh' has been launched in Nagpur. The Blind Relief Association Nagpur and Samdrushti Kshamata Vikas Avam Anusandhan Mandal (Saksham) are the pioneers of the concept. It will help the visually-impaired gain seamless access to education resources and audiobooks.

Hence, the correct option is (B).

**27.** Prasoon Joshi was appointed as the new chairman of the Central Board of Film Certification (CBFC) in August 2017.

- The Union Information and Broadcasting Ministry has appointed Prasoon Joshi. He replaced the Pahlaj Nihalani and shall have a tenure of three years.

- The central board of film certification film rating system is also known as the Censor board.

- It is a statutory censorship and classification body under the ministry of information and broadcasting, Govt of India.

- It is established with regulation and public exhibition of films under the provisions of the Cinematography act 1952.

Hence, the correct option is (D).

**28.** As on March 2018, Pratyush is the India's fastest supercomputer.

Pratyush is set up at the Indian Institute of Tropical Meteorology (IITM) in Pune and is used for weather and climate predictions.

India's most powerful supercomputer Pratyush, the first multi-petaflop device in the country which is being used to improve weather and climate predictions, has made it to the 39th spot on the Top 500 List of supercomputers in the world.

- The 4 petaflop supercomputer has improved India's ranking in the list from high 300s to under 50 for the first time.

- One petaflop is a million billion floating-point operations per second and is a reflection of the computing capacity of a system

- Pratyush will be used to do more accurate weather and climate forecasting, including the all-important monsoon predictions.

Hence, the correct option is (D).

**29.** San Jose is the capital of Costa Rica.

| Country | Costa Rica |
|---|---|
| Capital | San Jose |
| President | Carlos Alvarado Quesada |
| Currency | Costa Rican colón |

Hence, the correct option is (D).

**30.** According to article 202, the salaries and allowances of the judges of the High Court are charged on the Consolidated Fund of the State. The pension of the judges of the High Court is charged on the Consolidated Fund of India.

Hence, the correct option is (A).

**31.** Sitara Devi was an eminent Indian Kathak dancer. She is a recipient of Padma Shri, Sangeet Natak Akademi Award, Nritya Nipun, and Kalidas Samman.

Hence, the correct option is (B).

**32.** Mumbai mint is known for producing standardized weights and measures in India.

Mumbai has integrated facility of Gold Refining, processing and testing (assaying). Mumbai has installed and successfully commissioned the state-of-the-art technology in Gold Refining.

Hence, the correct option is (B).

**33.** "ATA' stands for Advanced Technology Attachment. It is a type of disk drive that integrates the drive controller directly on the drive itself. Computers can use ATA hard drives without a specific controller to support the drive.

Hence, the correct option is (A).

**34.** Reverse Repo rate is the short term borrowing rate at which RBI borrows money from banks. The Reserve bank uses this tool when it feels there is too much money floating in the banking system.

Hence, the correct option is (A).

**35.** SIDBI is a development financial institution which acts as the Principal Financial Institution for the Promotion, Financing, and Development of the Micro, Small and Medium Enterprises (MSME) sector.

| Bank | Headquarter | Formation | Chairman/MD |
| --- | --- | --- | --- |
| SIDBI | Lucknow | April, 2 1990 | Mohammad Mustafa |

Hence, the correct option is (D).

**36.**

| Article | Article is about |
| --- | --- |
| Article 52 | The President of India |
| Article 63 | The Vice-President of India |
| Article 76 | Attorney General of India |
| Article 110 | Money Bills |

Hence, the correct option is (C).

**37.** The Rourkela steel plant was built on the banks of the Brahmani river. It is the first integrated steel plant in the public sector in India. It was set up with West German collaboration with an installed capacity of 1 million tonnes in the 1960s. It is operated by the Steel Authority of India.

Hence, the correct option is (B).

**38.** Jallikatu is a traditional game of Tamil Nadu in which a bull is released into a crowd of people, and multiple human participants attempt to grab the large hump on the bull's back with both arms and hold on to it while the bull attempts to escape.

It is practiced as a part of Pongal celebrations on Mattu Pongal day, which takes place annually in January.

Hence, the correct option is (C).

**39.** Carolina Marin Martin is a professional badminton player from Spain who is the Olympic Champion. She is currently ranked 5 in the Badminton World Federation ranking. She is a two-time world champion and four times European Champion.

Hence, the correct option is (D).

**40.** Playing It My Way is the autobiography of former Indian cricketer Sachin Tendulkar. It was launched on 5 November 2014 in Mumbai. The book summarizes Tendulkar's early days, his 24 years of international career and aspects of his life that have not been shared publicly.

Hence, the correct option is (D).

**41.** The INC resolved in favour of the Non-Cooperation Movement in its Calcutta Session in 1920. It was decided that the INC would consider Swaraj as the ultimate aim. The movement mainly implied non-cooperation with the British Government in all the spheres of governance such as educational organizations, courts and offices etc.  The movement was called off by Mahatma Gandhi in 1922.

Hence, the correct option is (B).

**42. Ashoka's, Rock Edict No. 13(XIII) states:**

Beloved-of-the-Gods, King Priyadarsi, conquered the Kalingas eight years after his coronation. One hundred and fifty thousand were deported, one hundred thousand were killed and many more died (from other causes). After the Kalingas had been conquered, Beloved-of-the-Gods came to feel a strong inclination towards the Dharma, a love for the Dharma and for instruction in Dharma. Now Beloved-of-the-Gods feels deep remorse for having conquered the Kalingas.

Hence, the correct option is (B).

**43.**

| Oil seed production | Yellow Revolution |
| --- | --- |
| Crude Petroleum | Black revolution |

Hence, the correct option is (B).

**44.** Wilhelm Conrad Roentgen discovered X-Rays.

Wilhelm Conrad Röntgen was a German mechanical engineer and physicist born in 27th March 1845. In 1901, he was awarded the first Nobel Prize for Physics for the discovery of X-Rays.

Hence, the correct option is (C).

**45.** Sarojini Naidu was the first woman president from India of the Indian National Congress. She presided over the Kanpur Session of the INC in 1925. Annie Besant was the first woman president of the INC in the Calcutta Session in 1917.

Hence, the correct option is (A).

**46.** Trishna Wildlife Sanctuary is a Wildlife Sanctuary in Tripura, India. This sanctuary is situated in South Tripura District. Indian Gaur (Bison) is an attraction of this sanctuary. Apart from it, there are varieties of Birds, Deers, Hollock Gibbon, Golden Langur, Pheasant and many other animals and reptiles.

Hence, the correct option is (D).

**47.** World Humanitarian Day is observed across the world on August 19 to pay tribute to workers who risk their lives in humanitarian services and to gather support for people affected by crises around the world. The day was designated by the UN General Assembly to commemorate the 19 August 2003 bombing of the United Nations headquarters in Baghdad, Iraq.

Hence, the correct option is (C).

**48.** The United Nations General Assembly. has unanimously adopted a resolution on COVID-19, calling for intensified international cooperation to defeat the pandemic. Co-sponsored by 188 nations including India, the resolution is titled 'Global solidarity to fight the coronavirus disease 2019 (COVID-19)'. It is the first such document on the global pandemic to be adopted by the world organization.

Hence, the correct option is (B).

**49.** Ustad Bismillah Khan is famous for Shehnai and was awarded Bharat Ratna.

Bismillah Khan was an Indian musician who popularised the reeded woodwind instrument shehnai. Khan is recognised with boosting the shehnai's reputation and introducing it to the concert stage, despite the fact that it had long been revered as a folk instrument used largely in traditional ceremonies.

The Bharat Ratna is the Republic of India's highest civilian honour.

The award, which was established on January 2, 1954, is given in appreciation of excellent service/performance of the highest level, regardless of race, occupation, status, or sex.

The award was once restricted to achievements in the arts, literature, science, and public service, but in December 2011, the government broadened the requirements to include "any sphere of human endeavour."

Hence, the correct option is (A).

**50.** Mitchell Marsh won the Player of the Match award in the final match of T20 Men's Cricket World Cup 2021.

Mitchell Marsh scored 77 runs in 50 balls(not out) in the finals. Mitchell Marsh achieved this feat against New Zealand. He scored a total of 185 runs during the tournament. He is the 12th highest run-scorer in the recently concluded T20 Men's Cricket World Cup 2021.

Hence, the correct option is (D).

**51.** According to question:

$345.86 + 321.86 + 123.14 + 189.14 = ?$

$\Rightarrow ? = 980$

Hence, the correct option is (B).

**52.** Let Swati's monthly salary be Rs. ' $x$ '

Her monthly savings = 12% of $x = 0.12\ x$

But, she saved only Rs. 7020 which is 90% of her monthly savings

$\Rightarrow 90\%$ of $0.12\ x = 7020$

$\Rightarrow \dfrac{9}{10} \times 0.12\ x = 7020$

$\Rightarrow 0.108\ x = 7020$

$\Rightarrow x =$ Rs. 65000

$\therefore$ Swati's monthly salary = Rs. 65000

Hence, the correct option is (C).

**53.** Average marks before correction = 55

Total marks scored before correction

$= 60 \times 55 = 3300$

$\because$ The marks 6, 6, 3 were wrongly entered instead of 96, 60 and 39,

$\Rightarrow$ Total marks scored after correction

$= 3300 - 6 - 6 - 3 + 96 + 60 + 39 = 3480$

$\because$ No. of students = 60

$\therefore$ Correct average marks scored in examination

$= \dfrac{3480}{60} = 58$

Hence, the correct option is (C).

**54.** Let the number of filled and unfilled seats in the college be '7 $x$' and '3 $x$' respectively

$\Rightarrow$ Total no. of seats in college = 7 $x$ + 3 $x$ = 10 $x$

Now, if there were 60 seats more in college,

$\Rightarrow$ Total no. of seats would be = 10 $x$ + 60

$\Rightarrow$ No. of unfilled seats = 3 $x$ + 24

$\Rightarrow$ No. of filled seats = Total seats - Unfilled seats

= 10 $x$ + 60 - 3 $x$ - 24 = 7 $x$ + 36

$\because$ The ratio of filled to unfilled seats would be 9 : 4

$\Rightarrow \dfrac{(7x+36)}{(3x+24)} = \dfrac{9}{4}$

$\Rightarrow$ 28 $x$ + 144 = 27 $x$ + 216

$\Rightarrow x =$ 216 - 144 = 72

$\therefore$ Total no. of seats in college = 10 $x$ = 10(72) = 720

Hence, the correct option is (D).

**55.** Quantity of zinc in alloy

$\Rightarrow 1 = 28 \times \dfrac{3}{4} = 21$ kg

Quantity of copper in alloy

$\Rightarrow 1 = 28 - 21 = 7$ kg

Quantity of zinc in alloy

$\Rightarrow 2 = 28 \times \dfrac{5}{7} = 20$ kg

Quantity of copper in alloy

$\Rightarrow 2 = 28 - 20 = 8$ kg

Ratio of copper : zinc in new mixture

= total quantity of copper : total quantity of zinc

$\therefore$ Ratio of copper : zinc in new mixture

= (7 + 8) : (21 + 20) = 15 : 41

Hence, the correct option is (B).

**56.** When A runs 1000 m, B runs 900 m and when B runs 800 m, C runs 700 m.

When B runs 900 m, distance that C runs = $\dfrac{(900 \times 700)}{800}$

$= \dfrac{6300}{8}$

= 787.5 m.

In a race of 1000 m, A beats C by (1000 - 787.5)

= 212.5 m to C.

In a race of 600 m, the number of meters by which A beats C

$$= \frac{(600 \times 212.5)}{1000}$$

= 127.5 m.

Hence, the correct option is (B).

**57.** Given,

LCM of two numbers =32

HCF of two numbers is =8

First number is =8

The product of the two numbers =HCF $\times$ LCM

$\Rightarrow 8 \times$ Second number $= 8 \times 32$

$\Rightarrow$ Second number $= \frac{(8 \times 32)}{8}$

$\therefore$ Second number =32.

Hence, the correct option is (C).

**58.** Given:

$16 - [5 - 2\{14 \text{ of } 2 - (8 \div 4 \times 2 - 1 + 3)\}] = 16 - [5 - 2\{28 - 6\}]$

$$= 16 - [5 - 44] = 55$$

Hence, the correct option is (B).

**59.** Let the speed of slower bike be $x$ km/hr.

Speed of faster bike $= x + 9$

Relative speed $= 2x + 9$

$\Rightarrow 2x + 9 = \frac{324}{4}$

$\Rightarrow 2x + 9 = 81$

$\Rightarrow x = 36$ km/hr

$\therefore$ The speed of slower bike be 36 km/hr.

Hence, the correct option is (B).

**60.** Given:

Put ($x$ - 4) = m

$\Rightarrow x$ = m + 4

$\Rightarrow (m + 4)^2 - 12(m + 4) + 33 = 0$

$\Rightarrow m^2 + 16 + 8m - 12m - 48 + 33 = 0$

$\Rightarrow m^2 - 4m + 1 = 0$

On dividing the equation by m,

$\Rightarrow m + \dfrac{1}{m} = 4$

Now Putting ($x$ - 4) = m in ($x$ - 4)$^2$ + $\left[\dfrac{1}{(x-4)}\right]^2$

$\Rightarrow m^2 + \dfrac{1}{m^2} = \left(m + \dfrac{1}{m}\right)^2 - 2$

$\Rightarrow m^2 + \dfrac{1}{m^2} = 16 - 2 = 14$

$\therefore$ ($x$ - 4)$^2$ + $\left[\dfrac{1}{(x-4)}\right]^2$ = 14

Hence, the correct option is (B).

**61.** Given:

$x - 4 = 0$

$\Rightarrow x = 4$

Put $x = 4$ in equation $x^3 - 3x^2 + 63$

$\Rightarrow 4^3 - 3(4)^2 + 63$

$\Rightarrow 64 - 48 + 63$

$\Rightarrow 79$

$\therefore$ Unit digit of expression = 9

Hence, the correct option is (C).

**62.** All the face cards are removed.

$\therefore$ Number of remaining cards

$$= 52 - 12 = 40$$

Number of ace cards $= 4$

$\therefore$ Required Probability

$$= \frac{4}{40} = \frac{1}{10}$$

Hence, the correct option is (C).

**63.** Let the CP be $x$.

And gain % = 21%

SP = CP + Gain

SP = 1.21 $x$

If gain would have been 37%.

SP = CP + Gain

SP = 1.37 $x$

$\Rightarrow 1.37\, x - 1.21\, x = 640$

$\Rightarrow x = 4000$

So, the cost price of the article = Rs. 4000

Hence, the correct option is (B).

**64.** Given:

Total selling price with tax

= Selling price + 5% of selling price

$\Rightarrow 3024 = 1.05 \times$ selling price

$\Rightarrow$ Selling price $= \dfrac{3024}{1.05} = 2880$

Also, 80% of marked price = Selling price

$\Rightarrow 0.8 \times$ marked price = 2880

$\Rightarrow$ Marked price $= \dfrac{2880}{0.8} = 3600$

Hence, the correct option is (C).

**65.** Given:

$\Rightarrow$ Amount = Principal + Interest = 25000 + 8275 = 33275

We know,

Amount = Principal $\left[1 + \left(\dfrac{R}{100}\right)^{n}\right]$

$\Rightarrow 33275 = 25000 \left[1 + \left(\dfrac{R}{100}\right)^{n}\right]$

$\dfrac{33275}{25000} = \left(\dfrac{11}{10}\right)^{n}$

$\dfrac{1331}{1000} = \left(\dfrac{11}{10}\right)^{n} = \left(\dfrac{11}{10}\right)^{3}$

$\therefore n = 3$ years.

Hence, the correct option is (C).

**66.** We know that,

$SI = \left(\dfrac{P \times R \times T}{100}\right)$

$\Rightarrow SI = \dfrac{(3500 \times 16 \times 3)}{100}$

$\Rightarrow SI = 1680$

Amount = Principal + Interest

$\Rightarrow A = 3500 + 1680 = 5180$

Hence, the correct option is (C).

**67.** Time taken by bus to cross the bridge

$= \dfrac{\text{Sum of length of bus} \times \text{bridge}}{\text{Speed of bus}}$

$\Rightarrow 6 = \dfrac{(15 + 75)}{\text{Speed of bus}}$

$\Rightarrow$ Speed of bus

$= \dfrac{90}{6} = 15$ m/sec

Now,

Speed of man = 9 km/hr

$= \dfrac{9 \times 5}{18} = 2.5$ m/sec

$\because$ The man is running in the same direction as the bus, their relative speed is the difference of their individual speeds

$\Rightarrow$ Relative speed

= 15 - 2.5 = 12.5 m/sec

$\Rightarrow$ Time taken by bus to cross the man

$= \dfrac{\text{Length of bus}}{\text{Relative speed}}$

$\therefore$ Tome taken by bus to cross the man

$= \dfrac{15}{12.5} = 1.2$ seconds

Hence, the correct option is (D).

**68.** Given,

Speeds of a boat along the current and against the current are 12 km/hr and 6 km/hr respectively.

Speed downstream = 12km/hr

Speed upstream = 6km/hr

Speed of the current

$= \dfrac{1}{2} \times$ (speed downstream - speed upstream)

Speed of the current

$= \dfrac{1}{2} \times (12 - 6) = \dfrac{6}{2} = 3$

$\therefore$ Speed of the current is 3km/hr.

Hence, the correct option is (B).

**69.** Given:

$(3^5)^x \div (9)^{2x-1} = 243$

$\Rightarrow (3)^{5x} \div (3^2)^{2x-1} = (3)^5$

$\Rightarrow (3)^{5x} \div (3)^{4x-2} = (3)^5$

$\Rightarrow (3)^{5x-4x+2\}} = (3)^5$

$\Rightarrow (3)^{x+2} = (3)^5$

Equating powers,

$\Rightarrow x + 2 = 5$

$\Rightarrow x = 5 - 2 = 3$

Also, $(5)^{x-2y} \times (5)^{x+y} = 625$

$\Rightarrow (5)^{(x-2y+x+y)} = (5)^4$

$\Rightarrow (5)^{2x-y} = (5)^4$

Equating powers,

$\Rightarrow 2x - y = 4$

Substituting for '$x$'

$\Rightarrow 2(3) - y = 4$

$\Rightarrow y = 6 - 4 = 2$

$\therefore (x - y) = 3 - 2 = 1$

Hence, the correct option is (B).

**70.** Area of Rhombus = $\frac{1}{2}$ × (product of diagonals)

Given,

Side of a rhombus = 5cm and diagonal of rhombus = 8cm

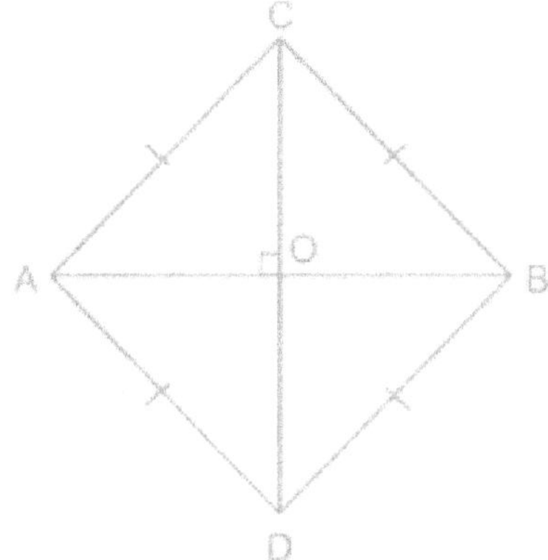

Angle between the diagonals is right angle triangle.

Using Pythagoras theorem,

⇒ (side of rhombus)² = (half of one diagonal)² + (half of other diagonal)²

⇒ $5^2 = \left(\frac{8}{2}\right)^2$ + (half of other diagonal)²

⇒ 25 = 4² + (half of other diagonal)²

⇒ 25 = 16 + (half of other diagonal)²

⇒ (half of other diagonal)² = 9

Half of other diagonal = 3

Length of other diagonal = 6cm

Area of a rhombus = $\frac{1}{2} \times (6 \times 8) = 24$

∴ Area of a rhombus 24 cm².

Hence, the correct option is (B).

**71.** Given,

Let r = radius of base and h = height

Volume of a cone = $\frac{(\pi r^2 h)}{3}$

Volume of a hemisphere = $(\pi r^3) \times \left(\frac{2}{3}\right)$

Volume of a cylinder = πr²h

Ratio of their volume

= $\left(\frac{1}{3}\right) : \left(\frac{2}{3}\right) : 1$

= 1 : 2 : 3

Hence, the correct option is (B).

**72.** The point where the triangle forms the right angle in the right-angled triangle is known as the ortho-centre.

The orthocenter is the point where all the three altitudes of the triangle cut or intersect each other. Here, the altitude is the line drawn from the vertex of the triangle and is perpendicular to the opposite side.

Hence, the correct option is (D).

**73.** Given:

A's share : B's share = A's investment : B's investment =24000: 8000=3 : 1.

Let be A's share $= 3x$ and B's share $= 1x$

According to the question

$$3x + x = 48000$$

$$\Rightarrow 4x = 48000$$

$$\Rightarrow x = 12000$$

Put the value of $x$ in A & B Share of B

=Rs .12000

Share of A=3 $x = 3 \times 12000$

=Rs .36000

∴ Share of A and B is Rs. 36,000 & Rs. 12,000

Hence, the correct option is (A).

**74.** Given:

Pipe A can fill tank =15 min

Pipe B can fill tank =45 min

One minute work of pipe A $= \frac{1}{15}$

One minute work of pipe B $= \frac{1}{45}$

One min work of both pipe $= \frac{1}{15} + \frac{1}{45} = \frac{4}{45}$

They can fill the full tank in = $\frac{45}{4}$ minute

∴ Both pipes can fill 50% of the tank in $\frac{45}{8}$ minutes.

Hence, the correct option is (C).

**75.** Given,

Length of train =500 m

Speed of train =90 km/hr

Speed = $\frac{\text{Distance}}{\text{time}}$

1 km/h = $\frac{5}{18}$ m/s

1 m/s = $\frac{18}{5}$ km/h

1 min = 60 seconds

3 min 20 seconds = 200 seconds

Let length of bridge be $x$ m.

According to the question

$$90 \times \left[\frac{5}{18}\right] = \frac{(x+500)}{60}$$

$$\Rightarrow 25 \times 60 = x + 500$$

$$\Rightarrow 1500 = x + 500$$

$$\Rightarrow x = 1500 - 500$$

$$\Rightarrow x = 1000$$

$\therefore$ Length of bridge is 1000 m

Let speed of person be km/sec

$$\Rightarrow k = \frac{1000}{200}$$

$$\Rightarrow k = 5 \times \left(\frac{18}{5}\right)$$

$\therefore$ k =18 km/hr

Hence, the correct option is (D).

**76.** Statements A and C suggest the ways in which the U.S. plans to 'shame' China by explicitly bringing its denial to list Azhar in front of the UNSC and UN General Assembly.

So, A and C are correct.

But; statement B does not explain the U.S. plan to shame China.

Hence, the correct option is (A).

**77.** The passage states that Chine could veto this proposal, moving further into Pakistan's corner and that India does not wish to sacrifice the bilateral relationship with China.

So, all statements are correct.

Hence, the correct option is (D).

**78.** The passage states that it is India that is justified in pursuing the listing of Azhar and not the U.S.

So, I is incorrect.

Statements II and III, however, find support from the passage as correct.

Hence, the correct option is (C).

**79.** Both Forums and Fora are correct plural forms of the word 'forum', although 'forums' is more commonly used.

The word 'Fora' is derived from Latin roots and is accepted as correct, even if it is not used too often.

Hence, the correct option is (D).

**80.** The passage states that India desires not to sacrifice the bilateral relationship with China over the issue.

None of the other conclusions can be drawn from the passage.

Hence, the correct option is (B).

**81.** The sentence uses the form Having seen which is correct and needs no improvement.

To faze is to disturb.

Having seen is a perfect participle, which is used to indicate a completed action. It is in the form- (present participle Having + past participle of the verb).

None of the alternatives can make the sentence meaningful.

Hence, the correct option is (D).

**82.** The error lies in part 2 of the sentence as the verb 'threatening' is incorrect here and must be replaced with the form 'threatened' as can be understood from the structure of the sentence. It should read as:'or threatened to leave a number of agreements'.

Hence, the correct option is (B).

**83.** The word 'ostentatious' means **to show off**. One would not give petition to a judge who shows off. Since they wanted justice, the judge must have known to be 'sagacious' or 'judicious'.

Hence, the correct option is (B).

**84.** The sentence suggests that the blank should contain a pronoun as it is referring to the pronoun, 'he'.

Whom and whose both refer to subjects other than 'he'; so they cannot be correct here.

The correct word here should be 'he 'who' loves' or 'he 'that' loves his fellow men'. Both of these refer to the subject; but since it is a person, it is more appropriate to use 'who'.

'That' can be a correct choice in case of a thing and not a person.

Hence, the correct option is (C).

**85.** The sentence is in active voice thus in passive voice the object 'shop' must be written before the subject 'you.'

In active voice :

Subject+verb+object

In passive voice:

Object+verb+subject

The tense here is simple past thus 'being looked' is the correct verb to be used here. The other options use incorrect tenses or are grammatically incorrect.

Hence, the correct option is (C).

**86.** There are four basic rules for converting sentences from active to passive voice:

1. The place of subject and object is interchanged.

2. 3rd form of verb is used.

**3.** Tense and form of the original sentence is not changed.

**4.** Helping verb (is, am, are, was, were) will be changed according to the tense.

The given sentence is in interrogative form of past perfect tense. So, the rule is:

- Active Voice – Sub + had + V3 + Obj .

- Passive Voice – Obj + had + been + V3+ by + Sub.

"Who" gets changed to "by whom" in the passive voice and the tense is kept unchanged.

Hence, the correct option is (A).

**87.** In indirect speech, the words of the speaker are not written in quotes. Usually, the word 'that' is used to convey the words of the speaker. The correct tense should be past perfect as the tense in direct speech is present perfect. The correct form of speech is: Ted said that the flowers were to be taken care of.

Hence, the correct option is (A).

**88.** When converting the sentence to direct speech form indirect speech, the punctuation '?' is added. The pronoun in 3rd person 'he; becomes 'you' in the 2nd person. The conjunction 'is' is dropped. The verb 'was' is replaced with the verb 'are'.

Thus, the sentence will be,

Changed verb 'are + changed pronoun 'you' + Catholic or Jewish + added punctuation '?' + The strange lady asked the man.

Hence, the correct option is (D).

**89.** Haste means speed or urgency.

The phrase 'To make haste' means doing something in a speedy and urgent manner.

The only option that can form this phrase is 'made'.

Hence, the correct option is (D).

**90.** The sentence suggests that the blank must contain a verb.

Also, given the context, the word should mean 'think or contemplate on'.

The only word that fits the blank is dwell.

Hence, the correct option is (B).

**91.** The sentence suggests that the blank must contain a noun.

Also, given the context, the word should mean an uncontrollable competitive spirit or wild behaviour.

The only word that fits the blank is frenzy.

Pallor is unhealthy paleness, succor means aid in the times of need.

Hence, the correct option is (C).

**92.** The sentence suggests that the blank must contain an adjective.

Also, given the context, the word should mean 'substantial'.

The only word that fits the blank is credible.

Hence, the correct option is (A).

**93.** The sentence suggests that the blank must contain an adjective for 'security'.

Also, given the context, the word should be close to 'stable' and planned.

The only word that fits the blank is strategic.

Note: 'prevalent' cannot be apt here as the passage talks about the future implications and uncertainty.

Hence, the correct option is (D).

**94.** The sentence suggests that the blank must contain a verb.

Also, given the context, the word should mean 'promote' space weaponization.

The only word that fits the blank is spur.

Hence, the correct option is (B).

**95.** The word 'benediction' means 'the utterance of a blessing'.

Let us find out the meanings of the following words-

Oppressive-inflicting harsh and authoritarian treatment

Clinch-confirm or settle

Curse-a cause of harm or misery

Deceitful-deceiving or misleading others

After looking at the meanings of the given words, it is understood that the most appropriate answer is option C i.e, 'curse'.

Hence, the correct option is (C).

**96.** The correct option is 'Sanguine'. A sanguine person is a very optimistic person especially when it comes to a difficulty. It may also be used to refer to the blood of a person.

E.g. Rachel as a person has a very sanguine disposition.

Hence, the correct option is (B).

**97.** Teetotaler: A person who does not drink alcohol.

Vegetarian: a person who does not eat meat or fish.

Faithful: True-hearted or devoted.

Religious: Spiritual or relating to religion.

Hence, the correct option is (D).

**98.** After reading the given sentences we can easily make out that the paragraph talks about 'Happiness'.

As sentence B is the only independent sentence and it introduces the subject, it is hence the starting point of the paragraph. Sentence D will follow B as it tells that the term is so common that even small kids can define it. Thus, a link is formed between the two. Sentence E will follow D as it takes the discussion further about the meaning of the term and the method to attain it.

Sentence C will follow E as it answers the question asked in sentence E. Sentence A will follow C as the pronoun 'they' is used for people discussed in sentence C. Thus, sentence A is linked with C.

Coherent paragraph- 'Happiness is a very simple term which is used commonly. Even a small kid can tell the meaning of happiness. But how many of us really know the meaning of true happiness and how to attain that state? Not many! Most people look for happiness outside. They believe that they can be happy if they possess certain things or be with certain people or reach a professional height'.

Hence, the correct option is (B).

**99.** After reading the given sentences we can easily make out that the paragraph talks about 'Cancer'.

Sentence C defines the subject, thus forms the perfect base of the paragraph. Sentence A will follow C as it links with A by telling that if not detected at an early stage, the problem can become severe. Sentence D links with A as it tells that not only the disease is severe, but its treatment is also equally agonizing. Sentence B links with D as it further takes the discussion by telling that since the treatment is also agonizing, it is important to detect the disease at an early stage. Conjunction, 'thus' links the two sentences. Sentence E tells what else is required to be taken care of, so will follow B.

Coherent paragraph- 'Cancer, a condition that is caused by excessive growth of cells, can be cured if detected at an early stage. However, as the severity of the problem increases it becomes more and more difficult to deal with it. As painful as the condition is, the treatments used to cure it are equally agonizing. It is thus important to be alert and avert the problem from arising in the first place. It is also essential not to neglect its symptoms to get rid of it at the earliest'.

Hence, the correct option is (D).

**100.** The meanings of the words are:

Nepotism=> Giving undue favours to one's own kith and kin

Patriotism=> Love for one's own country

Jingoism=> Patriotism

Hence, the correct option is (B).

# General Intelligence & Reasoning

**Q.1** In the following question have four options (1), (2), (3) and (4) are followed by a combination of letters and numbers. Choose the option that closely resembles the mirror image of the given combination.

ANS43Q12

(1) 2 1Q34SИA    (2) S 1Q34SИA

(3) 2ИA34QS 1    (4) 1 2Q34AИS

**A.** (1)    **B.** (2)    **C.** (3)    **D.** (4)

**Q.2** In the following question, select the odd letters from the given alternatives.

**A.** HFDA    **B.** VTQN    **C.** CAYV    **D.** OMKH

**Q.3** In the following question, select the odd letters words from the given alternatives.

**A.** Tunis    **B.** Maputo    **C.** Harare    **D.** Leeds

**Q.4** In the following question, select the related letters / numbers from the given alternatives.

KUNA34 : PFMZ14 :: MEGA41 : ?

**A.** NVUZ10    **B.** NVTZ10
**C.** NUTZ10    **D.** OVTZ10

**Q.5** In the following question, select the related word from the given alternatives.

Rabid : Friendly :: Quaint : ?

**A.** Aghast    **B.** Modern
**C.** Edgy    **D.** Disparaging

**Q.6** In the following question, select the related word pair from the given alternatives.

Iron : Metal : : Oxygen :

**A.** Respiration    **B.** Gas
**C.** Odourless    **D.** Living

**Q.7** In the following question, select the missing number from the given series.

39, 40, 42, 43, 45, ?

**A.** 47    **B.** 46    **C.** 48    **D.** 49

**Q.8** Select the missing number from the given series.

1, 4, 3, 9, 5, 16, 7, 25, 9, 36, 11, ?

**A.** 49    **B.** 13    **C.** 64    **D.** 17

**Q.9** In a certain code language,

"lower down like this" is written as "6%S 5*O 5*F 5*T"

"eyes are like clean" is written as "6*T 5%F 5*F 6%O"

"India is good country" is written as "7%B 4*T 5*E 8%Z"

How is "evaporation" written in that code language?

**A.** 12%O    **B.** 13%O    **C.** 13*O    **D.** 12*O

**Q.10** In a certain code language 'pi ma ti sa' means 'Neelam is watching TV', 'pi ta si' means 'school is there', 'ma ha ga si' means 'Neelam goes to school', 'ma pi ti mi' means 'neelam is watching movie'.

Which of the following means 'movie' in that code language?

**A.** mi    **B.** ha    **C.** ma    **D.** pi

**Q.11** In  the following question have given a combination of alphabets and/or numbers followed by four alternatives (1), (2), (3) and (4). Choose the alternative which is closely resembles the mirror image of the given combination.

MALAYALAM

(1) MALAYALAM    (2) MAJAYAJAM

(3) MAJAYAJAM    (4) MAΓAYAΓAM

**A.** (1)    **B.** (2)    **C.** (3)    **D.** (4)

**Q.12** In the following question have given a figure (X) followed by four alternative figures (1), (2), (3) and (4) such that figure (X) is embedded in one of them. Trace out the alternative figure which contains figure (X) as its part.

Find out the alternative figure which contains figure (X) as its part.

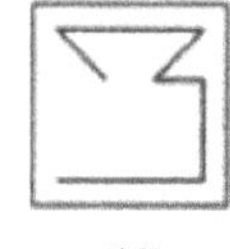

(X)    (1)    (2)    (3)    (4)

**A.** (1)    **B.** (2)    **C.** (3)    **D.** (4)

**Q.13** In the following question have given a figure (X) followed by four alternative figures (1), (2), (3) and (4) such that figure (X) is embedded in one of them. Trace out the alternative figure which contains figure (X) as its part.

Find out the alternative figure which contains figure (X) as its part.

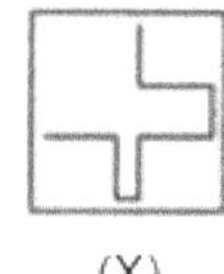
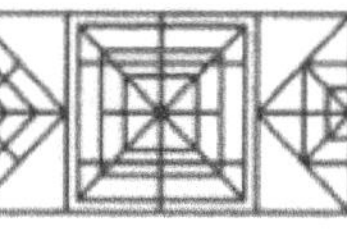
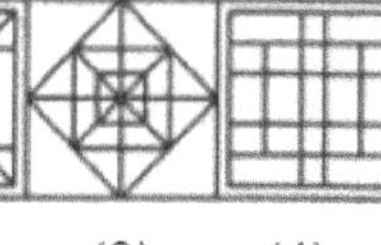

(X)    (1)    (2)    (3)    (4)

**A.** (1)    **B.** (2)    **C.** (3)    **D.** (4)

**Q.14** The question below consists of two statements labelled as I and II You have to decide whether the data provided in the statement are sufficient to answer the question given below. Read both the statements and select the correct option.

Is D the wife of M?

I) R is the son of D.

II) M is the mother of S.

**A.** Data in Statement I alone sufficient to answer the question.

**B.** Data in Statement II alone sufficient to answer the question.

**C.** Data in both Statement I and II are sufficient to answer the question.

**D.** Data in both Statement I and II are not sufficient to answer the question.

**Q.15** In the following question, find out which of the answer figures (1), (2), (3) and (4) completes the figure matrix?

Select a suitable figure from the four alternatives that would complete the figure matrix.

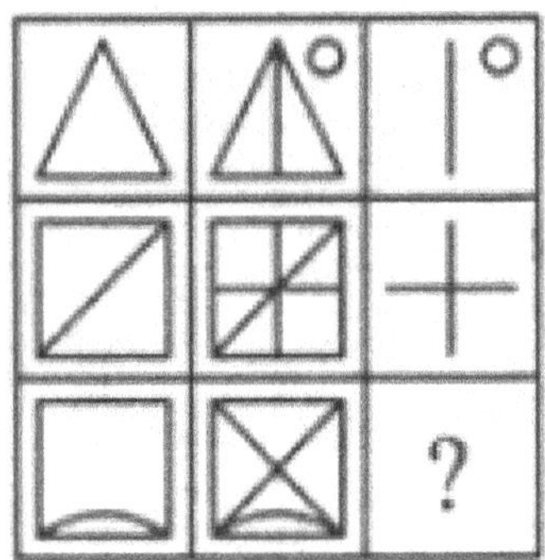

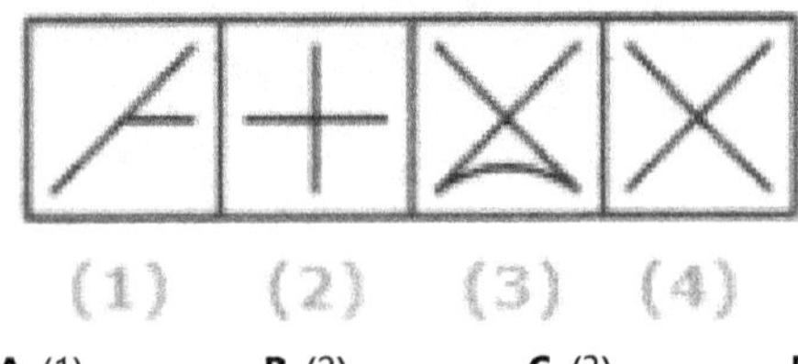

(1)    (2)    (3)    (4)

**A.** (1)    **B.** (2)    **C.** (3)    **D.** (4)

**Q.16** Identify the diagram that best represents the relationship among the given classes.

Cow, Dog, Animals

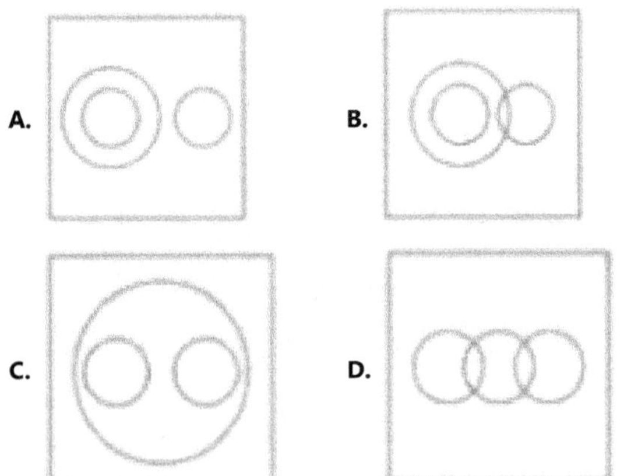

**Q.17** In the following question, find out which of the answer figures (1), (2), (3) and (4) completes the figure matrix?

Select a suitable figure from the four alternatives that would complete the figure matrix.

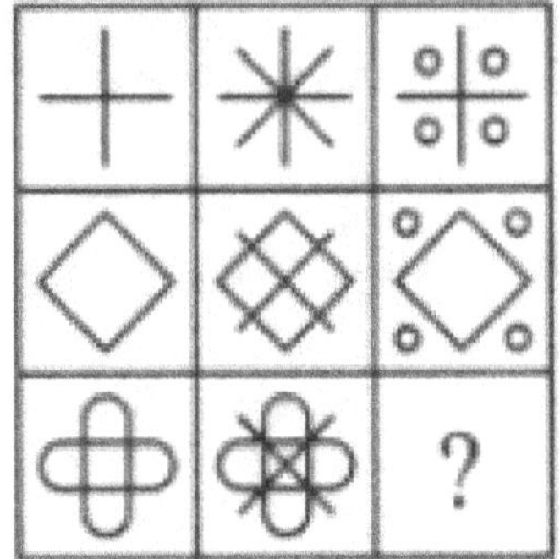

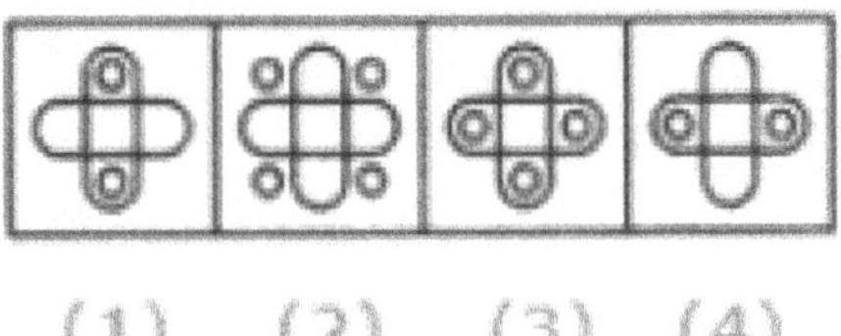

(1)    (2)    (3)    (4)

**A.** (1)    **B.** (2)    **C.** (3)    **D.** (4)

**Q.18** In the following question, select a figure from amongst the four alternatives, which when placed in the blank space of figure (X) would complete the pattern.

Identify the figure that completes the pattern.

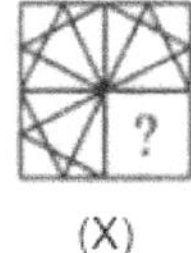

(X)    (1)    (2)    (3)    (4)

**A.** (1)    **B.** (2)    **C.** (3)    **D.** (4)

**Q.19** Select the correct combination of mathematical signs to replace * signs and to balance the given equation.

12 * 4 * 5 * 8

**A.** =, ×, -    **B.** ×, -, =    **C.** =, -, ×    **D.** -, ×, =

**Q.20** In the following question, select a figure from amongst the four alternatives, which when placed in the blank space of figure (X) would complete the pattern.

Identify the figure that completes the pattern.

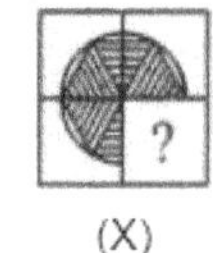

(X)    (1)    (2)    (3)    (4)

**A.** (1)    **B.** (2)    **C.** (3)    **D.** (4)

**Q.21**

Find the minimum number of straight lines required to make the given figure.

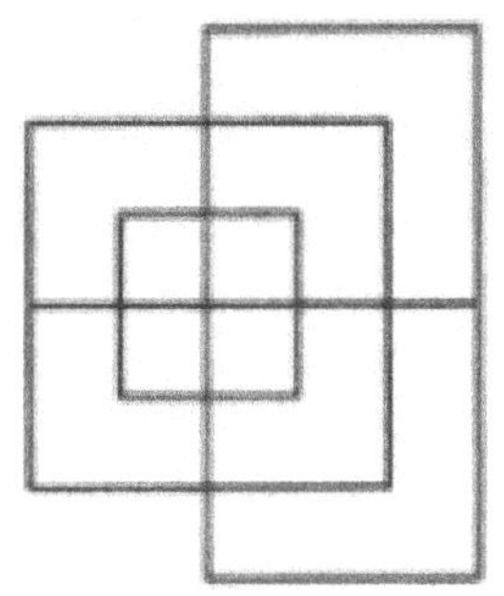

**A.** 13     **B.** 15     **C.** 17     **D.** 19

**Q.22** Find the number of triangles in the given figure.

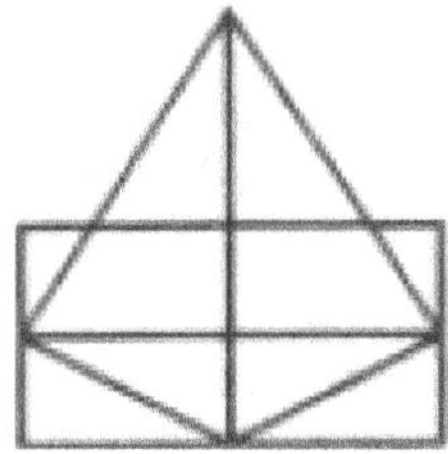

**A.** 11     **B.** 13     **C.** 15     **D.** 17

**Q.23** A piece of paper is folded and punched as shown below in the question figures. Form the given answer figures, indicate how it will appear when opened?

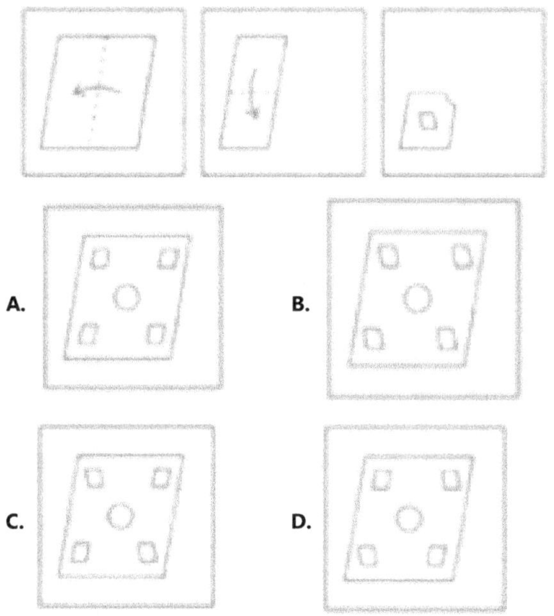

**Q.24** In the following question consists of two sets of figures. Figures A, B, C and D constitute the Problem Set while figures 1, 2, 3, 4 and 5 constitute the Answer Set. There is a definite relationship between figures A and B. Establish a similar relationship between figures C and D by selecting a suitable figure from the Answer Set that would replace the question mark (?) in fig. (D).

Select a suitable figure from the Answer Figures that would replace the question mark (?).

## Problem Figures:

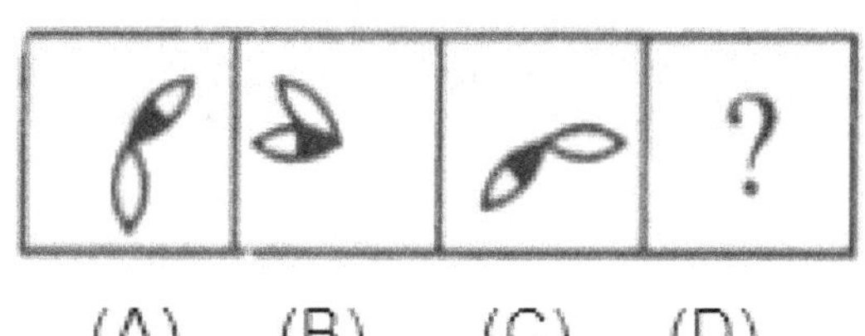



## Answer Figures:

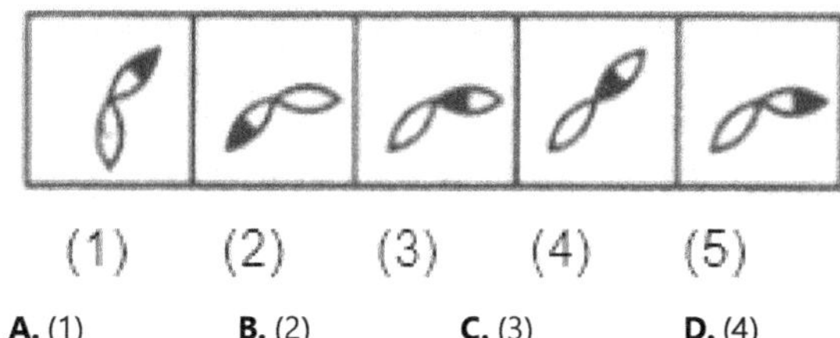



**A.** (1)     **B.** (2)     **C.** (3)     **D.** (4)

**Q.25** In the following question consists of two sets of figures. Figures A, B, C and D constitute the Problem Set while figures 1, 2, 3, 4 and 5 constitute the Answer Set. There is a definite relationship between figures A and B. Establish a similar relationship between figures C and D by selecting a suitable figure from the Answer Set that would replace the question mark (?) in fig. (D).

Select a suitable figure from the Answer Figures that would replace the question mark (?).

## Problem Figures:

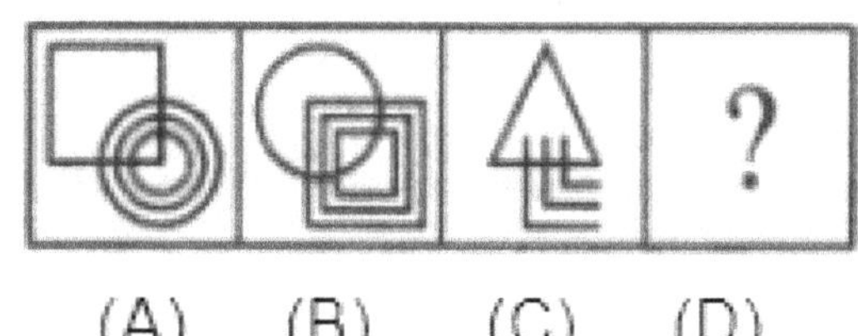



## Answer Figures:

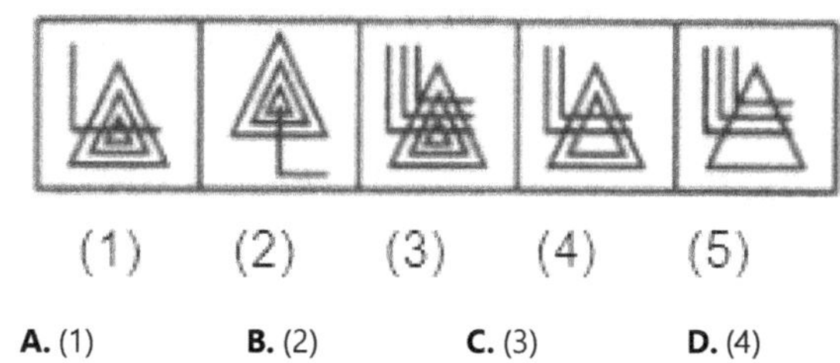



**A.** (1)     **B.** (2)     **C.** (3)     **D.** (4)

# General Awareness

**Q.26** The Prime Minister released a commemorative coin of Rs 100 denomination, to honour which personality?

**A.** Vijaya Raje Scindia

**B.** Syama Prasad Mukherjee

**C.** Deendayal Upadhyaya

**D.** M. S. Golwalkar

**Q.27** India's rank in Human Development Index, 2018 is:

[Super TET Paper - I, 2019]

**A.** 128th     **B.** 129th     **C.** 130th     **D.** 131st

**Q.28** The 44th International Advertising Association (IAA) Summit held in which city/UT?

**A.** New Delhi     **B.** Kochi
**C.** Pune     **D.** Chennai

**Q.29** The Siege of Arcot was a part of ______.

**A.** Second Carnatic War
**B.** First Anglo Mysore War
**C.** Battle of Wadgaon
**D.** First Carnatic War

**Q.30** When is World Water Day Celebrated annually?

**A.** 22 March     **B.** 5 March
**C.** 13 March     **D.** 20 March

**Q.31** Talley Valley wildlife sanctuary is located in which of the following state?

**A.** Assam     **B.** Arunachal Pradesh
**C.** Mizoram     **D.** Manipur

**Q.32** Who deciphered the Brahmi and Kharoshthi scripts?

**A.** Piyadassi
**B.** Colin Mackenzie
**C.** Alexander Cunningham
**D.** James Prinsep

**Q.33** How many sessions of the Lok Sabha take place in a year?

**A.** 1     **B.** 4     **C.** 6     **D.** 3

**Q.34** Which of the following two water bodies is connected by The Yucatan Strait?

**A.** Java Sea and the Indian Ocean
**B.** Gulf of Mexico and the Caribbean Sea
**C.** Red Sea and the Gulf of Aden
**D.** Arafura Sea & Gulf of Papua

**Q.35** Ms. Florence Nightingale was associated with ______.

**A.** Seven Years War     **B.** Thirty Years War
**C.** Crimean War     **D.** Hundred Years War

**Q.36** Which of the following focuses on the financial needs of the institutional clients and the industry?

**A.** Universal Banking     **B.** Virtual Banking
**C.** Wholesale Banking     **D.** Retail Banking

**Q.37** Indira Sagar Dam is located on which of the following rivers?

**A.** Godavari     **B.** Tapi
**C.** Narmada     **D.** Luni

**Q.38** Which of the following is not a part of India's Money Market?

**A.** Banks
**B.** Bill Markets
**C.** Call Money Market
**D.** Indian Gold Council

**Q.39** Which of the following is the only river integrated into the Indian Thar Desert?

**A.** Satluj     **B.** Luni     **C.** Narmada     **D.** Tapi

**Q.40** Which among the following is the capital of Colombia?

**A.** Yerevan     **B.** Podgorica
**C.** Nassau     **D.** Bogota

**Q.41** Who decides Bank Rate in India?

**A.** Finance Minister of India
**B.** President of India
**C.** Reserve Bank of India
**D.** State Bank of India

**Q.42** The Law of supply establishes a direct relationship between ______ and ______.

**A.** Customer and Price     **B.** Price and Supply
**C.** Supply and Market     **D.** None of the above

**Q.43** Who first discovered that the earth revolves around the sun?

**A.** Newton     **B.** Dalton
**C.** Copernicus     **D.** Einstein

**Q.44** In the Indian Constitution, the idea of Residual Powers has been borrowed from the ______ Constitution.

**A.** French     **B.** Canadian
**C.** Russian     **D.** British

**Q.45** Gangaur festival is related to which of the following God?

**A.** Hanuman     **B.** Shiv and Gauri
**C.** Ram     **D.** Krishna

**Q.46** Among the following, which type of banking system works on the principles of 'sharia'?

**A.** Corporate Banking System
**B.** Shadow Banking
**C.** Islamic Banking
**D.** Payments Bank System

**Q.47** Which type of banking system focuses on expansion through branches?

**A.** Internet Banking     **B.** Unit Banking
**C.** Branch Banking     **D.** Consumer Banking

**Q.48** In which city is the summer Olympic Games 2024 to be held?

[Bihar Police SI, 2019]

**A.** Los Angeles     **B.** London
**C.** Beijing     **D.** Paris

**Q.49** Who has been selected as one of the three recipients of the Fukuoka Prize 2021?

**A.** Jayati Ghosh     **B.** P. Sainath
**C.** Prabhat Patnaik     **D.** Umar Khalid

**Q.50** "BOB World Wave" launched by Bank of Baroda (BOB) is ____________.

**A.** Global debit card     **B.** Wearable device
**C.** AI Chatbot     **D.** Investment platform

# Quantitative Aptitude

**Q.51** In what ratio two types of liquid costing Rs. $52$ liter and Rs. $65$ liter should be mixed to obtain a mixture of Rs. $60$ liter?

**A.** $8:13$  **B.** $5:8$  **C.** $13:5$  **D.** $8:5$

**Q.52** The distance between two places can be covered in $3\frac{1}{2}$ hours at a speed of $62$ km/hr. If the speed is increased by $8$ km/hr, how much time would be saved?

**A.** 20 minutes  **B.** 24 minutes
**C.** 15 minutes  **D.** 30 minutes

**Q.53** The difference between compound interest and simple interest on Rs. $28560$ for $2$ years at $15\%$ per annum is:

**A.** 646.6  **B.** 622.6  **C.** 644.6  **D.** 642.6

**Q.54** The ratio of incomes of C and D is $3:2$. Ratio of income of D and E is $5:4$. If one- third of Cs income is Rs. $4000$ more than the half of E's income, then what is D's income (in Rs.)?

**A.** 40000  **B.** 43000  **C.** 50000  **D.** 60000

**Q.55** Which of the following is quadratic equation?

**A.** $x+\frac{1}{x}=2$  **B.** $x^2+3x^{-1}=2$
**C.** $x^3-x^2=5$  **D.** $3x^2-\frac{4}{x}=0$

**Q.56** $(x+2)^3=(x^2-1)2x$ What type of equation is there?

**A.** Unilateral equation  **B.** Quadratic equation
**C.** Cubic equation  **D.** Constant position

**Q.57** The selling price of an item inclusive of a $16\%$ profit was Rs. $435$. What would be the percentage loss if the item was sold for Rs. $330$?

**A.** 12.25%  **B.** 13%  **C.** 12.5%  **D.** 12%

**Q.58** If $\dfrac{9^n\times3^5\times(27)^3}{3}\times(81)^4=27$, then the value of $n$ is:

**A.** 0  **B.** 2  **C.** 3  **D.** 4

**Q.59** The efficiency of A is $50\%$ more than that of B. And the efficiency ratio of B to C is $2:1$. Then calculate in how much time A complete the whole work. If they together complete the work in 6 days.

**A.** 7 days  **B.** 12 days  **C.** 5 days  **D.** 4 days

**Q.60** If $5\%$ of $(P+Q)=20\%$ of $(P-Q)$, then $P$ is what percentage of $Q$?

**A.** 133.33%  **B.** 166.66%
**C.** 150%  **D.** 171.33%

**Q.61** What is the value of $\sqrt{13-4\sqrt{10}}$?

**A.** $\sqrt{8}-\sqrt{5}$  **B.** $\sqrt{8}+\sqrt{5}$
**C.** $\sqrt{6}-\sqrt{3}$  **D.** $\sqrt{6}+\sqrt{3}$

**Q.62** If $2^{n-1}+2^{n+1}=320$, then $n$ is equal to:

**A.** 6  **B.** 8  **C.** 5  **D.** 7

**Q.63** A $145$ m long train crosses a $655$ m long bridge in $36$ seconds. What is the speed of the train?

**A.** 75 km/h  **B.** 60 km/h  **C.** 80 km/h  **D.** 70 km/h

**Q.64** A milk vendor has $2$ cans of milk. The first contains $25\%$ water and the rest milk. The second contains $50\%$ water. How much milk should he mix from each of the containers so as to get $12$ liters of milk such that the ratio of water to milk is $3:5$?

**A.** 4 liters, 8 liters  **B.** 6 liters, 6 liters
**C.** 5 liters, 7 liters  **D.** 7 liters, 5 liters

**Q.65** If $p+\left(\frac{1}{p}\right)=8$, find the value of $p^2+\left(\frac{1}{p^2}\right)$?

**A.** 62  **B.** 64  **C.** 36  **D.** 44

**Q.66** The market price of a cooler is Rs. $1600$. The shopkeeper allows a discount of $10\%$ and gains $20\%$. Find the cost price of the cooler.

**A.** Rs. 1280  **B.** Rs. 1220
**C.** Rs. 1180  **D.** None of these

**Q.67** A bag contains $4$ red balls, $6$ blue balls and $8$ pink balls. One ball is drawn at random and replaced with $3$ pink balls. A probability that the first ball drawn was either red or blue in colour and the second drawn was pink in colour?

**A.** $\frac{12}{21}$  **B.** $\frac{13}{17}$
**C.** $\frac{11}{30}$  **D.** None of these

**Q.68** Find the unit place digit in $(192)^{102}+(193)^{103}$.

**A.** 0  **B.** 1  **C.** 3  **D.** 5

**Q.69** Prapti's age is $\frac{1}{7}^{th}$ of Rakhi's age. Rakhi's age will be twice of Tithi's age after $5$ years, If Tithi's thirteenth birthday was celebrated two years ago, the present age of Prapti is:

**A.** 8 years  **B.** 18 years  **C.** 5 years  **D.** 12 years

**Q.70** What is the average of first $8$ multiples of $5$?

**A.** 22.5  **B.** 21.8  **C.** 20  **D.** 24

**Q.71** H.C.F of 493,527 and 697 is:

**A.** 27  **B.** 51  **C.** 17  **D.** 23

**Q.72** The value of $\dfrac{1}{1+\sqrt{2}}+\dfrac{1}{\sqrt{2}+\sqrt{3}}+\dfrac{1}{\sqrt{3}+\sqrt{4}}+\cdots+\dfrac{1}{\sqrt{15}+\sqrt{16}}$.

*[Delhi Forest Guard, 2021]*

**A.** 0  **B.** 3  **C.** $-3$  **D.** 1

**Q.73** $\frac{98}{3}\%$ of $769.002+24\%$ of $160.89-67.9900=?$

**A.** 220  **B.** 224  **C.** 225  **D.** 226

**Q.74** Which of the following has the most number of divisors?

**A.** 99 **B.** 101 **C.** 176 **D.** 182

**Q.75**

The L.C.M. of two numbers is 48. The numbers are in the ratio 2 : 3. Then sum of the number is:

**A.** 28 **B.** 32 **C.** 40 **D.** 64

# English Comprehension

**Ques (76-80):Read the following passage and answer the question given below.**

U.S. President Donald Trump's decision to recognise Israel's sovereignty over the occupied Golan Heights hardly came as a surprise given his administration's blatant pro-Israel stance. It may sound ironic that a President who promised to facilitate a deal between Israelis and Palestinians has turned out to be the most pro-Israel President in U.S. history. Mr. Trump has already recognised as Israel's capital Jerusalem, a city it captured in parts in the 1948 and 1967 wars and which is claimed by both Israelis and Palestinians. Before he announced his intention to recognise Israeli sovereignty over Golan, a State Department report had dropped the word 'occupied' in references to Golan Heights and the Palestinian territories of Gaza and the West Bank, hinting at where the administration stood on the issue. Israel captured Golan, a strategically important plateau beside the Sea of Galilee, from Syria in the 1967 war. Among the territories it captured in the war, Israel has returned only the Sinai Peninsula, to Egypt. It annexed East Jerusalem and Golan Heights and continues to occupy the West Bank and the Gaza Strip. In 1981, as it passed the Golan annexation legislation, the Security Council passed a resolution that said, "the Israeli decision to impose its laws, jurisdiction and administration in the occupied Syrian Golan Heights is null and void and without international legal effect".

**Q.76** Which of the following stance has been taken by the Security Council regarding the Golan Heights issue?

**A.** It recognizes Israeli sovereignty over Golan Heights

**B.** It does not recognize Israel's sovereignty over Golan Heights

**C.** It has passed the Golan annexation legislation

**D.** It recognizes the joint rights of Israel and Syria over the territory

**Q.77** Consider the following pairs. Which of these is incorrect?

**A.** Capturing of Jerusalem by Israel - 1967

**B.** Capturing of Golan Heights by Israel - 1967

**C.** Capturing of Sinai Peninsula by Israel -1967

**D.** Annexation of Golan Heights by Israel - 1967

**Q.78** Consider the following word from the passage. Choose its antonym from the options.

Blatant

**A.** Flagrant **B.** Vagrant

**C.** Inconspicuous **D.** Intransigent

**Q.79** Which of the following territories continue to be appropriated by Israel?

**A.** Golan Heights **B.** West Bank

**C.** Gaza Strip **D.** All of the above

**Q.80** Which of the following actions have been undertaken by President Trump regarding Israel?

A. Facilitating a deal between Israelis and Palestinians

B. Recognition of the city of Jerusalem as Israel's capital

C. Supporting Israel's claim of sovereignty on Golan Heights

**A.** Only A **B.** B and C

**C.** A and C **D.** A, B and C

**Ques (81-82):The question below consists of a set of labelled parts. Out of the options given, select the most logical order of the parts to form a coherent sentence.**

**Q.81** A. when an individual is supported

B. unconditional positive regard

C. what the individual does or says

D. is offered in a social situation

E. and not judged regardless of

**A.** DACEB **B.** CBEDA **C.** BDAEC **D.** AEDBC

**Q.82** A. it is a game of

B. who think in black and white

C. making it difficult for those

D. to understand or appreciate

E. nuance and varying shades,

**A.** DCEAB **B.** CAEDB **C.** AECBD **D.** ECABD

**Ques (83-84):In the following question, one part of the sentence may have an error. Find out which part of the sentence has an error. If the sentence is free from error, click the 'No error' option.**

**Q.83** The biggest drawback to sales tax, in the eyes (a) / of many, is that they are a regressive tax - A tax on income in whose (b) / the proportion of tax paid relative to income decreases as income increases. (c) / No Error (d).

**A.** (a) **B.** (b) **C.** (c) **D.** No Error

**Q.84** The government backtracked on the face of this (a) / stunning unity but in other cases, it has acted vindictively, a trait (b) / made worse by the loud support it has received from the bulk of the TV media. (c) / No Error (d).

**A.** (a) **B.** (b) **C.** (c) **D.** No Error

**Q.85 Fill in the blanks.**

In order to _______ understand what motivates human beings, Maslow proposed that human needs can be organized into a hierarchy.

**A.** More **B.** Most **C.** Be **D.** Better

**Ques (86-87):In the following question, a sentence has been given in Active/Passive voice. Out of four alternatives suggested, select the one, which best expresses the same sentence in Passive/Active voice.**

**Q.86** Piano lessons are given here.

**A.** You give piano lessons here.

**B.** They give piano lessons here.

**C.** They gave piano lessons here.

**D.** They have given piano lessons here.

**Q.87** Sergei was embarrassed by the fact that Natasha gave him flowers.

**A.** Sergei embarrassed Natasha by the fact that he gave her flowers.

**B.** Natasha embarrassed Sergei by the fact that she gave him flowers.

**C.** Natasha will embarrass Sergei by the fact that she will give him flowers.

**D.** Natasha embarrasses Sergei by the fact that she gives him flowers.

**Ques (88-89):In the following question, out of the four alternatives, choose the one which can be substituted for the given sentence.**

**Q.88** A hater of knowledge and learning:

**A.** Bibliophile **B.** Philologist

**C.** Misogynist **D.** Misologist

**Q.89** Commencement of words with the same letter:

**A.** Pun **B.** Alliteration

**C.** Transferred epithet **D.** Oxymoron

**Q.90 Direction: Fill in the blank with an appropriate word.**

India's social fabric has been damaged to an _______ where repair seems impossible.

**A.** Portent **B.** Extent

**C.** Extant **D.** Extension

**Q.91 In the following sentence, a part of the sentence is underlined. Below are given alternatives to the underlined part, which may improve the sentence. Choose the correct alternative. In case no improvement is needed, choose the option 'No improvement'.**

Freud also believed that the girl develops a weaker superego because the resolution of the girl's complex isn't driven by something as concrete as castration anxiety in men.

**A.** Hasn't driven by **B.** Isn't driving for

**C.** Is to be driven **D.** No improvement

**Ques (92-96):In the following passage, some of the words have been left out. Read the passage carefully and select the correct answer for the given blank out of the given alternatives.**

As the countdown for elections to the 17th Lok Sabha begins, the world's largest democracy has a chance to re-imagine itself. Over the last 16 general elections and numerous elections at lower levels, the _(1)_ trust that the founding fathers of the Republic put in the parliamentary democratic system has been substantially proven wise. India did make some dangerous turns and show signs of_(2)_, especially during the Emergency in the 1970s, but in the long term it expanded the scope of its democracy through widening representation, _(3)_ of power and redistribution of resources. This is not to overlook the various _(4)_ that have afflicted the country's democracy, such as disinformation campaigns, corruption, disenfranchisement of the weaker sections of the society, the _(5)_ influence of money and muscle power in elections, and divisive majoritarian tendencies.

**Q.92** Which of the following word fits the blank labelled as (1)?

**A.** Resolute **B.** Reproachful

**C.** Profligate **D.** Retributive

**Q.93** Which of the following word fits the blank labelled as (2)?

**A.** Frolic **B.** Fragility

**C.** Frangipani **D.** Bucolic

**Q.94** Which of the following word fits the blank labeled as (3)?

**A.** Reciprocation **B.** Concentration

**C.** Evolution **D.** Devolution

**Q.95** Which of the following word fits the blank labeled as (4)?

**A.** Malodours **B.** Malice

**C.** Maladies **D.** Masts

**Q.96** Which of the following word fits the blank labelled as (5)?

**A.** Corroding **B.** Collaborating

**C.** Corroborating **D.** Confluent

**Q.97 In the following question, out of the four alternatives, select the word opposite in meaning to the word given.**

Exiguous

**A.** Ransom **B.** Diluted **C.** Humble **D.** Colossal

**Q.98 In the following question, a word has been written in 4 different ways out of which the only one correctly spelt. Select the correctly spelt word.**

**A.** Concured **B.** Concuured

**C.** Conccured **D.** Concurred

**Q.99 Rearrange the given 5 sentences A, B, C, D and E in proper sequence to form a meaningful paragraph and mark the correct sequence from the given options as your answer.**

A. Child labour interferes with the proper growth and development of the children in all aspects like mentally, physically, socially and intellectually.

B. Child labour is the service paid by the children in their childhood in any field of work.

C. Childhood is the great and happiest period of the lives of everyone during which one learns about the basic strategy of the life from parents, loved ones and nature.

D. This is done by the child due to the lack of resources for the survival of life and irresponsibility of the parents.

E. It does not matter what is the cause of child labour as all the causes force children to live their life without childhood.

**A.** ADECB **B.** CEADB **C.** BDECA **D.** EDABC

**Q.100 Choose the correct one-word substitute for:**

"One who is interested in the welfare of other people."

**A.** Philosopher **B.** Altruist

**C.** Dreamer **D.** Worker

# // Smart Answer Sheet //

**Correct** — Indicates percentage of students who answered questions correctly.

**Skipped** — Indicates percentage of students who skipped questions.

| Q. | Ans. | Correct / Skipped |
|---|---|---|
| 1 | B | 49.76 % / 49.57 % |
| 2 | B | 57.85 % / 41.16 % |
| 3 | D | 77.15 % / 18.8 % |
| 4 | B | 45.06 % / 33.2 % |
| 5 | B | 62.53 % / 32.36 % |
| 6 | B | 41.44 % / 42.83 % |
| 7 | B | 47.75 % / 30.63 % |
| 8 | A | 68.07 % / 31.66 % |
| 9 | B | 22.0 % / 73.61 % |
| 10 | A | 49.72 % / 34.44 % |
| 11 | B | 60.84 % / 30.66 % |
| 12 | A | 69.83 % / 30.15 % |
| 13 | D | 61.11 % / 38.29 % |
| 14 | D | 54.0 % / 45.67 % |
| 15 | D | 61.6 % / 32.26 % |
| 16 | C | 63.06 % / 35.12 % |
| 17 | B | 65.01 % / 30.28 % |
| 18 | D | 68.16 % / 31.21 % |
| 19 | A | 57.98 % / 33.38 % |
| 20 | C | 40.01 % / 58.06 % |
| 21 | A | 57.0 % / 38.99 % |
| 22 | C | 53.54 % / 43.22 % |
| 23 | D | 63.99 % / 31.51 % |
| 24 | C | 56.37 % / 42.13 % |
| 25 | A | 54.39 % / 33.34 % |
| 26 | A | 45.55 % / 36.71 % |
| 27 | C | 61.85 % / 35.69 % |
| 28 | B | 64.51 % / 33.25 % |
| 29 | A | 51.05 % / 45.17 % |
| 30 | A | 64.75 % / 33.93 % |
| 31 | B | 69.24 % / 30.64 % |
| 32 | D | 60.15 % / 33.63 % |
| 33 | D | 54.09 % / 42.97 % |
| 34 | B | 42.3 % / 53.59 % |
| 35 | C | 63.31 % / 31.78 % |
| 36 | C | 58.77 % / 33.25 % |
| 37 | C | 69.18 % / 30.7 % |
| 38 | D | 40.17 % / 51.08 % |
| 39 | B | 54.76 % / 36.64 % |
| 40 | D | 61.29 % / 34.6 % |
| 41 | C | 85.15 % / 13.44 % |
| 42 | B | 49.12 % / 46.08 % |
| 43 | C | 54.43 % / 34.74 % |
| 44 | B | 57.62 % / 38.29 % |
| 45 | B | 40.59 % / 35.73 % |
| 46 | C | 61.83 % / 33.21 % |
| 47 | C | 57.4 % / 30.35 % |
| 48 | D | 58.63 % / 31.04 % |
| 49 | B | 52.39 % / 45.74 % |
| 50 | B | 68.55 % / 31.35 % |
| 51 | B | 44.84 % / 30.87 % |
| 52 | B | 82.37 % / 17.05 % |
| 53 | D | 50.56 % / 43.4 % |
| 54 | A | 67.82 % / 31.8 % |
| 55 | A | 50.61 % / 31.15 % |
| 56 | C | 62.02 % / 35.54 % |
| 57 | D | 77.64 % / 15.47 % |
| 58 | C | 52.14 % / 32.13 % |
| 59 | B | 69.71 % / 30.24 % |
| 60 | B | 48.62 % / 35.92 % |
| 61 | A | 47.9 % / 39.41 % |
| 62 | D | 47.3 % / 37.77 % |
| 63 | C | 67.41 % / 30.02 % |
| 64 | B | 64.04 % / 31.22 % |
| 65 | A | 47.64 % / 51.79 % |
| 66 | D | 49.88 % / 34.09 % |
| 67 | D | 51.81 % / 32.6 % |
| 68 | B | 42.36 % / 51.86 % |
| 69 | C | 62.14 % / 37.01 % |
| 70 | A | 87.43 % / 11.51 % |
| 71 | C | 84.82 % / 13.41 % |
| 72 | B | 63.38 % / 31.89 % |
| 73 | D | 51.19 % / 35.16 % |
| 74 | C | 46.33 % / 35.89 % |
| 75 | C | 80.6 % / 17.32 % |
| 76 | B | 47.79 % / 35.21 % |
| 77 | D | 10.83 % / 82.2 % |
| 78 | C | 69.64 % / 30.33 % |
| 79 | D | 47.23 % / 39.18 % |
| 80 | B | 48.05 % / 40.46 % |

| Q. | Ans. | Correct | | Q. | Ans. | Correct | | Q. | Ans. | Correct | | Q. | Ans. | Correct | | Q. | Ans. | Correct |
|---|---|---|---|---|---|---|---|---|---|---|---|---|---|---|---|---|---|---|
| | | Skipped | | | | Skipped | | | | Skipped | | | | Skipped | | | | Skipped |
| 81 | C | 86.3 % | | 85 | D | 76.52 % | | 89 | B | 52.72 % | | 93 | B | 56.07 % | | 97 | D | 89.89 % |
| | | 13.01 % | | | | 21.17 % | | | | 36.77 % | | | | 38.14 % | | | | 10.08 % |
| 82 | C | 86.49 % | | 86 | B | 49.93 % | | 90 | B | 41.81 % | | 94 | D | 49.89 % | | 98 | D | 54.9 % |
| | | 10.05 % | | | | 43.95 % | | | | 48.84 % | | | | 46.93 % | | | | 36.79 % |
| 83 | B | 58.31 % | | 87 | B | 52.62 % | | 91 | D | 48.58 % | | 95 | C | 64.74 % | | 99 | C | 61.62 % |
| | | 35.42 % | | | | 41.53 % | | | | 36.22 % | | | | 34.63 % | | | | 33.32 % |
| 84 | A | 59.58 % | | 88 | D | 89.19 % | | 92 | A | 63.32 % | | 96 | A | 53.37 % | | 100 | B | 88.12 % |
| | | 38.15 % | | | | 10.76 % | | | | 34.79 % | | | | 44.4 % | | | | 11.04 % |

## Performance Analysis

| | |
|---|---|
| Avg. Score (%) | 36.0% |
| Toppers Score (%) | 67.0% |
| Your Score | |

# //Hints and Solutions//

**1.**

ANSWER 2

Hence, the correct option is (B).

**2.**

$$H \xrightarrow{-2} F \xrightarrow{-2} D \xrightarrow{-3} A$$

$$V \xrightarrow{-2} T \xrightarrow{-3} Q \xrightarrow{-3} N$$

$$C \xrightarrow{-2} A \xrightarrow{-2} Y \xrightarrow{-3} V$$

$$O \xrightarrow{-2} M \xrightarrow{-2} K \xrightarrow{-3} H$$

So, VTQN is different from the other three.

Hence, the correct option is (B).

**3.** Tunis, Maputo, Harare are cities in Africa. Leeds is the city in England.

So, England is the odd one from the given alternatives.

Hence, the correct option is (D).

**4.**

| A | B | C | D | E | F | G | H | I | J | K | L | M |
|---|---|---|---|---|---|---|---|---|---|---|---|---|
| 1 | 2 | 3 | 4 | 5 | 6 | 7 | 8 | 9 | 10 | 11 | 12 | 13 |

| N | O | P | Q | R | S | T | U | V | W | X | Y | Z |
|---|---|---|---|---|---|---|---|---|---|---|---|---|
| 14 | 15 | 16 | 17 | 18 | 19 | 20 | 21 | 22 | 23 | 24 | 25 | 26 |

1) K is 11th letter from the starting of alphabet and P is 11th letter from the end.

2) U is 21st letter from the starting and F is 21st letter from the end.

3) N is 14th letter from the starting and M is 14th letter from the end.

4) A is 1st letter from the starting and Z is 1st letter from the end.

$34 \to 3 + 4 = 7 \times 2 \to 14$.

Similarly,

1) M is 13th from the starting and N is 13th from the end.

2) E is 5th from the starting and V is 5th from the end.

3) G is 7th from the starting and T is 7th from the end.

4) A is 1st from the starting and Z is 1st from the end.

$41 \to 4 + 1 = 5 \times 2 \to 10$.

So, MEGA41 is related to NVTZ10.

Hence, the correct option is (B).

**5.** Rabid and Friendly are exactly opposite in meaning. Rabid means extremist or violent, whereas Friendly is opposite to being Violent.

Similarly, Quaint and modern are opposite to each other in meaning. Quaint means old fashioned whereas Modern is exactly opposite of Old fashioned.

Hence, the correct option is (B).

**6.** Here, the 2nd word denotes the category while the 1st word denotes the example of that category i.e.,

Iron: Metal → here Iron is an example of Metal.

Similarly,

Oxygen is an example of Gas.

So, Gas is the correct alternative.

Hence, the correct option is (B).

**7.** The logic followed is:

$39 + 1 \to 40$

$40 + 2 \to 42$

$42 + 1 \to 43$

$43 + 2 \to 45$

$45 + 1 \to 46$

Hence, the correct option is (B).

**8.** Given Series: 1, 4, 3, 9, 5, 16, 7, 25, 9, 36, 11, ?

Logic behind the series:

The series consist of two alternate series:

1, 3, 5, 7, 9, 11 are consecutive odd numbers starting from 1.

4, 9, 16, 25, 36 are square of consecutive even numbers starting from 2.

$2^2 > 4$

$3^2 > 9$

$4^2 > 16$

$5^2 > 25$

$6^2 > 36$

$7^2 > 49$

So, the next term will be 49.

Hence, the correct option is (A).

**9.** 1) 1st element is number that represents

Number of letters in word + 1 (if word starts with consonant).

Number of letters in word + 2 (if word starts with vowel).

2) 2nd element is symbol that represents

% → if odd number of letters in the word.

* → if even number of letters in the word.

3) 3rd element is letter that represents last letters next letter in its capital form.

Ex: 7%Z for "early"

Starts with vowel so,

$7 \rightarrow 5 + 2$

No. of letters in early is 5.

% → if odd number of letters.

Last letter is "y" and its next letter in its capital form is "Z".

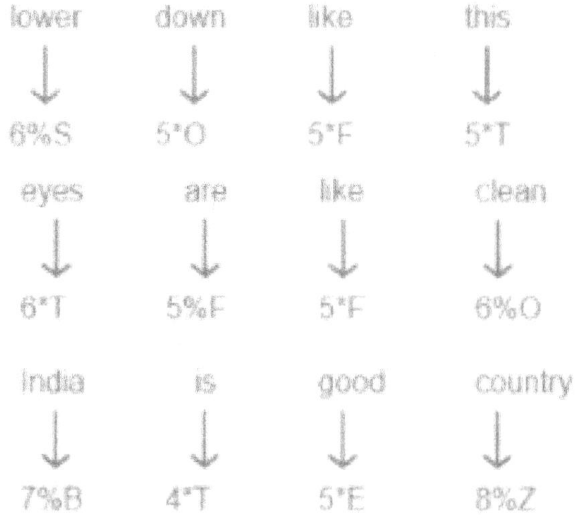

Code for "evaporation" is:

Starts with vowel so,

$13 \rightarrow 11 + 2$

No. of letters in "evaporation" is 11.

% → if odd number of letters.

Last letter is "n" and its next letter in its capital form is "O".

So, code for "independent" is "13%O".

Hence, the correct option is (B).

**10.**

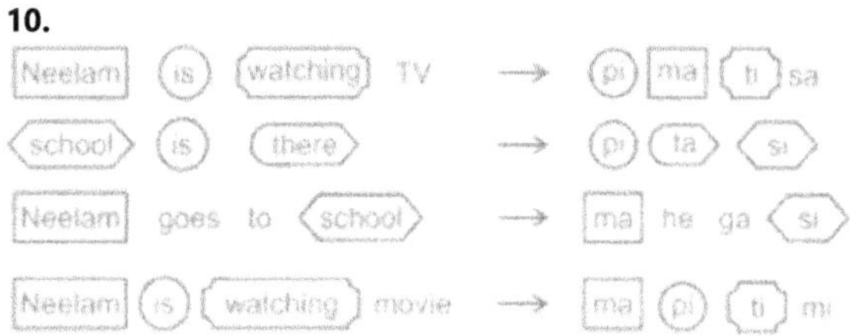

So, 'movie' is coded as 'mi'.

Hence, the correct option is (A).

**11.**

# MAJAYAJAM

Hence, the correct option is (B).

**12.**

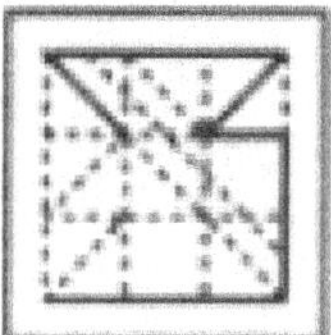

Hence, the correct option is (A).

**13.**

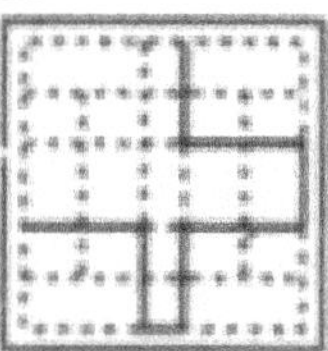

Hence, the correct option is (D).

**14.** From Statement I:

From Statement II:

From, combining Statement I and II, no relation can be established by combining both the statements.

So, none of the two statements is sufficient to answer the question.

Hence, the correct option is (D).

**15.** The third figure in each row comprises of parts which are not common to the first two figures.

Hence, the correct option is (D).

**16.**

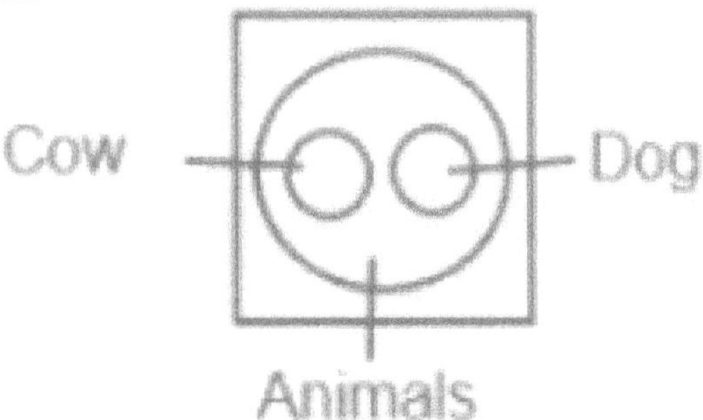


Hence, the correct option is (C).

**17.** In each row, the second figure is obtained from the first figure by adding two mutually perpendicular line segments at the center and the third figure is obtained from the first figure by adding four circles outside the main figure.

Hence, the correct option is (B).

**18.**

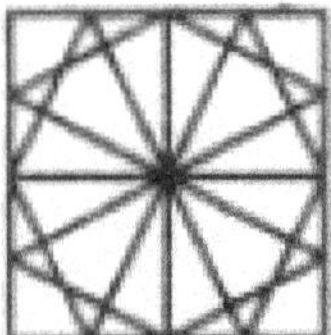

Hence, the correct option is (D).

**19.** Let us check each option,

1) 12 = 4 × 5 - 8, True

2) 12 × 4 - 5 = 8, False

3) 12 = 4 - 5 × 8, False

4) 12 - 4 × 5 = 8, False

So, '=, ×, -' is correct sequence.

Hence, the correct option is (A).

**20.**

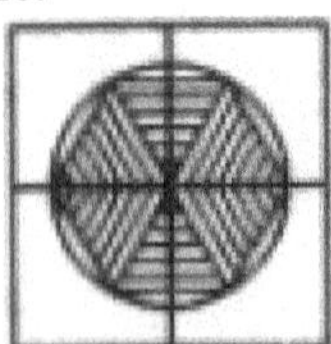

Hence, the correct option is (C).

**21.** The figure may be labelled as shown.

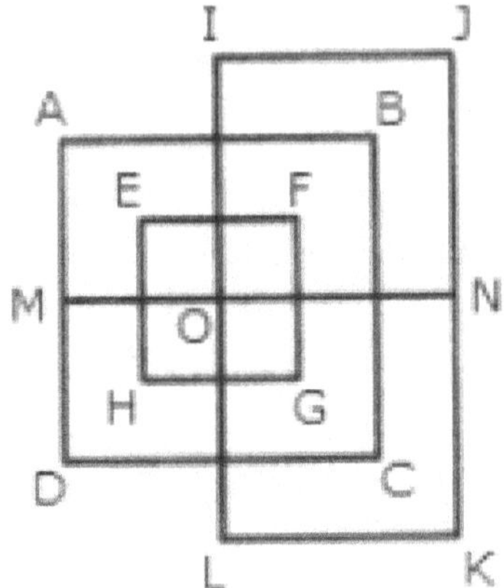

The horizontal lines are IJ, AB, EF, MN, HG, DC and LK i.e., 7 in number.

The vertical lines are AD, EH, IL, FG, BC and JK i.e., 6 in number.

Thus, there are 7 + 6 = 13 straight lines in the figure.

Hence, the correct option is (A).

**22.** The figure may be labelled as shown.

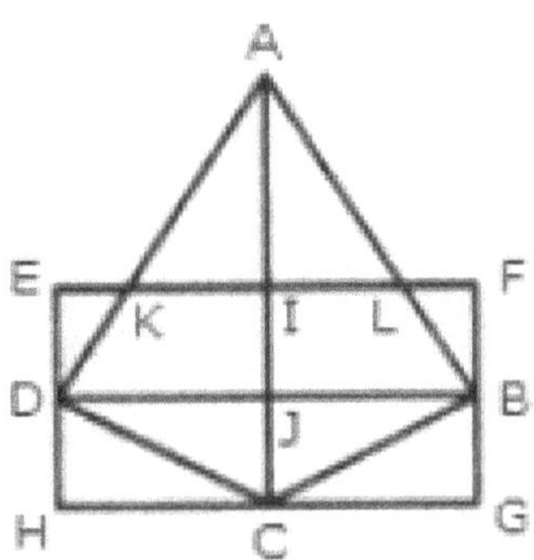

The simplest triangles are AKI, AIL, EKD, LFB, DJC, BJC, DHC and BCG i.e., 8 in number.

The triangles composed of two components each are AKL, ADJ, AJB and DBC i.e., 4 in number.

The triangles composed of the three components each are ADC and ABC i.e., 2 in number.

There is only one triangle i.e., ADB composed of four components.

Thus, there are 8+ 4 + 2 + 1= 15 triangles in the figure.

Hence, the correct option is (C).

**23.**

Hence, the correct option is (D).

**24.** The half-shaded leaf rotates 135° ACW and the unshaded leaf rotates 135° CW.

Hence, the correct option is (C).

**25.** The upper element is converted to an element similar to the lower elements and each one of the lower elements is converted to an element similar to the upper element.

Hence, the correct option is (A).

**26.** The Indian Prime Minister Narendra Modi released a commemorative Rs 100 coin as part of the end of birth centenary celebrations of Vijaya Raje Scindia.

She was also called as the Rajamata of Gwalior and was born on the same day in the year 1919. Vijaya Raje Scindia started her political career from the Congress and later joined the Swatantrata Party before becoming a member of the BJP's parent party, Jana Sangh.

Hence, the correct option is (A).

**27.** India's rank in Human Development Index, 2018 is 130th.

India has been positioned at 131 out of 189 countries and territories, according to the report. India had ranked 130 in 2018 in the index.

The United Nations Development Programme(UNDP) is the United Nations' global development network. UNDP works in about 170 countries and territories, helping to eradicate poverty, reduce inequalities and exclusion, and build resilience so countries can sustain progress. As the UN's development agency, UNDP plays a critical role in helping countries achieve Sustainable Development Goals.

Hence, the correct option is (C).

**28.** International Advertising Association (IAA), the integrated association of advertising agencies and the media, will organise the 44th edition of its global summit at Kochi. The three-day summit will see the participation of dignitaries from various fields and industries all over the world.

Hence, the correct option is (B).

**29.** The Siege of Arcot was part of the Second Carnatic War.

The Second Carnatic War (1749-54) was a struggle for power between various Indian claimants to power in southern India, each supported by the French or the British.

Hence, the correct option is (A).

**30.** World Water Day is celebrated annually on 22nd March. The day focuses attention on the importance of universal access to clean water, sanitation and hygiene (WASH) facilities in developing countries. The day also focuses on advocating for the sustainable management of freshwater resources.

Hence, the correct option is (A).

**31.** Talley Valley Wildlife Sanctuary is a wildlife sanctuary in Arunachal Pradesh, India. At the altitude of 2400 metres, Talley is a plateau with a dense forest of silver fir trees, a pine-clad plateau of beautiful grandeur, and a vast wasteland. The area has some of the most important endangered species including the clouded leopard.

Hence, the correct option is (B).

**32.** James Prinsep deciphered the Brahmi and Kharoshthi scripts.

Brahmi Script- It is the oldest writing styles in ancient India. The rock-cut edicts of Ashoka are the best examples of Brahmi script which were deciphered by an archaeologist of East India Company James Prinsep.

Kharoshthi scripts- It is used in Gandhara kingdom to write Gandhari Prakrit and Sanskrit in 4-3 century B.C.

Hence, the correct option is (D).

**33.** 3 sessions of the Lok Sabha take place in a year.

The period during which the House meets to conduct its business is called a session. The Constitution empowers the President to summon each House at such intervals that there should not be more than a six-month gap between the two sessions. So, the Parliament must meet at least twice a year. In India, the Parliament conducts 3 sessions each year:

- Budget session: January/February to May
- Monsoon session: July to August/September
- Winter session: November to December

Hence, the correct option is (D).

**34.** The Yucatan Strait connects The Gulf of Mexico and the Caribbean Sea.

When two large water bodies get naturally connected by a narrow waterway, then that waterway is termed as a Strait.

| **Yucatan Strait** | **The Gulf of Mexico and the Caribbean Sea** |
| --- | --- |
| Sunda Strait | The Java Sea and the Indian Ocean |
| Bab-el-Mandeb Strait | The Red Sea and the Gulf of Aden |
| Torres Strait | Arafura Sea & Gulf of Papua |

Hence, the correct option is (B).

**35.** Ms. Florence Nightingale was an English social reformer and the founder of modern nursing.

She was a manager and trainer of nurses during the Crimean War in which she organised to care for wounded soldiers.

Crimean War, (October 1853–February 1856), fought mainly on the Crimean Peninsula between the Russians and the British, French, and Ottoman Turkish, with support from January 1855 by the army of Sardinia-Piedmont.

The war arose from the conflict of great powers in the Middle East and was more directly caused by Russian demands to exercise protection over the Orthodox subjects of the Ottoman sultan.

Hence, the correct option is (C).

**36.** Wholesale banking is the provision of services by banks to organizations, such as mortgage brokers, large corporate clients, mid-sized companies, real estate developers and investors,

international trade finance businesses, institutional customers (such as pension funds and government entities/agencies), and services offered to other banks or other financial institutions.

Hence, the correct option is (C).

**37.** The Indira Sagar Dam is a multipurpose project of Madhya Pradesh on the Narmada River. In terms of storage of water, it withholds the largest reservoir in India, with a capacity of 12.22 billion cubic metres, followed by Nagarjuna Sagar between Telangana and Andhra Pradesh. The dam, built as a joint venture between Madhya Pradesh irrigation and National Hydroelectric Power Corporation. It was commissioned in May 2005.

Hence, the correct option is (C).

**38.** The Money market in India is the money market for short-term and long-term funds with maturity ranging from overnight to one year in India. The Indian money market consists of the unorganized sector: moneylenders, indigenous bankers and unregulated Non-Bank Financial Intermediaries (e.g. Finance Companies, Chit funds, Nidhi);

Hence, the correct option is (D).

**39.** Luni is the only river integrated into the Indian Thar Desert.

It originates in the Pushkar valley of the Aravalli Range, near Ajmer and ends in the marshy lands of Rann of Kutch in Gujarat.

It was first known as Sagarmati, then after passing Govindgarh, it meets its tributary Saraswati, which originates from PushkarLake, and from then on it gets its name Luni.

The Thar Desert is also known as the Great Indian Desert.

Hence, the correct option is (B).

**40.** Bogota is the capital of Colombia.

| Country | Colombia |
| --- | --- |
| Capital | Bogota |
| President | Iván Duque Márquez |
| Currency | Colombian Peso |

Hence, the correct option is (D).

**41.** In India, the Reserve Bank of India determines the bank rate, which is the standard rate at which it is prepared to buy or re-discount bills of exchange or other commercial bills eligible for purchase under the RBI Act 1934 (sec. 49).

Hence, the correct option is (C).

**42.** Law of supply states that other factors remaining constant, price and quantity supplied of a good are directly related to each other. In other words, when the price paid by buyers for a good rise, then suppliers increase the supply of that good in the market.

The Law of supply establishes a direct relationship between price and supply.

Hence, the correct option is (B).

**43.** Nicolaus Copernicus was an astronomer and mathematician who was the first to discover that the earth revolves around the sun giving birth to the heliocentric model in which the sun is at the center of the universe.

The Copernican Revolution was very important as it deviated from the Ptolemaic model, according to which the earth stationary at the center of the universe.

Hence, the correct option is (C).

**44.** The idea of Residual Power in the Indian Constitution has been borrowed from the Constitution of Canada.

According to Article 248 of the Indian Constitution, the Parliament has the exclusive power to formulate laws which are related to matters that have not been enumerated in the Concurrent List and State List.

Hence, the correct option is (B).

**45.** Gangaur is one of the most important festivals in Rajasthan. In some form or the other, it is celebrated all over Rajasthan. "Gan" is a synonym for Lord Shiva & "Gauri" or "Gaur" stands for Goddess Parvati, the heavenly consort of Lord Shiva. Gangaur celebrates the union of the two and is a symbol of conjugal & marital happiness.

Hence, the correct option is (B).

**46.** Islamic banking is banking or banking activity that is consistent with the principles of sharia (Islamic law) and it is a practical application through the development of Islamic economics.

Hence, the correct option is (D).

**47.** Branch banking is engaging in banking activities at facilities away from a bank's home office i.e. branches. Branch banking allows a financial institution to expand services to areas outside of the home location.

Hence, the correct option is (C).

**48.** The summer Olympic Games 2024 to be held in Paris.

Paris will become the second city to host the Olympics three times, after London (1908, 1948, and 2012). It was previously the host in the year 1900 and 1924. The year 2024 will mark the centenary of the Paris Games of 1924.

These will be the sixth Olympic Games hosted by France (three summers and three winters). Paris was elected as the host city on September 13, 2017, at the 131st IOC Session in Lima, Peru.

Hence, the correct option is (D).

**49.** Journalist P. Sainath has been selected as one of the three recipients of the Fukuoka Prize 2021.

Shri Sainath will receive the 'Grand Prize' of the Fukuoka Prize, while the Academic Award and the Art and Culture Award will be presented by Prof. Kishimoto Mio and Thailand-based filmmaker Prabda Yoon. In the last 30 years, 115 people from 28 countries have received the award.

Hence, the correct option is (B).

**50.** Bank of Baroda, India's leading public sector bank, has launched a solution for digital banking payments named BOB World Wave on December 13, 2021.

With the use of wearable technology across the globe, lenders are adopting it for a more convenient and cashless digital payment system. This innovative solution aims to fully deliver preventive health actions as well as easy payment transactions.

Hence, the correct option is (B).

**51.** Let $x$ litre of liquid costing Rs. $52/$ litre be mixed with $(1 - x)$ litre of liquid costing Rs. $65/$ litre making it a mixture of 1 litre

Cost of new liquid $= (x) \times 52 + (1 - x) \times 65 = 65 - 13x$

Cost of mixture $= 60/$ liter

$\Rightarrow 65 - 13x = 60$

$\Rightarrow 13x = 5$

$\Rightarrow \dfrac{x = 5}{13}$

$\Rightarrow (1 - x) = \dfrac{1 - 5}{13} = \dfrac{8}{13}$

The ratio in which liquids must be mixed $= \dfrac{x}{(1 - x)}$

$= \dfrac{\left(\frac{5}{13}\right)}{\left(\frac{8}{13}\right)}$

$= \dfrac{5}{8}$

$= 5 : 8$

Shortcut method:

$\dfrac{\text{Quantity of cheaper}}{\text{quantity of dearer}} = \dfrac{\text{(price of dearer - mean price)}}{\text{(mean price - price of cheaper)}}$

Price of cheaper = Rs. $52/$ liters

Price of dearer = Rs. 65 /liter

Mean price $=$ Rs. $60/$ liter

Required ratio $= \dfrac{\text{Quantity of cheaper}}{\text{quantity of dearer}}$

Required ratio $= \dfrac{(65 - 60)}{(60 - 52)}$

$= \dfrac{5}{8}$

$= 5 : 8$

Hence, the correct option is (B).

**52.** Distance between two places $= \text{time taken} \times speed$

$= \dfrac{7}{2} \times 62 = 217$ km

Increased speed $= 70$ km/hr

$\Rightarrow$ Time taken $= \dfrac{217}{70}$

$= 186$ minutes

$\therefore$ Time saved $= 210 - 186$

$= 24$ minutes

Hence, the correct option is (B).

**53.** Given that,

P $= 28560$

R $= 15\%$

T $= 2$ years

Simple Interest $= \dfrac{(P \times R \times T)}{100}$

$\Rightarrow$ Simple Interest $= \dfrac{(28560 \times 15 \times 2)}{100}$

$= 8568$

And,

Compound Interest $= P\left[\left(1 + \dfrac{R}{100}\right)^{T} - 1\right] =$ $28560\left[\left(1 + \dfrac{15}{10}\right)^{2} - 1\right]$

$\Rightarrow$ Compound Interest $= 28560\left(\dfrac{13225}{10000} - 1\right) =$ $28560 \times \dfrac{3225}{10000}$

$\Rightarrow$ Compound Interest $= 28560 \times 0.3225$

$= 9210.6$

So, Difference $= 9210.6 - 8568$

$= 642.6$

Hence, the correct option is (D).

**54.** Ratio of income of C and D $= 3 : 2 = 15 : 10$

Also,

Ratio of income of D and E $= 5 : 4 = 10 : 8$

Let income of C, D and E be $15x, 10x$ and $8x$ respectively

According to the question

$\Rightarrow \left(\dfrac{1}{3}\right)$ of $15x = \left(\dfrac{1}{2}\right)$ of $8x + 4000$

$\Rightarrow 5x = 4x + 4000$

$\Rightarrow x = 4000$

$\therefore$ D's income $= 10x = 10 \times 4000$

$= 40,000$

Hence, the correct option is (A).

**55.** $x + \dfrac{1}{x} = 2$

$\Rightarrow \frac{x^2+1}{x} = 2$

$\Rightarrow x^2 + 1 = 2x$

$\Rightarrow x^2 - 2x + 1 = 0$

Which is in the form of $ax^2 + bx + c = 0$.

Hence, the correct option is (A).

**56.** $(x + 2)^3 = (x^2 - 1)2x$

$\Rightarrow x^3 + 8 + 3 \cdot x \cdot 2(x + 2) = 2x^3 - 2x$

$\Rightarrow x^3 + 8 + 6x^2 + 12x = 2x^3 - 2x$

$\Rightarrow 2x^3 - x^3 - 6x^2 - 12x - 2x - 8 = 0$

$\Rightarrow x^3 - 6x^2 - 14x - 8 = 0$

Which is of the form $ax^3 + bx^2 + cx + d = 0$.

Hence, the correct option is (C).

**57.** Selling Price $=$ Rs. $435$ and profit $\% = 16\%$

Thus, Cost Price $=$ Selling Price $\times \frac{100}{(profit\%)}$

$= 435 \times \frac{100}{116} =$ Rs. $375$

Loss percentage when Selling Price $=$ Rs. $330$

$\therefore \text{loss}\% = \frac{(CostPrice - SellingPrice)}{CostPrice \times 100}$

$= \frac{(375 - 330)}{375 \times 100}$

$= 12\%$

Hence, the correct option is (D).

**58.** $\frac{\{9^n \times 3^5 \times (27)^3\}}{3} \times (81)^4$

$= 27 \Rightarrow \frac{\{(3^2)^n \times 3^5 \times (3^3)^3\}}{3 \times (3^4)^4}$

$= 3^3 \Rightarrow \frac{(3^{2n} \times 3^5 \times 3^{(3 \times 3)})}{3 \times 3^{(4 \times 4)}} = 3^3$

$\Rightarrow \frac{3^{2n+5+9}}{3 \times 3^{16}}$

$= 3^3 \Rightarrow \frac{3^{2n+14}}{3^{17}}$

$= 3^3 \Rightarrow 3^{(2n+14-17)} = 3^3$

$\Rightarrow 3^{2n-3} = 3^3$

From the equation powers:

$\Rightarrow 2n - 3 = 3$

$\Rightarrow 2n = 6$

$\Rightarrow n = 3.$

Hence, the correct option is (C).

**59.** The ratio of the efficiency of B to C $= 2x : x$

Efficiency of the A $= 2x \times \frac{150}{100} = 3x$

The ratio of the efficiency of A, B, and C $= 3 : 2 : 1$

Total efficiency $= (3 + 2 + 1) = 6$

Total work $= 6 \times 6 = 36$

$\therefore$ A alone can complete the whole work in $= \frac{36}{3}$

$= 12$ days

Hence, the correct option is (B).

**60.** According to the question

$\Rightarrow 5\%$ of $(P + Q) = 20\%$ of $(P - Q)$

$\Rightarrow \frac{5}{100} \times (P + Q) = \frac{20}{100} \times (P - Q)$

$\Rightarrow (P + Q) = 4 \times (P - Q)$

$\Rightarrow P + Q = 4P - 4Q$

$\Rightarrow 3P = 5Q$

$\Rightarrow \frac{P}{Q} = \frac{5}{3}$

Let $P = 5 \ \& \ Q = 3$

$\therefore$ Required $\% = \frac{5}{3} \times 100$

$= 166.66\%$

Hence, the correct option is (B).

**61.** Given expression:

$\Rightarrow \sqrt{13 - 4\sqrt{10}} = ?$

$\Rightarrow \sqrt{13 - 2\sqrt{10 \times 4}} = ?$

$\Rightarrow \sqrt{8 + 5 - 2\sqrt{10 \times 4}} = ?$

$\Rightarrow \sqrt{8 + 5 - 2\sqrt{5 \times 8}} = ?$

$\Rightarrow \sqrt{\left(\sqrt{8}\right)^2 - 2\sqrt{5 \times 8} + \left(\sqrt{5}\right)^2} = ?$

Using,

$(a + b)^2 = a^2 + 2ab + b^2$

$\Rightarrow \sqrt{\left(\sqrt{8} - \sqrt{5}\right)^2} = ?$

Taking square root,

$$= \sqrt{8} - \sqrt{5}$$

Hence, the correct option is (A).

**62.** Given equation:

$$2^{n-1} + 2^{n+1} = 320$$

$$\Rightarrow 2^{n-1}(1 + 2^2) = 320$$

$$\Rightarrow 5 \times 2^{n-1} = 320$$

$$\Rightarrow 2^{n-1} = \frac{320}{5}$$

$$\Rightarrow 2^{n-1} = 64$$

$$\Rightarrow 2^{n-1} = 2^6$$

$$\Rightarrow n - 1 = 6$$

$$n = 7$$

Hence, the correct option is (D).

**63.** Total distance covered by train $=$ Length of bridge $+$ length of train $= 655 + 145$

$$= 800 \text{ m}$$

$$= 0.8 \text{ km}$$

Time taken $= 36$ seconds

$$= \frac{36}{3600} \text{ hours}$$

$$= \frac{1}{100} \text{ hours}$$

$\therefore$ Speed of train $= \dfrac{\text{Distance covered}}{\text{Time taken}}$

$$= \frac{0.8}{\left(\frac{1}{100}\right)}$$

$$= 80 \text{ km/h}$$

Hence, the correct option is (C).

**64.** Let the cost of $1$ liter milk be Rs. $1$

Milk in $1$ liter mix. in $1^{\text{st}}$ can $= \dfrac{3}{4}$ litre, C.P. of 1 liter mix. in $1^{\text{st}}$ can Rs. $\dfrac{3}{4}$

Milk in $1$ liter mix. in $2^{\text{nd}}$ can $= \dfrac{1}{2}$ litre, C.P. of 1 litre mix. in $2^{\text{nd}}$ can Re.

Milk in $1$ liter of final mix. $= \dfrac{5}{8}$ litre, Mean price $=$ Rs. $\dfrac{5}{8}$

By the rule of alligation, we have:

C.P. of $1$ liter mixture in $1^{\text{st}}$ can C.P. of 1 liter mixture in $2^{\text{nd}}$ can

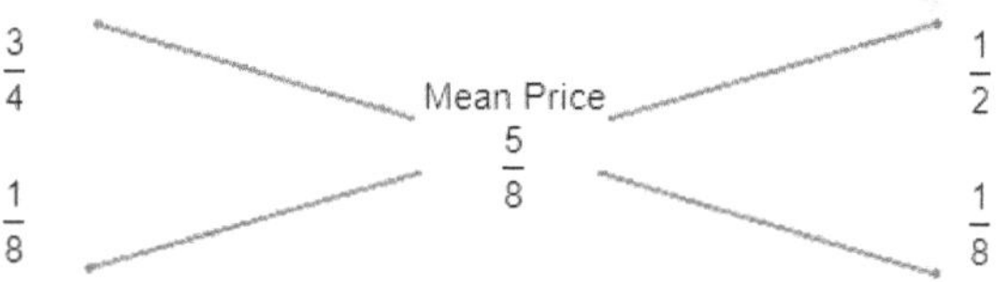


$\therefore$ Ratio of two mixtures $= \dfrac{1}{8} : \dfrac{1}{8} = 1 : 1$

So, quantity of mixture taken from each can $= \left(\dfrac{1}{2} \times 12\right) = 6$ liters.

Hence, the correct option is (B).

**65.** Given,

$$\Rightarrow p + \left(\frac{1}{p}\right) = 8 \quad - (1)$$

Squaring both the side in equation (1), we get

$$\Rightarrow p^2 + \left(\frac{1}{p}\right)^2 + 2 \times p \times \frac{1}{p} = 64$$

$$\Rightarrow p^2 + \left(\frac{1}{p^2}\right) + 2 = 64$$

$$\Rightarrow p^2 + \left(\frac{1}{p^2}\right) = 64 - 2$$

$$= 62$$

Hence, the correct option is (A).

**66.** Market price of cooler $= 1600$

Selling price $= 90\%$ of $1600 =$ Rs. $1440$

Profit $\% = 20\% = \dfrac{1}{5}$

Selling price $= 1 + 5 = 6$ units

$$= 1440$$

$1$ unit $=$ Rs. $240$

$\therefore$ Cost price of the cooler $= 5$ units

$$= 5 \times 240$$

$$= \text{Rs. } 1200$$

Hence, the correct option is (D).

**67.** Number of Red balls $= 4$

Number of Blue balls $= 6$

Number of Pink balls $= 8$

Total number of balls $= 4 + 6 + 8 = 18$

Required probability $= \dfrac{4}{18} \times \dfrac{11}{20} + \dfrac{6}{18} \times \dfrac{11}{20}$

$$= \frac{11}{20}\left[\frac{4}{18} + \frac{6}{18}\right]$$

$= \frac{11}{20} \times \frac{10}{18}$

$= \frac{11}{36}$

Hence, the correct option is (D).

**68.** $(192)^{102} + (193)^{103}$

We will consider the unit digit of each number

$\Rightarrow 2^{102} + 3^{103}$

$\Rightarrow 2^{4\times25+2} + 3^{4\times25+3}$

$\Rightarrow 2^2 + 3^3$ (consider only unit place digit of each sum)

$\Rightarrow 4 + 27$

$\Rightarrow 31$

$\therefore$ unit digit is 1

Hence, the correct option is (B).

**69.** After $5$ years the age of the Rakhi will be twice the age of the date, if the date's birthday was celebrated two years earlier.

So, present age of Tithi $= 13 + 2$

$= 15$ years.

After $5$ years, the age of Tithi $= 15 + 5$

$= 20$ years.

Let the present age of Rakhi be $x$ years.

After $5$ years, Rakhi's age $= (x + 5)$ years

Now we can write,

$x + 5 = 2 \times 20$

$\Rightarrow x = 40 - 5$

$\Rightarrow x = 35$

Then, the age of Rakhi $= 35$ years.

Prapti's age is $\frac{1}{7}^{th}$ of Rakhi's age.

$\therefore$ The age of Prapti $= 35 \times \left(\frac{1}{7}\right)$

$= 5$ years.

Hence, the correct option is (C).

**70.** First $8$ multiple of $5$ will be $5,10,15,20,25,30,35,40$

The sum $= 5 + 10 + 15 + 20 + 25 + 30 + 35 + 40$

$= 180$

The average $= \frac{180}{8}$

$= 22.5$.

Hence, the correct option is (A).

**71.** For H.C.F,

Factors of 493 = 17 × 29 = 1, 17, 29, 493

Factors of 527 = 17 × 31 = 1, 17, 31, 527

Factors of 697 = 17 × 41 = 1, 17, 41, 697

$\therefore$ H.C.F (493,527,697) = common factors of all three

= 17

Hence, the correct option is (C).

**72.** We have square root sign in the denominator. To remove it, rationalize the fractions. Use the opposite sign while rationalizing. On rationalizing we get:

$= \frac{1}{1+\sqrt{2}} \times \frac{1-\sqrt{2}}{1-\sqrt{2}} + \frac{1}{\sqrt{2}+\sqrt{3}} \times \frac{\sqrt{2}-\sqrt{3}}{\sqrt{2}-\sqrt{3}} \ldots + \frac{1}{\sqrt{15}+\sqrt{16}} \times \frac{\sqrt{15}-\sqrt{16}}{\sqrt{15}-\sqrt{16}}$

$= \frac{1-\sqrt{2}}{1-2} + \frac{\sqrt{2}-\sqrt{3}}{2-3} \ldots + \frac{\sqrt{15}-\sqrt{16}}{15-16} \rightarrow (a+b)(a-b)$
$= a^2 - b^2$

$= \frac{1-\sqrt{2}}{-1} + \frac{\sqrt{2}-\sqrt{3}}{-1} \ldots + \frac{\sqrt{15}-\sqrt{16}}{-1}$

$= -1 + \sqrt{2} - \sqrt{2} + \sqrt{3} - \cdots - \sqrt{15} + \sqrt{16}$

$= -1 + \sqrt{16} = -1 + 4 = 3$

Hence, the correct option is (B).

**73.** Divide the question into parts,

$(\frac{98}{3}\% \text{ of } 769.002) + (24\% of 160.89) - 67.9900$

$\Rightarrow \frac{98}{3}\% \text{ of } 769.002 = 33\% \times 769 = 254.77 = 255 - - (1)$

$\Rightarrow 24\% \text{ of } 160.89 = 24\% \times 161 = 38.64 = 39 - - (2)$

Finally,

$255 + 39 - 68 = 294 - 68 = 226$

Hence, the correct option is (D).

**74.** 99 = 1 x 3 x 3 x 11

101 = 1 x 101

176 = 1 x 2 x 2 x 2 x 2 x 11

182 = 1 x 2 x 7 x 13

So, divisors of 99 are 1, 3, 9, 11, 33, .99

Divisors of 101 are 1 and 101

Divisors of 176 are 1, 2, 4, 8, 11, 16, 22, 44, 88 and 176

Divisors of 182 are 1, 2, 7, 13, 14, 26, 91 and 182.

So, 176 has the most number of divisors.

Hence, the correct option is (C).

**75.** Let the numbers be 2x and 3x.

Then, their L.C.M. = 6x

So, 6x = 48 or x = 8

 The numbers are 16 and 24

So, required sum = (16 + 24) = 40

Hence, the correct option is (C).

**76.** The passage states that the Security Council passed a resolution in 1981 which considers the Israeli annexation as null and void. So, it does not recognize Israeli right over Golan Heights.

Hence, the correct option is (B).

**77.** According to the passage, Israel captured Jerusalem, Golan Heights and the Sinai Peninsula in the war of 1967.

But the annexation of Golan Heights happened in 1981.

Annexation –The act of adding extra territory to one's own by appropriation.

Hence, the correct option is (D).

**78.** Blatant means something bad done openly and unashamedly.

e.g. The government continued to supply them with blatant lies.

So, its antonym must mean something that is done secretly or something that is hidden and not very obvious.

Let's look at the meanings of the words:

Inconspicuous- not clearly visible or attracting attention.

Flagrant- conspicuously or obviously offensive.

Vagrant- a person without a settled home or regular work who wanders from place to place.

Intransigent- unwilling or refusing to change one's views or to agree about something.

Out of these, only Inconspicuous gives the opposite meaning to Blatant.

Hence, the correct option is (C).

**79.** The passage says that Israel continues to occupy the West Bank and the Gaza Strip and that it has also claimed sovereignty over Golan Heights.

Hence, the correct option is (D).

**80.** As per the passage, President Trump only promised but did not follow up on facilitating a deal between Israelis and Palestinians.

The passage states that he has recognized Jerusalem as Israel's capital and Golan Heights as being part of Israel.

Hence, the correct option is (B).

**81.** Instead of ordering the entire sentence, it is easier to find connections between one or two parts and then eliminating the options.

B talks about 'unconditional positive regard', which, in order to make a meaningful sentence, must be joined to the other parts by a verb.

D is the only part that begins with the verb 'is'.

Hence, the correct option is (C).

**82.** Instead of ordering the entire sentence, it is easier to find connections between one or two parts and then eliminating the options.

C talks about making something difficult 'for those', which must be logically followed by who think in black and white, as given by B.

Hence, the correct option is (C).

**83.** The sentence uses the incorrect form 'whose'.

'Whose' is a determiner/pronoun meaning 'belonging to someone'. As it refers to a person, it cannot be used here.

In the context of the sentence, the pronoun/determiner 'which' is more appropriate.

Hence, the correct option is (B).

**84.** The sentence uses the incorrect form 'on'.

The phrase 'on the face' does not make any sense. The correct preposition here should be 'in', which forms the phrase 'in the face of' something, meaning 'confronted with' something.

Hence, the correct option is (A).

**85.** The sentence suggests that the blank comes between the infinitive form 'to' and the verb 'understand'. This means that only an adverb can fit in the blank.

Given the context, the word should be 'better', as none of the other words can make the sentence meaningful.

Note here that 'to understand' is the verb and 'better' is the adverb. It can be used as both '**to better understand**' something or '**to understand something better**'. Both are correct forms.

Hence, the correct option is (D).

**86.** The sentence is in passive voice thus in active voice the subject 'they' must be written before the object 'piano lessons.' In active voice :

Subject+verb+object

In passive voice:

Object+verb+subject

The tense here is progressive present 'are given' thus 'give' is the correct verb to be used here.

Hence, the correct option is (B).

**87.** The original sentence is in passive voice so the answer should be in active voice. Thus, the pattern will be,

Subject (Sergei) + Verb (embarrass)+ Object (Natasha)

The original sentence is in the past perfect tense and this will change to simple past in the answer, this eliminated option c as it is in the future tense. Option d too is eliminated by the fact that it is in the present tense. Option a too cannot be the answer as it **changes the position** of the subject with the object and vice versa and thus cannot be the answer.

Hence, the correct option is (B).

**88.** One word-substitution is Misologist.

Misologist: A hater of knowledge and learning.

Bibliophile: a person who collects or has a great love for books.

Philologist: learner of the language, or linguist.

Misogynist: A person who hates women.

Hence, the correct option is (D).

**89.** The one word-substitution is Alliteration.

Alliteration: The occurrence of the same letter or sound at the beginning of adjacent or closely connected words.

Pun: A joke exploiting the different possible meanings of a word or the fact that there are words which sound alike but have different meanings.

Transferred epithet: A transferred epithet often involves shifting a modifier from the animate to the inanimate, as in the phrases.

Oxymoron: A figure of speech in which apparently contradictory terms appear in conjunction.

Hence, the correct option is (B).

**90.** The sentence suggests that the blank should contain a noun as it is used with the article 'an'.

Given the context, the word should mean 'level'.

Hence, the correct option is (B).

**91.** The sentence uses the form isn't driven by, which is correct and needs no improvement.

None of the alternatives can make the sentence meaningful.

Hence, the correct option is (D).

**92.** The sentence suggests that the blank must contain an adjective.

Also, given the context, the word should mean 'firm or strong', as it talks about the trust that our forefathers had in the democracy.

The only word that fits the blank is **resolute**

**Reproachable** means full of disapproval. **Profligate** means wasteful. **Retributive** means seeking revenge.

Hence, the correct option is (A).

**93.** The sentence suggests that the blank must contain a noun.

Also, given the context, the word should mean 'weakness or flaws'.

The only word that fits the blank is **fragility.**

**Frolic** are playful activities. **Frangipani** is a type of flower. **Bucolic** means rural.

Hence, the correct option is (B).

**94.** The sentence suggests that the blank must contain a noun.

Also, given the context, the word should mean a decentralisation or more equal distribution of power.

The only word that fits the blank is **devolution.**

Hence, the correct option is (D).

**95.** The sentence suggests that the blank must contain a noun.

Also, given the context, the word should mean 'disease or affliction'.

The only word that fits the blank is **maladies.**

**Malodour** is bad smell. **Malice** is ill will, **mast** is a tall upright pole, like of a ship.

Hence, the correct option is (C).

**96.** The sentence suggests that the blank must contain an adjective.

Also, given the context, the word should have a negative meaning as it refers to the negative effect of money, such as 'corrupting'.

The only word that fits the blank is **corroding.**

Hence, the correct option is (A).

**97.** The word **exiguous** means **very small in amount.**

The meanings of the other words are-

Colossal-large in amount

Ransom-a sum of money demanded the release of a captive

Diluted-make a liquid thin by adding water in it.

Humble-down to Earth

Hence, the correct option is (D).

**98.** The correct spelling is 'concurred'. To concur is to agree with someone or share the same opinion.

E.g. Almost all the directors on the board concurred with Steve on the idea that the company needed a total makeover.

Hence, the correct option is (D).

**99.** After reading the given sentences we can easily make out that the paragraph talks about 'Child Labour'.

'Child Labour' is defined in the sentence B, hence it is the starting point of the paragraph. Sentence D will follow B as it tells the cause of the matter concerned. And the pronoun 'this' used in D refers to 'child labour', thus D links with B. Sentence E also talks about 'cause' by saying that 'causes are irrelevant in this case', hence it will follow D. The last word of sentence E, i.e. 'childhood' is described in sentence C, hence C will follow E. Sentence A completes the paragraph by telling the negative aspects of the subject.

Hence, the correct option is (C).

**100.** One who is interested in the welfare of other people is called Altruist.

Philosopher - One who is engaged in philosophy and imparts wisdom to society or others.

Dreamer - One who keeps on dreaming.

Worker - One who works and achieves output.

Hence, the correct option is (B).

# General Intelligence & Reasoning

**Q.1 Direction:** Study the given information carefully and answer the given questions.

A, B, C, D, E, F, G and H are eight friends, Each of them likes different colour Green, Yellow, Pink, Red, Black, White, Blue and Grey, but not necessarily in the same order. Each of them has a different height.

The one who the tallest does not like black colour. The one who the shortest does not like red and pink. C is taller than A and D but shorter than H and E. A does not the shortest who likes the white colour. E who likes yellow is taller than G and is third to the tallest. B likes Black colour, is taller than E. F likes red colour, is shorter than G. The one who likes blue colour taller than G who likes Green colour. H does not like blue. The one who likes white is taller than F and smaller than G.

How many persons have more height than C?

**A.** One     **B.** Two     **C.** Three     **D.** Four

**Q.2** Solve the following?
If RAT = 9, GAME = 12, LIVER = 15, Then POLYSTER = ?
**A.** 17     **B.** 22     **C.** 24     **D.** 19

**Q.3** Which of the following shapes shows the best connection between the given classes?
Male, Guests, and Grandfather.

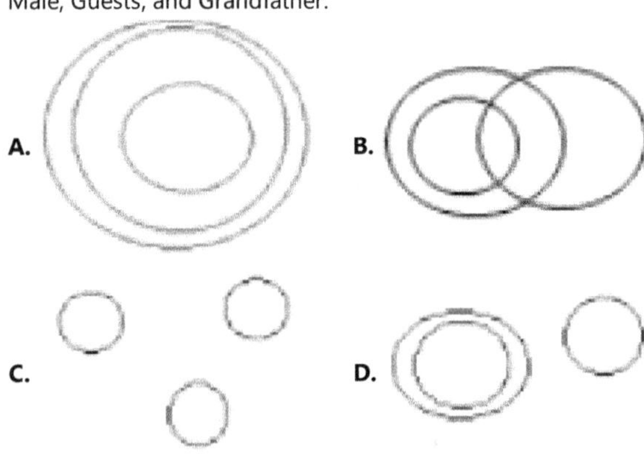

**Q.4 Direction:** In the following question, select the related word from the given alternatives.

HJIK : MONP : : PRQS : ?
**A.** UVWX     **B.** UWVX     **C.** UXWV     **D.** UWXV

**Q.5** Select a suitable figure from the Answer Figures that would replace the question mark (?).

**Problem Figures:**

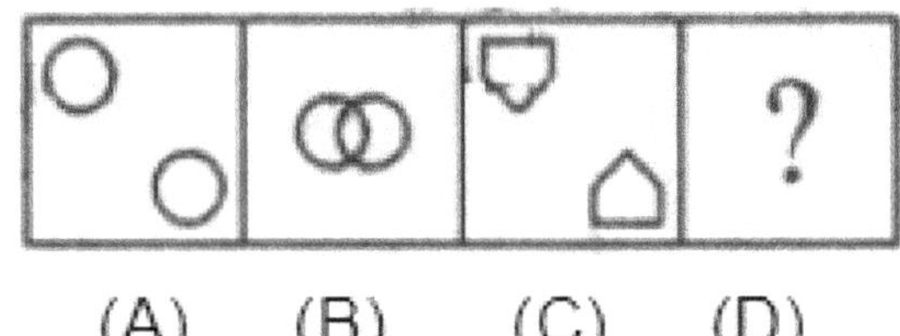

(A)     (B)     (C)     (D)

**Answer Figures:**

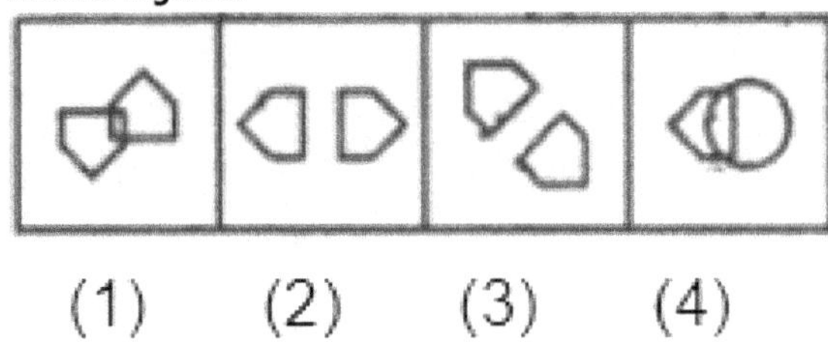

(1)     (2)     (3)     (4)

**A.** 1     **B.** 2     **C.** 3     **D.** 4

**Q.6** 664, 332, 340, 170, _____89. Find the missing number of this series.
**A.** 85     **B.** 97     **C.** 109     **D.** 178

**Q.7** In the following question, select the odd word pair from the given alternatives.

**A.** Square - Four     **B.** Hexagon - Six
**C.** Cone - Figure     **D.** Triangle - Three

**Q.8** Looking at a portrait of a man, Sanjay said, "His mother is the wife of my father's son. Brothers and sisters I have none." At whose portrait was Sanjay looking.
**A.** His son     **B.** His nephew
**C.** His cousin     **D.** His uncle

**Q.9** Pick out the odd one from the following:
**A.** Banana     **B.** Grape
**C.** Orange     **D.** Pomegranate

**Q.10** Find out the alternative figure which contains figure (X) as its part.

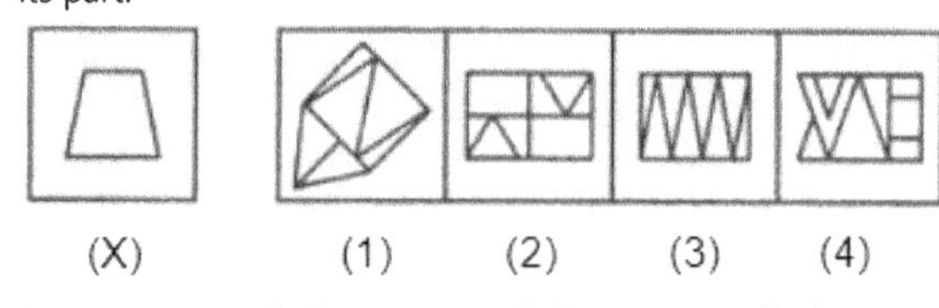

(X)     (1)     (2)     (3)     (4)

**A.** 1     **B.** 2     **C.** 3     **D.** 4

**Q.11** If the mirror is placed on the line AB, then which of the answer figure is the right image of the given figure?

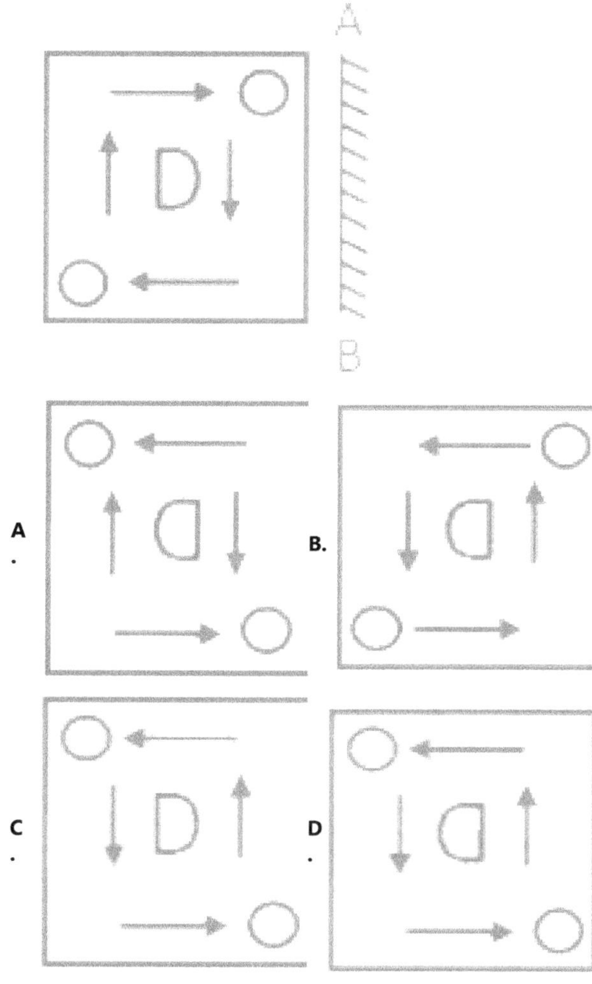

**A.**

**B.**

**C**

**D**

**Q.12** If 'A' means '+', 'B' means '×', 'P' means '÷' and 'Q' means '-', then 52 B 4 A 12 Q 75 P 5 =?

**A.** 221     **B.** 208     **C.** 224     **D.** 205

**Q.13 Direction:** Two statements are given, followed by two conclusions numbered I and II. Assuming the statements to be true, even if they seem to be at variance with commonly known facts, decide which of the conclusions logically follow(s) from the statements.

**Statements:**

No plant is a tree.

All ornaments are plants.

**Conclusions:**

I. no ornament is a tree.

II. Some plants are ornaments.

**A.** Either conclusion I or II follows

**B.** Both conclusions follow

**C.** Only conclusion II follows

**D.** Only conclusion I follows

**Q.14** In the following Venn diagram, the 'Circle' stands for 'Journalists', the 'Triangle' stands for 'Females' and the 'Rectangle' stands for 'Urban residents'. The given numbers represent the number of persons in that particular category. How many journalists are females but NOT urban residents?

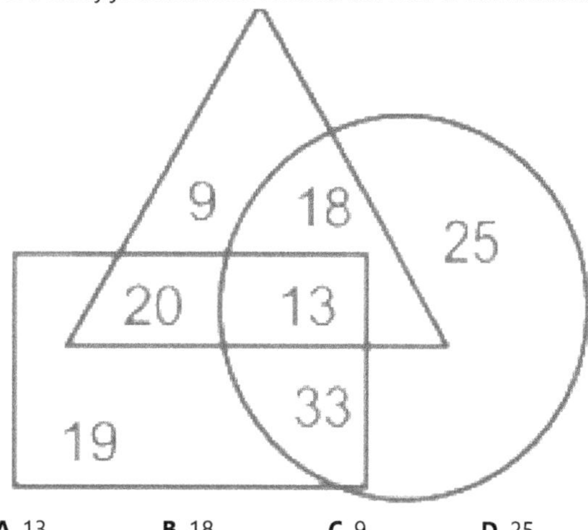

**A.** 13     **B.** 18     **C.** 9     **D.** 25

**Q.15 Directions:** In the question given below a statement followed by two conclusions are numbered I and II. You have to assume everything in the statement to be true, then consider the two conclusions together and decide which of them logically follow beyond a reasonable doubt from the information given in the statement. Give answer.

**Statement:** Millenials and Gen Z are heavily consuming content via apps such as Netflix while the ad revenue generated by TV channels is dropping.

**Conclusions:**

I. The ad revenue generated by apps such as Netflix is increasing.

II. TV ad revenue is decreasing due to people switching to apps.

**A.** Only Conclusion I follows

**B.** Only Conclusion II follows

**C.** Both the Conclusions I and II follow

**D.** Neither Conclusion I nor II follows

**Q.16** In the following question, select the odd word from the given alternatives.

**A.** Chikungunya     **B.** Malaria

**C.** Goitre     **D.** Dengue

**Q.17** From the given answer figures, select the one in which the question figure is hidden/embedded (Rotation not allowed).

*[SSC MTS, 2019]*

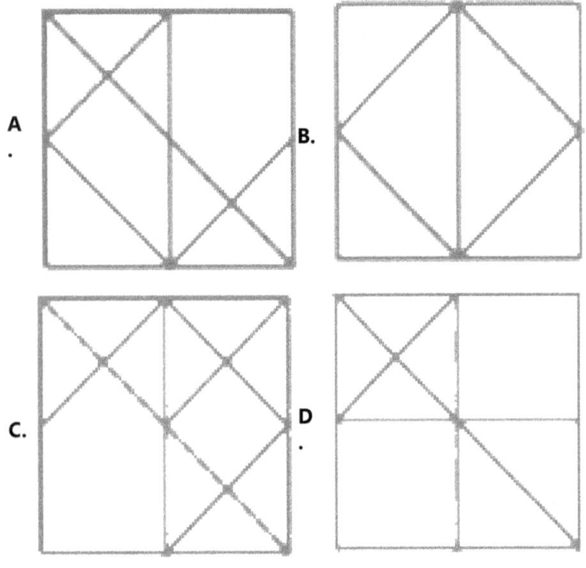

A.

B.

C.

D.

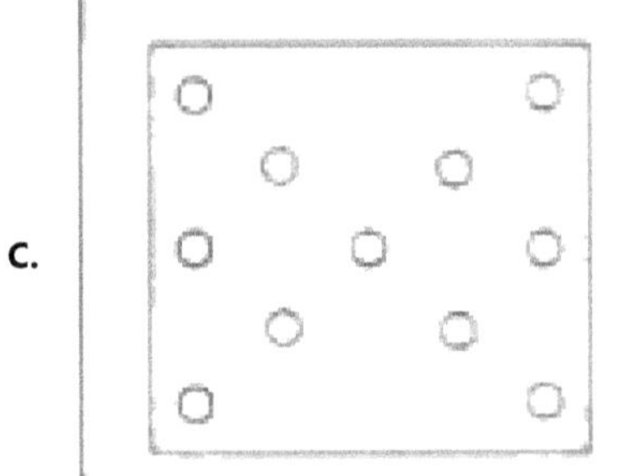

C.

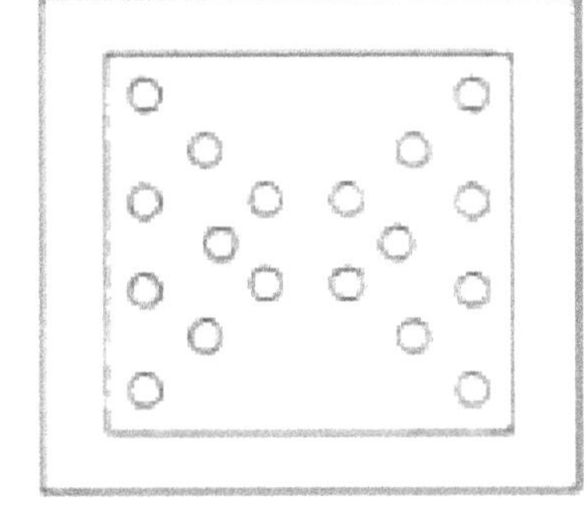

D.

**Q.18** A piece of paper is folded and punched as shown below in the question figures. From the given answer figures, indicate how it will appear when opened.

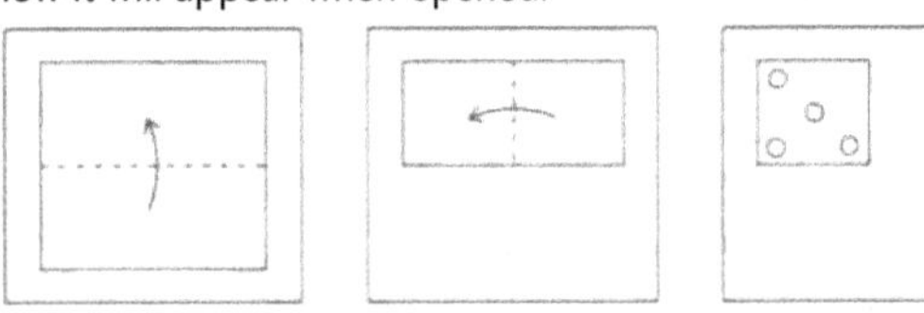

*[UP Police Constable, 2019], [SSC MTS, 2019]*

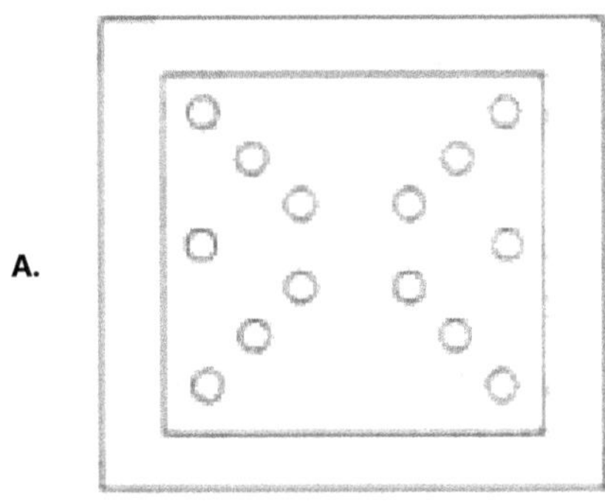

A.

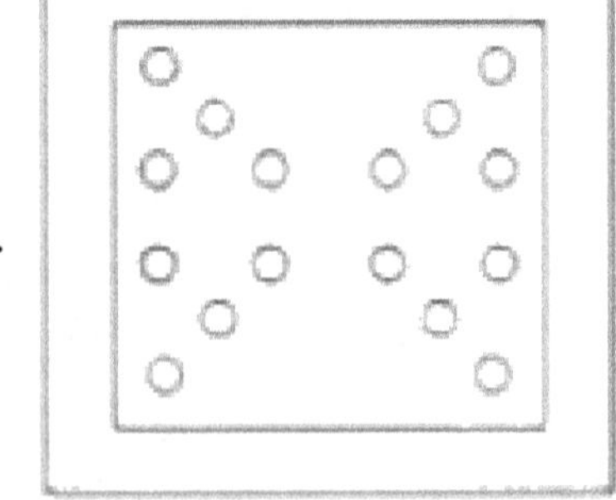

B.

**Q.19** Find the missing term in the following series ?

1440  240  ?  12  4

**A.** 89     **B.** 56     **C.** 48     **D.** 72

**Q.20** Find out which of the figures (1), (2), (3), and (4) can be formed from the pieces given in figure (X).

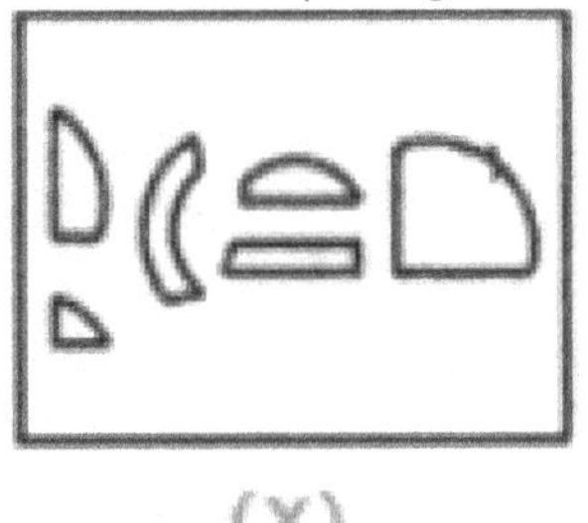

(X)

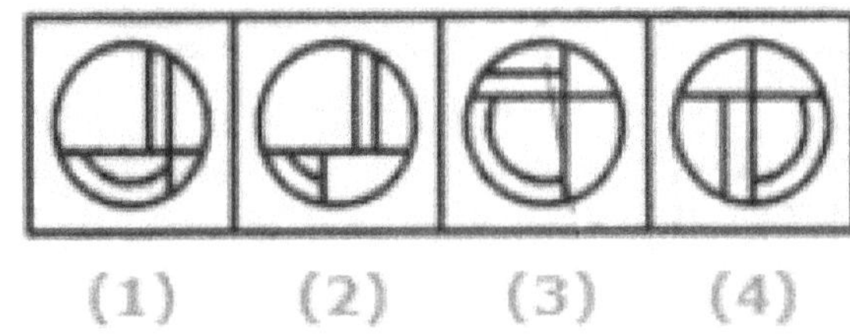

(1)     (2)     (3)     (4)

**A.** 1     **B.** 2     **C.** 3     **D.** 4

**Q.21 Direction:** In the following question, select the related word from the given alternatives.

Hour : Second :: Tertiary : ?

**A.** Intermediary     **B.** Primary

**C.** Ordinary     **D.** Secondary

**Q.22**

Choose the box that is similar to the box formed from the given sheet of paper (X).

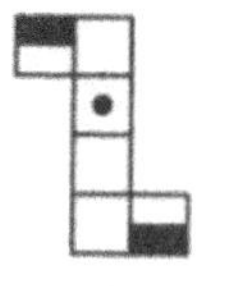    

(X)    (1)    (2)    (3)    (4)

**A.** 1 and 2 only
**B.** 2 and 3 only
**C.** 2 and 4 only
**D.** 1, 2, 3 and 4

**Q.23** In the given question if + means -, and - means +, then find out the answer of the following question.

15 + 5 - 6

**A.** 16
**B.** 12
**C.** 10
**D.** 19

**Q.24 Direction:** In the following question, select the related word from the given alternatives.

122 : 170 : : 290 : ?

**A.** 316
**B.** 344
**C.** 360
**D.** 362

**Q.25** Select the missing term based on the given related pair of terms.

COULD: BNTKC :: MOULD :_______

**A.** NITKH
**B.** CHMFI
**C.** LNKTC
**D.** LNTKC

# General Awareness

**Q.26** Who among the following became the Chief Minister of Uttarakhand in March 2021?

*[SSC CGL, 2022]*

**A.** Madan Kaushik
**B.** Dhan Singh Rawat
**C.** BC Khanduri
**D.** Tirath Singh Rawat

**Q.27** In January 2022, which country took over the G7 Presidency?

**A.** Netherlands
**B.** Germany
**C.** Austria
**D.** France

**Q.28** In which city, India's largest floating solar power plant was inaugurated in March 2022?

**A.** Srinagar
**B.** Udaipur
**C.** Ahmedabad
**D.** Tuticorin

**Q.29** Which Formula One racing driver won the British F1 Grand Prix on 3 July 2022?

**A.** Lewis Hamilton
**B.** Sergio Perez
**C.** Carlos Sainz
**D.** Max Verstappen

**Q.30** The ideal of 'Welfare State' in the Indian Constitution is enshrined in its:

**A.** Preamble
**B.** Directive Principles of State Policy
**C.** Fundamental Rights
**D.** Seventh Schedule

**Q.31** Who has the power to initiate the process of removal of the Election Commissioner?

**A.** Prime Minister
**B.** President
**C.** Supreme Court
**D.** Legislature

**Q.32** Who among the following laid the foundation of the Rashtrakuta Empire?

**A.** Dhruva
**B.** Dantidurga
**C.** Amoghavarsha I
**D.** Krishna I

**Q.33** A penalty stroke is used in which of the following given game?

**A.** Football
**B.** Field hockey and Football
**C.** Baseball
**D.** Rugby

**Q.34** Which is the highest gallantry award in India?

**A.** Param Vishisht Seva Medal
**B.** Param Vir Chakra
**C.** Kirti Chakra
**D.** Vir Chakra

**Q.35** Who took away the peacock throne built by Shah Jahan, from India?

**A.** Ahmad Shah Abdali
**B.** Zaman Shah
**C.** Nader Shah
**D.** Shah Suja

**Q.36** In terms of information and technology, what is the full form of ASCII in English?

**A.** American Standard Communication for Information Interchange
**B.** American Standard Code for Information Interchange
**C.** American Standard Code for Infrastructure Interchange
**D.** American Standard Code for International Interchange

**Q.37** Economic survey is published by:

**A.** Ministry of Finance
**B.** Planning Commission
**C.** Government of India
**D.** Indian Statistical Institute

**Q.38** Which of the following statement is correct about the NITI Aayog?

**A.** NITI Aayog was Formed 25 January 2016
**B.** NITI Aayog comes under the Ministry of Commerce and Industry
**C.** The full form of NITI Aayog is National institute for Transforming India
**D.** The NITI Aayog is a policy think tank of the Government of India

**Q.39** What does "Capitalism" refer to?

**A.** The use of market
**B.** Government ownership of capital
**C.** Private ownership of capital goods
**D.** Private ownership of homes and& cars

**Q.40** Who releases data of national income in India?

**A.** National statistics office
**B.** Central Statistics Office
**C.** NITI Aayog
**D.** None of the above

**Q.41** Pradhan Mantri Jan Dhan Yojana (PMJDY) provides access to which of the following financial services?

**A.** Pension

**B.** Credit

**C.** Banking Savings and Deposit Accounts

**D.** All the above

**Q.42** The largest part of the Gagnetic plain is covered by which of the following soil?

**A.** Bangar soil

**B.** Khadar soil

**C.** Bhur soil

**D.** Desert soil

**Q.43** Hot and dry winds blowing during the summer months in the Northern Plains is called:

**A.** Loo

**B.** Blossom Shower

**C.** Mango Shower

**D.** Kalbaisakhi

**Q.44** The Bhakra Nangal dam is situated on the _____ river.

*[SSC Selection Post Phase IX, 2019]*

**A.** Sutlej    **B.** Chenab    **C.** Ravi    **D.** Beas

**Q.45** Bidhan Chandra Roy Award is given in the field of:

**A.** Environment

**B.** Journalism

**C.** Music

**D.** Medicine

**Q.46** What is the Capital of Philippines?

**A.** Davao    **B.** Cebu    **C.** Surigao    **D.** Manila

**Q.47** Which instrument was played by "Ustad Bismillah Khan"?

**A.** Sitar    **B.** Flute    **C.** Shehnai    **D.** Santoor

**Q.48** When is Navy Day celebrated every year?

**A.** 1 December

**B.** 2 December

**C.** 3 December

**D.** 4 December

**Q.49** Who among the following organized the Harijan Sevak Sangh as a part of his constructive program for the removal of untouchability?

*[SSC Selection Post Phase IX, 2020]*

**A.** B.R. Ambedkar

**B.** Periyar EVR

**C.** Narayana Guru

**D.** Mahatma Gandhi

**Q.50** Who has been awarded Nobel in Peace 2021?

**A.** Syukuro Manabe and Klaus Hasselmann

**B.** Maria Ressa and Dmitry Muratov

**C.** Denis Mukwege and Nadia Murad

**D.** Ellen Johnson Sirleaf and Leymah Gbowee

# Quantitative Aptitude

**Q.51** A boat running upstream takes 8 hours 48 minutes to cover a certain distance, while it takes 4 hours to cover the same distance running downstream. What is the ratio between the speed of the boat and the speed of the water current respectively?

**A.** 2 : 1

**B.** 3 : 2

**C.** 8 : 3

**D.** Cannot be determined

**Q.52** What is the probability of getting a sum as 3 if a dice is thrown?

**A.** $\frac{2}{18}$    **B.** $\frac{1}{18}$    **C.** 4    **D.** $\frac{1}{36}$

**Q.53** If the roots of $ax^2 + bx + c = 0$ are in the ratio $m:n$, then:

**A.** $mna^2 = (m+n)c^2$

**B.** $mnb^2 = (m+n)ac$

**C.** $mnb^2 = (m+n)^2ac$

**D.** $mnb^2 = (m-n)^2ac$

**Q.54** In a group of 15 students, there are exactly 6 girls and 9 boys. Each day one student leaves the group. What is the probability that after four days there are exactly 8 boys in that group?

**A.** $\frac{12}{91}$    **B.** $\frac{13}{91}$    **C.** $\frac{15}{91}$    **D.** $\frac{18}{91}$

**Q.55** In a regiment, the ratio between the number of officers to soldiers was 3 : 31 before. In a battle, 6 officers and 22 soldiers were killed and the ratio become 1 : 13, the number of officers in the regiment before the battle was:

**A.** 31    **B.** 38    **C.** 21    **D.** 28

**Q.56** The average height of a family of three members is 140 cm and when two more members A and B added to that family, the average height is increased by 8 cm. If A is 36 cm taller than B, then what is the height of B?

**A.** 138 cm    **B.** 142 cm    **C.** 140 cm    **D.** 144 cm

**Q.57** A man gains 20% by selling an article for a certain price. If he sells it at double the price, the percentage of profit will be:

**A.** 130%    **B.** 140%    **C.** 150%    **D.** 160%

**Q.58** A mixture contains alcohol and water in the ratio 4 : 3. If 5 litres of water is added to the mixture, the ratio becomes 4 : 5. The quantity of alcohol in the given mixture is:

**A.** 3 litres    **B.** 4 litres    **C.** 15 litres    **D.** 10 litres

**Q.59** A train passes two bridges of lengths 300 m and 180 m in 82 seconds and 52 seconds respectively. Then find the length of the train.

**A.** 28 m    **B.** 32 m    **C.** 42 m    **D.** 48 m

**Q.60 Direction:** What approximate value will come in place of the question mark (?) in the following question? (You are not expected to calculate the exact value)

14.082 × 19.964 × 23.980 = ? ÷ 24.978

**A.** 162200    **B.** 158200    **C.** 168000    **D.** 159320

**Q.61** Anjali and Mohan can complete a work in 42 days and 56 days respectively. With the help of Laxmi, they completed the work in 12 days. In how many days Laxmi will complete the work working alone?

**A.** 32 days    **B.** 28 days    **C.** 24 days    **D.** 36 days

**Q.62** The radius of the base of a cone is 21 cm and its volume is 12.936 litres. What will be the difference between the curved surface area and the area of the base of the cone $(1cm^3 = 1ml$ and $\pi = \frac{22}{7})$?

**A.** 784 cm²      **B.** 876 cm²
**C.** 924 cm²      **D.** 1048 cm²

**Q.63** If each side of a cube is increased by 10%, then the volume of the cube will increase by:
**A.** 30%      **B.** 10%      **C.** 33.1%      **D.** 25%

**Q.64** A water tank has two pipes. The empty tank is filled in 12 min by the first and the full tank is emptied by the second in 20 min. The time required to fill the $\frac{1}{2}$ full tank when both pipes are in action, is:
**A.** 16 min      **B.** 15 min      **C.** 20 min      **D.** 30 min

**Q.65** Given that $10^{0.48} = x$, $10^{0.70} = y$ and $x^z = y^2$, then the value of $z$ is close to:
**A.** 1.45      **B.** 1.88      **C.** 2.9      **D.** 3.7

**Q.66** A, B, C subscribe Rs. 50000 for a business. A subscribes Rs. 4000 more than B and B Rs. 5000 more than C. Out of a total profit of Rs. 35000, A receives:
**A.** Rs. 8400      **B.** Rs. 11900
**C.** Rs. 13600      **D.** Rs. 14700

**Q.67** There is 40% increment in an amount in 8 years at simple interest. What will be the compound interest of Rs. 10000 after 3 years at the same rate?
**A.** Rs. 1576.25      **B.** Rs. 6305
**C.** Rs. 7881.25      **D.** Rs. 4728.75

**Q.68** Sum of two numbers is 384. HCF of the numbers is 48. The difference of the numbers is:
**A.** 100      **B.** 192      **C.** 288      **D.** 336

**Q.69** 15 months ago Tuhin's age was equal to three times the age of Sambit, who is 6 months older than Soumik. After 5 months from today Tuhin's age will be equal to 2.5 times Soumik's age. What is the sum of his present age?
**A.** 15 years 5 months      **B.** 15 years 11 months
**C.** 15 years 7 months      **D.** 15 years 9 months

**Q.70** The breadth of a rectangular hall is $\frac{3}{4}$ its length. If the area of the hall is 300 square metres, what is the difference between the length and breadth of the hall?
**A.** 15 m      **B.** 5 m      **C.** 4 m      **D.** 3 m

**Q.71** In a 1 km race, A beats B by 28 meters in 7 sec. Find A's time over the course.
**A.** 5 min 4 sec      **B.** 4 min 3 sec
**C.** 2 min 3 sec      **D.** 3 min 4 sec

**Q.72** Simplify:
$$1 + 2\left[3 - \left\{1 + \left(2 - \frac{1}{2} - \frac{\overline{5}}{2}\right)\right\}\right]$$
**A.** 2      **B.** 1      **C.** -3      **D.** 5

**Q.73** The diameter of the wheel of a bus is 140 cm, if the speed of the bus is 66 km/hr, then find how many revolutions it should make in one minute?
**A.** 500      **B.** 1000      **C.** 250      **D.** 750

**Q.74** 10% of the soldiers of an army are killed in the battle. 10% of the remaining soldiers died of disease and 10% of the remaining men were disabled. Now only 729000 soldiers are left in the army. How many soldiers were there in all in the army in the beginning?
**A.** 990000      **B.** 9900000      **C.** 9800000      **D.** 1000000

**Q.75** If a fixed sum of money amounts to Rs. 2400 in 2 years and Rs. 2800 in 3 years, then find the rate of interest?
**A.** 20%      **B.** 23%      **C.** 25%      **D.** 30%

# English Comprehension

**Ques (76-77):Directions:** In the following question, a sentence is divided into some parts. Find out which part of the sentence has an error. The number of that part is your answer. If there is no error, then choose (D) as your answer.

**Q.76** Four days have passed (A) / since (B) / he had gone missing (C) / No error (D).
**A.** (A)      **B.** (B)      **C.** (C)      **D.** (D)

**Q.77** No sooner (A) / I had started for college (B) / than it began to rain. (C)/ No error (D).
**A.** (A)      **B.** (B)      **C.** (C)      **D.** (D)

**Ques (78-79):Direction:** In the following questions, the 1st and the last sentences of the passage are numbered 1 and 6. The rest of the passage is split into four parts and named P, Q, R and S. These four parts are not given in their proper order. Read the sentence and find out which of the four combinations is correct. Then find the correct answer.

**Q.78** 1. He could not rise.
P. All at once, in the distance, he heard an elephant trumpet.
Q. He tried again with all his might but to no use.
R. The next moment he was on his feet.
S. He stepped into the river.
6. It was colder than usual.
**A.** PQSR      **B.** PRQS      **C.** QPRS      **D.** QPSR

**Q.79** 1. The crowd swelled around the thief.
P. Suddenly, he whipped out a knife from under his shirt.
Q. The thief stood quiet, his head hung in shame.
R. The two young men holding him were scared by the sight of the shining knife.
S. They took to their heels.
6. They were followed by the crowd which left the thief alone.
**A.** QPRS      **B.** SQPR      **C.** SPQR      **D.** RQSP

**Q.80 Direction:** In the following question, out of the four alternatives, select the word opposite in meaning to the given word.

Mitigate
**A.** Abate      **B.** Placate      **C.** Incite      **D.** Soften

**Q.81 Direction:** Select the most appropriate word for the given group of words.

A group of stars found close together.

**A.** Concoction  **B.** Conflagration
**C.** Confederation  **D.** Constellation

**Q.82 Direction:** Select the most appropriate word to fill in the blank.

Any account of the reign of King Harsha would remain _____ without a reference to Hiuen Tsang.

**A.** Incomplete  **B.** Famous
**C.** Eminent  **D.** Unknown

**Q.83 Direction:** Select the most appropriate word for the given group of words.

A place for collection of dried plant specimens

**A.** Green-house  **B.** Nursery
**C.** Warehouse  **D.** Herbarium

**Q.84** Select the wrongly spelt word.

**A.** Whimsical  **B.** Contiguous
**C.** Spectaculer  **D.** Adjacent

**Q.85 Direction:** In the following question, out of the four alternatives, select the word synonym in meaning to the given word.

Ostentatious

**A.** Distinct  **B.** Complete
**C.** Flashy  **D.** Trusted

**Ques (86-90):Direction:** In the following passage, some words have been deleted. Fill in the blanks with the help of the alternatives given. Select the most appropriate option for each blank.

It's turning out to be a tough summer for the State. With an alarming dip **(A)** _____ groundwater levels across **(B)** _____ state, experts fear residents **(C)** _____ soon have to battle an **(D)** _____ water crisis, along **(E)** _____ extremely high temperatures.

**Q.86** Select the most appropriate option to fill in the blank **(A)**.
**A.** from  **B.** in  **C.** on  **D.** with

**Q.87** Select the most appropriate option to fill in the blank **(B)**.
**A.** nearby  **B.** the  **C.** every  **D.** all

**Q.88** Select the most appropriate option to fill in the blank **(C)**.
**A.** might  **B.** should  **C.** shall  **D.** can

**Q.89** Select the most appropriate option to fill in the blank **(D)**.
**A.** unlikely  **B.** average
**C.** unknown  **D.** acute

**Q.90** Select the most appropriate option to fill in the blank **(E)**.
**A.** with  **B.** from  **C.** to  **D.** by

**Ques (91-95):Direction:** Read the passage and answer the following question.

By launching the GSAT-9 'South Asia satellite', India has reaffirmed the Indian Space Research Organisation's scientific prowess, but the messaging is perhaps more geopolitical than geospatial. To begin with, the Centre has kept its promise of considering India's "neighbourhood first". Within a month of taking over as Prime Minister in 2014, Narendra Modi went to Sriharikota for the launch of PSLV C-23 and "challenged" ISRO scientists to build this satellite for the South Asian Association for Regional Cooperation. The decision was then announced at the SAARC summit in Kathmandu, and the government has kept its commitment of gifting its neighbours at least one transponder each on the GSAT-9, a project that cost about ₹450 crore. India has no doubt gained goodwill across the subcontinent through the gesture, and the moment was neatly captured by the videoconference that followed the launch, showing all SAARC leaders (with the exception of Pakistan's) together on one screen as they spoke of the benefits they would receive in communication, telemedicine, meteorological forecasting and broadcasting. The message is equally strong to South Asia's other benefactor, China, at a time when it is preparing to demonstrate its global clout at the Belt and Road Forum on May 14-15. The Belt and Road Initiative is an infrastructure network that every SAARC nation other than India has signed on to. China has pledged billions of dollars in projects to each of the countries in the region; that, India is obviously not in a position to match.

Where India does excel is in its space programme, as it is the only country in South Asia that has independently launched satellites on **indigenously** developed launch vehicles. However, in recent years Pakistan and Sri Lanka have launched satellites with assistance from China, while Afghanistan, the Maldives and Nepal are also understood to have discussed satellite projects with China. Bangladesh, which will launch its first satellite Bangabandhu-1 this year, is working with a European agency. With the GSLV launch India is showing that where it is capable its commitment to the development of its neighbours is strong. Finally, by going ahead with the project despite Pakistan's decision to pull out, the Modi government is signalling that it will continue with its plans for the neighbourhood — 'SAARC minus one' — if necessary. This vision was dealt a minor blow recently when Bhutan pulled out of the 'mini-SAARC' alternative plan of a motor vehicles agreement for BBIN (Bangladesh, Bhutan, India Nepal), but the government's persistence indicates it will not be **deterred** by the obvious domestic constraints of the SAARC grouping. As Afghanistan President Ashraf Ghani, particularly aggrieved by Pakistan's refusal to grant transit rights for India-Afghanistan trade, said at the launch of the GSLV-F09: "If cooperation through land is not possible, we can be connected through space."

**Q.91** What according to the passage helped India gain goodwill across the subcontinent?

**A.** Launching the G-SAT 9 Satellite

**B.** Challenging ISRO scientists to build satellite for SAARC nations

**C.** Keeping promise of gifting it's neighbours one transponder each on G-SAT 9

**D.** For Launching G-SAT 9 at a mere cost of 450 Crore Rupees.

**Q.92** Why is India trying to so hard to woo its counterpart SAARC nations?

**A.** India wants to prove that it is committed to the development of it's neighbours in all fields

**B.** India wants to form allies against China

**C.** India wants to stand apart as a nation that has a strong space programme

**D.** Cannot be determined

**Q.93** In the phrase "India is obviously not in a position to match", what is being talked about?

**A.** The infrastructure of China and India

**B.** India assuring huge investments in SAARC nations

**C.** The inability of India to carve the road structure for the SAARC nations

**D.** Pledging of billions of dollars by China in projects world wide

**Q.94** Which countries have launched satellite with China's help?

**A.** Pakistan

**B.** Afghanistan

**C.** Sri Lanka

**D.** Both (A) and (C)

**Q.95** Choose the word which has its meaning most similar to the word 'indigenously' used in the passage.

**A.** Migrant

**B.** Expatriate

**C.** Adventitious

**D.** Native

**Q.96 Directions:** In the following question, a sentence is divided into some parts. Find out which part of the sentence has an error. The number of that part is your answer. If there is no error, then choose (D) as your answer.

He has been issued a summon to appear (1) in court at 8:30 a.m before (2) Judge Charles Pater. (3) No error (4)

**A.** 1

**B.** 2

**C.** 3

**D.** 4

**Q.97 Direction:** A sentence/a part of the sentence is underlined. Five alternatives are given to the underlined part which may improve the meaning of the sentence. Choose the correct alternative and click the button corresponding to it. In case no improvement is needed, click the option corresponding to "No improvement".

The manager and receptionist is careless of their duty.

**A.** cared about their

**B.** careful of their

**C.** careless of his

**D.** No improvement

**Ques (98-99):Direction:** The question below contains five scattered segments of a sentence. Indicate the sequence which correctly assembles the segments and completes the sentence.

**Q.98** A) in India have

B) as per Unesco's estimates,

C) over 280 million children

D) school closures due to Covid-19

E) been impacted by

**A.** BCDAE

**B.** BCAED

**C.** ABDCE

**D.** CBDEA

**Q.99** A) taking their children

B) and putting them in private schools

C) even lower middle class

D) out of government schools

E) parents have been

**A.** CEADB

**B.** CBDAE

**C.** EABCD

**D.** EBCDA

**Q.100 Direction:** A sentence/a part of the sentence is underlined. Five alternatives are given to the underlined part which will improve the meaning of the sentence. Choose the correct alternative and click the button corresponding to it.

The United States of America are a rich country.

**A.** United States of America is

**B.** United States of Americas are

**C.** United States of America can

**D.** United States of Americas were

# // Smart Answer Sheet //

**Correct** Indicates percentage of students who answered questions correctly.

**Skipped** Indicates percentage of students who skipped questions.

| Q. | Ans. | Correct / Skipped |
|---|---|---|
| 1 | C | 61.78 % / 31.26 % |
| 2 | C | 68.94 % / 30.73 % |
| 3 | B | 59.9 % / 37.54 % |
| 4 | B | 46.11 % / 51.78 % |
| 5 | A | 64.84 % / 31.81 % |
| 6 | D | 42.24 % / 51.24 % |
| 7 | C | 88.06 % / 10.88 % |
| 8 | A | 44.32 % / 42.98 % |
| 9 | B | 41.35 % / 36.2 % |
| 10 | C | 60.85 % / 38.11 % |
| 11 | D | 60.37 % / 37.09 % |
| 12 | D | 47.06 % / 42.78 % |
| 13 | B | 58.1 % / 33.06 % |
| 14 | B | 40.81 % / 32.75 % |
| 15 | B | 20.51 % / 72.36 % |
| 16 | C | 51.49 % / 30.86 % |
| 17 | D | 68.64 % / 30.06 % |
| 18 | B | 47.35 % / 40.39 % |
| 19 | C | 56.9 % / 30.74 % |
| 20 | A | 65.93 % / 31.43 % |
| 21 | B | 52.42 % / 42.68 % |
| 22 | D | 57.71 % / 33.3 % |
| 23 | A | 68.65 % / 31.34 % |
| 24 | D | 42.69 % / 44.42 % |
| 25 | D | 67.0 % / 32.99 % |
| 26 | D | 50.68 % / 47.05 % |
| 27 | B | 45.73 % / 35.52 % |
| 28 | D | 46.68 % / 39.36 % |
| 29 | C | 47.72 % / 31.99 % |
| 30 | B | 88.76 % / 10.88 % |
| 31 | B | 45.09 % / 43.4 % |
| 32 | B | 69.98 % / 30.01 % |
| 33 | B | 50.1 % / 33.1 % |
| 34 | B | 54.68 % / 44.77 % |
| 35 | C | 50.86 % / 34.44 % |
| 36 | B | 63.0 % / 36.05 % |
| 37 | A | 52.37 % / 44.63 % |
| 38 | D | 65.43 % / 33.09 % |
| 39 | C | 48.04 % / 42.49 % |
| 40 | B | 63.77 % / 31.81 % |
| 41 | D | 58.87 % / 32.16 % |
| 42 | A | 55.18 % / 36.53 % |
| 43 | A | 13.84 % / 77.11 % |
| 44 | A | 59.73 % / 31.95 % |
| 45 | D | 64.67 % / 31.23 % |
| 46 | D | 68.2 % / 30.31 % |
| 47 | C | 48.29 % / 39.99 % |
| 48 | D | 67.59 % / 32.31 % |
| 49 | D | 51.13 % / 32.46 % |
| 50 | B | 49.48 % / 47.23 % |
| 51 | C | 66.28 % / 31.19 % |
| 52 | B | 55.08 % / 41.44 % |
| 53 | C | 12.42 % / 82.56 % |
| 54 | A | 24.53 % / 73.11 % |
| 55 | C | 13.95 % / 71.38 % |
| 56 | B | 69.8 % / 30.06 % |
| 57 | B | 54.9 % / 43.24 % |
| 58 | D | 46.87 % / 30.92 % |
| 59 | A | 28.83 % / 67.79 % |
| 60 | C | 67.94 % / 30.38 % |
| 61 | C | 24.93 % / 72.57 % |
| 62 | C | 18.68 % / 73.89 % |
| 63 | C | 64.84 % / 30.59 % |
| 64 | B | 45.16 % / 34.16 % |
| 65 | C | 62.9 % / 36.12 % |
| 66 | D | 23.82 % / 71.35 % |
| 67 | A | 26.78 % / 70.31 % |
| 68 | C | 53.47 % / 35.53 % |
| 69 | D | 48.22 % / 35.56 % |
| 70 | B | 42.87 % / 34.95 % |
| 71 | B | 40.77 % / 47.21 % |
| 72 | C | 57.38 % / 39.05 % |
| 73 | C | 47.89 % / 34.8 % |
| 74 | D | 18.48 % / 79.03 % |
| 75 | C | 50.15 % / 48.65 % |
| 76 | D | 57.1 % / 30.12 % |
| 77 | B | 55.89 % / 42.17 % |
| 78 | C | 63.35 % / 34.12 % |
| 79 | A | 25.95 % / 70.02 % |
| 80 | C | 47.46 % / 49.75 % |

| Q. | Ans. | Correct | | Q. | Ans. | Correct | | Q. | Ans. | Correct | | Q. | Ans. | Correct | | Q. | Ans. | Correct |
|----|------|---------|---|----|------|---------|---|----|------|---------|---|----|------|---------|---|----|------|---------|
| | | Skipped | | | | Skipped | | | | Skipped | | | | Skipped | | | | Skipped |
| 81 | D | 40.37 % | | 85 | C | 42.03 % | | 89 | D | 59.84 % | | 93 | D | 29.63 % | | 97 | C | 58.0 % |
| | | 49.76 % | | | | 42.8 % | | | | 31.49 % | | | | 68.75 % | | | | 34.79 % |
| 82 | A | 49.61 % | | 86 | B | 52.36 % | | 90 | A | 44.94 % | | 94 | D | 56.02 % | | 98 | B | 41.66 % |
| | | 39.84 % | | | | 47.46 % | | | | 49.96 % | | | | 31.74 % | | | | 30.38 % |
| 83 | D | 53.5 % | | 87 | B | 42.92 % | | 91 | C | 68.23 % | | 95 | D | 46.78 % | | 99 | A | 21.55 % |
| | | 36.75 % | | | | 41.91 % | | | | 30.54 % | | | | 32.1 % | | | | 74.68 % |
| 84 | C | 67.3 % | | 88 | A | 50.61 % | | 92 | D | 60.68 % | | 96 | A | 62.18 % | | 100 | A | 56.67 % |
| | | 32.27 % | | | | 39.16 % | | | | 34.04 % | | | | 33.53 % | | | | 34.47 % |

## Performance Analysis

| | |
|---|---|
| **Avg. Score (%)** | 47.0% |
| **Toppers Score (%)** | 64.0% |
| **Your Score** | |

# //Hints and Solutions//

**1.** H (Pink) > B (Black) > E (Yellow) > C (Blue) > G (Green) > A (White) >F (Red) > D (Grey)

Hence, the correct option is (C).

**2.** RAT = 9,

Here logic is:

The total numbers of letters in a word × 3

RAT (3 × 3) = 9

GAME = 12,

The total numbers of letters in a word × 3

GAME (4 × 3) = 12

LIVER = 15,

The total numbers of letters in a word × 3

LIVER (5 × 3) = 15

Thus,

POLYSTER (8 × 3) = 24

Hence, the correct option is (C).

**3.**

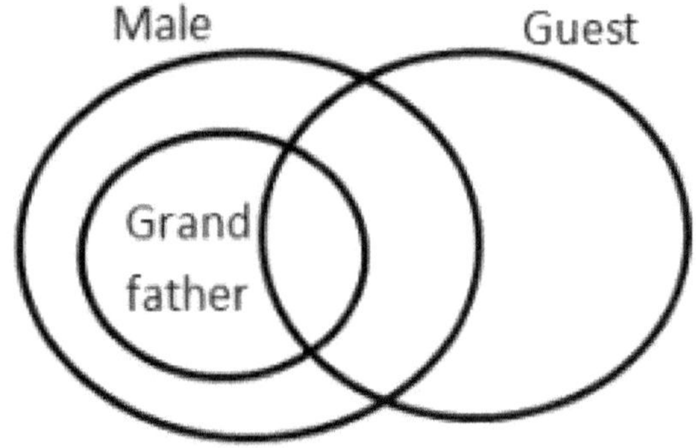


Hence, the correct option is (C).

**4.** The given word follow this pattern:

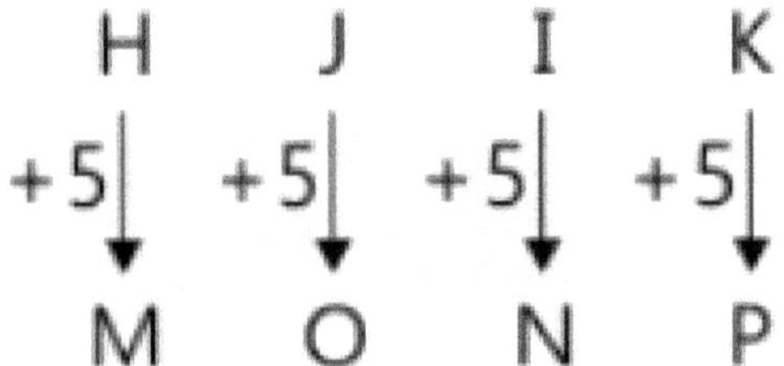


Similarly,



Hence, the correct option is (B).

**5.** The two elements approach each other and get overlapped.

Hence, the correct option is (A).

**6.** This is an alternating division and addition series: First, divide by 2, and then add 8.

664 ÷ 2 = 332

332 + 8 = 340

340 ÷ 2 = 170

170 + 8 = 178

178 ÷ 2 = 89

Hence, the correct option is (D).

**7.** All options except 'Cone – Figure' represent a geometric figure and number of sides that particular figure is made of.

Hence, the correct option is (C).

**8.** Since, Sanjay has neither a sister nor a brother, therefore, Sanjay is the only son of his father.

Hence, the mother of the portrait is wife of Sanjay.

Therefore, portrait was of Sanjay's son.

Hence, the correct option is (A).

**9.** Bananas, Oranges and Pomegranates are peeled before they are eaten. Grapes are not.

Hence, the correct option is (B).

**10.**

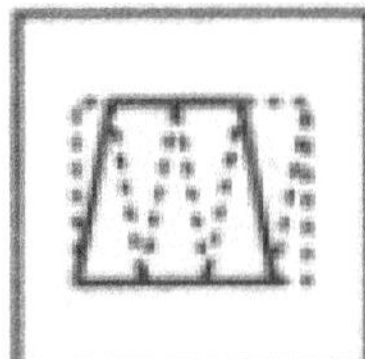

Hence, the correct option is (C).

**11.** The mirror image of the figure,

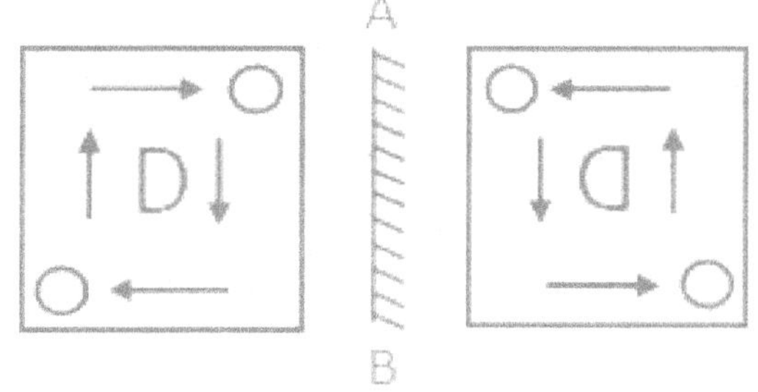

Hence, the correct option is (D).

**12.** 52 B 4 A 12 Q 75 P 5 = ?

After converting the symbols with the given code the equations will be;

$\Rightarrow 52 \times 4 + 12 - 75 \div 5$

$\Rightarrow 208 + 12 - 15$

$\Rightarrow 220 - 15$

$\Rightarrow 205$

Hence, the correct option is (D).

**13.** The possible venn diagram is as follows:

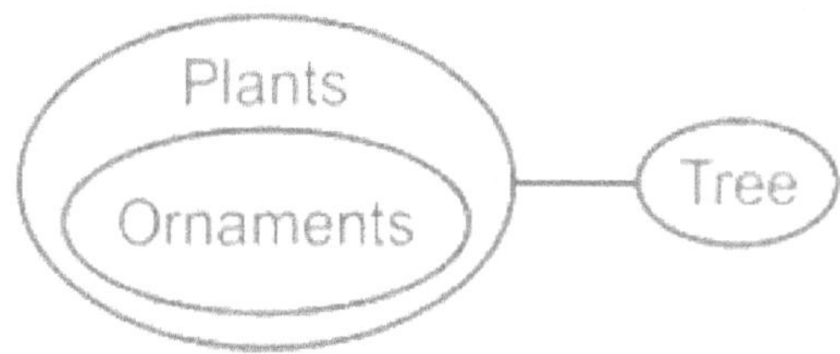


For conclusions:

I. No ornament is a tree → True (All ornaments are plants and no plant is a tree. Therefore, no ornament is a tree)

II. Some plants are ornaments → True (All ornaments are planted is given. Therefore, some plants are ornaments)

Hence, the correct option is (B).

**14.** The below given diagram shows the above stated statements:

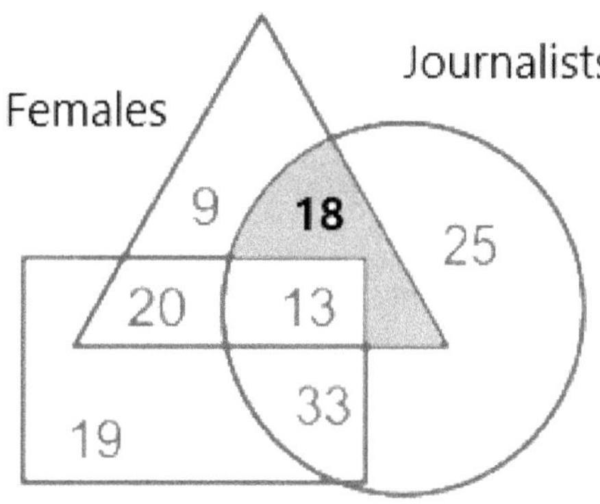


The highlighted portion in the above figure shows the female journalists, who are not urban residents i.e. 18

Hence, the correct option is (B).

**15.** Whether the ad revenue is being diverted from TV to the apps is debatable as the advertisers may be switching to other platforms as well as eliminating Option (A) and Option (C). The fact that TV channels' viewership has reduced due to the apps eating into their market has led to a lesser audience for the advertisers causing them to advertise lesser and consequently decreasing the ad revenues generated by the channels. This conclusion can be safely drawn by the information provided, eliminating option (D) and making option (B) as the correct answer.

Hence, the correct option is (B).

**16.** Chikungunya, Malaria, and Dengue are the names of human diseases that spread through mosquitoes. Goitre is caused due to the lack of dietary iodine.

Hence, the correct option is (C).

**17.** The question figure is embedded in,

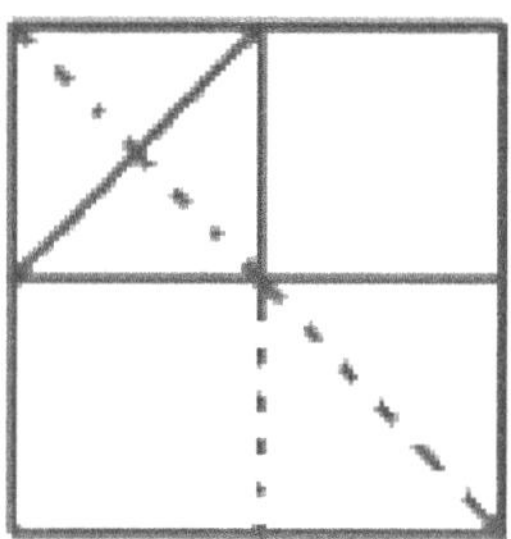

Hence, the correct option is (D).

**18.**

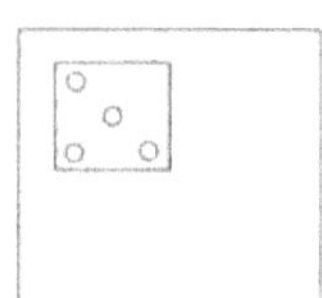 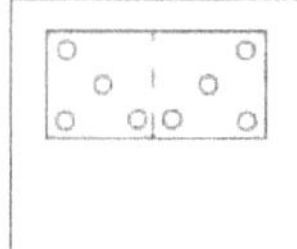 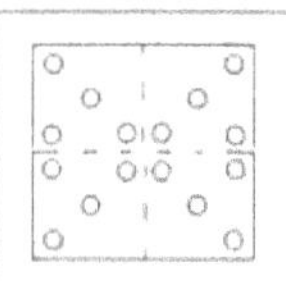

When we will open punched sheet of paper as it is folded it will appear as it is shown in the above diagram.

Hence, the correct option is (B).

**19.** The pattern followed here is:

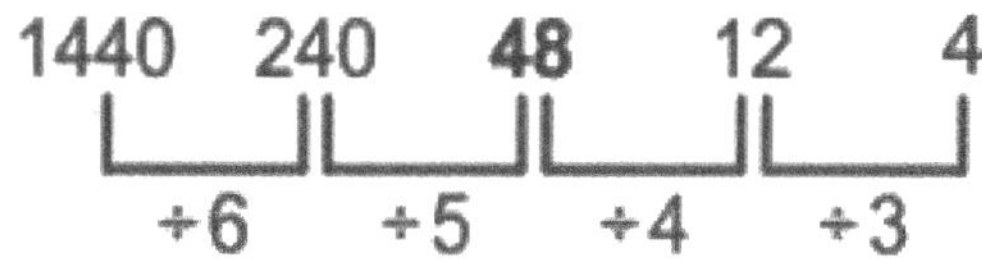


Hence, the correct option is (C).

**20.**

Hence, the correct option is (A).

**21.** Second, minutes and hours are the three units of time - seconds is the smallest unit and hours is the third unit in succession. Similarly, 'primary' represents the initial stage and 'tertiary' represents the third stage in a process.

Hence, the correct option is (B).

**22.** Figure (X) is similar to Form II. So, when a cube is formed by folding the sheet shown in figure (X), then the two half-shaded faces lie opposite to each other and one. of the three blank faces appears opposite to the face bearing a dot. Clearly, each one of the four cubes shown in figures (1), (2), (3), and (4) can be formed by folding the sheet shown in figure (X).

Hence, the correct option is (D).

**23.** After changing the sign according to the question,

15 - 5 + 6 = 16

Hence, the correct option is (A).

**24.** As, $122 : 170 \Rightarrow (11^2 + 1) = 122$

and $(11 + 2)^2 + 1 = 170$

Similarly,

$290 : ? \Rightarrow (17^2 + 1) = 290$

and $(17 + 2)^2 + 1 = ?$

$\Rightarrow ? = 19^2 + 1$

$\Rightarrow = 361 + 1$

$\therefore ? = 362$

Hence, the correct option is (D).

**25.** According to the alphabetical positions of the letters,

C - 1 = B

O - 1 = N

U - 1 = T

L - 1 = K

D - 1 = C

Similarly,

M - 1 = L

O - 1 = N

U - 1 = T

L - 1 = K

D - 1 = C

Hence, the correct option is (D).

**26.** Tirath Singh Rawat became the Chief Minister of Uttarakhand in March 2021.

- He is a former Chief Minister of Uttarakhand and a serving Member of Parliament in India.
- In the 2019 Indian general election, he was elected to the 17th Lok Sabha from the Garhwal constituency as a member of the Bharatiya Janata Party.
- From 9 February 2013 until 31 December 2015, he was the party head of the Bharatiya Janata Party Uttarakhand and a former member of the Uttarakhand Legislative Assembly from the Chaubattakhal constituency from 2012 to 2017.
- He was also Uttarakhand's first Education Minister.

Hence, the correct option is (D).

**27.** In January 2022, Germany took over the G7 Presidency.

On 1 January, Germany takes over the G7 Presidency. The G7, or "Group of Seven," consists of the US, Canada, Japan, France, the UK, Italy, and Germany. In June 2021 Summit, the G7 leaders agreed to distribute 2.3 billion vaccine doses. Germany is the second-largest donor in the COVAX vaccination alliance.

Hence, the correct option is (B).

**28.** Southern Petrochemicals Industries Corporation Limited (SPIC) inaugurated and fully operationalised India's largest floating solar power plant, in March 2022.

Situated in the SPIC factory's premises in Tuticorin, Tamil Nadu, this 48-acre floating solar power plant has been set up on a large water reservoir that spans 62-acres.

It is capable of generating 42 million units of power per year.

Hence, the correct option is (D).

**29.** Ferrari's Carlos Sainz won his career's first Formula One race on 3 July 2022 with a victory at the British Grand Prix.

Red Bull's Sergio Perez and Mercedes' Lewis Hamilton finished second and third respectively. Championship leader Max Verstappen finished seventh. Sainz has moved up to fourth in the 2022 Driver standings.

Hence, the correct option is (C).

**30.** Articles (36-51) of Part-IV of the Indian Constitution deals with Directive Principles of State Policy (DPSP). They are borrowed from the constitution of Ireland.

A welfare state is a concept of government where the state plays a key role in protecting and promoting the economic and social welfare of its citizens. DPSPs promote the welfare state's ideal by emphasizing the state to promote the welfare of people by providing them with basic facilities like shelter, food, and clothing.

Hence, the correct option is (B).

**31.** The Chief Election Commissioner of India may be removed from his office by a resolution passed by both houses of Parliament with a two-thirds majority in both the Lok Sabha and Rajya Sabha from his office on grounds of misbehavior or incapacity.

Hence, the correct option is (B).

**32.** Dantidurga (735 - 756)-He was the founder of the Rashtrakuta Empire of Manyakheta. His capital was based in the Gulbarga region of Karnataka.

Dhruva (780 - 793)-He is among the most notable rulers of the Rashtrakuta Empire, under whose reign Rashtrakutas emerged as a true pan-India power.

Amoghavarsha I (814 - 878)-He was the greatest ruler of the Rashtrakuta dynasty whose reign of 64 years is one of the longest precisely dated monarchical reigns on record.

Krishna I (756 - 774)-He succeeded Dantidurga who patronized the famous Jain logician Akalanka Bhatta, the author of Rajavartika.

Hence, the correct option is (B).

**33.** A penalty stroke is the most severe penalty given in field hockey and football.

It is predominantly awarded when a foul has prevented a certain goal from being scored or for a deliberate infringement by a defender in the penalty circle.

Other terms associated with field hockey are Artificial turf, Attacker, Breakaway, Corner flag, etc.

Hence, the correct option is (B).

**34.** The Param Vir Chakra (PVC) is India's highest military decoration awarded for the highest degree of valor or self-sacrifice in the presence of the enemy, similar to the British Victoria Cross, US Medal of Honor, Pakistani Nishan-e-Haider, or French Legion of Honor or Russian Cross of St. George.

Hence, the correct option is (B).

**35.** Nader Shah took away the peacock throne built by Shah Jahan, from India.

Nader Shah, the Ruler of Iran, stole the valuable jewels bound to him during the invasion of 1739.

A famous jeweled throne that was the seat of the Mughal Emperors of India was the Peacock Throne. It was commissioned by Emperor Shah Jahan in the early 17 century and was housed in the Diwan-i-Khas (Hall of Private Audiences) in the Delhi Red Fort.

Hence, the correct option is (C).

**36.** The American Standard Code for Information Interchange (ASCII) is a standard table of seven-bit designations for digital representation of uppercase and lowercase Roman letters, numbers, and special control characters in teletype, computer, and word processor systems.

Hence, the correct option is (B).

**37.** The Department of Economic Affairs, Finance Ministry of India presents the Economic Survey in the parliament every year, just before the Union Budget. It is prepared under the guidance of the Chief Economic Adviser, Finance Ministry. It is the ministry's view on the annual economic development of the country.

Hence, the correct option is (A).

**38.** The NITI Aayog is a policy think tank of the Government of India. This statement is correct. NITI Aayog was Formed 1 January 2015.

NITI Aayog (National Institute of Transformation of India) is a new institute set up by the Government of India, which has been replaced by the Planning Commission The institute will serve as a think tank of the government and provide it with directional and policy dynamism.

Hence, the correct option is (D).

**39.** Capitalism, also called free market economy or free enterprise economy, economic system, dominant in the Western world since the breakup of feudalism, in which most means of production are privately owned and production is guided and income distributed largely through the operation of markets.

Hence, the correct option is (C).

**40.** The GDP figures in India are released by the Central Statistics Office (CSO), which comes under the Ministry of Statistics and Program Implementation (MOSPI).

Hence, the correct option is (B).

**41.** Pradhan Mantri Jan Dhan Yojana's (PMJDY) objective is to provide access to various financial services including Remittance, Credit, Insurance, Pension, Banking Savings & Deposit Accounts in an affordable manner. Pradhan Mantri Jan-Dhan Yojana (PMJDY) is National Mission for Financial Inclusion to ensure access to financial services, namely, basic savings & deposit accounts, remittance, credit, insurance, pension in an affordable manner. Under the scheme, a basic savings bank deposit (BSBD) account can be opened in any bank branch or Business Correspondent (Bank Mitra) outlet, by persons not having any other account.

Hence, the correct option is (D).

**42.** The largest part of the Gagnetic soil is covered by the Bangar soil. It is found in those high plain regions which are free from floodwater. It is not very fertile in nature due to kankars. Kankars are calcareous deposits. It has a low upland covered by laterite deposits. It is old and matured alluvial soil. It is not renewed frequently as compared to the khaddar soil. It is known by various names like clay, sandy, loam. The fertility of the soil has been lost due to the continuous use of this soil for agriculture since ancient times.

Hence, the correct option is (A).

**43.** Loo is a strong, dusty, scorching, hot, and dry summer breeze from the west that runs across the western Indo-Gangetic plains of North India and Pakistan. It is particularly hot in the months of May and June.

Hence, the correct option is (A).

**44.** Bhakra Dam is a concrete gravity dam on the Sutlej River in Bilaspur, Himachal Pradesh in northern India. The dam forms the

Gobind Sagar reservoir. The dam, located at a gorge near the (now submerged) upstream Bhakra village in Bilaspur district of Himachal Pradesh of height approximately 226 m.

Hence, the correct option is (A).

**45.** Bidhan Chandra Roy Award was instituted in 1962 in memory of B. C. Roy by Medical Council of India. The Award is given annually in each of the following categories: Statesmanship of the Highest Order in India, Medical man-cum-Statesman, Eminent Medical Person, Eminent person in Philosophy, Eminent person in Science and Eminent person in Arts.

Hence, the correct option is (D).

**46.** The Philippines is a country located in Southeast Asia. Its official name is 'Republic of Philippines' and the capital is Manila. The country is made up of 7106 islands located in the western Pacific Ocean. The Philippine Islands are bounded on the east by the Philippines Ocean, on the west by the South China Sea, and on the south by the Celebes Sea.

Hence, the correct option is (D).

**47.** Ustad Bismillah Khan (Born Qamaruddin Khan, 21 March 1916 – 21 August 2006), often referred to by the title Ustad, was an Indian musician credited with popularizing the shehnai, a subcontinental wind instrument of the oboe class. While the shehnai had long held importance as a folk instrument played primarily in traditional ceremonies, Khan is credited with elevating its status and bringing it to the concert stage.

Hence, the correct option is (C).

**48.** Navy Day is celebrated every year on 4 December.

The day is celebrated in honor of the Indian Navy's role during the war with Pakistan in 1971 when Indian warships attacked Karachi port.

The day is also celebrated to highlight the role the Navy plays in securing the country's marine borders during peacetime and carrying out humanitarian missions.

Hence, the correct option is (D).

**49.** The Harijan Sevak Sangh was a non-profit organization founded by Mahatma Gandhi in 1932 to eradicate untouchability in India, work for Harijan or Dalit people, and uplift the Dalit. It is headquartered at Kingsway Camp in Delhi, with branches in 26 states across India.

Hence, the correct option is (D).

**50.** The Nobel Peace Prize in Peace for 2021 was awarded to Maria Ressa and Dmitry Muratov.

For their efforts to safeguard freedom of expression, which is a precondition for democracy and lasting peace. Ms. Ressa and Mr. Muratov are receiving the Peace Prize for their courageous fight for freedom of expression in the Philippines and Russia. The award was presented by Berit Reiss-Andersen, Chair of the Norwegian Nobel Committee, on 8 October 2021.

Hence, the correct option is (B).

**51.** Let the boat rate upstream be $x$ kmph and that downstream be $y$ kmph.

Then, distance covered upstream in $8$ hrs $48$ min $=$ Distance covered downstream in $4$ hrs

$$\Rightarrow x \times 8\frac{4}{5} = y \times 4$$

$$\Rightarrow \frac{44}{5}x = 4y$$

$$\Rightarrow y = \frac{11}{5}x$$

$\therefore$ Required ratio

$$= \frac{y+x}{2} : \frac{y-x}{2}$$

$$= \left(\frac{16x}{5} \times \frac{1}{2}\right) : \left(\frac{6x}{5} \times \frac{1}{2}\right)$$

$$= \frac{8}{5} : \frac{3}{5}$$

$$= 8 : 3$$

Hence, the correct option is (C).

**52.** In two throws a dice, n (S) = 6 × 6 = 36

Let E is the event of getting a sum of three.

E = (1, 2), (2, 1)

So, n (E) = 2

So, P (E) $= \dfrac{n(E)}{n(S)}$

$$= \frac{2}{36}$$

or $\dfrac{1}{18}$

Hence, the correct option is (B).

**53.** We have $\dfrac{\alpha}{\beta} = \dfrac{m}{n}$

$$\Rightarrow \frac{\alpha}{m} = \frac{\beta}{n}$$

$$\Rightarrow \frac{\alpha+\beta}{m+n} = \sqrt{\frac{\alpha\beta}{mn}} \text{ by ratio proportion}$$

$$\therefore mn(\alpha + \beta)^2 = \alpha\beta(m + n)^2$$

$$\Rightarrow mn\left(\frac{-b}{a}\right)^2 = (m + n)^2 \frac{c}{a}$$

$$\therefore mnb^2 = (m + n)^2 ac$$

Hence, the correct option is (C).

**54.** In 4 days 4 students will leave the group but still there are exactly 8 boys are remaining in the group it means 1 boy and 3 girls left the group.

Girls or boy can leave the group on any of the four days.

Probability $P(E) = \dfrac{{}^9C_1 \times {}^6C_3}{{}^{15}C_4}$

$= \dfrac{12}{91}$

Hence, the correct option is (A).

**55.** Let the number of officers and soldiers (before battle) $= 3x$, and $31x$

According to the question,

$\Rightarrow \dfrac{3x-6}{31x-22} = \dfrac{1}{13}$

$\Rightarrow 39x - 78 = 31x - 22$

$\Rightarrow 8x = 56$

$\Rightarrow x = 7$

So, number of officer before battle

$\Rightarrow 3x = 3 \times 7$

$= 21$

Hence, the correct option is (C).

**56.** Sum of heights of three persons = 140 × 3 = 420 cm

Sum of heights of five persons = 5 × (140 + 8) = 740 cm

Let the height of A and B be x and (x - 36) respectively.

Sum of heights of A and B = x + (x - 36) = 740 - 420

$\Rightarrow$ 2x - 36 = 320

$\Rightarrow$ x = 178

Hence height of B = x - 36 = 142 cm

Hence, the correct option is (B).

**57.** Let the cost price $= x$

Then selling price $= \left(\dfrac{120}{100}\right)x = \dfrac{6x}{5}$

New selling price $= 2\left(\dfrac{6x}{5}\right) = \dfrac{12x}{5}$

Profit $= \dfrac{12x}{5} - x = \dfrac{7x}{5}$

Profit% $= \dfrac{\text{Profit}}{\text{Cost price}} \times 100$

$\Rightarrow \dfrac{7x}{5} \times \dfrac{1}{x} \times 100 = 140\%$

Hence, the correct option is (B).

**58.** Let the quantity of alcohol and water be $4x$ litres and $3x$ litres respectively

$\dfrac{4x}{(3x+5)} = \dfrac{4}{5}$

$\Rightarrow 20x = 4(3x + 5)$

$\Rightarrow 8x = 20$

$\Rightarrow x = 2.5$

Quantity of alcohol

$= 4 \times 2.5$ litres

$= 10$ litres

Hence, the correct option is (D).

**59.** Let the speed of the Train $= x$ m/s and the length of the Train $= L$ metre

When a Train crosses a bridge, it covers a distance equal to its Length + length of bridge.

$\therefore$ According to the data in the question, we get the following equations

$x = \dfrac{300+L}{82}$ ......(1)

Also, $x = \dfrac{180+L}{52}$ ......(2)

Equating the above equations, we get:

$\dfrac{300+L}{82} = \dfrac{180+L}{52}$

$\Rightarrow 15600 + 52L = 14760 + 82L$

$\Rightarrow 30L = 840$

$\Rightarrow L = 28m$

Hence, the length of the train is $28$ m.

Hence, the correct option is (A).

**60.** Given,

14.082 × 19.964 × 23.980 = ? ÷ 24.978

By approximation, we get:

? ÷ 25 = 14 × 20 × 24

$\Rightarrow$ ? ÷ 25 = 6720

$\Rightarrow$ ? = 25 × 6720 = 168000

Hence, the correct option is (C).

**61.** Total work $=$ L.C.M of $(42, 56) = 168$ units

Efficiency of Anjali $= \dfrac{168}{42} = 4$

Efficiency of Mohan $= \dfrac{168}{56} = 3$

Efficiency of Anjali, Mohan and Laxmi $= \dfrac{168}{12} = 14$

$\therefore$ Efficiency of Laxmi $= 14 - 4 - 3 = 7$

Hence, the required number of days $= \dfrac{168}{7} = 24$ days

Hence, the correct option is (C).

**62.** Height of the cone $= h$

Volume of the cone $= \frac{1}{3} \times \pi r^2 h$

$= \frac{1}{3} \times \frac{22}{7} \times (21)^2 \times h$

$= 12936 \, ml = 12936 \, cm^3$

$\Rightarrow h = 28 \, cm$

Slant height of the cone $= L$

$L = \sqrt{r^2 + h^2}$

$= \sqrt{21^2 + 28^2}$

$= 35 \, cm$

Required difference $=$ curved surface area $-$ area of the base

Required difference $= \pi r L - \pi r^2$

$= \frac{22}{7}(35 \times 21 - 21 \times 21)$

$= 924 \, cm^2$

Hence, the correct option is (C).

**63.** Suppose, each side of cube $= a$ unit

Thus, volume of cube $= a^3$

Now, new side of cube $= a \times \frac{110}{100}$

$= 1.1a$ unit

Thus, new volume of cube $= (1.1a)^3$

$= 1.331a^3$

Thus, required increase percentage $= \frac{1.331a^3 - a^3}{a^3} \times 100$

$= \frac{0.331a^3}{a^3} \times 100$

$= 33.1$

Hence, the correct option is (C).

**64.** Since, first pipe takes 12 min to completely fill tank

Thus, tank filled by first pipe in 1 min $= \frac{1}{12}$

Now, second pipe takes 20 min to empty the full tank.

Thus time taken by both pipes to fill complete tank

$= \frac{1}{12} - \frac{1}{20}$

$= \frac{5-3}{60}$

$= \frac{2}{60}$

$= \frac{1}{30}$

Since, total tank will be filled in $30$ min.

Hence, time taken to fill the half tank

$= \frac{30}{2}$

$= 15$ min

Hence, the correct option is (B).

**65.** Given,

$x^z = y^2$

$\Rightarrow 10^{(0.48z)} = 10^{2 \times 0.70} = 10^{1.40}$

$\Rightarrow 0.48z = 1.40$

$\Rightarrow z = \frac{140}{48}$

$= \frac{35}{12}$

$= 2.9$ (approx)

Hence, the correct option is (C).

**66.** Let $C = x$

Then, $B = x + 5000$

And $A = x + 5000 + 4000 = x + 9000$

So, $x + x + 5000 + x + 9000 = 50000$

$\Rightarrow 3x = 36000$

$\Rightarrow x = 12000$

$A:B:C = 21000:17000:12000 = 21:17:12$

So $A$'s Share $=$ Rs. $35000 \times \frac{21}{50}$

$=$ Rs. $14700$

Hence, the correct option is (D).

**67.** Let principal $(P) = 100$

So, simple interest $(SI) = 40$

Time $(T) = 8$ years

And rate $= r\%$

$SI = \frac{P \times R \times T}{100}$

So, $40 = \frac{100 \times 8 \times r}{100}$

So, $r = 5\%$

Now, compound interest $(CI) = A\left(1 + \frac{r}{100}\right)^n - P$

$$\Rightarrow CI = 10000\left(1 + \frac{5}{100}\right)^3 - 10000$$

$$\Rightarrow CI = 10000 \times \frac{21}{20} \times \frac{21}{20} \times \frac{21}{20} - 10000$$

$$\Rightarrow CI = 11576.25 - 10000$$

$$\Rightarrow CI = \text{Rs. } 1576.25$$

Hence, the correct option is (A).

**68.** $HCF = 48$

Let number are $48x$ and $48y$ respectively

According to question,

$$\Rightarrow 48x + 48y = 384$$

$$(x + y) = \frac{384}{48} = 8$$

So, possible pairs of co-prime number are (1,7) (3,5) numbers are (48, 336) or (144, 240)

$\therefore$ Difference between numbers is $= 336 - 48 = 288$ and $240 - 144 = 96$

Hence, the correct option is (C).

**69.** 15 months ago,

Let Tuhin's age = x

Sambit's age = y

Soumik's age = z

According to the question,

x = 3y ... (i)

y – z = 6 ... (ii)

x + 20 = 2.5 (z + 20)

$\Rightarrow$ x - 2.5z = 30 ... (iii)

Put value of x = 3y in equation (iii) we get,

y - z = 6

3y - 5z = 30

On solving these equations,

$\Rightarrow$ x = 90, y = 30, z = 24

Present age of all three = 90 + 30 + 24 + 45 = 189 months = 15 years 9 months

Hence, the correct option is (D).

**70.** Let the length of the hall be $L$ m

Then, breadth $= \frac{3}{4}L$

According to question,

Area $=$ Length $\times$ Breadth

$$\Rightarrow L \times \frac{3}{4}L = 300$$

$$\Rightarrow L^2 = 400$$

$$\Rightarrow L = 20 \text{ m}$$

$\therefore$ Breadth $= \frac{3}{4} \times 20 = 15$ m

Hence, required difference $= (20 - 15) = 5$ m

Hence, the correct option is (B).

**71.** B covers 28 meters in 7sec

So, B's time over the course $= \dfrac{7}{28} \times 100 = 250$ sec

Whereas A's time over the course = 250 -7 = 243 sec

i.e., A's time over the course is 4 min 3 sec

Hence, the correct option is (B).

**72.** Here, we have a vinculum bar ($\overline{\phantom{x}}$). Simply treat it like a bracket.

$$1 + 2\left[3 - \left\{1 + \left(2 - \frac{1}{2} - \overline{\frac{5}{2}}\right)\right\}\right]$$

$$\Rightarrow 1 + 2[3 - \{1 + (2 - (-2))\}]$$

$$\Rightarrow 1 + 2[3 - \{1 + 4\}]$$

$$\Rightarrow 1 + 2[3 - 5]$$

$$\Rightarrow 1 + 2(-2)$$

$$\Rightarrow 1 - 4$$

$$\Rightarrow -3$$

Hence, the correct option is (C).

**73.** $2\pi r \times n = $ Distance travelled

$$\Rightarrow 2 \times \frac{22}{7} \times \frac{70}{100} \times n = 66 \times \frac{1000}{60}$$

$$\Rightarrow 4 \times \frac{n}{10} = 100$$

$$\Rightarrow n = \frac{1000}{4} = 250 \text{ Revolutions}$$

Hence, the correct option is (C).

**74.** Let the total number of soldiers in all in the army in the beginning $= 100$

$\therefore$ Number of soldiers killed in the battle $= \dfrac{10}{100} \times 100 = 10$

$\therefore$ Remaining soldiers $= 100 - 10 = 90$

Number of soldiers who died of disease $= \dfrac{10}{100} \times 90 = 9$

$\therefore$ Remaining soldiers $= 90 - 9 = 81$

Number of disabled soldiers $= \dfrac{10}{100} \times 81 = \dfrac{81}{10}$

$\therefore$ Remaining soldiers $= 81 - \dfrac{81}{10}$

$= \dfrac{810 - 81}{10}$

$= \dfrac{729}{10}$

If $\dfrac{729}{10}$ soldiers are left

Then total number of soldiers $= 100$

If $1$ soldier is left, then total number of soldiers $= \dfrac{100 \times 10}{729}$

If $729000$ soldiers are left, then total number of soldiers $=$
$\dfrac{100 \times 10 \times 729000}{729}$

$= 1000000$

Hence, the correct option is (D).

**75.** According to the given condition,

Simple interest (SI) for 1 year  = 2800 - 2400 = Rs. 400

Simple interest for two years = Rs.800

It means,

Principal (P) amount = 2400 - 800 = Rs. 1600

Therefore,

By using the formula,

$SI = \dfrac{P \times R \times T}{100}$

$\therefore R = \dfrac{SI \times 100}{P \times T}$

The required rate of interest

$= \dfrac{100 \times 400}{1600 \times 1}$

$= 25\%$

Hence, the correct option is (C).

**76.** No error.

Using the present perfect, we can define a period of time before now by considering its duration, with for + a period of time, or by considering its starting point, with since + a point in time.

Hence, the correct option is (D).

**77.** When we begin a sentence with a negative word, we put the auxiliary verb before the subject. No sooner had I started for college than it began to rain.

Hence, the correct option is (B).

**78.** The correct sequence is:

1. He could not rise.

Q. He tried again with all his might but to no use.

P. All at once, in the distance, he heard an elephant trumpet.

R. The next moment he was on his feet.

S. He stepped into the river.

6. It was colder than usual.

Hence, the correct option is (C).

**79.** The correct sequence is:

1. The crowd swelled around the thief.

Q. The thief stood quiet, his head hung in shame.

P. Suddenly, he whipped out a knife from under his shirt.

R. The two young men holding him were scared by the sight of the shining knife.

S. They took to their heels.

6. They were followed by the crowd which left the thief alone.

Hence, the correct option is (A).

**80.** Mitigate, Abate, Placate and Soften are synonyms which mean lessen the seriousness or extent of something while Incite means provoke or stir up. Therefore, Incite is the antonym of Mitigate.

Hence, the correct option is (C).

**81.** Constellation (n)- A group of stars found close together

Concoction (n)-  Mixture

Conflagration (n)- Fire

Confederation (n)- An organization which consists of a number of parties

Hence, the correct option is (D).

**82.** Any account of the reign of King Harsha would remain **incomplete** without a reference to Hiuen Tsang.

Hence, the correct option is (A).

**83.** Herbarium (n) - A place for collection of dried plant specimens

Green-house (n)- A glass building in which plants that need protection from cold weather are grown

Nursery (n)- A place where young plants and trees are grown for sale

Warehouse (n)- A large building where raw materials may be stored

Hence, the correct option is (D).

**84.** The correct spelling is 'spectacular', which means 'beautiful in a dramatic and eye-catching way'.

Hence, the correct option is (C).

**85.** Ostentatious: Expensive or noticeable in a way that is intended to impress other people

Flashy: Attracting attention by being very big, bright and expensive

Distinct: Being not of the same kind

Complete: Having or including all parts; with nothing missing

Trusted: To believe that somebody is good, sincere, honest, etc. and that he/she will not trick you or try to harm you

Hence, the correct option is (C).

**86.** Dip in/into – lower or move (something) downwards.

Hence, the correct option is (B).

**87.** 'The' is used to specify the noun 'state'.

Hence, the correct option is (B).

**88.** 'Might' shows the remote possibility.

Hence, the correct option is (A).

**89.** Acute (adj.)- severe

Hence, the correct option is (D).

**90.** 'Along with' means in company with or at the same time as.

Hence, the correct option is (A).

**91.** Keeping the promise of gifting it's neighbours one transponder each on G-SAT 9 helped India gain goodwill across the subcontinent.

Hence, the correct option is (C).

**92.** It is said in the passage that launch India is showing that where it is capable its commitment to the development of its neighbours is strong. Why is India showing so isn't mentioned.

Hence, the correct option is (D).

**93.** It is clearly mentioned in the passage that: China has pledged billions of dollars in projects to each of the countries in the region; that, India is obviously not in a position to match.

Hence, the correct option is (D).

**94.** Pakistan & Sri Lanka have launched the satellite with China's assistance.

Hence, the correct option is (D).

**95.** Indigenously - produced or occurring locally.

originating in and characteristic of a particular region or country; native (often followed by to):

Hence, the correct option is (D).

**96.** In part a, 'summon' should be replaced with 'summons'.

Some nouns look plural but have a singular meaning. A singular verb is used with them.

Hence, the correct option is (A).

**97.** If two singular nouns are joined by 'and' and if an article is used before the first singular noun, then it denotes 'one person/thing'.

Singular pronouns he, himself, his, him, etc. will come for human beings(when singular nouns are used), and it, itself, its will come for non-living things.

In the given sentence, two singular nouns 'manager' and 'receptionist' are joined by 'and', and the article 'The' is used before the first singular noun.

Hence, the correct option is (C).

**98.** First is B as it states the source of the findings i.e. UNESCO. This part could have come at the end of the sentence but notice how a comma is used after this segment. Hence, it has to be placed in the beginning.

Next is C as it indicates the number of children.

A follows C as it tells us the children where these children are i.e. India.

Next is E as it starts with 'been'. This should come after A to form the proper verb tense 'have been'.

Last is D as it tells as E ends with 'by' and D indicates the reason for this situation.

Hence, the correct option is (B).

**99.** First is C as it is the only logical opener of the sentence.

Next is E as it specifies the group of lower middle class people that are being talked about i.e. the parents.

A follows E as 'have been' should be followed by the main verb i.e. taking.

Next is D as it tells from where the children are being taken out.

Last is B as it starts with 'and' and states where these children are being relocated to.

Hence, the correct option is (A).

**100.** In the above sentence, the noun is 'United States of America.'

A basic rule in grammar is that, even when a 'proper noun' is a plural name, the verb must be singular.

In this case, the noun is 'the United States of America' and is considered as singular, but the plural verb 'are' is used which is grammatically incorrect.

Hence, the correct option is (A).

## General Intelligence & Reasoning

**Q.1** If in the given number, "695423574892" one is added to every even digit and two is subtracted from every odd digit, then how many numbers appear more than twice after the rearrangement?

**A.** One     **B.** Two     **C.** Three     **D.** Four

**Q.2** M is the son of R's Father's sister. A is the son of S, who is the mother of D, and the grandmother of R. N is the father of F, and the grandfather of M. S is the wife of N. A has no daughter. How many grandchildren does S have?

**A.** One     **B.** Two     **C.** Three     **D.** Four

**Q.3** Select the related shape from the given option.

   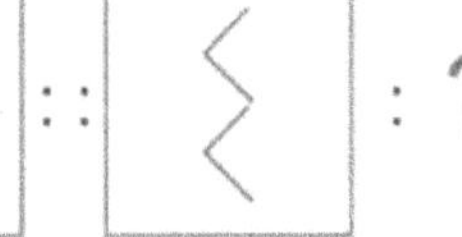

A. 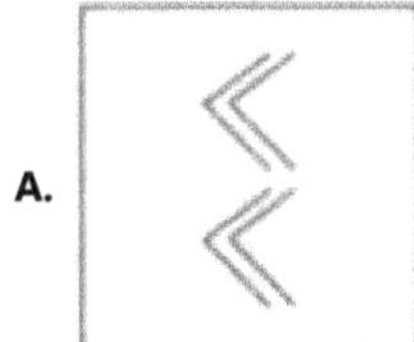    B. 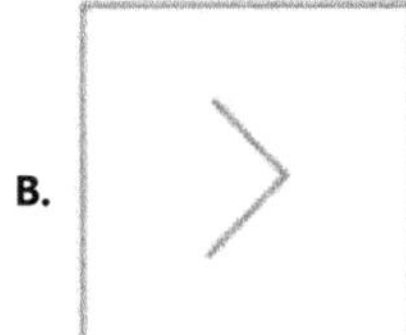

C. 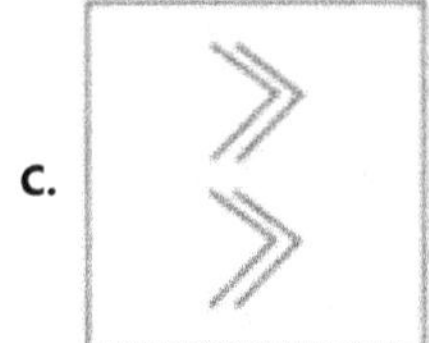    D. 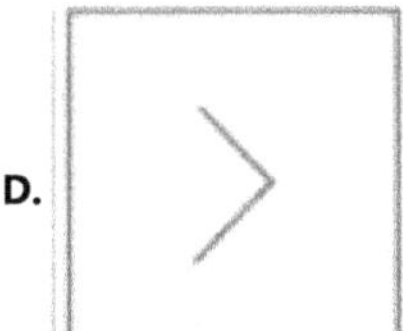

**Q.4** Select the related shape from the given option.

 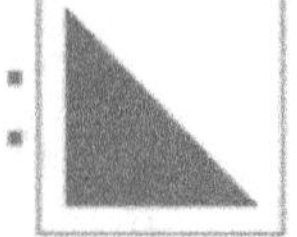 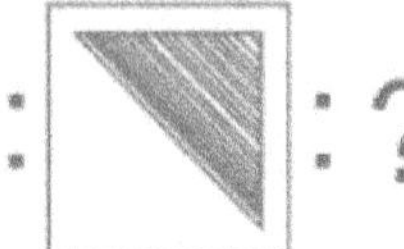

A.     B. 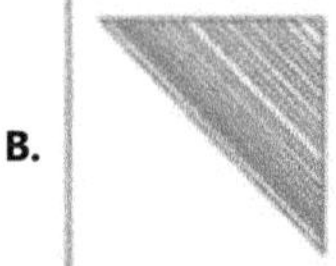

C. 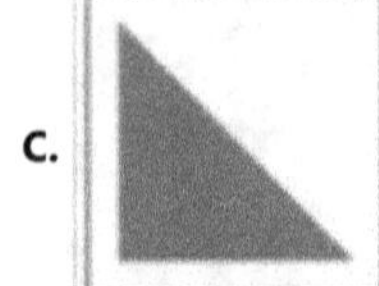    D. 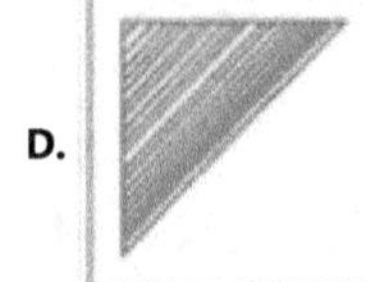

**Q.5 Direction:** In the following question, a word is represented by only one set of numbers are given in any one of the alternatives. The sets of numbers given in the alternatives are represented by two classes of alphabets as in the two given matrices. The column and row of Matrix I are numbered from 0 to 4 and those of Matrix II from 5 to 9. A letter from these matrices can be represented first by row and then the column number e.g. in the matrices for questions 1 to 5, K can be represented by 65,77, etc. H can be represented by 30,11 etc. Similarly, you have to identify the correct set for the word given in each question.

**Matrix I**

|   | 0 | 1 | 2 | 3 | 4 |
|---|---|---|---|---|---|
| 0 | A | E | S | T | H |
| 1 | T | H | A | E | S |
| 2 | E | S | T | H | A |
| 3 | H | A | E | S | T |
| 4 | S | T | H | A | E |

**Matrix II**

|   | 5 | 6 | 7 | 8 | 9 |
|---|---|---|---|---|---|
| 5 | P | O | R | K | L |
| 6 | K | L | P | O | R |
| 7 | O | R | K | L | P |
| 8 | L | P | O | R | K |
| 9 | R | K | L | P | O |

*HORSE*

**A.** 86,32,67,13,44     **B.** 57,95,02,24,87

**C.** 95,75,32,02,59     **D.** 04,75,88,21,32

**Q.6** In the following question, select the missing letter from the series:

| 9 | 5 | 6 | 4 |
|---|---|---|---|
| 8 | 7 | 8 | 8 |
| 6 | 3 | ? | 7 |
| 78 | 38 | 56 | 39 |

**A.** 7     **B.** 8     **C.** 6     **D.** 5

**Q.7** If LABOURED is written as LOBAERUD, then which among the following can be written as BROTHERS?

**A.** BTOEHRTS     **B.** BTORHETS

**C.** BTORREHS     **D.** BOTREHTS

**Q.8** Which figure will come in the given figure series?

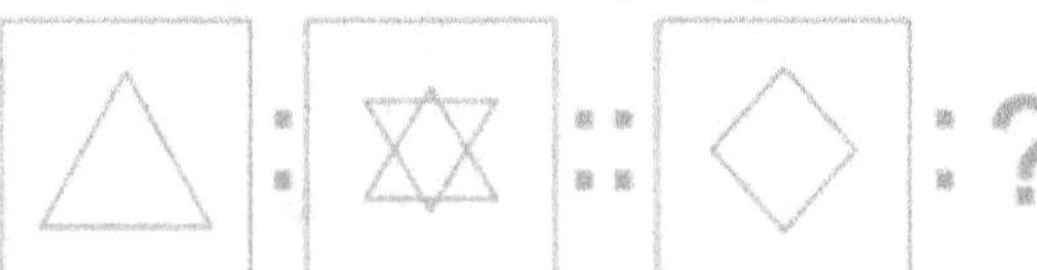

 **A.**

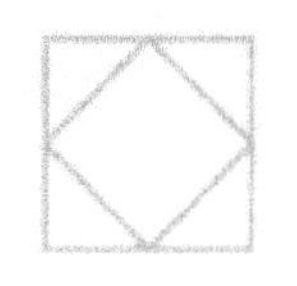 **B.**

**C.** 

**D.**

**B.** 

**C.** 

**D.** 

**Q.9** If in a certain language, "SANITY" is coded as "< + = * & ?" and "MURPHY" is coded as " # $ @ ! % ?". How is "TRIUMPH" coded in that code?

**A.** # > + < ! = $

**B.** & @ * $ # ! ?

**C.** & @ * $ # ! %

**D.** # > < + ! = $ %

**Q.10** What will come in the place of the question mark (?).

$$\frac{2}{3} : \frac{19}{29} :: \frac{8}{7} : ?$$

**A.** $\frac{89}{79}$

**B.** $\frac{79}{79}$

**C.** $\frac{79}{69}$

**D.** $\frac{80}{70}$

**Q.11** What will come in the place of the question mark (?).

91 : ? :: 64 : 54

**A.** 63

**B.** 101

**C.** 32

**D.** 70

**Q.12** Take a look at the image below and then choose the correct mirror image from the options provided below:

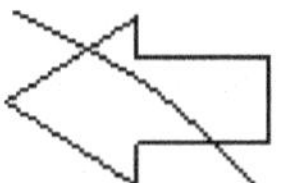

**A.** 

**B.** 

**C.** 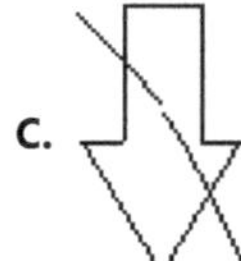

**D.** None of these

**Q.13** Which of the following diagrams best depicts the relationship among Doctors, Lawyers, and Professionals?

**A.** 

**Q.14** Which of the following diagrams best depicts the relationship among Water, Atmosphere and Hydrogen?

**A.** 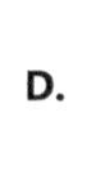

**B.** 

**C.** 

**D.** 

**Q.15** Unscrambled the letters in the given word and find the odd one.

**A.** PLPAE

**B.** RAORCT

**C.** AUVAG

**D.** NOONI

**Q.16** Find the odd one out.

**A.** Cathedral

**B.** Mosque

**C.** Monastery

**D.** Temple

**Q.17** Choose the word which is different from the rest.

**A.** Frog      **B.** Snake
**C.** Swan      **D.** Crocodile

**Q.18** In this question, four words are given, out of which, choose the odd one:

**A.** Potassium      **B.** Silicon
**C.** Zirconium      **D.** Gallium

**Q.19** In this question, four words have been given, choose out the odd one.

**A.** Raid    **B.** Attack    **C.** Assault    **D.** Defence

**Q.20** Which figure can be placed in the place of the question mark (?).

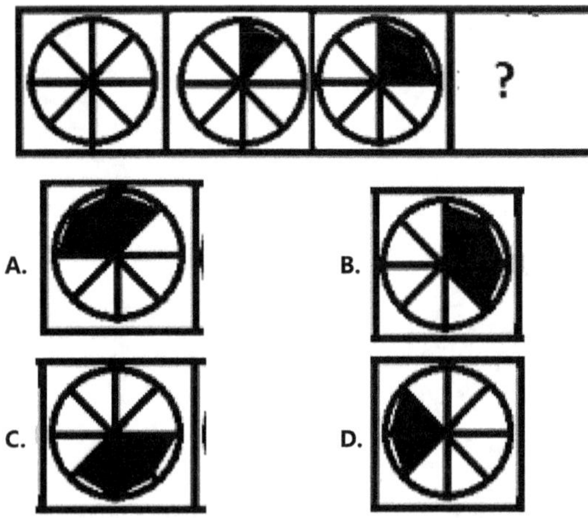

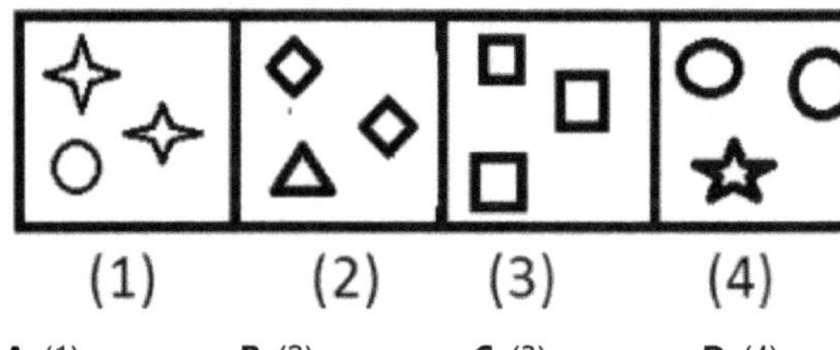

**Q.21** Which figure is different from others?

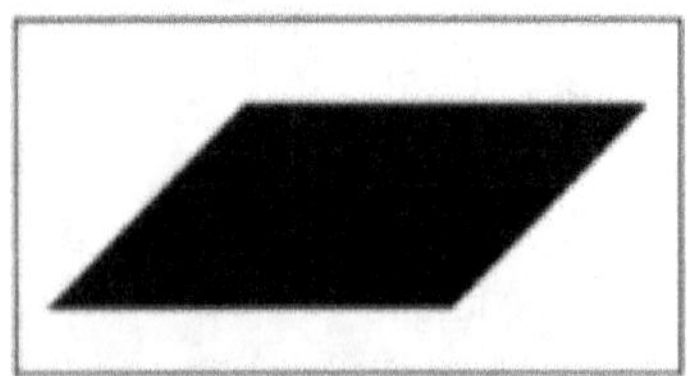

**A.** (1)      **B.** (2)      **C.** (3)      **D.** (4)

**Q.22** If, 50 * 34 = 28, 32 * 22 = 18 and 28 * 14 = 14, then what should 80 * 67 = ?

**A.** 34      **B.** 27      **C.** 49      **D.** 29

**Q.23** Find the odd one out:

**A.** 64      **B.** 48      **C.** 85      **D.** 92

**Q.24** Which group of shapes, which are shown in the answer figure, can be included to form the shape shown in the question figure?

**Question figure**

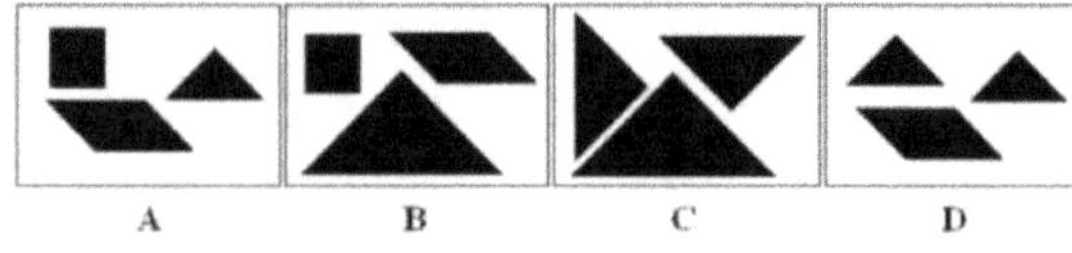

**Answer figure**

**A.** A      **B.** B      **C.** C      **D.** D

**Q.25** If TOUR is written in a certain code as 1234, CLEAR as 56784 and SPARE as 90847, what will be the $5^{th}$ digit for SCULPTURE in the same code?

**A.** 3      **B.** 4      **C.** 6      **D.** 0

# General Awareness

**Q.26** In April 2022, the Mazagon Dock Shipbuilders launched _______, the last of the six submarines under Project 75.

**A.** INS Vela      **B.** INS Vagsheer
**C.** INS Kalvari      **D.** INS Vagir

**Q.27** Which of the following launched a report titled 'India's Booming Gig and Platform Economy'?

**A.** NITI Aayog      **B.** RBI
**C.** FICCI      **D.** NASSCOM

**Q.28** Who addressed the CoWin Global Conclave in July 2021?

**A.** Narendra Modi      **B.** Amit Shah
**C.** Hardeep Singh Puri      **D.** Nitin Gadkari

**Q.29** What is the venue of the 'Semicon India Conference-2022'?

**A.** Mumbai      **B.** New Delhi
**C.** Chennai      **D.** Bengaluru

**Q.30** Which of the following is the Mascot of Indian Railways?

*[RRB (NTPC), 2017]*

**A.** Morris, the cat
**B.** Murugan, the peacock
**C.** Nandi, the bull
**D.** Bholu, the elephant

**Q.31** In which state of India, tarnetar fair is held every year?

**A.** Telangana      **B.** Manipur
**C.** Madhya Pradesh      **D.** Gujarat

**Q.32** Which of the following states is the largest jute producing state in India?

**A.** Rajasthan      **B.** Karnataka
**C.** West Bengal      **D.** Nagaland

**Q.33** Which was India's first full-length 'Talkie' film?

**A.** Indra Sabha      **B.** Sheree Farhad
**C.** Devout Prahlada      **D.** Alam Ara

**Q.34** Which of the following is the largest coal field in India?

**A.** Talcher    **B.** Ranchi    **C.** Rampur    **D.** Jharia

**Q.35** World Hindi Day or Vishwa Hindi Divas is celebrated on _______ every year.

**A.** January 10      **B.** December 10
**C.** January 11      **D.** December 11

**Q.36** What is the capital of Tripura?
A. Udaipur
B. Agartala
C. Aizawl
D. Kanchanpur

**Q.37** What is the capital of Mizoram?
A. Jaipur
B. Gangtok
C. Aizawl
D. Khwajvel

**Q.38** How much loan amount has been approved by the Asian Development Bank for urban sector projects in Rajasthan and Madhya Pradesh?
A. 570 million dollars
B. 650 million dollars
C. 590 million dollars
D. 410 million dollars

**Q.39** The Braille version of the Indian Constitution was unveiled in which state?
A. Goa
B. Karnataka
C. Uttar Pradesh
D. Maharashtra

**Q.40** Sultan Azlan Shah Cup is related to which game?
A. Badminton
B. Hockey
C. Table tennis
D. Golf

**Q.41** Pay attention to the following: -
1- Introduction
2- Fundamental Rights
3- Fundamental duties
4- Directive Principles of State Policy
Which of the following is the principle of gender equality?
A. only 1
B. 1 & 2
C. 1, 2 & 3
D. 1, 2, 3 & 4

**Q.42** Which Indian Institute has developed 'MOUSHIK', an indigenously-made microprocessor for the Internet of things devices?
A. IIT Kanpur
B. IIT Kharagpur
C. IIT Madras
D. IIT Guwahati

**Q.43** Which of the following laws was not enacted by the Parliament of India?
A. AFSPA
B. POTA
C. MCOCA
D. FEMA

**Q.44** Navelish is the historical name of which country?
A. India
B. Myanmar
C. China
D. Egypt

**Q.45** In which state is the Nohkalikai waterfall?
A. Kerala
B. Assam
C. Manipur
D. Meghalaya

**Q.46** Which of the following Indian kings appointed Dharma Mahamatta?
A. Ashoka
B. Samudragupta
C. Chandragupta I
D. Chandra Gupta Mourya

**Q.47** Who was the 22nd Tirthankara of Jainism?
A. Rishabhdev
B. Arishtanemi
C. Parshvanath
D. Mahavir

**Q.48** On which date is the birthday of Nobel laureate Ravindra Nath Tagore celebrated?
A. 6 May
B. 7 May
C. 8 May
D. 9 May

**Q.49** Which country will host the 2023 Cricket World Cup?
A. England
B. South Africa
C. Australia
D. India

**Q.50** The Public Accounts Committee (PAC) of Parliament completed how many years of inception?
A. 50
B. 60
C. 75
D. 100

# Quantitative Aptitude

**Q.51** What will come in place of question mark (?).
$$179.994\% \times 139.98 + 300.07\% \text{ of } 50.015 + 420.020\% \text{ of } 59.921 - ? = 145.023 \times 2.019$$
A. 346
B. 468
C. 364
D. 356

**Q.52 Direction:** What approximate value will come in place of the question mark (?) in the given questions?
$$45.014\% \text{ of } 239.97 + 325.089\% \times 199.936 - ? = 950.032 \div 19.012$$
A. 708
B. 698
C. 824
D. 584

**Q.53 Direction:** What approximate value will come in place of the question mark (?) in the given questions.
$$\sqrt{36.07 \times 16.083 \times 4.07 \times 323.95} = ? - 149.958 \times 179.9\%$$
A. 984
B. 1064
C. 1134
D. 1122

**Q.54** The ratio of length and breadth is 7: 4. The difference between length and breadth is 33 cm. What is the area of the rectangle?
A. 3388
B. 4455
C. 8866
D. 1122

**Q.55** The 480 m long train can cross the same length of the train with the same speed in opposite direction in 8 seconds. What is the speed of the train?
A. 60 m/sec
B. 10 m/sec
C. 12 m/sec
D. 15 m/sec

**Q.56** Sidhant buys some pen drives at Rs. 500 per piece and an equal number of Keyboards at Rs. 1500 per piece. He sold pen drives at $x\%$ profit and markup keyboard $2x\%$ above the cost price and gave $x\%$ discount at the time of the sale. By this Sidhant earned a total $(x - 6)\%$ profit in overall transitions. Find the value of $x$.
A. 15%
B. 18%
C. 25%
D. 20%

**Q.57** Vessel A has 88 litres of pure milk and vessel B has 88 litres of water. 22 litres milk is transferred from A to B. Then 22 litres is transferred from B to A. This process is repeated two times more. What is the ratio of milk and water in A at the end?
A. 64:63
B. 19:21
C. 64:61
D. 17: 8

**Q.58** The base of a right prism is an equilateral triangle on a side $6$ cm long. If the volume of the prism is $108\sqrt{3}$ cm³, its height is
A. 9 cm
B. 10 cm
C. 11 cm
D. 12 cm

**Q.59** A boats takes 9 hours more to travel $65$ km in upstream then to travel $60$ km in downstream. If speed of boat in still water is $2\frac{7}{9}\ m/sec$ then find speed of stream in (km/hr).

**A.** 7     **B.** 4     **C.** 8     **D.** 5

**Q.60** A man invested Rs. 3300 on Simple Interest for two years at the rate of 12 % p.a and Rs. $x$ on Compound Interest at the rate of 20% p.a. for two years. If the ratio of Simple Interest to Compound Interest get by man after two years is 9: 10, then find $x$?

**A.** Rs. 2050     **B.** Rs. 2000     **C.** Rs. 2450     **D.** Rs. 2300

**Q.61** The curved surface area of a cone whose radius is 42 cm, is 7656 cm². If the height of the cone is half of the perimeter of a square, then find the area of the square?

**A.** 400 cm²     **B.** 441 cm²
**C.** 1600 cm²     **D.** 900 cm²

**Q.62** How many permutations of the letters of the word APPLE are there?

**A.** 600     **B.** 120     **C.** 240     **D.** 60

**Q.63** The ratio of the present age of Abhi and Sam is 5:3, respectively. If the age of sam after 12 years will be 50% more than age of Abhi 4 years ago from now, then find the value of $x$.

**A.** 4     **B.** 2     **C.** 6     **D.** 5

**Q.64** If the volume of a sphere is 2304π cm³ and the radius of a hemisphere is 75% of the radius of the sphere, then find the volume of the hemisphere?

**A.** $456\pi$ cm³     **B.** $476\pi$ cm³
**C.** $486\pi$ cm³     **D.** $496\pi$ cm³

**Q.65** A train can cross a 150 m long platform in 20 seconds and a pole in 12.5 seconds. What is the speed of the train?

**A.** 63 km/h     **B.** 72 km/h
**C.** 90 km/h     **D.** 108 km/h

**Q.66** A boat takes some time to cover a distance of 240 km and takes 18 hours less to return back. If the speed of the stream is $\frac{2}{3}$ times the speed of the boat in still water, then find the speed of the boat in still water.

**A.** 24 km/hr     **B.** 36 km/hr     **C.** 28 km/hr     **D.** 32 km/hr

**Q.67** What will come in the place of question mark (?) in the given expression?

$$? +727-93 = 20\% \text{ of } 50\% \text{ of } 20000$$

**A.** 1369     **B.** 1366     **C.** 1768     **D.** 1665

**Q.68** What will come in the place of question mark (?) in the given expression?

$$4\frac{2}{5} + 3\frac{1}{3} - 6\frac{1}{2} =?$$

**A.** $2\frac{7}{30}$     **B.** $1\frac{7}{30}$     **C.** $1\frac{11}{30}$     **D.** $2\frac{13}{30}$

**Q.69** In the question, two equations I and II are given. You have to solve both the equations to establish the correct relation between $x$ and $y$ and choose the correct option.

I. $x^2 - 20x + 96 = 0$

II. $y^2 + 6y - 91 = 0$

**A.** $x > y$     **B.** $x \geq y$     **C.** $x < y$     **D.** $x \leq y$

**Q.70** In the question, two equations I and II are given. You have to solve both the equations to establish the correct relation between $x$ and $y$ and choose the correct option.

I. $x^2 + 5x - 36 = 0$

II. $y^2 + 24y + 135 = 0$

**A.** $x > y$     **B.** $x \geq y$     **C.** $x < y$     **D.** $x \leq y$

**Q.71** A sum of Rs. 15360 at 12.5% rate of interest compounded annually, then what is the interest earned after 3 years?

**A.** Rs. 6750     **B.** Rs. 6480     **C.** Rs. 4840     **D.** Rs. 6510

**Q.72** A is 8 years younger than B and 6 years elder than C. If the present age of B and D is 30 years and 24 years, respectively, then find the ratio of the present age of C to the present age of D.

**A.** 1:2     **B.** 2:5     **C.** 1:4     **D.** 2:3

**Q.73** 'A' can complete a work in 32 days while 'B' takes 8 days less than 'A' to complete the work. If the total wage received by them is Rs. 1050 then find the wage received by 'A'.

**A.** Rs. 600     **B.** Rs. 450     **C.** Rs. 750     **D.** Rs. 900

**Q.74** A bag contains 3 red, 4 blue, and 3 green balls. If 2 balls are drawn at random then what is the probability that none is green.

**A.** $\frac{6}{11}$     **B.** $\frac{8}{15}$     **C.** $\frac{11}{15}$     **D.** $\frac{7}{15}$

**Q.75** Find the number of ways in which $8$ different beads can be arranged to form a necklace.

**A.** 2520     **B.** 40320     **C.** 20160     **D.** 5040

# English Comprehension

**Ques (76-80):Direction**: In the following passage some words have been omitted. Select the most appropriate option for each blank.

When things go as ________**(A)**, we feel comfortable. But when life throws a curveball, it creates anxiety and stress. The current Covid-19 pandemic has ________**(B)** the carpet from under our feet. It has increased ________**(C)** over the economy, employment, finances, relationships, and, of course, physical and mental health. Yet as human beings, we crave security. Fear and diffidence make you powerless and drain you emotionally.

Many people can ________**(D)** some levels of uncertainty in life. Some enjoy taking risks. Others get overwhelmed by the ________**(E)** of life. No matter how bad the situation may be, there are steps you can take to better ________**(F)** yourself to face the unknown with courage.

The world consists of pairs of opposites. Pleasure and pain, joy and sorrow, honour and dishonour are an________**(G)** part of life. So, things will change, and for the better.

_______________(H), the world is constantly changing. And this change is unpredictable.

**Q.76** Select the most appropriate option for blank **(A)**.

A. planned    B. normal    C. berserk    D. good

**Q.77** Select the most appropriate option for blank **(B)**.

A. placed    B. pulled    C. snatched    D. pushed

**Q.78** Select the most appropriate option for blank **(C)**.

A. uncertainty    B. turmoil
C. grip    D. momentum

**Q.79** Select the most appropriate option for blank **(D)**.

A. forecast    B. expect    C. tolerate    D. testify

**Q.80** Select the most appropriate option for blank (E).

A. harmony    B. pacification
C. egalitarianism    D. unpredictability

**Q.81 Direction:** In the following question, some part of the sentence may have errors. Find out which part of the sentence has an error and select the appropriate option.

We should never (a)/look down to (b)/ a person merely (c)/because he is poor. (d)

A. (a)    B. (b)    C. (c)    D. (d)

**Q.82 Direction:** In the following question, some part of the sentence may have errors. Find out which part of the sentence has an error and select the appropriate option.

The voyager took rest (a)/below the shade (b)/ of a large (c)/ banyan tree. (d)

A. (a)    B. (b)    C. (c)    D. (d)

**Q.83** Find the synonym of the given word.

Boast

A. Dry    B. Revive    C. Pride    D. Sly

**Q.84** Find the synonym of the given word.

Haste

A. Fiat    B. Murky    C. Impact    D. Hurry

**Q.85** Improve the bracketed part of the sentence.

Pensions are linked to inflation, (besides) they should be linked to the cost of living.

A. and    B. whereas
C. where    D. as long as

**Q.86** Improve the bracketed part of the sentence.

I went to the last lecture, (no sooner then) I got reminded of it.

A. almost as soon as    B. as sooner as
C. so quickly as    D. as quickly as

**Q.87** Fill in the blanks.

The Western Ghats have infested ___ different snakes.

A. of    B. in    C. with    D. by

**Q.88** Fill in the blank.

You take a decision. The ball is in _________now

A. your court    B. your pocket
C. your garden    D. your net

**Q.89** Fill in the blanks with a suitable verb.

The cold breath of autumn had _______the ivy leaves from the vine and the branches remained almost bare.

A. striking    B. stricken    C. strike    D. struck

**Q.90** Improve the bold part of the sentence.

M Venkaiah Naidu **has appointed as the** Vice President of India in a smooth transition after the term of Hamid Ansari ended on August 9.

A.    takes the post of
B.    took over as the
C.    has taken the post of
D.    had taken over the

**Q.91** Improve the bold part of the sentence.

There are two facets to the National Climate Assessment **that can craft** distinguished brains in America's science fraternity.

A.    which is crafted as
B.    that is crafted through
C.    which have crafted
D.    that has been crafted by

**Q.92** What is an antonym for "coarse"?

A. Fine    B. Gritty    C. Gravelly    D. Grainy

**Q.93** What is the antonym for "Apathetic".

A. Agitated    B. Happy
C. Concerned    D. Surprised

**Q.94** Improve the bracketed part of the sentence.

I (regret for) using objectionable words against a man so mighty.

A. repent for    B. sorry for
C. regret    D. No improvement

**Q.95** Given below is a sentence. Identify the part of speech of the underlined word. Choose the response which is the most appropriate expression.

Calcium is essential for strong bones.

A. Abstract noun    B. Adjective
C. Material Noun    D. Adverb

**Q.96** Given below is an/a idiom/phrase followed by four alternative meanings. Choose the response which is the most appropriate expression.

Cook the books

A.    To alter facts dishonestly
B.    To do something that spoils someone's plan
C.    To tell an interesting story
D.    To be very angry

**Q.97** Given below is an/a idiom/phrase followed by four alternative meanings. Choose the response which is the most appropriate expression.

To vote with your feet

A.    To show that you do not support something
B.    To replace something important
C.    To change something you must do

**D.** To express a particular opinion

**Q.98** Choose the correct preposition to fill the blank in the given sentence.

I lived in America _______ 2016.

**A.** until      **B.** from      **C.** for      **D.** with

**Q.99** Substitute one word for the group of the words given below.

A person who renounces the world and practices self-discipline in order to attain salvation

**A.** Sceptic      **B.** Ascetic

**C.** Devotee      **D.** Antiquarian

**Q.100** Find the correctly spelled word.

**A.** Accomplish      **B.** Acomplush

**C.** Ackmplesh      **D.** Accompalish

# // Smart Answer Sheet //

**Correct** — Indicates percentage of students who answered questions correctly.

**Skipped** — Indicates percentage of students who skipped questions.

| Q. | Ans. | Correct / Skipped | Q. | Ans. | Correct / Skipped | Q. | Ans. | Correct / Skipped | Q. | Ans. | Correct / Skipped | Q. | Ans. | Correct / Skipped |
|---|---|---|---|---|---|---|---|---|---|---|---|---|---|---|
| 1 | C | 44.46 % / 51.9 % | 17 | C | 89.09 % / 10.9 % | 33 | D | 56.62 % / 30.2 % | 49 | D | 43.05 % / 39.18 % | 65 | B | 46.33 % / 49.64 % |
| 2 | B | 69.61 % / 30.16 % | 18 | A | 46.01 % / 40.85 % | 34 | D | 64.76 % / 31.11 % | 50 | D | 59.64 % / 34.18 % | 66 | D | 52.21 % / 45.6 % |
| 3 | C | 83.03 % / 15.02 % | 19 | D | 47.57 % / 46.1 % | 35 | A | 84.64 % / 12.63 % | 51 | C | 50.87 % / 45.08 % | 67 | B | 56.08 % / 39.57 % |
| 4 | D | 68.91 % / 30.56 % | 20 | B | 45.96 % / 54.01 % | 36 | B | 45.14 % / 41.96 % | 52 | A | 64.38 % / 35.21 % | 68 | B | 80.71 % / 17.17 % |
| 5 | D | 17.39 % / 75.07 % | 21 | C | 65.35 % / 32.28 % | 37 | C | 55.8 % / 31.49 % | 53 | C | 42.15 % / 32.01 % | 69 | A | 44.02 % / 52.72 % |
| 6 | B | 61.59 % / 33.16 % | 22 | C | 56.12 % / 35.29 % | 38 | A | 61.46 % / 30.59 % | 54 | A | 65.29 % / 31.72 % | 70 | B | 65.97 % / 31.35 % |
| 7 | C | 54.28 % / 39.6 % | 23 | C | 44.84 % / 40.39 % | 39 | D | 50.51 % / 42.33 % | 55 | A | 42.63 % / 32.06 % | 71 | D | 66.15 % / 30.42 % |
| 8 | C | 47.06 % / 43.75 % | 24 | C | 25.05 % / 73.1 % | 40 | B | 42.26 % / 41.42 % | 56 | D | 28.2 % / 70.16 % | 72 | D | 47.71 % / 45.7 % |
| 9 | C | 44.82 % / 42.8 % | 25 | D | 64.74 % / 33.95 % | 41 | D | 15.37 % / 68.97 % | 57 | D | 51.94 % / 30.55 % | 73 | B | 65.01 % / 30.69 % |
| 10 | C | 49.14 % / 44.05 % | 26 | B | 42.76 % / 51.02 % | 42 | C | 53.69 % / 30.99 % | 58 | D | 60.64 % / 38.29 % | 74 | D | 52.01 % / 34.95 % |
| 11 | A | 55.04 % / 42.3 % | 27 | A | 46.76 % / 35.66 % | 43 | C | 66.28 % / 30.85 % | 59 | D | 46.47 % / 33.91 % | 75 | A | 47.86 % / 40.37 % |
| 12 | A | 81.4 % / 12.45 % | 28 | A | 55.15 % / 41.65 % | 44 | A | 53.25 % / 38.16 % | 60 | B | 41.69 % / 35.0 % | 76 | A | 18.95 % / 73.7 % |
| 13 | B | 62.31 % / 32.58 % | 29 | D | 61.81 % / 32.12 % | 45 | D | 63.02 % / 36.15 % | 61 | A | 48.53 % / 31.49 % | 77 | B | 10.11 % / 77.37 % |
| 14 | D | 48.54 % / 45.68 % | 30 | D | 42.24 % / 33.28 % | 46 | A | 59.36 % / 38.31 % | 62 | D | 56.49 % / 40.87 % | 78 | A | 29.91 % / 67.04 % |
| 15 | D | 61.92 % / 34.27 % | 31 | D | 51.67 % / 46.0 % | 47 | B | 57.2 % / 41.63 % | 63 | A | 68.97 % / 30.98 % | 79 | C | 68.48 % / 30.61 % |
| 16 | C | 46.77 % / 45.59 % | 32 | C | 65.78 % / 33.08 % | 48 | D | 48.64 % / 50.58 % | 64 | C | 64.39 % / 30.56 % | 80 | D | 20.83 % / 74.54 % |

| Q. | Ans. | Correct |
|---|---|---|
| | | Skipped |
| 81 | B | 47.26 % |
| | | 33.97 % |
| 82 | A | 40.58 % |
| | | 46.4 % |
| 83 | C | 82.79 % |
| | | 13.24 % |
| 84 | D | 55.46 % |
| | | 33.51 % |

| Q. | Ans. | Correct |
|---|---|---|
| | | Skipped |
| 85 | B | 53.72 % |
| | | 43.34 % |
| 86 | A | 40.12 % |
| | | 41.63 % |
| 87 | C | 48.96 % |
| | | 37.16 % |
| 88 | A | 49.78 % |
| | | 37.9 % |

| Q. | Ans. | Correct |
|---|---|---|
| | | Skipped |
| 89 | D | 52.59 % |
| | | 37.29 % |
| 90 | B | 41.04 % |
| | | 44.78 % |
| 91 | D | 54.84 % |
| | | 44.91 % |
| 92 | A | 48.58 % |
| | | 46.58 % |

| Q. | Ans. | Correct |
|---|---|---|
| | | Skipped |
| 93 | C | 48.02 % |
| | | 46.05 % |
| 94 | C | 45.04 % |
| | | 41.6 % |
| 95 | C | 60.15 % |
| | | 36.42 % |
| 96 | A | 56.38 % |
| | | 35.8 % |

| Q. | Ans. | Correct |
|---|---|---|
| | | Skipped |
| 97 | A | 45.75 % |
| | | 49.57 % |
| 98 | A | 46.58 % |
| | | 38.59 % |
| 99 | B | 48.78 % |
| | | 41.43 % |
| 100 | A | 49.52 % |
| | | 38.61 % |

## Performance Analysis

| | |
|---|---|
| Avg. Score (%) | 47.5% |
| Toppers Score (%) | 70.0% |
| Your Score | |

# //Hints and Solutions//

**1.** The given number is,

6 9 5 4 2 3 5 7 4 8 9 2

After the rearrangement,

7 7 3 5 3 1 3 5 5 9 7 3

Then three numbers appear more than twice after the rearrangement.

Hence, the correct option is (C).

**2.**

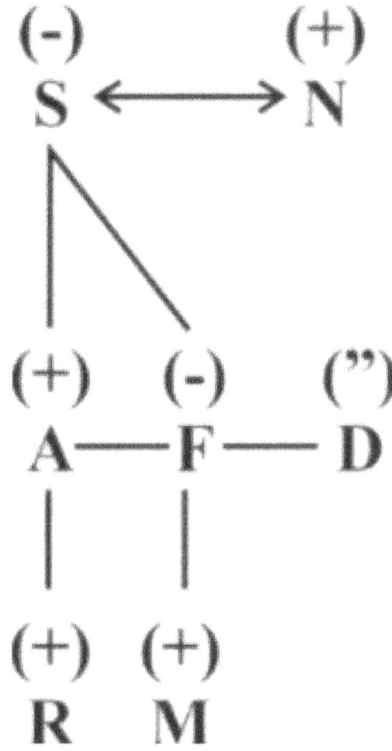

Hence, the correct option is (B).

**3.**

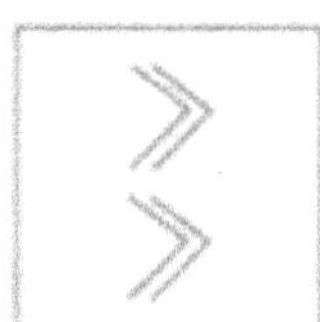

Hence, the correct option is (C).

**4.**

Hence, the correct option is (D).

**5.** $H \to 04,11,23,30,42$

$O \to 56,68,75,87,99$

$R \to 57,69,76,88,95$

$S \to 02,14,21,33,40$

$E \to 01,13,20,32,44$

$HORSE \to 04,75,88,21,32$

Hence, the correct option is (D).

**6.** The pattern followed here is:

9 × 7 + 6 = 78

5 × 7 + 3 = 38

6 × 8 + 8 = 56

**4 × 8 +7 = 39**

Hence, the correct option is (B).

**7.** Leaving the first letter, the next three letters of the word are written in reverse followed by the next three letters written in reverse, and no change is done to the first and the last letter of the word.

LABOURED → LOBAERUD

BROTHERS → BTORREHS

Hence, the correct option is (C).

**8.**

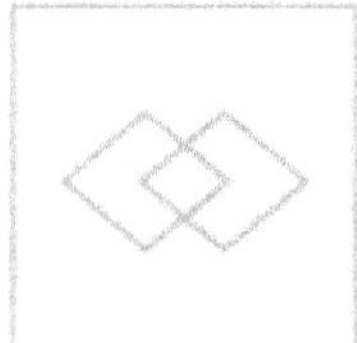

Hence, the correct option is (C).

**9.** In **"SANITY"**,

S represents <

A represents +

N represents =

I represents *

T represents &

Y represents ?

Similarly,

In **"MURPHY"**,

M represents #

U represents $

R represents @

P represents !

H represents %

Y represents ?

So, **"TRIUMPH"** would be coded as "**& @ * $ # ! %**"

Hence, the correct option is (C).

**10.** As shown below:

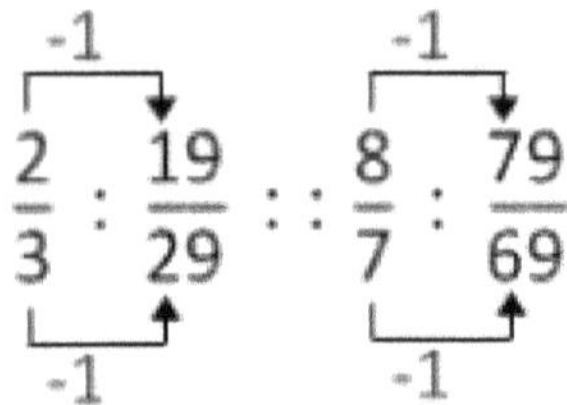

Hence, the correct option is (C).

**11.** As shown,

64 : 54

⇒ (6 + 4) : (5 + 4)

⇒ 10 : 9

Similarly,

91 : 63

⇒ (9 + 1) : (6 + 3)

⇒ 10 : 9

Hence, the correct option is (A).

**12.**

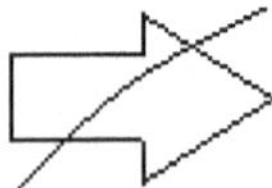

Hence, the correct option is (A).

**13.** Doctors and lawyers are entirely different. But, both are Professionals.

Hence, the correct option is (B).

**14.** Hydrogen is a constituent of both Water and the Atmosphere. Water is present in the Atmosphere.

Hence, the correct option is (D).

**15.** First, unscrambling the letters, we get

PLPAE - APPLE

RAORCT – CARROT

AUVAG – GUAVA

NOONI – ONION

Now, except onion all others are fruits.

Hence, the odd man out is onion.

**16.** Except, monastery all others are places of worship. Monastery is a housing complex of the numns and monks.

Hence, the correct option is (C).

**17.** Except Swan, no other can fly.

Therefore, the odd one out is Swan.

Hence, the correct option is (C).

**18.** All except Potassium are metals used in semiconductor devices.

Hence, the correct option is (A).

**19.** All except Defence are forms of attacks.

Hence, the correct option is (D).

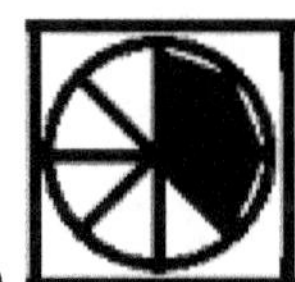

**20.**

Hence, the correct option is (B).

**21.** Each box has three figures of two types, of which two are the same while the other is different.

Hence, the correct option is (C).

**22.** The pattern is,

50 * 34 = 50 + 34 = 84

84 ÷ 3 = 28

Similarly,

80 * 67 = 80 + 67 = 147

147 ÷ 3 = 49

Hence, the correct option is (C).

**23.** Except 85, all others are multiples of 4.

$64 = 16 \times 4$

$48 = 12 \times 4$

$92 = 23 \times 4$

**$85 = 17 \times 5$**

Hence, the correct option is (C).

**24.**

Hence, the correct option is (C).

**25.** By, comparing letters and digit, we get

T = 1

O = 2

U = 3

R = 4

C = 5

L = 6

E = 7

A = 8

S = 9

P = 0

As the 5th letter is SCULPTURE is P and '0' is used for P, therefore, 5th digit is the required code which is '0'.

Hence, the correct option is (D).

**26.** The Mazagon Dock Shipbuilders on 20 April 2022, launched INS Vagsheer, the last of the six submarines under Project 75. The submarine was launched by Defence Secretary Ajay Kumar.

Named after sandfish, a deadly deep water sea predator of the Indian Ocean, the first submarine 'Vagsheer' was commissioned in Indian navy December 1974. It was decommissioned in Indian navy April 1997.

Hence, the correct option is (B).

**27.** NITI Aayog launched a report titled 'India's Booming Gig and Platform Economy', on 27 June 2022.

It is a first-of-its-kind study that presents comprehensive perspectives and recommendations on the gig–platform economy in India.

The report provides a scientific methodological approach to estimate the current size and job-generation potential of the sector.

Hence, the correct option is (A).

**28.** Prime Minister Narendra Modi addressed the CoWin Global Conclave on 5 July 2021.

India offers CoWin as a digital public good to the world to combat COVID-19. COVID-19 Vaccine registration portal, CoWin has become very popular, and foreign countries are showing interest in this technology. Over 50 countries from across Central Asia, Latin America, and Africa are interested in it.

Hence, the correct option is (A).

**29.** Prime Minister Narendra Modi inaugurated Semicon India Conference-2022 in Bengaluru.

To make India a global hub for Semiconductor Design, Manufacturing, and Technology Development which will help propel the vision of the India Semiconductor Mission.

Semiconductors are materials with electrical conductivity values falling between a conductor and an insulator.

Hence, the correct option is (D).

**30.** Bholu, the Elephant is the mascot of Indian Railways, represented as a cartoon of an elephant holding a signal lamp with a green ring in one hand. It is designed by the National Institute of Design, to commemorate the 150th anniversary of the Indian Railways and was unveiled on 16 April 2002 in Bangalore.

Hence, the correct option is (D).

**31.** Tarnetar fair is celebrated every year in Saurashtra, Gujarat. Whose tribal youths and girls adorn themselves. And choose their living partner.

Hence, the correct option is (D).

**32.** The state of West Bengal is the largest jute producing state in India. The temperature of 20 to 40 degree Celsius and hot and high humid climate is considered suitable for jute crops.

Hence, the correct option is (C).

**33.** Alam Ara was a 1931 Indian film directed by Ardeshir Irani. It was the first sound film in India. Alam Ara was India's first full-length 'Talkie' film.

Hence, the correct option is (D).

**34.** Jharia was the largest city in the state of Jharkhand. Jharia is famous for its rich coal resources. Which is used to make coke.

Hence, the correct option is (D).

**35.** World Hindi day is celebrated every year on January 10. This day is celebrated to mark the First World Hindi Conference, which was held from January 10 to January 12, 1975, at Nagpur. The first Hindi Conference was inaugurated by Indira Gandhi. The first World Hindi day was observed on January 10, 2006. The Day aims to promote the Hindi language around the world.

Hence, the correct option is (A).

**36.** The capital of Tripura is Agartala. Bengali and Tripuri are the main languages here. Tripura is an Indian state in the northeast, bordering Mizoram, Assam and Bangladesh. It is bounded by Bangladesh in the north, south and west and 84% of its total border area i.e., 856 km is in the form of international border.

Hence, the correct option is (B).

**37.** Aizawl is the capital of Mizoram. There are 8 districts in Mizoram, Aizawl is the largest district in the population of the state with a population of 400309, Aizawl is the largest district in the area. Mizoram became a Union Territory when the Northeast Region Reorganization Act came into force in 1972.

Hence, the correct option is (C).

**38.** The Manila-headquartered Asian Development Bank (ADB) has approved two loan totaling 570 million dollars (about Rs 4,200 crore) for urban sector projects in Rajasthan and Madhya Pradesh. It has approved a 300 million dollars to develop Rajasthan's secondary towns and a USD 270 million dollars loans for Madhya Pradesh Urban Services Improvement Project.

Hence, the correct option is (A).

**39.** Maharashtra Social Justice Minister Dhananjay Munde unveiled a Braille version of the Indian Constitution at an event in Mumbai. The Braille version of the Constitution has been prepared on behalf of Thane-based NGO Astitva Foundation.

Hence, the correct option is (D).

**40.** Sultan Azlan Shah Cup is an international hockey competition. It started in 1983. It occurs in Malaysia and is named after the 9th King of Malaysia, Sultan Azlan Shah.

Hence, the correct option is (B).

**41.** All of the above parts talk about gender equality. The constitution not only guarantees equality to women but also empowers the state to adopt measures of positive discrimination in favor of women. Please note that fundamental duties speak for abandoning abusive practices for the dignity of women, leading to an implicit idea rather than a clear declaration.

Hence, the correct option is (D).

**42.** The Indian Institute of Technology (IIT) Madras has successfully developed 'MOUSHIK', an indigenously-made microprocessor for the Internet of things (IoT) devices. 'MOUSHIK' is a processor cum a system-on-chip that can cater to the rapidly-growing IoT devices, an integral part of smart cities of a digital India.

Hence, the correct option is (C).

**43.** MCOCA (Maharashtra Control of Organised Crime Act) is an act of the Government of Maharashtra. The Act provides the State Government with special powers to deal with these issues, including powers of surveillance, clear evidence standards, and procedural safeguards, and setting additional criminal penalties, including the death penalty.

Hence, the correct option is (C).

**44.** Nabhivarsha is the historical name of the country of India. According to historical sources, the old name of Bharatvarsha was Nabhivarsha. Which was earlier named after King Nabhi, father of Jain Tirthankara Rishabhdev.

Hence, the correct option is (A).

**45.** The Nohkalikai waterfall is in Cherrapunji, Meghalaya. It is 1115 ft (340 m) high. Its width is 75 feet. It is one of the highest waterfalls in India. Cherrapunji has been famous for heavy rains, this is the source of the water of this waterfall.

Hence, the correct option is (D).

**46.** Ashoka appointed Dharma Mahamatta to propagate his Dhamma or Dharma. Who preached his religion. Its information comes from the inscription of Ashoka.

Hence, the correct option is (A).

**47.** The 22nd Tirthankara of Jainism was Arishtanemi. His description is in Rigveda. The first Tirthankara of Jainism was Rishabhdev. There were a total of 24 Tirthankaras in Jainism, of which the first Rishabhdev and the 22nd Arishtanemi are named in the Rigveda.

Hence, the correct option is (B).

**48.** Asia's first Nobel laureate Rabindra Nath Tagore's birthday is celebrated on 9 May. Ravindra Jayanti is popularly called Pochishi Boishakh, and is formally and celebrated throughout West Bengal and Bangladesh. He composed over 2230 songs. His songs are called Ravindra Geet. Ravindra Nath Tagore composed the national anthems of India and Bangladesh. Tagore was highly influential in introducing Indian culture to the West and is generally regarded as an outstanding creative artist of modern India. He was awarded the 1913 Nobel Prize for Gitanjali, an English translation of Tagore's Bengali poems. His literature has been translated into English, Dutch, German, Spanish, and other European languages.

Hence, the correct option is (D).

**49.** India will host the 2023 Cricket World Cup.

The 2023 ICC Men's Cricket World Cup will be the 13th edition of the men's Cricket World Cup, scheduled to be hosted by India during October and November 2023. This will be the first time the competition is held entirely in India.

Hence, the correct option is (D).

**50.** President Ram Nath Kovind had addressed at the centenary celebration of the Public Accounts Committee (PAC) of the Parliament. He said that the PAC ensures "administrative accountability of the executive towards the legislature". The President released a souvenir depicting the 100 glorious years of the PAC's journey and 67 articles, including 15 from the Commonwealth countries.

Hence, the correct option is (D).

**51.** $179.994\% \times 139.98 + 300.07\%$ of $50.015 + 420.020\%$ of $59.921 - ? = 145.023 \times 2.019$

Taking approximate value of each number, we get

$$\Rightarrow \frac{140 \times 180\% + 50 \times 300\% + 60 \times 420\% - ?}{145 \times 2} =$$

$\Rightarrow 252 + 150 + 252 - 290 =?$

$\Rightarrow ? = 364$

Hence, the correct option is (C).

**52.** $45.014\%$ of $239.97 + 325.089\% \times 199.936 - ? = 950.032 \div 19.012$

Taking approximate value of each number, we get

$\Rightarrow 240 \times 45\% + 200 \times 325\% - ? = 950 \div 19$

$\Rightarrow 108 + 650 - ? = 50$

$\Rightarrow 758 - 50 =?$

$\Rightarrow ? = 708$

Hence, the correct option is (C).

**53.** $\sqrt{36.07 \times 16.083 \times 4.07 \times 323.95} =? - 149.958 \times 179.9\%$

Taking approximate value of each number, we get

$\Rightarrow \sqrt{36 \times 16 \times 4 \times 324} =? -150 \times 180\%$

$\Rightarrow 6 \times 4 \times 2 \times 18 + 270 =?$

$\Rightarrow 24 \times 36 + 270 =?$

$\Rightarrow ? = 1134$

Hence, the correct option is (C).

**54.** Let the length and breadth of the rectangle be $7x$ and $4x$.

Given,

The ratio of length and breadth of the rectangle $= 7:4$

Difference in length and breadth of rectangle $= 33$ cm

$7x - 4x = 33$

$\Rightarrow 3x = 33$

$\Rightarrow x = 11$

Length $= 11 \times 7 = 77$ cm

Breadth $= 11 \times 4 = 44$ cm

$\therefore$ Area of the rectangle $= 44$ cm $\times 77$ cm

$= 3388$ cm$^2$

Hence, the correct option is (A).

**55.** Let the speed of the train is $x$.

Given,

Length of the train = 480 m

Length of the second train coming from opposite direction = 480 m

Time is taken to cross the second train = 8 second

$\dfrac{\text{(Length of first train + Length of second train)}}{\text{(Speed of first train + Speed of second train)}} = 8$

$\Rightarrow \dfrac{480+480}{x+x} = 8$

$\Rightarrow x = 60$ m/sec

Hence, the correct option is (A).

**56.** Pen drives Cost Price $= 500$

Profit $\% = x\%$

Profit $= 5x$

Keyboards Cost Price $= 1500$

$\Rightarrow$ Marked Price $= 1500 \left(1 + \dfrac{2x}{100}\right)$

$\Rightarrow$ Selling Price $= 1500 \left(1 + \dfrac{2x}{100}\right)\left(1 - \dfrac{x}{100}\right)$

Profit $= \left[\left(1 + \dfrac{2x}{100}\right)\left(1 - \dfrac{x}{100}\right) - 1\right] 1500$

According to question, over all profit

$\Rightarrow \dfrac{\left[\left(1 + \frac{x}{50}\right)\left(1 - \frac{x}{100}\right) - 1\right] 1500 + 5x}{\left(\frac{1500+500}{100}\right)} = (x - 6)$

$\Rightarrow \left[1 + \dfrac{x}{50} - \dfrac{x}{100} - \dfrac{x^2}{5000} - 1\right] 1500 + 5x = (x - 6)(20)$

$\Rightarrow \left(\dfrac{x}{100} - \dfrac{x^2}{5000}\right) 1500 + 5x = 20x - 120$

$\Rightarrow 15x - \dfrac{3x^2}{10} + 5x = 20x - 120$

$\Rightarrow x^2 = 400$

$\Rightarrow x = 20\%$

Hence, the correct option is (D).

**57.** Given,

Pure milk in vessel A = 88 liters

Water in pot B = 88 liters

Milk transferred from A to B = 22 liters

Water transferred from B to A = 22 liters

Final concentration of Milk in vessel A

$\Rightarrow \left(88 \times \dfrac{3}{4} + 88 \times \dfrac{1}{4} \times \dfrac{1}{5}\right)\dfrac{3}{4} + \left[\left(88 \times \dfrac{3}{4} + 88 \times \dfrac{1}{4} \times \dfrac{1}{5}\right)\dfrac{1}{4} + 88 \times \dfrac{1}{4} \times \dfrac{4}{5}\right]\dfrac{1}{5}$

$\Rightarrow (66 + 4.4)\dfrac{3}{4} + \left((66 + 4.4)\dfrac{1}{4} + 17 - 6\right)\dfrac{1}{5}$

$\Rightarrow (70.4) \times \dfrac{3}{4} + \dfrac{70.4}{5 \times 4} + \dfrac{17.6}{5}$

$$\Rightarrow 17.6 \times 3 + \frac{17.6}{5} + \frac{17.6}{5}$$

$$\Rightarrow \frac{17.6 \times 17}{5} = 59.84$$

Concentration of wate $= 88 - 59.84 = 28.16$

Milk: Water in vessel $A$

$$\Rightarrow 59.84 : 28.16 = 17 : 8$$

Hence, the correct option is (D).

**58.** Let the height of the prism be $h$.

Given,

The side of an equilateral triangle $= 6$ cm

Volume of a prism $= 108\sqrt{3}$ cm $^3$

Area of the base $= \frac{\sqrt{3}}{4}$ side $^2$

$$= \frac{\sqrt{3}}{4} \times 6 \times 6 = 9\sqrt{3} \text{ cm } ^2$$

: Volume of prism = Area of base $\times$ height

$$\Rightarrow 108\sqrt{3} = 9\sqrt{3} \times h$$

$$\Rightarrow h = \frac{108\sqrt{3}}{9\sqrt{3}} = 12 \text{ cm}$$

Hence, the correct option is (D).

**59.** Speed of boat in still water $= \frac{25}{9} \times \frac{18}{5} = 10 \ km/hr$

Let the speed of stream be $x$ km /hr.

Total time taken to go in upstream $= 10 - x$

Total time taken to go in downstream $= 10 + x$

So,

$$\Rightarrow 65(10 + x) - 60(10 - x) = 9(100 - x^2)$$

$$\Rightarrow 650 + 65x - 600 + 60x = 900 - 9x^2$$

$$\Rightarrow 125x + 50 = 900 - 9x^2$$

$$\Rightarrow 9x^2 + 125x - 850 = 0$$

$$\Rightarrow 9x^2 + 170x - 45x - 850 = 0$$

$$\Rightarrow x(9x + 170) - 5(9x + 170)$$

$$\Rightarrow x = 5 \text{ km/hr}$$

Hence, the correct option is (D).

**60.** Given,

A man invested Rs. 3300 on Simple Interest for two years at the rate of 12 % p.a.

Rs. $x$ on Compound Interest at the rate of 20% p.a. for two years.

If the ratio of Simple Interest to Compound Interest get by man after two years is 9: 10.

Simple Interest $= 3300 \times \frac{12 \times 2}{100} = 792$

$$\frac{\text{Simple Interest}}{\text{Compound Interest}} = \frac{9}{10}$$

Compound Interest $= 792 \times \frac{10}{9} = 880$

$$\Rightarrow x \times \frac{44}{100} = 880$$

$$\Rightarrow x = \text{Rs. } 2000$$

Hence, the correct option is (B).

**61.** Given,

The curved surface area of a cone whose radius is 42 cm, is 7656 cm $^2$.

Curved surface of cone $= \frac{22}{7} \times r \times l = 7656 \ cm^2$

Where $'r'$ is radius and $'l'$ is slant height of cone

$$l = \frac{7656}{22} \times \frac{7}{42} = 58 \ cm$$

Height of cone $= \sqrt{58^2 - 42^2}$

$$h = \sqrt{1600} = 40 \text{ cm}$$

Perimeter of square $= 40 \times 2 = 80$ cm

Side of square $= \frac{80}{4} = 20$ cm

Area of square $= 20^2 = 400$ cm $^2$

Hence, the correct option is (A).

**62.** APPLE $= 5$ letters

But two letters $PP$ is of same kind.

Thus, required permutations,

$$\Rightarrow \frac{5!}{2!}$$

$$\Rightarrow \frac{120}{2}$$

$$\Rightarrow 60$$

Hence, the correct option is (D).

**63.** As given, the ratio of the present age of Abhi and Sam is 5:3.

Let the present ages of Abhi and Sam be $5x$ and $3x$ respectively.

Sam's age after 12 years $= 3x + 12$

According to the question,

$$1.5(5x - 4) = 3x + 12$$

Or, $4.5x = 18$

Or, $x = \dfrac{18}{4.5}$

$\Rightarrow x = 4$

Hence, the correct option is (A).

**64.** Let the radius of sphere be $r$ cm.

Given,

The volume of a sphere $= 2304\pi$ cm

$$\dfrac{4}{3} \times \pi \times r^3 = 2304\pi$$

$\Rightarrow r^3 = 1728$

$\Rightarrow r = 12$ cm

Radius of hemisphere $= 12 \times \dfrac{3}{4} = 9$ cm

Volume of hemisphere $= \dfrac{2}{3} \times \pi \times r^3$

$\Rightarrow \dfrac{2}{3} \times \pi \times 9 \times 9 \times 9$

$\Rightarrow 486\pi$ cm $^3$

Hence, the correct option is (C).

**65.** Given, A train can cross a 150 m long platform in 20 seconds and a pole in 12.5 seconds.

Let the length of the train = $x$ m

According to the question,

$$\dfrac{x}{12.5} = \dfrac{150+x}{20}$$

$\Rightarrow 20x = 12.5x + 1875$

$\Rightarrow 7.5x = 1875$

$\Rightarrow x = 250$

Speed of the train $= \dfrac{250}{12.5}$

$\Rightarrow 20$ m/s or $20 \times \dfrac{18}{5}$

$\Rightarrow 72$ km/h

Hence, the correct option is (B).

**66.** Let the speed of the boat in still water $= a$ km/hr

Then, stream speed $= \dfrac{2a}{3}$ km/h

Now, upstream speed $= a - \dfrac{2a}{3} = \dfrac{a}{3}$

And, downstream speed $= a + \dfrac{2a}{3} = \dfrac{5a}{3}$

Then, $\dfrac{240}{\frac{a}{3}} - \dfrac{240}{\frac{5a}{3}} = 18$

$\Rightarrow a = 32$ km/hr

Hence, the correct option is (D).

**67.** Given,

$? + 727 - 93 = 20\%$ of $50\%$ of $20000$

$\Rightarrow ? + 727 - 93 = .20 \times .50 \times 20000$

$\Rightarrow ? = 2000 - 634$

$\Rightarrow ? = 1366$

Hence, the correct option is (B).

**68.** Given,

$\Rightarrow 4\dfrac{2}{5} + 3\dfrac{1}{3} - 6\dfrac{1}{2} = ?$

$\Rightarrow 4 + 3 - 6 + \left(\dfrac{2}{5} + \dfrac{1}{3} - \dfrac{1}{2}\right) = ?$

$\Rightarrow 1\dfrac{7}{30} = ?$

Hence, the correct option is (B).

**69.** From I:

$\Rightarrow x^2 - 20x + 96 = 0$

$\Rightarrow x^2 - 8x - 12x + 96 = 0$

$\Rightarrow x(x - 8) - 12(x - 8) = 0$

$\Rightarrow (x - 8)(x - 12) = 0$

$\Rightarrow x = 8, 12$

From II:

$\Rightarrow y^2 + 6y - 91 = 0$

$\Rightarrow y^2 - 7y + 13y - 91 = 0$

$\Rightarrow y(y - 7) + 13(y - 7) = 0$

$\Rightarrow (y - 7)(y + 13) = 0$

$\Rightarrow y = 7, -13$

Therefore, $x > y$

Hence, the correct option is (A).

**70.** From I:

$\Rightarrow x^2 + 5x - 36 = 0$

$\Rightarrow x^2 + 9x - 4x - 36 = 0$

$\Rightarrow x(x + 9) - 4(x + 9) = 0$

$\Rightarrow (x + 9)(x - 4) = 0$

$\Rightarrow x = -9, 4$

From II:

$$\Rightarrow y^2 + 24y + 135 = 0$$

$$\Rightarrow y^2 + 9y + 15y + 135 = 0$$

$$\Rightarrow y(y + 9) + 15(y + 9) = 0$$

$$\Rightarrow (y + 9)(y + 15) = 0$$

$$\Rightarrow y = -9, -15$$

Therefore, $x \geq y$

Hence, the correct option is (B).

**71.** Given,

A sum of Rs. 15360 at a 12.5% rate of interest compounded annually.

Principal $=$ Rs. 15360

Rate $= 12.5\%$ per annum

Time $= 3$ years

Compound Interest $= 15360 \times \left[ \left(1 + \frac{12.5}{100}\right)^3 - 1 \right]$ = Rs. $6510$

Hence, the correct option is (D).

**72.** Given,

A is 8 years younger than B and 6 years elder than C.

And the present age of B and D is 30 years and 24 years.

According to the question,

Present age of A = 30 – 8 = 22 years

Present age of C = 22 – 6 = 16 years

Required ratio = 16:24 = 2:3

Hence, the correct option is (D).

**73.** Given,

Time is taken by A to complete the work = 32 days

Time taken by B to complete the work = 32 – 8 = 24 days

The ratio of efficiencies is the inverse of the number of days taken

Therefore, ratio of efficiencies of A to B = 24 : 32 = 3 : 4

Wage received by A $= 1050 \times \frac{3}{7} =$ Rs. $450$

Hence, the correct option is (B).

**74.** Given,

A bag contains 3 red, 4 blue and 3 green balls.

Total balls = 10

Required probability,

$$\Rightarrow \frac{^7C_2}{^{10}C_2}$$

$$\Rightarrow \frac{7}{15}$$

Hence, the correct option is (D).

**75.** We know that, ' $n$' different objects can be arranged in a circle in $(n - 1)!$ ways

$\therefore$ Number of ways to arrange 8 different beads to form a necklace

$$= (8 - 1)! = 7! = 7 \times 6 \times 5 \times 4 \times 3 \times 2 \times 1 = 5040$$

But, in case of arranging beads to form necklace, both clockwise and anticlockwise arrangement will be same.

$\therefore$ Actual number of ways to arrange $8$ different beads to form a necklace

$$= \frac{5040}{2} = 2520$$

Hence, the correct option is (A).

**76.** The blank 'A' will take the word "planned" because the context of the passage is the planning, from the execution of that we get comfortable. All other options fail to convey any appropriate meaning.

Hence, the correct option is (A).

**77.** The blank 'B' will take the word "pulled" as carpet cannot be pushed but pulled and the intended meaning is to disbalance someone if the carpet under them get pulled, so since we all got disbalanced in 2020 so 'pulled' is the appropriate word.

Hence, the correct option is (B).

**78.** The blank 'C' will take the word "uncertainty" because the context is of disbalancing, disbalancing of economy employment etc for which the word that need to be used is 'uncertainty'.

Hence, the correct option is (A).

**79.** The blank 'D' will take the word "tolerate", since the context is of uncertainty which is not a good thing to experience is life but people have to face it, and to express this the word that need to be used is to 'tolerate' is we tolerate the uncertainty.

Hence, the correct option is (C).

**80.** The blank (E) will take the word "Unpredictability" overwhelm has the context of expressing 'difficult to fight against', and the thing which needed to be fought with is 'unpredictability', the unpredictability of life.

Hence, the correct option is (D).

**81.** The correct phrase is 'look down on' which means to regard (someone) with a feeling of superiority.

Then the sentence is,

We should never look down **on** a person merely because he is poor.

Hence, the correct option is (B).

**82.** Replace "below' with "under" as it is used to show something directly below something, whereas below or above is used to show level in the context of comparison.

Then the sentence,

The voyager took rest **under** the shade of a large banyan tree.

Hence, the correct option is (A).

**83.** Boast: talk with excessive pride and self-satisfaction about one's achievements, possessions, or abilities

Pride: Vanity

Dry: Seared

Revive: Soothe

Sly: Mischievous

Hence, the correct option is (C).

**84.** Haste: Excessive speed or urgency of movement or action

Hurry: Spank

Fiat: Prospect

Murky: Faded

Impact: Effect

Hence, the correct option is (D).

**85.** 'whereas' is used in contrast or comparison with the fact that is previously stated.

Then the sentence is

Pensions are linked to inflation, whereas they should be linked to the cost of living.

Hence, the correct option is (B).

**86.** "almost as soon as" will be used in place of "no sooner then".

Then the sentence is,

"I went to the last lecture, almost as soon as I got reminded of it."

Hence, the correct option is (A).

**87.** To show the context of possession or having 'with' is used, and since the Western Ghats have different snakes, thus for that 'with' is the correct preposition to use.

The sentence is,

The Western Ghats have infested **with** different snakes.

Hence, the correct option is (C).

**88.** The ball is in your court is the correct idiom which means 'it is your responsibility to take action next'.

Hence, the correct option is (A).

**89.** The use of 'had' clearly indicates that the third form of the verb is required here. 'Stricken' is an adjective and the verb forms of strike are - strike - struck - struck. But 'stricken' is also used as the past participle of 'strike'.

The sentence,

The cold breath of autumn had **struck** the ivy leaves from the vine and the branches remained almost bare.

Hence, the correct option is (D).

**90.** "took over as the" is the correct phrase to make the sentence grammatically correct. Read the sentence carefully, later part of the sentence suggests that "took over" is the correct phrasal verb to add meaning to the sentence. The phrasal verb "take over" means an act of assuming control of something.

The sentence is,

M Venkaiah Naidu **took over as the** Vice President of India in a smooth transition after the term of Hamid Ansari ended on August 9.

Hence, the correct option is (B).

**91.** "that has been crafted" is the correct phrase to make the sentence grammatically correct. It is to be noted that the sentence is in Passive form. Moreover the preposition "by" is correct usage as it signifies the action performed by distinguished brains in America's science fraternity.

The sentence is

There are two facets to the National Climate Assessment **that has been crafted** by distinguished brains in America's science fraternity.

Hence, the correct option is (D).

**92.** Coarse: Consisting of large pieces; rough, not smooth

Fine: Happy and comfortable

Gritty: Showing bravery and spirit

Gravelly: Resembling, containing, or consisting of gravel

Grainy: Not smooth or fine

Hence, the correct option is (A).

**93.** Apathetic: Lacking interest or desire to act

Concerned: Worried and feeling concern about something

Agitated: Worried or excited

Happy: Feeling or showing pleasure; pleased

Surprised: Feeling or showing surprise

Hence, the correct option is (C).

**94.** The bracketed part is incorrect because "regret" is not followed by any preposition. So, 'regret for' needs to be replaced with 'regret' to make the sentence grammatically correct.

Hence, the correct option is (C).

**95.** The underlined word is a noun. It is a Material Noun. Material Noun refers to a material or substance from which things are made.

Hence, the correct option is (C).

**96.** The phrase "cook the books" means alter facts or figures dishonestly or illegally.

Example: He was an accountant, he could have cooked the books and made himself a lot more money.

Hence, the correct option is (A).

**97.** The phrase "to vote with your feet" means "to show your opinion by leaving an organization or by no longer supporting, using, or buying something."

Example:

When the price of skiing doubled, tourists voted with their feet and just stopped going.

Hence, the correct option is (A).

**98.** 'Until' is the most appropriate preposition to fill the blank, as the preposition until is describing the time span of an action or occurrence of something before a specific time.

Hence, the correct option is (A).

**99.** One word substitution is Ascetic.

Ascetic: Characterized by severe self-discipline and abstention from all forms of indulgence, typically for religious reasons

Sceptic: A person inclined to question or doubt accepted opinions

Devotee: A person who is very interested in and enthusiastic about someone or something

Antiquarian: Relating to or dealing in antiques or rare books

Hence, the correct option is (B).

**100.** The correct spelling is 'Accomplish'.

Accomplish: To succeed in doing something difficult that you planned to do

Example: I managed to accomplish my goal of writing ten letters a day.

Hence, the correct option is (A).

## General Intelligence & Reasoning

**Q.1** Each question given below consists of a statement, followed by two arguments numbered I and II. Decide which of the arguments is a 'strong' argument and which is a 'weak' argument and choose the corresponding option as your answer.

Should breakfast be provided by schools to its students?

I. Yes, schools are the best places to ensure good nutrition.

II. No, a school breakfast for all is a greater cost on schools.

**A.** I only

**B.** II only

**C.** I and II both

**D.** Neither I nor II

**Q.2 Direction:** Consider the given statement and decide which of the given assumptions is(are) implicit.

**Statement:** Ramesh said to Mahesh, "Nowadays it is cheaper to take a flight than to take a train".

**Assumptions:**

1. Mahesh usually takes the train.

2. Ramesh makes travel arrangements for people.

**A.** Only assumption 1 is implicit

**B.** Only assumption 2 is implicit

**C.** Both assumptions are implicit

**D.** Neither assumption 1 nor assumption 2 is implicit

**Q.3** Find the one from option figures, which will replace the question mark from question figures.

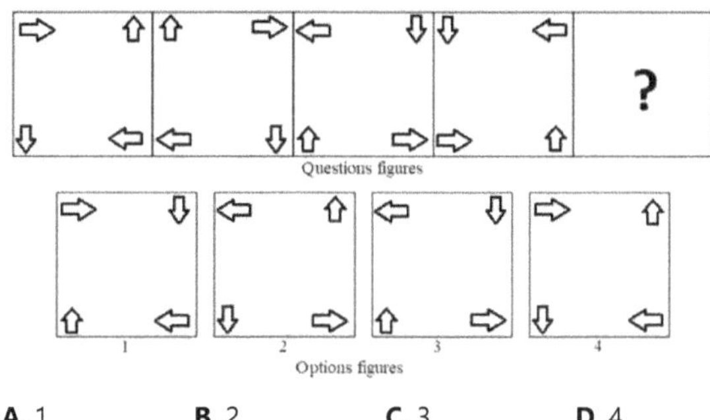

**A.** 1    **B.** 2    **C.** 3    **D.** 4

**Q.4** Identify the diagram that best represents the relationship among classes given below:

Beverage, Aerated drink, Coke

a)

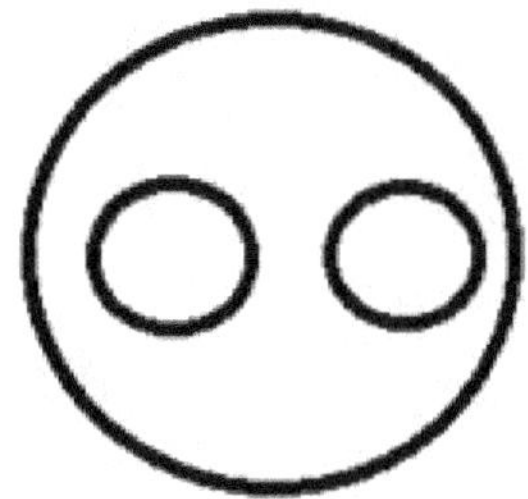

b)

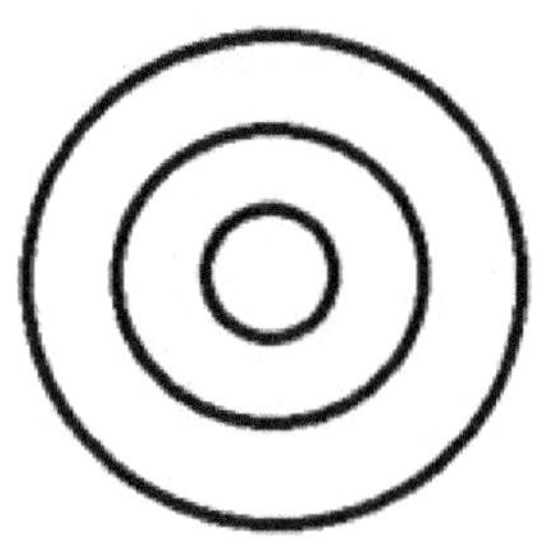

c)

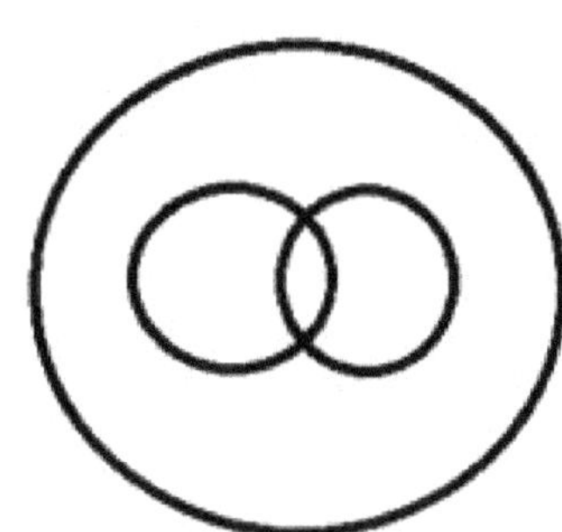

d)

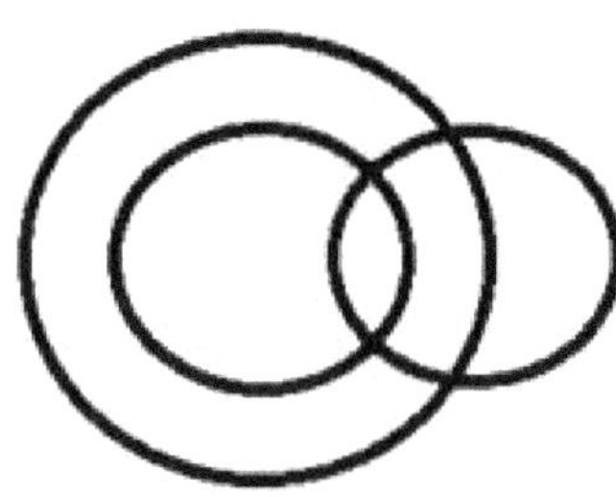

**A.** a    **B.** b    **C.** c    **D.** d

**Q.5** One figure is not like the other three. Choose the figure which is different from the rest.

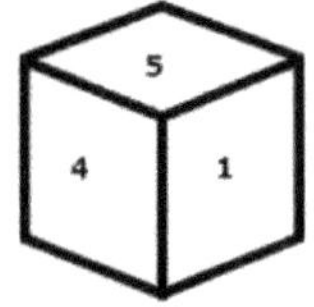 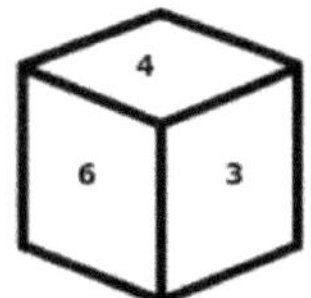 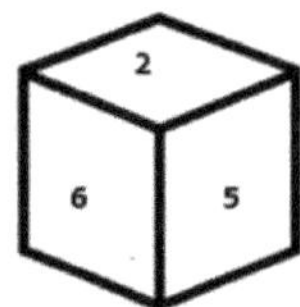

(A)    (B)    (C)    (D)

**A.** A     **B.** B     **C.** C     **D.** D

**Q.6 Direction**: Answer according to the analogy given:

Ornithologist : Bird :: Archaeologist : ?

**A.** Islands     **B.** Mediators
**C.** Archaeology     **D.** Aquatic

**Q.7** If "Lion" is called "Rabbit", Tiger is called "Hen", Wolf is called "Cow" and Deer is called "Leopard" then which of the following represents a herbivore?

**A.** Rabbit     **B.** Cow     **C.** Leopard     **D.** Hen

**Q.8** The questions below are to be answered on the basis of the three views of a cube given as follows:

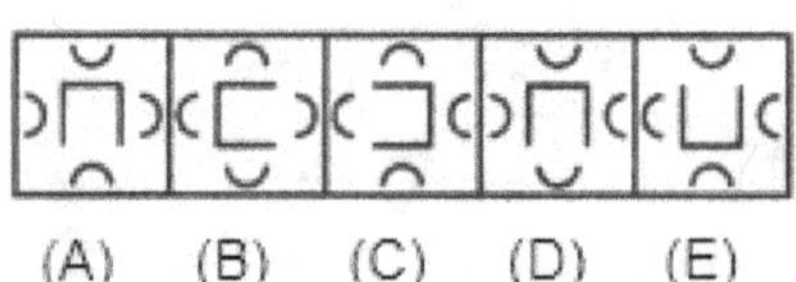

Which number is on the face opposite to 4?

**A.** 3     **B.** 2
**C.** 6     **D.** None of the above

**Q.9** If '%' means 'x', '$' means '-', '&' means '÷', and '@' means '+' then 65 % 7 & 13 @ 8 % 6 $ 5 = ?

**A.** 87     **B.** 78     **C.** 48     **D.** 44

**Q.10** In an organization, If Operational officer decides to quit his job; How the management of the organization has to deal with this situation:

**A.** The management should immediately offer him a very good hike in salary

**B.** The management should ask him to put his papers and leave

**C.** The management should ask him to put his papers and leave

**D.** The management should conduct a formal farewell for the person

**Q.11** Select a figure from amongst the Answer Figures which will continue the same series as established by the five Problem Figures.

**Problem Figures:**

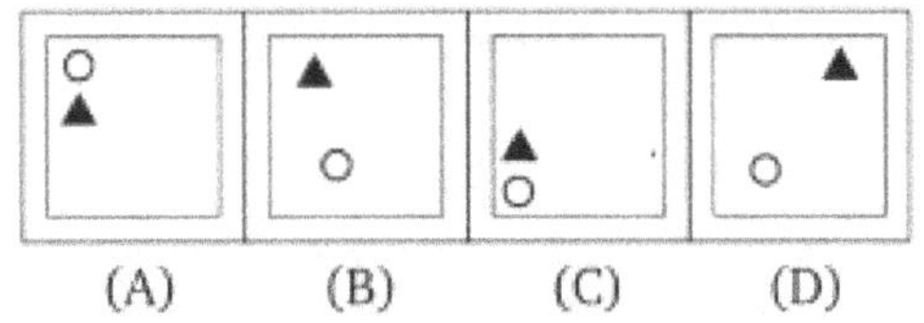

(A)    (B)    (C)    (D)    (E)

**Answer Figures:**

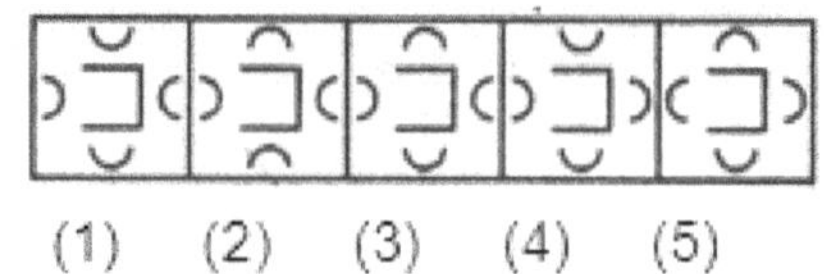

(1)    (2)    (3)    (4)    (5)

**A.** 1     **B.** 2     **C.** 3     **D.** 5

**Q.12** Find the odd one out:

**A.** 147     **B.** 159     **C.** 379     **D.** 579

**Q.13** Find the odd one out:

**A.** ABB     **B.** BCF     **C.** CDL     **D.** DES

**Q.14** If a mirror is placed on the given line, then which of the following answer figure is right image of the given figure?

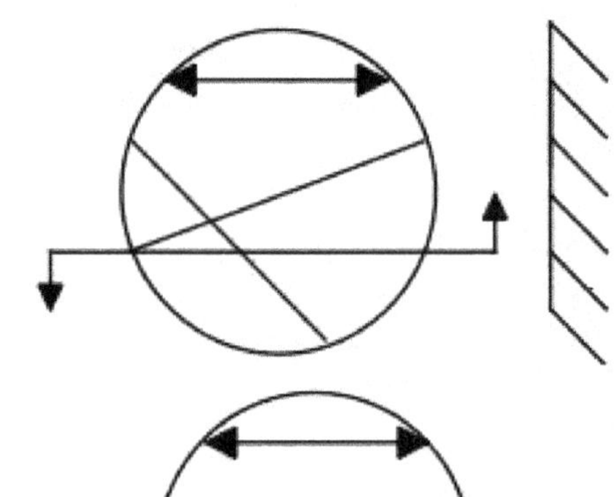

**A.** 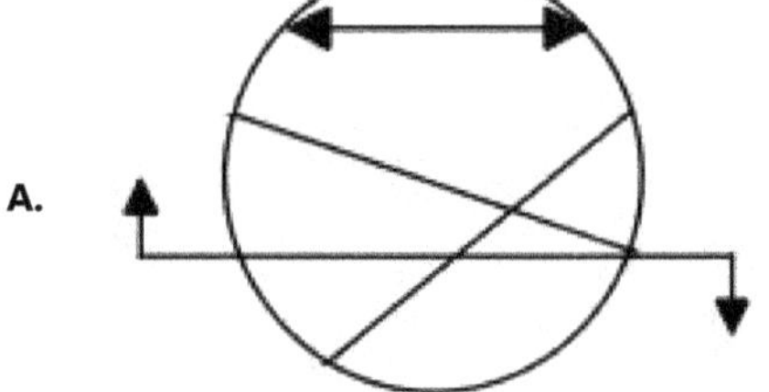

**B.** 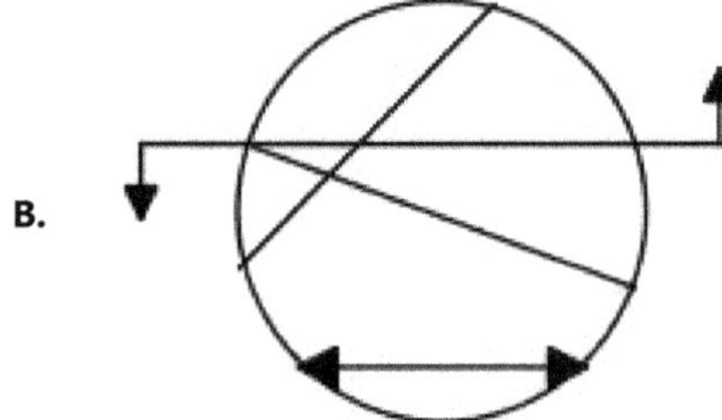

**C.** 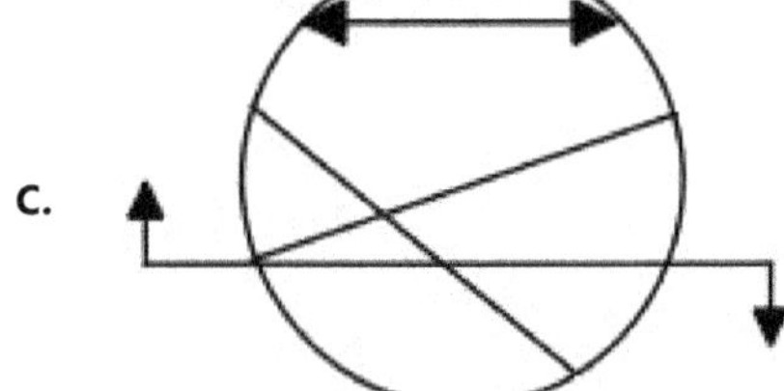

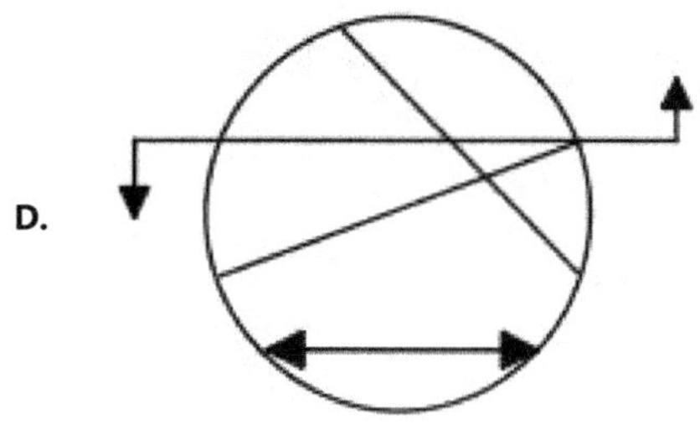

**D.**

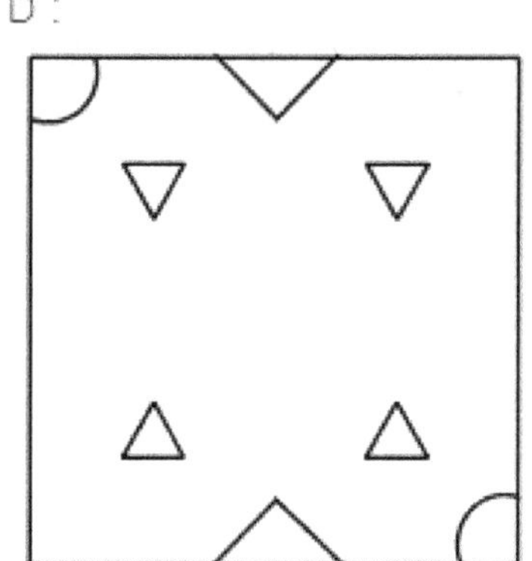

D :

**Q.15** A piece of paper is folded and cut as shown in the question figures. From the given answer figures, indicate how it will appear when opened.

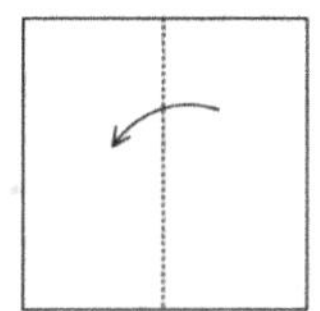 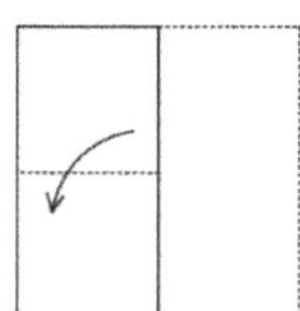 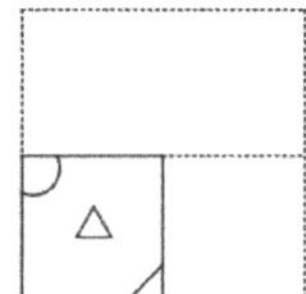

A

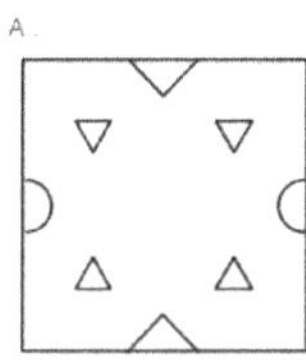

B :

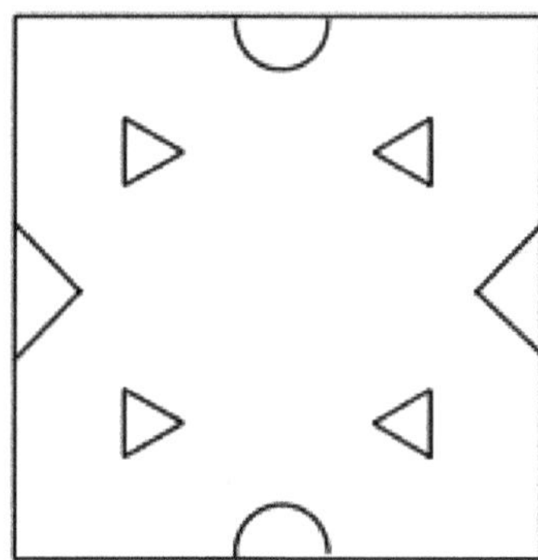

C :

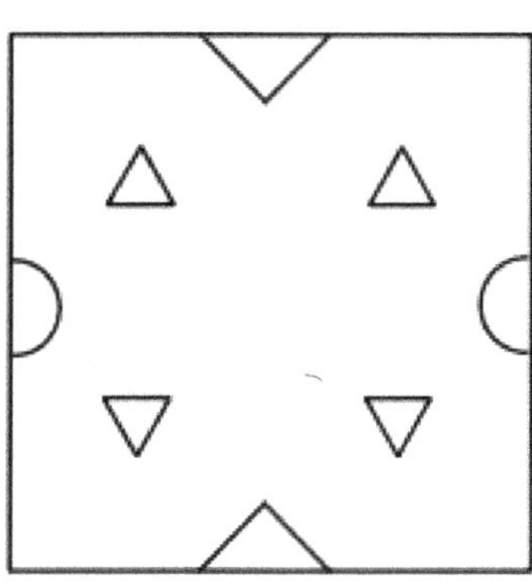

**A.** A      **B.** B      **C.** C      **D.** D

**Q.16** A bag contains an equal number of one rupee, 25 paise and 20 paise coins respectively. If the total value is Rs 58, how many coins of each type are there?

**A.** 40 coins    **B.** 18 coins    **C.** 22 coins    **D.** 55 coins

**Q.17** P is mother of Q and R, where P has no sons. S and T are daughters of Q, where U is father of S and T. How is S and T related to R?

**A.** Daughters      **B.** Cousin
**C.** Brother      **D.** Niece

**Q.18** Find the odd one out:

**A.** Bats: Screech      **B.** Snakes: Hiss
**C.** Turkeys: Squeak      **D.** Whales: Sing

**Q.19** Complete the series:
24, 13, 15, 34, ?

**A.** 142    **B.** 144    **C.** 146    **D.** 140

**Q.20** Complete the series:
3, 4, 8, 17, 33, ?

**A.** 68    **B.** 57    **C.** 58    **D.** 63

**Q.21** Count the number of triangles in the following figure.

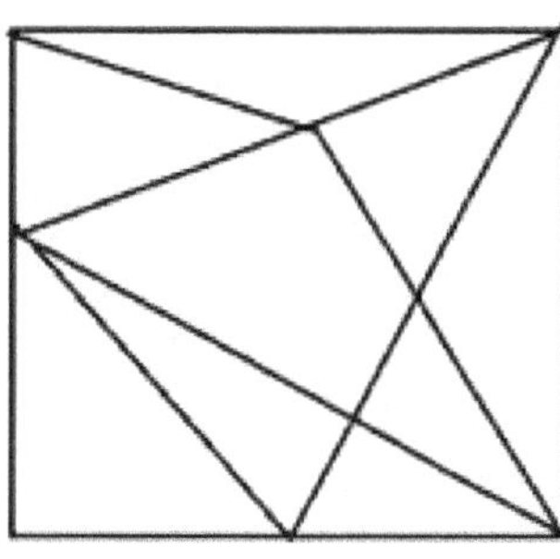

**A.** 16    **B.** 18    **C.** 20    **D.** 24

**Q.22** In a certain code 'STONE' is coded as '36521' and 'RAIN' is coded as '7842'. In the same code how will 'STATION' be coded as?

**A.** 3685462    **B.** 3686452    **C.** 3686425    **D.** 3676352

**Q.23** In each of the following questions, you are given a figure (X) followed by four alternative figures (a), (b), (c) and (d) such that figure (X) is embedded in one of them. Trace out the alternative figure which contains fig. (X) as its part.

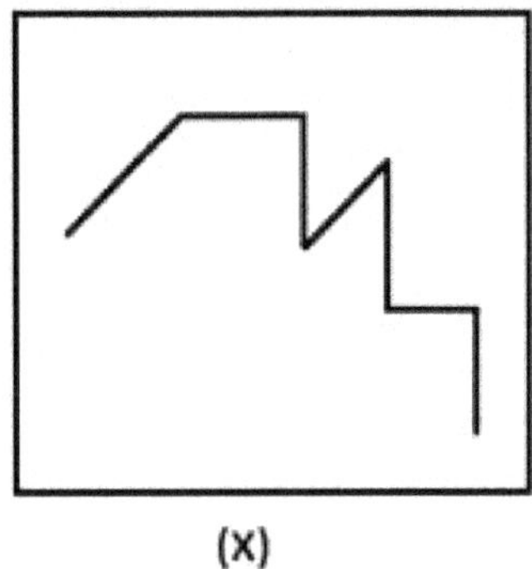

(X)

a)

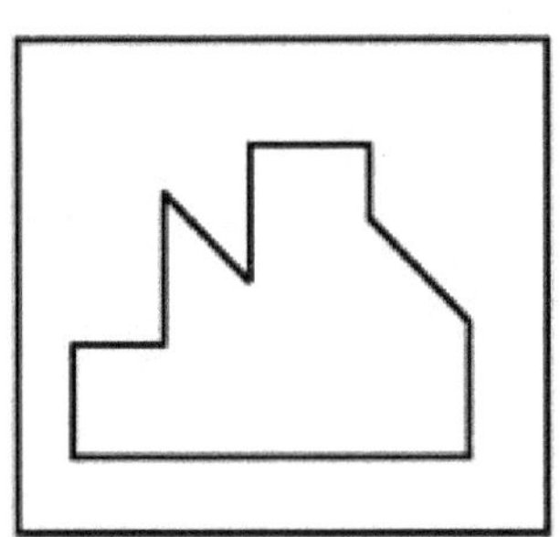

b)

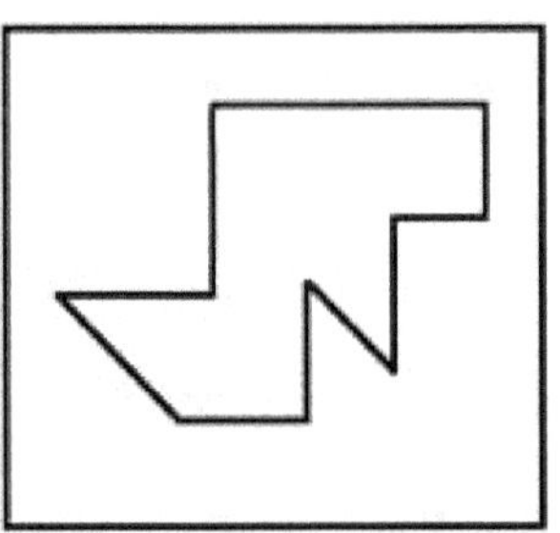

c)

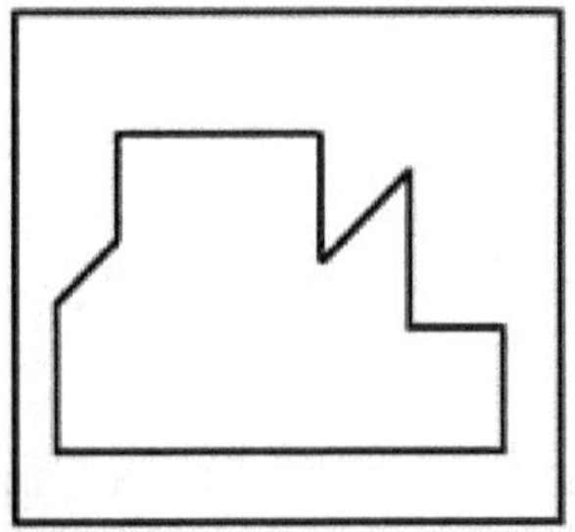

d)

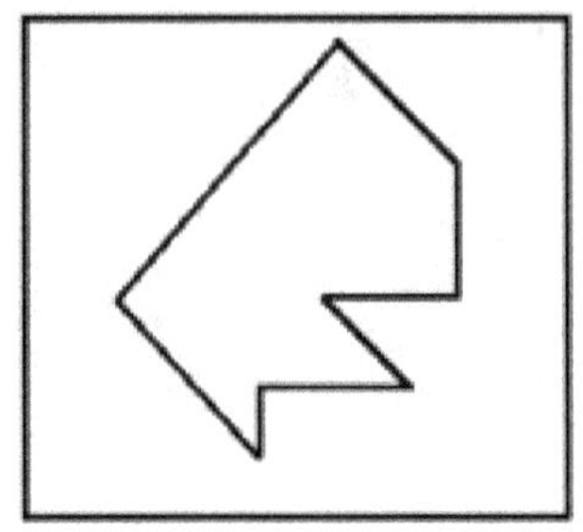

**A.** a)     **B.** b)     **C.** c)     **D.** d)

**Q.24** In a certain code if 'HUMAN' is coded as 'OZNTI' and 'STORY' is coded as 'ZQPST' then how will 'BREAD' be coded as in the same code?

**A.** EZDQC     **B.** EZFSC     **C.** EZFQC     **D.** EBFSC

**Q.25** If DRIBBLE is related to FOOTBALL, in the same way RALLY is related to _____ .

**A.** CHESS            **B.** BADMINTON

**C.** BASKETBALL      **D.** HOCKEY

# General Awareness

**Q.26** Who assassinated W.C. Rand, the Plague Commissioner of Pune in 1897?

**A.** Ganesh Savarkar

**B.** Chapekar Brothers

**C.** Vasudev Balwant Phadke

**D.** Chiplunkar Brothers

**Q.27** What is the minimum net worth required for Scheduled Commercial Banks to issue Credit Cards?

**A.** Rs 10 Crores       **B.** Rs 50 Crores

**C.** Rs 100 Crores     **D.** Rs 500 Crores

**Q.28** Jharkhand CM Hemant Soren has launched Jharkhand ____ Policy 2022 in Ranchi on 13th September 2022?

**A.** Farmer's         **B.** Sports

**C.** Unskilled Labour    **D.** All of the above

**Q.29** The Nobel Memorial Prize in Economic Sciences 2022 was awarded to three scientists for their research in which field?

**A.** Behavioural Economics

**B.** Global Poverty

**C.** Banks and Financial Crises

**D.** Quantitative Methods

**Q.30** Financial Assistance to Non-School Going Disabled Children (less than 18 years) is the Financial Assistance Scheme of which Department of State Government of Haryana?

*[Haryana Police Constable Commando Wing, 2021]*

**A.** Finance

**B.** Women and Child Development

**C.** Social Justice and Empowerment

**D.** Health and Family Welfare

**Q.31** Who among the following has received the first ever Philip Kotler Presidential Award?

A. Piyush Goyal
B. Narendra Modi
C. Manmohan Singh
D. Ram Nath Kovind

**Q.32** The time duration during which one can return the purchased policy to the insurer is called _______.
A. Recurring period
B. Vesting period
C. Free look period
D. Waiting period

**Q.33** Which among the following covers the monetary and asset losses due to fraudulent employee action?
A. Fidelity Bond
B. Surety Bond
C. Guarantee Bond
D. Fiduciary Bond

**Q.34** In the Economical terms, what does 'P' mean in WPI?
A. Price     B. Point     C. Plan     D. Paying

**Q.35** The Attorney General is the Law officer of Government of India. He/She is appointed by _______.
A. President of India
B. Chief justice of India
C. Vice President of India
D. Prime Minister of India

**Q.36** Which article of Indian Constitution describes the Abolition of Untouchability?
A. Article 19
B. Article 17
C. Article 24
D. Article 21

**Q.37** What is the maximum age limit of a Chief Judge of a High Court?
A. 60 years     B. 65 years     C. 62 years     D. 67 years

**Q.38** Which type of inflation is an extremely fast or out-of-control inflation?
A. Stagflation
B. Creeping Inflation
C. Super Inflation
D. Hyperinflation

**Q.39** Nyokum Festival is celebrated in which among the following states?
A. Arunachal Pradesh
B. Bihar
C. Jammu and Kashmir
D. Assam

**Q.40** Pritzker Prize is associated with which field?
A. Science and technology
B. Architecture
C. Sports
D. Journalism

**Q.41** The layer below earth's crust is called _________.
A. Inner Core
B. Outer Core
C. Mantle
D. Sedimentary layer

**Q.42** Who invented the first-ever safety elevator?
A. Bill Gates
B. Elisha Otis
C. Paul Allan
D. Dave Hyatt

**Q.43** Ain-i-Akbari was written in the 16th century Mughal India by whom among the following?
A. Birbal
B. Todar Mal

C. Abul Fazl
D. Fa-Hien

**Q.44** Under whose rule the Mughal arts and painting reached to its zenith?
A. Humayun
B. Akbar
C. Jahangir
D. Shah Jahan

**Q.45** Krishna river originates from which among the following states?
A. Chhattisgarh
B. Madhya Pradesh
C. Maharashtra
D. Karnataka

**Q.46** Who was the first Indian to become the Governor-General of Independent India?
A. Jawahar Lal Nehru
B. Mahatma Gandhi
C. C Rajagopalachari
D. Rajendra Prasad

**Q.47** Match the following cultural dances with their respective states.

| A. Kathakali | a. Assam |
|---|---|
| B. Bharatnatyam | b. Rajasthan |
| C. Sattriya | c. Tamil Nadu |
| D. Ghoomar | d. Kerala |

A. A-d, B-a, C-c, D-b
B. A-c, B-d, C-a, D-b
C. A-d, B-c, C-a, D-b
D. A-d, B-c, C-b, D-a

**Q.48** Dublin is the capital of which of the following nation?
A. Bulgaria     B. Ireland     C. Norway     D. Spain

**Q.49** When is World Consumer Rights Day celebrated?
A. June 20
B. April 22
C. September 27
D. March 15

**Q.50** Which Indian Pace bowler achieved the milestone of 200 Test wickets recently?
A. Mohammed Shami
B. Ravichandran Ashwin
C. Ravindra Jadeja
D. Jasprit Bumrah

# Quantitative Aptitude

**Q.51** A shopkeeper bought shampoo packets of 2 varieties. First variety cost him 11 for Rs 10 and Second variety cost him 9 for Rs 10. He sells both at the rate of 1 for Rs.1. Then in the whole transaction, he:
A. Gains 1
B. Loss 1%
C. Gains 2%
D. Loss 2%

**Q.52** A number 1a2b3c is divisible by 11. What are the values possible for (a, b, c)?
A. (4, 0, 2)     B. (4, 5, 3)     C. (5, 2, 7)     D. (5, 3, 6)

**Q.53** Select the correct option:
Convert decimal 131 to binary.
A. 10001101
B. 1000011
C. 10000011
D. 1100001

**Q.54** Person P takes 36 days to finish a work alone while to finish 75% of that work person Q takes $41\left(\frac{2}{3}\right)\%$ of time taken by P to finish the complete work. Q is 20% more efficient than R, then in how many days persons P and R together can finish that work?

**A.** 14.4 days  **B.** 16.2 days
**C.** 12.8 days  **D.** 18.2 days

**Q.55** What is the value of:
7 x 4 ÷ 204 x 120 x 20 - 18 x 3 - 2 x 34
**A.** 678  **B.** 644  **C.** 632  **D.** 625

**Q.56** What is the unit digit of $312^{86} + 125^{29}$?
**A.** 7  **B.** 9  **C.** 1  **D.** 3

**Q.57** Find the value of 'b' in the equation given below.
30% of b% of 296 = 40% of 50% of 5% of 1480
**A.** $\frac{50}{3}$  **B.** $\frac{40}{3}$  **C.** $\frac{125}{3}$  **D.** $\frac{80}{3}$

**Q.58** 100 cards are numbered from 1 to 100. Find the probability of getting a prime number.
**A.** $\frac{3}{4}$  **B.** $\frac{27}{50}$  **C.** $\frac{1}{4}$  **D.** $\frac{29}{100}$

**Q.59** The H.C.F and L.C.M of two numbers is 11 and 7700. If one of the numbers is 275, find the other number:
**A.** 279  **B.** 283  **C.** 308  **D.** 318

**Q.60** The quadratic equation whose one rational root is $3 + \sqrt{2}$ is:
**A.** $x^2 - 7x + 5 = 0$  **B.** $x^2 + 7x + 6 = 0$
**C.** $x^2 - 7x + 6 = 0$  **D.** $x^2 - 6x + 7 = 0$

**Q.61** P and Q started a business in the ratio of 2 : 3. After 1 year P left the business but Q continues. After 2 years he had profit of Rs. 26000. What is the profit of Q?
**A.** Rs. 10400  **B.** Rs. 13000
**C.** Rs. 15600  **D.** None of these

**Q.62** If $x = y = 2z$ and $xyz = 32$, find the value of $x$:
**A.** 4  **B.** 8  **C.** 32  **D.** 64

**Q.63** The cost of an orange is $33\frac{1}{3}\%$ less than the cost of 1 mango. If a man sells four oranges at the cost price of 5 mangoes, what is his percentage of profit?
**A.** 75%  **B.** 81%  **C.** 87.5%  **D.** 90%

**Q.64** If a right circular cone of height 24 cm has a volume of 1232 cm³, then the area of its curved surface (take $\pi = \frac{22}{7}$ is):
**A.** 1254 cm²  **B.** 704 cm²
**C.** 550 cm²  **D.** 154 cm²

**Q.65** 3 years ago, the average age of Rahul's family consisting of 6 members was 35 years. One year ago a new baby born in this family. Four years hence the average age of the family will be?
**A.** $36\frac{5}{7}$ years  **B.** 40 years
**C.** 37 years  **D.** 68 years

**Q.66** The cost of fencing a rectangular park is Rs. 20 per meter. Find the total cost of fencing if the area is 2420 m² and ratio of sides is 4 : 5-
**A.** Rs. 3980  **B.** Rs. 3960  **C.** Rs. 1980  **D.** Rs. 7920

**Q.67** Priyanka travels at the speed of 45 kmph for 5.4 hours and 39 kmph for 7 hours. In this way she covers four-fifths of the distance. At what average speed should she travel to cover the remaining distance in 3 hours?
**A.** 52 kmph  **B.** 38 kmph  **C.** 43 kmph  **D.** 48 kmph

**Q.68** Garima Garg deposited ₹5000 for 6 years, ₹4500 for 8 years, and ₹6500 for 4 years with same rate of simple interest. She received a total simple interest of ₹4600. What is the rate of interest per annum?
**A.** 8%  **B.** 7%  **C.** 6%  **D.** 5%

**Q.69** The total salary of two employees, A and B, in an organization is Rs. 40,000. After increasing salary of A by 9% and B by 11%, the total salary becomes Rs. 44100. Calculate the salary of A.
**A.** Rs. 25000  **B.** Rs. 15000
**C.** Rs. 18000  **D.** None of the above

**Q.70** Ratio of two numbers is 3 : 8. On adding 5 to both numbers, the ratio becomes 2 : 5. Which is the smaller number out of the two?
**A.** 64  **B.** 120  **C.** 45  **D.** 105

**Q.71** How many litres of water should be added to a 30 litre mixture of milk and water containing milk and water in the ratio of 7 : 3 such that the resultant mixture has 40% water in it?
**A.** 5  **B.** 2  **C.** 3  **D.** 8

**Q.72** In a colony, there are 55 members. Every member posts a greeting card to all the members. How many greeting cards were posted by them?
**A.** 990  **B.** 890  **C.** 2970  **D.** 1980

**Q.73** Three pipes A, B and C can fill a tank from empty to full in 30 minutes, 20 minutes, and 10 minutes respectively. When the tank is empty, all the three pipes are opened. A, B and C discharge chemical solutions P, Q and R respectively. What is the proportion of the solution R in the liquid in the tank after 3 minutes?
**A.** $\frac{5}{11}$  **B.** $\frac{6}{11}$  **C.** $\frac{7}{11}$  **D.** $\frac{8}{11}$

**Q.74** A boat can travel with a speed of 13 km/hr in still water. If the speed of the stream is 4 km/hr, find the time taken by the boat to go 68 km downstream.
**A.** 2 hours  **B.** 3 hours  **C.** 4 hours  **D.** 5 hours

**Q.75** In how much time will the 100-meter long train cross the 140-meter long bridge at a speed of 60 km per hour?
**A.** 3.6 sec  **B.** 7.2 sec  **C.** 14.4 sec  **D.** 21.6 sec

# English Comprehension

**Ques (76-80):Direction:** For the question below, a passage is given with five blanks. Choose the correct words to be filled in each blank.

She is one of the first ______(1) I started following on YouTube. She makes content on vegan food, finding balance, motivation, and all lifestyle things. Her ______(2) of content creation is very ______(3), and her vlogs are to die for. What I particularly like about her is that she actively talks about mental health and issues that are generally considered a ______(4). So, if you haven't checked out her channel yet, please do so ______(5).

**Q.76** Fill in the correct word which fits blank 1?

**A.** human    **B.** person    **C.** persons    **D.** woman

**Q.77** Fill in the blank which fits the blank 2?

**A.** produce    **B.** style    **C.** address    **D.** make

**Q.78** Fill in the blank which fits the blank 3?

**A.** innovate        **B.** style

**C.** absorbent       **D.** interesting

**Q.79** Fill in the blank which fits blank 4?

**A.** taboo        **B.** encouragement

**C.** acceptance     **D.** legal

**Q.80** Fill in the blank which fits blank 5?

**A.** directly        **B.** exactly

**C.** immediately     **D.** squarely

**Q.81** Which of the following sentence is correct?

**A.** Ritu was carrying the glasses in a tray.

**B.** I have allot of money with me.

**C.** The so-called 'hotel' was just an old shed.

**D.** Close the door at once.

**Q.82** In the below question, a sentence has been given in **Active/Passive Voice.** Out of the four alternatives suggested, select the one which best expresses the same sentence in Passive/Active Voice.

You should have done the assignment weeks ago.

**A.** The assignment should have been doing by you weeks ago.

**B.** The assignment should have done by you weeks ago.

**C.** The assignment should be done by you weeks ago.

**D.** The assignment should have been done by you weeks ago.

**Q.83** In the following question, some part of the sentence may have errors. Find out which part of the sentence has an error and select the appropriate option. If a sentence is free from error, select 'No Error'.

The journey was a great undertaking (1)/ in those days, especially (2)/ to people of small means. (3)/ No error (4)

**A.** 1    **B.** 3    **C.** 2    **D.** 4

**Q.84** A part of the sentence is bracketed. Below are given alternatives to the bracketed part which may improve the sentence. Choose the correct alternative. In case no improvement is required, choose **"No Improvement"** option.

She is living (independent from) her parents now.

**A.** independent off      **B.** independent of

**C.** independent on      **D.** No improvement

**Q.85** In the following question, some part of the sentence may have errors. Find out which part of the sentence has an error and select the appropriate option. If a sentence is free from error, select 'No Error'.

Between the men who fought for the South (1)/ were some of the bravest soldiers (2)/ and truest men in all history. (3)/ No error (4)

**A.** 4    **B.** 3    **C.** 2    **D.** 1

**Q.86** Sentence/passage is split into four/five parts and named A, B, C, D & E. These four parts are not given in their proper order. Read the sentence or passage and find out which of the four combinations is correct. Then find the correct answer.

A. they find some

B. industrious as these peasants are

C. in their spare time

D. minor occupations

**A.** ADCB    **B.** BCDA    **C.** DCAB    **D.** BADC

**Q.87** Choose the option that best fits the blanks in the sentence.

When writers ______ ideas or things, they ______ them with human-like characteristics.

**A.** Enunciate, Undo      **B.** Inculcate, Deride

**C.** Acclimatize, Bribe     **D.** Personify, Endow

**Ques (88-92):Directions:** Read the passage given below and then answer the question given below the passage.

The worst days of any summer are the rainy ones. We spend all year looking forward to nice weather and long, hot days. And then, summer comes, and it rains. As a child, I would wake up to rainy summer days and come close to crying. On those rainy summer days, I had nothing fun to do and could only sit inside, staring out at the rain like a Dickensian orphan. I was an only child, so there was no one else to play with. I'd crawl through the day and pray each night that the rain would not be there the next day. As an adult, though, my opinion of summer rain has changed. When you have to work every day, summer is not as eagerly anticipated. Everything seems monotonous and dull, and an ennui or listlessness kicks in. Such a mind set makes you cheer for anything new or different. Rainy days are still the worst days of the summer, but summer rain today means positively beautiful - and considerably cooler - weather tomorrow.

**Q.88** The passage makes use of language that is -

**A.** Metaphorical      **B.** Rhetorical

**C.** Formal           **D.** Ambiguous

**Q.89** According to the passage, summer is different for adults because -

**A.** rain brings with it cold temperatures for the following days

**B.** the weather is much warmer than it is for children

**C.** they do not get a long time off from work for the season

**D.** they better know how to occupy their downtime

**Q.90** According to the passage, which of the following is a true statement about the narrator as a child?

**A.** He or she was often bored on summer days.

**B.** He or she preferred cooler weather.

**C.** He or she liked staying indoors.

**D.** He or she had no siblings.

**Q.91** Compared to how he or she was as a child, the narrator as an adult is:

**A.** More realistic      **B.** Less excitable
**C.** More idealistic      **D.** Less calm

**Q.92** Which of the following generalisations can be made, based on the passage?

**A.** For an adult, summer rains are welcome.
**B.** For a child, summer rains are a bad thing.
**C.** For an adult, life seems monotonous.
**D.** All the above.

**Q.93** In the following question, choose the word opposite in meaning to the given word.
Robust

**A.** Sturdy      **B.** Frail      **C.** Eager      **D.** Glum

**Q.94** Select the word which is opposite in meaning to the word given.
Flabby

**A.** Long      **B.** Firm
**C.** Weak      **D.** Stretched

**Q.95** In each of the question below, a phrase is given. From the options, choose the one that sums up the meaning of the given phrase in one word.
An unconventional style of living

**A.** Cynosure      **B.** Apostate
**C.** Debonair      **D.** Bohemian

**Q.96** In the following options, four words are given, out of which only one word is correctly spelt. Find the correctly spelt word.

**A.** Arguement      **B.** Concensus
**C.** Independant      **D.** Embarrass

**Q.97** In the following options, four words are given, out of which only one word is correctly spelt. Find the correctly spelt word.

**A.** Inadvertant      **B.** Indispensable
**C.** Persaverance      **D.** Privelege

**Q.98 In the following question, a sentence given with a blank to be filled in with an appropriate word. Four alternatives are suggested for the question. Choose the correct alternative out of the four and indicate it by selecting the appropriate option.**
One thing that tends to happen with telecommuters is that their entire _______ becomes their office space.

**A.** forebode      **B.** forbade      **C.** abode      **D.** remote

**Q.99** In the following question, out of the four alternatives, choose the one which best expresses the meaning of the given word.
Astute

**A.** Brood      **B.** Crude      **C.** Shrewd      **D.** Impolite

**Q.100 Direction:** Select the word which means the same as the group of words given.

A movement or action of the hands or face

**A.** Action      **B.** Gesture      **C.** Anima      **D.** Posture

# // Smart Answer Sheet //

**Correct** — Indicates percentage of students who answered questions correctly.

**Skipped** — Indicates percentage of students who skipped questions.

| Q. | Ans. | Correct | Skipped |
|----|------|---------|---------|
| 1 | B | 66.57 % | 31.93 % |
| 2 | D | 44.93 % | 51.69 % |
| 3 | D | 52.4 % | 36.85 % |
| 4 | B | 51.07 % | 46.12 % |
| 5 | A | 41.1 % | 57.46 % |
| 6 | C | 68.53 % | 30.43 % |
| 7 | C | 42.24 % | 54.04 % |
| 8 | B | 62.99 % | 36.27 % |
| 9 | B | 63.53 % | 31.2 % |
| 10 | C | 41.49 % | 40.19 % |
| 11 | D | 30.36 % | 68.7 % |
| 12 | C | 66.24 % | 32.92 % |
| 13 | D | 87.78 % | 11.23 % |
| 14 | A | 60.74 % | 32.09 % |
| 15 | A | 53.35 % | 41.8 % |
| 16 | A | 42.21 % | 30.54 % |

| Q. | Ans. | Correct | Skipped |
|----|------|---------|---------|
| 17 | D | 40.06 % | 45.29 % |
| 18 | C | 63.9 % | 30.85 % |
| 19 | B | 82.26 % | 15.82 % |
| 20 | C | 58.82 % | 30.3 % |
| 21 | B | 63.19 % | 35.26 % |
| 22 | B | 47.05 % | 38.76 % |
| 23 | B | 47.32 % | 43.58 % |
| 24 | C | 66.9 % | 30.79 % |
| 25 | B | 79.31 % | 10.42 % |
| 26 | B | 57.0 % | 37.35 % |
| 27 | C | 56.15 % | 34.34 % |
| 28 | B | 54.73 % | 30.87 % |
| 29 | C | 43.34 % | 49.38 % |
| 30 | C | 66.81 % | 30.11 % |
| 31 | B | 54.28 % | 41.53 % |
| 32 | C | 79.49 % | 17.81 % |

| Q. | Ans. | Correct | Skipped |
|----|------|---------|---------|
| 33 | A | 62.87 % | 34.89 % |
| 34 | A | 54.27 % | 38.73 % |
| 35 | A | 50.35 % | 33.81 % |
| 36 | B | 49.63 % | 37.88 % |
| 37 | C | 54.02 % | 37.8 % |
| 38 | D | 53.07 % | 45.87 % |
| 39 | A | 65.01 % | 33.73 % |
| 40 | B | 64.72 % | 33.92 % |
| 41 | C | 86.55 % | 10.26 % |
| 42 | B | 68.15 % | 30.75 % |
| 43 | C | 56.73 % | 42.01 % |
| 44 | C | 59.59 % | 31.77 % |
| 45 | C | 55.01 % | 44.74 % |
| 46 | C | 48.81 % | 40.31 % |
| 47 | C | 43.16 % | 34.66 % |
| 48 | B | 47.35 % | 39.97 % |

| Q. | Ans. | Correct | Skipped |
|----|------|---------|---------|
| 49 | D | 45.41 % | 33.34 % |
| 50 | A | 64.25 % | 34.77 % |
| 51 | B | 60.83 % | 31.89 % |
| 52 | A | 45.82 % | 37.26 % |
| 53 | C | 79.4 % | 18.22 % |
| 54 | A | 18.26 % | 70.92 % |
| 55 | A | 48.62 % | 46.28 % |
| 56 | B | 53.68 % | 43.92 % |
| 57 | A | 52.84 % | 45.57 % |
| 58 | C | 46.62 % | 49.5 % |
| 59 | C | 82.73 % | 11.5 % |
| 60 | D | 56.67 % | 36.89 % |
| 61 | D | 62.41 % | 32.73 % |
| 62 | A | 40.16 % | 38.14 % |
| 63 | C | 66.48 % | 33.43 % |
| 64 | C | 45.32 % | 36.46 % |

| Q. | Ans. | Correct | Skipped |
|----|------|---------|---------|
| 65 | A | 67.27 % | 30.93 % |
| 66 | B | 52.38 % | 42.0 % |
| 67 | C | 32.94 % | 67.04 % |
| 68 | D | 57.94 % | 40.5 % |
| 69 | B | 48.03 % | 38.5 % |
| 70 | C | 62.29 % | 36.33 % |
| 71 | A | 69.63 % | 30.15 % |
| 72 | C | 60.88 % | 32.5 % |
| 73 | B | 44.13 % | 30.33 % |
| 74 | C | 41.07 % | 35.89 % |
| 75 | C | 27.81 % | 67.98 % |
| 76 | C | 44.87 % | 36.71 % |
| 77 | B | 54.94 % | 31.0 % |
| 78 | D | 59.88 % | 38.55 % |
| 79 | A | 88.51 % | 10.38 % |
| 80 | C | 57.04 % | 32.14 % |

| Q. | Ans. | Correct | | Q. | Ans. | Correct | | Q. | Ans. | Correct | | Q. | Ans. | Correct | | Q. | Ans. | Correct |
|---|---|---|---|---|---|---|---|---|---|---|---|---|---|---|---|---|---|---|
| | | Skipped | | | | Skipped | | | | Skipped | | | | Skipped | | | | Skipped |
| 81 | C | 40.14 % | | 85 | D | 42.54 % | | 89 | C | 42.47 % | | 93 | B | 61.43 % | | 97 | B | 62.94 % |
| | | 46.6 % | | | | 52.05 % | | | | 30.87 % | | | | 37.6 % | | | | 33.01 % |
| 82 | D | 40.14 % | | 86 | D | 40.8 % | | 90 | D | 43.63 % | | 94 | B | 46.13 % | | 98 | C | 41.53 % |
| | | 45.96 % | | | | 37.95 % | | | | 48.09 % | | | | 30.59 % | | | | 46.41 % |
| 83 | D | 68.29 % | | 87 | D | 62.38 % | | 91 | B | 67.51 % | | 95 | D | 52.66 % | | 99 | C | 44.76 % |
| | | 30.4 % | | | | 31.48 % | | | | 31.43 % | | | | 32.33 % | | | | 44.9 % |
| 84 | B | 65.1 % | | 88 | A | 67.03 % | | 92 | D | 46.99 % | | 96 | D | 45.21 % | | 100 | B | 45.84 % |
| | | 32.18 % | | | | 32.08 % | | | | 48.3 % | | | | 40.79 % | | | | 36.62 % |

## Performance Analysis

| | |
|---|---|
| Avg. Score (%) | 57.5% |
| Toppers Score (%) | 70.0% |
| Your Score | |

# //Hints and Solutions//

**1.** Option II: It can be said with surety that if schools start providing breakfast, it will be additional cost to them which can be a good enough reason not to provide breakfast. Hence, it's a strong argument.

Option I: The word 'best' is subjective in nature and cannot be said with certainty that schools are the best places to ensure good nutrition (Kind of vague and ambiguous). Hence, it's a weak argument.

Hence, the correct option is (B).

**2.** (D) should be the appropriate answer. we can not assume anything about Mahesh from the given statement.

Hence, the correct option is (D).

**3.** By clockwise rotation of the arrow we get the correct figure as follows:

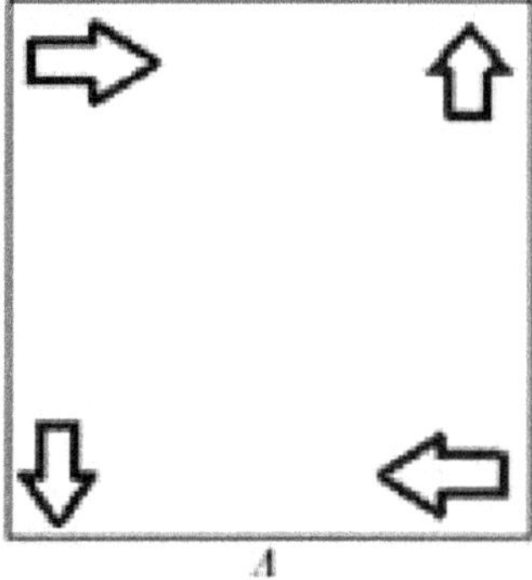

Hence, the correct option is (D).

**4.** All Aerated drinks are beverages and all coke are aerated drinks. Therefore correct venn diagram is:

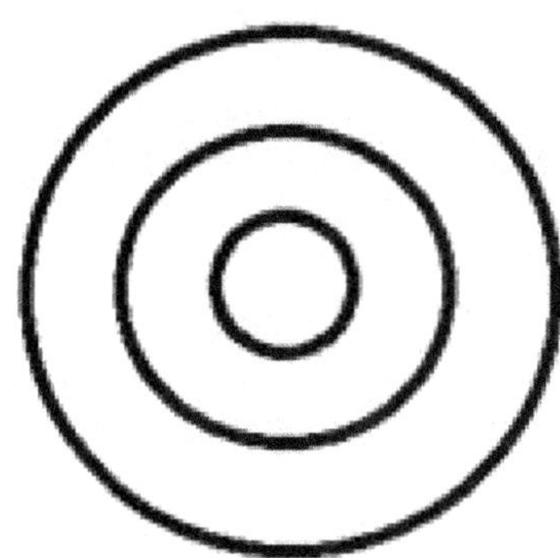

Hence, the correct option is (B).

**5.** Only in figure(A), the triangle is below the circle.

So, option (A) is the odd one.

Hence, the correct option is (A).

**6.** As Ornithologist is a specialist of Birds similarly Archaeologist is a specialist of Archaeology.

Hence, the correct option is (C).

**7.** Herbivore is an animal that eats plants. In the given question the only herbivore is Deer and that is called "Leopard".

Hence, the correct option is (C).

**8.** From 1st cube, we know that 5 and 1 are immediate neighbors of 4.

From 2nd cube, we know that 6 and 3 are immediate neighbors of 4.

So, from these two cubes only, we can say that 2 will be opposite to 4.

Hence, the correct option is (B).

**9.** Given:

65 % 7 & 13 @ 8 % 6 $ 5 = ?

After changing the signs, we get,

65 x 7 ÷ 13 + 8 x 6 - 5

$\Rightarrow$ 5 x 7 + 48 - 5

$\Rightarrow$ 35 + 48 - 5

$\Rightarrow$ 83 - 5

$\Rightarrow$ 78

Hence, the correct option is (B).

**10.** In an organization, If an Operational officer decides to quit his job then,

Statement (A) is a very random call and the instant hike is not the best option.

Statement (B) is a very harsh call,

Statement (D) can be a way to deal with the situation, but should be performed after the proper evaluation and statement (C) is the apt way to deal with the situation.

Hence, the correct option is (C).

**11.** Three and two arcs are inverted alternately. The central element rotates 90° ACW and 180° alternately. Therefore the correct answer figure will be:

Hence, the correct option is (D).

**12.** The middle term is the average of the terms at the extreme end of the number, therefore,

(A) 147 = $\dfrac{(1+7)}{2}$ = 4

(B) 159 = $\dfrac{(1+9)}{2}$ = 5

(C) 379 = $\dfrac{(3+9)}{2}$ = 6 not 7 as given in option.

(D) $579= \dfrac{(5+9)}{2} = 7$

Hence, the correct option is (C).

**13.** Given:

| Alphabets | A | B | C | D | E | F | G | H | I | J | K | L | M |
|---|---|---|---|---|---|---|---|---|---|---|---|---|---|
| Positional value | 1 | 2 | 3 | 4 | 5 | 6 | 7 | 8 | 9 | 10 | 11 | 12 | 13 |
| Positional value | 26 | 25 | 24 | 23 | 22 | 21 | 20 | 19 | 18 | 17 | 16 | 15 | 14 |
| Alphabets | Z | Y | X | W | V | U | T | S | R | Q | P | O | N |

From the table positional vaues are given:

$\Rightarrow A \times B = 1 \times 2 = 2 = B$

$\Rightarrow B \times C = 2 \times 3 = 6 = F$

$\Rightarrow C \times D = 3 \times 4 = 12 = L$

$\Rightarrow D \times E = 4 \times 5 = 20 = T$ and not S(19).

Hence, the correct option is (D).

**14.** Option (B) and (D) can easily be eliminated as we can clearly see that the position of both the horizontal lines is wrong. In option (C), the two inclined lines are drawn wrong. Option (A) is the correct mirror image of the given question figure.

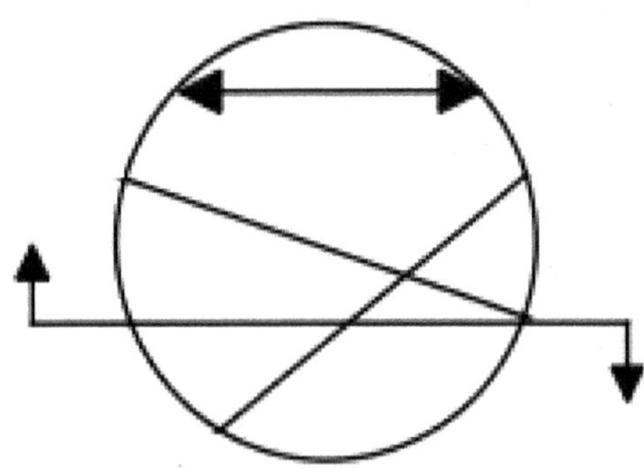

Hence, the correct option is (A).

**15.** In option (B), the position of the outer semicircles and the two triangles is wrong, also the orientation of the four inner triangles is wrong. In option (C), the orientation of the four inner triangles is wrong. In option (D), position of 2 semicircles is wrong. Option (A) is the correct figure which would appear when the given sheet of paper is unfolded.

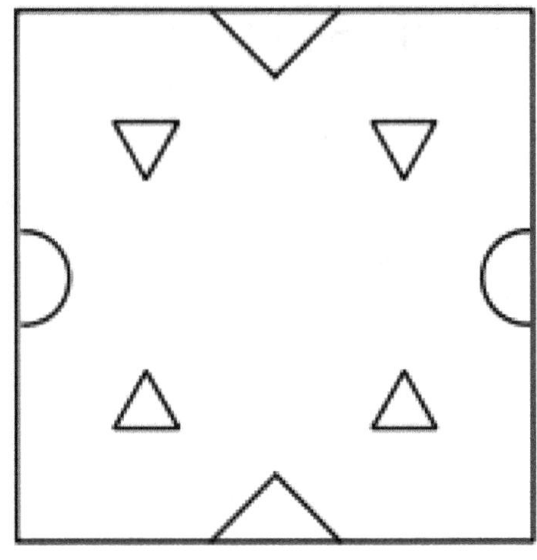

Hence, the correct option is (A).

**16.** Here, the number of each type of coins is same.

Therefore, number of each type of coins $= \dfrac{\text{total amount}}{\text{sum of value of each coin}}$

$= \dfrac{58}{(1+0.2+0.25)}$

$= \dfrac{58}{1.45} = 40$

Therefore, 40 coins of each type.

Hence, the correct option is (A).

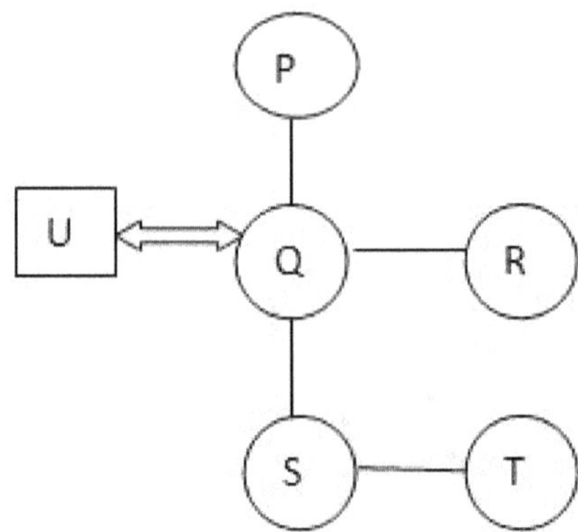

**17.**

In the above figure, square elements are male and circles are female.

$\therefore$ S and T are niece of R.

Hence, the correct option is (D).

**18.** Sound/noises made by the animals is given.

The noise made by turkey is gobble and rest of them are true.

Hence, the correct option is (C).

**19.** According to the series given in the question:

24, 13, 15, 34, ?

Series follow this sequence:

$\Rightarrow 24 \times 0.5 + 1 = 13$

$\Rightarrow 13 \times 1 + 2 = 15$

$\Rightarrow 15 \times 2 + 4 = 34$

$\therefore 34 \times 4 + 8 = 144$

Hence, the correct option is (B).

**20.** Given Series: 3, 4, 8, 17, 33, ?

Now the sequence followed is square of the consecutive values:

$3 + 1^2 = 4,$

$4 + 2^2 = 8,$

$8 + 3^2 = 17,$

$17 + 4^2 = 33,$

$33 + 5^2 = 58$

Therefore, the missing number is 58.

Hence, the correct option is (C).

**21.**

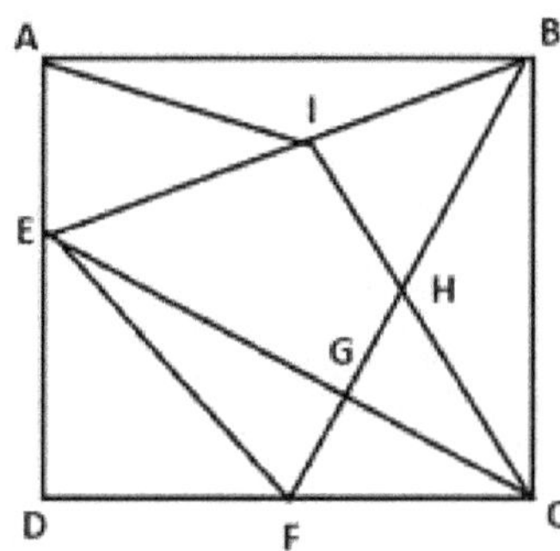

With A: AIB, AIE, AEB

With B: BIH, BHC, BGC, BFC, BEF, BEG, BIC

With C: CGH, CEI, CHF, CED, CFE, CGF,

With D: DEF

With E: EFG

Therefore, the Number of triangles is 18.

Hence, the correct option is (B).

**22.** The code is as follows:

STONE is coded as 36521, RAIN is coded as 7842

Similarly, STATION is coded as 3685462

Hence, the correct option is (B).

**23.** By observation and analysis, we get,

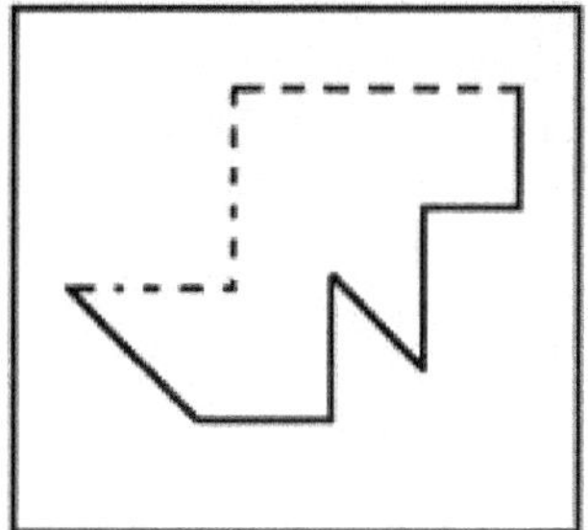

Hence, the correct option is (B).

**24.** According to the question, we draw the following diagrams,

The pattern is followed as:

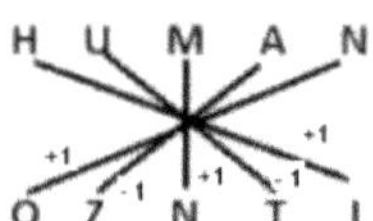
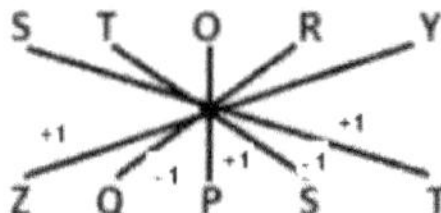

Similarily,

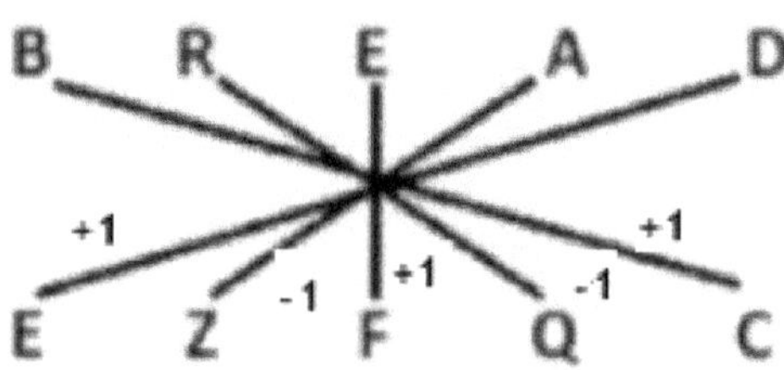

Therefore, the code for BREAD is EZFQC.

Hence, the correct option is (C).

**25.** DRIBBLE is a terminology used in FOOTBALL similarly RALLY is a terminology used in BADMINTON.

Hence, the correct option is (B).

**26.** Chapekar Brothers assassinated W.C. Rand, the Plague Commissioner of Pune in 1897.

On 22 June 1897, brothers Damodar Hari Chapekar and Balkrishna Hari Chapekar assassinated British officer W.C. Rand and his military escort, Lieutenant Ayerst, in Pune, Maharashtra. This was the first case of militant nationalism in India after the revolt of 1857.

Hence, the correct option is (B).

**27.** Reserve Bank of India (Credit Card and Debit Card – Issuance and Conduct) Directions, 2022 was released recently by the RBI.

Scheduled Commercial Banks (SCBs) with a net worth of Rs. 100 crores can issue credit cards. Regional Rural Banks need to collaborate with other banks. Urban Cooperative Banks (UCBs) and NBFCs registered with the Reserve Bank with a net worth of more than Rs. 100 crores can issue cards subject to certain guidelines.

Hence, the correct option is (C).

**28.** Jharkhand CM Hemant Soren has launched Jharkhand Sports Policy 2022 in Ranchi on 13th September 2022.

- This policy is aimed at reducing bottlenecks in the path of sportspersons in excelling at national and international events.
- The sports policy made for five years is the second such policy framework in Jharkhand.
- The last such policy was made in 2007.

Hence, the correct option is (B).

**29.** The Nobel Memorial Prize in Economic Sciences was awarded to Ben S Bernanke, the former chair of the US Federal Reserve, Douglas W Diamond and Philip H Dybvig of USA for research into banks and financial crises.

As per the committee, 'the laureates have provided a foundation for our modern understanding of why banks are needed, why they're vulnerable, and what to do about it'.

Hence, the correct option is (C).

**30.** Financial Assistance to Non-School Going Disabled Children (less than 18 years) is the Financial Assistance Scheme of Social Justice and Empowerment Department of State Government of Haryana.

The Ministry of Social Justice and Empowerment is a Government of India ministry. It is responsible for welfare, social justice and empowerment of disadvantaged and marginalised sections of society, including scheduled castes (SC), Other Backward Classes (OBC), Manual Scavengers, the disabled, the elderly, and the victims of drug abuse.

Hence, the correct option is (C).

**31.** Narendra Modi has received the first ever Philip Kotler Presidential Award.

He has been selected for his outstanding leadership and selfless service towards India, combined with his tireless energy.

The award focuses on the triple bottom-line of 'people, profit and planet. It will be given annually to the leader of a nation.

Hence, the correct option is (B).

**32.** A time frame during which anyone can return the purchased policy to the insurer is known as Free Look Period.

It is applicable to all new life insurance policies. IRDAI recommended free look period in life insurance is 15 or 30 days after receiving the policy document.

Hence, the correct option is (C).

**33.** Fidelity bond is a form of insurance that offers an employer protection against losses caused by its employees' fraudulent or dishonest actions.

Fidelity bonds are held by insurance companies which are specifically required to carry protection proportional to their net capital.

Hence, the correct option is (A).

**34.** Wholesale Price Index is the full form of WPI.

Wholesale Price Index measure the changes in the price of goods in the stages before the retail level.

WPI is used as an important measure of inflation in India.

Hence, the correct option is (A).

**35.** The Attorney General is appointed by the President of India under Article 76(1) of the Constitution.

The 15th and current Attorney General is K. K. Venugopal. The tenure period of his is 3 years.

The Attorney General is necessary for giving advice to the Government of India in legal matters referred to him. He also performs other legal duties assigned to him by the President.

Hence, the correct option is (A).

**36.** Article 17 of Indian Constitution describes the Abolition of Untouchability.

Untouchability is abolished and its practice in any form is forbidden the enforcement of any disability arising out of Untouchability shall be an offence punishable in accordance with law.

Hence, the correct option is (B).

**37.** The maximum age limit of a Chief Judge of a High Court is 62 years.

The High court is the head of judiciary in the state. Judge of High court is appointed by the President.

Article 217 of Constitution reads the appointment and conditions of the office of a Judge of a High Court.

Hence, the correct option is (C).

**38.** When the prices of good and services rise rapidly, hyperinflation occurs.

Hyperinflations are caused by extremely rapid growth in the supply of paper money.

When there is a significant increase in the money supply not supported by the country's gross domestic product growth which results the Hyperinflation.

Hence, the correct option is (D).

**39.** Nyokum Festival is celebrated in Arunachal Pradesh.

Nyokum is a very colourful festival and reflects the interesting cultural heritage and ethnicity of the Nyishi tribe.

Assam - Bihu

Jammu and Kashmir - Hemis

Bihar - Chhath Puja

Hence, the correct option is (A).

**40.** Pritzker Prize is related to Architecture. Also, Striling Prize is given for excellence the in Architecture.

Shanti Swarup Bhatnagar Prize is given for outstanding Indian work in science & technology.

Arjuna Award, Dhayan Chand Award, Rajiv Gandhi Khel Ratna Award are related to sports.

Hence, the correct option is (B).

**41.** Mantle lies just below the thin outer layer of the earth called crust. It lies between the crust and the thick dense core of the earth.

It is about 2,900 kilometres (1,802 miles) thick and makes up a whopping 84% of Earth's total volume.

Hence, the correct option is (C).

**42.** A safety elevator was a modification of primitive elevators which prevented the platform from falling in case the cable broke. It was invented by Elisha Otis in 1852. On 23rd March 1857, the first passenger safety elevator was installed at 488 Broadway in New York.

Hence, the correct option is (B).

**43.** Abul Fazl who was the court historian of Emperor Akbar in the Mughal era wrote the treatise Ain-i-Akbari, the 3rd volume of Akbarnama.

This work of Abul Fazl throws light on the administrative aspect of the Emperor Akbar, as he has given the rules and regulations framed and put into effect for proper administration by Akbar at that time.

Hence, the correct option is (C).

**44.** Mughal painting emerged from the Persian miniature painting tradition, with additional Hindu, Buddhist, and Jain influences, it usually took the form of book illustrations or single sheets preserved in albums. The emperor Jahangir was influenced by European art and encouraged his atelier to emulate the single point perspective favored by European painters, unlike the flattened, multi-layered style traditionally used in miniature painting.

Hence, the correct option is (C).

**45.** The river Krishna originates from Maharashtra.

It is the one of the longest rivers in India. It flows through the state of Karnataka before entering Telangana State.

It is one of the major sources of irrigation for Maharashtra, Karnataka, Telangana and Andhra Pradesh.

Hence, the correct option is (C).

**46.** C Rajagopalachari was the first Governor General of Independent India.

He held the position from the period of 21 June 1948- 26 January 1950, till the day the new constitution of India came into existence.

After the constitution came into effect, the Post of Governor General was replaced with the President and powers established as per the constitution.

Hence, the correct option is (C).

**47.**

| A. Kathakali | d. Kerala |
|---|---|
| B. Bharatnatyam | c. Tamil Nadu |
| C. Sattriya | a. Assam |
| D. Ghoomar | b. Rajasthan |

Hence, the correct option is (C).

**48.** Dublin is the Capital of Ireland. The currency of Ireland is Euro.

Hence, the correct option is (B).

**49.** World Consumer Rights Day is celebrated every year on March 15.

It is a day marked to raise global awareness about consumer rights and needs.

The theme of promoted World Consumer Rights Day 2021 is 'Tackle plastic pollution'.

Hence, the correct option is (D).

**50.** Mohammed Shami recently achieved the milestone of 200 Test wickets, during the first Test against South Africa.

The 31-year-old bowler is third-fastest among Indian pacers to reach the landmark, as he achieved this feat in his 55th Test match. He is only behind Kapil Dev (434), Ishant Sharma (311), Zaheer Khan (311), and Javagal Srinath (236), at present.

Hence, the correct option is (A).

**51.** $\Rightarrow$ C.P of 11 shampoo of 1st type = 10

$\Rightarrow$ C.P of $9 \times 11$ shampoo of 1st type $= 9 \times 10$

$= 90$

$\Rightarrow$ C.P of 9 shampoo of 2nd type = Rs 10

$\Rightarrow$ C.P of $9 \times 11$ shampoo of 2nd type = Rs $10 \times 11$

$=$ Rs 110

$\Rightarrow$ Total C.P of 99 + 99 shampoos

$=$ Rs 110 + Rs 90

$\Rightarrow$ Total C.P of 198 shampoos = Rs 200

$\Rightarrow$ And S.P of 198 shampoos = Rs 198

$\Rightarrow$ Loss = 200 - 198 = 2

$\Rightarrow$ Loss % = $2 \times \dfrac{100}{200}$

$\Rightarrow$ 1 %

Hence, the correct option is (B).

**52.** For a number to be divisible by 11.

(Sum of digits at odd positions) - (Sum of digits at even positions) should be divisible by 11

i.e. (1 + 2 + 3) - (a + b + c) should be divisible by 11

$\therefore$ 6 - (a + b + c) should be divisible by 11.

This is possible when a + b + c = 6.

This is only in option A when a = 4, b = 0, c = 2.

Hence, the correct option is (A).

**53.** Divide the decimal number (131)10 successively by 2, until the quotient becomes 0. And, then the remainders (i.e. 1 and 0 written on the right side) taken in reverse order is the binary equivalent for the given decimal number.

| 2 | 131 | |
|---|-----|---|
| 2 | 65 | 1 |
| 2 | 32 | 1 |
| 2 | 16 | 0 |
| 2 | 8 | 0 |
| 2 | 4 | 0 |
| 2 | 2 | 0 |
| 2 | 1 | 0 |
| | 0 | 1 |

Thus, $(131)_{10} = (10000011)_2$

Hence, the correct option is (C).

**54.** Time taken by P alone to finish the work = 36 days

Time taken by Q alone to finish the 75% of the work = $41\left(\frac{2}{3}\right)$% of 36

= 15 days

Time taken by Q alone to finish the complete work =

$15 \times \left(\frac{100}{75}\right)$

$= 20$ days

Ratio of efficiency of Q to R = 120% : 100%

= 6 : 5

Time taken by R alone to finish the work $= 20 \times \left(\frac{6}{5}\right)$

$= 24$ days

Time taken by P and R together to finish the work $= \frac{1}{\left(\frac{1}{36}\right)} + \left(\frac{1}{24}\right)$

= 14.4 days

Hence, the correct option is (A).

**55.** Given:

17 x 4 ÷ 204 x 120 x 20 - 18 x 3 - 2 x 34

By solving, the above expression:

⇒ 800 - 54 - 68

⇒ 678

Hence, the correct option is (A).

**56.** The concept of cyclicity is used to identify the last digit of the number.

Cyclicity chart:

| Number | Cyclicity | Unit digit values | | | |
|--------|-----------|---------|---------|---------|---------|
| | | Power 1 | Power 2 | Power 3 | Power 4 |
| 0 | 1 | 0 | | | |
| 1 | 1 | 1 | | | |
| 2 | 4 | 2 | 4 | 8 | 6 |
| 3 | 4 | 3 | 9 | 7 | 1 |
| 4 | 2 | 4 | 6 | | |
| 5 | 1 | 5 | | | |
| 6 | 1 | 6 | | | |
| 7 | 4 | 7 | 9 | 3 | 1 |
| 8 | 4 | 8 | 4 | 2 | 6 |
| 9 | 2 | 9 | 1 | | |

(Note: remainder = power. When remainder is 0, power = cyclicity)

In $312^{86}$:

Unit digit of 312 is 2.

$2^{86}$: From the cyclicity chart, cyclicity of 2 is 4.

$\Rightarrow \frac{86}{4}$, remainder = 2

= power 2

So, unit digit of $312^{86} = 4$

In $125^{29}$:

Unit digit of 125 is 5.

$5^{29}$: From the cyclicity chart, cyclicity of 5 is 1.

Unit digit of $125^{29} = 5$

Therefore, unit digit of $312^{86} + 125^{29}$

= unit digit of (4 + 5) = 9

Hence, the correct option is (B).

**57.** Given: 30% of b% of 296 = 40% of 50% of 5% of 1480

$\Rightarrow \left(\frac{30}{100}\right) \times \left(\frac{b}{100}\right) \times 296 = \left(\frac{40}{100}\right) \times \left(\frac{50}{100}\right) \times \left(\frac{5}{100}\right) \times 1480$

$\Rightarrow b = \frac{(40\times50\times5\times1480)}{(30\times296\times100)}$

$\Rightarrow b = \frac{50}{3}$

Hence, the correct option is (A).

**58.** Total prime numbers from 1 to 100 are:

2, 3, 5, 7, 11, 13, 17, 19, 23, 29, 31, 37, 41, 43, 47, 53, 59, 61, 67, 71, 73, 79, 83, 89, 97

That means 25 out of 100

So, probability is:

$$P \text{ (prime)} = \frac{25}{100}$$

$$\Rightarrow P \text{ (prime)} = \frac{1}{4}$$

Hence, the correct option is (C).

**59.** Given: One of the Number=275, HCF= 11, LCM=7700

Let the other number be $x$.

We know,

H.C.F × L.C.M = Product of two numbers

$\Rightarrow$ H.C.F × L.C.M = 275 × $x$

$\Rightarrow 11 \times 7700 = 275 \times x$

$\Rightarrow x = \frac{(11 \times 7700)}{275}$

$\Rightarrow x = 308$

Therefore, the number is 308.

Hence, the correct option is (C).

**60.** $\because$ one root is $3 + \sqrt{2}$

$\therefore$ other root is $3 - \sqrt{2}$

$\therefore$ Sum of roots $= 3 + \sqrt{2} + 3 - \sqrt{2} = 6$

Product of roots $= \left(3 + \sqrt{2}\right)\left(3 - \sqrt{2}\right)$

$= (3)^2 - \left(\sqrt{2}\right)^2 = 9 - 2 = 7$

We know, Quadratic equation is:

$ax^2+bx+c=0$,

$\therefore$ Required quadratic equation is,

$\Rightarrow x^2 - 6x + 7 = 0$

Hence, the correct option is (D).

**61.** Let the initial capital of P and Q be Rs. $2x$ and Rs. $3x$ respectively

Then, ratio of profits $= (2x \times 12) : (3x \times 24)$

$= 24x : 72x$

$= 1 : 3$

$\therefore$ Q's share $= $ Rs. $\left(26000 \times \frac{3}{4}\right)$

$= $ Rs. 19500

Hence, the correct option is (D).

**62.** Given: x=y=2z , xyz= 32-----(1)

$\therefore z = \dfrac{x}{2}$, y=x-------(2)

Putting the value of $y$ and $z$ in terms of $x$ from (2) in (1) we get

$\Rightarrow x \times x \times \dfrac{x}{2} = 32$

$\Rightarrow x^3 = 64$

$\Rightarrow x = 4$

Hence, the correct option is (A).

**63.** Let the cost of 1 mango be Rs. 1

Then the cost of an orange $= \dfrac{200}{3}$ % of 1

$= $ Rs. $\dfrac{2}{3}$

According to the question:

Selling price of 4 oranges $= $ Rs. 5

Cost price of 4 oranges $= 4 \times \dfrac{2}{3}$

$= $ Rs. $\dfrac{8}{3}$

Profit= S.P.-C.P.

Profit $= 5 - \dfrac{8}{3}$

$= $ Rs. $\dfrac{7}{3}$

Percentage of profit $= \dfrac{\left(\frac{7}{3}\right)}{\left(\frac{8}{3}\right)} x$

$\Rightarrow$ Percentage of profit $= \dfrac{7}{8} \times 100 = 87.5\%$

Hence, the correct option is (C).

**64.** Volume of the cone $= \dfrac{1}{3}\pi r^2$ h

$\Rightarrow 1232 = \dfrac{1}{3} \times \dfrac{22}{7} \times r^2 \times 24$

$\Rightarrow r^2 = \dfrac{(1232 \times 3 \times 7)}{(22 \times 24)} = 49$

$\Rightarrow r = 7$

Slant height, $l = \sqrt{(r^2 + h^2)}$

$l = \sqrt{(7)^2 + (24)^2}$

$= \sqrt{(49 + 576)}$

$= \sqrt{625} = 25$ cm

Area of curved surface $= \pi r l$

$= \frac{22}{7} \times 7 \times 25$

$= 550$ cm$^2$

Hence, the correct option is (C).

**65.** Three years ago, the total age of 6 members = 6 x 35

= 210 years

At the time of birth of new baby, the total age of family = 210 + 2 × 6

= 222 years

The present age of family = 222 + (1 x 7)

= 229 years

4 years thus, the average age of family $= \frac{(229+4\times7)}{7}$

$= 36\frac{5}{7}$ years

Hence, the correct option is (A).

**66.** Let length $= 4x$

Breath $= 5x$

We know,

Area= length × breadth

$\Rightarrow 4x \times 5x = 2420$

$\Rightarrow x = 11$

Now, perimeter= 2 (length+breadth) $= 2(4x + 5x) = 18x$

$\Rightarrow Perimeter = 18 \times 11 = 198$ cm

$\Rightarrow$ Cost of fencing = Rs. $20 \times 198$

= Rs. 3960

Hence, the correct option is (B).

**67.** Let the total distance $= x$km

She travels the distance $= 45 \times 5.4 + 39 \times 7$

$= 516$ km

According to the question, 516 km is four-fifths of the total distance.

Therefore, $\frac{4x}{5} = 516$ km

$\Rightarrow x = 516 \times \frac{5}{4} = 645$ km

Remaining distance = 645 - 516 = 129 km

$\therefore$ average speed $= \frac{129}{3}$

$= 43$ kmph

Hence, the correct option is (C).

**68.** Let the rate of interest be $r\%$ per annum.

We know,

Simple interest= $\frac{P \times R \times T}{100}$

$\therefore 4600 = \left(\frac{5000\times6\times r}{100}\right) + \left(\frac{4500\times8\times r}{100}\right) + \left(\frac{6500\times4\times r}{100}\right)$

$\Rightarrow 4600 = 300r + 360r + 260r$

$\Rightarrow 4600 = 920r$

$\Rightarrow r = 5\%$

Hence, the correct option is (D).

**69.** Given: A + B = 40000

According to question:

44100 = 1.09A + 1.11B --- (1)

So, 1.09A + 1.09B = 43600 --- (2)

Solving (1) and (2),

Salary of A = Rs 15000, B = Rs. 25000

Hence, the correct option is (B).

**70.** Ratio of original numbers =3 : 8

Common factor helps in finding actual values easily

So, take 'M' as common factor.

$\therefore$ Original numbers will be 3M and 8M

Adding 5 to them, we get (3M+5) and (8M+5)

$\frac{3M+5}{8M+5} = \frac{2}{5}$  → (Ratio of new numbers is 2 : 5)

$\therefore 15M + 25 = 16M + 10$

$\therefore$ M=15

Smaller Number is $3M = 3 \times 15 = 45$

Hence, the correct option is (C).

**71.** Total quantity of mixture $= \frac{7}{7+3} \times 30$ litres

$= 21$ litres

And quantity of water in the mixture $= \frac{3}{7+3} \times 30$ litres

$= 9$ litres

Let water to be mixed be ' $a$' litre

Then,

$\Rightarrow (30 + a) \times \frac{40}{100} = 9 + a$

$\Rightarrow 120 + 4a = 90 + 10a$

$\Rightarrow 120 - 90 = 10a - 4a$

$\Rightarrow 30 = 6a$

$\Rightarrow a = 5$

So, 5 litres water mixed in the mixture.

Hence, the correct option is (A).

**72.** First player can post greeting cards to the remaining 54 players in 54 ways. Second player can post greeting card to the 54 players. Similarly, it happens with the rest of the players. The total numbers of greeting cards posted are,

54 + 54 + 54............54 (55 times)

∴ 54 (55times) = 54 x 55 = 2970.

Hence, the correct option is (C).

**73.** Part filled by (A + B + C) in 3 minutes $= 3\left(\dfrac{1}{30} + \dfrac{1}{20} + \dfrac{1}{10}\right)$

$= 3 \times \dfrac{11}{60} = \dfrac{11}{20}$

Part filled by C in 3 minutes $= \dfrac{3}{10}$

∴ Required ratio $= \dfrac{3}{10} \times \dfrac{20}{11}$

$= \dfrac{6}{11}$

Hence, the correct option is (B).

**74.** We know,

Speed of downstream = (Boat speed+ Speed of stream)

Speed of downstream = (13 + 4) km/hr

= 17 km/hr

We know,

Time $= \dfrac{Distance}{Speed}$

Time taken to travel 68 km downstream $= \dfrac{68}{17}$ hours

$= 4$ hours

Hence, the correct option is (C).

**75.** Speed $= \left(60 \times \dfrac{5}{18}\right)$ m/sec (By changing km/hr to m/sec.)

$= \dfrac{50}{3}$ m/sec

Total distance covered, $= (100 + 140)$m

=240 m

∴ Required time $= \left(240 \times \dfrac{3}{50}\right)$ sec

$= \dfrac{72}{5}$ sec

=14.4 sec

Hence, the correct option is (C).

**76.** The phrase 'one of the first' is always followed by the plural form of the noun. 'Persons' would be correct.

Hence, the correct option is (C).

**77.** Options (A), (C) and (D) doesn't make sense here. The sentence is saying that the person's method/way of content creation; and 'style' makes perfect sense for this.

Hence, the correct option is (B).

**78.** (A) and (C) doesn't make any sense. 'Very' being an adverb should qualify a verb, adjective or another adverb and not a noun (style); thus, (B) is eliminated. (D) fits in perfectly.

Hence, the correct option is (D).

**79.** Taboo- a social or religious custom prohibiting or restricting a particular practice or forbidding association with a particular person, place, or thing. While other options give out opposite meaning to the sentence and do not fit in contextually. Option (A) fits here as per the context.

Hence, the correct option is (A).

**80.** 'Directly', 'exactly' and 'squarely' do not make sense here. 'Immediately' fits here perfectly.

Hence, the correct option is (C).

**81.** Option (A) is incorrect because of the usage of preposition 'in' (we keep things 'on' a tray). Option (B) is incorrect because it uses 'allot' (allocate or assign), which is a contextual misfit; here, the phrase 'a lot' should be used. Option (D) is incorrect as 'close' is an adjective, while we need a verb to describe the action, thus, 'shut' should be used in place of 'close'. The sentence given in option (C) is correct grammatically and contextually.

Hence, the correct option is (C).

**82.** Option (D) is the right answer. Option (A) is eliminated as it is grammatically incorrect; the part participle 'done' should be used here. Option (B) is eliminated as it is grammatically incorrect; it omits the use of the verb 'been'. Option (C) is eliminated as it uses the future tense, while the original sentence has used the present perfect tense.

Hence, the correct option is (D).

**83.** In part 3 of the question, usage of "to" is correct. 'to' is also used for identifying the person or thing affected by or receiving something. Therefore, the sentence is correct and free of error.

Hence, the correct option is (D).

**84.** Independent should be followed by 'of' not 'from'. The phrase means to be self-sufficient or separate. The difference between 'Independent from' and 'independent of' is as follows:

Independent from = [not ruled by another country]

The rebel republic has already declared itself independent from the Soviet Union

Independent of = [unaffected by]

Personal conversations are not independent of media news.

Their decisions are quite independent of any other arguments.

Hence, the correct option is (B).

**85.** The preposition 'among' should be used here instead of 'between', as more than two people are being referred to. 'Between' is used when referring to only two persons.

Hence, the correct option is (D).

**86.** Arranging the parts according to option (D): 'Industrious as these peasants are, they find some minor occupations in their spare time'- is a well formed sentence. None of the other options can result in a meaningful sentence.

Hence, the correct option is (D).

**87.** "Human-like characteristics" is the key phrase here. Among the given choices, the word personify refers to giving human-like characteristics to inanimate objects. Also, the second blank must contain a word that means the same as providing with a quality. Hence, endow is appropriate. Enunciate- say or pronounce clearly; Inculcate- generate or instil; Deride- express contempt for; Acclimatize- adjust or adapt.

Hence, the correct option is (D).

**88.** Throughout the passage, the narrator uses language that is figurative and not literal. He or she refers to "soaking in the bright and burning sun," needing to "crawl through the day" when it was raining outside. All of these are examples of figurative or metaphorical language. Because of this, choice (A) is correct. Rhetorical language is a language used to try to persuade someone or to impress someone. There is no effort made to convince the reader to agree with him or her. As such, the passage does not use rhetorical language, so choice (B) is incorrect. The passage does not use formal language. Such language would sound stiff and polite, and it would be completely free of figurative language. Choice (C) is incorrect. Ambiguous language is a language that is unclear in meaning.

Hence, the correct option is (A).

**89.** The narrator explains his or her views of summer as an adult. Since adults do not get time off from work for the summer, it is different for them than it is for children.

Hence, the correct option is (C).

**90.** To answer this detail question, look for the parts of the passage that describe the narrator as a child. The narrator states that he or she "was an only child." This makes it clear that he or she had no siblings, and choice (D) is, therefore, correct.

Hence, the correct option is (D).

**91.** The passage makes it clear the narrator looked forward to summer as a child, while the last few lines of the paragraph state that all days seem "monotonous and dull" and cause him or to feel "ennui or listlessness." It also states that "summer is not as eagerly anticipated" as an adult. All of this implies that the narrator is less excitable as an adult than he or she was as a child.

Hence, the correct option is (B).

**92.** All of the above generalisations can be made from the passage. Short statements given is clearly stated in the passage.

Hence, the correct option is (D).

**93.** Robust/ sturdy - strong and hardy. Frail - weak.

Eager - keen. Glum - unhappy.

Hence, the correct option is (B).

**94.** Flabby means soft and loose. Therefore, the word opposite in meaning is "Firm".

Hence, the correct option is (B).

**95.** Bohemian - an unconventional lifestyle.

Cynosure - One who is a centre of attraction.

Apostate - A person who has changed his faith.

Debonair - A person having a sophisticated charm.

D is the right answer.

Hence, the correct option is (D).

**96.** The incorrect spellings of the other words are: Argument, consensus and independent. Correct spelling is Embarrass.

Hence, the correct option is (D).

**97.** The incorrect spellings of the other words are: Inadvertent, Perseverance and Privilege. Correct spelling is indispensable.

Hence, the correct option is (B).

**98.** Forebode - predict something unpleasant. Forbade - to prohibit. Abode - a place where one lives. Remote - distant. We need a noun here, so, only (C) is correct. (A) and (B) are verbs, while (D) is an adjective.

Hence, the correct option is (C).

**99.** Astute - having sharp powers of judgment.

Shrewd - good at judging people or situations.

Brood - complain.

Crude - rude or vulgar.

Impolite - rude.

Hence, the correct option is (C).

**100.** Gesture- a movement of part of the body, especially a hand or the head, to express an idea or meaning.

Action- the way in which something works or moves.

Anima- (In psychology) the feminine part of a man's personality.

Posture- the position in which someone holds their body when standing or sitting.

Out of these, only Gesture shows the same meaning as the given phrase.

Hence, the correct option is (B).

## General Intelligence & Reasoning

**Q.1** Pick out the odd one from the following:

**A.** George W. Bush      **B.** Emmanuel Macron

**C.** Vladimir Putin      **D.** Narendra Modi

**Q.2** In the following question, select the odd word from the given alternatives.

Demographer : Population :: Philatelist : ?

**A.** Fossils      **B.** Stamps

**C.** Photography      **D.** Music

**Q.3** A,B,C,D,E are five brothers. A is greater than D, C is greater than B, B is younger than D, E is greater than B, A is younger than E, C is younger than A. Who is the eldest and youngest?

**A.** E and B    **B.** D and E    **C.** A and E    **D.** E and C

**Q.4** A series is given with one term missing. Select the correct alternative from the given ones that will complete the series.

97,77,59, ? ,29,17

**A.** 54      **B.** 55      **C.** 43      **D.** 56

**Q.5** Which number will be in the middle of the following numbers are arranged in descending order?

7756, 7765, 7655, 7665, 7565

**A.** 7756      **B.** 7765      **C.** 7565      **D.** 7665

**Q.6** A word is represented by only one set of numbers as given in any one of the alternatives. The sets of numbers given in the alternatives are represented by two classes of alphabets as in two matrices given below. The columns and rows of Matrix I are numbered – form 0 to 4 and that Matrix II are numbered from 5 to 9. A letter from these matrices can be represented first by its row and next by its column, e.g., 'U' can be represented by 01, 14, etc. and E can be represented by 55, 66 etc. Similarly, you have to identify the set for the word 'JUDGE'.

### Matrix - I

|   | 0 | 1 | 2 | 3 | 4 |
|---|---|---|---|---|---|
| 0 | J | U | G | R | Z |
| 1 | G | R | Z | J | U |
| 2 | Z | J | U | G | R |
| 3 | U | G | R | Z | J |
| 4 | R | Z | J | U | G |

### Matrix - II

|   | 5 | 6 | 7 | 8 | 9 |
|---|---|---|---|---|---|
| 5 | E | M | D | N | O |
| 6 | D | E | O | M | N |
| 7 | O | N | E | D | M |
| 8 | N | O | M | E | D |
| 9 | M | D | N | O | E |

**A.** 13, 31, 96, 10, 88      **B.** 00, 30, 56, 31, 99

**C.** 42, 43, 65, 21, 55      **D.** 34, 01, 89, 23, 66

**Ques (7-8):Direction:** In the following question, a word is represented by only one set of numbers are given in anyone of the alternatives. The sets of numbers given in the alternatives are represented by two classes of alphabets as in the two given matrices. The column and row of Matrix I are numbered from 0 to 4 and those of Matrix II from 5 to 9. A letter from these matrices can be represented first by row and then the column number e.g. in the matrices for questions 1 to 5, K can be represented by 65, 77 etc. H can be represented by 30, 11 etc. Similarly you have to identify the correct set for the word in the given question.

**Q.7** LEAST

### Matrix-I

|   | 0 | 1 | 2 | 3 | 4 |
|---|---|---|---|---|---|
| 0 | A | E | S | T | H |
| 1 | T | H | A | E | S |
| 2 | E | S | T | H | A |
| 3 | H | A | E | S | T |
| 4 | S | T | H | A | E |

### Matrix-II

|   | 5 | 6 | 7 | 8 | 9 |
|---|---|---|---|---|---|
| 5 | P | O | R | K | L |
| 6 | K | L | P | O | R |
| 7 | O | R | K | L | P |
| 8 | L | P | O | R | K |
| 9 | R | K | L | P | O |

**A.** 85, 01, 00, 40, 41      **B.** 32, 21, 44, 87, 44

**C.** 10, 34, 21, 32, 97      **D.** 00, 66, 33, 20, 34

**Q.8** POLAR

## Matrix-I

|   | 0 | 1 | 2 | 3 | 4 |
|---|---|---|---|---|---|
| 0 | A | E | S | T | H |
| 1 | T | H | A | E | S |
| 2 | E | S | T | H | A |
| 3 | H | A | E | S | T |
| 4 | S | T | H | A | E |

## Matrix-II

|   | 5 | 6 | 7 | 8 | 9 |
|---|---|---|---|---|---|
| 5 | P | O | R | K | L |
| 6 | K | L | P | O | R |
| 7 | O | R | K | L | P |
| 8 | L | P | O | R | K |
| 9 | R | K | L | P | O |

**A.** 66, 31, 95, 33, 43

**B.** 86, 97, 24, 88, 11

**C.** 79, 87, 59, 31, 76

**D.** 00, 86, 32, 89, 57

**Q.9** In a code language, the word 'TRIP' is denoted by the code 'QJSU'. The corresponding word for the code 'LSPD' is:

**A.** ROCK  **B.** EQTM  **C.** PORK  **D.** RUCK

**Q.10 Direction:** In the following question presents a situation and asks you to make a judgment regarding that particular circumstance. Choose an answer based on given information.

Eileen is planning a special birthday dinner for her husband's 35th birthday. She wants the evening to be memorable, but her husband is a simple man who would rather be in jeans at a baseball game than in a suit at a fancy restaurant. Which restaurant below should Eileen choose?

**A.** Alfredo's offers fine Italian cuisine and an elegant Tuscan decor. Patrons will feel as though they've spent the evening in a luxurious Italian villa.

**B.** Pancho's Mexican Buffet is an all-you-can-eat family style smorgasbord with the best tacos in town.

**C.** The Parisian Bistro is a four-star French restaurant where guests are treated like royalty. Chef Dilbert Olay is famous for his beef bourguignon.

**D.** Marty's serves delicious, hearty meals in a charming setting reminiscent of a baseball clubhouse in honor of the owner, Marty Lester, a former major league baseball all-star.

**Q.11** Which of the following numbers is different from the others?

19, 13, 27, 37, 17

**A.** 27  **B.** 19  **C.** 17  **D.** 13

**Q.12** Which of the following diagrams best depicts the relationship between various items/objects gives in these question?

Train, Motor Car, Engine

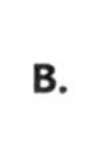

A.  B.

C.  D.

**Q.13** In a certain code 'PRINCE' is coded as 'SPLLFC'. In the same code how will 'RESPECTIVELY' be coded as?

**A.** RWGYCOWJWPCJ

**B.** RJJWPWGYCOWC

**C.** WGYCOWWPCJRJ

**D.** UCVNHAWGYCOW

**Q.14 Direction:** Dr. Miller has a busy pediatric dentistry practice and she needs a skilled, reliable hygienist to keep things running smoothly. The last two people she hired were recommended by top dentists in the area, but they each lasted less than one month. She is now in desperate need of a hygienist who can competently handle the specific challenges of her practice. Which one of the following candidates should Dr. Miller consider most seriously?

**A.** Marilyn has been a hygienist for fifteen years, and her current employer, who is about to retire, says she is the best in the business. The clientele she has worked with consists of some of the wealthiest and most powerful citizens in the county.

**B.** Lindy recently graduated at the top of her class from one of the best dental hygiene programs in the state. Prior to becoming a dental hygienist, Lindy spent two years working in a day care center.

**C.** James has worked as a dental hygienist for three years in a public health clinic. He is very interested in securing a position in a private dental office.

**D.** Kathy is an experienced and highly recommended dental hygienist who is also finishing up a degree in early childhood education, which she hopes will get her a job as a preschool teacher. She is eager to find a job in a paediatric practice, since she has always wanted to work with children.

**Q.15**

Find out the alternative figure which contains figure (X) as its part.

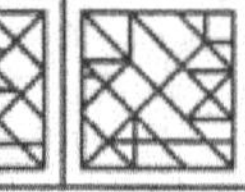

(X)  (1)  (2)  (3)  (4)

**A.** (1)  **B.** (2)  **C.** (3)  **D.** (4)

**Q.16**

Find out which of the figures (1), (2), (3) and (4) can be formed from the pieces given in figure (X).

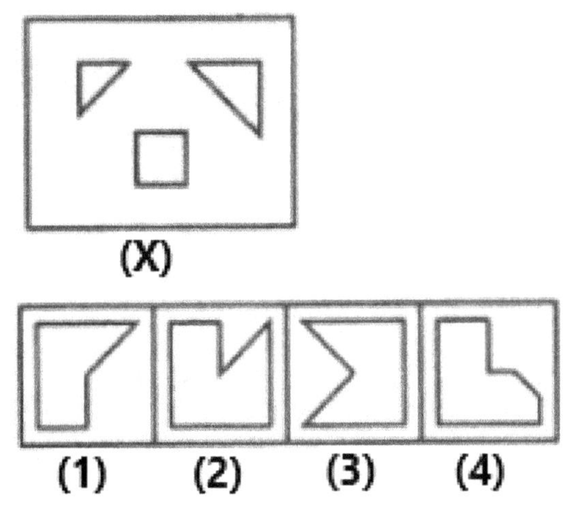

**(X)**

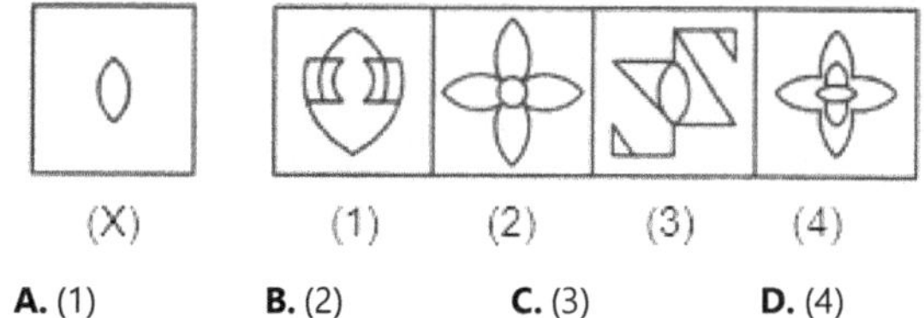

**(1)**    **(2)**    **(3)**    **(4)**

**A.** (1)    **B.** (2)    **C.** (3)    **D.** (4)

**Q.17**

Find out the alternative figure which contains figure (X) as its part.

(X)    (1)    (2)    (3)    (4)

**A.** (1)    **B.** (2)    **C.** (3)    **D.** (4)

**Q.18** Babli and Babita are siblings. Babita is the mother of Ayush. Ayush has two Children namely Rekha and Rupa. How's Babli related to Rupa?

**A.** Mother
**B.** Sister
**C.** Grand Mother
**D.** Can't be determined

**Q.19** In the following question, select the odd number from the given alternatives.

**A.** 85431    **B.** 23870    **C.** 99300    **D.** 11559

**Q.20** In the following question, select the related group of letters from the given alternatives.

RIDE : LNBE :: HELP : ?

**A.** NINP    **B.** BAJP    **C.** JPCH    **D.** BJJP

**Q.21** A series is given with one term missing. Select the correct alternative from the given ones that will complete the series.

LC, OF, RI, UC, ?

**A.** YS    **B.** XL    **C.** ZL    **D.** XF

**Ques (22-23):** In the following question, a set of five alternative figures 1, 2, 3 and 4 followed by a set of four alternatives (A), (B), (C) and (D) is provided. It is required to select the alternative which represents three out of the five alternative figures which when fitted into each other would form a complete square.

**Q.22**

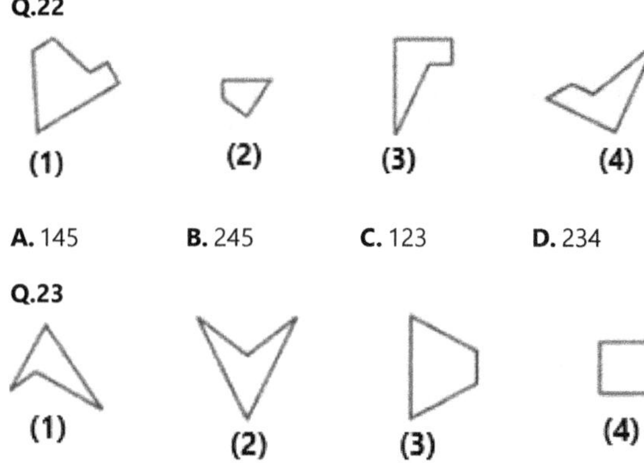

**(1)**    **(2)**    **(3)**    **(4)**

**A.** 145    **B.** 245    **C.** 123    **D.** 234

**Q.23**

**(1)**    **(2)**    **(3)**    **(4)**

**A.** 124    **B.** 345    **C.** 123    **D.** 135

**Q.24** In the question below is given a statement followed by three courses of action numbered (A), (B) and (C.) A course of action is a step or administrative decision to be taken for. improvement, follow-up or further action in regard to the problem, policy, etc. On the basis of the information given in the statement, you have to assume everything in the statement to be true, then decide which of the suggested courses of action logically follow(s) for pursuing.

**Statement:**

A large private bank has decided to retrench one-third of its employees in view of the huge losses incurred by it during the past three quarters.

**Courses of action:**

(A) The Government should issue a notification to general public to immediately: stop all transactions with the bank.
(B) The Government should direct the bank to refrain from retrenching its employees.
(C) The Government should ask the central bank of the country to initiate an enquiry into the bank's activities and submit its report.

**A.** None    **B.** Only (A)    **C.** Only (B)    **D.** Only (C)

**Q.25** Identify the diagram that best represents the relationship among the given classes.

India, Maharashtra and Kerala

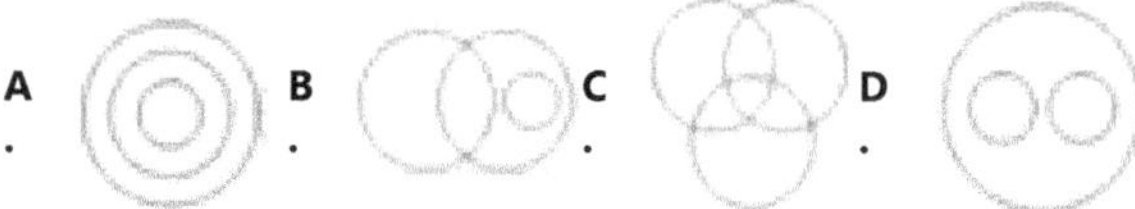

**A**    **B**    **C**    **D**

# General Awareness

**Q.26** Who among the following introduced the Preventive Detention Bill in 1950 in the Indian parliament?

**A.** Baldev Singh
**B.** Narahar Vishnu Gadgil
**C.** Sardar Patel
**D.** Jawahar Lal Nehru

**Q.27** Who has won the Best Male actor award in the International Indian Film Academy Awards 2022 held in Abu Dhabi?

A. Salman Khan
C. Vicky Kaushal
B. Shah Rukh Khan
D. Varun Dhawan

**Q.28** Which company has signed a Memorandum of Understanding (MoU) with SIDBI to accelerate e-commerce for small industries in August 2022?

A. Flipkart   B. Zomato   C. Myntra   D. ONDC

**Q.29** Who has become the first Indian to win gold in the World Cadet Judo Championship 2022?

A. Avtar Singh
B. Linthoi Chanambam
C. Poonam Chopra
D. Kalpana Devi

**Q.30** On the advice of which committee the Railway Budget was merged with the General Budget?

A. Ashok Mehta Committee
B. Mandal Committee
C. Bibek Debroy Committee
D. None of these

**Q.31** Which fundamental right has been abolished by the 44th Amendment?

A. Right to Liberty
B. Right to Property
C. Right to Equality
D. Right to Religion

**Q.32** Which award is given to the coaches of sportspersons?

A. Dronacharya Award
B. Arjun Award
C. Kalidas Samman
D. Rajiv Gandhi Khel Ratna

**Q.33** Who was the Private Secretary of Mahatma Gandhi?

A. Gopal Krishna Gokhale
B. Mahadev Desai
C. Bipin Chandra Pal
D. Dadabhai Naoroji

**Q.34** Exam Warriors is an inspiring book for the youth Written by:

A. Narendra Modi
B. Yogi Adityanath
C. Manmohan Singh
D. None of these

**Q.35** With which of the following countries, India shares maximum length of border?

A. Pakistan
B. China
C. Bangladesh
D. Nepal

**Q.36** India's only active volcano is located at which among the following places?

A. Car Nicobar
B. Barren island
C. Maya Bunder
D. Lakshdweep

**Q.37** Where is the headquarter of ADB (Asian Development Bank)?

A. Manila, Philippines
B. Washington, USA
C. Manhattan, USA
D. Geneva, Switzerland

**Q.38** The First Indian satellite is:

A. Aryabhata spacecraft
B. Bhaskara-1
C. Rohini RS-1
D. INSAT-1A

**Q.39** Who discovered X-Ray?

A. Wilhelm Conrad Rontgen
B. William Lee
C. X Rollswick
D. I. Thompson

**Q.40** The tax levied by the union government on income of individuals is known as:

A. Personal income tax
B. Interest tax
C. Wealth tax
D. Corporation tax

**Q.41** Which of the following commission was appointed by the Central Government on Union-State relations in 1983?

A. Sarkariya commission
B. Dutt commission
C. Setalvad commission
D. Rajamannar commission

**Q.42** Quit India Movement Started in?

A. August 1945
B. August 1942
C. June 1942
D. July 1943

**Q.43** Who was called the Akbar of Kashmir?

A. Zain-ul-Abidin
B. Hussain Shah
C. Balban
D. Sujauddaulla

**Q.44** Which of the following is the overall literacy rate of India (Census 2011)? (Approximately)

A. 68%   B. 70%   C. 74%   D. 78%

**Q.45** The First Election Commissioner of India was?

A. S.P. Sen Verma
B. Dr Nagendra Singh
C. K.V.K. Sundram
D. Sukumar Sen

**Q.46** India's first National War Memorial is built in which city?

A. Amritsar
B. Mumbai
C. Allahabad
D. Delhi

**Q.47** Who among the following held the office of Vice President of India for two consecutive terms?

A. Dr. R Venkatramanan
B. Dr. Shankar Dayal Sharma
C. Dr. VV Giri
D. Dr. S Radhakrishnan

**Q.48** Which of the following taxes are levied by the Union government but collected and appropriated by the states?

A. Stamp duties
B. Excise duties on medical and toilet materials
C. Sales tax
D. (A) and (B)

**Q.49** Holkar Trophy is associated with which sport?

A. Bridge
B. Hockey

**C.** Football      **D.** Badminton

**Q.50** Who among the following received Padma Award 2021 for his Social Work?

**A.** Kangana Ranaut      **B.** P.V Sindhu

**C.** Tulsi Gowda      **D.** Oinam Bembem

## Quantitative Aptitude

**Q.51** Find the quadratic equations whose roots are the reciprocals of the roots of $2x^2 + 5x + 3 = 0$?

**A.** $3x^2 + 5x - 2 = 0$      **B.** $3x^2 + 5x + 2 = 0$

**C.** $3x^2 - 5x + 2 = 0$      **D.** $3x^2 - 5x - 2 = 0$

**Q.52** The total cost of a chair and table is Rs. $600$ and the ratio of cost of one chair and table is $7:5$. Find the cost of chair.

**A.** Rs. $400$    **B.** Rs. $350$    **C.** Rs. $250$    **D.** Rs. $450$

**Q.53** Find value of $M - \dfrac{1}{M}$, if $M + \dfrac{1}{M} = 4$?

**A.** $3\sqrt{2}$    **B.** $2$    **C.** $2\sqrt{3}$    **D.** $-4$

**Q.54** $\dfrac{5}{8}$ of $\dfrac{3}{10}$ of $\dfrac{4}{9}$ of a number is $60$. What is the number?

**A.** $270$    **B.** $702$    **C.** $720$    **D.** $506$

**Q.55** In a rally of $256$ students, boys and girls are in the ratio $9:7$. Find the number of girls.

**A.** $120$    **B.** $114$    **C.** $112$    **D.** $115$

**Q.56** Find the value of $\dfrac{a}{b} + \dfrac{b}{a}$, if a and $b$ are the roots of the quadratic equation $x^2 + 8x + 4 = 0$?

**A.** $15$    **B.** $14$    **C.** $24$    **D.** $26$

**Q.57** A bag contains Rs. $187$ in the form of Rs. $1, 50$ paise and $10$ paise coins in the ratio $3:4:5$. Then, the number of each type of coins is:

**A.** $102,136$ and $170$      **B.** $100,128$ and $150$

**C.** $101,135$ and $169$      **D.** None of these

**Q.58** $70$ is what percentage of $210$?

**A.** $33\dfrac{1}{3}\%$    **B.** $66\dfrac{2}{3}\%$    **C.** $40\%$    **D.** $30\%$

**Q.59** Simplify the fraction into simplest terms.

$$\dfrac{3258}{6822}$$

**A.** $\dfrac{7}{17}$    **B.** $\dfrac{181}{379}$    **C.** $\dfrac{181}{369}$    **D.** $\dfrac{8}{17}$

**Q.60** Circumference of a circle A is $1\dfrac{4}{7}$ times perimeter of a square. Area of the square is $784$ sq/cm. What is the area of another circle B whose diameter is half the radius of the circle A?

**A.** $154$ sq/cm      **B.** $156$ sq/cm

**C.** $35.8$ sq/cm      **D.** $616$ sq/cm

**Q.61** The average monthly salary or $A$ and $B$ is Rs. $14000$, that of $B$ and $C$ is Rs. $15600$, and that of $A$ and $C$ is Rs. $14400$. Monthly salary of B is:

**A.** Rs. $12400$      **B.** Rs. $12800$

**C.** Rs. $15200$      **D.** Rs. $16000$

**Q.62** A sum of money at simple interest amount to Rs. $720$ after $2$ years and to Rs. $1020$ after a further period of $5$ years. The sum is:

**A.** Rs. $600$    **B.** Rs. $450$    **C.** Rs. $650$    **D.** Rs. $500$

**Q.63** Cost Price of $22$ articles is same as the Selling Price of $18$ articles, find the profit percentage?

**A.** $33.33\%$    **B.** $22.22\%$    **C.** $11.11\%$    **D.** $1\%$

**Q.64** A certain sum of money amounts to Rs. $1008$ in $2$ years and to Rs. $1164$ in $\dfrac{7}{2}$ years. Find the sum and the rate of interest.

**A.** $10\%$    **B.** $11\%$    **C.** $12\%$    **D.** $13\%$

**Q.65** What is the present worth of Rs. $132$ due in $2$ years at $5\%$ simple interest per annum?

**A.** Rs. $123$    **B.** Rs. $132$    **C.** Rs. $120$    **D.** Rs. $119$

**Q.66** In a compound, the ratio of carbon and oxygen is $1:4$. Find the percentage of carbon in the compound.

**A.** $20\%$    **B.** $10\%$    **C.** $5\%$    **D.** $80\%$

**Q.67** Simplify: $\left(\dfrac{\frac{3}{2+\sqrt{3}} - \frac{2}{2-\sqrt{3}}}{2-5\sqrt{3}}\right) = ?$

**A.** $\dfrac{1}{2} - 5\sqrt{3}$      **B.** $2 - 5\sqrt{3}$

**C.** $1$      **D.** $0$

**Q.68** What will come in the place of question mark (?).

$$(25)^{7.5} \times (5)^{2.5} \div (125)^{1.5} = 5^{?}$$

**A.** $8.5$    **B.** $13$    **C.** $16$    **D.** $17.5$

**Q.69** The value of $\left(\dfrac{9^2 \times 18^4}{3^{16}}\right)$ is $= ?$

**A.** $\dfrac{3}{2}$    **B.** $\dfrac{4}{9}$    **C.** $\dfrac{16}{81}$    **D.** $\dfrac{32}{243}$

**Q.70** The length of the diagonal AC of a square ABCD is 10 cm. Find the length of each side of the square:

**A.** $7.07\ cm$    **B.** $6.05\ cm$    **C.** $8\ cm$    **D.** $9.12\ cm$

**Q.71** A train $270$ metres long is running at a speed of $36$ km per hour, How long will it take to cross a bridge of length $180$ m.

**A.** $40$ second      **B.** $45$ second

**C.** $50$ second      **D.** $35$ second

**Q.72** One third of a certain journey is covered at the rate of $25\ km/$ hour, one-fourth at the rate of $30\ km/$ hour and the rest at $50\ km/$ hour. The average speed for the whole journey is:

**A.** $35\ km/hr$      **B.** $33\dfrac{1}{3}\ km/hr$

**C.** $30\ km/hr$      **D.** $37\frac{1}{12}\ km/hr$

**Q.73** A is $30\%$ more efficient than B. How much time will they, working together, take to complete a job which A alone could have done in $23$ days?

**A.** 11 days      **B.** 13 days

**C.** $20\frac{3}{17}$ days      **D.** None of these

**Q.74** $8$ men can do work in $12$ days. After $6$ days of work, $4$ more men were engaged to finish the work. In how many days would the remaining work be completed?

**A.** 2 days    **B.** 3 days    **C.** 4 days    **D.** 5 days

**Q.75** In a race of $300$ m, P can beat Q by $25$ m, and in another race of $250$ m, Q can beat R by $30$ m. Then by how many meters will P beat Q in a race of $200$ meters?

**A.** $\frac{116}{3}$    **B.** $\frac{118}{3}$    **C.** $\frac{120}{3}$    **D.** $\frac{119}{3}$

# English Comprehension

**Ques (76-80):Direction: Read the passage given below and answer the question given under it.**

The strength of the electronics industry in Japan is the Japanese ability to organize production and marketing rather than their achievements in original research. The British are generally recognized as a far more inventive collection of individuals but never seem able to exploit what they invent. There are many examples, from the TSR Z hovercraft, high-speed train and Sinclair scooter to the Triumph, BSA and Norton motorcycle which all prove this sad rule. The Japanese were able to exploit their strength in marketing and development many years ago, and their success was at first either not understood in the West or was dismissed as something which could have been produced only at their low price. They were sold because they were cheap copies of other peoples' ideas churned out of a workhouse which was dedicated to hard grind above all else.

**Q.76** The main theme of this passage is:

**A.** Electronics industry in Japan

**B.** Industrial comparison between Japan and Britain

**C.** The importance of Original Research in industry

**D.** The Role of Marketing Efficiency in Industrial Prosperity

**Q.77** The TSR Z hovercraft, high-speed train, Sinclair Scooter, etc. are the symbols of Marketing:

**A.** Failure of Japanese      **B.** Success of Japanese

**C.** Failure of British      **D.** Success of British

**Q.78** The sad rule mentioned in this passage refers to:

**A.** The lack of variety in Japanese inventions

**B.** The inability of the Japanese to be inventive like the British the poorer marketing ability of the British

**C.** The poorer marketing ability of the British

**D.** The inability of the British to be industrious like the Japanese

**Q.79** According to the passage, prosperity in industry depends upon:

**A.** Marketing ability      **B.** Productivity

**C.** Official patronage      **D.** Inventiveness

**Q.80** It is evident from this passage that the strength of a country's industry depends upon:

**A.** Electronic development

**B.** Dedicated work force

**C.** Original research

**D.** International cooperation

**Ques (81-85):Direction:** In the following passage there are blanks, each of which has been numbered. These members are printed below the passage and against each, five words are suggested, one of which fits the blank appropriately. Find out the appropriate words.

Thought is the response of memory that has been stored through knowledge; knowledge is gathered through experience. That is experience, knowledge, memory stored in the brain, then_____ (1), then action. This_______ (2) our pattern of living, and the whole process is based on this movement. Man has done this for the last million years. He______ (3) caught in the cycle, which is the movement of thought. And within this area, he has choice. He can go from one corner to the other and say, "This is my choice, this is my movement of freedom" — but it is always within the_____ (4) field of the known. And knowledge is always accompanied by______ (5) because there is no complete knowledge about anything.

**Q.81** Memory stored in the brain, then ________(1), then action.

**A.** confused    **B.** thought    **C.** sarcastic    **D.** honest

**Q.82** This ______(2) our pattern of living,

**A.** is      **B.** are      **C.** have      **D.** has

**Q.83** He _________(3) caught in the cycle,

**A.** was being      **B.** were being

**C.** has been      **D.** have been

**Q.84** it is always within the _______(4) field of the known.

**A.** limited      **B.** unfettered

**C.** unlimited      **D.** cosmic

**Q.85** Knowledge is always accompanied by ________(5) because there is no complete knowledge about anything.

**A.** cognizance      **B.** ignorance

**C.** wisdom      **D.** competence

**Q.86 Given below is a set of five sentences, numbered 1 to 5 which are not in a meaningful order. Choose from the options given, the order which will be acceptable and meaningful.**

1. The Great Recession has had an immense role in the working of the Federal Reserve Bank as it highlighted some of the faults in the system.

2 Various minimal expenditure related firms took a great deal of propel, inability to pay it back made the market fall.

3. It was called the most observably terrible overall withdraw since World War II.

4. The faults were later corrected and it marked the arrival of the modern Federal Bank. The Great Recession was a period some place around 2000 and mid-2010 in which the world economy declined at an especially disturbing pace.

5. The clarification behind the subsidence was later found to be the failure of the Federal Reserve Bank to stop the tide of unsafe home credits.

**A.** 12435     **B.** 14352     **C.** 13452     **D.** 54321

**Q.87 Given below is a set of five sentences, numbered 1 to 5 which are not in a meaningful order. Choose from the given options, the order which will be acceptable and meaningful.**

1. Advertising is also advantageous to the consumers if it increases the sale of goods, industry prospers and prices may be reduced.

2. There is no obvious connection, for example, between a picture of a smiling girl and a certain brand sweet.

3. The advertiser's assumption is that by looking at such pictures, the consumer would be influenced to buy his products.

4. On the other hand, much of the canvassing, of which the consumer is the object, does not convey information but endeavours merely to draw the public attention to certain products.

5. But most people like looking at the pictures of pretty girls.

**A.** 54321     **B.** 12345     **C.** 14253     **D.** 24531

**Q.88 Direction: In the following question, some parts of the sentence may have an error. The error, if any, will be in one part of the sentence. Find out which part of the sentence has an error and select the appropriate option. If a sentence is free from errors, select 'No error' as your answer.**

The worker's union wanted /(a) she to take over /(b) as the new chairman /(c) of its coveted board /(d) No Error.

**A.** (a)     **B.** (b)     **C.** (c)     **D.** (d)

**Q.89** Given below is an ungrammatical, defective sentence and there are 4 options given. One of them is the correct and improved form of the sentence. Choose the one which improves the given sentence.

**Therein lie the danger of too much information.**

**A.** Therein lays the danger of too much information.

**B.** Therein lies a danger of much too information.

**C.** Therein lies the danger of much too information.

**D.** Therein lies the danger of too much information.

**Q.90** Given below is an ungrammatical, defective sentence and there are 4 options given. One of them is the correct and improved form of the sentence. Choose the one which improves the given sentence.

**A bird to the hand is worth two in the bushes.**

**A.** A bird in the hand is worth two in the bush.

**B.** Two birds in the hand are worth two in the bushes.

**C.** Birds in the hand are worthy of two in the bush.

**D.** A bird in the hands is worthy of two in the bush.

**Q.91** In the following question, a sentence has been given in Active Voice/Passive Voice. Out of the four alternatives suggested, select the one which best expresses the same sentence in Passive/Active Voice.

**By 1829, British goods worth seven crore rupees were being exported to India by Britain.**

**A.** India was exporting British goods worth seven crore rupees to Britain, by 1829.

**B.** By 1829, Britain exported British goods worth seven crore rupees to India.

**C.** By 1829, Britain was exporting British goods worth seven crore rupees to India

**D.** Britain exported British goods to India worth seven crore rupees by 1829.

**Q.92** Given below is a sentence which is to be transformed and rewritten as indicated in brackets and there are four options given. Choose the one which 'correctly' transforms the given sentence.

**Did she like putting her mother's old china in the dishwasher?**

**A.** She didn't like putting her mother's old china in the dishwasher.

**B.** She didn't like to put her mother's old china in the dishwasher.

**C.** She liked putting her mother's old china in the dishwasher.

**D.** She didn't like putting her mother's old china in the dishwasher.

**Q.93 Direction:** Read the sentence to find out whether there is an error in it. The error, if any, will be in one part of the sentence. The number of that part is the answer. If there is no error, the answer is:

This year (a) on my birthday (b) my parents gifted me the book (c) that I am fond with (d) No error.

**A.** (a)     **B.** (b)     **C.** (c)     **D.** (d)

**Q.94** Read the sentence given below. Pay attention to the words/phrase/segments in italics. Choose the appropriate ONE WORD substitutes for the phrase and clauses italicized.

**The volume of the TV was very loud; so I asked her to turn it down but she turned down my request.**

**A.** The volume of the TV was very loud; so I asked her to increase it but she accepted my request.

**B.** The volume of the TV was very loud; so I asked her to lower the volume but she declined my request.

**C.** The volume of the TV was very loud; so I asked her to turn it off but she refused my request.

**D.** The volume of the TV was very loud; so I asked her to change the channel but she accepted my request.

**Q.95** Given below is a sentence which divided into four parts labelled a, b, c and d. One of these parts contains an error. Choose the part that has the error.

**Lay your books (a)/ aside and (b)/ lay down to rest (c)/ for a while (d)/no error.**

**A.** (a)     **B.** (b)     **C.** (c)     **D.** (d)

**Q.96** Fill in the blanks with the correct form of idioms/proverbs by choosing the correct option given.

I only _______ to the gym __________.
A. goes, once in a silver moon
B. go, once in a blue moon
C. gone, once in a blue moon
D. did go, once in a black moon

**Q.97** Fill in the blanks with the correct form of idioms/proverbs by choosing the correct option given.

Keyneslan economic theory differs ___________ from Marrxian.
A. Variably                 B. Markedly
C. Literally                D. Usually

**Q.98** Choose the word SIMILAR in meaning to the given word.

Hide

A. Reveal        B. Conceal        C. Display        D. Exhibit

**Q.99** A keyword is given below. Choose the word which indicates the contradictory or opposite meaning (antonym) of the keyword.

Melody

A. Chant                  B. Lyric
C. Cacophony             D. Inflection

**Q.100** Given below is a set of four words. One of the four words is spelled wrongly. Choose the word that has been spelled wrongly.

A. Aparently              B. Aggressive
C. Ambassador            D. Attention

# // Smart Answer Sheet //

**Correct** — Indicates percentage of students who answered questions correctly.

**Skipped** — Indicates percentage of students who skipped questions.

| Q. | Ans. | Correct / Skipped | Q. | Ans. | Correct / Skipped | Q. | Ans. | Correct / Skipped | Q. | Ans. | Correct / Skipped | Q. | Ans. | Correct / Skipped |
|---|---|---|---|---|---|---|---|---|---|---|---|---|---|---|
| 1 | D | 81.45 % / 13.67 % | 17 | C | 53.57 % / 41.85 % | 33 | B | 45.96 % / 39.07 % | 49 | A | 40.87 % / 51.27 % | 65 | C | 47.8 % / 50.31 % |
| 2 | B | 62.08 % / 34.69 % | 18 | D | 60.24 % / 38.79 % | 34 | A | 57.46 % / 30.76 % | 50 | C | 40.05 % / 30.54 % | 66 | A | 79.44 % / 12.06 % |
| 3 | A | 67.55 % / 32.05 % | 19 | B | 58.88 % / 38.47 % | 35 | C | 49.53 % / 37.08 % | 51 | B | 63.77 % / 32.4 % | 67 | C | 76.02 % / 12.15 % |
| 4 | C | 43.77 % / 55.63 % | 20 | D | 60.73 % / 32.48 % | 36 | B | 23.76 % / 68.75 % | 52 | B | 68.18 % / 31.49 % | 68 | B | 55.1 % / 42.63 % |
| 5 | D | 83.96 % / 10.1 % | 21 | D | 59.03 % / 33.97 % | 37 | A | 46.23 % / 37.13 % | 53 | C | 55.59 % / 42.89 % | 69 | C | 83.81 % / 10.29 % |
| 6 | D | 53.02 % / 42.56 % | 22 | B | 45.0 % / 44.11 % | 38 | A | 68.4 % / 30.08 % | 54 | C | 79.41 % / 12.24 % | 70 | A | 43.64 % / 56.29 % |
| 7 | A | 62.68 % / 32.65 % | 23 | D | 42.42 % / 35.53 % | 39 | A | 87.41 % / 10.68 % | 55 | C | 84.94 % / 10.06 % | 71 | B | 64.59 % / 30.49 % |
| 8 | C | 46.2 % / 32.67 % | 24 | D | 41.43 % / 37.15 % | 40 | A | 43.49 % / 33.82 % | 56 | B | 48.19 % / 48.72 % | 72 | B | 59.06 % / 39.86 % |
| 9 | B | 66.71 % / 33.29 % | 25 | D | 51.86 % / 34.76 % | 41 | A | 44.79 % / 34.07 % | 57 | A | 54.95 % / 38.79 % | 73 | B | 46.57 % / 40.5 % |
| 10 | D | 40.85 % / 55.51 % | 26 | C | 51.53 % / 35.21 % | 42 | B | 89.17 % / 10.3 % | 58 | A | 86.92 % / 12.96 % | 74 | C | 77.8 % / 21.29 % |
| 11 | A | 78.07 % / 17.54 % | 27 | C | 66.87 % / 30.23 % | 43 | A | 78.1 % / 19.19 % | 59 | B | 81.05 % / 11.76 % | 75 | A | 68.22 % / 31.7 % |
| 12 | D | 61.23 % / 30.82 % | 28 | D | 43.68 % / 52.2 % | 44 | C | 51.43 % / 31.51 % | 60 | A | 62.61 % / 34.11 % | 76 | D | 55.17 % / 39.68 % |
| 13 | D | 52.4 % / 40.25 % | 29 | B | 46.54 % / 51.88 % | 45 | D | 49.66 % / 37.15 % | 61 | C | 47.78 % / 35.17 % | 77 | C | 64.75 % / 32.55 % |
| 14 | B | 55.44 % / 35.82 % | 30 | C | 45.12 % / 45.69 % | 46 | D | 53.86 % / 37.89 % | 62 | A | 66.3 % / 31.14 % | 78 | C | 47.97 % / 45.69 % |
| 15 | A | 68.69 % / 30.9 % | 31 | B | 49.17 % / 36.81 % | 47 | D | 69.01 % / 30.67 % | 63 | B | 40.56 % / 43.98 % | 79 | A | 50.53 % / 44.93 % |
| 16 | A | 67.27 % / 32.05 % | 32 | A | 68.91 % / 30.07 % | 48 | D | 58.05 % / 37.86 % | 64 | D | 64.96 % / 31.22 % | 80 | B | 45.95 % / 49.21 % |

| Q. | Ans. | Correct / Skipped |
|---|---|---|
| 81 | B | 51.96 % |
|  |  | 44.53 % |
| 82 | A | 40.2 % |
|  |  | 34.87 % |
| 83 | C | 67.82 % |
|  |  | 31.43 % |
| 84 | A | 64.46 % |
|  |  | 33.0 % |

| Q. | Ans. | Correct / Skipped |
|---|---|---|
| 85 | B | 59.96 % |
|  |  | 31.6 % |
| 86 | B | 30.8 % |
|  |  | 68.56 % |
| 87 | C | 48.93 % |
|  |  | 45.5 % |
| 88 | B | 86.4 % |
|  |  | 11.24 % |

| Q. | Ans. | Correct / Skipped |
|---|---|---|
| 89 | D | 77.83 % |
|  |  | 10.84 % |
| 90 | A | 55.82 % |
|  |  | 41.58 % |
| 91 | C | 53.97 % |
|  |  | 44.87 % |
| 92 | D | 45.3 % |
|  |  | 47.99 % |

| Q. | Ans. | Correct / Skipped |
|---|---|---|
| 93 | D | 18.07 % |
|  |  | 72.85 % |
| 94 | B | 55.63 % |
|  |  | 34.76 % |
| 95 | C | 59.79 % |
|  |  | 35.13 % |
| 96 | B | 79.68 % |
|  |  | 18.93 % |

| Q. | Ans. | Correct / Skipped |
|---|---|---|
| 97 | B | 57.79 % |
|  |  | 37.58 % |
| 98 | B | 68.55 % |
|  |  | 30.16 % |
| 99 | C | 63.56 % |
|  |  | 31.69 % |
| 100 | A | 64.86 % |
|  |  | 34.03 % |

## Performance Analysis

| | |
|---|---|
| Avg. Score (%) | 51.5% |
| Toppers Score (%) | 68.0% |
| Your Score | |

# //Hints and Solutions//

**1.** Bush, Macron and Putin are the Presidents of the US, Russia and France, whereas Narendra Modi is the Prime Minister of India.

Hence, the correct option is (D).

**2.** As Demographer is the study of the characteristics of human populations.

Similarly philatelist is collection of stamps and postages and thus it is related to stamps.

Hence, the correct option is (B).

**3.** From the given question:

A > D

C > B

B < D

E > B

E > A

C < A

From the above relations, we get two orders.

1st- E> A > C > B

2nd- E > A > D > B

From the above two orders, E is eldest and B is youngest.

Hence, the correct option is (A).

**4.** From the given series, we get

$$97 - 77 = 20$$

$$77 - 59 = 18$$

The difference between two successive terms in the sequence is decreasing by 2. So, after 20,18 the next difference should be 16.

$$\therefore 59 - x = 16$$

$$\Rightarrow x = 43$$

Hence, the correct option is (C).

**5.** Given series is:

7756, 7765, 7655, 7665, 7565

Arranging in descending order, we get

7765, 7756, 7665, 7655, 7565

Hence, the correct option is (D).

**6.**

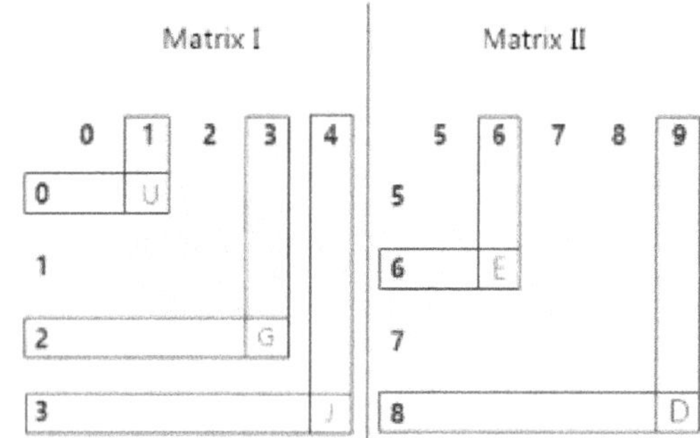


Hence, the correct option is (D).

**7.** L= 59, 66, 78, 85, 97

E= 01, 13, 20, 32, 44

A= 00, 12, 24, 31, 43

S= 02, 14, 21, 33, 40

T= 03, 10, 22, 34, 41

LEAST= 85, 01, 00, 40, 41

Hence, the correct option is (A).

**8.** P= 55, 67, 79, 86, 98

O= 56, 68, 75, 87, 99

L= 59, 66, 78, 85, 97

A= 00, 12, 24, 31, 43

R= 57, 69, 76, 88, 95

POLAR= 79, 87, 59, 31, 76

Hence, the correct option is (C).

**9.** The coding of DINE in question is based on the following pattern

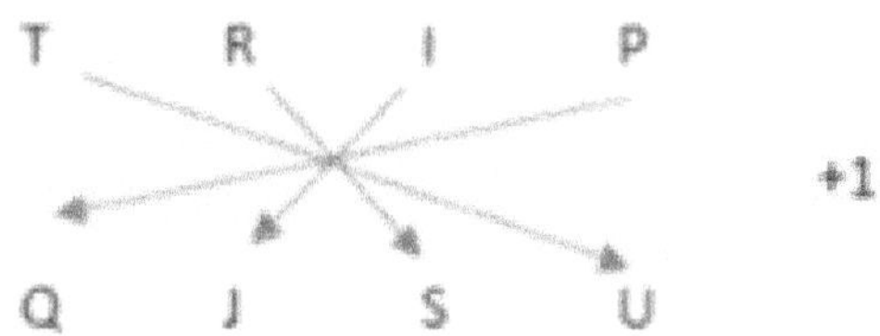


Repeating the same pattern, the code for LSPD will be EQTM.

Hence, the correct option is (B).

**10.** Since Eileen's husband does not enjoy fancy restaurants, options (A) and (C) can be ruled out. Option (B), although casual, doesn't sound as though it would be the kind of special and memorable evening that Eileen is looking for. Option (D), which is owned by a former baseball star and is described as "charming" and "reminiscent of a baseball clubhouse", sounds perfect for

Eileen's husband, who is described as a baseball fan and a man with simple tastes.

Hence, the correct option is (D).

**11.** Except 27, rest of all are the prime numbers, as 27 is a composite number.

Hence, the correct option is (A).

**12.** The diagram that best depicts the relationship between Train, Motor Car, and Engine is shown below:

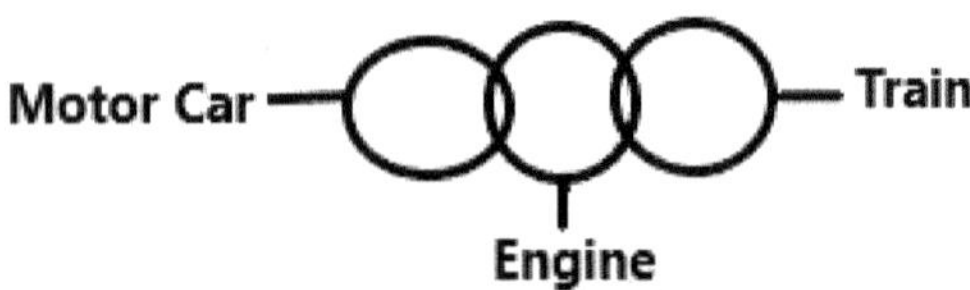


Both train and motor car runs on an engine.

Hence, the correct option is (D).

**13.**

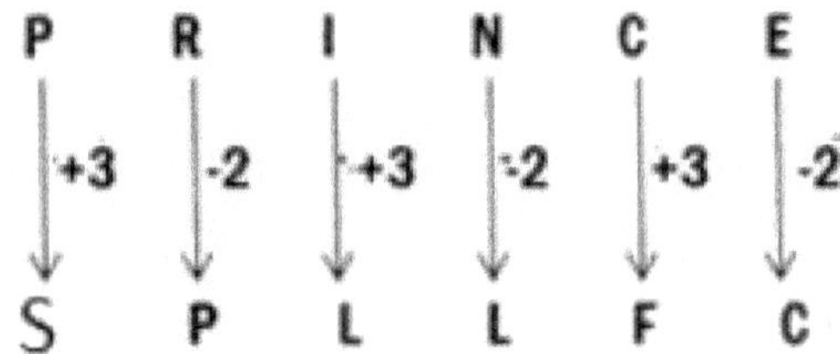


Similarily

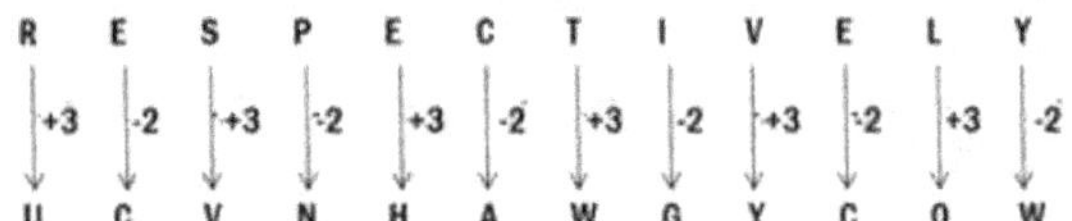


Hence, the correct option is (D).

**14.** The situation described indicates that Dr. Miller's practice presents some specific challenges, namely that it is a busy environment with a child clientele. There is also some indication that even highly recommended, experienced hygienists might not be cut out for Dr. Miller's office. There is nothing to suggest that Marilyn option (A) or James option (C) would be a good fit for Dr. Miller's practice. Kathy (choice D) has experience and she is also interested in working with children. However, the fact that she hopes to become a preschool teacher in the not-too-distant future indicates that she might not be the kind of committed, long-term employee that Dr. Miller needs. Lindy option (B), with her hands-on experience working with children as well as a degree from a prestigious dental hygiene program, is the most attractive candidate for the position based on the situation described.

Hence, the correct option is (B).

**15.**

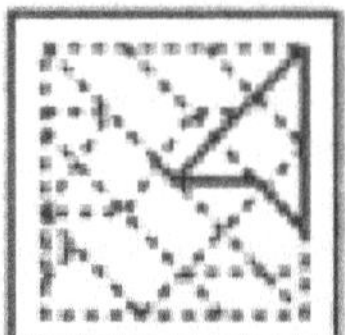

Hence, the correct option is (A).

**16.**

Hence, the correct option is (A).

**17.**

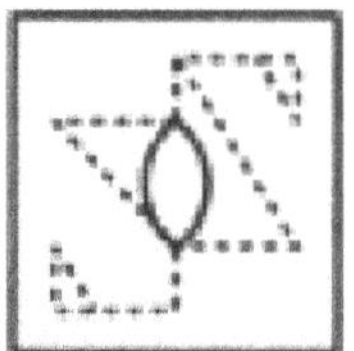

Hence, the correct option is (C).

**18.**

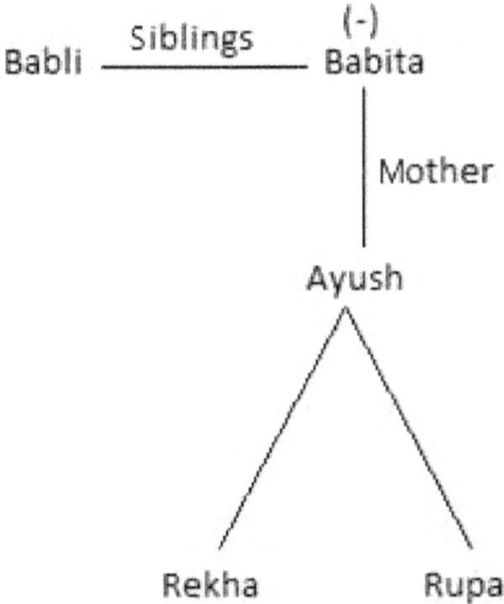


Since we do not know the gender of Babli in the given figure.

Therefore, We can not find the correct answer.

Hence, the correct option is (D).

**19.** The series will be,

8 + 5 + 4 + 3 + 1 = 21

2 + 3 + 8 + 7 + 0 = 20

9 + 9 + 3 + 0 + 0 = 21

1 + 1 + 5 + 5 + 9 = 21

Hence, the correct option is (B).

**20.** As

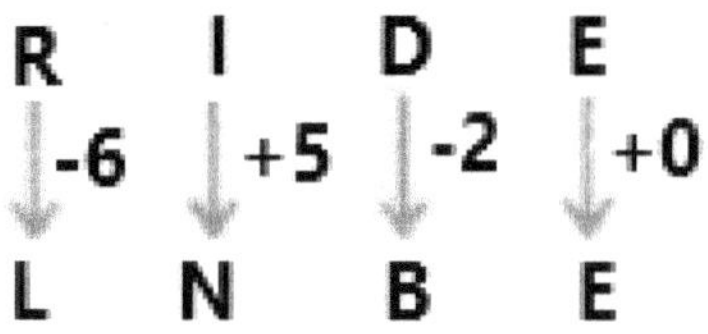

Similarily,

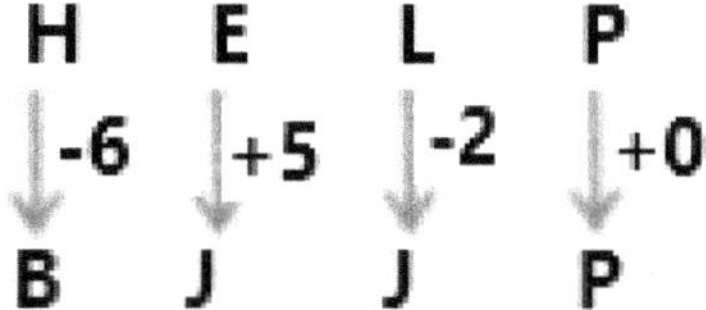

Hence, the correct option is (D).

**21.**

Hence, the correct option is (D).

**22.**

Hence, the correct option is (B).

**23.**

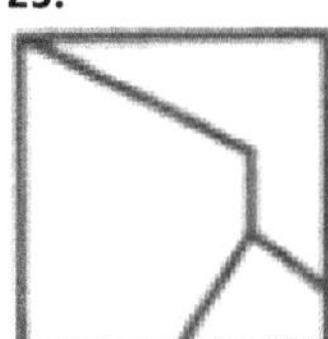

Hence, the correct option is (D).

**24.** The Government should ask the central bank of the country to initiate an enquiry into the bank's activities and submit its report.

Hence, the correct option is (D).

**25.** Maharashtra and Kerala both are states of India.

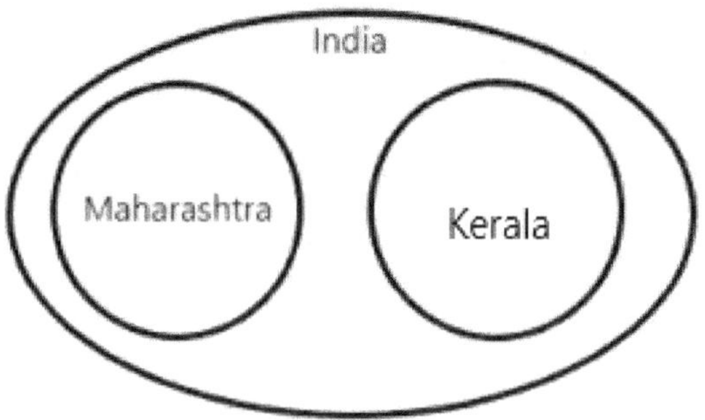


Hence, the correct option is (D).

**26.** The first preventive detention bill of Independent India was moved in 1950 by Sardar Patel. Patel had said that he had several sleepless nights before deciding if it was necessary to introduce the bill. Consequently, the Preventive Detention Act, 1950 was enacted by the Parliament on 26th February 1950.

Hence, the correct option is (C).

**27.** Vicky Kaushal has won the Best Male actor award in the International Indian Film Academy Awards held in Abu Dhabi. He has bagged the award for the best performance for a leading role (Male) at the IIFA 2022 held in Abu Dhabi. He won the award for the film Sardar Udham, directed by Shoojit Sircar.

Hence, the correct option is (C).

**28.** ONDC has signed a Memorandum of Understanding (MoU) with SIDBI for the coordination of functions of institutions engaged in similar activities in August 2022.

- The partnership is aimed to change the landscape of MSMEs by bringing them into the ONDC network and accelerating their participation in eCommerce.
- The MoU was signed by Sivasubramanian Ramanan, Chairman & MD of SIDBI and T Koshy, MD & CEO of ONDC.

Hence, the correct option is (D).

**29.** Indian judo player Linthoi Chanambam scripted history by winning a gold medal in the women's 57 kg category at the World Cadet Judo Championship 2022 in Sarajevo, Bosnia. 16-year-old Channambam has become the first Indian to win a gold medal at the World Judo Championships in any category.

Hence, the correct option is (B).

**30.** On the advice of the Bibek Debroy Committee, the Railway Budget was merged with the General Budget. Since 2017, Railway Budget has been merged with General Budget. Ministry of Railways will continue to function as a departmentally run commercial undertaking.

Hence, the correct option is (C).

**31.** The Right to property was abolished by the 44th amendment. The right was abolished due to a controversy that centred upon the questions: who is deemed to have property rights protected (e.g. human beings or also corporations), the type of property which is protected (property used for the purpose of consumption or production), and the reasons for which a property can be restricted (for instance, for regulations, taxation or nationalisation in the public interest).

Hence, the correct option is (B).

**32.** Dronacharya Award is given to the coaches of a sportsperson.

Dronacharya Award is an award presented by the Ministry of Youth Affairs and Sports, Government of India for excellence in sports coaching.

Hence, the correct option is (A).

**33.** Mahadev Desai was the Private Secretary of Mahatma Gandhi. He was an Indian Independence activist and writer. He has variously been described as "Gandhi's Boswell, a Plato to Gandhi's Socrates, as well as an Ananda to Gandhi's Buddha.

Hence, the correct option is (B).

**34.** Exam Warriors by PM Narendra Modi is an inspiring book for the youth. Written in a fun and interactive style, with illustrations, activities and yoga exercises, this book will be a friend not only in acing exams but also in facing life.

Hence, the correct option is (A).

**35.** India has 15106.7 Km of land border running through 92 districts in 17 States and a coastline of 7516.6 Km touching 13 States and Union Territories (UTs). The length of India's land borders with neighbouring countries is as under.

- Bangladesh- 4,096.7 km
- China- 3,488 km
- Pakistan- 3,323 km
- Nepal- 1,751 km
- Myanmar- 1,643 km
- Bhutan-699 km
- Afghanistan- 106 km

India shares 4096.7 Km of its land border with Bangladesh. West Bengal, Assam, Meghalaya, Tripura and Mizoram are the States which share the border with Bangladesh.

Hence, the correct option is (C).

**36.** The Barren Island is located in the Union Territory of Andaman and Nicobar Islands and is the only confirmed active volcano in South Asia.

Hence, the correct option is (B).

**37.** The headquarter of ADB (Asian Development Bank) is in Manila, Philippines. The Asian Development Bank (ADB) is a regional development bank established on 19 December 1966. A centre of operations, as of the police or a business, from which orders are issued, the chief administrative office of an organization.

Hence, the correct option is (A).

**38.** Aryabhata spacecraft was India's first satellite, named after the famous Indian astronomer of the same name. Contents Aryabhatta, which was launched by the Soviet Union on 19 April 1975.

Hence, the correct option is (A).

**39.** Wilhelm Conrad Rontgen discovered X-rays. Rontgen's discovery occurred accidentally when he was testing whether cathode rays could pass through glass when he noticed a glow coming from a nearby chemically coated screen. X-rays are electromagnetic energy waves that act similarly to light rays but at wavelengths approximately 1,000 times shorter than those of light.

Hence, the correct option is (A).

**40.** It is based on the principle of ability to pay. The tax levied by the union government on income of individuals is known as income tax.

Hence, the correct option is (A).

**41.** Sarkaria Commission was set up in 1983 by the central government of India to examine the central-state relationship on various portfolios. Justice Ranjit Singh Sarkaria (Chairman of the commission), was a retired judge of the Supreme Court of India.

Hence, the correct option is (A).

**42.** Quit India Movement or the India August Movement, was a movement launched at the Bombay session of the All-India Congress Committee by Mahatma Gandhi on 8 August 1942, during World War II, demanding an end to British Rule of India.

The Cripps Mission had failed, and on August 1942, Gandhi made a call to Do or Die in his Quit India speech delivered in Bombay at the Gowalia Tank Maidan.

Hence, the correct option is (B).

**43.** Emperor Zain-ul Abidin was known as "Akbar of Kashmir". He was called so because he was one of the greatest rulers of Kashmir. Like Emperor Akbar, he was also a generous and liberal king.

Hence, the correct option is (A).

**44.** The Literacy rate in India has improved a lot over the last decade. As per the data published by the 2011 census. India had managed to achieve an effective literacy rate of 74.04 % in 2011. In the 2001 Census, the country's literacy rate stood at 64.8%.

Hence, the correct option is (C).

**45.** Sukumar Sen (1899–1961) was an Indian civil servant who was the first Chief Election Commissioner of India, serving from 21 March 1950 to 19 December 1958.

Hence, the correct option is (D).

**46.** Prime Minister Narendra Modi will inaugurate the National War Memorial in Delhi, on February 25, 2019. It has been built on 40 acres of land at India Gate C-Hexagon. It has been built for honouring about 26,000 soldiers who had laid down their lives in wars and operations since Independence. National War Memorial has been prepared at a cost of 176 crores. The Central Government approved this amount in October 2015.

Hence, the correct option is (D).

**47.** Dr. S. Radhakrishnan was elected as the first Vice-President of India in 1952, and elected as the second Vice-President of India (1962–1967).

Hence, the correct option is (D).

**48.** The revenue generated from the Stamp duties, Excise duties on medical and toilet materials is imposed by the Central Government but collected and kept by the respective state government.

Hence, the correct option is (D).

**49.** Holkar Trophy is associated with Bridge sport. The bridge is the ultimate tricky card game that four people can play with a pack of 52 cards. It is the greatest source of enjoyment.

Hence, the correct option is (A).

**50.** President Ram Nath Kovind presents Padmashri to Smt Tulsi Gowda for social work.

She is an environmentalist from Karnataka. She has planted more than 30000 saplings. She has been involved in environmental conservation activities for the past six decades.

Hence, the correct option is (C).

**51.** The quadratic equation whose roots are reciprocal of $2x^2 + 5x + 3 = 0$ can be obtained by replacing $x$ by $\frac{1}{x}$.

So, $2\left(\frac{1}{x}\right)^2 + 5\left(\frac{1}{x}\right) + 3 = 0$

$\Rightarrow 3x^2 + 5x + 2 = 0$

Hence, the correct option is (B).

**52.** Given, cost of a chair and table is Rs. $600$ and the ratio of cost of one chair and table is $7:5$.

Let the cost of one chair be $a$ and one table be $b$.

$\therefore \frac{a}{b} = \frac{7}{5}$

$\Rightarrow a = \frac{7b}{5}$

Now, $a + b = 600$

$\Rightarrow \left(\frac{7b}{5} + b\right) = 600$

$\Rightarrow 12b = 3000$

$\Rightarrow b = $ Rs. $250$

$\therefore a = $ Rs. $350$

Hence, the correct option is (B).

**53.** Given,

$M + \frac{1}{M} = 4$

Squaring given equation we get,

$\left(M + \frac{1}{M}\right)^2 = 4^2 = 16$

$\therefore M^2 + 2 + \frac{1}{M^2} = 16$

$\therefore M^2 + \frac{1}{M^2} = 14$

Similarly, $\left(M - \frac{1}{M}\right)^2 = M^2 - 2 + \frac{1}{M^2}$

$= 14 - 2 = 12$

Taking square root,

$\Rightarrow M - \frac{1}{M} = \sqrt{12}$

$= 2\sqrt{3}$

Hence, the correct option is (C).

**54.** $\left(\frac{5}{8}\right) \times \left(\frac{3}{10}\right) \times \left(\frac{4}{9}\right) \times x = 60$

$\therefore x = 60 \times \frac{8}{5} \times \frac{10}{3} \times \frac{9}{4}$

$= 720$

Hence, the correct option is (C).

**55.** Given,

In a rally of $256$ students, boys and girls are in the ratio $9:7$.

$\therefore$ Number of girls $= \left(\frac{7}{16}\right) \times 256$.

$= 112$

Hence, the correct option is (C).

**56.** Given,

$x^2 + 8x + 4 = 0$

We know that the

Sum of zeros $= -\dfrac{\text{coefficient of } x}{\text{coefficient of } x^2}$

$\Rightarrow a + b = -\frac{8}{1} = -8$

Also we know that,

Product of the zeros $= \dfrac{\text{constant}}{\text{coefficient of } x^2}$

$\Rightarrow$ product of the zeros $= \frac{4}{1}$

$\Rightarrow ab = 4$

Now, we will be finding value of the following:-

$\frac{a}{b} + \frac{b}{a}$

$= \frac{a^2 + b^2}{ab}$

$$= \frac{(a+b)^2 - 2ab}{ab}$$

$$= \frac{64 - 8}{4}$$

$$= \frac{56}{4}$$

$$= 14$$

Hence, the correct option is (B).

**57.** Let number of Rs. $1, 50$ paise and $10$ paise coins be $3x, 4x$ and $5x$, respectively, then

$$3x + 4x \times \frac{50}{100} + 5x \times \frac{10}{100} = 187$$

$$\Rightarrow 3x + 2x + \frac{x}{2} = 187$$

$$\Rightarrow \frac{11x}{2} = 187$$

$$\Rightarrow x = 187 \times \frac{2}{11} = 34$$

$$\therefore 3x = 3 \times 34 = 102,$$

And $4x = 4 \times 34 = 136$

And $5x = 5 \times 34 = 170$

$\therefore$ Number of $1$ rupee coins is $102, 50$ paise coins is $136, 10$ paise coins $170$.

Hence, the correct option is (A).

**58.** $70$ of $210$ can be written as:

$$= \frac{70}{210}$$

To find percentage, we need to find an equivalent fraction with denominator $100$. Multiply both numerator & denominator by $100$

$$= \frac{70}{210} \times \frac{100}{100}$$

$$= \left( \frac{70 \times 100}{210} \right) \times \frac{1}{100}$$

$$= \frac{33.33}{100}$$

Hence, the correct option is (A).

**59.** Reducing the fraction

$$\frac{3258}{6822}$$

$$= \frac{18 \times 181}{18 \times 379}$$

$$= \frac{181}{379}$$

Hence, the correct option is (B).

**60.** Given,

Side of square $= \sqrt{784}$

$= 28$ cm

$\therefore$ Circumference of circle A

$$= 4 \times 28 \times \frac{11}{7}$$

$$\Rightarrow 2\pi r = 16 \times 11$$

$$\Rightarrow 2 \times \frac{22}{7} \times r = 16 \times 11$$

$$\Rightarrow r = \frac{16 \times 11 \times 7}{2 \times 22} = 28$$

Radius of circle $B = \frac{28}{4}$

$$= 7$$

$\therefore$ Area $= \pi r^2$

$$= \frac{22}{7} \times 7 \times 7$$

$$= 154 \text{ sq/cm}$$

Hence, the correct option is (A).

**61.** Given,

Salary of $A$ and $B$ is Rs. $14000$

Then,

$$\Rightarrow \frac{(A+B)}{2} = \text{Rs. } 14000$$

$$\Rightarrow A + B = \text{Rs. } 28000 \rightarrow \text{Eqn (i)}$$

Similarly $B + C = \text{Rs. } 31200 \rightarrow \text{Eqn (ii)}$

$A + C = \text{Rs. } 28800 \rightarrow \text{Eqn (iii)}$

Adding equation (i), (ii) and (iii),

We get $2(A + B + C) = \text{Rs. } 88000$

$A + B + C = \text{Rs. } 44000 \ldots \ldots \text{Eqn (iv)}$

On subtracting Eqn. (iv) with Eqn. (iii)

We will get $A + B + C - (A + C) = \text{salary of } B$

$44000 - 28800 = \text{Salary of } B$

Salary of $B = \text{Rs. } 15200$

So, Monthly salary of $B = \text{Rs. } 15200$

Hence, the correct option is (C).

**62.** Amount for $2$ years is Rs. $720$ and after a further $5$ years is Rs. $1020$.

Means Rs. $1020$ is a Amount in $7$ years.

So, to find Simple Interest for $5$ years, you need to subtract it.

As, for next $5$ years, $P = 720$

$A = 1020$

And

Simple Interest $=$ Amount $-$ Principal

Simple Interest for $5$ years $=$ Amount in $7$ years $-$ principal for further $5$ years.

Simple Interest for $5$ years $= 1020 - 720 = 300.$

So, Simple Interest per year $= \dfrac{300}{5}$

$= 60$

Thus, Simple Interest for $2$ years $= 60 \times 2 = 120.$

Now, Actual principal $=$ Amount for $2$ years $-$ Simple Interest for $2$ years.

$= 720 - 120$

$=$ Rs. 600

Hence, the correct option is (A).

**63.** Let the Cost Price of $1$ article $=$ Rs. $1$

From the given data,

Then, the Selling Price of $1$ article $= \dfrac{22}{18}$

$= \dfrac{11}{9}$

Then, Profit $=$ Selling Price $-$ Cost Price $= \frac{11}{9} - 1$

$= \dfrac{2}{9}$

Required, profit $\% = \dfrac{Profit}{CP} \times 100$

$= [\dfrac{\left(\frac{2}{9}\right)}{1}] \times 100$

$= \dfrac{200}{9}$

$= 22.222\%$

Hence, the correct option is (B).

**64.** Given,

$=$ Simple Interest for $3\frac{1}{2}$ years $-$ Simple Interest for $2$ years

$=$ Rs. $(1164 - 1008)$

$=$ Rs. $156$

Simple Interest for $1$ years $=$ Rs. $\left(156 \times \dfrac{2}{3}\right)$

$=$ Rs. $104$

Simple Interest for $2$ years $=$ Rs. $104 \times 2$

$=$ Rs. $208$

So, principal $=$ Amount of $2$ years $-$ Simple Interest of $2$ years.

$=$ Rs. $(1008 - 208)$

$=$ Rs. $800$

Now $P = 800,$ T $= 2$ years and

Simple Interest $=$ Rs. $208$

So, Rate $= \left(\dfrac{100 \times 208}{800 \times 2}\right)$

$= 13\%$

Hence, the correct option is (D).

**65.** Let the present worth be Rs. $x$.

Then, Simple Interest $=$ Rs. $(132 - x).$

Applying a formula,

Simple Interest $= \dfrac{P \times R \times T}{100}$

$\therefore \left(\dfrac{x \times 5 \times 2}{100}\right) = 132 - x$

$\Rightarrow 10x = 13200 - 100x$

$\Rightarrow 110x = 13200$

$\Rightarrow x = 120$

Hence, the correct option is (C).

**66.** Given:

The ratio of carbon and oxygen $= 1:4$

Formula used:

Percentage of carbon $= \left(\dfrac{\text{Value of carbon}}{\text{sum of ratio}}\right) \times 100$

Sum of ratio $= 1 + 4 = 5$

Percentage of carbon $= \left(\dfrac{1}{5}\right) \times 100$

$\Rightarrow 20\%$

The percentage of carbon is $20\%$

Hence, the correct option is (A).

**67.** Given,

$= \dfrac{\frac{3}{2+\sqrt{3}} - \frac{2}{2-\sqrt{3}}}{2 - 5\sqrt{3}}$

$= \dfrac{\frac{3(2-\sqrt{3}) - 2(2+\sqrt{3})}{(2+\sqrt{3})(2-\sqrt{3})}}{2 - 5\sqrt{3}}$

$$= \frac{6-3\sqrt{3}-4-2\sqrt{3}}{(2+\sqrt{3})(2-\sqrt{3})(2-5\sqrt{3})}$$

$$= \frac{2-5\sqrt{3}}{2-5\sqrt{3}}$$

$$= 1$$

Hence, the correct option is (C).

**68.** Let,

$$(25)^{7.5} \times (5)^{2.5} \div (125)^{1.5} = 5^x$$

Then,

$$\frac{\left(5^2\right)^{7.5} \times (5)^{2.5}}{(5^3)^{1.5}} = 5^x$$

$$\Rightarrow \frac{5^{(2 \times 7.5)} \times 5^{2.5}}{5^{(3 \times 1.5)}} = 5^x$$

$$\Rightarrow \frac{5^{15} \times 5^{2.5}}{5^{4.5}} = 5^x$$

$$\Rightarrow 5^x = 5^{(15+2.5-4.5)}$$

$$\Rightarrow 5^x = 5^{13}$$

$$\therefore x = 13$$

Hence, the correct option is (B).

**69.** Given,

$$\left(\frac{9^2 \times 18^4}{3^{16}}\right)$$

$$= \frac{9^2 \times (9 \times 2)^4}{3^{16}}$$

$$= \frac{\left(3^2\right)^2 \times \left(3^2\right)^4 \times 2^4}{3^{16}}$$

$$= \frac{3^4 \times 3^8 \times 2^4}{3^{16}}$$

$$= \frac{3^{(4+8)} \times 2^4}{3^{16}}$$

$$= \frac{3^{12} \times 2^4}{3^{16}}$$

$$= \frac{2^4}{3^{(16-12)}}$$

$$= \frac{2^4}{3^4}$$

$$= \frac{16}{81}$$

Hence, the correct option is (C).

**70.** $AC = 10\ cm$

We know that all sides of a square are equal. $\therefore AB = BC = CD = DA$

And each angle measures $90°$.

$$\therefore \angle ABC = \angle BCD = \angle CDA = \angle DAB = 90°$$

Now, in right angles $\Delta ABC\ \ AC^2 = AB^2 + BC^2$

(By Pythagorean theorem) $\Rightarrow 10^2 = AB^2 + AB^2$

$$\Rightarrow 100 = 2AB^2$$

$$\Rightarrow \frac{100}{2} = AB^2$$

$$\Rightarrow AB^2 = 50$$

$$AB = \sqrt{50} = 7.07(\text{ approx. })$$

Since all the sides of a square are equal, therefore, $AB = BC = CD = DA = 7.07$ cm (approx.)

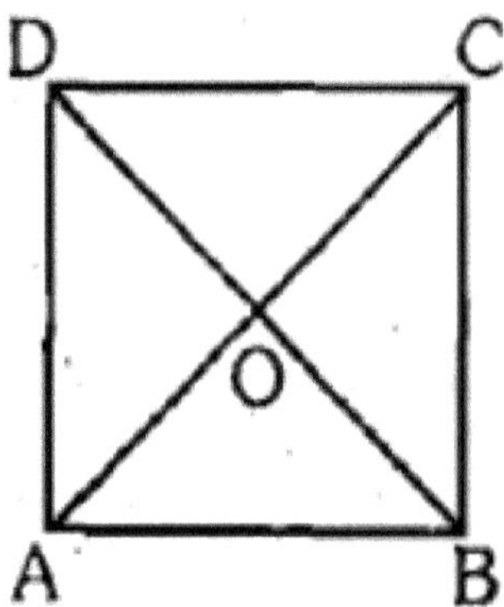

Hence, the correct option is (A).

**71.** Length of the train $= 270$ m

Speed of the train $= 36$ km/h

Length of the bridge $= 180$ m

Total Distance $=$ Length of train $+$ Length of bridge

$\Rightarrow$ Total Distance $= 270$ m $+ 180$ m

$\Rightarrow$ Total Distance $= 450$ m

Now the speed of the train is in km/h.

So we need to convert it into m/s.

For that we need to multiply with $\left(\frac{5}{18}\right)$.

$$\Rightarrow \text{Speed} = 36 \times \left(\frac{5}{18}\right)$$

$$\Rightarrow \text{Speed} = 10\ m/s$$

We know that, Speed $= \dfrac{\text{Distance}}{\text{Time}}$

$$\Rightarrow \text{Time} = \frac{\text{Distance}}{\text{Speed}}$$

$$\Rightarrow \text{Time} = \frac{450}{10}$$

$\Rightarrow$ Time $= 45$ seconds

So, it will takes $45$ second to cross bridge.

Hence, the correct option is (B).

**72.** Here, $x = 3, u = 25, y = 4, v = 30$

$z = \dfrac{12}{5}, w = 50$

Average Speed $= \dfrac{1}{\frac{1}{xu} + \frac{1}{yv} + \frac{1}{zw}}$

$= \dfrac{1}{\frac{1}{3 \times 25} + \frac{1}{4 \times 30} + \frac{1}{(12/5) \times 50}}$

$= \dfrac{1}{\frac{1}{75} + \frac{1}{120} + \frac{1}{120}}$

$= \dfrac{1}{\frac{1}{75} + \frac{1}{60}}$

$= \dfrac{1}{\frac{4+5}{300}}{300}$

$= \dfrac{300}{9} = \dfrac{100}{3}$

$= 33\dfrac{1}{3} \ km/hr$

Hence, the correct option is (B).

**73.** Ratio of times taken by A and B $= 100 : 130 = 10 : 13$

Suppose B takes $x$ days to do the work Then, $10 : 13 : : 23 : x$

$\Rightarrow x = \dfrac{23 \times 13}{10}$

$\Rightarrow x = \dfrac{299}{10}$

A's 1 day's work $= \dfrac{1}{23}$

B's 1 day's work $= \dfrac{10}{299}$

A $+$ B 's $1$ day's work

$= \dfrac{1}{23} + \dfrac{10}{299}$

$= \dfrac{23}{299}$

$= \dfrac{1}{13}$

A and B together can complete the work in $13$ days.

Hence, the correct option is (B).

**74.** Let, $1$ men does $1$ unit of work per day.

Total work: $8 \times 12 = 96$ units

$6$ days work of $8$ men

$= 8 \times 6 = 48$ units

work lelt $= 96 - 48 = 48$ units

After $6$ days $4$ men join.

So total men is $12$ men $(8 + 4)$ they will do $12$ unit of work per day.

Now, remaining work completed in

$= \dfrac{48}{12}$

$= 4$ days

Hence, the correct option is (C).

**75.** When P runs $300$ m,

Then Q runs $(300 - 25) = 275$ m

Now, When Q runs $250$ m,

Then R runs $(250 - 30) = 220$ m

When Q runs $275$ m then C runs $= 220 \times \dfrac{275}{250}$

$= 242$ m

When P runs $300$ m then C runs $242$ m,

Now in a $200$ meters race, when P runs $200$ runs, C will run:

$\Rightarrow \dfrac{242}{300} \times 200 = \dfrac{484}{3}$ m

$P$ beats R in a $200$ m race by $\left(200 - \dfrac{484}{3}\right)$

$= \dfrac{(600 - 484)}{3}$

$= \dfrac{116}{3}$ m

Hence, the correct option is (A).

**76.** The passage is about the role of marketing efficiency in industrial prosperity. The author has taken the example of Japanese who were very good in their marketing strategy. The British were great in inventing something however, they were really bad at marketing. The author's motive behind the comparison was to draw out attention towards the importance of marketing for a business perspective.

Hence, the correct option is (D).

**77.** It can be inferred from the following statements of the passage, 'The British are generally recognized as a far more inventive collection of individuals but never seem able to exploit what they invent. There are many examples, from the TSR Z hovercraft, high-speed train and Sinclair scooter to the Triumph, BSA and Norton motorcycle which all prove this sad rule.'

Hence, the correct option is (C).

**78.** The author believed that inspite of inventing more things than the Japanese, the British were unable to market their product like the Japanese did. This is also reflected in the following lines of the passage, "they are generally recognized as a far more inventive collection of individuals but never seem able to exploit what they invent".

Hence, the correct option is (C).

**79.** It can be well inferred from the theme of the passage. The passage has highlighted the fact that though British were the ones to invent things, they could however, not exploit them well since they were not good at marketing. The productivity and official patronage are out of context.

Hence, the correct option is (A).

**80.** The passage proves that if you have a dedicated workforce which knows how and when to bring tactics in play and take a lead ahead, success is guaranteed. Had the British had a dedicated workforce which could think of ways of exploiting their inventions they would have been the ones to have written the success stories, which was not the case.

Hence, the correct option is (B).

**81.** A Noun is required in the blank. Out of the given options only thought is a noun which means an idea. All the other options confused, sarcastic and honest are adjectives. Also from the first sentence of the passage, we can see a process that is mentioned in the first sentence is arranged in reverse order in the 2nd one.

Hence, the correct option is (B).

**82.** "This" is a singular pronoun and it will take singular helping verb "is" after it. Thus, "are" and "have" are eliminated. Also the sentence is in simple present tense thus "has" is also eliminated.

Hence, the correct option is (A).

**83.** "He" is a singular pronoun and it will take singular helping verb after it. Thus, "were being" and "have been" are eliminated. Also the sentence is in active voice thus "was being" is also eliminated. Thus "has been" is the correct option.

Hence, the correct option is (C).

**84.** In context of the sentence a word is required to compliment the word "within" which means inside or surrounded by. Thus limited is the best option. Unfettered means lose which does not fit in context of the sentence. Similarly, cosmic and unlimited are in contrast with the word "within".

Hence, the correct option is (A).

**85.** Ignorance which means lack of knowledge is the most appropriate option as in the latter part of the sentence it is mentioned that "there is no complete knowledge about anything." Thus, "ignorance" is the word complementing this part. Cognizance means knowledge or awareness, wisdom means knowledge, competence means ability. All the other options are in contrast with the latter part of the sentence.

Hence, the correct option is (B).

**86.** Sentence 1 should be the first sentence as it introduces the theme of the passage which is the Great Recession. Sentence 4 should be the second sentence since it continues to talk about the "fault" which is mentioned in sentence 1. The word "it" in

sentence 3 signifies what has been discussed in sentence 4. Therefore, 3 would be the next sentence. Sentence 5 should be next since it clarifies the reason for the great recession. Sentence 2 would be the last sentence as it concludes the passage.

Hence, the correct option is (B).

**87.** Sentence 1 should be the first sentence as it mentions the advantages of advertisement to the consumers. It should be followed by sentence 4 which provides some other perspective that is also true at the same time. Next sentence should be 2 as it gives an example to the already stated fact mentioned in sentence 4. Sentence 5 is in continuation with 2, so, it comes next. Sentence 3 concludes the passage stating that the motive behind these advertisements is to prompt a consumer to buy their products.

Hence, the correct option is (C).

**88.** The word she is a pronoun. The word wanted is a verb. The pronoun she is also used here as an object of the verb wanted. Hence, she must be replaced with her as it is an accusative case.

Hence, the correct option is (B).

**89.** The given sentence is incorrect due to the following reasons:

"Therein" is an adverb that means in that place, document, or respect. Whenever a sentence begins with "therein", it takes singular verb which means the use of plural form "lie" is incorrect and should be changed to "lies".

Hence, the correct option is (D).

**90.** The given sentence is a famous proverb and it is incorrectly written here. The correct form is "a bird in the hand is worth two in the bush.

Hence, the correct option is (A).

**91.** The given sentence is in passive voice of past continuous tense. The structures for active/passive voices are:

Passive: Object + was/were + being + verb (IIIrd from) + by + subject...

Active: Subject + was/were + verb (ing) + object...

So, with the help of the above structures, we can convert the given sentence into active voice:

By 1829, Britain was exporting British goods worth seven crore rupees to India.

Hence, the correct option is (C).

**92.** If the interrogative sentence is affirmative in nature, the assertive sentence will be negative.

Hence, the correct option is (D).

**93.** The preposition should be 'of' instead of 'with'. In case of relative pronoun being the object of the preposition in the sentence, the sentence generally ends with the preposition.

Hence, the correct option is (D).

**94.** The given sentence uses the same phrasal verb two times; however, it has a different meaning in the given contexts. Turn down means to lower the volume of something and it also means to refuse to accept a request, to decline. The first context is to lower the volume and the second context is to decline the request. The correct meanings have been used in option (B).

Hence, the correct option is (B).

**95.** The error is in part (C) of the sentence. The use of verb "lay" is incorrect and should be replaced by "lie". It is because "lay" means place some object on the ground or on a surface while "lie" means to place yourself on the ground or on a surface. Lay requires an object however, lie does not require any object. So you lie down on the sofa (no direct object), but you lay the book down on the table (the book is the direct object).

Hence, the correct option is (C).

**96.** The pronoun "I" is followed by a plural noun. So, the correct verb is "go". Also, the correct form of the idiom is "once in a blue moon".

Hence, the correct option is (B).

**97.** Markedly = prominently

Variably = inconstant

Literally = in literal context

Usually = under normal conditions; generally.

Whether the two theories differ in content or its intent is unclear from the given sentence; hence literally can't be the answer. 'Differs' and 'variably' are used to provide the same meaning; hence can't be used together. Usually is a structural misfit.

Hence, the correct option is (B).

**98.** Hide means to put or keep something out of sight.

Conceal means to not allow to be seen; to hide something.

Reveal means to make previously unknown or secret information known to others.

Display means to put something in a prominent place in order that it may readily be seen.

Exhibit means to publicly display a work of art in a museum.

Hence, the correct option is (B).

**99.** Melody means a sequence of single notes that is musically satisfying, a tune.

Cacophony means a harsh mixture of sounds.

Chant means a repeated rhythmic phrase, typically one shouted or sung in unison by a crowd.

Lyric means (of poetry) expressing the writer's emotions, usually briefly and in stanzas or recognized forms.

Inflection means the variation of the pitch of a musical note.

Hence, the correct option is (C).

**100.** The correct spelling is 'apparently'. It means as far as one knows or can see.

The meanings of the other words are:

Aggressive means ready or likely to attack or confront.

Ambassador is an accredited diplomat sent by a state as its permanent representative in a foreign country.

Attention is a notice taken of someone or something, the regarding of someone or something as interesting or important.

Hence, the correct option is (A).

**Q.1 Direction:** In the following question a statement is given, followed by two conclusions. Give answer.

**Statements:** The old order changed yielding place to new.

**Conclusions:**

I. Change is the law of nature.

II. Discard old ideas because they are old.

**A.** Only conclusion I follows

**B.** Only conclusion II follows

**C.** Either I or II follows

**D.** Neither I nor II follows

**Ques (2-3):Direction:** In the following question, select the related word from the given alternatives.

**Q.2** Eloquent : Inarticulate :: Obsolete : ?

**A.** Current    **B.** Bereave    **C.** Divest    **D.** Bleak

**Q.3** Trivial : Essential :: Outrage : ?

**A.** Agile    **B.** Bereft    **C.** Tranquil    **D.** Berate

**Q.4** In the following question, select the one which is different from the other three responses.

**A.** 1234 – 2345    **B.** 2467 – 4182

**C.** 2023 – 2001    **D.** 3123 – 2042

**Q.5** In question given below find the odd one from the given responses.

**A.** H160T    **B.** E70N    **C.** K198R    **D.** G109O

**Q.6 Direction:** In the following question, select the missing number from the given series.

13, 17, ?, 28, 35, 43

**A.** 20    **B.** 22    **C.** 25    **D.** 26

**Q.7 Direction:** In the given series one number is missing. Select the correct alternative from the given ones that will complete the series.

7, ?, -2, -8, -15

**A.** 4    **B.** 2    **C.** 3    **D.** 0

**Q.8** In a certain code language, "GOAT" is written as "45" and "COAT" is written as "41". How is "BOAT" written in that code language?

**A.** 40    **B.** 41    **C.** 42    **D.** 43

**Q.9** In a certain code language 'KEYBOARD' is written as 'FMGADQCT'. How will be 'TOUCHPAD' written in that code language?

**A.** FUQEBSJR    **B.** FVQWEJSB

**C.** FVQWEJRC    **D.** FVQWEJSC

**Q.10** In a drama, two characters are related to each other. One of them is the section mother of the other's daughter. How are the two related to each other?

**A.** Grandmother – Granddaughter

**B.** Mother – Daughter

**C.** Aunt – Niece

**D.** Husband – Wife

**Q.11** X told Y, "It is true that I am your real brother, but you are not my sister". How would Y be possibly related to X?

**A.** Cousin

**B.** Friend

**C.** Brother

**D.** Cannot be determined

**Q.12** In the given figure, how many people speak only Italian and only French Language?

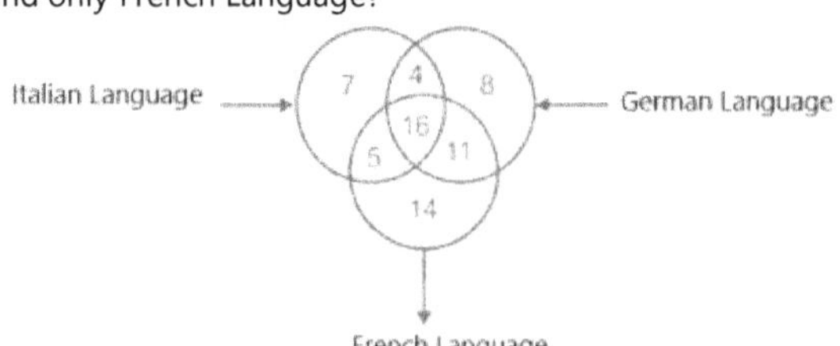


**A.** 21    **B.** 16    **C.** 27    **D.** 20

**Q.13** In the following figure, the square represents Teachers, the triangle represents swimmers, the circle represents Nurses and the rectangle represents Women. Which set of letters represents Teachers who are either swimmers or nurses?

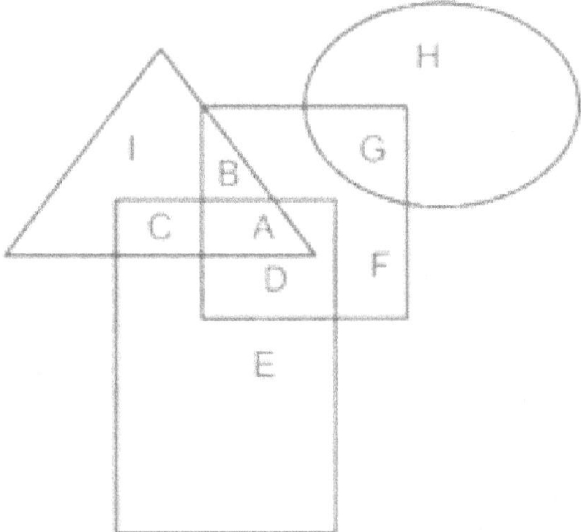


**A.** D, F    **B.** A, B, D, F, G

**C.** A, B, G    **D.** I, C, H

**Q.14** From amongst the figures marked (A), (B), (C) and (D), select the figure which satisfies the same conditions of placement of the dots as in figure (X).

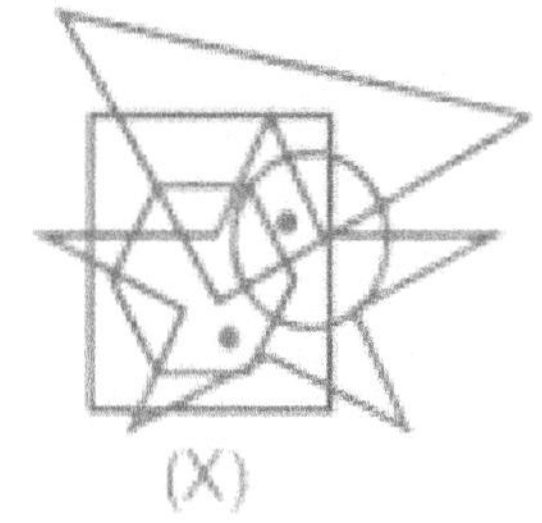

(X)

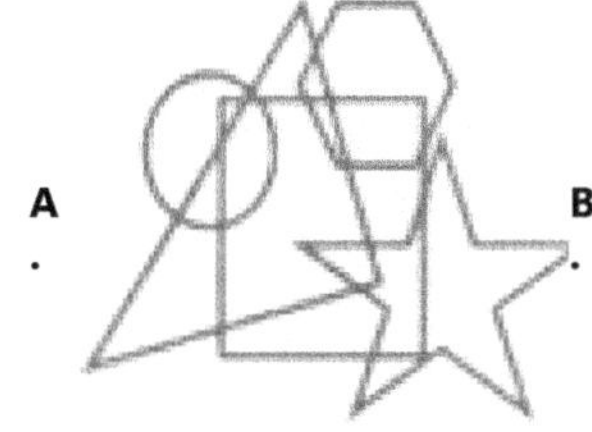

A.

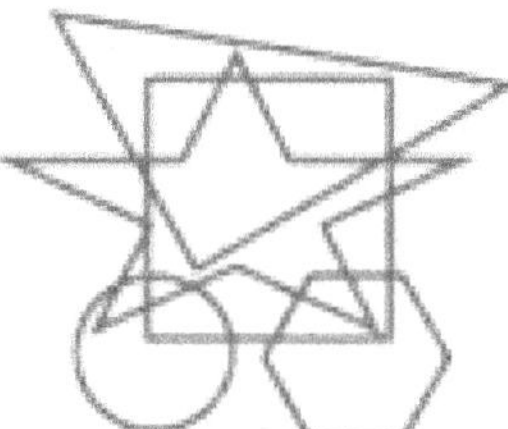

B.

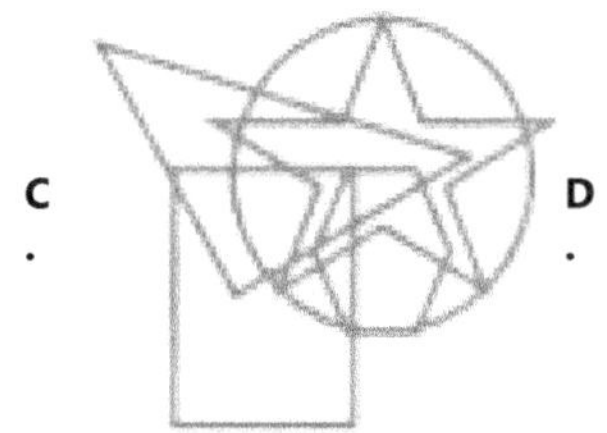

C.

D.

**Q.15** Select the option that depicts the correct mirror image for the given word.

A. ИƎTƎЯ

B. ƎƎTИЯ

C. ƎЯИƎT

D. ЯƎTИƎ

**Q.16** Select a figure from amongst the Answer Figures which will continue the same series as established by the five Problem Figures.

**Problem Figures:**

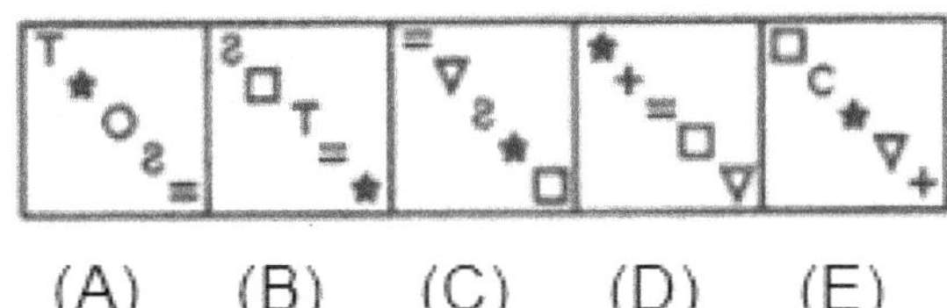

(A)   (B)   (C)   (D)   (E)

**Answer Figures:**

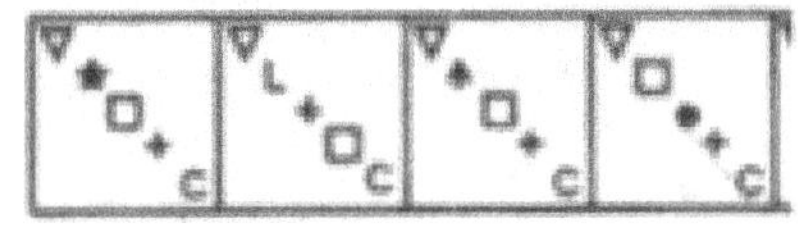

(1)   (2)   (3)   (4)

**A.** 1    **B.** 2    **C.** 3    **D.** 4

**Q.17** Select a figure from amongst the Answer Figures which will continue the same series as established by the five Problem Figures.

**Problem Figures:**

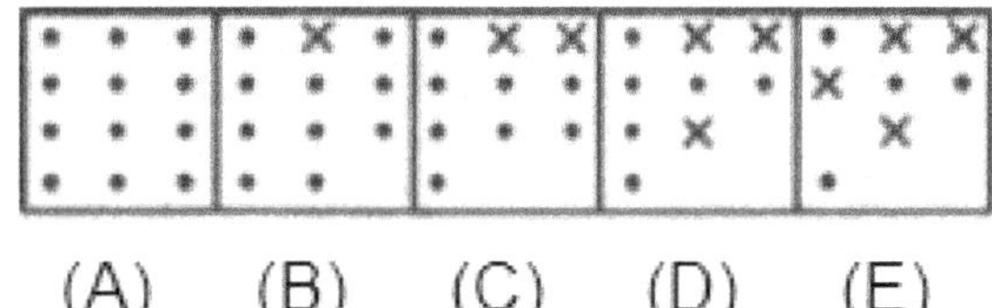

(A)   (B)   (C)   (D)   (E)

**Answer Figures:**

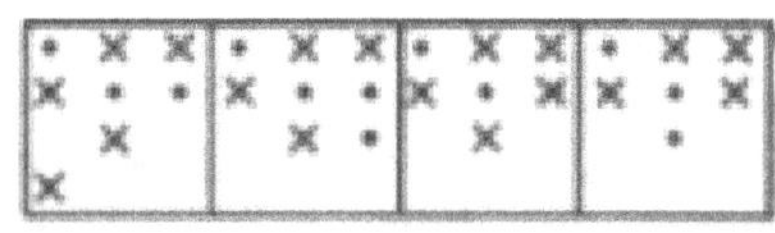

(1)   (2)   (3)   (4)

**A.** 1    **B.** 2    **C.** 3    **D.** 4

**Ques (18-19):Direction:** In the following question, select the related word from the given alternatives.

**Q.18** 11 : GO :: 14.5 : ?
**A.** CF    **B.** KM    **C.** IT    **D.** LP

**Q.19** Ammeter : Current :: Barometer : ?
**A.** Pressure    **B.** Thickness
**C.** Mass    **D.** Speed

**Q.20** Select the one which is different from the other three responses.
**A.** 919-949    **B.** 646-686    **C.** 828-848    **D.** 434-464

**Q.21** One day Ramesh tried to notice the shadow of a pole while coming home at 12:00 noon. In which direction could he find the shadow of the pole?
**A.** No shadow formed    **B.** West
**C.** East    **D.** South

**Q.22** One morning Mahesh was standing in front of a pole. The shadow of the pole falls exactly to his right. To which direction was he facing?
**A.** North    **B.** West    **C.** East    **D.** South

**Q.23** In the following question, select the number which can be placed at the sign of question mark (?) from the given alternatives.

| 2 | 5 | 625 |
|---|---|-----|
| 1 | 3 | 169 |
| 1 | 1 | ? |

**A.** 235     **B.** 121     **C.** 432     **D.** 226

**Q.24** In the following question, find the missing number from the given responses.

| 5 | 12 | 17 |
|---|----|----|
| 15 | 13 | 8 |
| 10 | 69 | 47 |
| 65 | 87 | ? |

**A.** 85     **B.** 87     **C.** 89     **D.** 83

**Q.25** In a certain code HEALING is written as BFIKHOJ. How is BEDTIME written in that code?

**A.** EFCSJNF     **B.** EFCSFNJ

**C.** EFCUFNS     **D.** CFESFNJ

# // Smart Answer Sheet //

**Correct** — Indicates percentage of students who answered questions correctly.

**Skipped** — Indicates percentage of students who skipped questions.

| Q. | Ans. | Correct / Skipped |
|----|------|-------------------|
| 1 | A | 13.38 % / 74.93 % |
| 2 | A | 43.19 % / 35.58 % |
| 3 | C | 43.38 % / 56.43 % |
| 4 | D | 40.38 % / 56.1 % |
| 5 | D | 19.41 % / 79.07 % |
| 6 | B | 41.63 % / 48.12 % |
| 7 | C | 57.72 % / 32.58 % |
| 8 | A | 69.43 % / 30.42 % |
| 9 | C | 59.05 % / 36.19 % |
| 10 | D | 41.68 % / 32.63 % |
| 11 | C | 40.7 % / 47.98 % |
| 12 | A | 67.2 % / 30.32 % |
| 13 | C | 13.77 % / 77.51 % |
| 14 | D | 49.97 % / 46.68 % |
| 15 | D | 64.8 % / 32.9 % |
| 16 | C | 53.68 % / 41.31 % |
| 17 | C | 67.61 % / 31.27 % |
| 18 | C | 57.26 % / 37.96 % |
| 19 | A | 85.92 % / 11.12 % |
| 20 | A | 65.06 % / 34.82 % |
| 21 | A | 40.28 % / 56.95 % |
| 22 | D | 61.39 % / 36.01 % |
| 23 | B | 43.87 % / 53.63 % |
| 24 | C | 43.35 % / 41.62 % |
| 25 | B | 52.15 % / 31.36 % |

| Performance Analysis | |
|----------------------|----------|
| Avg. Score (%) | 56.0% |
| Toppers Score (%) | 56.0% |
| Your Score | |

# //Hints and Solutions//

**1.** The old order changed, yielding place to new.

Conclusions -

I: Change is the law of nature - This is an implicit assumption as new replaces old as time changes need and demands changes.

II: Discard old ideas because they are old - Change of ideas could have many reasons as maybe they were not meeting with current needs and demands, so this is far fetched conclusion.

Clearly, I directly follows from the given statement. Also, it is mentioned that old ideas are replaced by new ones, as thinking changes with the progressing time. So, II does not follow.

Hence, the correct option is (A).

**2.** Eloquent and Inarticulate are exactly opposite in meaning. Eloquent means fluent or persuasive in speaking or writing, whereas Inarticulate means unable to express one's ideas or feelings clearly or easily, opposite of Inarticulate.

Similarly, Obsolete and Current are opposite to each other in meaning. Obsolete means no longer produced or used; out of date, whereas Current is up to date, exactly opposite to Obsolete.

Hence, the correct option is (A).

**3.** Trivial and Essential are exactly opposite in meaning. Trivial means 'of little value or importance', whereas Essential means 'important'.

Similarly,

Outrage and Tranquil are opposite to each other in meaning. Outrage means 'an extremely strong reaction of anger, shock', whereas Tranquil is the opposite of outrage meaning 'in a peaceful state'.

Hence, the correct option is (C).

**4.** (A) 1234 = 1 + 2 + 3 + 4 = 10,

2345 = 2 + 3 + 4 + 5 = 14;

14 − 10 = 4

(B) 2467 = 2 + 4 + 6 + 7 = 19,

4182 = 4 + 1 + 8 + 2 = 15;

19 − 15 = 4

(C) 2023 = 2 + 0 + 2 + 3 = 7,

2001 = 2 + 0 + 0 + 1 = 3;

7 − 3 = 4

(D) 3123 = 3 + 1 + 2 + 3 = 9,

2042 = 2 + 0 + 4 + 2 = 8;

9 − 8 = 1

Hence, the correct option is (D).

**5.** Here the places of letters in English alphabet are multiplied and written in the middle of letters.

H160T → The value of H is 8 and value of T is 20 so the multiplication is 160.

E70N → The value of E is 5 and value of N is 14 so the multiplication is 70.

K198R → The value of K is 11 and the value of R is 18 so the multiplication is 198.

G109O → The value of G is 7 and the value of O is 15 so the multiplication is 105.

Hence, the correct option is (D).

**6.**

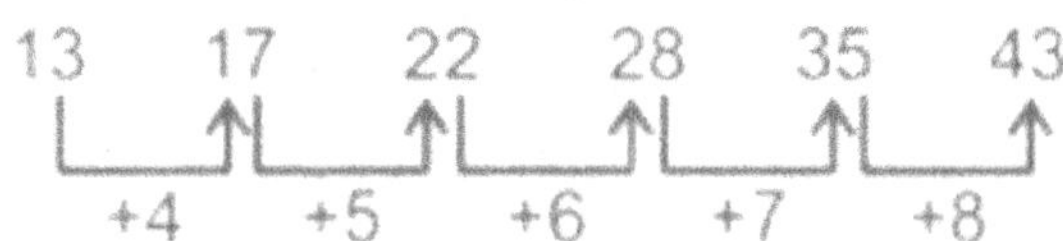


Hence, the correct option is (B).

**7.** Here, the logic followed is:

7 − 4 = 3;

3 − 5 = -2;

-2 − 6 = -8;

-8 − 7 = -15;

Hence, 3 is the missing number in the series.

Hence, the correct option is (C).

**8.** Consider the position of letters of the English Alphabet:

A B C D E F G H I J K L M N O P Q R S T U V W X Y Z

'GOAT' can be written as

'COAT' can be written as

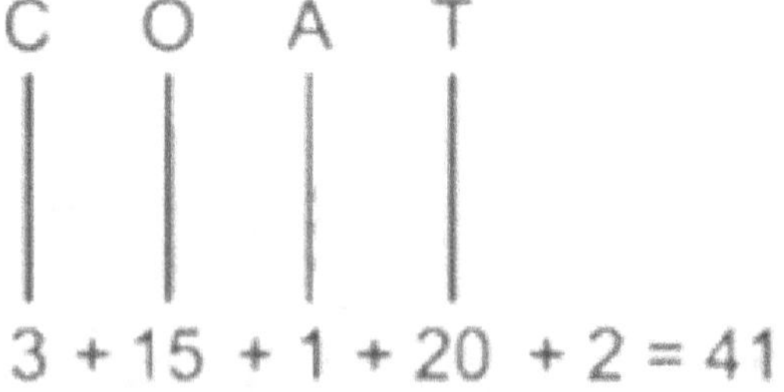


Similarly, 'BOAT' can be written as

$$2 + 15 + 1 + 20 + 2 = 40$$

Hence, the correct option is (A).

**9.** The pattern followed for coding KEYBOARD is as follows,

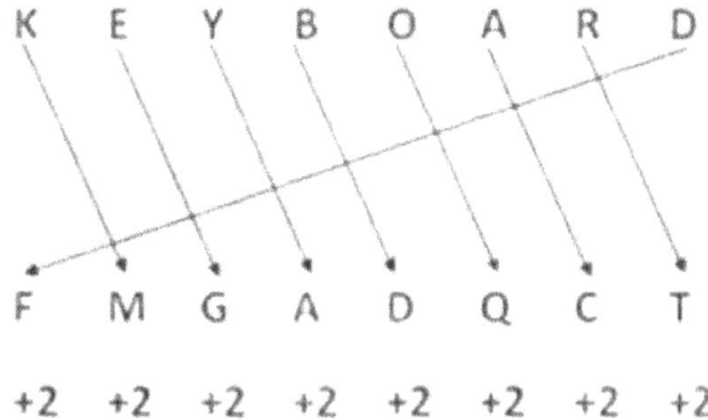

Following the same pattern,

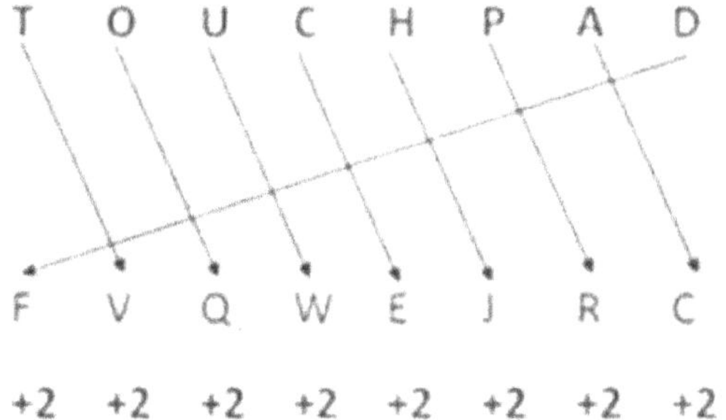

Hence, the correct option is (C).

**10.** The character is the mother of the other character's daughter. This means that they are both parents of the same child, and hence are husband and wife.

Hence, the correct option is (D).

**11.** Here X told Y that he is real brother of Y.

So gender of X is male.

Y can be male or female.

But then again X says that Y is not his sister.

That means Y is also a male and thus brother of X.

Hence, the correct option is (C).

**12.** According to question,

People who speak only in Italian = 7

People who speak only in French = 14

So, Total number of people = 7 + 14 = 21

Hence, 21 people can speak in Italian and French.

Hence, the correct option is (A).

**13.**

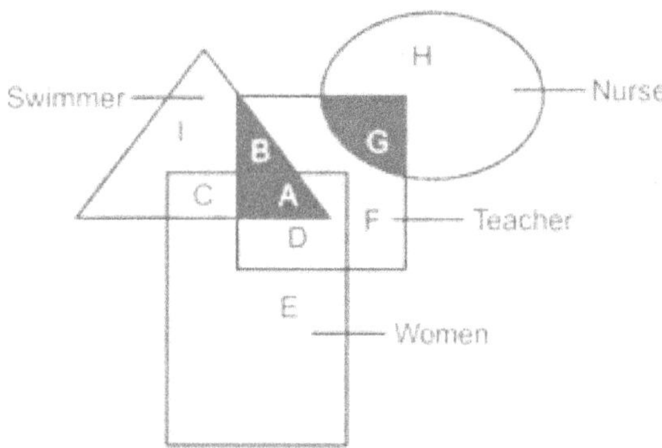


Teachers who are either swimmers or nurses represented by shaded part i.e., A, B and G.

Hence, the correct option is (C).

**14.** In figure (X), one of the dots lies in the region common to the hexagon, the star and the square only and the other dot lies in the region common to all the geometrical shapes expect hexagon. Only figure (D) consists of both types of regions.

Hence, the correct option is (D).

**15.** The correct mirror image of the given word is as follows,

So, mirror image of ENTER is ЯƎTИƎ.

Hence, the correct option is (D).

**16.** In each step, the symbols move in the sequence

and the symbol that reaches the encircled position gets replaced by a new one.

Hence, the correct option is (C).

**17.** In each step, one dot is lost while another dot is replaced by a cross.

Hence, the correct option is (C).

**18.** Consider, A =1, B = 2, C = 3,.........., Y = 25, Z = 26

G is 7th and O is 15th in the alphabetical order.

GO = 7 + 15 = 22 → 22/2 = 11

Similarly,

CF = 3 + 6 = 9 → 9/2 = 4.5 ≠ 14.5

KM = 11 + 13 = 24 → 24/2 = 12 ≠ 14.5

IT = 9 + 20 = 29 → 29/2 = 14.5 = 14.5

LP = 12 + 16 = 28 → 28/2 = 14 ≠ 14.5

Hence, the correct option is (C).

**19.** Current is measured by Ammeter.

Similarly, Pressure is measured by Barometer.

Hence, the correct option is (A).

**20.** The pattern followed is that the middle term of 2nd number is twice the middle term of 1st number in each pair

6$\underline{4}$6-6$\underline{8}$6 ⇒ 4 × 2 = 8

8$\underline{2}$8-8$\underline{4}$8 ⇒ 2 × 2 = 4

4$\underline{3}$4-4$\underline{6}$4 ⇒ 3 × 2 = 6

But in 9$\underline{1}$9-9$\underline{4}$9 ⇒ 1 × 2 = 2 ≠ 4

Hence, the correct option is (A).

**21.** At 12:00 noon, the rays are vertically downward hence there will be no shadow.

Hence, the correct option is (A).

**22.** In the morning sun rises in the east.

So the shadow will fall toward the west.

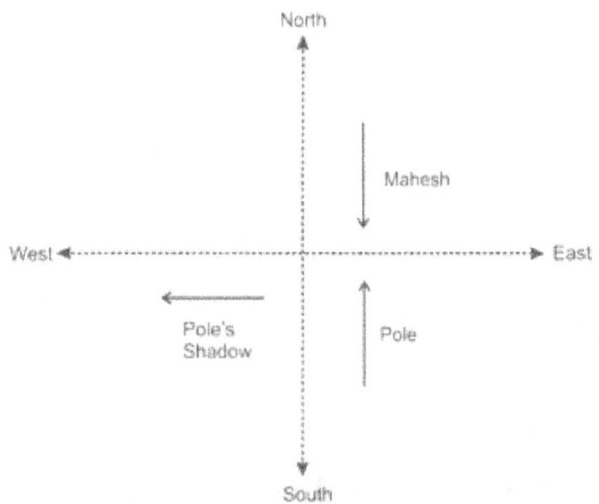


Since the shadow falls toward his right. It means the shadow is toward the left of the pole it means Mahesh is facing towards South.

Hence, the correct option is (D).

**23.** The pattern followed here is:

$25^2 = 625$

$13^2 = 169$

So, $11^2 = 121$

Hence, the correct option is (B).

**24.** The given logic is as follows:

(Row 1 × Row 2) – Row 3 = Row 4,

5 × 15 = 75 – 10 = 65

12 × 13 = 156 – 69 = 87

17 × 8 = 136 – 47 = 89

Hence, the correct option is (C).

**25.** The pattern is as follows,

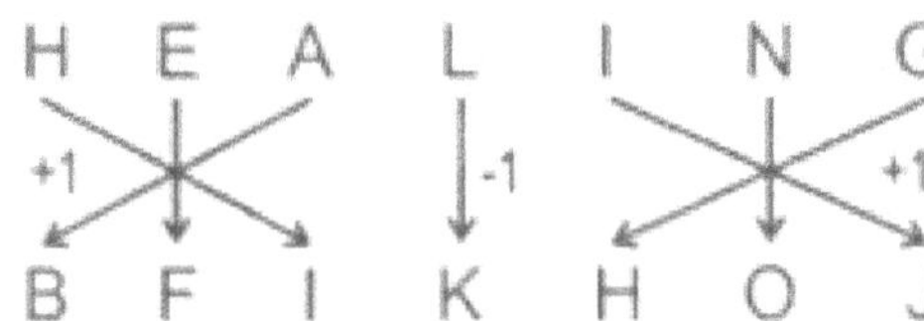


Similarly,

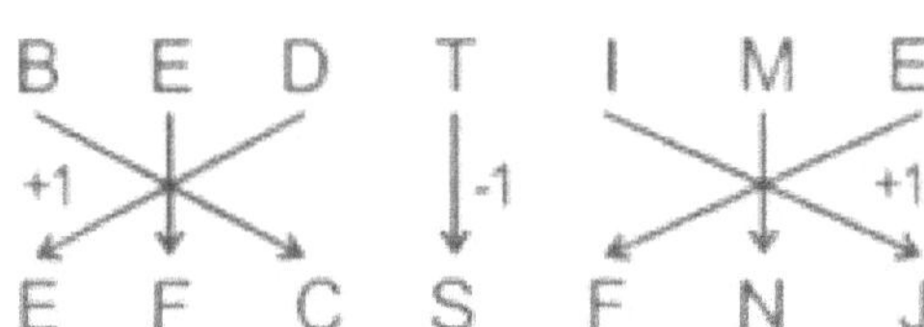


So, BEDTIME is coded as EFCSFNJ.

Hence, the correct option is (B).

**Ques (1-2):Direction:** In the following question, various terms of a number series are given with one term missing as shown by (?). Choose the missing term out of the given alternatives.

**Q.1** 31, 93, 90, 270, 267, ?
**A.** 667     **B.** 801     **C.** 934     **D.** 720

**Q.2** 8, 24, 12, 36, 18, ?
**A.** 72     **B.** 56     **C.** 54     **D.** 96

**Ques (3-4):Direction:** In the following question, various terms of a letter series are given with one or more terms missing as shown by (?). Choose the missing term(s) out of the given alternatives.

**Q.3** ab_ba_babd_acb_bdba_b
**A.** cdabc     **B.** dcabc     **C.** dcbac     **D.** acbcd

**Q.4** ABC, BDF, CFI, ?, EJO
**A.** DHL     **B.** DKM     **C.** EHM     **D.** DIM

**Q.5** Pointing to a boy a woman says, "His father is the father-in-law of that person whose father is the father-in-law of mine". Then how is the boy related to the woman?
**A.** Son     **B.** Brother
**C.** Son-in -law     **D.** Brother-in-law

**Q.6** If white is called red, red is called black, black is called green, and green is called blue. In this language, what will be the color of milk?
**A.** White     **B.** Red     **C.** Black     **D.** Green

**Q.7** If water is called air, the air is called a sea, the sea is called sky, the sky is called a road, the road is called a cloud. In this language, where do birds fly?
**A.** Sky     **B.** Sea     **C.** Cloud     **D.** Road

**Ques (8-10):Direction:** The following question based on analogy, a particular relationship between words/letters/numbers is given and another similar relationship has to be identified from the alternatives provided.

**Q.8** ACFG: 2478 :: HDRT:?
**A.** 851919     **B.** 951920     **C.** 951921     **D.** 851921

**Q.9** 9 : 24 :: ? : 6
**A.** 5     **B.** 3     **C.** 2     **D.** 1

**Q.10** DYTR : 67 :: HTBF : ?
**A.** 38     **B.** 36     **C.** 32     **D.** 40

**Q.11** Ratan introduces Sonu as his mother's only son's son. How is Sonu related to Ratan?
**A.** Uncle     **B.** Son     **C.** Nephew     **D.** Father

**Q.12** If '+' means '÷', '-' means 'x', '÷' means '-' and 'x' means '+', then –
42 ÷ 24 + 6 × 4 – 3 =?

**A.** 22     **B.** 50     **C.** 58     **D.** 26

**Q.13 Direction:** Select the option that correctly represents the relationship among the following:

Badminton, Baseball, Outdoor games

A.
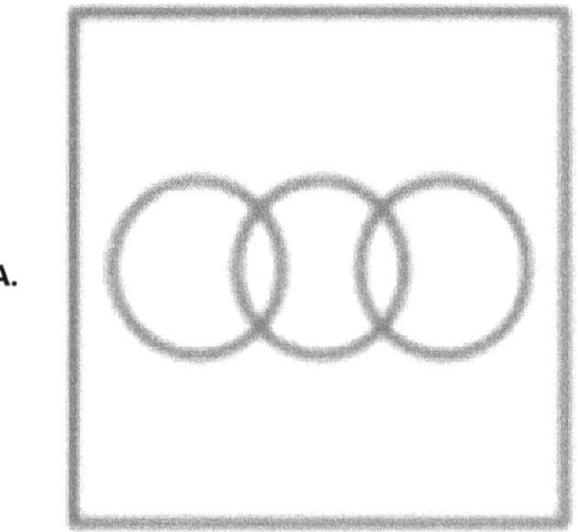

B.
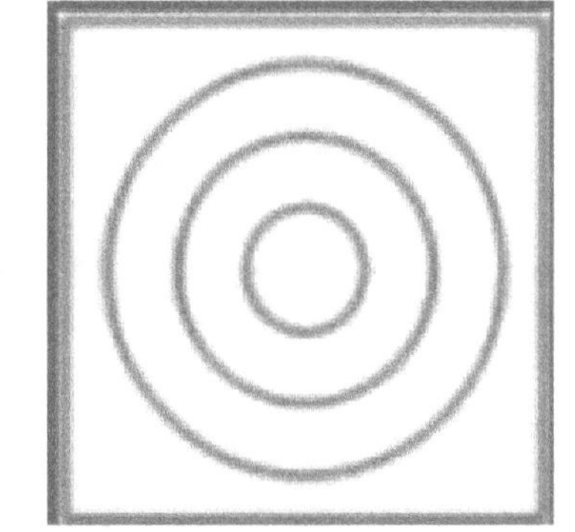

C.
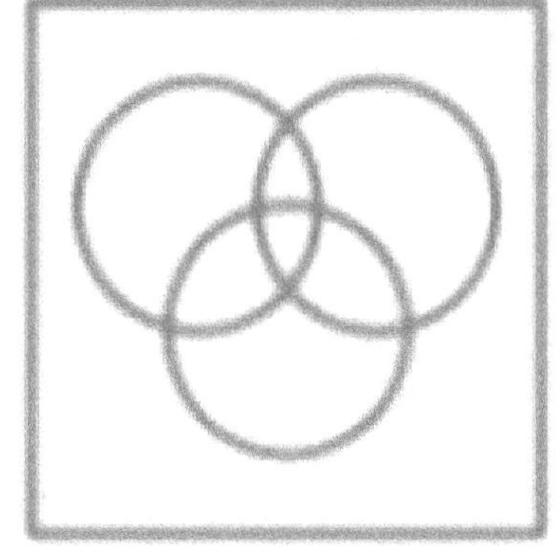

**D.**

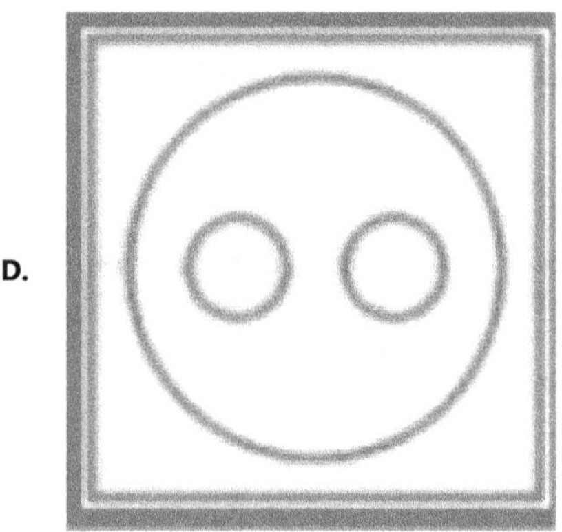

**Q.14 Direction:** Which numbered space in the figure below represents doctors who are players as well artists?

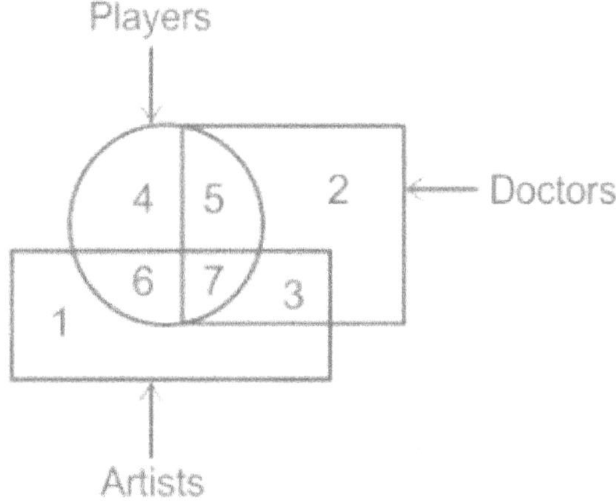

**A.** 2     **B.** 3     **C.** 6     **D.** 7

**Q.15 Direction:** There is 6 surface of dice which is A, B, C, D, E and F. Different position of dice is shown below. Which word will be on the opposite surface of D?

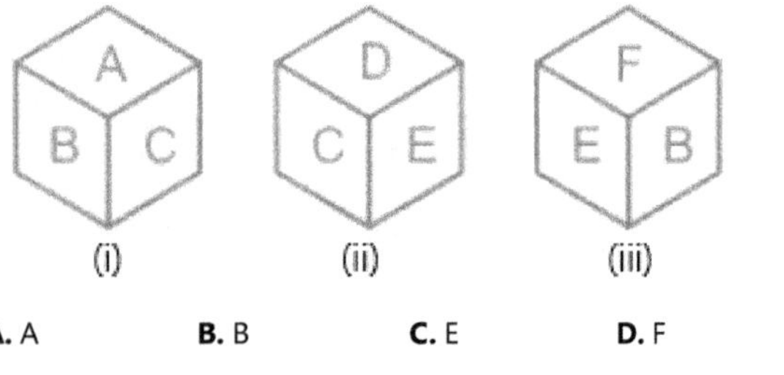

**A.** A     **B.** B     **C.** E     **D.** F

**Ques (16-17):Direction:** Select a suitable figure from the four alternatives that would complete the figure matrix.

**Q.16**

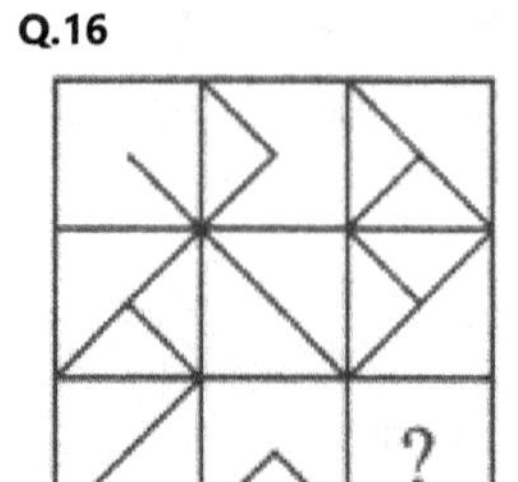

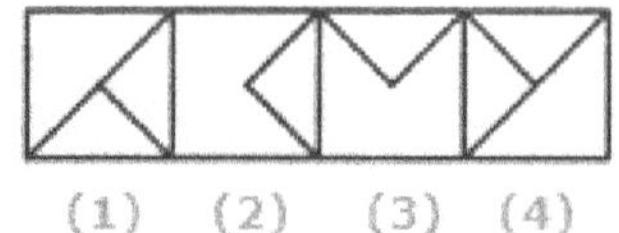

**A.** (1)     **B.** (2)     **C.** (3)     **D.** (4)

**Q.17**

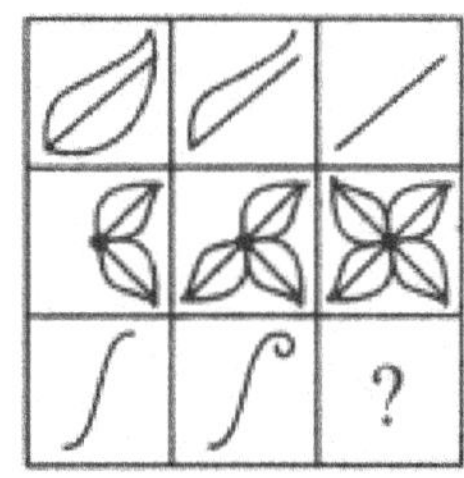

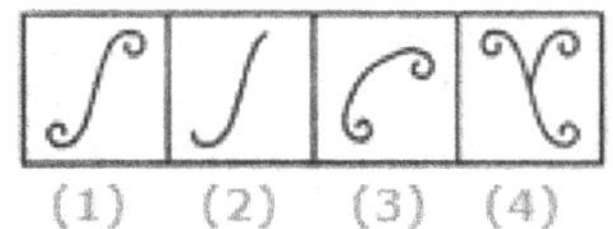

*[UP Police Sub Inspector, 2021]*

**A.** (1)     **B.** (2)     **C.** (3)     **D.** (4)

**Ques (18-19):Direction:** In the following question, select a figure from amongst the four alternatives, which when placed in the blank space of figure (X) would complete the pattern.

**Q.18**

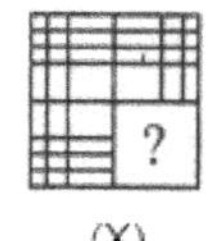

*[Telangana Police Constable, 2015]*

**A.** (1)     **B.** (2)     **C.** (3)     **D.** (4)

**Q.19**

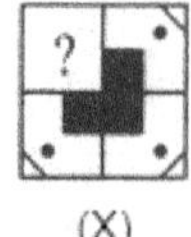

*[SSC Sub Inspector (CPO), 2020]*

**A.** (1)     **B.** (2)     **C.** (3)     **D.** (4)

**Q.20** If A = 4, K = 3, N = 2, P = 1, then the sum of which set of the letters makes the highest number?

| **A.** KANPK | **B.** NPAKN | **C.** PKANA | **D.** NAKNA | **A.** 11 | **B.** 18 | **C.** 20 | **D.** 21 |
|---|---|---|---|---|---|---|---|

**Q.21** If TOUR is coded as 1234, CLEAR is coded 56784 and SPARE as 90847, how will the word SCULPTURE be coded as:

**A.** 953601347  
**B.** 567903417  
**C.** 953016347  
**D.** 953603741

**Q.22** If in a certain language SISTER is coded as 535301 , UNCLE is coded as 84670 and BOY as 129 , how son is coded?

**A.** 923    **B.** 524    **C.** 342    **D.** 872

**Q.23 Direction:** If a mirror is placed on line AB, then which of the answer figures is the right image of the given figure?

**A.** 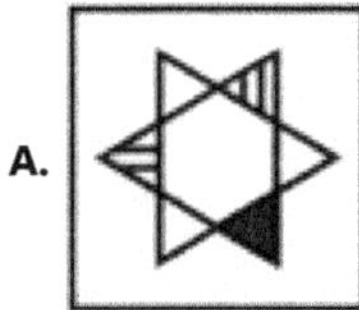    **B.** 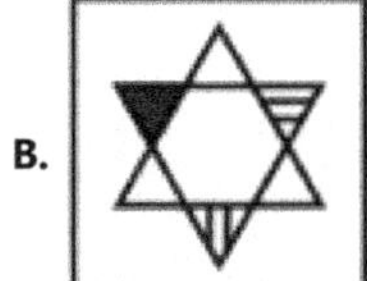

**C.** 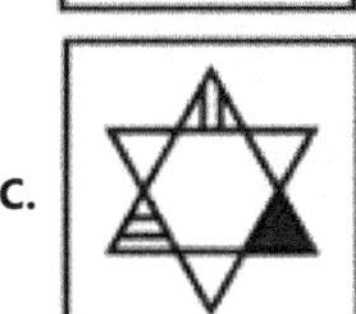    **D.** 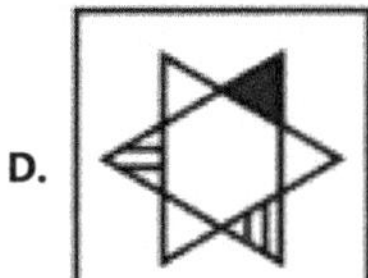

**Q.24 Direction:** From the given answer figures, select the one in which the question figure is hidden/embedded.

**A.** 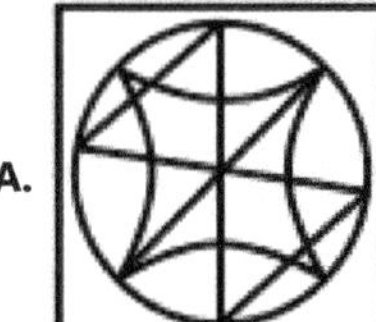    **B.** 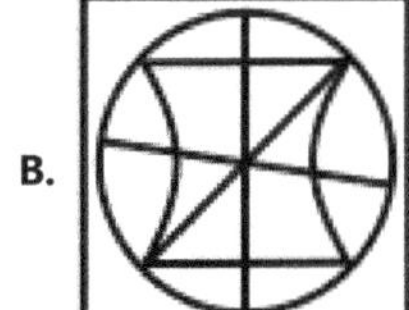

**C.** 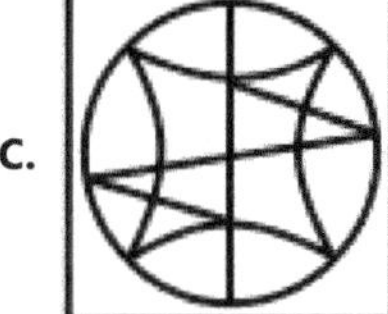    **D.** 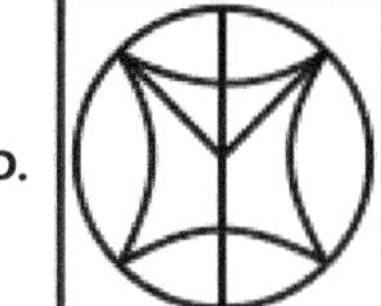

**Q.25** If you write down all the numbers from 1 to 100, then how many times do you write 3?

*[TNUSRB Sub Inspector, 2020]*

# // Smart Answer Sheet //

**Correct** — Indicates percentage of students who answered questions correctly.

**Skipped** — Indicates percentage of students who skipped questions.

| Q. | Ans. | Correct / Skipped |
|----|------|-------------------|
| 1 | B | 79.89 % / 17.57 % |
| 2 | C | 78.72 % / 14.91 % |
| 3 | C | 86.76 % / 11.04 % |
| 4 | A | 43.09 % / 43.97 % |
| 5 | B | 58.95 % / 32.62 % |
| 6 | B | 50.96 % / 40.94 % |
| 7 | D | 83.55 % / 10.69 % |
| 8 | C | 77.68 % / 18.63 % |
| 9 | B | 85.24 % / 10.52 % |
| 10 | B | 57.22 % / 31.89 % |
| 11 | B | 58.42 % / 35.84 % |
| 12 | B | 69.42 % / 30.19 % |
| 13 | D | 40.61 % / 32.97 % |
| 14 | D | 43.54 % / 55.72 % |
| 15 | B | 54.98 % / 35.99 % |
| 16 | B | 79.61 % / 14.32 % |
| 17 | A | 61.51 % / 30.2 % |
| 18 | C | 52.89 % / 39.51 % |
| 19 | D | 85.16 % / 12.68 % |
| 20 | D | 47.51 % / 43.86 % |
| 21 | A | 42.27 % / 35.62 % |
| 22 | B | 66.04 % / 32.37 % |
| 23 | B | 41.15 % / 48.13 % |
| 24 | A | 60.2 % / 34.29 % |
| 25 | C | 45.81 % / 40.73 % |

| Performance Analysis | |
|---|---|
| Avg. Score (%) | 38.0% |
| Toppers Score (%) | 60.0% |
| Your Score | |

# //Hints and Solutions//

**1.** The pattern followed here is:

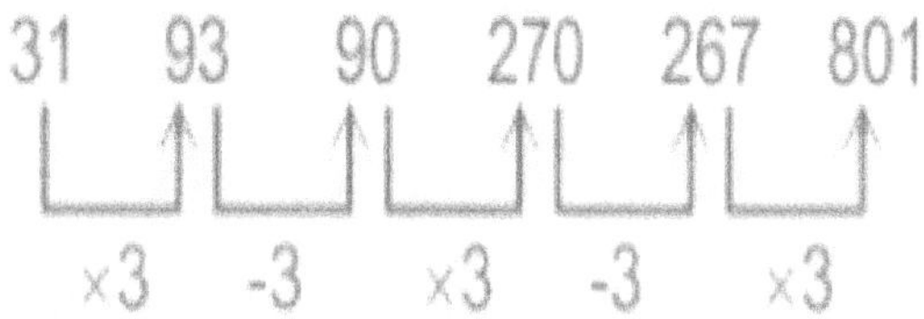

Hence, the correct option is (B).

**2.** The pattern followed here is:

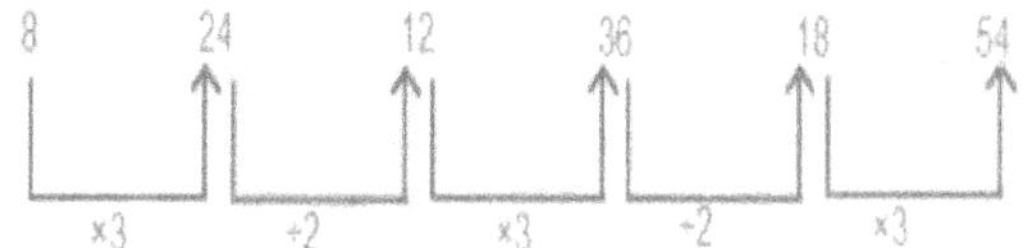

Hence, the correct option is (C).

**3.** 1) abcbadbabdaacbbbdbacb → doesn't follow any pattern

2) abdbacbabdaacbbbdbacb → doesn't follow any pattern

3) abdbacb/abdbacb/abdbacb → follows a pattern i.e. abdbacb

4) ababacbabdbacbcbdbadb → doesn't follow any pattern

Hence, the correct option is (C).

**4.** The pattern followed here is:

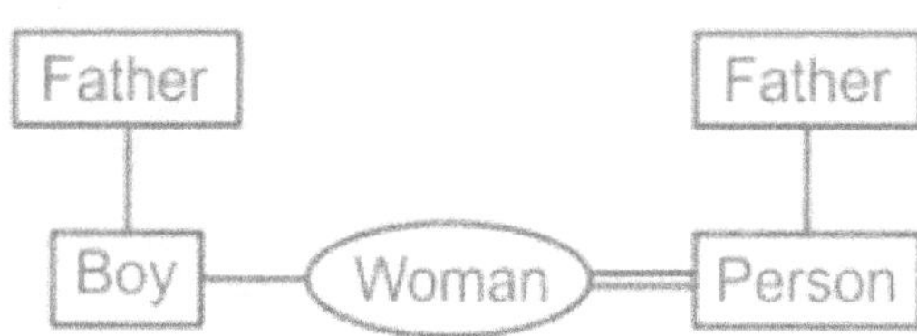

Hence, the correct option is (A).

**5.** Pointing to a boy a woman says, "His father is the father-in-law of that person whose father is the father-in-law of mine".

Hence, the boy is the brother of the woman.

Hence, the correct option is (B).

**6.** We know the color of the milk is white.

But, White is called red.

Hence, the correct option is (B).

**7.** We know the birds fly in the sky.

But, The sky is called road.

Hence, the correct option is (D).

**8.** $2 \rightarrow A + 1$

$4 \rightarrow C + 1$

$7 \rightarrow F + 1$

$8 \rightarrow G + 1$

Similarly,

$9 \rightarrow H + 1$

$5 \rightarrow D + 1$

$19 \rightarrow R + 1$

$21 \rightarrow T + 1$

Hence, the correct option is (C).

**9.** The pattern followed is,

For 9: 24,

$9 \times 3 - 3 = 24$

Similarly,

$3 \times 3 - 3 = 6$

Hence, the correct option is (B).

**10.** $D + Y + T + R = 4 + 25 + 20 + 18 = 67$

Similarly, $H + T + B + F = 8 + 20 + 2 + 6 = 36$

Hence, the correct option is (B).

**11.** Given:

Ratan introduces Sonu as his mother's only son's son.

The word his indicates that Ratan is a male.

Ratan's mother's only son means Ratan himself

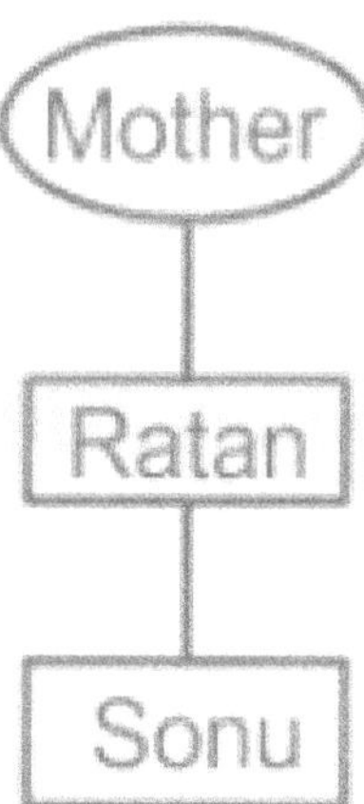


According to the tree diagram, Sonu is the son of Ratan.

Hence, the correct option is (B).

**12.** $42 \div 24 + 6 \times 4 - 3$

$\Rightarrow$ Converting

$42 - 24 \div 6 + 4 \times 3$

Using BODMAS rule:

$42 - 4 + 4 \times 3$

$\Rightarrow 42 - 4 + 12$

$= 54 - 4 = 50$

Hence, the correct option is (B).

**13.** Baseball and badminton both are outdoor games.

The correct Venn diagram representation is,

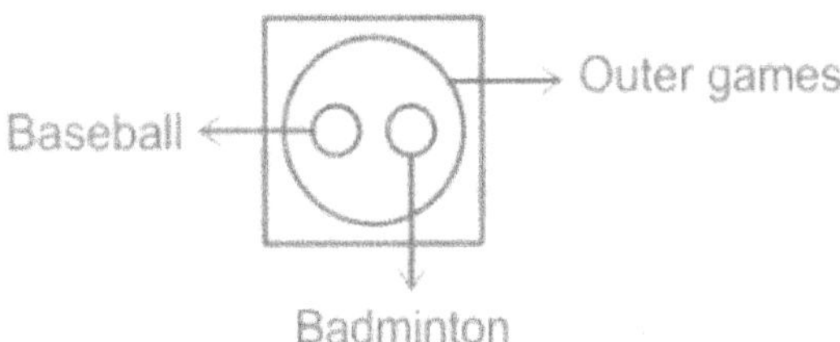



Hence, the correct option is (D).

**14.** The space in the figure which represents doctors who are players as well artists is shown below:

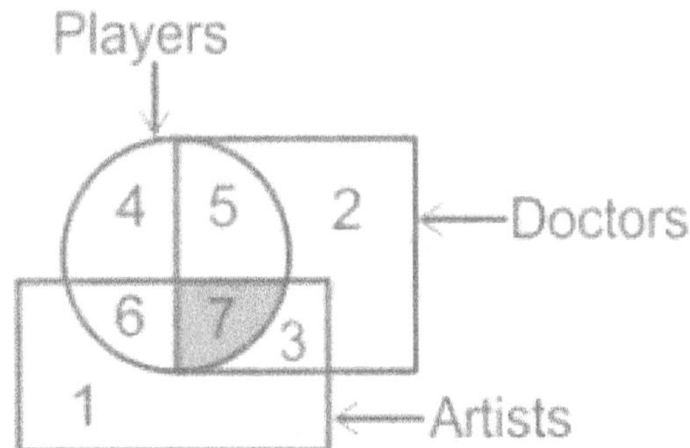



Hence, the correct option is (D).

**15.** Here 3 figures are given and there is one common letter C in both dice (i) and (ii). So we can find the opposite surface by going clockwise from the common side in both dice. It is called one common trick. Below is the figure:

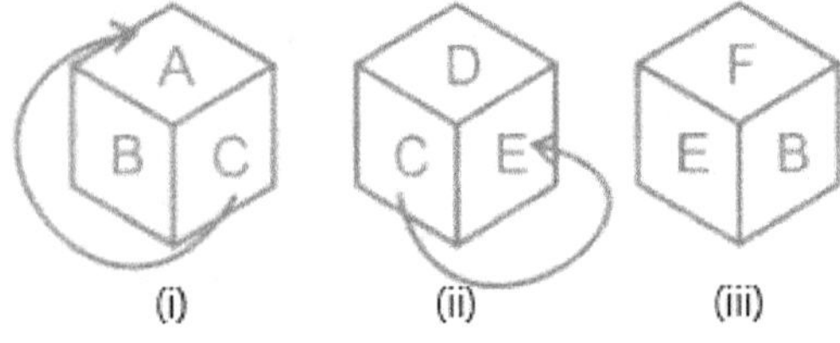



So opposite surfaces are:-

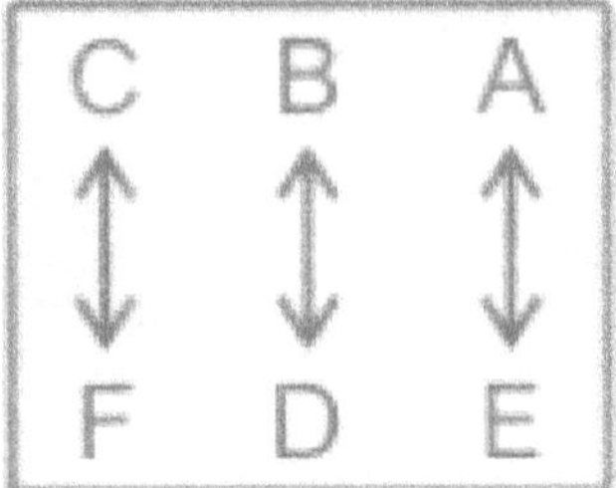



So the number opposite to D is B.

Hence, the correct option is (B).

**16.** The third figure in each row comprises parts that are not common to the first two figures.

Hence, the correct option is (B).

**17.** The number of components in each row either increases or decreases from left to right. In the third row, it increases.

Hence, the correct option is (A).

**18.**

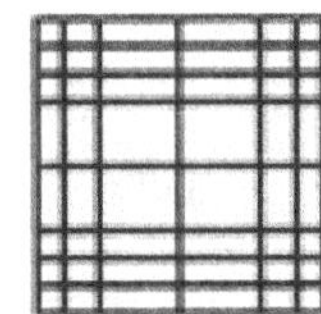

Hence, the correct option is (C).

**19.**

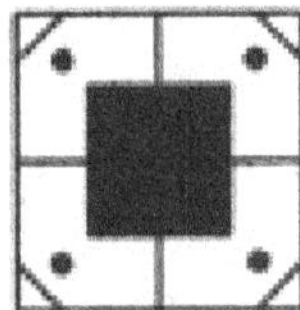

Hence, the correct option is (D).

**20.** Given, A = 4, K = 3, N = 2, P = 1.

Sum of first Set,

$= K + A + N + P + K = 3 + 4 + 2 + 1 + 3 = 13.$

Sum of the second set,

$N + P + A + K + N = 2 + 1 + 4 + 3 + 2 = 12.$

Sum of the third set,

$P + K + A + N + A = 1 + 3 + 4 + 2 + 3 = 13.$

Sum of the fourth set,

$N + A + K + N + A = 2 + 4 + 3 + 2 + 4 = 15.$

Hence, the correct option is (D).

**21.** T = 1

O = 2

U = 3

R = 4

C = 5

L = 6

E = 7

A = 8

S = 9

P = 0.

Hence, SCULPTURE = 953601347

Hence, the correct option is (A).

**22.** We have, S = 5

I = 3

T = 3

E = 0

R = 1

U = 8

N = 4

C = 6

L = 7

B = 1

O = 2

Y = 9.

So,

SON = 524.

Hence, the correct option is (B).

**23.** Since a vertical mirror is placed, thus the top and bottom positions will remain same, while the left and right positions will be swapped.

The black triangle at the top right will appear at top left and thus the first, third and fourth figure will be eliminated.

Hence, the correct option is (B).

**24.**

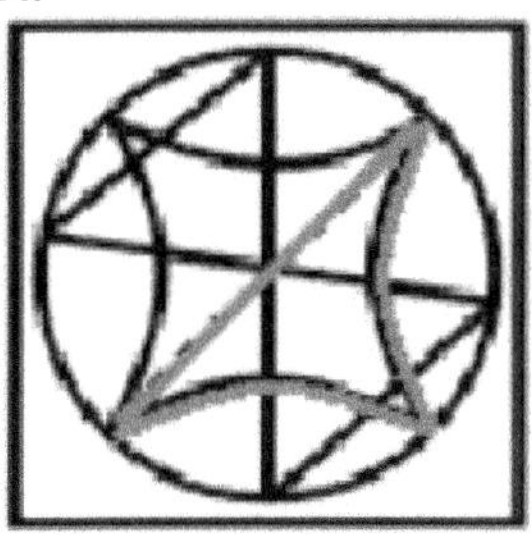

Hence, the correct option is (A).

**25.** Clearly, From 1 to 100, there are ten numbers with 3 as the unit's digit - 3, 13, 23, 33, 43, 53, 63, 73, 83, 93 and ten numbers with 3 as the ten's digit - 30, 31, 32, 33, 34, 35, 36, 37, 38, 39.

So, required number = 10 + 10 = 20.

Hence, the correct option is (C).

**Q.1** Which answer figure will complete the pattern in the figure?

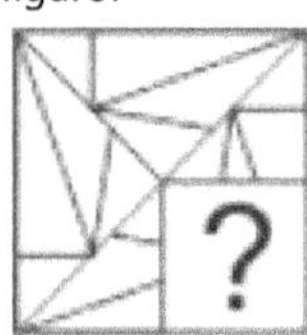

 A.     B.    C.     D.

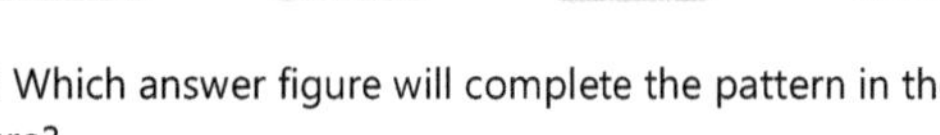

**Q.2** Which answer figure will complete the pattern in the figure?

 A.     B.     C.     D.

**Q.3** From the given options, select a figure in which the question figure is hidden/embedded.

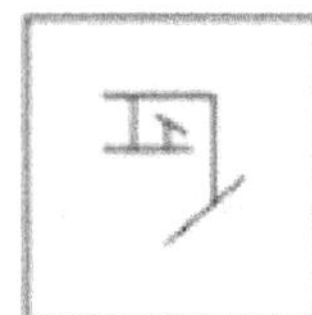

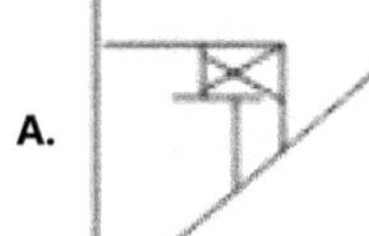 A.

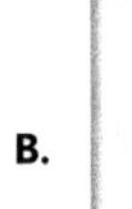 B.

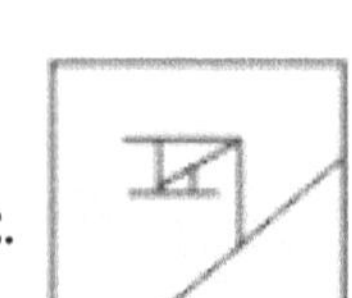 C.

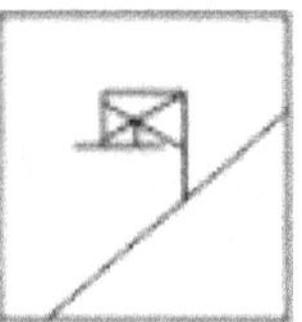 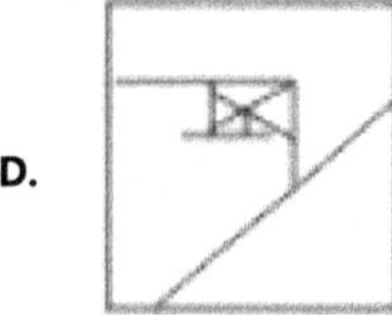 D.

**Q.4** From the given options, select a figure in which the question figure is hidden/embedded.

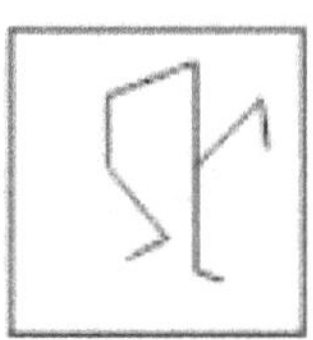

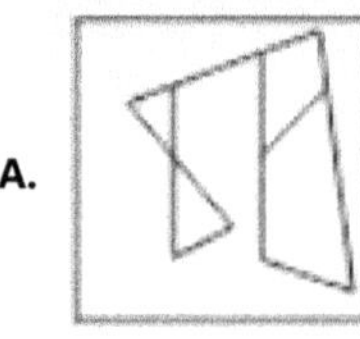 A.    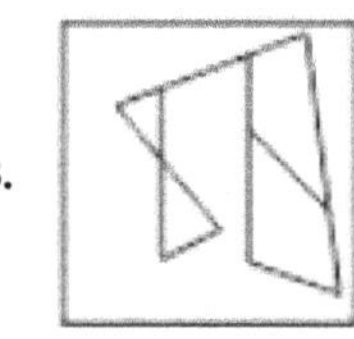 B.

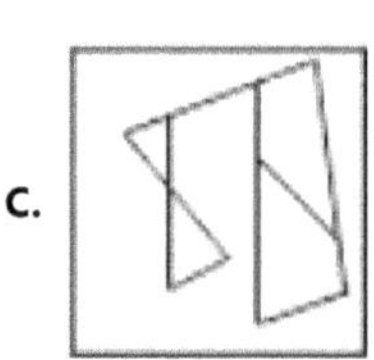 C.    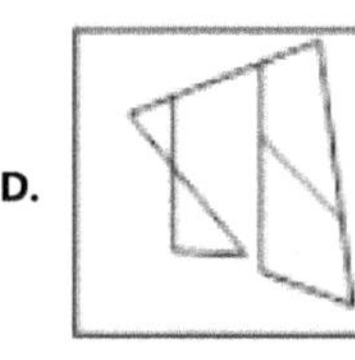 D.

**Q.5** A mirror is placed on the line MN, and then which of the Answer Figures is the right image of the given Question Figure?

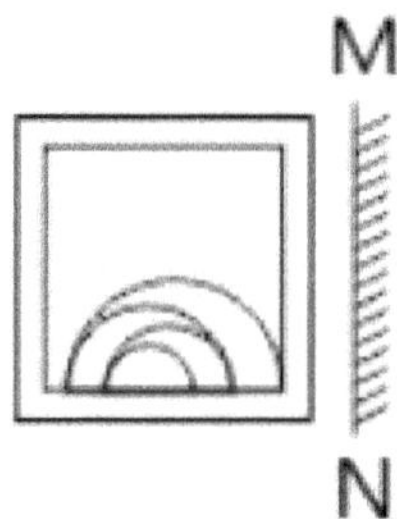



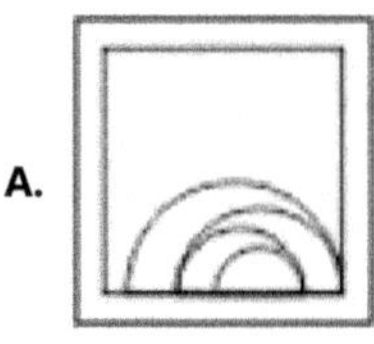 A.    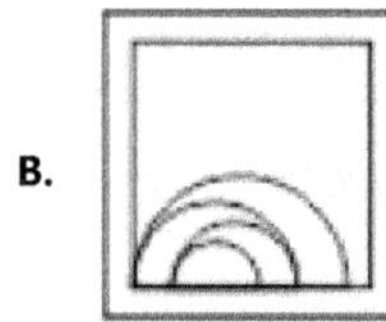 B.

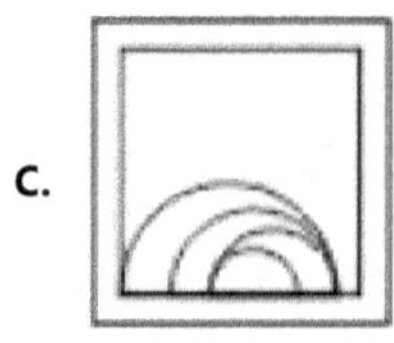 C.    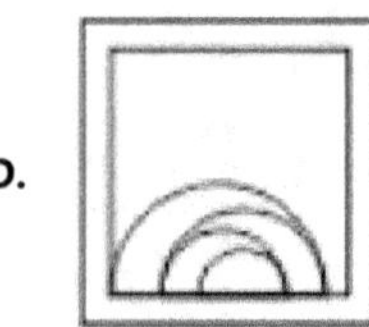 D.

**Q.6** A mirror is placed on the line MN, and then which of the Answer Figures is the right image of the given Question Figure?

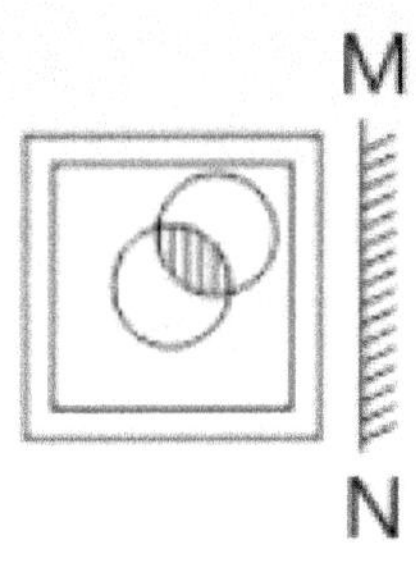

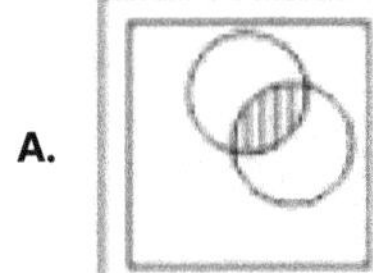

A.

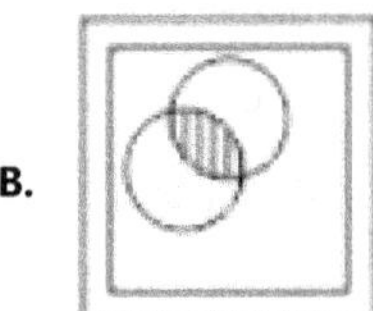

B.

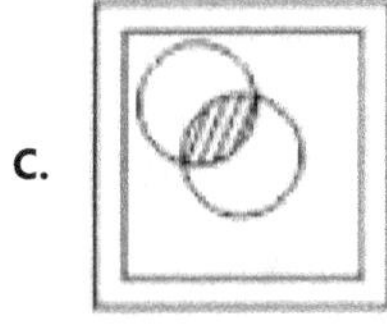

C.

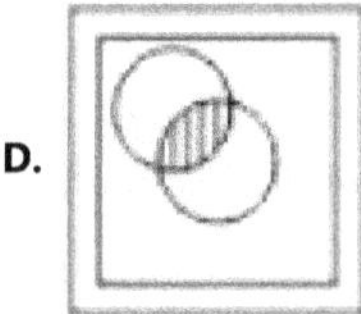

D.

**Q.7** Which of the following diagrams best depicts the relationship among Tie, Shirt, and Shoe?

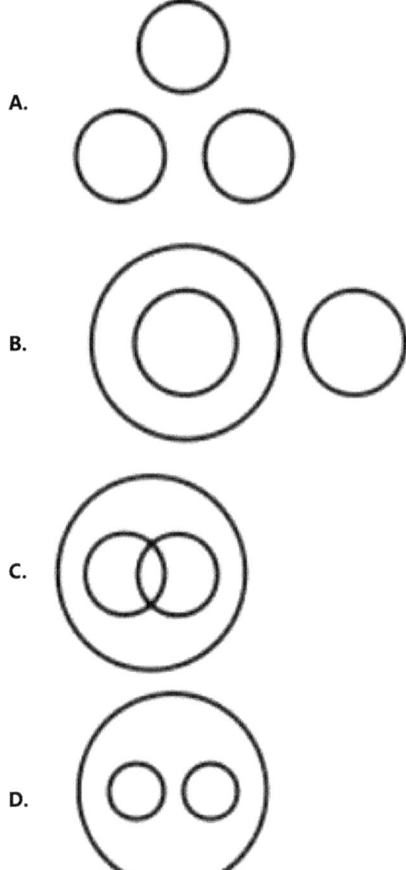

A.

B.

C.

D.

**Q.8** Which of the following diagrams best depicts the relationship among Book, Dictionary, and Printer?

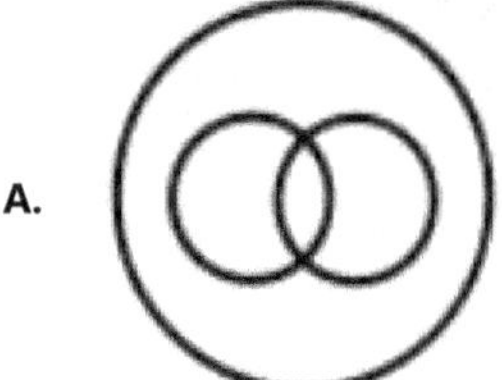

A.

B.

C.

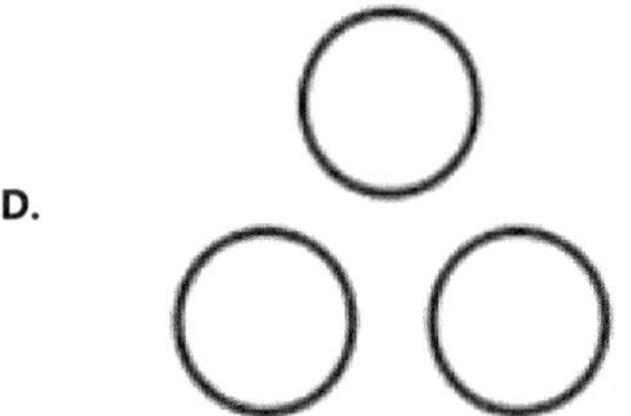

D.

**Q.9 Direction:** In the following question, a word is represented by only one set of numbers are given in any one of the alternatives. The sets of numbers given in the alternatives are represented by two classes of alphabets as in the two given matrices. The column and row of Matrix I are numbered from 0 to 4 and those of Matrix II from 5 to 9. A letter from these matrices can be represented first by row and then the column number e.g. in the matrices for questions 1 to 5, K can be represented by 65,77, etc. H can be represented by 30,11 etc. Similarly, you have to identify the correct set for the word given in each question.

| | 0 | 1 | 2 | 3 | 4 |
|---|---|---|---|---|---|
| 0 | A | E | S | T | H |
| 1 | T | H | A | E | S |
| 2 | E | S | T | H | A |
| 3 | H | A | E | S | T |
| 4 | S | T | H | A | E |

Matrix I

| | 5 | 6 | 7 | 8 | 9 |
|---|---|---|---|---|---|
| 5 | P | O | R | K | L |
| 6 | K | L | P | O | R |
| 7 | O | R | K | L | P |
| 8 | L | P | O | R | K |
| 9 | R | K | L | P | O |

Matrix II

TASTE

A. 32,02,31,04,12

B. 34,00,40,22,44

C. 76,10,14,12,13

D. 44,32,21,33,31

**Q.10 Direction**: In the following question, a word is represented by only one set of numbers are given in any one of the alternatives. The sets of numbers given in the alternatives are represented by two classes of alphabets as in the two given matrices. The column and row of Matrix I are numbered from 0 to 4 and those of Matrix II from 5 to 9. A letter from these matrices can be represented first by row and then the column number e.g. in the matrices for questions 1 to 5, K can be represented by 65,77, etc. H can be represented by 30,11 etc. Similarly, you have to identify the correct set for the word given in each question.

|   | 0 | 1 | 2 | 3 | 4 |
|---|---|---|---|---|---|
| 0 | A | E | S | T | H |
| 1 | T | H | A | E | S |
| 2 | E | S | T | H | A |
| 3 | H | A | E | S | T |
| 4 | S | T | H | A | E |

Matrix I

|   | 5 | 6 | 7 | 8 | 9 |
|---|---|---|---|---|---|
| 5 | P | O | R | K | L |
| 6 | K | L | P | O | R |
| 7 | O | R | K | L | P |
| 8 | L | P | O | R | K |
| 9 | R | K | L | P | O |

Matrix II

LAKE

**A.** 85,31,77,44

**B.** 77,00,41,12

**C.** 58,40,66,12

**D.** 02,76,43,31

**Q.11** What will come in the place of the question mark (?) ?
8 : 39 :: 72 : ?

**A.** 64 **B.** 312 **C.** 351 **D.** 300

**Q.12** What will come in the place of the question mark (?).
123 : 4 :: 726 : ?

**A.** 23 **B.** 26 **C.** 14 **D.** 12

**Q.13** In a certain code, VISHWANATHAN is written as NAAWTHHSANIV. How is KARUNAKARANA written in that code?

**A.** AKNUARRANKA

**B.** KAANRAURNAAK

**C.** NKRANKRAUK

**D.** RURNKAAUNAK

**Q.14** In a certain code language, ' $STAY$ ' is written as ' $RTSUZBXZ$ '. How will ' $DESK$ ' be written in that language?

**A.** $CEDERTJL$    **B.** $CEDFQTJL$

**C.** $CEDFRTJL$    **D.** $ECFDTQLJ$

**Q.15** Eight persons – Sarin, Rahi, Akasa, Pavi, Preet, Gunjan, Taran, and Namya belong to a family which consists of three generations and two married couples. Preet is the sister of the only son of Akasa. Pavi is the daughter-in-law of Sarin. Rahi is the mother of Akasa. Sarin is the grandfather of Taran who is the daughter of Pavi. Namya is the maternal uncle of Gunjan. How many male members are there in the family?

**A.** 3 **B.** 4 **C.** 5 **D.** 6

**Q.16** Select the one which is different from the other three responses.

**A.** 8 – 11 **B.** 1 – 4 **C.** 7 – 10 **D.** 3 – 5

**Q.17** Select the one which is different from the other three responses.

**A.** (96, 24) **B.** (39, 18) **C.** (81, 54) **D.** (82, 64)

**Q.18** Which interchange of signs will make the following equation correct?
(8 – 8) + 8 × 32 = 64

**A.** ×, +, –    **B.** –, ÷, +    **C.** +, ÷, +    **D.** +, ÷,×

**Q.19** Which of the following interchange of sign would make the given equation correct?
64 – 8 × 9 ÷ 8 = 64

**A.** + and –    **B.** ÷ and ×    **C.** + and ÷    **D.** – and ÷

**Q.20** Choose the correct alternative from the given one that will complete the series.
AD EI IN OS ?

**A.** UX **B.** XY **C.** WY **D.** UY

**Q.21** Choose the correct alternative from the given one that will complete the series.
MN QR UV ?

**A.** XY **B.** WX **C.** YX **D.** YZ

**Q.22** Choose the number which is DIFFERENT from the rest?

**A.** 7851 **B.** 6432 **C.** 5789 **D.** 1325

**Q.23** Which of the following words can be formed using the letters of the word "SQUIRREL" only?

**A.** Square **B.** Quarrel **C.** Liar **D.** Lure

**Q.24** Find the missing number from the given options.

| 15 | 5 | 7 | 10 |
|---|---|---|---|
| 64 | 4 | 5 | ? |
| 91 | ? | 9 | 22 |

**A.** 21, 7 **B.** 12, 4 **C.** 24, 8 **D.** 35, 5

**Q.25** Find the odd word from the given alternatives.

**A.** Swimming    **B.** Sailing

**C.** Diving    **D.** Driving

# // Smart Answer Sheet //

**Correct** Indicates percentage of students who answered questions correctly.

**Skipped** Indicates percentage of students who skipped questions.

| Q. | Ans. | Correct / Skipped |
|---|---|---|
| 1 | A | 63.95 % / 32.84 % |
| 2 | B | 62.47 % / 34.02 % |
| 3 | D | 51.73 % / 43.64 % |
| 4 | A | 41.4 % / 57.7 % |
| 5 | D | 60.47 % / 37.81 % |

| Q. | Ans. | Correct / Skipped |
|---|---|---|
| 6 | D | 45.13 % / 47.82 % |
| 7 | A | 43.81 % / 51.69 % |
| 8 | C | 69.01 % / 30.13 % |
| 9 | B | 27.78 % / 70.98 % |
| 10 | A | 18.69 % / 80.11 % |

| Q. | Ans. | Correct / Skipped |
|---|---|---|
| 11 | C | 84.0 % / 11.58 % |
| 12 | D | 48.34 % / 32.25 % |
| 13 | B | 58.01 % / 37.53 % |
| 14 | C | 65.85 % / 33.67 % |
| 15 | B | 54.99 % / 33.3 % |

| Q. | Ans. | Correct / Skipped |
|---|---|---|
| 16 | D | 40.78 % / 35.94 % |
| 17 | D | 56.85 % / 34.56 % |
| 18 | D | 48.44 % / 35.3 % |
| 19 | D | 50.74 % / 35.88 % |
| 20 | A | 61.03 % / 31.21 % |

| Q. | Ans. | Correct / Skipped |
|---|---|---|
| 21 | D | 52.71 % / 34.94 % |
| 22 | B | 60.48 % / 32.53 % |
| 23 | D | 45.45 % / 34.3 % |
| 24 | A | 47.68 % / 31.71 % |
| 25 | D | 57.18 % / 34.3 % |

| Performance Analysis | |
|---|---|
| Avg. Score (%) | 36.0% |
| Toppers Score (%) | 72.0% |
| Your Score | |

# //Hints and Solutions//

**1.**

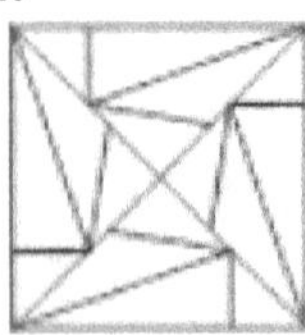

Hence, the correct option is (A).

**2.**

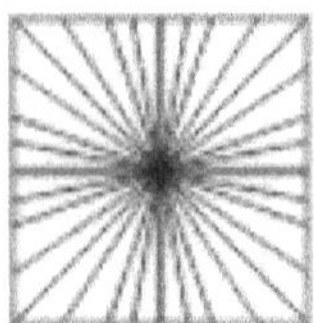

Hence, the correct option is (B).

**3.**

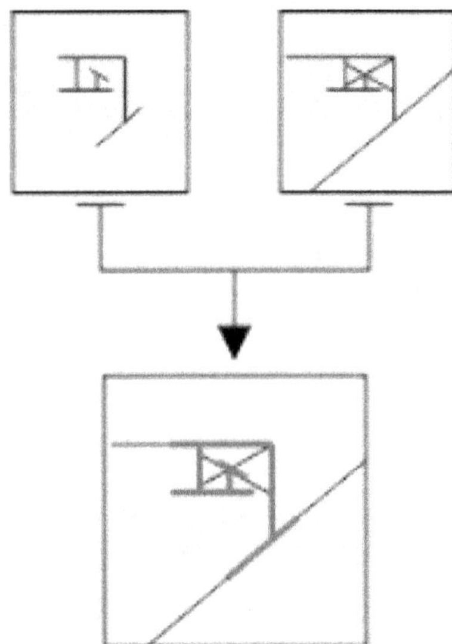

Hence, the correct option is (D).

**4.**

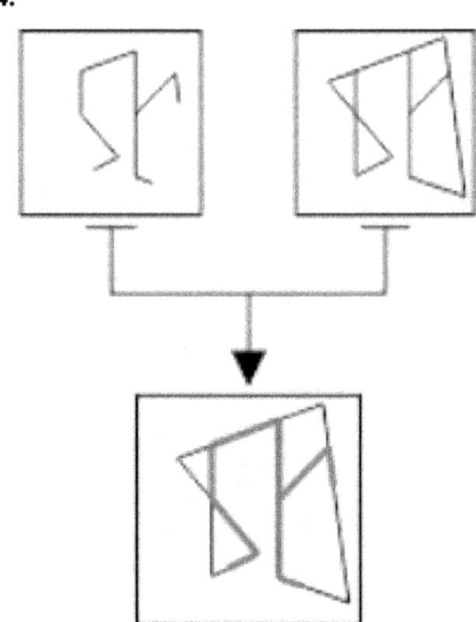

Hence, the correct option is (A).

**5.**

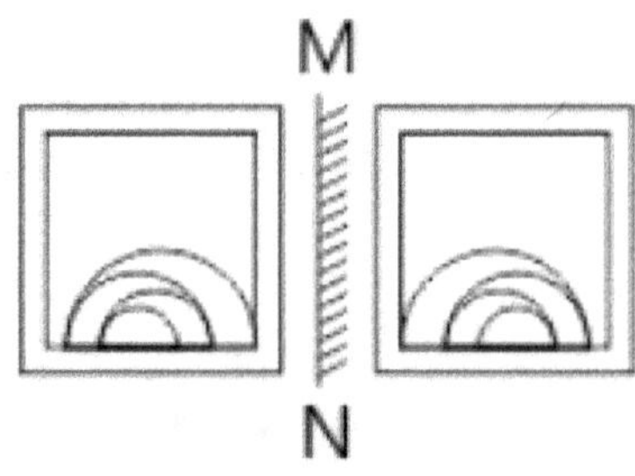

Hence, the correct option is (D).

**6.**

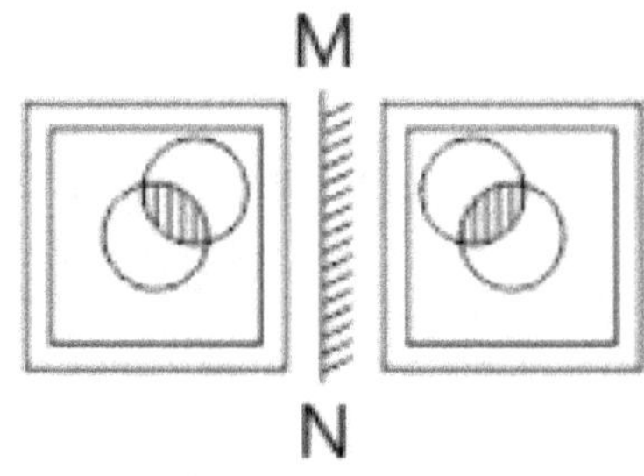

Hence, the correct option is (D).

**7.** Tie, Shirt, and Shoe are all separate items, entirely different from each other.

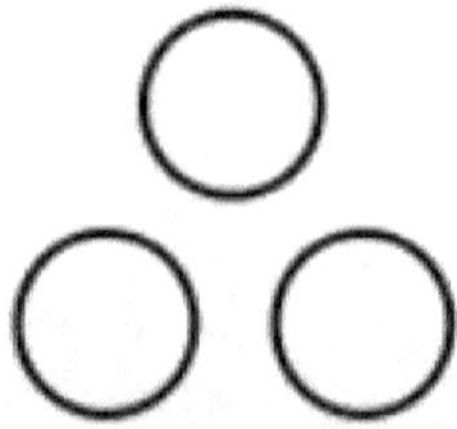

Hence, the correct option is (A).

**8.** Dictionary is also a type of Book. But printer has a separate identity.

Hence, the correct option is (C).

**9.** $T \rightarrow 03,10,22,34,41$

$A \rightarrow 00,12,24,31,43$

$S \rightarrow 02,14,21,33,40$

$T \rightarrow 03,10,22,34,41$

$E \rightarrow 01,13,20,32,44$

TASTE $\rightarrow 34,00,40,22,44$

Hence, the correct option is (B).

**10.** $L \rightarrow 59,66,78,85,97$

$A \rightarrow 00,12,24,31,43$

$K \rightarrow 58,65,77,89,96$

$E \rightarrow 01,13,20,32,44$

TASTE $\rightarrow 85,31,77,44$

Hence, the correct option is (A).

**11.** $\Rightarrow 8 \times 5 - 1 = 39$

Similarly,

$\Rightarrow 72 \times 5 - 9 = 351$

Hence, the correct option is (C).

**12.** Here, first two digits of the given number are divided by the third one.

$$123 \Rightarrow \frac{12}{3} = 4$$

Similarly,

$$726 \Rightarrow \frac{72}{6} = 12$$

Hence, the correct option is (D).

**13.** Divide the word into six sets of two letters each and label these sets from 1 to 6. Then, the code contains these sets in the order 4, 3, 5, 2, 6, 1 with the letters of sets 3, 2, 1 written in reverse order.

Given,

VI SH WA NA TH AN $\Rightarrow$ NA AW TH HS AN IV

Thus

KA RU NA KA RA NA $\Rightarrow$ KA AN RA UR NA AK

Hence, the correct option is (B).

**14.** The logic is:

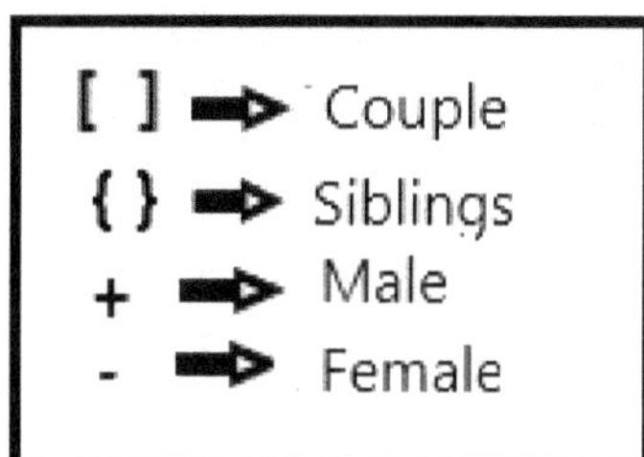

Similarly,

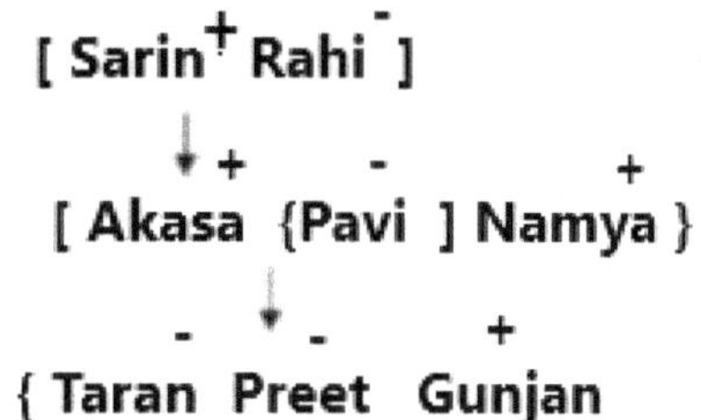

Therefore ' $CEDFRTJL$ ' is the correct answer.

Hence, the correct option is (C).

**15.**





Hence, 4 male members are there in the family.

Hence, the correct option is (B).

**16.** From the options, we get

$8 - 11 = 3$

$1 - 4 = 3$

$7 - 10 = 3$

But,

$3 - 5 = 2$

Thus, option (D) is different.

Hence, the correct option is (D).

**17.** Except the number pair (82, 64), in all other number pairs both the numbers are multiples of 3.

⇒ 96 = 32 × 3;   24 = 8 × 3

⇒ 39 = 13 × 3;   18 = 6 × 3

⇒ 81 = 27 × 3;   54 = 18 × 3

Hence, the correct option is (D).

**18.** Given,

⇒ (8 – 8) + 8 × 32 = 64

According to option (D), by inchanging the signs, we get

⇒ (8 + 8) ÷ 8 × 32 = 64

⇒ 16 ÷ 8 × 32 = 64

⇒ 2 × 32 = 64

Hence, the correct option is (D).

**19.** Given,

64 – 8 × 9 ÷ 8 = 64

According to option (D), on exchange of signals, we get

⇒ 64 ÷ 8 × 9 – 8 = 64

⇒ 8 × 9 – 8 = 64

⇒ 72 – 8 = 64

⇒ 64 = 64

Hence, the correct option is (D).

**20.** A – E – I – O – U ⇒ Vowels

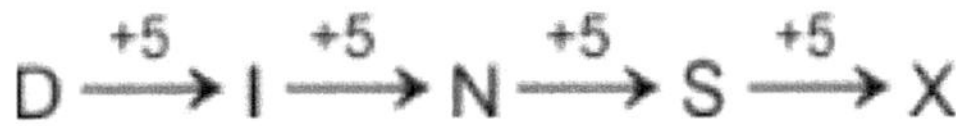


Hence, the correct option is (A)

**21.**

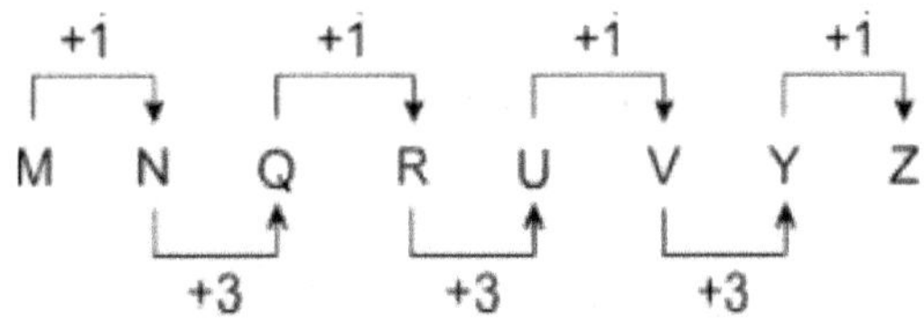


Hence, the correct option is (D)

**22.** Each of the numbers except 6432, is an odd number.

Hence, the correct option is (B).

**23.** Only "Lure" can be formed using the letters of the word "SQUIRREL".

Rest words possess some extra letters.

Hence, the correct option is (D).

**24.** The pattren is,

⇒ 15 ÷ 5 + 7 = 10

⇒ 64 ÷ 4 + 5 = 21

⇒ 91 ÷ ? + 9 = 22

⇒ ? = 91 ÷ 13

⇒ 7

Hence, the correct option is (A).

**25.** Swimming, Sailing and Diving is related to water. So, Driving is an odd one. Driving is the act of controlling and steering the movement of a vehicle or animal.

Hence, the correct option is (D)

**Q.1** The Ministry of Women and Child Development had extended the PM Cares for Children Scheme till 28th __________.

**A.** February  2022    **B.** March  2022
**C.** February  2022    **D.** December  2022

**Q.2** Who clinched the gold medal in weightlifting at the ongoing Singapore International?

*[Delhi Forest Guard, 2021]*

**A.** Mirabai Chanu    **B.** Swati Singh
**C.** Kunjarani Devi    **D.** Karnam Malleswari

**Q.3** The winner of US Open Tennis Tournament, 2018 (Women's Singles) was:

*[Delhi Forest Guard, 2020], [Super TET Paper - I, 2019]*

**A.** Caroline Wozniacki    **B.** Simona Halep
**C.** Naomi Osaka    **D.** Serena Williams

**Q.4** In the year 2022, which edition of International Yoga Day was celebrated on June 21?

**A.** 4th    **B.** 5th    **C.** 8th    **D.** 7th

**Q.5** The division of powers and the independent judiciary are two important characteristics of:

**A.** Democratic form of government
**B.** Federal form of government
**C.** Socialist form of government
**D.** Unitary form of government

**Q.6** The Constitution Amendment Act to prevent misuse of the National Emergency Declaration is-

**A.** 42nd Amendment Act
**B.** 43rd Amendment Act
**C.** 44th Amendment Act
**D.** 45th Amendment Act

**Q.7** Who among the following first introduced Europe to India?

**A.** Alexander (Alexander)
**B.** Arab
**C.** Greek
**D.** Iranian

**Q.8** In 1612 AD, the English fleet defeated the Portuguese in which war?

**A.** Surat    **B.** Kerala
**C.** Ahmedabad    **D.** Malacca

**Q.9** On which river is Hirakud Dam located?

**A.** Rihand    **B.** Mahanadi
**C.** Subarnarekha    **D.** Bhargavi

**Q.10** How many countries share India's terrestrial border?

**A.** 6    **B.** 7    **C.** 8    **D.** 9

**Q.11** The largest revenue in India is obtained from __________.

**A.** Sales tax    **B.** Direct taxes
**C.** Excise duties    **D.** None of the above

**Q.12** What does the Lorenz Curve indicate?

**A.** Relationship between the price of a certain commodity and its demand
**B.** Income distribution
**C.** Taxable income elasticity
**D.** Rate of employment

**Q.13** Which of the following is the regulator of the credit rating agencies in India?

**A.** RBI    **B.** SBI    **C.** SIDBI    **D.** SEBI

**Q.14** Which constitutional amendment is done to pass the GST bill in India?

**A.** 101st    **B.** 115th    **C.** 120th    **D.** 122nd

**Q.15** Match list I with list II and select the correct answer using the codes given below.

|     | List I |     | List II |
| --- | --- | --- | --- |
| (a) | National Maritime Day | (1) | 21 June |
| (b) | World Health Day | (2) | 22 May |
| (c) | International Yoga Day | (3) | 7 April |
| (d) | World Homeopathy day | (4) | 10 April |

**A.** (a)-(1), (b)-(2), (c)-(3), (d)-(4)
**B.** (a)-(3), (b)-(4), (c)-(1), (d)-(2)
**C.** (a)-(4), (b)-(3), (c)-(2), (d)-(1)
**D.** (a)-(2), (b)-(3), (c)-(1), (d)-(4)

**Q.16** Which article of Indian constitution was Dr. B.R. Ambedkar called "the heart and soul of the Indian Constitution"?

**A.** Article 356    **B.** Article 32
**C.** Article 14    **D.** Article 19

**Q.17** Through which rights are the fundamental rights enshrined in India?

**A.** Right to equality
**B.** Right against exploitation
**C.** Right to constitutional remedies
**D.** Educational and cultural rights

**Q.18** What is a secular state?

**A.** Who has no religion of his own
**B.** Who is an atheist
**C.** Who is anti religious
**D.** Which takes into account the religious sentiments of the people

**Q.19** The full form of CNBC is:

**A.** Consumer News and Business Channel
**B.** Consumer Network and Business Channel
**C.** Cosmopolitan Network and Business Channel

**D.** Crystalline News and Business Channel

**Q.20** Who was the last Mauryan emperor?
**A.** Ashoka
**B.** Brihadratha
**C.** Samprati
**D.** None of these

**Q.21** Which of the following hills serve as a connecting link between the Himalayas and Plains?
**A.** Tipra Hills
**B.** Morni Hills
**C.** Aravali Hills
**D.** Ambala Hills

**Q.22** The Carnatic wars (1740-1763) were fought between which of the following European powers?
**A.** Dutch and Portuguese
**B.** British and French
**C.** French and Dutch
**D.** British and Dutch

**Q.23** Who has been awarded Nobel in literature 2021?
**A.** Abdulrazak Gurnah
**B.** Peter Handke
**C.** Olga Tokarczuk
**D.** Kazuo Ishiguro

**Q.24** 'Ibonia', which was seen in the news recently, is a similar version of Ramayana found in which country?
**A.** Nepal
**B.** Madagascar
**C.** Sri Lanka
**D.** Mauritius

**Q.25** Which country won the Davis Cup Title in December 2021?
**A.** Spain
**B.** Russia
**C.** Croatia
**D.** Serbia

# // Smart Answer Sheet //

**Correct** — Indicates percentage of students who answered questions correctly.

**Skipped** — Indicates percentage of students who skipped questions.

| Q. | Ans. | Correct / Skipped |
|----|------|-------------------|
| 1 | A | 43.17 % / 47.66 % |
| 2 | A | 61.9 % / 34.48 % |
| 3 | C | 60.71 % / 33.43 % |
| 4 | C | 63.42 % / 35.12 % |
| 5 | B | 63.37 % / 31.51 % |
| 6 | C | 31.17 % / 67.46 % |
| 7 | A | 47.18 % / 49.57 % |
| 8 | A | 25.1 % / 74.02 % |
| 9 | B | 63.76 % / 35.0 % |
| 10 | B | 68.1 % / 31.18 % |
| 11 | C | 30.62 % / 68.12 % |
| 12 | B | 58.74 % / 39.71 % |
| 13 | D | 59.87 % / 33.8 % |
| 14 | D | 26.77 % / 67.52 % |
| 15 | D | 42.14 % / 40.91 % |
| 16 | B | 67.58 % / 31.75 % |
| 17 | C | 20.79 % / 73.58 % |
| 18 | A | 65.01 % / 33.16 % |
| 19 | A | 47.9 % / 30.61 % |
| 20 | B | 45.95 % / 33.31 % |
| 21 | B | 48.66 % / 43.83 % |
| 22 | B | 45.86 % / 52.22 % |
| 23 | A | 65.54 % / 30.82 % |
| 24 | B | 58.68 % / 35.3 % |
| 25 | B | 68.69 % / 30.94 % |

| Performance Analysis | |
|----------------------|----------|
| Avg. Score (%) | 28.0% |
| Toppers Score (%) | 56.0% |
| Your Score | |

# //Hints and Solutions//

**1.** The Ministry of Women and Child Development had extended the PM Cares for Children Scheme till 28th February 2022. Earlier the scheme was valid till 31st December 2021. The scheme covers all children who have lost both parents, surviving parents, or legal guardian/adoptive parents/single adoptive parent due to COVID 19 pandemic, starting from 11 March 2020.

Hence, the correct option is (A).

**2.** Mirabai Chanu clinched the gold medal in weightlifting at the Singapore International.

The 2020 Tokyo Olympics silver medallist in weightlifting, Mirabai Chanu, clinched the gold medal at the ongoing Singapore International on 25 February 2022. This win also helped her secure a slot at the upcoming 2022 Commonwealth Games in Birmingham. Competing in a new weight category- 55 kg, Chanu lifted a total of 191 kg- 86 kg in Snatch and 105 kg in Clean and Jerk, to clinch the gold.

Hence, the correct option is (A).

**3.** The winner of US Open Tennis Tournament, 2018 (Women's Singles) was Naomi Osaka.

- Naomi Osaka beats Serena Williams in the dramatic U.S Open final.
- She became the first Japanese woman to win a Grand Slam title.
- She registered an emphatic 6-2, 6-4 win over Serena Williams in the finals.

Hence, the correct option is (C).

**4.** The 8th edition of International Yoga Day was celebrated on June 21, 2022, it was guided by the theme of yoga for humanity.' Choosing the right yoga asanas and practicing them with awareness during the post-COVID-19 recovery period helps to build immunity with a relaxed body and mind for faster healing.

Hence, the correct option is (C).

**5.** The division of powers between the Union and the states is a fundamental element of the federal constitution. This division is usually done by a constitution, which is the highest law of the country. Since the powers of governments are divided by a written constitution, different governments should not interfere in each other's area of work. This requires an institution that can deal with disputes between the central and state governments fairly, being independent and impartial.

Hence, the correct option is (B).

**6.** Article 352 of the 44th Constitutional Amendment made in 1978 to prevent misuse of the National Emergency Declaration, now provides that the National Emergency can be proclaimed only when the Cabinet in writing asks the President to make such a proclamation. By this amendment, the term 'armed rebellion' has been replaced by 'internal unrest'. Therefore, emergency declaration can now be done only if there is internal disturbance from armed rebellion.

Hence, the correct option is (C).

**7.** Alexander's real name was Alexander III. In India, he is called as Alexander. Through the Iranians, the Greeks came to know about the immense wealth of India, which resulted in Alexander's invasion. Alexander's invasion of India was the second foreign and first European invasion.

Hence, the correct option is (A).

**8.** In 1600 AD, some British merchants obtained permission from Queen Elizabeth of England to do business with India. For this, he formed a company called East India Company. By that time, Portuguese travelers had found a sea route to travel to India. The Surat War of 1612 AD took place between the Portuguese and the English, in which the British won.

Hence, the correct option is (A).

**9.** Hirakud Dam is a dam built on the Mahanadi in Odisha. It is 15 km from Sambalpur. There is a huge reservoir behind this dam. This project is one of the few initial projects undertaken in India. Built on the Mahanadi in 1957, this dam is one of the longest dams in the world. Its total length is 25.8 km.

Hence, the correct option is (B).

**10.** India has a total terrestrial border of 15,106 km, comprising 92 districts and 17 states. India's terrestrial border is Pakistan, Bangladesh, China, Nepal, Myanmar, Bhutan and Afghanistan.

Hence, the correct option is (B).

**11.** An excise or excise tax (sometimes called an excise duty) is a type of tax charged on goods produced within the country (as opposed to customs duties, charged on goods from outside the country). It is a tax on the production or sale of a good. This tax is now known as the Central Value Added Tax (CENVAT).

Hence, the correct option is (C).

**12.**

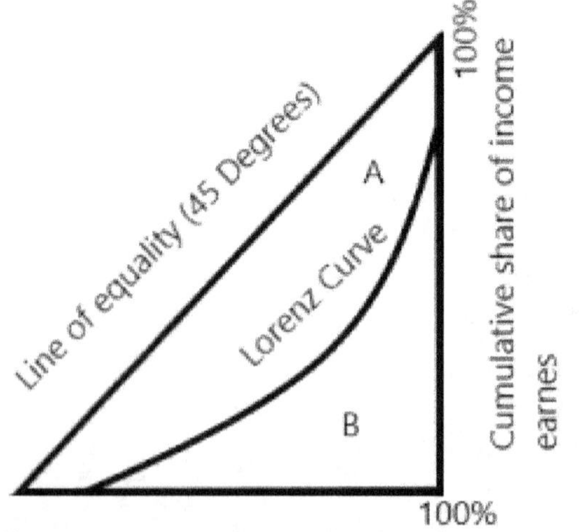


Cumulative share of people from lowest to highest incomes

A Lorenz curve is a graph used in economics to show inequality in income spread or wealth. It was developed by Max Lorenz in 1905, and is primarily used in economics. However, it may also be used to show inequality in other systems. The Gini index can be calculated from a Lorenz curve by taking the integral of the curve and subtracting from 0.5.

Hence, the correct option is (B).

**13.** SEBI stands for Securities Exchange Board of India. It is known as the regulator of the credit rating agencies in India. It is established by the Act of Parliament in 1992 to protect the interests of investors in securities, to promote the development of and to regulate the securities market.

Hence, the correct option is (D).

**14.** The Constitution (101 Amendment) Act, 2016, this amendment introduced a national Goods and Services Tax (GST) in India from 1 July 2017. It was introduced as the 122nd Amendment Bill of the Constitution of India,

The Goods and Services Tax (GST) is a Value added Tax (VAT) proposed to be a comprehensive indirect tax levy on manufacture, sale and consumption of goods as well as services at the national level. It replaces all indirect taxes levied on goods and services by the Indian Central and state governments. It is aimed at being comprehensive for most goods and services.

Hence, the correct option is (D).

**15.** The correct match is:

|     | List I                |     | List II  |
| --- | --------------------- | --- | -------- |
| (a) | National Maritime Day | (2) | 22 May   |
| (b) | World Health Day      | (3) | 7 April  |
| (c) | Internmational Yoga Day | (1) | 21 June |
| (d) | World Homeopathy day  | (4) | 10 April |

Hence, the correct option is (D).

**16.** Article 32 of the Constitution of India Ambedkar has called it "the heart and soul of the Indian Constitution." The right to apply to the Supreme Court has been given by appropriate proceedings to enforce fundamental rights under this Article.

Hence, the correct option is (B).

**17.** Fundamental rights in India are ensured by the right to constitutional remedies (Article 32). Under this, the right of inclusion in the Supreme Court has been guaranteed by appropriate proceedings to enforce the fundamental rights.

Hence, the correct option is (C).

**18.** A secular state refers to a state that has no religion of its own. Do not encourage any particular religion. In the preamble to the Indian Constitution, the word secular was added by the 42nd Constitution Amendment, 1976.

Hence, the correct option is (A).

**19.** With the full name "Consumer News and Business Channel" dropped, the network's daytime business programming was branded "CNBC/FNN Daytime," although this was phased out by 1992.

Hence, the correct option is (A).

**20.** The last Mauryan emperor was Brihadratha, who was killed by his commander Emperor Pushyamitra Sunga and established the kingdom of Sunga.

Hence, the correct option is (B).

**21.** Morni Hills serves as a connecting link between the Himalayas and Plains.

Morni is a village and tourist attraction in the Morni Hills at the height of 1,267 meters (4,157 ft) in the Panchkula district of the Indian state of Haryana. The Morni Hills are offshoots of the Shivalik range of the Himalayas, which run in two parallel ranges.

Hence, the correct option is (B).

**22.** It coincided with the wars between the British and French in Europe for primarily. For the protection of commercial interests.

Political developments in South India and Europe provided pretexts to contest their claims which culminated in the three Carnatic Wars. First Carnatic War (1744-48)- It was an extension of the Anglo-French rivalry in Europe and ended in 1748 with the treaty of Aix-La-Chapelle. Second Carnatic War (1749-54) - Although inconclusive, it undermined the French power in south India vis-a-vis the British. Third Carnatic War (1758-63) - A decisive war, known for the Battle of Wandiwash.

Hence, the correct option is (B).

**23.** The Nobel Prize in Literature 2021 was awarded to Abdulrazak Gurnah "for his uncompromising and compassionate penetration of the effects of colonialism and the fate of the refugee in the gulf between cultures and continents."

Gurnah, 73, is the author of 10 novels, including Paradise and Desertion. He was born in Zanzibar in 1948, Gurnah arrived in England as a refugee in the late 1960s.

Hence, the correct option is (A).

**24.** Indian Poet and Diplomat Abhay K has found that the 'Ibonia' of Madagascar resembles the Indian epic 'Ramayana' in its grand plot.

Ibonia is an epic poem of Madagascar, which narrates the story of birth, betrothal, struggle and death of its hero Ibonia. His betrothed wife Rampela was abducted by Ravato in similar lines with Ramayana. There are over $300$ similar words between Sanskrit and the Malagasy Language.

Hence, the correct option is (B).

**25.** Russia won the Davis Cup title in 2021 by defeating Croatia, after a brilliant performance from Daniil Medvedev. The 25-year-old player defeated Marin Cilic in the second singles match, to make the country win its first Davis Cup title since 2006.

It was also the fifth consecutive straight-set victory in the Davis Cup for the No. 2 Medvedev. Russia's first Davis Cup title was in 2002.

Hence, the correct option is (B).

# Sectional Test 05

**Q.1** In which of the following city, the first-ever edition of the India Global Forum (IGF) was held in March 2022?

*[Delhi Forest Guard, 2021]*

**A.** Bengaluru     **B.** Panaji
**C.** Mumbai     **D.** Chennai

**Q.2** Who clinched the gold medal in weightlifting at the Singapore International on 25 February 2022 ?

**A.** Mirabai Chanu     **B.** Swati Singh
**C.** Kunjarani Devi     **D.** Karnam Malleswari

**Q.3** L&T collaborated with _____ to develop Green Hydrogen Technology.

**A.** IIT Bombay     **B.** IIT Delhi
**C.** IIT Kanpur     **D.** IIT Madras

**Q.4** In April 2022, who has been appointed as the Chairman of the Union Public Service Commission (UPSC)?

**A.** Vikram Singh Mehta
**B.** Dr. Manoj Soni
**C.** Gopal Sharma
**D.** Sanjay Sharma

**Q.5** When was the insignia (₹) selected for the Indian currency?

**A.** 2009    **B.** 2010    **C.** 2012    **D.** 2013

**Q.6** What is the Capital of Cambodia?

**A.** Phnom Penh     **B.** Phnom Kravanh
**C.** Krong Kampot     **D.** Bakan

**Q.7** When is National Voters Day celebrated?

**A.** 17 December     **B.** 17 March
**C.** 21 June     **D.** 25 January

**Q.8** When is World Hindi Day celebrated?

**A.** 16 August     **B.** 14 September
**C.** 25 January     **D.** 11 July

**Q.9** In which country is Shakespeare Beach located?

**A.** France    **B.** England    **C.** Canada    **D.** Italy

**Q.10** The Sankosh river forms the boundary between which two states?

**A.** Bihar and West Bengal
**B.** Assam and Arunachal Pradesh
**C.** Assam and West Bengal
**D.** Bihar and Jharkhand

**Q.11** What type of forests are found mostly in India?

**A.** Tropical deciduous forest
**B.** Savannah and Desert forest
**C.** Equatorial evergreen forest
**D.** Tropical rain forest

**Q.12** In which state is the ancient Bhima Devi temple located?

**A.** Punjab     **B.** Haryana
**C.** Uttar Pradesh     **D.** Bihar

**Q.13** Where is Rumtek monastery located?

**A.** Arunachal Pradesh     **B.** Himachal Pradesh
**C.** Sikkim     **D.** Jammu Kashmir

**Q.14** In which state is the Lingaraja temple?

**A.** Odisha     **B.** Andhra Pradesh
**C.** Uttar Pradesh     **D.** Karnataka

**Q.15** Who has Babur described as the most powerful king of India?

**A.** Krishna Dev Rai
**B.** Rana Sanga
**C.** Muhammad Shah Rangeela
**D.** None of these

**Q.16** Who came to India with Mahmud Ghaznavi?

**A.** Al-Biruni     **B.** Amir Khusro
**C.** Ibn Batuta     **D.** None of these

**Q.17** What was the official language of the Satavahana rulers?

**A.** Pali     **B.** Sanskrit
**C.** Prakrit     **D.** None of the above

**Q.18** In which state was the poll monitoring system first introduced?

**A.** Goa    **B.** Manipur    **C.** Assam    **D.** Tripura

**Q.19** How many candidates can an EVM have?

**A.** 16    **B.** 32    **C.** 38    **D.** 64

**Q.20** Price theory is also known as:

**A.** Macro Economics
**B.** Development Economics
**C.** Public Economics
**D.** Micro Economics

**Q.21** An expert committee has been constituted by RBI to look into measures for the economic and financial stability of micro, small and medium enterprises (MSMEs). This committee is headed by ____.

**A.** G. N. Bajpai     **B.** C. B. Bhave
**C.** M. Damodaran     **D.** U. K. Sinha

**Q.22** _________ is the work of the Reserve Bank of India.

**A.** Money regulation
**B.** Credit control
**C.** Acting banker to the government
**D.** All of the above

**Q.23** Tokyo Paralympics medallist Avani Lekhara will be conferred the Khel Ratna 2021, she is from which state?

**A.** Uttar Pradesh     **B.** Rajasthan
**C.** Gujarat     **D.** Maharashtra

**Q.24** Who has received 2021 UNESCO/Guillermo Cano World Press Freedom Prize?

**A.** Paul Mescal

**B.** Tsitsi Dangarembga

**C.** Maria Ressa

**D.** Roberto Benigni

**Q.25** Who is the first Indian male badminton player to reach the final of BWF World Badminton Championships?

**A.** K. Srikanth

**B.** Parupalli Kashyap

**C.** Sai Praneeth

**D.** Nandu Natekar

# // Smart Answer Sheet //

**Correct** — Indicates percentage of students who answered questions correctly.

**Skipped** — Indicates percentage of students who skipped questions.

| Q. | Ans. | Correct / Skipped |
|---|---|---|
| 1 | A | 60.68 % / 38.26 % |
| 2 | A | 50.36 % / 41.02 % |
| 3 | A | 66.45 % / 31.48 % |
| 4 | B | 59.0 % / 34.41 % |
| 5 | B | 52.92 % / 46.4 % |
| 6 | A | 78.74 % / 17.96 % |
| 7 | D | 62.23 % / 31.12 % |
| 8 | B | 63.35 % / 34.67 % |
| 9 | B | 51.87 % / 42.59 % |
| 10 | B | 68.65 % / 31.17 % |
| 11 | A | 47.8 % / 40.42 % |
| 12 | B | 47.64 % / 41.01 % |
| 13 | C | 69.61 % / 30.18 % |
| 14 | A | 59.95 % / 32.15 % |
| 15 | A | 40.82 % / 43.24 % |
| 16 | A | 64.14 % / 31.86 % |
| 17 | C | 31.01 % / 67.18 % |
| 18 | A | 64.61 % / 32.54 % |
| 19 | D | 21.22 % / 70.9 % |
| 20 | D | 42.19 % / 44.92 % |
| 21 | D | 47.24 % / 50.39 % |
| 22 | D | 48.84 % / 41.82 % |
| 23 | B | 45.03 % / 31.29 % |
| 24 | C | 42.26 % / 39.17 % |
| 25 | A | 40.32 % / 52.14 % |

## Performance Analysis

| Performance Analysis | |
|---|---|
| Avg. Score (%) | 56.0% |
| Toppers Score (%) | 70.0% |
| Your Score | |

# //Hints and Solutions//

**1.** The India Global Forum (IGF) at Bengaluru was held on 7th and 8th March 2022.

IGF is the agenda-setting forum for international business and global leaders.

Minister of State for Skill Development and Entrepreneurship Mr Rajeev Chandrasekhar will be taking part in it.

This is the first ever edition of IGF at Bengaluru. The previous editions were hosted at Dubai and UK.

Hence, the correct option is (A).

**2.** Mirabai Chanu clinched the gold medal in weightlifting at the Singapore International on  25 February 2022 .

The 2020 Tokyo Olympics silver medallist in weightlifting, Mirabai Chanu, clinched the gold medal at the Singapore International on 25 February 2022. This win also helped her secure a slot at the upcoming 2022 Commonwealth Games in Birmingham. Competing in a new weight category - 55 kg, Chanu lifted a total of 191 kg - 86 kg in Snatch and 105 kg in Clean and Jerk, to clinch the gold.

Hence, the correct option is (A).

**3.** Larsen & Toubro (L&T) signed a pact with the Indian Institute of Technology in Bombay, Maharashtra to co-research and develop green hydrogen technology. Under this partnership, L&T will utilize its engineering expertise, product scale-up, and commercialization know-how, while IIT Bombay will use its cutting-edge research in hydrogen technologies and world-class technologists to develop indigenous globally-competitive technologies.

Hence, the correct option is (A).

**4.** Dr. Manoj Soni has been appointed as the Chairman of the Union Public Service Commission (UPSC). He is currently a member of the UPSC. He served as the country's youngest Vice-Chancellor in 2005, of MS University. He also served as the Vice-Chancellor of Dr. Babasaheb Ambedkar Open University in Ahmedabad between August 2009 to July 2015.

Hence, the correct option is (B).

**5.** The rupee symbol is also a metaphor for India's ethos. This new rupee symbol is made by combining the letter 'R' in Devanagari script and the letter 'R' in Roman script, which also has a horizontal line. This line reflects our national flag and equal sign. The Indian government selected the insignia for the Indian currency on 15 July 2010.

Hence, the correct option is (B).

**6.** Cambodia is largely a land of plains and great rivers and lies amid important overland and river trade routes linking China to India and Southeast Asia. The Capital of Cambodia is Phnom Penh.

Hence, the correct option is (A).

**7.** In India, National Voters Day is celebrated on 25 January every year. In the largest democracy like India in the world, National Voters' Day was being observed in view of the declining trend regarding voting. Mrs. Pratibha Devi Singh Patil inaugurated the 'National Voters Day'.

Hence, the correct option is (D).

**8.** World Hindi Day is celebrated on 14 September and World Hindi Week is observed from 14 September to 20 September. Its purpose is to create awareness for the promotion and propagation of Hindi in the world and to introduce Hindi as an international language. The first World Hindi Conference was held in Nagpur on 10 January 1975, since then this day is celebrated as 'World Hindi Day'.

Hence, the correct option is (B).

**9.** Shakespeare Beach is located west of the port of Dover in England, the distance between France and England being the shortest. Dover is a city and major ferry port in the domestic county of Kent in southeast England.

Hence, the correct option is (B).

**10.** The Sankosh river originates from northern Bhutan, in Assam, it joins the Brahmaputra. This river forms the border between Assam and Arunachal Pradesh. Sankosh River or Gadadhar River is a river in Northeast India. In Bhutan, its name is Puna Tsang Choo.

Hence, the correct option is (B).

**11.** Most tropical deciduous forests are found in India, they are also called monsoon forests. These forests are found in areas with 70 to 200 cm of rainfall. Sandal, rosewood, mahua, sal, teak, and bamboo trees are found in these forests.

Hence, the correct option is (A).

**12.** The ancient Bhima Devi Temple is called Khajuraho of North India. It is in the Panchkula district of Haryana. This temple is a panchayatan style temple. A temple complex in this style consists of 5 temples dedicated to 5 deities.

Hence, the correct option is (B).

**13.** Rumtek monastery is also known as Dharmachakra Kendra. It is located at a distance of 24 km from Gangtok, the capital of Sikkim. This monastery is about three hundred years old. Rumtek is considered to be the oldest Buddhist monastery in Sikkim. The monastery has a school and a separate section for meditation and meditation. The monastery was rebuilt in the 1960s.

Hence, the correct option is (C).

**14.** The Lingaraja Temple is in Bhubaneswar, the capital of Odisha. It was built by Jajati Keshari. It was built in the 11th century but still some parts of it are 1400 years old.

Hence, the correct option is (A).

**15.** Krishna Dev Rai was the greatest king of the Vijayanagara Empire. His kingdom was spread over present-day Tamil Nadu, Kerala, Orissa, Karnataka, Andhra Pradesh. Babur has described Krishna Dev Rai as the most powerful king of India.

Hence, the correct option is (A).

**16.** Al-Biruni was a proud scholar in the court of Mahmud Ghaznavi. He came to India at the time of his invasion of India. Al-Biruni was a Persian scholar writer, scientist, theologian and thinker. Al-Biruni was said to be the first person of Indian history. Al-Biruni's compositions are in Arabic but he had knowledge of three other languages besides his mother tongue, Persian - Syrian, Sanskrit, Greek.

Hence, the correct option is (A).

**17.** 'Prakrit language' is an ancient form of Indian Arya language. The time of its use was 500 BC. It is believed to be from 1000 AD. When Sanskrit began to lose its importance due to religious reasons, 'Prakrit language' began to be more practiced. Its four forms are particularly notable.

- Ardhmagdhi Prakrit
- Paishachi Prakit
- Maharashtri Prakrit
- Shaurseni Prakrit

Hence, the correct option is (C).

**18.** The poll monitoring system was first implemented in Goa. Under the system, voters' fingerprints will be recorded by web cameras mounted on computers with fingerprint reading machines along with their photographs.

Hence, the correct option is (A).

**19.** EVM can cater to a maximum of 64 candidates. The balloting unit has provision for 16 candidates. If the total number of candidates exceeds 16, the second balloting unit can be added parallel to the first balloting unit. Similarly, if the total number of candidates is more than 32, the third balloting unit can be added and if the total number of candidates exceeds 48, the fourth balloting unit can be added to cater for a maximum of 64 candidates.

Hence, the correct option is (D).

**20.** An economic theory contends that the price for any specific goods/service is the relationship between the forces of supply and demand. It is also known as Micro Economics.

Hence, the correct option is (D).

**21.** An eight-member expert committee headed by U. K. Sinha to suggest long-term measures to micro, small and medium enterprises (micro, small and medium enterprises-MSMEs) in terms of timely lending and their economic and financial strength. Is formed.

Hence, the correct option is (D).

**22.** The Reserve Bank of India (RBI) is the central bank of India. RBI performs many functions such as overseeing monetary policy, issuing currency, managing foreign exchange, acting as the banker of government and banker of scheduled commercial banks, etc. It does not accept deposits and gives loans and advances to the public.

Hence, the correct option is (D).

**23.** Avani Lekhara is from Jaipur, Rajasthan.

As 19-year-old Avani Lekhara won the gold medal in women's 10 m air rifle Standing event in the SH 1 category at the Tokyo Paralympics. She became the first Indian woman to win a gold medal at the Paralympics. Avani shot 249.6 points in the R2 women's 10m air rifle SH1 category for a Paralympic Record and equal the World Record.

Hence, the correct option is (B).

**24.** Investigative journalist and media executive Maria Ressa of the Philippines has received the 2021 laureate of the UNESCO/Guillermo Cano World Press Freedom Prize.

The Award Ceremony took place on 2 May in Windhoek, Namibia, on the occasion of the World Press Freedom Day Global Conference. Over a career spanning more than thirty years, Ressa has worked as CNN's lead investigative reporter for Asia and the head of ABS-CBN News and Current Affairs. She has also been involved in many international initiatives to promote press freedom.

Hence, the correct option is (C).

**25.** Indian badminton champion K.Srikanth has become the very first Indian man to reach the final match of BWF World badminton championship. But unfortunately, K.Srikanth lost against Singapore's Loh Kean Yew at the final match and ended up winning a silver-medal.

K.Srikanth was ranked world number 1 at the Badminton World Federation (BWF) ranking in April 2018 and is the recipient of Arjuna award in 2015 and Padma Shri in 2018.

Hence, the correct option is (A).

**Q.1** Tarkari Express was started from which of the following cities in Bihar?

**A.** Darbhanga
**B.** Patna
**C.** Gaya
**D.** Munger

**Q.2** The International Financial Services Centres Authority (IFSCA) and _________ has signed an MoU in April 2022.

**A.** Bajaj Finance Limited
**B.** Aditya Birla Finance Ltd
**C.** Muthoot Finance Ltd
**D.** GVFL Limited

**Q.3** Which city has been chosen by the Union of European Football Associations (UEFA) as a replacement of St Petersburg for the Champions League 2022 ?

*[Delhi Forest Guard, 2021]*

**A.** Paris
**B.** Brussels
**C.** London
**D.** Munich

**Q.4** Which institution released the 'Women and girls left behind: Glaring gaps in pandemic responses' report?

*[Delhi Forest Guard, 2021]*

**A.** World Economic Forum
**B.** World Bank
**C.** UN Women
**D.** NITI Aayog

**Q.5** Who among the following has won the Mexican open 2022 held in Acapulco, Mexico?

**A.** Rafael Nadal
**B.** Novak Djokovic
**C.** Roger Federer
**D.** Alexander Zverev

**Q.6** Nitish Kumar broke the record of which former Chief Minister of flag hoisting 14 times by hoisting the flag for the 15th time at Gandhi Maidan after independence on 15th August 2021?

**A.** Gopal
**B.** Shri Krishna Singh
**C.** Diksha
**D.** Jagannath Mishra

**Q.7** Benjamin Netanyahu has been nominated for the 2021 Nobel Peace Prize. He is the Prime Minister of which country?

**A.** Israel
**B.** Turkey
**C.** Yemen
**D.** Oman

**Q.8** Moin-ud-Dowlah Gold Cup Tournament is related to which sports?

*[AFCAT, 2021]*

**A.** Cricket
**B.** Football
**C.** Hockey
**D.** Kabaddi

**Q.9** Where is the capital of Croatia?

*[AFCAT, 2021]*

**A.** Kiev
**B.** Warsaw
**C.** Dubrovnik
**D.** Zagreb

**Q.10** What is the currency of Malaysia?

**A.** Malaysian Dinar
**B.** Malaysian Dollars
**C.** Malaysian Euro
**D.** Malaysian Ringgit

**Q.11** What is the currency of Iran?

**A.** Iranian Rial
**B.** Iranian Rubel
**C.** Iranian Diner
**D.** Iranian Dollar

**Q.12** Which of the following Ministry was renamed the Ministry of Education in the year 2020?

**A.** Ministry of Labour
**B.** Ministry of Human Resource Development
**C.** Ministry of Tribal Affairs
**D.** Ministry of Skill Development

**Q.13** Kuchipudi dance has its origin from which of the following states?

**A.** Telangana
**B.** Andhra Pradesh
**C.** Tamilnadu
**D.** Kerala

**Q.14** Who among the following is a famous Sarod player of India?

**A.** Nusrat Fateh Ali Khan
**B.** Amjad Ali Khan
**C.** Shiv Kumar Sharma
**D.** Hari Prasad Chaurasia

**Q.15** Paravur Assembly Constituency is located in _________

**A.** Kerala
**B.** Karnataka
**C.** Tamil Nadu
**D.** Andhra Pradesh

**Q.16** Shahid parvez is related to _________.

*[Punjab And Sind Bank Clerk, 2021], [UCO Bank Clerk, 2021], [Bank of India Clerk, 2021]*

**A.** Sitar
**B.** Tabla
**C.** Flute
**D.** Shenai

**Q.17** When is World Sparrow Day observed?

**A.** 18 March
**B.** 20 March
**C.** 22 March
**D.** 24 March

**Q.18** Which of the following day is observed as the Zero Discrimination Day?

**A.** 3rd March
**B.** 1st March
**C.** 2nd March
**D.** 28th February

**Q.19** The headquarter of the Asian Development Bank is located in which of the following cities?

**A.** Bangkok
**B.** Singapore
**C.** Shanghai
**D.** Metro Manila

**Q.20** Consider the following statements:

1. The office of Chief Justice of India comes under the purview of the Right to Information (RTI) Act.

2. The Chief Information Commissioner and an Information Commissioner shall hold office for such term as prescribed by the Central Government or until they attain the age of 65 years, whichever is earlier.

Which of the above statements is/are correct?

**A.** 1 only      **B.** 2 only

**C.** Both 1 and 2      **D.** Neither 1 nor 2

**Q.21** Who has been conferred with the Swami Brahmanand Award 2021?

**A.** Anand Kumar

**B.** Asha Bhosle

**C.** Dr Rajendra Kishore Panda

**D.** P Sainath

**Q.22** The Abel Prize for 2021 was jointly awarded to___.

**A.** Prof. Shankar Balasubramanian and Prof. David Klenerman

**B.** László Lovász and Avi Wigderson

**C.** Alfred V. Aho and Jeffrey David Ullman

**D.** Nitin Rakesh and Jerry Wind

**Q.23** Who is the author of "Tamil Thai Vazhathu" declared as the state song of Tamil Nadu?

**A.** Subramania Bharathi

**B.** Bharathidasan

**C.** Manonmaniam Sundaram

**D.** None of these

**Q.24** Who won the 'Global Entrepreneur of the Year Award' from The Indus Entrepreneurs (TIE)?

**A.** Ratan Tata

**B.** Kumar Mangalam Birla

**C.** Uday Kotak

**D.** Adi Godrej

**Q.25** Which of the following is the winner of the Padma Bhushan Award 2021?

**A.** M.C Mary Kom      **B.** P.V Sindhu

**C.** Kangna Ranaut      **D.** Adnan Sami

# // Smart Answer Sheet //

**Correct**   Indicates percentage of students who answered questions correctly.

**Skipped**   Indicates percentage of students who skipped questions.

| Q. | Ans. | Correct / Skipped |
|---|---|---|
| 1 | B | 67.37 % / 31.55 % |
| 2 | D | 56.93 % / 38.5 % |
| 3 | A | 61.98 % / 31.66 % |
| 4 | C | 53.74 % / 45.67 % |
| 5 | A | 60.25 % / 37.95 % |

| Q. | Ans. | Correct / Skipped |
|---|---|---|
| 6 | B | 53.69 % / 35.64 % |
| 7 | A | 61.07 % / 31.52 % |
| 8 | A | 82.01 % / 14.12 % |
| 9 | D | 69.08 % / 30.92 % |
| 10 | D | 82.46 % / 13.59 % |

| Q. | Ans. | Correct / Skipped |
|---|---|---|
| 11 | A | 77.5 % / 22.05 % |
| 12 | B | 49.91 % / 38.13 % |
| 13 | B | 61.12 % / 38.2 % |
| 14 | B | 49.41 % / 50.37 % |
| 15 | A | 45.14 % / 44.58 % |

| Q. | Ans. | Correct / Skipped |
|---|---|---|
| 16 | A | 55.45 % / 36.54 % |
| 17 | B | 77.27 % / 17.17 % |
| 18 | B | 44.7 % / 47.42 % |
| 19 | D | 55.91 % / 37.01 % |
| 20 | C | 45.95 % / 53.38 % |

| Q. | Ans. | Correct / Skipped |
|---|---|---|
| 21 | A | 65.05 % / 33.43 % |
| 22 | B | 42.58 % / 32.24 % |
| 23 | C | 44.19 % / 36.33 % |
| 24 | B | 44.26 % / 48.62 % |
| 25 | B | 67.76 % / 30.11 % |

| Performance Analysis | |
|---|---|
| Avg. Score (%) | 50.0% |
| Toppers Score (%) | 66.0% |
| Your Score | |

# //Hints and Solutions//

**1.** Bihar Cooperation Minister Subhash Singh launched Tarkari Express on August 24,2021. It is a service to deliver vegetables to the residents of Patna at their doorstep at half prices. The vegetables are obtained directly from farmers' fields and reaches all the neighbourhoods of Patna on e-rickshaws.

Hence, the correct option is (B).

**2.** The International Financial Services Centres Authority (IFSCA) and GVFL Limited signed an MoU at IFSCA's office at Gift City, Gujarat.

It has been signed for cooperation and collaboration to support and facilitate the FinTech ecosystem in GIFT IFSC. IFSCA is a unified regulator responsible for the development and regulation of financial products, financial services and institutions in the IFSCs.

Hence, the correct option is (D).

**3.** Russia was stripped of hosting the Champions League final by UEFA on 25 Feb 2022 with St. Petersburg replaced by Paris after Russia's invasion of Ukraine. France last hosted the Champions League final 16 years ago, when Barcelona beat Arsenal in the 2006 final.

Hence, the correct option is (A).

**4.** United Nations Women recently released a new report titled 'Women and girls left behind: Glaring gaps in pandemic responses'.

As per the report, women were less likely to receive COVID-19 relief from government. At least 29 per cent of working mothers living with children lost their jobs compared to 20 per cent of working men living with children. Single women living with children were left behind more, as per the report.

Hence, the correct option is (C).

**5.** Rafael Nadal has won the Mexican Open 2022 held in Acapulco, Mexico. Nadal, who first won the title in 2005 and took it again in 2013 and 2020, stormed through the Acapulco draw without dropping a set, to claim his third straight title of 2022.

Hence, the correct option is (A).

**6.** Nitish Kumar broke the record of 14 times of former Chief Minister Shri Krishna Singh by hoisting the flag for the 15th time at Gandhi Maidan after independence on 15 August 2021.

On 15th August, Bihar Chief Minister Nitish Kumar hoisted the tricolor flag for the 15th time. Earlier, Shri Krishna Singh had the record of hoisting the flag for the maximum number of times as the Chief Minister of Bihar.

Hence, the correct option is (B).

**7.** Israeli Prime Minister Benjamin Netanyahu and Abu Dhabi Crown Prince Mohammed bin Zayed Al Nahyan have been nominated for the 2021 Nobel Peace Prize. They have been nominated for their roles in establishing diplomatic ties between their countries It was announced in September 2020 that Donald Trump has been nominated for the Prize following his efforts to broker peace between Israel and the UAE.

Hence, the correct option is (A).

**8.** The non-first-class competition was of three-day matches until 1989-90. After a break, it resumed in 1993-94, as one day 50 over competition. Now held every year in August and September at various grounds in Hyderabad and Secunderabad, with the final at the Rajiv Gandhi international cricket stadium in Hyderabad. Teams from the various regional associations of cricket in India to compete. Hyderabad Cricket Association XI won in 2017-18.

Hence, the correct option is (A).

**9.**

| Croatia | Located in Europe |
|---|---|
| Capital | Zagreb |
| Currency | Kuna |
| Legislature | Sabor |

Hence, the correct option is (D).

**10.** The currency of Malaysia is the Malaysian ringgit. It is further divided into 100 sen. The Malaysian ringgit is issued by the central bank of Malaysia (Bank Negara Malaysia). Dinar is a monetary unit used in several Middle Eastern countries, including Algeria, Bahrain, Iraq, Jordan, Kuwait, Libya, and Tunisia.

Hence, the correct option is (D).

**11.** The Parliament of Iran has decided to change its currency from Rial to Toman. But, the decision has not been implemented yet. Thus, currently, Rial is the official currency of Iran.

Hence, the correct option is (A).

**12.** President Ram Nath Kovind gave assent to the change in name of the Ministry of Human Resource Development (MHRD) as Ministry of Education. The name change was among the key recommendations of the draft new National Education Policy (NEP). The Ministry of Education was renamed the HRD ministry in 1985 during the tenure of then prime minister Rajiv Gandhi. The National Education Policy was introduced in 1986 and was later amended in 1992.

Hence, the correct option is (B).

**13.** Kuchipudi, one of the major dance forms of India was originated from Andhra Pradesh.

It grew largely as a product of the Bhakti movement beginning in the 7th Century AD.

Kuchipudi derives its name from the village Kuchelapuram, where it was nurtured by great scholars and artists who built up the repertoire and refined the dance technique.

Hence, the correct option is (B).

**14.** Amjad Ali Khan Bangash is an Indian classical sarod player, best known for his clear and fast 'ekhara taans'.

He was awarded India's second-highest civilian honour Padma Vibhushan in 2001.

Amjad Ali Khan was awarded 21st Rajiv Gandhi National Sadbhavna Award, Padma Shri in 1975 and Padma Bhushan in 1991.

Hence, the correct option is (B).

**15.** The EVMs were used for the first time in 1982 during the by-election to North Paravur Assembly Constituency in Kerala.

An EVM can record a maximum of 3840 votes and 2000 votes in the new version.

The EVMs or Electronic Voting Machines were designed in 1980 by the Technical Experts Committee of the Election Commission in collaboration with Bharat Electronics Ltd, Bangalore, and Electronics Corporation of India Ltd, Hyderabad.

Hence, the correct option is (A).

**16.** Shahid Parvez is related to Sitar.

Ustaad Allarakha Qureshi popularly known as Alla Rakha was an Indian tabla player who specialized in Hindustani classical.

Pandit Bhimsen Gururaj Joshi was a legendary Hindustani classical vocalist.

Hence, the correct option is (A).

**17.** World Sparrow Day is observed on 20 March every year to raise awareness about the bird. The initiative was started by Nature Forever Society (NFS) of India, founded by Mohammed Dilawar, an Indian conservationist. The first World Sparrow Day was celebrated in 2010 in different parts of the world.

Hence, the correct option is (B).

**18.** The United Nations and other international organisations commemorate Zero Discrimination Day on March 1st each year. Zero Discrimination Day is observed to uphold and celebrate the rights of all people, regardless of their age, gender, race, nationality, race, skin colour, or other factors. The aim of Zero Discrimination Day is to raise consciousness about the right to live a dignified life, regardless of one's values, views, occupation, education, disability, or disease. "End Inequalities" is the slogan of Zero Discrimination Day 2021.

Hence, the correct option is (B).

**19.** The headquarter of the Asian Development Bank is located in Metro Manila. It is a regional development bank. ADB is an official United Nations Observer. The current President is Masatsugu Asakawa. It has 31 field offices in Asia and the Pacific and representative offices in Washington, Frankfurt, Tokyo and Sydney.

Hence, the correct option is (D).

**20.** RTI applicable to the Supreme Court of India in 2019, upheld the decision of the Delhi High Court bringing the office of Chief Justice of India under the purview of the Right to Information (RTI) Act. So, statement 1 is correct. Currently, Political parties are not under the ambit of the RTI act.

The Central Information Commission was established by the Central Government in 2005. It was constituted through an Official Gazette Notification under the provisions of the Right to Information Act (2005). Hence, it is not a constitutional body. The Central Information Commission is a high-powered independent body that inter alia looks into the complaints made to it and decides the appeals. The Chief Information Commissioner/Information Commissioner shall hold office for a term of 5 (five) years or till he attains the age of 65 years. Therefore, statement 2 is correct.

Hence, the correct option is (C).

**21.** Mathematician Anand Kumar has been conferred with the Swami Brahmanand Award 2021 for his contribution in the field of education through his Super 30 initiative.

The award carries Rs. 10,000 in cash, a bronze medal, a bronze statue of Swami Brahmanand, and a certificate. The award is given every year to people who have done special work in the education sector or for the welfare of the cow.

Hence, the correct option is (A).

**22.** The Abel Prize 2021 was awarded to Avi Wigderson, and Laszlo Lovasz.

László Lovász is a mathematician of Alfréd Rényi Institute of Mathematics (ELKH, MTA Institute of Excellence) and Eötvös Loránd University in Budapest, Hungary, and Avi Wigderson a mathematician of the Institute for Advanced Study, Princeton, USA.

Hence, the correct option is (B).

**23.** The state anthem of Tamil Nadu is Tamil Thai Vazhathu, also known as Thamiz Thai Vazhathu Invocation of Mother Tamil. Manonmaniam Sundaram Pillai composed the song, which he wrote. As per the order given by the Chief Minister of the state, Mr. M.K. Stalin, except the persons with disabilities, all those present during the singing of the song will standing position.

Hence, the correct option is (C).

**24.** Indus Entrepreneurs (TIE) has named Aditya Birla Group Chairman Kumar Mangalam Birla as the Global Entrepreneur of the Year in Business Transformation for his leadership during the COVID-19 pandemic.

He is also the first Indian industrialist to receive this award. Other award winners are Elon Musk (Global Entrepreneur of the Year – Immigrant Entrepreneur), Jeff Bezos (Global Entrepreneur of the Year-First Generation) and Satya Nadella (Global Entrepreneur of the Year Entrepreneurial CEO).

Hence, the correct option is (B).

**25.** President Ram Nath Kovind presents Padma Bhushan to shuttler PV Sindhu.

She is the first Indian to become a badminton World champion. She has also won the silver medal at Rio Olympics.

Hence, the correct option is (B).

**Q.1** $A \times B$ implies $A^2 + B^2$. What is the value of $6 \times (2 \times 4)$?

**A.** 999 **B.** 3616 **C.** 324 **D.** 436

**Q.2** If $\left(\dfrac{a}{b}\right)^{x-1} = \left(\dfrac{b}{a}\right)^{x-3}$, then the value of $x$ is:

**A.** $\dfrac{1}{2}$ **B.** 1 **C.** 2 **D.** $\dfrac{7}{2}$

**Q.3** Three unbiased coins are tossed. What is the probability of getting at most two heads?

**A.** $\dfrac{3}{4}$ **B.** $\dfrac{1}{4}$ **C.** $\dfrac{3}{8}$ **D.** $\dfrac{7}{8}$

**Q.4** If the simple interest for 6 years be equal to 30% of the principal, it will be equal to the principal after:

**A.** 20 years **B.** 30 years **C.** 10 years **D.** 22 years

**Q.5** A certain some of money and Rs. 2420 in 2 years and Rs. 2662 in 3 years at same rate of compound interest, compounded annually. The rate of interest per annum is:

**A.** 6% **B.** 8% **C.** 9% **D.** 10%

**Q.6** Father is aged three times more than his son Ronit. After 8 years, he would be two and a half times of Ronit's age. After further 8 years, how many times would he be of Ronit's age?

**A.** 2 times **B.** $2\dfrac{1}{2}$ times
**C.** $2\dfrac{3}{4}$ times **D.** 3 times

**Q.7** A can contains a mixture of two liquids A and B is the ratio 7 : 5. When 9 litres of mixture are drawn off and the can is filled with B, the ratio of A and B becomes 7 : 9. How many litres of liquid A was contained by the can initially?

**A.** 10 **B.** 20 **C.** 21 **D.** 25

**Q.8** Find the average of first 97 natural numbers.

*[Delhi Forest Guard, 2021]*

**A.** 47 **B.** 37 **C.** 48 **D.** 49

**Q.9** If 4 (P's Capital) = 6 (Q's Capital) = 10 ( R's Capital ), then out of the total profit of Rs. 4650, R will receive:

**A.** Rs. 600 **B.** Rs. 700 **C.** Rs. 800 **D.** Rs. 900

**Q.10** A hollow iron pipe is 21 cm long and its external diameter is 8 cm. If the thickness of the pipe is 1 cm and iron weighs 8 g/cm³, then the weight of the pipe is:

**A.** 3.6 kg **B.** 3.696 kg **C.** 36 kg **D.** 36.9 kg

**Q.11** Two trains running in opposite directions cross a man standing on the platform in 27 seconds and 17 seconds respectively and they cross each other in 23 seconds. The ratio of their speeds is:

**A.** 1 : 3 **B.** 3 : 2
**C.** 3 : 4 **D.** None of these

**Q.12** On decreasing the price of a colour TV by 30% its sale is increased by 20% The effect on the revenue is:

**A.** 16% decrease **B.** 16% increase
**C.** 20% increase **D.** 20% decrease

**Q.13** Pipe A can fill a tank in 5 hours, pipe B in 10 hours, and pipe C in 30 hours. If all the pipes are open, in how many hours will the tank be filled?

**A.** 2.5 hours **B.** 2 hours
**C.** 3.5 hours **D.** 3 hours

**Q.14** If $x + \dfrac{1}{x} = 6$, then the value of $\dfrac{2x}{3x^2-4x+3}$ is:

**A.** 1 **B.** $1\dfrac{1}{7}$ **C.** $\dfrac{1}{7}$ **D.** $\dfrac{3}{7}$

**Q.15** Sum of the digits of a two-digit number is 10. If 18 is added to the number, then the digits are reversed. What is the number?

**A.** 46 **B.** 27 **C.** 37 **D.** 62

**Q.16** A car was sold at a gain of 20%. Had it been sold for Rs. 50,000 more, the gain would have been 25%. The cost price of the car is:

**A.** Rs. 10,00,000 **B.** Rs. 15,00,000
**C.** Rs. 5,00,000 **D.** Rs. 2,50,000

**Q.17** Prabhat has done $\dfrac{1}{2}$ of a job in 12 days. Santhosh completes the rest of the job in 6 days. In how many days can they together do the job?

**A.** 12 days **B.** 4 days **C.** 8 days **D.** 16 days

**Q.18** The length of two parallel sides of a trapezium are 53 cm and 68 cm respectively, and the distance between the parallel sides is 16 cm. Find the area of the trapezium.

**A.** 968 cm² **B.** 972 cm²
**C.** 988 cm² **D.** 1024 cm²

**Q.19** A, B, and C start at the same time in the same direction to run around a circular stadium. A completes a round in 252 seconds, B in 308 seconds, and C in 198 seconds, all starting the same point. After what time will they again at the starting point?

**A.** 26 minutes 18 seconds
**B.** 42 minutes 36 seconds
**C.** 45 minutes
**D.** 46 minutes 12 seconds

**Q.20** The number of students in 3 classes is in the ratio 2 : 3 : 4. If 12 students are increased in each class this ratio changes to 8 : 11 : 14. The total number of students in the three classes in the beginning was:

**A.** 162 **B.** 108 **C.** 96 **D.** 54

**Q.21** The speed of the boat in still water is 5 km/h. The river is flowing with a speed of 2 km/h and the time taken to cover a certain distance upstream is 2 hrs more than the time is taken to cover the same distance downstream. Find the distance.

**A.** 10.5 km **B.** 11 km **C.** 10.9 km **D.** 15 km

**Q.22** In how many ways 4 boys and 3 girls can be seated in a row so that they are alternate?

**A.** 144 **B.** 288 **C.** 12 **D.** 256

**Q.23** The value of $\sqrt{6 + \sqrt{6 + \sqrt{6 \ldots \ldots}}}$ :

**A.** 3.5 **B.** 4 **C.** 3 **D.** -3

**Q.24** A man sold his watch at a loss of 5%. Had he sold it for Rs. 56.25 more, he would have gained 10%. What is the cost price of the watch (in Rs.)?

**A.** 365 **B.** 370 **C.** 375 **D.** 390

**Q.25** On a certain principal if the simple interest for two years is Rs. 1400 and compound interest for the two years is Rs. 1449, what is the rate of Interest?

**A.** 7% **B.** 3.5% **C.** 1.4% **D.** 10.5%

# // Smart Answer Sheet //

**Correct** — Indicates percentage of students who answered questions correctly.

**Skipped** — Indicates percentage of students who skipped questions.

| Q. | Ans. | Correct / Skipped |
|---|---|---|
| 1 | D | 55.88 % / 41.76 % |
| 2 | C | 31.71 % / 67.67 % |
| 3 | D | 55.05 % / 30.31 % |
| 4 | A | 41.8 % / 37.61 % |
| 5 | D | 21.19 % / 77.94 % |
| 6 | A | 42.78 % / 47.7 % |
| 7 | C | 59.86 % / 39.77 % |
| 8 | D | 42.71 % / 33.15 % |
| 9 | D | 66.48 % / 30.02 % |
| 10 | B | 20.93 % / 76.43 % |
| 11 | B | 49.68 % / 33.28 % |
| 12 | A | 65.53 % / 30.57 % |
| 13 | D | 53.01 % / 46.71 % |
| 14 | C | 63.34 % / 31.22 % |
| 15 | A | 12.85 % / 70.65 % |
| 16 | A | 48.59 % / 40.15 % |
| 17 | C | 60.0 % / 30.31 % |
| 18 | A | 59.42 % / 35.83 % |
| 19 | D | 59.15 % / 36.11 % |
| 20 | A | 46.98 % / 45.78 % |
| 21 | A | 53.92 % / 39.37 % |
| 22 | A | 43.05 % / 49.42 % |
| 23 | C | 21.44 % / 76.21 % |
| 24 | C | 59.19 % / 36.43 % |
| 25 | A | 16.48 % / 75.98 % |

## Performance Analysis

| | |
|---|---|
| Avg. Score (%) | 40.0% |
| Toppers Score (%) | 64.0% |
| Your Score | |

# //Hints and Solutions//

**1.** Here, $A \times B$ does not mean multiplication. It only signifies the expression $A^2 + B^2$. So,

$6 \times (2 \times 4)$

$= 6 \times (2^2 + 4^2)$

$= 6 \times (4 + 16)$

$= 6 \times 20$

$= 6^2 + 20^2$

$= 36 + 400$

$= 436$

Hence, the correct option is (D).

**2.** Given,

$$\left(\frac{a}{b}\right)^{x-1} = \left(\frac{b}{a}\right)^{x-3}$$

$$\Rightarrow \left(\frac{a}{b}\right)^{x-1} = \left(\frac{a}{b}\right)^{-(x-3)} = \left(\frac{a}{b}\right)^{(3-x)}$$

$\Rightarrow x - 1 = 3 - x$

$\Rightarrow 2x = 4$

$\Rightarrow x = 2$

Hence, the correct option is (C).

**3.** Getting at most Two heads means 0 to 2 but not more than 2

Here S = {TTT, TTH, THT, HTT, THH, HTH, HHT, HHH}

Let E = event of getting at most two heads

Then E = {TTT, TTH, THT, HTT, THH, HTH, HHT}

$$\therefore P(E) = \frac{n(E)}{n(S)}$$

$$= \frac{7}{8}$$

Hence, the correct option is (D).

**4.** Let principal $= 10P$

Interest $= 10P \times \dfrac{30}{100}$

$= 3P$

According to the question,

Case (I)

$$\Rightarrow 3P = \frac{10P \times R \times 6}{100}$$

$\Rightarrow R = 5\%$

Case (II)

Interest $=$ Principal $= 10P$

$$\Rightarrow 10P = \frac{10P \times 5 \times t}{100}$$

$\Rightarrow t = 20$ years

Hence, the correct option is (A).

**5.** Amount after three years = Rs. 2662

Amount after two years = Rs. 2420

Net interest earned in the 3rd year = 2662–2420

= Rs. 242

Rate of interest (r) $= \dfrac{242}{2420} \times 100 = 10\%$   ($\because$ 2nd year's amount is principal for 3rd year)

Hence, the correct option is (D).

**6.** Let Ronit's present age be $x$ years

Then, father's present age $= (x + 3x)$ years $= 4x$ years

$\therefore (4x + 8) = \dfrac{5}{2}(x + 8)$

$\Rightarrow 8x + 16 = 5x + 40$

$\Rightarrow 3x = 24$

$\Rightarrow x = 8$

Hence, required ratio $= \dfrac{(4x+16)}{(x+16)}$

$\dfrac{48}{24}$

$= 2$ times

Hence, the correct option is (A).

**7.** Suppose the can initially contains $7x$ and $5x$ of mixtures A and B respectively.

Quantity of A in mixture left

$= \left(7x - \dfrac{7}{12} \times 9\right)$ litres

$= \left(7x - \dfrac{21}{4}\right)$ litres

Quantity of B in mixture left

$= \left(5x - \dfrac{5}{12} \times 9\right)$ litres

$= \left(5x - \dfrac{15}{4}\right)$ litres

$\therefore \dfrac{\left(7x - \dfrac{21}{4}\right)}{\left(5x - \dfrac{15}{4}\right) + 9} = \dfrac{7}{9}$

$\Rightarrow \dfrac{28x - 21}{20x + 21} = \dfrac{7}{9}$

$\Rightarrow 252x - 189 = 140x + 147$

$\Rightarrow 112x = 336$

$\Rightarrow x = 3$

So, the can contained $21$ litres of A.

Hence, the correct option is (C).

**8.** Average of 1st $n$ natural number is given by

$$= \frac{\frac{n \times (n+1)}{2}}{n}$$

Average of 1st $97$ natural number is given by

$$= \frac{\frac{97 \times (97+1)}{2}}{97}$$

$$= 49$$

Hence, the correct option is (D).

**9.** Let

P's capital $= p$,

Q's capital $= q$ and

R's capital $= r$

Then

$4p = 6q = 10r$

$\Rightarrow 2p = 3q = 5r$

$\Rightarrow q = \dfrac{2p}{3}$

$\Rightarrow r = \dfrac{2p}{5}$

$P:Q:R = p:\dfrac{2p}{3}:\dfrac{2p}{5}$

(Multiply by $15$)

$= 15:10:6$

R's share $= 4650 \times \dfrac{6}{31}$

$= 150 \times 6$

$= $ Rs. $900$

Hence, the correct option is (D).

**10.** External radius $(r_1) = 4$ cm,

Internal radius $(r_2) = 3$ cm,

Height of pipe $(h) = 21$ cm

Volume of iron $(V) = \pi(r_1^2 - r_2^2) \times h$

$= \left(\dfrac{22}{7} \times [(4)^2 - (3)^2] \times 21\right)$ cm³

$= \left(\dfrac{22}{7} \times 7 \times 1 \times 21\right)$ cm³

$= 462$ cm³

$\therefore$ Weight of iron $= (462 \times 8) = 3696$ gm

$= 3.696$ kg

Hence, the correct option is (B).

**11.** Let the speeds of the two trains be $x$ m/sec and $y$ m/sec respectively

Then, length of the first train $= 27x$ metres,

and length of the second train $= 17y$ metres

According to question;

$\therefore \dfrac{27x + 17y}{x + y} = 23$

$\Rightarrow 27x + 17y = 23x + 23y$

$\Rightarrow 4x = 6y$

$\Rightarrow \dfrac{x}{y} = \dfrac{3}{2} = 3:2$

Hence, the correct option is (B).

**12.** Let the price of $1$ color TV $=$ Rs. $x$ and the number of TV sold $= y$

$\therefore$ The total original sell price $= xy$

Now, the price after $30\%$ reduction $= x - \dfrac{30x}{100} = \dfrac{7x}{10}$

The number of sold TV after it was increased by $20\%$

$= y + \dfrac{20y}{100} = \dfrac{6y}{5}$

$\therefore$ The total of the new sell price $= \dfrac{7x}{10} \times \dfrac{6y}{5}$

$= \dfrac{21xy}{25} < xy$

$\therefore$ It is a loss

$\therefore$ Loss $= xy - \dfrac{21xy}{25}$

$= \dfrac{4xy}{25}$

So, the per colour TV of loss $= \dfrac{\frac{4xy}{25}}{xy} \times 100$

$= 16\%$ per colour TV

Hence, the correct option is (A).

**13.** Part filled by A in $1$ hour $= \dfrac{1}{5}$

Part filled by B in $1$ hour $= \dfrac{1}{10}$

Part filled by C in $1$ hour $= \dfrac{1}{30}$

Part filled by A+B+C in $1$ hour $= \dfrac{1}{5} + \dfrac{1}{10} + \dfrac{1}{30}$

$= \dfrac{1}{3}$

So all pipes will fill the tank in 3 hours.

Hence, the correct option is (D).

**14.** $x + \dfrac{1}{x} = 6$

$\Rightarrow x^2 + 1 = 6x$

Now,

$\dfrac{2x}{3x^2 - 4x + 3}$

$= \dfrac{2x}{3(x^2 + 1) - 4x}$

$= \dfrac{2x}{3 \times 6x - 4x}$

$= \dfrac{2x}{14x}$

$= \dfrac{1}{7}$

Hence, the correct option is (C).

**15.** Let the digit on one's place be y and the digit in ten's place be x

$\therefore$ The number is = 10x + y

Sum of the digits is 10

$\therefore$ x + y = 10

Now, when 18 is added, the digits are reversed

$\therefore$ New number = 10y + x

$\therefore$ (10x + y) + 18 = 10y + x

$\Rightarrow$ 9x + 18 = 9y

$\Rightarrow$ x + 2 = y

$\therefore$ x + y = 10

$\Rightarrow$ x + (x + 2) = 10

$\Rightarrow$ 2x + 2 = 10

$\Rightarrow$ 2x = 8

$\Rightarrow$ x = 4

$\therefore$ y = 10 − x = 10 − 4 = 6

$\therefore$ The number is 10x + y = (10 × 4) + 6 = 46

Hence, the correct option is (A).

**16.** Let CP of car be x

SP at 20% gain = x + 0.20x = 1.2x

SP at 25% gain = x + 0.25x = 1.25x

According to question,

1.25x − 1.2x = 50000

$\Rightarrow$ 0.05x = 50000

$\Rightarrow$ x = $\dfrac{5000}{0.05}$

$\Rightarrow$ x = Rs.10,00,000

Hence, the correct option is (A).

**17.** Prabhat has done $\dfrac{1}{2}$ of job in 12 days.

Prabhat has done in $\dfrac{1}{24}$ part of job in 1 day.

Santhosh complete rest $\dfrac{1}{2}$ part of job in 6 days.

Santhosh has done in $\dfrac{1}{12}$ part of job in 1 days.

Santhosh and Prabhat complete part of job in 1 day = $\left(\dfrac{1}{24}\right)$ + $\left(\dfrac{1}{12}\right) = \dfrac{1}{8}$

Santhosh and Prabhat complete $\dfrac{1}{8}$ part of job in 1 day.

Santhosh and Prabhat will complete job in 8 day.

Hence, the correct option is (C).

**18.** Area of the Trapezium = $\dfrac{1}{2}$ × (Sum of the parallel sides) × (Distance between parallel sides)

$\Rightarrow \dfrac{1}{2}$ × (53 + 68) × 16

$\Rightarrow \dfrac{1}{2}$ × 121 × 16

$\therefore$ Area of the Trapezium = 968 cm²

Hence, the correct option is (A).

**19.** A complete his round in 252 seconds

B completes his round in 308 seconds

C completes his round in 198 seconds

They will again at starting together after,

LCM of 252, 308 and 198

252 = 2 × 2 × 3 × 3 × 7

308 = 2 × 2 × 7 × 11

198 = 2 × 3 × 3 × 11

Required LCM = 2 × 2 × 3 × 3 × 7 × 11 = 2772 seconds

= 46 minutes 12 seconds

Hence, the correct option is (D).

**20.** Let the number of students in the classes be $2x, 3x$ and $4x$ respectively.

Total students $= 2x + 3x + 4x = 9x$

According to the question,

$$\frac{2x+12}{3x+12} = \frac{8}{11}$$

or, $24x + 96 = 22x + 132$

or, $2x = 132 - 96$

or, $x = \frac{36}{2} = 18$

Hence, Original number of students,

$$9x = 9 \times 18$$

$$= 162$$

Hence, the correct option is (A).

**21.** Let distance be $x$ km

Speed downstream $= 5 + 2 = 7$ km /hr

Speed upstream $= 5 - 2 = 3$ km /hr

So, $\frac{x}{3} - \frac{x}{7} = 2$

$$\Rightarrow 7x - 3x = 2 \times 21$$

$$\Rightarrow 4x = 42$$

$$\Rightarrow x = \frac{42}{4} = 10.5 \text{ km}$$

Hence, the correct option is (A).

**22.** Let the arrangement be,

B G B G B G B

4 boys can be seated in 4! Ways

Girl can be seated in 3! Ways

Required number of ways,

$= 4! \times 3!$

$= 144$

Hence, the correct option is (A).

**23.** Let $\sqrt{6 + \sqrt{6 + \sqrt{6 \ldots \ldots}}} = y$

Then

$$\sqrt{6 + \sqrt{6 + \sqrt{6 \ldots \ldots}}} = y$$

$$\Rightarrow \sqrt{6 + y} = y$$

$$\Rightarrow 6 + y = y^2$$

$$\Rightarrow y^2 - y - 6 = 0$$

$$\Rightarrow y^2 - (3 - 2)y - 6 = 0$$

$$\Rightarrow y^2 - 3y + 2y - 6 = 0$$

$$\Rightarrow y(y - 3) + 2(y - 3) = 0$$

$$\Rightarrow (y - 3)(y + 2) = 0$$

$$\Rightarrow y = 3, -2$$

Since $y$ cannot be negative as negative square root is not real so $y = 3$.

Hence, the correct option is (C).

**24.** He sold his watch at loss of 5%. If he sells his watch for Rs. 56.25 more, he would gain 10%. It means that

15% = Rs. 56.25

So,

$1\% = \dfrac{56.25}{15}$

$100\% = \dfrac{56.25 \times 100}{15}$ = Rs. 375

Therefore, the cost price of the watch is Rs. 375

Hence, the correct option is (C).

**25.** Let the principal amount $=$ Rs. $100x$ and rate of interest $= r\%$

Time period $= 2$ years

Simple Interest $= \dfrac{P \times R \times T}{100} = 1400$

$$\Rightarrow \frac{100x \times r \times 2}{100} = 1400$$

$$\Rightarrow 2rx = 1400$$

$$\Rightarrow x = \frac{1400}{2r} = \frac{700}{r}$$

Compound Interest $= P\left[\left(1 + \dfrac{R}{100}\right)^T - 1\right] = 1449$

$$\Rightarrow 100x\left[\left(1 + \frac{r}{100}\right)^2 - 1\right] = 1449$$

$$\Rightarrow 100x\left[\left(1 + \frac{r^2}{100^2} + 2\frac{r}{100}\right) - 1\right] = 1449$$

$$\Rightarrow \left(100 \times \frac{700}{r}\right)\left[\frac{r^2}{10000} + \frac{2r}{100}\right] = 1449$$

$$\Rightarrow 7r + 1400 = 1449$$

$$\Rightarrow 7r = 1449 - 1400 = 49$$

$$\Rightarrow r = \frac{49}{7} = 7\%$$

Hence, the correct option is (A).

**Q.1 Direction:** In the question, two equations (I) and (II) are given. You have to solve both the equations and give the answer.

I. $x^2 - 19x + 88 = 0$

II. $y^2 - 12y + 35 = 0$

**A.** If $x > y$      **B.** If $x > y$      **C.** If $x \geq y$      **D.** If $x < y$

**Q.2 Direction:** In the questions, two equations (I) and (II) are given. You have to solve both the equations and give the answer.

I. $x^2 - 11x + 24 = 0$

II. $y^2 - 16y + 63 = 0$

**A.**  If $x > y$

**B.**  If $x \leq y$

**C.**  If $x \geq y$

**D.**  If $x = y$ or relationship between $x$ and $y$ can't be established

**Q.3 Direction:** What approximate value should come in place of the question mark (?).

17.92 × 10.97 – 52.11 = ?

**A.** 146      **B.** 196      **C.** 216      **D.** 228

**Q.4 Direction:** What approximate value should come in place of the question mark (?).

127.93 × 4.1 – 116.01 × 2.95 = ?

**A.** 106      **B.** 164      **C.** 98      **D.** 196

**Q.5** Amit, Anil, and Ajit ride from home to their common office with speeds in the ratio 5: 4 : 3. If in total they take 94 minutes (sum of the individual time taken) to cover the individual distance (which is the same for all), then find the time taken by 'Anil' to cover his distance.

**A.** 30 min      **B.** 48 min      **C.** 24 min      **D.** 40 min

**Q.6** The average age of 36 students in a group is 14 years. When the teacher's age is included the average increases by one. What is the teacher's age?

**A.** 31 years      **B.** 36 years      **C.** 51 years      **D.** 41 years

**Q.7** The average marks of a student in seven subjects were 75. His average marks in six subjects, excluding Maths, was 73. How many marks did he score in Maths?

**A.** 81      **B.** 84      **C.** 87      **D.** 91

**Q.8** The average age of X and Y is 33 years. If Z's age is added the average of their ages becomes 31 years. What is the age of Z ?

**A.** 24 years      **B.** 27 years      **C.** 30 years      **D.** 33 years

**Q.9** A man lent Rs. 4500 at 30% compound interest per annum for 3 years. What is the difference between the interest earned by the man in the 2nd year only and the interest earned by the man in the 3rd year only?

**A.** Rs. 545.5      **B.** Rs. 502

**C.** Rs. 526.5      **D.** Rs. 532

**Q.10** Mahesh can complete a job in 5 days. Mahesh is twice as fast as Akhilesh while Akhilesh is thrice as fast as Nimesh. If all of them work together, in how many days would the job get completed?

**A.** 5 days      **B.** 9 days      **C.** 12 days      **D.** 3 days

**Q.11** 100 Men were employed to finish work in 180 days. After 60 days it was found that only $\frac{1}{5}$ of the work was done. How many more men must be employed to finish the work in the stipulated time?

**A.** 100      **B.** 200      **C.** 300      **D.** 150

**Q.12** A shopkeeper deals in milk and 45 litre mixture is to be distributed in Milk & Water in the ratio of 4 : 1. If 4 litre milk & 3 litre water will be added in the mixture then what will be the new ratio of water and milk?

**A.** 5 : 6      **B.** 3 : 10      **C.** 4 : 5      **D.** 7 : 8

**Q.13** The ratio between the speed of the boat in still water to the speed of the stream is 5: 2. If 224 km is traveled by downstream in 4 hours then find the difference between the speed of the boat in still water and the speed of the stream?

**A.** 24 km/hr      **B.** 22 km/hr      **C.** 28 km/hr      **D.** 26 km/hr

**Q.14** A shop sells 10 tube lights out of which 3 are defective. Salman buys four tube lights. Find the probability that all of Salman's tube lights work.

**A.** $\frac{1}{15}$      **B.** $\frac{1}{25}$      **C.** $\frac{1}{30}$      **D.** $\frac{1}{6}$

**Q.15** From a box containing 8 yellow and 5 white pens, three are drawn one after the other. Find the probability of all three pens being yellow if the pens drawn are not replaced?

**A.** $\frac{336}{1716}$      **B.** $\frac{128}{429}$      **C.** $\frac{113}{1716}$      **D.** $\frac{336}{2197}$

**Q.16** In how many ways can the letters of the word 'PARAGLIDING' be arranged such that all the vowels occur together?

**A.** 88322 ways      **B.** 120960 ways

**C.** 740 ways      **D.** 144868 ways

**Q.17** The boys and girls in a school are in the ratio 9: 5. If the total strength of the school is 448, find the number of girls.

**A.** 160      **B.** 100      **C.** 200      **D.** 150

**Q.18** What will come in place of question mark (?) in the following question?

$$\sqrt[3]{(126 + 392 \div 7 - 35 + 14^2)} = ?$$

**A.** 8      **B.** 7      **C.** 9      **D.** 5

**Q.19** What will come in place of question mark (?) in the following question?

$$120\% \text{ of } 200 + \frac{16^2 - 12^2}{2} - 15 = ?$$

**A.** 312      **B.** 281      **C.** 408      **D.** 292

**Q.20** The cost price of an article is Rs. 480. If it is to be sold at a profit of 6.25%, how much would be its selling price?

**A.** Rs. 510      **B.** Rs. 530      **C.** Rs. 503      **D.** Rs. 519

**Q.21** A tradesman marks his goods at 35% above its cost price and allows a discount of 17.5% for purchase in cash. What profit percent does he make?

**A.** 11.25      **B.** 12.125      **C.** 11.125      **D.** 11.375

**Q.22** The total number of students in a school is 2140. If the number of girls in the school is 1200, then what is the respective ratio of the total number of boys to the total number of girls in the school?

**A.** 26 : 25      **B.** 47 : 60      **C.** 18 : 13      **D.** 31 : 79

**Q.23** The income of A is 150% of the income of B and the income of C is 120% of the income of A. If the total income of A, B and C together is Rs. 86000, what is C's income?

**A.** Rs. 30000      **B.** Rs. 32000

**C.** Rs. 20000      **D.** Rs. 36000

**Q.24** In a town the ratio of men, women, and children is 9 : 8 : 3. 80% men are literate and 30% women are illiterate. If 90% of children are literate, then the illiteracy rate of that town is:

**A.** $22\frac{1}{2}\%$      **B.** $25\frac{1}{2}\%$      **C.** 27%      **D.** 30%

**Q.25** The population of a town is 126800. It increases by 15% in the first year, and decreases by 20% in the second year. What is the population of the city at the end of 2 years?

**A.** 174984      **B.** 135996      **C.** 116656      **D.** 145820

# // Smart Answer Sheet //

**Correct**    Indicates percentage of students who answered questions correctly.

**Skipped**    Indicates percentage of students who skipped questions.

| Q. | Ans. | Correct / Skipped | Q. | Ans. | Correct / Skipped | Q. | Ans. | Correct / Skipped | Q. | Ans. | Correct / Skipped | Q. | Ans. | Correct / Skipped |
|----|------|-------------------|----|------|-------------------|----|------|-------------------|----|------|-------------------|----|------|-------------------|
| 1 | A | 55.68 % / 30.33 % | 6 | C | 60.04 % / 37.52 % | 11 | A | 55.59 % / 42.17 % | 16 | B | 32.54 % / 67.24 % | 21 | D | 50.43 % / 38.09 % |
| 2 | D | 51.68 % / 45.67 % | 7 | C | 68.65 % / 30.19 % | 12 | B | 42.13 % / 44.53 % | 17 | A | 53.84 % / 32.62 % | 22 | B | 79.26 % / 17.39 % |
| 3 | A | 89.69 % / 10.28 % | 8 | B | 45.78 % / 38.04 % | 13 | A | 60.72 % / 37.95 % | 18 | B | 46.35 % / 42.51 % | 23 | D | 53.5 % / 31.8 % |
| 4 | B | 65.58 % / 33.76 % | 9 | C | 25.53 % / 70.04 % | 14 | D | 54.65 % / 38.93 % | 19 | B | 49.35 % / 35.9 % | 24 | A | 30.19 % / 67.99 % |
| 5 | A | 41.46 % / 42.0 % | 10 | D | 51.16 % / 38.12 % | 15 | A | 55.32 % / 42.22 % | 20 | A | 69.99 % / 30.0 % | 25 | C | 43.85 % / 32.39 % |

| Performance Analysis | |
|---|---|
| Avg. Score (%) | 34.0% |
| Toppers Score (%) | 70.0% |
| Your Score | |

# //Hints and Solutions//

**1.** According to the given equations,

I. $x^2 - 19x + 88 = 0$

$\Rightarrow x^2 - 11x - 8x + 88 = 0$

$\Rightarrow x(x - 11) - 8(x - 11) = 0$

$\Rightarrow (x - 8)(x - 11) = 0$

$x = 8, 11$

II. $y^2 - 12y + 35 = 0$

$\Rightarrow (y^2 - 7y - 5y + 35 = 0$

$\Rightarrow y(y - 7) - 5(y - 7) = 0$

$\Rightarrow (y - 7)(y - 5) = 0$

$y = 7, 5$

After a comparison of both equations, the conclusion is $x > y$. Hence, the correct option is (A).

**2.** According to the given equations,

I. $x^2 - 11x + 24 = 0$

$\Rightarrow x^2 - 3x - 8x + 24 = 0$

$\Rightarrow x(x - 3) - 8(x - 3) = 0$

$\Rightarrow (x - 3)(x - 8) = 0$

$x = 3, 8$

II. $y^2 - 16y + 63 = 0$

$\Rightarrow y^2 - 7y - 9y + 63 = 0$

$\Rightarrow y(y - 7) - 9(y - 7) = 0$

$\Rightarrow (y - 7)(y - 9) = 0$

$y = 7, 9$

While comparing the root values of $x$ and $y$, we find that one root value of $x$ lies between the root values of $y$. Hence, the relation between $x$ and $y$ can't be established.
Hence, the correct option is (D).

**3.** Given,

$17.92 \times 10.97 - 52.11 = ?$

Taking approximate value, we get

$\Rightarrow ? \approx 18 \times 11 - 52$

$\Rightarrow ? = 146$

Hence, the correct option is (A).

**4.** Given,

$127.93 \times 4.1 - 116.01 \times 2.95 = ?$

By taking approximate value, we get

$\Rightarrow ? \approx 128 \times 4 - 116 \times 3$

$\Rightarrow ? = 512 - 348$

$\Rightarrow ? = 164$

Hence, the correct option is (B).

**5.** Given,

Ratio of the speeds = 5 : 4 : 3

Total time = 94 sec

For a given distance, speed and time are inversely proportional.

So, their respective time will be in the ratio of $\dfrac{1}{5} : \dfrac{1}{4} : \dfrac{1}{3}$.

Multiplying with their LCM which is 60, we get the ratio as 12 : 15 : 20.

Let be the time taken by Amit, Anil and Ajit to go to the same office from home is $12x, 15x,$ and $20x$ respectively.

Total time = 94 sec

$\Rightarrow 12x + 15x + 20x = 94$

$\Rightarrow x = 2$

Time taken by Anil to cover the distance $= 2 \times 15 = 30$ min

Hence, the correct option is (A).

**6.** Given, the average age of 36 students in a group is 14 years.

Total age of 36 students = 14 × 36 = 504 years

Given that when teacher's age is included the average increases by one

∴ Total age along with the teacher = 15 × 37 = 555 years

Now, the teacher's age = 555 – 504 = 51 years
Hence, the correct option is (C).

**7.** Given, the average marks of a student in seven subjects was 75.

And his average marks in six subjects, excluding Maths, was 73.

Total marks in seven subjects = 7 × 75 = 525

Now, excluding Maths

∴ Total marks in six subjects = 6 × 73 = 438

∴ Marks in Maths = 525 – 438 = 87
Hence, the correct option is (C).

**8.** Given,

The average age of X and Y is 33 years.

Total age of X and Y = 2 × 33 = 66 years

Now, Z's age is added

∴ Total age of X, Y and Z = 3 × 31 = 93 years

$\therefore$ Z's age = Total age of X, Y, and Z - Total age of X and Y

$\Rightarrow$ 93 − 66 = 27 years

Hence, the correct option is (B).

**9.** As given, A man lent Rs. 4500 at 30% compound interest per annum for 3 years.

$P =$ Rs. $4500$

$r = 30\%$

Interest earned by the man on 2nd year $= P[\left(1 + \frac{r}{100}\right)^2 - 1] - \frac{P \times r \times 2}{100}$

$\Rightarrow 4500 \times \left[\left\{1 + \left(\frac{30}{100}\right)\right\}^2 - 1\right] - \left(\frac{4500 \times 30 \times 1}{100}\right)$

$\Rightarrow 4500 \times \left(\frac{69}{100}\right) - 1350$

$\Rightarrow 3105 - 1350$

$\Rightarrow$ Rs. $1755$

Interest earned by the man on 3rd year $= P[\left(1 + \frac{r}{100}\right)^3 - 1] - P[\left(1 + \frac{r}{100}\right)^2 - 1]$

$\Rightarrow 4500 \times \left[\left\{1 + \left(\frac{30}{100}\right)\right\}^3 - 1\right] - 4500 \times \left[\left\{1 + \left(\frac{30}{100}\right)\right\}^2 - 1\right]$

$\Rightarrow 4500 \times \left(\frac{1197}{1000}\right) - 4500 \times \frac{69}{100}$

$\Rightarrow 5386.5 - 3105$

$\Rightarrow$ Rs. $2281.5$

Therefore, required difference $= 2281.5 - 1755 =$ Rs. $526.5$

Hence, the correct option is (C).

**10.** As given, Mahesh can do a piece of work in 5 days, Akhilesh can do the same work in 10 days, Nimesh can do the same work in 30 days.

Mahesh works in a day $= \frac{1}{5}$

Nimesh works in a day $= \frac{1}{10}$

Akhilesh works in a day $= \frac{1}{30}$

So together they can do the piece of work in 1 day

$= \left(\frac{1}{5} + \frac{1}{10} + \frac{1}{30}\right)$

$= \left(\frac{12+6+2}{60}\right) + \frac{20}{60} = \frac{1}{3}$

In a day they finsih $\frac{1}{3}$ rd of the work.

Hence, together they will finish the piece of work in 3 days.

Hence, the correct option is (D).

**11.** As given, 100 Men were employed to finish a work in 180 days.

By product constancy,

$\frac{M_1 \times D_1}{W_1} = \frac{M_2 \times D_2}{W_2}$

$M_1 = 100$

$D_1 = 180$

$W_1 = \frac{1}{5}$

$M_2 = a$

$D_2 = 60$

$W_2 = \left(1 - \frac{1}{5}\right)$

$\Rightarrow \frac{100 \times 60}{\frac{1}{5}} = \frac{a \times 60}{1 - \frac{1}{5}}$

$\Rightarrow a = 200$

Total workers = 200

Extra men required = 200 - 100 = 100

Hence, the correct option is (A).

**12.** As given, a shopkeeper deals in milk and 45 litre mixture is to be distributed in Milk & Water in the ratio of 4: 1.

In the mixture of 45 litre,

Milk $= \frac{45}{5} \times 4 = 36$ litre,

Water $= \frac{45}{5} \times 1 = 9$ litre

New ratio,

$= 9 + 3 : 36 + 4$

$= 12 : 40 = 3 : 10$

Hence, the correct option is (B).

**13.** As given, the ratio between the speed of the boat in still water to the speed of the stream is 5: 2.

Let the speed of the boat in still water and speed of the stream be $5x$ and $2x$ respectively.

According to the question,

$\frac{224}{4} = 5x + 2x$

$\Rightarrow x = \frac{224}{7} \times 4$

$\Rightarrow x = \dfrac{32}{4} = 8$

Required difference $= 5x - 2x$

$= 3x$

$= 24$ km/hr

Hence, the correct option is (A).

**14.** As given, a shop sells 10 tube lights out of which 3 are defective.

$n(S) = {}^{10}C_4 = 210$

7 of the 10 lamps are not defective.

$\therefore$ If $T$ is the event that all of Salman's tube lights work,

$n(T) = {}^{7}C_4 = 35$

$\therefore$ Probability that all of Salman's tube lights work $= \dfrac{n(S)}{n(T)}$

$\Rightarrow \dfrac{35}{210} = \dfrac{1}{6}$

Hence, the correct option is (D).

**15.** Given,

From a box containing 8 yellow and 5 white pens, three are drawn one after the other.

If the pens are being drawn one after another, the probability of drawing any color of pens for every fresh draw changes.

$\therefore$ Required probability $= \dfrac{8}{13} \times \dfrac{7}{12} \times \dfrac{6}{11} = \dfrac{336}{1716}$

Hence, the correct option is (A).

**16.** In the word "PARAGLIDING", there are 11 letters in which there are 4 vowels (i.e., 2 A and 2 I) and 7 consonants (i.e., 2 G and each of P, R, L, D, N).

Considering vowel as one letter, the number of letters becomes 8 which can be arranged as,

$\Rightarrow frac8!2! = \dfrac{40320}{2} = 20160$

Total vowel = 4

Vowel A and I appear twice, so vowels can be arranged as,

$\Rightarrow \dfrac{4!}{(2! \times 2!)} = \dfrac{24}{4} = 6$

Hence the required number of ways in which the letters of the word "PARAGLADING" be arranged so that all the vowels occur together $= 20160 \times 6 = 120960$

Hence, the correct option is (B).

**17.** Given,

Number of boys: number of girls $= 9:5$

Total strength $= 448$

Let number of boys be $9x$ and number of girls be $5x$.

According to the question,

$9x + 5x = 448$

$\Rightarrow 14x = 448$

$\Rightarrow x = \dfrac{448}{14}$

$\Rightarrow x = 32$

$\therefore$ Number of girls are $160$.

Hence, the correct option is (A).

**18.** Given,

$\sqrt[3]{(126 + 392 \div 7 - 35 + 14^2)} =?$

$\Rightarrow \sqrt[3]{(126 + 56 - 35 + 196)} =?$

$\Rightarrow \sqrt[3]{(378 - 35)} =?$

$\Rightarrow \sqrt[3]{343} =?$

$\Rightarrow ? = 7$

Hence, the correct option is (B).

**19.** Given,

$120\% \text{ of } 200 + \dfrac{16^2 - 12^2}{2} - 15 =?$

$\Rightarrow 240 + \dfrac{256 - 144}{2} - 15 =?$

$\Rightarrow 240 + \dfrac{112}{2} - 15 =?$

$\Rightarrow 240 + 56 - 15 =?$

$\Rightarrow ? = 296 - 15$

$\Rightarrow ? = 281$

Hence, the correct option is (B).

**20.** Given,

The cost price of an article is Rs. 480.

Profit = 6.25%

Profit % $= \dfrac{(SP - CP) \times 100}{CP}$

$SP =$ Selling price

$CP =$ Cost price

$SP - CP =$ Profit % $\times \dfrac{CP}{100}$

$SP = CP +$ Profit % $\times \dfrac{CP}{100}$

$\Rightarrow 480 + \dfrac{6.25 \times 480}{100}$

$\Rightarrow 480 + 30$

$\Rightarrow$ Rs. $510$

Hence, the correct option is (A).

**21.** Given,

A tradesman marks his goods at 35% above its cost price and allows a discount of 17.5% for purchase in cash.

For solving, we can apply the formula,

$$x + y + \frac{xy}{100}$$

Let's take $x = 35\%$ and $y = -17.5\%$

By the above formula, we get

$$\text{Profit } \% = \left(35 - 17.5 - \frac{35 \times 17.5}{100}\right)\%$$

$$\Rightarrow (17.5 - 6.125)\%$$

$$\Rightarrow 11.375\%$$

Hence, the correct option is (D).

**22.** Given,

The total number of students in a school is 2140 and the number of girls in the school is 1200.

Total number of boys $= 2140 - 1200 = 940$

Respective ratio $= 940 : 1200 = 47 : 60$

Hence, the correct option is (B).

**23.** Given,

The income of A is 150% of the income of B and the income of C is 120% of the income of A.

And the total income of A, B and C together = Rs. 86000

Let's take B's income = Rs. 100

Then

$$A : B : C = 150 : 100 : \frac{120 \times 150}{100}$$

$$\Rightarrow 15 : 10 : 18$$

$\therefore$ The income of C $= \dfrac{18}{43} \times 86000$

$$\Rightarrow \text{Rs. } 36000$$

Hence, the correct option is (D).

**24.** Given,

The ratio of men, women, and children $= 9 : 8 : 3$

Suppose, Men $= 90$, Women $= 80$, Children $= 30$

Total population $= 200$

Now, the number of literate men $= \dfrac{90 \times 80}{100} = 72 \text{.....(i)}$

The number of literate women $= \dfrac{80 \times 70}{100} = 56 \text{.....(ii)}$

The number of literate children $= \dfrac{30 \times 90}{100} = 27 \text{.....(iii)}$

Total literate $= 155$

Total illiterate $200 - 155 = 45$

So, illiteracy rate $= \dfrac{45}{200} \times 100$

$$\Rightarrow 22\frac{1}{2}\%$$

Hence, the correct option is (A).

**25.** Given,

The population of a town is 126800.

To solve this, we can apply the formula,

$$x + y + \frac{xy}{100}\%$$

$x = 15\%$ and $y = -20\%$

From the above formula, we get

$$= 15 - 20 - \frac{15 \times 20}{100} = -8\%$$

So, $(100 - 8)\%$ of $126800$

$$\Rightarrow 92\% \text{ of } 126800$$

$$\Rightarrow \frac{92 \times 126800}{100}$$

$$\Rightarrow 92 \times 1268$$

$$\Rightarrow 116656$$

Hence, the correct option is (C).

**Q.1** What will come in the place of the question mark '?' in the following question?

$[90 \div 6 \times (24 - 8 \div 4) \div 3] - 90 \div 5 + 34 = ?$

**A.** 181     **B.** 154     **C.** 126     **D.** 135

**Q.2** What value will come in place of the question mark?

$6 \times 12 + 8 \times 11 - 48 \div 6 + 23 \times 8 \div 4 - 2 = ?^2$

**A.** 14     **B.** 15     **C.** 196     **D.** 24

**Q.3** What will come in place of the question mark (?) in the following question?

$$(12)^4 \times (144)^8 \div (24)^3 = (?)^{17} \times 2^{(-3)}$$

**A.** 18     **B.** 12     **C.** 24     **D.** 6

**Q.4** Find the average of four numbers $2\frac{1}{4}, 5\frac{2}{3}, 4\frac{5}{6}, 8\frac{2}{3}$.

**A.** $5\frac{3}{16}$     **B.** $3\frac{13}{16}$     **C.** $3\frac{16}{5}$     **D.** $5\frac{17}{48}$

**Q.5** An average price of pen, pencil, rubber is Rs. 33. If their prices are in the ratio 5 : 3 : 1, then their prices are respectively:

**A.** Rs. 55, Rs. 33, Rs. 11
**B.** Rs. 65, Rs. 39, Rs. 13
**C.** Rs. 60, Rs. 48, Rs. 12
**D.** Rs. 25, Rs.15, Rs. 5

**Q.6** The present age of P and Q is 2 : 7. 18 yr ago, this ratio was 1 : 26. What is the sum of the present age of P and Q?

**A.** 70 yr     **B.** 80 yr     **C.** 90 yr     **D.** 60 yr

**Q.7** The income of A and B is in the ratio 7 : 8 and that of B and C is 4 : 3. The ratio of savings of A and C is 4 : 3 and the difference between the savings of B and C together to the savings A is Rs. 32,000. Find the salary of B if it is given their expenditure is equal.

**A.** Rs. 56,000
**C.** Rs. 49,000
**B.** Rs. 58,000
**D.** Rs. 64,000

**Q.8** The ratio between fourth proportional to 14, 18, 26 and third proportional of 14, 21 is:

**A.** 52 : 49     **B.** 49 : 51     **C.** 51 : 49     **D.** 52 : 47

**Q.9** A, B and C can do a work in 40 days, 50 days, and 60 days respectively. They finished together that work and gained Rs. 7400 as wage. Find the wages (in Rs.) of A, B, and C respectively.

**A.** 4500, 2400 , 5000
**C.** 4400 , 5500 , 3000
**B.** 3000 , 2400 , 2000
**D.** 2400 , 2000 , 3000

**Q.10** Sahil, Nikhil, and Akhil can complete work in 10 days. Sahil alone takes 20 days to complete work while Nikhil takes 5 more days than Sahil to finish the work. They were paid Rs 60,000 for it. What is the share of Akhil in the earnings?

**A.** Rs. 8000     **B.** Rs. 5000     **C.** Rs. 7500     **D.** Rs. 6000

**Q.11** Aditya sells goods at 5% loss on cost price but uses 15% less weight. Find the profit or loss percent.

**A.** $\frac{200}{17}\%$     **B.** $\frac{150}{13}\%$     **C.** $\frac{210}{19}\%$     **D.** $\frac{190}{11}\%$

**Q.12** A toy when sold for Rs. 750 fetches 25 percent profit. What would be the percentage profit/loss if 5 such toys are sold for Rs. 3,300?

**A.** 10 % loss
**C.** 10 % profit
**B.** 11 % loss
**D.** 11 % profit

**Q.13** If 24 carat gold is hundred percent pure gold and price of 50% pure gold is 30,000. Then find the price of pure gold in 22 carat gold.

**A.** Rs. 55000
**C.** Rs. 57000
**B.** Rs. 56000
**D.** Rs. 58000

**Q.14** Evaluate: $\dfrac{\sqrt{0.01 + \sqrt{0.0064}}}{0.01 \times 0.3}$

**A.** 1     **B.** 10     **C.** 100     **D.** 1000

**Q.15** If the base and height of a parallelogram are increased by 30% and 45% respectively, what will be the percentage change in the area of the parallelogram?

**A.** 74.8% cm
**C.** 88.5% cm
**B.** 79.5% cm
**D.** 89.8% cm

**Q.16** The parallel side of a trapezium is 30 cm and 18 cm. The perpendicular distance between the parallel sides is 8 cm. Find the area of the trapezium (in cm²).

**A.** 129     **B.** 192     **C.** 219     **D.** 291

**Q.17** The length and breadth of a rectangle are 14.6 cm and 19.2 cm respectively. Find the difference between the areas of the squares whose sides are two more and two less than the length and breadth respectively of the rectangle?

**A.** 22.08 cm²
**C.** 28.02 cm²
**B.** 20.28 cm²
**D.** 22.82 cm²

**Q.18** A box contains three types of rings. Four square rings, three circular rings and three hexagonal rings. 3 rings are drawn randomly. What is the probability that rings drawn contain 2 square rings?

**A.** 0.2     **B.** 0.3     **C.** 0.1     **D.** 0.5

**Q.19** A card is drawn at random from a pack of 52 cards. What is the probability that the card drawn is a digit card?

**A.** $\frac{9}{13}$     **B.** $\frac{2}{13}$     **C.** $\frac{4}{13}$     **D.** $\frac{5}{13}$

**Q.20** A pack contains 4 blue, 2 red and 3 black pens. If 2 pens are drawn at random from the pack, not replaced and then another pen is drawn. What is the probability of drawing 2 blue pens and 1 black pen?

**A.** $\frac{2}{9}$     **B.** $\frac{1}{14}$     **C.** $\frac{2}{63}$     **D.** $\frac{2}{14}$

**Q.21** $(1000)^{12} \div (10)^{30} = ?$

**A.** $(1000)^2$    **B.** 10    **C.** 100    **D.** $(100)^{12}$

**Q.22** Simplify:

$$\frac{1.5^3+4.7^3+3.8^3-3\times1.5\times4.7\times3.8}{1.5^2+4.7^2+3.8^2-1.5\times4.7-4.7\times3.8-3.8\times1.5}=?$$

**A.** 0    **B.** 1    **C.** 10    **D.** 30

**Q.23** Simplify:

$$\frac{0.41\times0.41\times0.41+0.69\times0.69\times0.69}{0.41\times0.41-0.41\times0.69+0.69\times0.69}=?$$

**A.** 0.28    **B.** 1.41    **C.** 1.1    **D.** 2.8

**Q.24** In how many years will Rs. 2000 amounts to Rs. 2420 at 10% per annum compound interest?

**A.** 3 years    **B.** $2\frac{1}{2}$ years

**C.** 2 years    **D.** $1\frac{1}{2}$ years

**Q.25** If the difference between the compound interest and simple interest on a sum of $5\%$ rate of interest per annum for three years is Rs. $36.60$, then the sum is:

**A.** Rs. 8000    **B.** Rs. 8400    **C.** Rs. 4400    **D.** Rs. 4800

# // Smart Answer Sheet //

**Correct**    Indicates percentage of students who answered questions correctly.

**Skipped**    Indicates percentage of students who skipped questions.

| Q. | Ans. | Correct | Skipped |
|----|------|---------|---------|
| 1 | C | 58.67 % | 32.12 % |
| 2 | A | 54.17 % | 37.44 % |
| 3 | B | 13.26 % | 74.46 % |
| 4 | D | 32.0 % | 67.18 % |
| 5 | A | 55.79 % | 37.96 % |

| Q. | Ans. | Correct | Skipped |
|----|------|---------|---------|
| 6 | C | 68.24 % | 30.45 % |
| 7 | D | 20.79 % | 71.74 % |
| 8 | A | 49.1 % | 33.37 % |
| 9 | B | 68.44 % | 30.89 % |
| 10 | D | 28.46 % | 67.74 % |

| Q. | Ans. | Correct | Skipped |
|----|------|---------|---------|
| 11 | A | 42.83 % | 33.09 % |
| 12 | C | 60.03 % | 31.47 % |
| 13 | A | 67.54 % | 30.13 % |
| 14 | C | 25.23 % | 71.17 % |
| 15 | C | 25.33 % | 69.16 % |

| Q. | Ans. | Correct | Skipped |
|----|------|---------|---------|
| 16 | B | 57.67 % | 36.56 % |
| 17 | B | 60.66 % | 30.31 % |
| 18 | B | 48.44 % | 48.61 % |
| 19 | A | 43.84 % | 37.43 % |
| 20 | B | 65.61 % | 30.91 % |

| Q. | Ans. | Correct | Skipped |
|----|------|---------|---------|
| 21 | A | 40.7 % | 38.74 % |
| 22 | C | 11.98 % | 68.93 % |
| 23 | C | 48.55 % | 39.58 % |
| 24 | C | 54.3 % | 31.58 % |
| 25 | D | 29.23 % | 68.39 % |

## Performance Analysis

| | |
|----|----|
| Avg. Score (%) | 58.0% |
| Toppers Score (%) | 62.0% |
| Your Score | |

# //Hints and Solutions//

**1.** Given,

$[90 \div 6 \times (24 - 8 \div 4) \div 3] - 90 \div 5 + 34$

Using the BODMAS rule

$\Rightarrow [90 \div 6 \times (24 - 8 \div 4) \div 3] - 90 \div 5 + 34 = ?$

$\Rightarrow [90 \div 6 \times (24 - 2) \div 3] - 90 \div 5 + 34 = ?$

$\Rightarrow [90 \div 6 \times (22) \div 3] - 90 \div 5 + 34 = ?$

$\Rightarrow [90 \div 6 \times \dfrac{22}{3}] - 90 \div 5 + 34 = ?$

$\Rightarrow [15 \times \dfrac{22}{3}] - 90 \div 5 + 34 = ?$

$\Rightarrow [110] - 90 \div 5 + 34 = ?$

$\Rightarrow 110 - 18 + 34 = ?$

$\Rightarrow 110 + 16 = ?$

$\Rightarrow ? = 126$

∴ In place of '?' 126 will come.

Hence, the correct option is (C).

**2.** Given,

$6 \times 12 + 8 \times 11 - 48 \div 6 + 23 \times 8 \div 4 - 2 = ?^2$

Using BODMASS rule,

$6 \times 12 + 8 \times 11 - 48 \div 6 + 23 \times 8 \div 4 - 2 = ?^2$

$\Rightarrow 6 \times 12 + 8 \times 11 - 8 + 23 \times 2 - 2 = ?^2$

$\Rightarrow 72 + 88 - 8 + 46 - 2 = ?^2$

$\Rightarrow 72 + 80 + 44 = ?^2$

$\Rightarrow 196 = ?^2$

$\Rightarrow 14^2 = ?^2$

$\Rightarrow 14 = ?$

∴ Required value of '?' is 14.

Hence, the correct option is (A).

**3.** $\Rightarrow (12)^4 \times (144)^8 \div (24)^3 = (?)^{17} \times 2^{(-3)}$

$\Rightarrow 12^4 \times (12^2)^8 \div (12 \times 2)^3 = (?)^{17} \times 2^{(-3)}$

$\Rightarrow 12^{20} \div (12^3 \times 2^3) = (?)^{17} \times 2^{(-3)}$

$\Rightarrow 12^{17} \div 2^3 = (?)^{17} \times 2^{(-3)}$

$\Rightarrow 12^{17} \times 2^{(-3)} = (?)^{17} \times 2^{(-3)}$

$\therefore = 12$

Hence, the correct option is (B).

**4.** $\Rightarrow 2\dfrac{1}{4} = \dfrac{9}{4}$

$\Rightarrow 5\dfrac{2}{3} = \dfrac{17}{3}$

$\Rightarrow 4\dfrac{5}{6} = \dfrac{29}{6}$

$\Rightarrow 8\dfrac{2}{3} = \dfrac{26}{3}$

The sum of given numbers

$= \dfrac{9}{4} + \dfrac{17}{3} + \dfrac{29}{6} + \dfrac{26}{3}$

$= \dfrac{27 + 68 + 58 + 104}{12}$

$= \dfrac{257}{12}$

∴ The average of given four numbers

$= \left(\dfrac{257}{12}\right) \div 4$

$= \dfrac{257}{48}$

$= 5\dfrac{17}{48}$

Hence, the correct option is (D).

**5.** The average price of pen, pencil and rubber = 33

$\text{Average} = \dfrac{\text{Total price of items}}{\text{Number of items}}$

∴ Total price for pen, pencil and rubber = 33 × 3 = 99

Let the price of pen, pencil and rubber be 5x, 3x and x.

$\Rightarrow 99 = 5x + 3x + x$

$\Rightarrow 99 = 9x$

$\Rightarrow x = 11$

∴ The price of rubber = Rs. 11

The price of pen and pencil (5x and 3x) = Rs. 55 and Rs. 33.

∴ The price of pen, pencil and rubber is Rs. 55, Rs. 33, Rs. 11 respectively.

Hence, the correct option is (A).

**6.** Given:

Present age of $P$ and $Q = 2 : 7$

$18$ yrs ago age of $P$ and $Q = 1 : 26$

Let the present age of $P$ be $2x$.

Let the present age of $Q$ be $7x$.

∴ According to the question

$\Rightarrow \dfrac{(2x - 18)}{(7x - 18)} = \dfrac{1}{26}$

$\Rightarrow 26(2x - 18) = (7x - 18)$

$\Rightarrow 52x - 468 = 7x - 18$

$\Rightarrow 52x - 7x = -18 + 468$

$\Rightarrow 45x = 450$

$\Rightarrow x = \dfrac{450}{45}$

$\Rightarrow x = 10$

P's present age $= 2 \times 10 = 20$ yr

Q's present age $= 7 \times 10 = 70$ yr

$\therefore$ The sum of the present age of $P$ and $Q = 20 + 70 = 90$ yr

Hence, the correct option is (C).

**7.** Given,

The income of A and B is in the ratio 7 : 8

The income of B and C is 4 : 3.

The ratio of savings of A and C is 4 : 3

The difference between the savings of B and C together to the savings A is Rs. 32,000.

Income of A, B and C is 7 $x$, 8 $x$, 6 $x$

Let their expenditure be $y$

Income = Expenditure + Saving

Savings of A = 7 $x - y$

Savings of C = 6 $x - y$

Ratio of A: B = 7 : 8

Ratio of B : C = 4 : 3

Now equating ratios of B we get

B: C $\times$ 2 = 8: 6

A: B: C = 7: 8: 6

$\Rightarrow$ Ratio of saving A and C = $\dfrac{(7x-y)}{(6x-y)} = \dfrac{4}{3}$

$\Rightarrow 21x - 3y = 24x - 4y$

$\Rightarrow y = 3x$

$\Rightarrow$ Saving of A $= 7x - 3x = 4x$

$\Rightarrow$ Saving of B $= 8x - 3x = 5x$

$\Rightarrow$ Saving of C $= 6x - 3x = 3x$

Difference between the savings of B and C together to the savings A is 32,000

$\Rightarrow (5x + 3x) - (4x) = 32,000$

$\Rightarrow 4x = 32,000$

$\Rightarrow x = 8000$

$\therefore$ Income of B $= 8x = 8 \times 8000$

Rs. $64,000$

Hence, the correct option is (D).

**8.** Given:

We need to find the ratio between fourth proportional to $14,18,26$ and third proportional of $14,21$.

Fourth proportional of $a, b, c$ is $\dfrac{bc}{a}$

Third proportional to $a, b$ is $\dfrac{b^2}{a}$

$\Rightarrow$ Fourth proportional to $14,18,26 = \dfrac{(18 \times 26)}{14} = \dfrac{234}{7}$

$\Rightarrow$ Third proportional of $14,21 = \dfrac{21^2}{14} = \dfrac{63}{2}$

$\therefore$ Required ratio $= \dfrac{\frac{234}{7}}{\frac{63}{2}}$

$= \dfrac{52}{49}$

$= 52 : 49$

Hence, the correct option is (A).

**9.** The time required to complete the work by A = 40 days,

The time required to complete the work by B = 50 days,

The time required to complete the work by C = 60 days

$\Rightarrow$ Wages of A + B + C = Rs.7400

If A, B, and C can do a piece of work in $x, y,$ and $z$ days respectively. The contract for the work is Rs. $r$ and all of them work together.

Then,

Share of A = Rs. $\dfrac{ryz}{xy+yz+zx}$

Share of B = Rs. $\dfrac{rzx}{xy+yz+zx}$

Share of C = Rs. $\dfrac{rxy}{xy+yz+zx}$

Share of A = Rs. $\dfrac{7400 \times 50 \times 60}{40 \times 50 + 50 \times 60 + 60 \times 40}$

$\Rightarrow$ Rs. 3000

Share of B = Rs. $\dfrac{7400 \times 60 \times 40}{40 \times 50 + 50 \times 60 + 60 \times 40}$

$\Rightarrow$ Rs. 2400

$\Rightarrow$ Share of C = Rs. $\dfrac{7400 \times 40 \times 50}{40 \times 50 + 50 \times 60 + 60 \times 40}$

$\Rightarrow$ Rs. 2000

∴ The wages of A, B, and C respectively are Rs. 3000, Rs. 2400, Rs. 2000.

Hence, the correct option is (B).

**10.** Given:

Time taken by Sahil, Nikhil and Akhil to complete a work = 10 days

Time taken by Sahil alone to complete a work = 20 days

Time taken by Nikhil alone to complete a work = 25 days

Earnings from the work = Rs. 60,000

Work done by Sahil, Nikhil and Akhil in 1 day = $\dfrac{1}{10}$

Work done by Sahil alone in 1 day = $\dfrac{1}{20}$

Work done by Nikhil alone in 1 day = $\dfrac{1}{25}$

Work done by Akhil in 1 day = $\dfrac{1}{10} - \left[\dfrac{1}{20} + \dfrac{1}{25}\right]$

$= \dfrac{1}{10} - \dfrac{9}{100} = \dfrac{1}{100}$

Ratio of time taken by Sahil, Nikhil and Akhil in 1 day = $\dfrac{1}{20} : \dfrac{1}{25} : \dfrac{1}{100} = 5 : 4 : 1$

Share of Akhil in earnings = $\dfrac{1}{10} \times 60,000 = $ Rs 6,000

Hence, the correct option is (D).

**11.** Given:

Aditya sells goods at 5% loss

He uses 15% less weight

Let the cost price of 1000 gm be Rs. 100

Loss % = 5%

S.P = C.P × $\dfrac{(100 - loss\%)}{100}$

So, S.P = 100 × $\dfrac{95}{100}$

⇒ S.P = Rs. 95

Now, he is using weight 15% less

So, weight he is using = 1000 × $\dfrac{1000 - 15}{100}$

⇒ Weight he is using = 850 gm

So, the cost price will be on 850 gm only

So, Total cost price of 850 gm = Rs. 100 × $\dfrac{850}{100}$

⇒ Rs. 85

And, total selling price of 1000 gm = Rs. 95 × $\dfrac{1000}{1000}$

⇒ Rs. 95

Gain = S.P – C.P

⇒ Gain = Rs. 95 – Rs. 85

⇒ Rs. 10

Gain % = $\dfrac{Gain}{C.P.} \times 100$

⇒ $\dfrac{10}{85} \times 100$

⇒ $\dfrac{200}{17}\%$

∴ Total Profit percent of Aditya is $\dfrac{200}{17}\%$

Hence, the correct option is (A).

**12.** Let C.P. of the toy be 'x'.

Profit = Profit% × C.P. = $\dfrac{25}{100}$ × C.P. = 0.25C.P

S.P. of the toy = Rs. 750

⇒ x + 0.25x = 750

⇒ 1.25x = 750

⇒ x = $\dfrac{750}{1.25}$ = Rs. 600

C.P. of 5 such toys = 5 × 600 = Rs. 3,000

S.P. of 5 such toys = Rs. 3,300

Profit on 5 such toys = S. P. of 5 such toys - C.P. of 5 such toys = 3300 – 3000 = Rs. 300

Profit % on 5 such toys = $\dfrac{300}{3000} \times 100 = 10\%$

Hence, the correct option is (C).

**13.** Given:

24 carat gold is hundred percent pure gold.

Price of 50% pure gold is Rs. 30,000

So, price of 1% pure gold = Rs. 600

In 22 carat gold pure gold is 22 parts out of 24 parts.

Percent of pure gold in 22 carat gold $= \dfrac{22}{24} \times 100\% = 91\dfrac{2}{3}\%$

Since, price of $1\%$ pure gold $=$ Rs. 600

∴ Price of pure gold in 22 carat Gold $= 600 \times 91\dfrac{2}{3}\%$

⇒ Price of pure gold in 22 carat Gold = Rs. 55,000

Hence, the correct option is (A).

**14.** The square root of $64 = 8$

If there are 4 decimals in square, square root has $\frac{4}{2} = 2$ decimals

$$\therefore \sqrt{0.0064} = 0.08$$

$$\therefore \frac{\sqrt{0.01 + \sqrt{0.0064}}}{0.01 \times 0.3}$$

$$= \frac{\sqrt{0.01 + 0.08}}{0.01 \times 0.3}$$

$$= \frac{\sqrt{0.09}}{0.01 \times 0.3}$$

$$= \frac{0.3}{0.01 \times 0.3}$$

$$= \frac{1}{0.01}$$

$$= 100$$

Hence, the correct option is (C).

**15.** Let the base and height of the parallelogram be 'b' and 'h' respectively

$\Rightarrow$ Formula for Area of the parallelogram = Base × Height

$\Rightarrow$ Area of the parallelogram = bh

Given the base and height of a parallelogram are increased by 30% and 45% respectively

$\Rightarrow$ Area of the parallelogram = bh × (1 + 30%) × (1 + 45%)

$\Rightarrow$ Area of the parallelogram = bh × (1 + 0.3) × (1 + 0.45)

$\Rightarrow$ Area of the parallelogram = bh × 1.3 × 1.45

$\Rightarrow$ Area of the parallelogram = 1.885bh

$\Rightarrow$ Percentage change = $\dfrac{\text{New Area - Old Area}}{\text{Old Area}} \times 100\%$

$\Rightarrow$ Percentage change = $\dfrac{1.885bh - bh}{bh} \times 100\%$

$\Rightarrow$ Percentage change = $\dfrac{0.885bh}{bh} \times 100\%$

$\Rightarrow$ Percentage change = 88.5%

$\therefore$ Percentage change in area = 88.5%

Hence, the correct option is (C).

**16.**

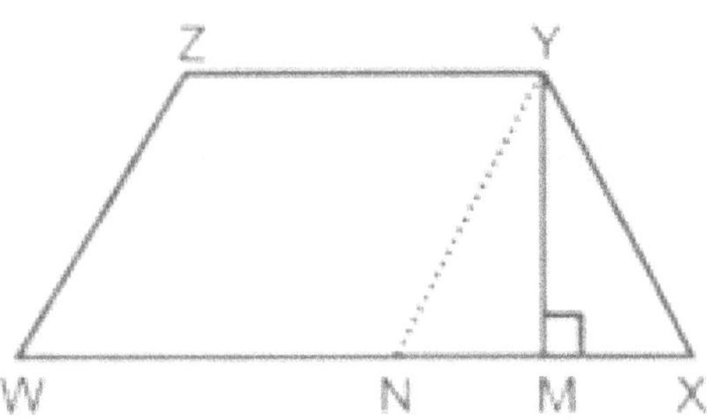


Area of trapezium WXYZ, A = $\frac{1}{2}$ × (sum of parallel sides) × (distance between them)

$\Rightarrow$ A = $\frac{1}{2}$ × (30 + 18) × 8 cm²

$\therefore$ A = 192 cm²

Hence, the correct option is (B).

**17.** Side of the first square = Length of the rectangle + 2 = 16.6 cm

Area of the first square = 16.6 × 16.6 = 275.56 cm²

Side of the second square = Breadth of the rectangle - 2 = 17.2 cm

Area of the second square = 17.2 × 17.2 = 295.84 cm²

Difference in area of the two squares = 295.84 − 275.56 = 20.28 cm²

$\therefore$ Difference in areas of the two squares is 20.28 cm²

Hence, the correct option is (B).

**18.** Given:

Total number of rings: 10

$P(E) = \dfrac{\text{no. of favorable outcomes}}{\text{total number of outcomes}}$

Let 'E' is an event of favorable outcomes.

Number of favorable outcomes $= {}^{4}C_2 \times {}^{6}C_1 \Rightarrow 36$

Total number of outcomes $= {}^{10}C_3 \Rightarrow 120$

$$P(E) = \frac{36}{120}$$

$$= \frac{3}{10}$$

$$= 0.3$$

Hence, the correct option is (B).

**19.** Given:

Total number of cards = 52

$P(E) = \dfrac{\text{no. of favorable outcomes}}{\text{total number of outcomes}}$

(Digit cards are from 2 to 10. Each suit contains 4 cards. Therefore, total number of digit cards are 36 i.e. 4 × 9)

Let 'E' is an event of favorable outcomes.

Number of favorable outcomes = 36

$P(E) = \dfrac{36}{52}$

$= \dfrac{9}{13}$

Hence, the correct option is (A).

**20.** Given,

Total Blue Pens: $4$

Total Red Pens: $2$

Total Black Pens: $3$

Total Pens: $4 + 2 + 3 = 9$

Probability of drawing pens $= \dfrac{^4C_2}{^9C_2} = \dfrac{4\times3}{9\times8} = \dfrac{1}{6}$

After this, the pens are not replaced, which reduces the number of pens in the pack to $7$

So, the probability of drawing $1$ black pen from a pack of $7$ pens would be $\dfrac{^3C_1}{^7C_1} = \dfrac{3}{7}$

Probability of drawing $2$ blue pens and $1$ black pen $=$
$\dfrac{1}{6} \times \dfrac{3}{7} = \dfrac{1}{14}$

Hence, the correct option is (B).

**21.** $\dfrac{(1000)^{12}}{(10)^{30}}$

$= \dfrac{(10^3)^{12}}{(10)^{30}}$

$= \dfrac{(10)^{(3\times12)}}{(10)^{30}}$

$= \dfrac{(10)^{36}}{(10)^{30}}$

$= (10)^{(36-30)}$

$= 10^6$

$= (10^3)^2$

$= (1000)^2$

Hence, the correct option is (A).

**22.** $\dfrac{1.5^3+4.7^3+3.8^3-3\times1.5\times4.7\times3.8}{1.5^2+4.7^2+3.8^2-1.5\times4.7-4.7\times3.8-3.8\times1.5}$

$= \dfrac{(1.5+4.7+3.8)\{1.5^2+4.7^2+3.8^2-1.5\times4.7-4.7\times3.8-3.8\times1.5\}}{\{1.5^2+4.7^2+3.8^2-1.5\times4.7-4.7\times3.8-3.8\times1.5\}}$

$\left[\because a^3 + b^3 + c^3 - 3abc = (a+b+c)\right.$
$\left.(a^2 + b^2 + c^2 - ab - bc - ca)\right]$

$= 1.5 + 4.7 + 3.8$

$= 10.0$

$= 10$

Hence, the correct option is (C).

**23.** $\dfrac{0.41\times0.41\times0.41+0.69\times0.69\times0.69}{0.41\times0.41-0.41\times0.69+0.69\times0.69}$

$= \dfrac{(0.41)^3+(0.69)^3}{(0.41)^2-0.41\times0.69+(0.69)^2}$  $\left[\because a^3 + b^3 =\right.$
$\left.(a+b)(a^2 + b^2 - ab)\right]$

$= 0.41 + 0.69$

$= 1.1$

Hence, the correct option is (C).

**24.** Principal $=$ Rs. 2000

Amount $=$ Rs. 2420

Rate $= 10\%$

By using formula,

$A = P\left(1 + \dfrac{r}{100}\right)^n$

$\Rightarrow 2420 = 2000\left(1 + \dfrac{10}{100}\right)^n$

$\Rightarrow \dfrac{2420}{2000} = \left(1 + \dfrac{10}{100}\right)^n$

$\Rightarrow \dfrac{121}{100} = \left(\dfrac{11}{10}\right)^n$

$\Rightarrow \left(\dfrac{11}{10}\right)^2 = \left(\dfrac{11}{10}\right)^n$

$\Rightarrow n = 2$

Hence, required time $= 2$ years

Hence, the correct option is (C).

**25.** Given that,

Difference $=$ Compound Interest $-$ Simple Interest

$= 36.60$

Time $= 3$ years,

Rate $= 5\%$

Using the given formula.

Difference of Simple interest and Compound interest for $3$ years

$= \dfrac{PR(300+R)}{100^3}$

$$\because \frac{P \times 25 \times 305}{100 \times 100 \times 100}$$

$$= 36.60$$

$$\Rightarrow P = \frac{36.60 \times 100 \times 100 \times 100}{25 \times 305}$$

$$= 4800$$

Hence, the correct option is (D).

**Q.1 Direction:** In the following question, out of the four alternatives, select the alternative which best expresses the meaning of the Idiom/Phrase.

Hear it on the grapevine

**A.** To hear rumours

**B.** To find out the truth

**C.** To know something through unexpected sources

**D.** To know something which is already a big news

**Q.2** Find the correct word.

**A.** Condone
**B.** Aprobate
**C.** Conceede
**D.** Currtail

**Q.3 Direction:** In the following sentence, the given blank is to be filled with the appropriate words. Four alternatives are suggested for each question. Choose the correct alternative and mark your answer:

Just as I began to get _______ about the surroundings, she applied the brakes.

**A.** Elusive     **B.** Inclusive     **C.** Effusive     **D.** Evasive

**Q.4 Direction:** Read each sentence to find out whether there is any error in it. The error, if any, will be in one part of the sentence. Mark the part with the error as your answer.

Summer is the holiday peak for rural India, but for urban Indians, there's one peak in August, and then a few similar highs in May, September and October, possibly reflecting regional festivals.

**A.** Summer is the holiday peak for rural India

**B.** but for urban Indians, there's one peak

**C.** in August, and then a few similar highs in May, September

**D.** and October, possibly reflecting regional festivals.

**Q.5 Direction:** In the following questions, the first and the last parts of the sentence are numbered 1 and 6. The rest of the sentence is split into four parts named, P, Q, R, and S. These four parts are not given in their proper order. Read the parts, arrange them properly and find out which of the four combinations given below is appropriate, and mark it as your answer.

1. The psychology professor

P. to an auditorium

Q. stress management principles

R. walked around on a

S. stage while teaching

6. filled with students

**A.** RPSQ     **B.** SRPQ     **C.** RSQP     **D.** RQSP

**Ques (6-10):Direction:** Read the passage given below and answer the questions that follow based on it.

Two decades after signing the UN Convention against Torture and Other Cruel, Inhuman or Degrading Treatment or

Punishment, India is yet to **ratify** it. There can be little justification for such a prolonged delay in passing legislation to give effect to the convention. In recent times there is a fresh note of urgency attached to the need for early ratification, as the country has pending requests for the extradition of its nationals from other countries. For, as pointed out by the Supreme Court, the absence of a stand-alone law prohibiting torture may prevent many countries from agreeing to India's extradition requests. Such a law may be in the national interest, the Chief Justice of India observed during the course of a hearing on a public interest petition seeking the enactment of an anti-torture law in accordance with the country's commitment. The court also noted that India was subjected to close questioning during the Universal Periodic Review of its human rights obligations at the UN Human Rights Council in Geneva. It cannot be forgotten that an extradition request relating to Purulia arms drop case suspect Kim Davy failed owing to the apprehension that he may be ill-treated in India. In an era of increasing international cooperation on criminal matters, India will be better served if it is seen as adhering to international treaties, especially its obligations under the Convention Against Torture, which it signed in 1997.

There may be some doubt whether India needs a fresh law to prevent and punish torture. Provisions relating to causing hurt or grievous hurt, especially with a view to extracting a confession, criminal intimidation, and wrongful confinement already exist in the Indian Penal Code. However, the idea of a stand-alone law ought to be ultimately seen as a more tangible way of expressing commitment to eliminating torture. A concrete step towards enacting a law was made when the Prevention of Torture Bill, 2010, was passed by the Lok Sabha in 2010, but it was referred to a Select Committee in the Rajya Sabha. In its report submitted in the same year, the committee recommended exhaustive amendments to the Bill to make it consistent with the language and intent of the Convention. Thereafter the Bill lapsed. The government now says it has referred the matter to the Law Commission for an authoritative view. Given the pervasive nature of custodial violence and its complex policing requirements, the present legislative and administrative framework is obviously inadequate to prevent torture in a country of India's size. It is imperative that a strong law that criminalises torture, imposes stringent punishment for it, and contains liberal provisions for those suffering torture to complain against their perpetrators, prosecute them, and be compensated and rehabilitated, is passed at the earliest.

**Q.6** What according to the Supreme Court, might inhibit countries from agreeing to India's extradition requests?

**A.** Non ratification of the convention

**B.** The delay in bringing the convention to effect

**C.** The non-existence of a self-contained law which acts against torture

**D.** A large list of pending extradition requests

**Q.7** Why does the author feel that the present administrative framework is inadequate to prevent torture?

A. The violence occurring when a person is in custody is inescapable

B. The requirements pertaining to 'policing' being of a very complicated nature

C. The law commission hasn't given an authoritative view on the present framework

D. Both (A) and (B)

**Q.8** Why did the bill lapse in the first place?

A. It was debated in Lok Sabha for a long time

B. The Select Committee in the Rajya Sabha took very long to respond

C. The select committee strong amendments in the bill

D. Cannot be determined

**Q.9** Why did the extradition request against the accused in the Purulia arms drop case fail?

A. Because of the close questioning of India's human rights obligations at the UN Human Rights Council

B. Because Geneva was apprehensive of ill treatment of the accused

C. Because India is not seen as adhering to international treaties

D. None of the above

**Q.10** Choose the word which has its meaning most similar to the word '**ratify**' used in the passage.

A. Defy                     B. Endorse
C. Confront                 D. Controvert

**Ques (11-15):Direction:** Below, a passage is given with five blanks labelled (A)-(E). Below the passage, four options are given for each blank. Choose the word that fits each blank most appropriately in the context of the passage, and mark the corresponding answer.

The thermometer is an instrument for measuring temperature. The __(A)__ form consists of a __(B)__ tube with a fine __(C)__. One end of the __(D)__ is blown to form __(E)__ bulb and the other is closed.

**Q.11** Which of these words most appropriately fits the blank labelled **(A)**?

A. Common                   B. Seen
C. Unseen                   D. Heard

**Q.12** Which of these words most appropriately fits the blank labelled **(B)**?

A. Metal        B. Brass        C. Glass        D. Rubber

**Q.13** Which of these words most appropriately fits the blank labelled **(C)**?

A. Bore         B. Boar         C. Cavity       D. Mole

**Q.14** Which of these words most appropriately fits the blank labelled **(D)**?

A. Place        B. Tube         C. Edge         D. Centre

**Q.15** Which of these words most appropriately fits the blank labelled **(E)**?

A. An           B. That         C. A            D. All

**Q.16 Direction:** In the following question, a sentence has been given in Active/Passive Voice. Out of the four alternatives suggested, select the one which best expresses the same sentence in Passive/Active Voice.

She died in 2012.

A. She died.                 B. In 2012, she died.
C. She is dead.             D. None of the above

**Q.17 Direction:** In the following question, out of the four alternatives, select the word which best expresses the meaning of the given word.

Exiguous

A. Bombastic                 B. Petite
C. Conventional             D. Erroneous

**Q.18 Direction:** In the following question, out of the four alternatives, select the word opposite in meaning to the given word.

Temerity

A. Audacity                  B. Effrontery
C. Impudence                D. Wariness

**Q.19 Direction:** Out of four alternatives, choose the one which can be substituted for the given words/sentences.

Spread negative information about someone

A. Vociferous                B. Vilify
C. Vituperative             D. Winsome

**Q.20 Direction:** The 1st and the last parts of the sentence/ paragraph are numbered 1 and 6. The rest of the sentences are split into four parts and named P, Q, R, and S. These four parts are not given in their proper order. Read the sentence/ paragraph and find out which of the four combinations is correct.

1. It has been suggested
P. so called Pasupati seal
Q. may go back to
R. that the roots of Shiva worship
S. on the basis of the
6. the Harappan civilization.

A. SPRQ         B. PQSR         C. SRQP         D. RSPQ

**Q.21 Directions:** The 1st and the last parts of the paragraph are numbered 1 and 6. The rest of the paragraph are split into four parts and named P, Q, R, and S. These four parts are not given in their proper order. Read the sentence/ paragraph and find out which of the four combinations is correct.

1. More organisations today seek a transformation in their businesses, yet most of them think of and talk about managing change.
P. Change is characterised by 'reactivity'.
Q. Most of us live in the domain of change both as individuals and as organisations.

R. The characteristics of transformation are positive and actually creative. They stem from a new found sense of purposefulness, once a higher purpose is discovered.

S. The implications of this conflict will not be fully appreciated until we learn to distinguish between change and transformation.

6. Clearly, we all aspire to live in the domain of transformation even if we presently are in the domain of change.

**A.** SRQP      **B.** PQSR      **C.** SPRQ      **D.** SPQR

**Q.22 Direction:** A sentence/a part of the sentence is underlined. Five alternatives are given to the underlined part which may improve the meaning of the sentence. Choose the correct alternative. In case no improvement is needed, click the option corresponding to "No improvement".

When it was feared that the serfs might go too far and gain their freedom from serfdom, the protestant leaders joined the princess <u>at crushing</u> them.

**A.** into crushing      **B.** in crushing
**C.** without crushing      **D.** No improvement

**Q.23 Direction:** Improve the bracketed part of the sentence

Ganesh was by his side, (dressing in) his master's best suit.

**A.** Dressed in      **B.** Dressed with
**C.** Dressed of      **D.** No improvement

**Q.24 Direction:** In the following question, out of the four alternatives, select the word opposite in meaning to the given word.

Loquacious

**A.** Reticent      **B.** Talkative
**C.** Verbose      **D.** Chatty

**Q.25 Direction:** Out of four alternatives, choose the one which can be substituted for the given words/sentences.

To remove an objectionable part from a book.

**A.** Exterminate      **B.** Expurgate
**C.** Extirpate      **D.** Eradicate

# // Smart Answer Sheet //

**Correct**   Indicates percentage of students who answered questions correctly.

**Skipped**   Indicates percentage of students who skipped questions.

| Q. | Ans. | Correct / Skipped | Q. | Ans. | Correct / Skipped | Q. | Ans. | Correct / Skipped | Q. | Ans. | Correct / Skipped | Q. | Ans. | Correct / Skipped |
|---|---|---|---|---|---|---|---|---|---|---|---|---|---|---|
| 1 | A | 60.28 % / 30.83 % | 6 | C | 23.49 % / 71.23 % | 11 | A | 65.5 % / 33.23 % | 16 | D | 45.96 % / 33.7 % | 21 | D | 58.19 % / 32.37 % |
| 2 | A | 59.61 % / 34.62 % | 7 | D | 42.62 % / 39.14 % | 12 | C | 62.15 % / 30.2 % | 17 | B | 66.14 % / 32.31 % | 22 | B | 66.06 % / 32.94 % |
| 3 | D | 55.0 % / 44.95 % | 8 | D | 46.88 % / 52.85 % | 13 | A | 53.88 % / 39.72 % | 18 | D | 57.59 % / 32.38 % | 23 | A | 53.15 % / 31.77 % |
| 4 | B | 60.15 % / 31.07 % | 9 | D | 55.43 % / 32.44 % | 14 | B | 29.98 % / 68.49 % | 19 | B | 14.83 % / 76.46 % | 24 | A | 43.91 % / 52.97 % |
| 5 | C | 40.77 % / 53.44 % | 10 | B | 43.01 % / 43.88 % | 15 | C | 86.12 % / 10.21 % | 20 | A | 57.81 % / 30.16 % | 25 | B | 45.67 % / 46.72 % |

| Performance Analysis | |
|---|---|
| Avg. Score (%) | 64.0% |
| Toppers Score (%) | 64.0% |
| Your Score | |

# //Hints and Solutions//

**1.** To hear it on the grapevine is an idiomatic expression which means to hear some news from someone who heard it from someone else.

Hence, the correct option is (A).

**2.** The correct spellings are -

Approbate

Concede

Curtail

Hence, the correct option is (A).

**3.** Elusive – subtle, intangible, vague, abstract, mysterious.

Inclusive – comprehensive, complete, broad.

Effusive – demonstrative, fulsome, lavish, expansive.

Evasive – elusive, slippery, shifty, indirect, ambiguous.

Evasive: trying to avoid something; not direct

Hence, the correct option is (D).

**4.** When 'rural India' is used, 'urban India' should be used instead of 'urban Indians'.

Hence, the correct option is (B).

**5.** The psychology professor walked around on a stage while teaching stress management principles to an auditorium filled with students.

Hence, the correct option is (C).

**6.** The author points out clearly in the passage that: 'For, as pointed out by the Supreme Court, the absence of a stand-alone law prohibiting torture may prevent many countries from agreeing to India's extradition requests. Such a law may be in the national interest, the Chief Justice of India observed during the course of a hearing on a public interest petition seeking the enactment of an anti-torture law in accordance with the country's commitment'.

Hence, the correct option is (C).

**7.** It is clearly mentioned in the passage that: 'Given the pervasive nature of custodial violence and its complex policing requirements, the present legislative and administrative framework is obviously inadequate to prevent torture in a country of India's size. It is imperative that a strong law that criminalises torture, imposes stringent punishment for it and contains liberal provisions for those suffering torture to complain against their perpetrators, prosecute them and be compensated and rehabilitated, is passed at the earliest'.

Hence, the correct option is (D).

**8.** There is no such information provided by the author in the given passage that could give any clarity regarding this.

Hence, the correct option is (D).

**9.** The author has stated in the passage that: 'An extradition request relating to Purulia arms drop case suspect Kim Davy failed owing to the apprehension that he may be ill-treated in India'.

Hence, the correct option is (D).

**10.** Ratify means giving formal consent or making something officially valid.

Endorse means to say publicly that you give official support or agreement to a plan, statement, decision, etc.

Hence, the correct option is (B).

**11.** The word 'common' needs to be used to demonstrate the normal kind of thermometer. The other three options are inappropriate as they fail to demonstrate any meaning.

Hence, the correct option is (A).

**12.** A thermometer has to be made up of glass as it needs to be transparent for the readings to be read properly. It cannot be brass or metal or rubber.

Hence, the correct option is (C).

**13.** The word 'bore' means a hollow part inside a tube. The rest of the words do not demonstrate any meaning. 'boar' is a kind of animal. We cannot use the word 'cavity' here, which means an empty space within a solid object. 'Mole' means a spy or a kind of animal.

Hence, the correct option is (A).

**14.** The bulb is formed at one end and the other side of it is closed. Thus 'it' has to be the tube. The other three options fail to have a proper meaning.

Hence, the correct option is (B).

**15.** We need to use the article 'a' to mean that a bulb is formed in the other end. 'an' or 'all' are incorrect here. 'That' is incorrect too as there is nothing to specify here.

Hence, the correct option is (C).

**16.** The given sentence has intransitive verb 'died'. The sentences having intransitive verb can't be converted into Passive voice as they don't have any clear known object.

Hence, the correct option is (D).

**17.** The meanings of the words are:

Exiguous - small

Petite - small

Bombastic - pompous

Conventional - old

Erroneous - wrong

Hence, the correct option is (B).

**18.** Effrontery, Impudence, Audacity and Temerity are synonyms and mean insolence/ boldness /impertinence, all of which are related to bad manners.

'Wariness' means to be 'careful', 'cautious', and 'alert' and best expresses the opposite meaning of the given word.

Hence, the correct option is (D).

**19.** Vilify: defame someone

Vociferous: conspicuously and offensively loud

Vituperate: use abusive language

Winsome: charming in a childlike or naive way

Hence, the correct option is (B).

**20.** The given sentence begins with the phrase 'it has been suggested'.

S should succeed 'Part 1' as it tells that on a certain basis something has been suggested.

Following it, the part P provides the thing on the basis of which the suggestion has been made.

After this, the sentence R begins to talk about the suggestion that has been made, a concept which is then completed by part Q and part 6 respectively.

Although option 4 may seem correct, we have to tell on what basis something is suggested which is directly given in S. Thus, (D) cannot be true.

Hence, the correct option is (A).

**21.** The first sentence talks of 'transformation in the organization and its effects'. The next sentence is S which talks more on sentence 1 and presents two factors 'change' and 'transformation'. The next sentence is P which talks out change and sentence Q extends P and tells us about our current domain. The next sentence is R which talks about the characteristics of transformation. Finally 6 tells our aspiration to live in the domain of transformation.

Hence, the correct option is (D).

**22.** When it was feared that the serfs might go too far and gain their freedom from serfdom, the protestant leaders joined the princess in crushing them.

Hence, the correct option is (B).

**23.** The correct verb here must be simple past 'dressed' and the preposition 'in' is the correct one to follow it. 'Dressed in' means 'attired in.'

Hence, the correct option is (A).

**24.** Loquacious: Someone who talks too much.

Reticent: An introvert, who speaks very little.

Talkative: A person who loves to talk.

Verbose: A person who makes long lengthy explanations.

Chatty: Readily engaging in an informal talk.

Hence, the correct option is (A).

**25.** 'Exterminate' means to kill.

'Extirpate' means to destroy.

'Eradicate' is similar in meaning to 'exterminate'.

'Expurgate' means to purge or clean up.

Hence, the correct option is (B).

**Ques (1-5):Direction:** Read the following passage carefully and answer the question that follow.

Smiling a lot is a valued trait: People who often smile sincerely radiate likeability, connect easily with others, and are appreciated more. By smiling, you make a positive impression that will assist in making contacts and reaching your goals. Moreover, smiling makes you feel good. However, not all smiles are created equal, and it is not a good idea to smile in every situation. Let's face it, smiling is not always as easy as it looks, which might be why we often indulge in it so **sparingly**. When all is said and done, it takes a bit of practice to turn smiling into a habit. Management is serious business! However, most managers are aware of the positive effect a well-meant smile can have on others. In most situations, your smile will contribute to your success. On the other hand, there are moments when you'd better not smile: Imagine that you are receiving some bad news, or you're in the middle of a difficult negotiation.

In addition, not all smiles are created equal: When someone smiles, we think of pleasure and happiness first, but that interpretation is not always correct. Imagine, for example, that you **stumble** on the street and almost knock into someone. Are you happy? No! But the chances are high that you will smile at the other person, and that the other person will immediately answer with a smile. The meaning of the smile here is more by way of an apology. Finding the right balance between showing a happy or serious facial expression is an art in itself. We want to come across as relaxed and friendly, but be taken seriously at the same time. However, If we contemplate this for too long, a **frown** will soon appear on our faces. In the end, with a smile, you will achieve the most and you will feel most happy with it. Nevertheless, smiling isn't always that easy; sometimes a lot of courage is needed to do it. Especially in situations where when it's preferable to smile, we tend to clench our jaws and look too tense.

Many job applicants miss out on a promising career because they were too tense to conjure a spontaneous smile on their faces. Many lovers miss out on their life partner because they didn't dare smile during the first meeting. And many managers have possibly lost the deal of their dreams because they couldn't smile spontaneously. A well-meant smile is almost something you cannot do too much of. Most people respond positively to this friendly gesture. And if they do not do that, it probably says more about their own fear of smiling. That said, smiling at someone who does not smile back can evoke a feeling of discomfort and shame. We naturally fear losing face. That's why we perhaps do not always dare to smile.

**Q.1** What does the author mean by the statement "smiling is not always as easy as it looks"?

**A.** It needs a lot of practice to perfect the art of smiling.

**B.** All smiles are not equal and our indulgence in it depends upon the nature of the situation.

**C.** Always Keep smiling.

**D.** It is very difficult to make smiling a habit.

**Q.2** Choose the word/group of words which is most SIMILAR in meaning to the word/group of words printed in bold as used in the passage.

Sparingly

**A.** Satiate

**B.** Aversion

**C.** Meagerly

**D.** Exacerbate

**Q.3** Choose the word/group of words which is most SIMILAR in meaning to the word/group of words printed in bold as used in passage.

Stumble

**A.** Falter

**B.** Extort

**C.** Fretful

**D.** Condone

**Q.4** Choose the word/group of words which is most OPPOSITE in meaning to the word/group of words printed in bold as used in passage.

Evoke

**A.** Compel

**B.** Sneer

**C.** Scrupulous

**D.** Quell

**Q.5** Choose the word/group of words which is most OPPOSITE in meaning to the word/group of words printed in bold as used in passage.

Frown

**A.** Accredit

**B.** Rife

**C.** Summon

**D.** Grin

**Q.6 Direction:** In the question given below, a sentence is given with one blank, followed by four options, each having a word which may or may not fit in the blank. From the given options, choose the one that gives the correct word that fits in the blank.

_________________ factors influence the way these circuits operate, for better or worse.

**A.** Explicit

**B.** Scores

**C.** Plethora

**D.** Myriad

**Q.7 Direction:** In the question given below, a sentence is given with one blank, followed by four options, each having a word which may or may not fit in the blank. From the given options, choose the one that gives the correct word that fits in the blank.

Fewer people on Southwest Florida beaches may have ________ to more sea turtle nests this season.

**A.** led

**B.** lead

**C.** leading

**D.** causing

**Q.8 Direction:** Select the correct option that identifies the noun in the sentence.

It will take all of your energy and will to be able to walk again.

**A.** Take

**B.** All

**C.** Your

**D.** Energy

**Q.9 Direction:** In the following question, out of the four alternatives, select the alternative which is the best substitute for the given group of the words.

A remedy for all diseases

**A.** Stoic

**C.** Panacea

**B.** Marvel

**D.** Recompense

**Q.10 Direction:** In the following question, out of the four alternatives, select the alternative which is the best substitute for the given group of the words.

One who is fond of fighting

**A.** Bellicose

**C.** Belligerent

**B.** Aggressive

**D.** Militant

**Q.11 Direction:** In the following question, out of the four alternatives, select the alternative which is the best substitute of the idiom/phrase, given in underlined part.

The captain played with determination because the honour of the team was **at stake.**

**A.** very low

**C.** in danger

**B.** at the top

**D.** appropriate

**Q.12 Direction**: In the following question, out of the four alternatives, select the alternative which is the best substitute of the idiom/phrase, given in underlined part.

Dishonesty is **at a premium** in almost all spheres of public life.

**A.** prevalent

**C.** encouraged

**B.** practised openly

**D.** valued highly

**Q.13 Direction:** In the following question six words are given which are denoted by A, B, C D, E, and F. By using all the six words, each only once, you have to frame a meaningful and grammatically correct sentence. The correct order of words is the answer. Choose from the four alternatives the one having the correct order of words.

A. eat

B. does

C. raw

D. not

E. meat

F. man

**A.** FBDAER

**C.** FBADCE

**B.** BDAFCE

**D.** FBDACE

**Q.14 Direction:** In the following question six words are given which are denoted by A, B, C D, E, and F. By using all the six words, each only once, you have to frame a meaningful and grammatically correct sentence. The correct order of words is the answer. Choose from the four alternatives the one having the correct order of words.

A. different

B. there

C. of

D. vehicles

E. kinds

F. are

**A.** BFEACD

**C.** DCAEBF

**B.** AECDBF

**D.** BFAECD

**Q.15 Direction:** In the following question, a sentence has been given in Active/Passive voice. Out of four alternatives suggested, select the one, which best expresses the same sentence in Passive/Active voice.

They are not meeting us.

**A.** We have not being met by them.

**B.** We are not being met by them.

**C.** We are being not met by them.

**D.** We have being not met by them.

**Q.16** Find out that word, the spelling of which is wrong.

**A.** Assailant

**C.** Ancestry

**B.** Appeasment

**D.** Aerobatics

**Q.17** Find out that word, the spelling of which is wrong.

**A.** Tuberculosis

**C.** Tincture

**B.** Trachery

**D.** Thwart

**Q.18** Choose the word SIMILAR in meaning to the given word.

CORPULENT

**A.** Lean

**C.** Emaciated

**B.** Gaunt

**D.** Obese

**Q.19** Choose the word SIMILAR in meaning to the given word.

BRIEF

**A.** Limited

**B.** Small

**C.** Little

**D.** Short

**Q.20** Choose the opposite word to the given word.

FRAUDULENT

**A.** Candid

**C.** Forthright

**B.** Direct

**D.** Genuine

**Q.21** Choose the opposite word to the given word.

FLAGITIOUS

**A.** Innocent

**C.** Ignorant

**B.** Vapid

**D.** Frivolous

**Q.22 Direction:** In the following question, some part of the sentence may have errors. Find out which part of the sentence has an error and select the appropriate option.

Suganya opened a almirah (a) / full of books (b) / and took one of them (c) / for reading (d).

**A.** Suganya opened a almirah

**B.** full of books

**C.** and took one of them

**D.** for reading

**Q.23 Direction:** In the following question, some part of the sentence may have errors. Find out which part of the sentence has an error and select the appropriate option.

As I was to reach (a) / early I left in aeroplane (b) / instead of (c) / going by train (d).

**A.** As I was to reach

**B.** early I left in aeroplane

**C.** instead of

**D.** going by train

**Q.24** Choose the suitable part of speech for a given word boldly.

Andy knocked on the door **but** nobody answered.

**A.** Adverb

**B.** Adjective

**C.** Conjunction      **D.** Verb

**Q.25** Choose the suitable part of speech for a given word boldly.

**After** lunch let's go out for a coffee.

**A.** Pronoun      **B.** Preposition

**C.** Verb      **D.** Adverb

# // Smart Answer Sheet //

**Correct** — Indicates percentage of students who answered questions correctly.

**Skipped** — Indicates percentage of students who skipped questions.

| Q. | Ans. | Correct / Skipped |
|---|---|---|
| 1 | B | 69.9 % / 30.09 % |
| 2 | C | 31.34 % / 67.18 % |
| 3 | A | 21.37 % / 75.76 % |
| 4 | D | 32.28 % / 67.44 % |
| 5 | D | 54.88 % / 39.71 % |
| 6 | D | 47.06 % / 32.03 % |
| 7 | A | 41.87 % / 40.27 % |
| 8 | D | 50.86 % / 42.7 % |
| 9 | C | 49.06 % / 49.75 % |
| 10 | A | 53.34 % / 35.08 % |
| 11 | C | 65.88 % / 32.13 % |
| 12 | D | 41.12 % / 47.0 % |
| 13 | D | 69.93 % / 30.0 % |
| 14 | D | 55.54 % / 40.57 % |
| 15 | B | 55.55 % / 44.12 % |
| 16 | B | 86.96 % / 11.54 % |
| 17 | B | 58.25 % / 36.12 % |
| 18 | D | 41.47 % / 50.03 % |
| 19 | D | 69.56 % / 30.22 % |
| 20 | D | 60.95 % / 38.57 % |
| 21 | A | 67.91 % / 30.0 % |
| 22 | A | 65.24 % / 31.18 % |
| 23 | B | 66.48 % / 30.3 % |
| 24 | C | 65.07 % / 33.93 % |
| 25 | B | 50.16 % / 41.28 % |

## Performance Analysis

| | |
|---|---|
| Avg. Score (%) | 34.0% |
| Toppers Score (%) | 62.0% |
| Your Score | |

# //Hints and Solutions//

**1.** Refer to the first paragraph of the passage where it is mentioned that Smiling is not always as easy as it looks as it is not a good idea to smile in every situation. Smiling a lot is a valued trait: People who often smile sincerely radiate likeability, connect easily with others, and are appreciated more. By smiling, you make a positive impression that will assist in making contacts and reaching your goals.

Hence. the correct option is (B).

**2.** Sparingly means in a restricted or infrequent manner; in small quantities. Hence it has the same meaning as meagerly.

Satiate means to completely satisfy yourself or a need, especially with food or pleasure.

Aversion means a strong dislike or disinclination.

Exacerbate means make (a problem, bad situation, or negative feeling) worse.

Hence. the correct option is (C).

**3.** Stumble means trip or momentarily lose one's balance; almost fall. Hence it has same meaning as falter.

Extort means obtain (something) by force, threats, or other unfair means.

Condone means approve or sanction (something), especially with reluctance.

Fretful means feeling or expressing distress or irritation.

Hence. the correct option is (A).

**4.** Evoke means bring or recall (a feeling, memory, or image) to the conscious mind. Hence it has opposite meaning to quell.

Compel means to force somebody to do something.

Sneer means a contemptuous or mocking smile, remark, or tone.

Scrupulous means very careful or paying great attention to detail.

Hence. the correct option is (D).

**5.** Frown means to furrow one's brows in an expression indicating disapproval, displeasure, or concentration. Hence it has opposite meaning to grin.

Rife means if something unpleasant is rife, it is very common or happens a lot.

Accredit means give credit to (someone) for something.

Summon means to order a person to come to a place.

Hence. the correct option is (D).

**6.** Myriad means a countless or extremely great number of people or things.

Explicit means stated clearly and in detail, leaving no room for confusion or doubt.

Scores means a group or set of twenty or about twenty.

Plethora means a large or excessive amount of something.

Hence. the correct option is (D).

**7.** The blank is preceded by 'have' which indicates that the verb occupying the blank will be used in the past participle form. According to this, options (B) are negated because these are the base forms of verbs, and (C) and (D) are negated because these are present participle forms of verbs. Option (A) satisfies the grammatical condition mentioned above and brings out a meaningfully correct sentence.

Hence, the correct option is (A).

**8.** Energy is a noun, as is will here. Take (A) is a verb. All (B) is an adverb modifying take. Your (C) is an adjective modifying energy and will.

Hence, the correct option is (D).

**9.** One word substitution is **Panacea**.

**Panacea**: a solution or remedy for all difficulties or diseases.

**Stoic**: a person who can endure pain or hardship without showing their feelings or complaining.

**Marvel**: be filled with wonder or astonishment.

**Recompense**: make amends to or reward someone for (loss, harm, or effort).

Hence, the correct option is (C).

**10.** One word substitution is **Bellicose.**

**Bellicose:** demonstrating aggression and willingness to fight.

**Aggressive:** ready or likely to attack or confront

**Belligerent:** engaged in a war or conflict, as recognized by international law.

**Militant:** favouring confrontational or violent methods in support of a political or social cause.

Hence, the correct option is (A).

**11.** "At stake" means "in danger". This phrase uses stake in the sense of something that is wagered.

**Example:**

She has to manage getting the contract this time since her job is at stake if she fails.

Hence, the correct option is (C).

**12.** 'At a premium" means "valued highly". Touts sell the tickets at a premium.

**Example:**

Difficult to get because there is little available We bought bunk beds because space in the apartment is at a premium.

Hence, the correct option is (D).

**13.** The correct sequence is FBDACE.

The meaningful sentence will be: **"Man does not eat raw meat."**

Hence, the correct option is (D).

**14.** The correct sequence is BFAECD.

The meaningful sentence will be: "**There are different kinds of vehicles.**"

Hence, the correct option is (D).

**15.** The action takes place in the present progressive, and the doer of the action is shown as lesser important than the addressee.

In the passive voice,

"We are not being met by them".

Hence, the correct option is (B).

**16.** Appeasment will be Appeasement.

Appeasement means giving people what they want to prevent them from harming you or being angry with you.

**Example:**

Music is an appeasement to shattered nerves.

Hence, the correct option is (B).

**17.** Trachery will be Treachery.

Treachery means the act of causing harm to somebody who trusts you.

**Example:**

The treachery of a foreign guide also added to his difficulties. But soon afterwards the king.

Hence, the correct option is (B).

**18.** Synonym of **Corpulent** is **Obese.**

**Obese :** grossly fat or overweight

**Lean :** be in or move into a sloping position

**Gaunt :** (of a person) lean and haggard, especially because of suffering, hunger, or age

**Emaciated :** abnormally thin or weak, especially because of illness or a lack of food

Hence, the correct option is (D).

**19.** Synonym of **Brief** is **Short.**

**Short :** lasting or taking a small amount of time

**Limited :** restricted in size, amount, or extent

**Small :** of a size that is less than normal or usual

**Little :** small in size, amount, or degree

**Brief :** of short duration; not lasting for long

Hence, the correct option is (D).

**20. Fradulent:** Obtained, done by, or involving deception, especially criminal deception.

Antonym of **Fradulent** is **Genuine.**

**Genuine**: Truly what something is said to be

**Candid:** Truthful and straight forward

**Direct:** Extending or moving from one place to another without changing direction or stopping

**Forthright:** Direct and outspoken

Hence, the correct option is (D).

**21. Flagitious**: Criminal

Antonym of **Flagitious** is **Innocent.**

**Innocent:** Not guilty of a crime or offenc

**Vapid**: Offering nothing that is stimulating or challenging

**Ignorant**: Lacking knowledge or awareness in general

**Frivolous:** Not having any serious purpose or value

Hence, the correct option is (A).

**22.** 'An' is used before words that begin with a vowel sound. For example, the word "European" begins with the vowel letter 'e' but it is pronounced with the consonant sound.

**Example:**

"He's British but he thinks of himself as a European."

So for the above sentence:

Suganya opened **an** almirah full of books and took one of them for reading.

Hence, the correct option is (A).

**23.** 'An' is used before words that begin with a vowel sound. For example, the word "European" begins with the vowel letter 'e' but it is pronounced with the consonant sound.

**Example:**

"He's British but he thinks of himself as a European."

So for the above sentence:

As I was to reach early I left in **an** aeroplane instead of going by train.

Hence, the correct option is (B).

**24.** A conjunction is a glue that holds words, phrases, and clauses (both dependent and independent) together. Here "but" is used as a conjunction.

Then the sentence is,

Andy knocked on the door **but** nobody answered.

Hence, the correct option is (C).

**25.** A preposition is a word that indicates the relationship between a noun and the other words of a sentence. Here "after" is used as a preposition.

Then the sentence is,

**After** lunch let's go out for a coffee.

Hence, the correct option is (B).

**Q.1** Select the most appropriate synonym of the given word.

Enthral

**A.** Disgust
**B.** Free
**C.** Mesmerise
**D.** Repel

**Q.2** The sentence is divided into four parts. Find out which part has an error mark it as your answer. If there is no error, mark 'No error' as your answer.

Neither of the two swimmers /(a) was good enough /(b) to break Shikha Tandon's records, /(c) one of India's finest swimmers. /(d) no error.

**A.** (a)
**B.** (b)
**C.** (c)
**D.** No error

**Q.3** Find the antonyms of the following word:

Foremost

**A.** Hindmost
**B.** Unimportant
**C.** Mature
**D.** Disposed

**Q.4** Find the antonyms of the following word:

Protects

**A.** Defends
**B.** Deprives
**C.** Deserts
**D.** Devises

**Q.5** Find the synonym of the following word:

Cease

**A.** Begin
**B.** Stop
**C.** Create
**D.** Dull

**Q.6** Find the synonym of the following word:

Pious

**A.** Religious
**B.** Sympathetic
**C.** Afraid
**D.** Faithful

**Q.7 Direction:** Choose an option, which can be substituted for a given word/sentence/phrase out of given options.

Ram speaks less in the forum. Ram is

**A.** unintelligible
**B.** reticent
**C.** garrulous
**D.** banal

**Q.8 Direction:** Choose an option, which can be substituted for a given word/sentence/phrase out of given options.

One who cannot easily pleased

**A.** Cosmopolitan
**B.** Frightening
**C.** Fastidious
**D.** Feminist

**Q.9 Direction:** Choose an option, which can be substituted for a given word/sentence/phrase out of given options.

The murder of Brother:

**A.** Homicide
**B.** Regicide
**C.** Fratricide
**D.** Suicide

**Ques (10-11):Direction:** In the question given below, a part of the sentence is underlined. Below are given alternatives to the italicised part which may improve the sentence. Choose the correct alternative.

**Q.10** Hoping not to be disturbed, I sat down in my easy chair to read the book. <u>I won as a prize.</u>

**A.** I had won as a prize
**B.** I have won as prize
**C.** I had to win as a prize
**D.** No improvement

**Q.11** No one could explain how a calm and balanced person like him could <u>penetrate</u> such a mindless act on his friends.

**A.** Perpetuate
**B.** Perpetrate
**C.** Precipitate
**D.** No improvement

**Ques (12-13):Direction:** Choose the alternative which best expresses the meaning of the given idiom/phrase/ word.

**Q.12** The thief was caught red-handed.

**A.** In the every act of committing the theft
**B.** On red tape
**C.** After being given a warning
**D.** With blood on his hands

**Q.13** He decided to jump the gun and apply for the job before it was advertised in the press.

**A.** Play safe
**B.** Fake his credentials
**C.** Be overhasty
**D.** Use influence

**Q.14**

From the given group of words, choose the word wrongly spelt:

**A.** Imperative
**B.** Ilicit
**C.** Imminent
**D.** Immature

**Q.15** Fill in the blank with an appropriate word.

The ship _____ Robinson arrived on the Island.

**A.** had been broken
**B.** having been broken
**C.** having broken
**D.** has broken

**Q.16** Fill in the blank with an appropriate word.

Our armed forces are ______ those of any other country in the world.

**A.** Superior than
**B.** Superior to
**C.** Superior from
**D.** Superior of

**Q.17 Direction:** In the following question, choose the correctly spelt word.

**A.** Commettee
**B.** Committe
**C.** Comittee
**D.** Committee

**Q.18 Direction:** In the following question, four words are given out of which one word is incorrectly spelt. Select the incorrectly spelt word.

**A.** Succulent
**B.** Palaeolithic
**C.** Omellete
**D.** Enthusiastic

**Ques (19-23):Direction: Read the passage given below and then answer the question given below the passage. Some**

**words may be highlighted for your attention. Read carefully.**

Music can be divided into genres (e.g., country music) and genres can be further divided into subgenres (e.g., country blues and pop country are two of the many country subgenres), although the dividing lines and relationships between music genres are often subtle, sometimes open to personal interpretation, and occasionally controversial. For example, it can be hard to draw the line between some early 1980 s hard rock and heavy metal. Within the arts, music may be classified as performing art, fine art, or auditory art. Music may be played or sung and heard live at a rock concert or orchestra performance, heard live as part of a dramatic work (a music theater show or opera), or it may be recorded and listened to on a radio, MP3 player, CD player, smartphone or as film score or TV show.

By bringing music to the classrooms, schools are doing an important job by encouraging children to sing or play an instrument, thereby giving them a gift that will last for a lifetime. Students of music are better suited to face the world once they leave school. Here is what JoAnn Hood, Music Teacher, Nashville Forum, has to say about the impact of music on children. "I have found, during my 18 years of teaching, that music students tend to score better on tests, have better communication skills, and are better-disciplined students. They tend to be more prepared for the workforce and are more readily hired by businesses. I have also seen several instances where music kept a student in school who would have otherwise dropped out." Learning music at a young age can also equip people with skills that will benefit them when they grow old. John Ratey, MD, in his book titled "The User's Guide to the Brain," talks about how music benefits elders by helping the brain organize information and allow for selfexpression. Even Albert Einstein, the renowned physicist who learned to play the violin and piano in his childhood, continued to play and enjoy music till his very last days, commenting that he got most of his joy in life out of music.

**Q.19** Which of the following can be inferred from the second paragraph of the passage?

**A.** Music can be recorded

**B.** Music is of different types

**C.** Music enriches a person for life

**D.** Music adds joy to life

**Q.20** As per the passage, which of the following are two sub-country genres of music?

**A.** Folk and cowboy

**B.** Pop music and jazz

**C.** Classic blues and gospel music

**D.** Country blues and pop country

**Q.21** As per the passage, how is music classified within art?

**A.** Within the arts, music may be classified as performing art, sophisticated art, or auditory art.

**B.** Within the arts, music may be classified as performing art, virtual, or auditory art.

**C.** Within the arts, music may be classified as performing art, fine art, or museum art.

**D.** Within the arts, music may be classified as performing art, fine art, or auditory art.

**Q.22** Which of the following is true as per the passage?

**A.** Music may be played or sung and heard live at a rock concert or orchestra performance

**B.** Music can be heard live as part of a dramatic work (a music theater show or opera)

**C.** Music may be recorded and listened to on a radio, MP3 player, CD player, smartphone or as film score or TV show

**D.** All are true

**Q.23** Which of the following is true as per the given passage?

**A.** Students of music are better suited to face the world once they leave school

**B.** Students of music are better suited to face the world once they leave college

**C.** Students of music are better suited to face the world once they leave university

**D.** Students of music are better suited to face the world once they leave premises

**Q.24 Direction:** Select the segment of the sentence that contains the grammatical error. If there is no error, mark 'No error' as your answer

She is ten years old (a) and you twelve still you (b) are acting like a child and (c) creating a nuisance all over the place (d) No error.

**A.** (a)     **B.** (b)     **C.** (c)     **D.** (d)

**Q.25 Direction:** Select the part of the sentence which has an error from the given options. Select 'No error' if all are correct

Justin is the most fastest runner on the track team (a) He has won the nationals (b) twice, but there has been a (c) deterioration in his form over the years. (d) No error.

**A.** (a)     **B.** (b)     **C.** (c)     **D.** (d)

# // Smart Answer Sheet //

**Correct** — Indicates percentage of students who answered questions correctly.

**Skipped** — Indicates percentage of students who skipped questions.

| Q. | Ans. | Correct / Skipped |
|---|---|---|
| 1 | C | 84.24 % / 13.2 % |
| 2 | B | 77.13 % / 14.47 % |
| 3 | B | 79.38 % / 13.39 % |
| 4 | C | 89.41 % / 10.19 % |
| 5 | B | 76.52 % / 19.71 % |
| 6 | A | 86.24 % / 10.98 % |
| 7 | B | 65.1 % / 34.59 % |
| 8 | C | 55.07 % / 33.56 % |
| 9 | C | 42.85 % / 38.59 % |
| 10 | A | 78.04 % / 11.56 % |
| 11 | B | 85.82 % / 13.37 % |
| 12 | A | 46.03 % / 47.97 % |
| 13 | C | 88.57 % / 11.12 % |
| 14 | B | 86.3 % / 13.63 % |
| 15 | C | 83.6 % / 14.41 % |
| 16 | B | 80.89 % / 15.37 % |
| 17 | D | 48.64 % / 34.15 % |
| 18 | C | 88.32 % / 10.92 % |
| 19 | C | 44.46 % / 55.51 % |
| 20 | D | 53.88 % / 39.57 % |
| 21 | D | 66.13 % / 33.71 % |
| 22 | D | 65.14 % / 33.39 % |
| 23 | A | 21.34 % / 76.72 % |
| 24 | B | 80.57 % / 17.48 % |
| 25 | A | 85.78 % / 10.37 % |

| Performance Analysis | |
|---|---|
| Avg. Score (%) | 46.0% |
| Toppers Score (%) | 58.0% |
| Your Score | |

# //Hints and Solutions//

**1.** Enthral means to capture and hold one's attention, fascinate or mesmerise. Mesmerise is the most appropriate synonym of the given word.

Disgust and Repel mean strong dislike.

Free means costing nothing.

Hence, the correct option is (C).

**2.** The error lies in the wrong usage of the verb 'were' in Part B. 'Were' should be replaced by 'was' because a singular verb always comes after 'neither', 'each', 'either', 'everyone', 'many a'.

For example- Neither of the two applicants has the desired qualification.

Therefore, the singular verb 'was' should be used instead of the plural verb 'were' to make the sentence correct.

Hence, the correct option is (B).

**3.** Foremost: most prominent in rank, importance, or position.

Unimportant: lacking in importance or significance.

Hindmost: furthest back, latest or ultramodern.

Mature: fully developed physically, full-grown.

Disposed: inclined or willing.

Hence, the correct option is (B).

**4.** Protects: keep safe from harm

Deserts: to abandon that is to stop supporting or looking after

Defends: protect from harm or danger.

Deprives: prevent (a person or place) from having or using something

Devises: plan or invent (a complex procedure, system, or mechanism) by careful thought.

Hence, the correct option is (C).

**5.** Cease: come to an end, cease to happen.

Stop: come to an end, cease to happen.

Begin: perform or undergo the first part of (an action or activity).

Create: bring (something) into existence.

Dull: lacking interest or excitement.

Hence, the correct option is (B).

**6.** Pious: devoutly religious.

Religious: relating to or believing in a religion.

Sympathetic: feeling, showing, or expressing sympathy.

Afraid: feeling fear or anxiety; frightened.

Faithful: remaining loyal and steadfast.

Hence, the correct option is (A).

**7.** Not open or communicative is reticent. A garrulous person is excessively talkative. A banal remark is devoid of freshness or originality.

Hence, the correct option is (B).

**8.** The one-word substitution is Fastidious.

Fastidious: very attentive to and concerned about accuracy and detail.

Cosmopolitan: familiar with and at ease in many different countries and cultures.

Frightening: making someone afraid or anxious; terrifying.

Feminist: a person who supports feminism.

Hence, the correct option is (C).

**9.** Fratricide - the killing of one's brother or sister.

Homicide - the killing of one person by another.

Regicide - the action of killing a king.

Suicide - intentionally causing one's own death.

Hence, the correct option is (C).

**10.** While crossing the highway a five-year-old child was knocked down by a car.

Hence, the correct option is (A).

**11.** No one could explain how a calm and balanced person like him could perpetrate such a mindless act on his friends.

Hence, the correct option is (B).

**12.** In the very act of committing the theft.

The boys were trying to steal a car and the police caught them red-handed.

Hence, the correct option is (A).

**13.** Be overhasty

The new executive jumped the gun by sending out the appointment letter too soon.

Hence, the correct option is (C).

**14.** The word wrongly spelt is Ilicit.

It is used about an activity or substance) not allowed by law or by the rules of society.

Hence, the correct option is (B).

**15.** "The ship having broken, Robinson arrived on the Island." means the ship was broken and therefore Robinson arrived on the island which is a complete sentence.

Hence, the correct option is (C).

**16.** The adjective like superior is normally used with to. "Superior than" would therefore form a wrong sentence.

Hence, the correct option is (B).

**17.** The correctly spelt word is a committee.

It means a group of people who have been chosen to discuss something or decide something.

Hence, the correct option is (D).

**18.** 'Omellete' is spelt incorrectly which have the correct spelling as 'omelette'.

Omelette - A dish of beaten eggs cooked in a frying pan and served plain or with a savoury or sweet topping or filling.

Hence, the correct option is (C).

**19.** An inference can always be logically deduced from the information given in the passage. It is never directly stated in the passage. The author has explained how the learnings from music last for a lifetime.

Hence, the correct option is (C).

**20.** "Music can be divided into genres (e.g., country music) and genres can be further divided into subgenres (e.g., country blues and pop country are two of the many country subgenres)".

Hence, the correct option is (D).

**21.** Within the arts, music may be classified as performing art, fine art, or auditory art.

Hence, the correct option is (D).

**22.** Music may be played or sung and heard live at a rock concert or orchestra performance, heard live as part of a dramatic work (a music theatre show or opera) or it may be recorded and listened to on a radio, MP3 player, CD player, smartphone or as film score or TV show.

Hence, the correct option is (D).

**23.** The sentence is "Students of music are better suited to face the world once they leave school".

Hence, the correct option is (A).

**24.** There is an error in part (b) of the sentence (a) single verb can be used for two subjects only if the form of the verb is the same for both subjects. Here, She is a singular subject and is in the third person. 'You' is also a singular subject but it is in the second person. The verb 'is' is used for the subject she. The verb is missing for the subject you. Therefore are should be used after you in part (b) of the sentence.

Hence, the correct option is (B).

**25.** The superlative degree (or superlative) compares more than two things to show which has the least or greatest degree of the quality (e.g., brightest, most bright).

The use of "most" is incorrect as 'fastest' is in the superlative degree. We avoid the use of double superlative. Justin is the fastest runner on the track team.

Hence the correct option is (A).

# // Notes //

# // Notes //

www.ingramcontent.com/pod-product-compliance
Lightning Source LLC
La Vergne TN
LVHW080615200726
843509LV00007B/316